Cancer
SOURCEBOOK
for Women

Fifth Edition

Health Reference Series

Fifth Edition

Cancer
SOURCEBOOK
for Women

Basic Consumer Health Information about Gynecological Cancers and Other Cancers of Special Concern to Women, Including Cancers of the Breast, Cervix, Colon, Esophagus, Lung, Ovaries, Thyroid, and Uterus

Along with Facts about Benign Conditions of the Female Reproductive System, Cancer Risk Factors, Screening and Prevention Programs, Women's Issues in Cancer Treatment and Survivorship, Research Initiatives, a Glossary of Cancer Terms, and a Directory of Resources for Additional Help and Information

OMNIGRAPHICS

155 W. Congress, Suite 200 Detroit, MI 48226

Bibliographic Note
Because this page cannot legibly accommodate all the copyright notices, the Bibliographic
Note portion of the Preface constitutes an extension of the copyright notice.

* * *

Omnigraphics, Inc.
Editorial Services provided by Omnigraphics, Inc.,
a division of Relevant Information, Inc.

Keith Jones, *Managing Editor*

* * *

Copyright © 2016 Relevant Information, Inc.
ISBN 978-0-7808-1379-3
E-ISBN 978-0-7808-1403-5

Table of Contents

Part V: Other Cancers of Special Concern to Women

Part VI: Diagnosing and Treating Cancer

Part VII: Coping with the Side Effects of Cancer and Cancer Treatments

Part VIII: Clinical Trials and Cancer Research

Part IX: Additional Help and Information

Preface

About This Book

According to the National Cancer Institute and Centers for Disease Control, cancer continues to take a devastating toll. In the United States, cancer is the second-leading cause of death among women after heart disease. However, medical researchers fighting against cancer have made significant progress. In recent years, cancer incidence rates have been stable, and—although the annual rate of decline in cancer death rates among men have been twice as large as the declines in women—mortality has decreased for ten of the top 15 cancers in women. With improved cancer screening programs and innovative treatments, women receiving a cancer diagnosis today have a better chance of overcoming their disease than ever before.

Cancer Sourcebook for Women, Fifth Edition provides updated information about breast cancer, gynecological cancers and other cancers of special concern to women, including cancers of the female reproductive organs and cancers responsible for the highest number of deaths in women. It explains cancer risks—including lifestyle factors, inherited genetic abnormalities, and hormonal medications—and methods used to diagnose and treat cancer. Practical suggestions for coping with side effects of the treatment are provided, and a section on cancer survivorship discusses methods for maintaining quality of life during and after treatment. The book concludes with a glossary of cancer-related terms, a directory of resources, and facts about locating support groups.

How to Use This Book

This book is divided into parts and chapters. Parts focus on broad areas of interest. Chapters are devoted to single topics within a part.

Part I: Cancer Overview defines what cancer is and what women must know about cancer. It also gives brief insight into cancer types, metastatic cancer and cancer clusters. Common questions related to cancer misconceptions are also included.

Part II: Cancer Risks and Prevention offers an overview of the factors that are known to increase the risk of cancer such as cigarette smoking and drinking alcohol. It also provides details on cancer risks associated with pregnancy, contraceptives, menopausal hormones and psychological stress. In addition to risk factors, it also provides a broad overview on cancer prevention.

Part III: Breast Cancer offers facts about breast health and breast cancer, including information about risk factors, prevention, screening and diagnostic methods, treatment options, and a list of approved drugs. Screening tools, including mammography and clinical breast exams, are discussed, and facts about the steps involved in diagnosing, staging, and treating breast cancer are included.

Part IV: Gynecological Cancer discusses cancers of a woman's reproductive organs. Individual chapters include information about symptoms, diagnosis, and treatment of cervical cancer, endometrial cancer, gestational trophoblastic tumors, ovarian cancer, uterine cancer, vaginal cancer, and vulvar cancer.

Part V: Other Cancers of Special Concern to Women discusses cancers other than gynecologic cancers that have a higher prevalence among women than men or those cancer types responsible for the most cancer-related deaths among women. It provides detailed information on anal cancer, bladder cancer, colorectal cancer, esophageal cancer, gallbladder cancer, extrahepatic bile duct cancer, lung cancer, pancreatic cancer, skin cancer, and thyroid cancer.

Part VI: Diagnosing and Treating Cancer covers tests and procedures involved in cancer diagnosis, as well as staging and general treatment options including chemotherapy, radiation therapy, biological therapy, targeted cancer therapies, stem cell transplant, immunotherapy and nutrition therapy. It also highlights complementary and alternative medicine (CAM) practices in cancer care. Information on cancer drugs and vaccines are also included.

Part VII: Coping with the Side Effects of Cancer and Cancer Treatments discusses the many side effects of chemotherapy and radiation and how to cope with it. The part concludes with a brief overview of the role of support groups and caregivers in helping cancer survivors.

Part VIII: Clinical Trials and Cancer Research gives a brief introduction to clinical trials and their importance, and also focuses on the development of research methods for cancer treatment.

Part IX: Additional Help and Information includes a glossary of cancer-related terms and a directory of national cancer organizations that provide information about specific cancers.

Bibliographic Note

This volume contains documents and excerpts from publications issued by the following U.S. government agencies: National Cancer Institute (NCI), Centers for Disease Control and Prevention (CDC), Food and Drug Administration (FDA), National Institutes of Health (NIH), National Institute on Alcohol Abuse and Alcoholism (NIAAA), National Institute on Aging (NIA), Office On Women's Health (OWH), and U.S. Food and Drug Administration (FDA).

About the Health Reference Series

The *Health Reference Series* is designed to provide basic medical information for patients, families, caregivers, and the general public. Each volume takes a particular topic and provides comprehensive coverage. This is especially important for people who may be dealing with a newly diagnosed disease or a chronic disorder in themselves or in a family member. People looking for preventive guidance, information about disease warning signs, medical statistics, and risk factors for health problems will also find answers to their questions in the *Health Reference Series*. The *Series*, however, is not intended to serve as a tool for diagnosing illness, in prescribing treatments, or as a substitute for the physician/patient relationship. All people concerned about medical symptoms or the possibility of disease are encouraged to seek professional care from an appropriate health care provider.

A Note about Spelling and Style

Health Reference Series editors use *Stedman's Medical Dictionary* as an authority for questions related to the spelling of medical terms and the *Chicago Manual of Style* for questions related to grammatical structures, punctuation, and other editorial concerns. Consistent adherence is not always possible, however, because the individual volumes within the *Series* include many documents from a wide variety of different producers, and the editor's primary goal is to present material from each source as accurately as is possible. This sometimes means that information in different chapters or sections may follow other guidelines and alternate spelling authorities.

Our Advisory Board

We would like to thank the following board members for providing guidance to the development of this Series:

- Dr. Lynda Baker, Associate Professor of Library and Information Science, Wayne State University, Detroit, MI

- Nancy Bulgarelli, William Beaumont Hospital Library, Royal Oak, MI

- Karen Imarisio, Bloomfield Township Public Library, Bloomfield Township, MI

- Karen Morgan, Mardigian Library, University of Michigan-Dearborn, Dearborn, MI

- Rosemary Orlando, St. Clair Shores Public Library, St. Clair Shores, MI

Health Reference Series Update Policy

The inaugural book in the *Health Reference Series* was the first edition of Cancer Sourcebook published in 1989. Since then, the Series has been enthusiastically received by librarians and in the medical community. In order to maintain the standard of providing high-quality health information for the layperson the editorial staff at Omnigraphics felt it was necessary to implement a policy of updating volumes when warranted.

Medical researchers have been making tremendous strides, and it is the purpose of the *Health Reference Series* to stay current with the most recent advances. Each decision to update a volume is made on an individual basis. Some of the considerations include how much new information is available and the feedback we receive from people who use the books. If there is a topic you would like to see added to the update list, or an area of medical concern you feel has not been adequately addressed, please write to:

Managing Editor
Health Reference Series
Omnigraphics, Inc.
155 W. Congress, Ste. 200
Detroit, MI 48226

Part One

Cancer Overview

Chapter 1

Introduction to Cancer

Chapter Contents

Section 1.1

Cancer – An Overview

This section includes excerpts from "What Is Cancer?," National
Cancer Institute (NCI), February 9, 2015

A Collection of Related Diseases

Cancer is the name given to a collection of related diseases. In all
types of cancer, some of the body's cells begin to divide without stopping
and spread into surrounding tissues.

Cancer can start almost anywhere in the human body, which is
made up of trillions of cells. Normally, human cells grow and divide to
form new cells as the body needs them. When cells grow old or become
damaged, they die, and new cells take their place.

When cancer develops, however, this orderly process breaks down.
As cells become more and more abnormal, old or damaged cells survive
when they should die, and new cells form when they are not needed.
These extra cells can divide without stopping and may form growths
called tumors. Many cancers form solid tumors, which are masses of
tissue. Cancers of the blood, such as leukemia, generally do not form
solid tumors.

Cancerous tumors are malignant, which means they can spread
into, or invade, nearby tissues. In addition, as these tumors grow,
some cancer cells can break off and travel to distant places in the body
through the blood or the lymph system and form new tumors far from
the original tumor.

Unlike malignant tumors, benign tumors do not spread into, or
invade, nearby tissues. Benign tumors can sometimes be quite large,
however. When removed, they usually don't grow back, whereas malignant tumors sometimes do. Unlike most benign tumors elsewhere in
the body, benign brain tumors can be life threatening.

Differences between Cancer Cells and Normal Cells

Cancer cells differ from normal cells in many ways that allow
them to grow out of control and become invasive. One important
difference is that cancer cells are less specialized than normal cells.

4

That is, whereas normal cells mature into very distinct cell types with specific functions, cancer cells do not. This is one reason that, unlike normal cells, cancer cells continue to divide without stopping. In addition, cancer cells are able to ignore signals that normally tell cells to stop dividing or that begin a process known as programmed cell death, or apoptosis, which the body uses to get rid of unneeded cells. Cancer cells may be able to influence the normal cells, molecules, and blood vessels that surround and feed a tumor—an area known as the microenvironment. For instance, cancer cells can induce nearby normal cells to form blood vessels that supply tumors with oxygen and nutrients, which they need to grow. These blood vessels also remove waste products from tumors. Cancer cells are also often able to evade the immune system, a network of organs, tissues, and specialized cells that protects the body from infections and other conditions. Although the immune system normally removes damaged or abnormal cells from the body, some cancer cells are able to "hide" from the immune system. Tumors can also use the immune system to stay alive and grow. For example, with the help of certain immune system cells that normally prevent a runaway immune response, cancer cells can actually keep the immune system from killing cancer cells.

How Cancer Arises

Cancer is a genetic disease—that is, it is caused by changes to genes that control the way our cells function, especially how they grow and divide.

Genetic changes that cause cancer can be inherited from our parents. They can also arise during a person's lifetime as a result of errors that occur as cells divide or because of damage to DNA caused by certain environmental exposures. Cancer-causing environmental exposures include substances, such as the chemicals in tobacco smoke, and radiation, such as ultraviolet rays from the sun.

Each person's cancer has a unique combination of genetic changes. As the cancer continues to grow, additional changes will occur. Even within the same tumor, different cells may have different genetic changes.

In general, cancer cells have more genetic changes, such as mutations in DNA, than normal cells. Some of these changes may have nothing to do with the cancer; they may be the result of the cancer, rather than its cause.

"Drivers" of Cancer

The genetic changes that contribute to cancer tend to affect three main types of genes—proto-oncogenes, tumor suppressor genes, and DNA repair genes. These changes are sometimes called "drivers" of cancer. Proto-oncogenes are involved in normal cell growth and division. However, when these genes are altered in certain ways or are more active than normal, they may become cancer-causing genes (or oncogenes), allowing cells to grow and survive when they should not. Tumor suppressor genes are also involved in controlling cell growth and division. Cells with certain alterations in tumor suppressor genes may divide in an uncontrolled manner. DNA repair genes are involved in fixing damaged DNA. Cells with mutations in these genes tend to develop additional mutations in other genes. Together, these mutations may cause the cells to become cancerous. As scientists have learned more about the molecular changes that lead to cancer, they have found that certain mutations commonly occur in many types of cancer. Because of this, cancers are sometimes characterized by the types of genetic alterations that are believed to be driving them, not just by where they develop in the body and how the cancer cells look under the microscope.

When Cancer Spreads

A cancer that has spread from the place where it first started to another place in the body is called metastatic cancer. The process by which cancer cells spread to other parts of the body is called metastasis. Metastatic cancer has the same name and the same type of cancer cells as the original, or primary cancer. For example, breast cancer that spreads to and forms a metastatic tumor in the lung is metastatic breast cancer, not lung cancer. Under a microscope, metastatic cancer cells generally look the same as cells of the original cancer. Moreover, metastatic cancer cells and cells of the original cancer usually have some molecular features in common, such as the presence of specific chromosome changes. Treatment may help prolong the lives of some people with metastatic cancer. In general, though, the primary goal of treatments for metastatic cancer is to control the growth of the cancer or to relieve symptoms caused by it. Metastatic tumors can cause severe damage to how the body functions, and most people who die of cancer die of metastatic disease.

Tissue Changes That Are Not Cancer

Not every change in the body's tissues is cancer. Some tissue changes may develop into cancer if they are not treated, however. Here are some examples of tissue changes that are not cancer but, in some cases, are monitored: Hyperplasia occurs when cells within a tissue divide faster than normal and extra cells build up, or proliferate. However, the cells and the way the tissue is organized look normal under a microscope. Hyperplasia can be caused by several factors or conditions, including chronic irritation. Dysplasia is a more serious condition than hyperplasia. In dysplasia, there is also a build-up of extra cells. But the cells look abnormal and there are changes in how the tissue is organized. In general, the more abnormal the cells and tissue look, the greater the chance that cancer will form. Some types of dysplasia may need to be monitored or treated. An example of dysplasia is an abnormal mole (called a dysplastic nevus) that forms on the skin. A dysplastic nevus can turn into melanoma, although most do not. An even more serious condition is carcinoma in situ. Although it is sometimes called cancer, carcinoma in situ is not cancer because the abnormal cells do not spread beyond the original tissue. That is, they do not invade nearby tissue the way that cancer cells do. But, because some carcinomas in situ may become cancer, they are usually treated.

Types of Cancer

There are more than 100 types of cancer. Types of cancer are usually named for the organs or tissues where the cancers form. For example, lung cancer starts in cells of the lung, and brain cancer starts in cells of the brain. Cancers also may be described by the type of cell that formed them, such as an epithelial cell or a squamous cell. You can search National Cancer Institute's (NCI) website for information on specific types of cancer based on the cancer's location in the body or by using our A to Z List of Cancers. We also have collections of information on childhood cancers and cancers in adolescents and young adults. Here are some categories of cancers that begin in specific types of cells:

Carcinoma

Carcinomas are the most common type of cancer. They are formed by epithelial cells, which are the cells that cover the inside and outside surfaces of the body. There are many types of epithelial cells, which often have a column-like shape when viewed under a microscope. Carcinomas that begin in different epithelial cell types have specific names: Adenocarcinoma is a cancer that forms in epithelial cells that produce fluids or mucus. Tissues with this type of epithelial cell are sometimes called glandular tissues. Most cancers of the breast, colon, and prostate are adenocarcinomas. Basal cell carcinoma is a cancer that begins in the lower or basal (base) layer of the epidermis, which is a person's outer layer of skin. Squamous cell carcinoma is a cancer that forms in squamous cells, which are epithelial cells that lie just beneath the outer surface of the skin. Squamous cells also line many other organs, including the stomach, intestines, lungs, bladder, and kidneys. Squamous cells look flat, like fish scales, when viewed under a microscope. Squamous cell carcinomas are sometimes called epidermoid carcinomas. Transitional cell carcinoma is a cancer that forms in a type of epithelial tissue called transitional epithelium, or urothelium. This tissue, which is made up of many layers of epithelial cells that can get bigger and smaller, is found in the linings of the bladder, ureters, and part of the kidneys (renal pelvis), and a few other organs. Some cancers of the bladder, ureters, and kidneys are transitional cell carcinomas.

Sarcoma

Sarcomas are cancers that form in bone and soft tissues, including muscle, fat, blood vessels, lymph vessels, and fibrous tissue (such as tendons and ligaments). Osteosarcoma is the most common cancer of bone. The most common types of soft tissue sarcoma are leiomyosarcoma, Kaposi sarcoma, malignant fibrous histiocytoma, liposarcoma, and dermatofibrosarcoma protuberans.

Leukemia

Cancers that begin in the blood-forming tissue of the bone marrow are called leukemias. These cancers do not form solid tumors. Instead, large numbers of abnormal white blood cells (leukemia cells and leukemic blast cells) build up in the blood and bone marrow, crowding out normal blood cells. The low level of normal blood cells can make it harder for the body to get oxygen to its tissues, control bleeding, or fight infections. There are four common types of leukemia, which are grouped based on how quickly the disease gets worse (acute or chronic) and on the type of blood cell the cancer starts in (lymphoblastic or myeloid).

Lymphoma

Lymphoma is cancer that begins in lymphocytes (T cells or B cells). These are disease-fighting white blood cells that are part of the immune system. In lymphoma, abnormal lymphocytes build up in lymph nodes and lymph vessels, as well as in other organs of the body. There are two main types of lymphoma:

Hodgkin lymphoma – People with this disease have abnormal lymphocytes that are called Reed-Sternberg cells. These cells usually form from B cells.

Non-Hodgkin lymphoma – This is a large group of cancers that start in lymphocytes. The cancers can grow quickly or slowly and can form from B cells or T cells.

Multiple Myeloma

Multiple myeloma is cancer that begins in plasma cells, another type of immune cell. The abnormal plasma cells, called myeloma cells, build up in the bone marrow and form tumors in bones all through the body. Multiple myeloma is also called plasma cell myeloma and Kahler disease.

Melanoma

Melanoma is cancer that begins in cells that become melanocytes, which are specialized cells that make melanin (the pigment that gives skin its color). Most melanomas form on the skin, but melanomas can also form in other pigmented tissues, such as the eye.

Brain and Spinal Cord Tumors

There are different types of brain and spinal cord tumors. These tumors are named based on the type of cell in which they formed and where the tumor first formed in the central nervous system. For example, an astrocytic tumor begins in star-shaped brain cells called astrocytes, which help keep nerve cells healthy. Brain tumors can be benign (not cancer) or malignant (cancer).

Other Types of Tumors

Germ Cell Tumors

Germ cell tumors are a type of tumor that begins in the cells that give rise to sperm or eggs. These tumors can occur almost anywhere in the body and can be either benign or malignant.

Neuroendocrine Tumors

Neuroendocrine tumors form from cells that release hormones into the blood in response to a signal from the nervous system. These tumors, which may make higher-than-normal amounts of hormones, can cause many different symptoms. Neuroendocrine tumors may be benign or malignant.

Carcinoid Tumors

Carcinoid tumors are a type of neuroendocrine tumor. They are slow-growing tumors that are usually found in the gastrointestinal system (most often in the rectum and small intestine). Carcinoid tumors may spread to the liver or other sites in the body, and they may secrete substances such as serotonin or prostaglandins, causing carcinoid syndrome.

Section 1.2

Common Cancer Myths and Misconceptions

This section includes excerpts from "Common Cancer Myths and Misconceptions," National Institute of Cancer (NCI), February 3, 2014.

Is cancer a death sentence?

In the United States, the likelihood of dying from cancer has dropped steadily since the 1990s. Five-year survival rates for some cancers, such as breast, prostate, and thyroid cancers, now exceed 90 percent. The 5-year survival rate for all cancers combined is currently about 66 percent.

It is important to note, however, that these rates are based on data from large numbers of people. How long an individual cancer patient will live and whether he or she will die from the disease depend on many factors, including whether the cancer is slow or fast growing, how much the cancer has spread in the body, whether effective treatments are available, the person's overall health, and more.

Will eating sugar make my cancer worse?

No. Although research has shown that cancer cells consume more sugar (glucose) than normal cells, no studies have shown that eating sugar will make your cancer worse or that, if you stop eating sugar, your cancer will shrink or disappear. However, a high-sugar diet may contribute to excess weight gain, and obesity is associated with an increased risk of developing several types of cancer.

Do artificial sweeteners cause cancer?

No. Researchers have conducted studies on the safety of the artificial sweeteners (sugar substitutes) saccharin (Sweet 'N Low®, Sweet Twin®, NectaSweet®); cyclamate; aspartame (Equal®, NutraSweet®); acesulfame potassium (Sunett®, Sweet One®); sucralose (Splenda®); and neotame and found no evidence that they cause cancer in humans. All of these artificial sweeteners except for cyclamate have been approved by the Food and Drug Administration for sale in the United States.

Is cancer contagious?

In general, no. Cancer is not a contagious disease that easily spreads from person to person. The only situation in which cancer can spread from one person to another is in the case of organ or tissue transplantation. A person who receives an organ or tissue from a donor who had cancer in the past may be at increased risk of developing a transplant-related cancer in the future. However, that risk is extremely low—about two cases of cancer per 10,000 organ transplants. Doctors avoid the use of organs or tissue from donors who have a history of cancer. In some people, cancers may be caused by certain viruses (some types of *human papillomavirus*, or HPV, for example) and bacteria (such as *Helicobacter pylori*). While a virus or bacterium can spread from person to person, the cancers they sometimes cause cannot spread from person to person.

Does my attitude—positive or negative—determine my risk of, or likely recovery from, cancer?

To date, there is no convincing scientific evidence that links a person's "attitude" to his or her risk of developing or dying from cancer. If you have cancer, it's normal to feel sad, angry, or discouraged sometimes and positive or upbeat at other times. People with a positive attitude may be more likely to maintain social connections and stay active, and physical activity and emotional support may help you cope with your cancer.

Can cancer surgery or a tumor biopsy cause cancer to spread in the body?

The chance that surgery will cause cancer to spread to other parts of the body is extremely low. Following standard procedures, surgeons use special methods and take many steps to prevent cancer cells from spreading during biopsies or surgery to remove tumors. For example, if they must remove tissue from more than one area of the body, they use different surgical tools for each area.

Will cancer get worse if exposed to air?

No. Exposure to air will not make tumors grow faster or cause cancer to spread to other parts of the body.

Do cell phones cause cancer?

No, not according to the best studies completed so far. Cancer is caused by genetic mutations, and cell phones emit a type of low-frequency energy that does not damage genes.

Do power lines cause cancer?

No, not according to the best studies completed so far. Power lines emit both electric and magnetic energy. The electric energy emitted by power lines is easily shielded or weakened by walls and other objects. The magnetic energy emitted by power lines is a low-frequency form of radiation that does not damage genes.

Are there herbal products that can cure cancer?

No. Although some studies suggest that alternative or complementary therapies, including some herbs, may help patients cope with the side effects of cancer treatment, no herbal products have been shown to be effective for treating cancer. In fact, some herbal products may be harmful when taken during chemotherapy or radiation therapy because they may interfere with how these treatments work. Cancer patients should talk with their doctor about any complementary and alternative medicine products—including vitamins and herbal supplements—they may be using.

If someone in my family has cancer, am I likely to get cancer, too?

Not necessarily. Cancer is caused by harmful changes (mutations) in genes. Only about 5 to 10 percent of cancers are caused by harmful mutations that are inherited from a person's parents. In families with an inherited cancer-causing mutation, multiple family members will often develop the same type of cancer. These cancers are called "familial" or "hereditary" cancers. The remaining 90 to 95 percent of cancers are caused by mutations that happen during a person's lifetime as a natural result of aging and exposure to environmental factors, such as tobacco smoke and radiation. These cancers are called "non-hereditary" or "spontaneous" cancers.

If no one in my family has had cancer, does that mean I'm risk-free?

No. Based on the most recent data, about 40 percent of men and women will be diagnosed with cancer at some point during their lives. Most cancers are caused by genetic changes that occur throughout a person's lifetime as a natural result of aging and exposure to environmental factors, such as tobacco smoke and radiation. Other factors, such as what kind of food you eat, how much you eat, and whether you exercise, may also influence your risk of developing cancer.

Do antiperspirants or deodorants cause breast cancer?

No. The best studies so far have found no evidence linking the chemicals typically found in antiperspirants and deodorants with changes in breast tissue.

Does hair dye use increase the risk of cancer?

There is no convincing scientific evidence that personal hair dye use increases the risk of cancer. Some studies suggest, however, that hairdressers and barbers who are regularly exposed to large quantities of hair dye and other chemical products may have an increased risk of bladder cancer.

Chapter 2

What Women Need to Know about Cancer

Cancer and Women

Every year, cancer claims the lives of more than a quarter of a million women in America. You can lower your cancer risk in several ways.

What You Can Do

- **Don't smoke, and avoid secondhand smoke.** More women in the United States die from lung cancer than any other kind of cancer, and cigarette smoking causes most cases.

- **Get recommended screening tests for breast, cervical, and colorectal cancer.** Screening tests are the best way to find these cancers early, when they are easier to treat.

- **Protect your skin from the sun and avoid indoor tanning.** Skin cancer is the most common cancer in the United States. Most cases of melanoma, the deadliest kind of skin cancer, are

This chapter includes excerpts from "Cancer and Women," Centers for Disease Control and Prevention (CDC), September 2, 2014; text from "Cancer Among Women," Centers for Disease Control and Prevention (CDC), September 2, 2014; and text from "Healthy Choices," Centers for Disease Control and Prevention (CDC), July 21, 2015.

caused by exposure to ultraviolet (UV) light from the sun and tanning devices.

- **Stay active and keep a healthy weight.** Adopting a lifestyle that includes healthy eating and regular physical activity can help lower your risk for several kinds of cancer.

Fast Facts about Cancer and Women

- The most common kinds of cancer among women in the U.S. are skin cancer, breast cancer, lung cancer, colorectal cancer, and uterine cancer.

- Cancer survivors largely consist of people who are 65 years of age or older and women. Of the 11.7 million people living with cancer in 2007, 6.3 million were women, and the largest group of cancer survivors were breast cancer survivors (22%).

- People who have cancer often live at home and get help from informal caregivers—people who help them without being paid. The majority of caregivers are women.

- Some HPV-associated cancers can be prevented. The HPV vaccine is available for girls and women who are 9 to 26 years old. It protects against the types of HPV that most often cause cervical cancer.

- Most breast cancers are found in women who are 50 years old or older, but breast cancer also affects younger women.

Cancer Among Women

Three Most Common Cancers Among Women

Note: The numbers in parentheses are the rates per 100,000 women of all races and Hispanic origins combined in the United States.

Breast cancer (122.0)

First among women of all races and Hispanic origin populations.

Lung cancer (52.0)

Second among white, black, and American Indian/Alaska Native women. Third among Asian/Pacific Islander and Hispanic women.

Colorectal cancer (34.9)

Second among Asian/Pacific Islander and Hispanic women. Third among white, black, and American Indian/Alaska Native women.

Leading Causes of Cancer Death Among Women

Lung cancer (37.0)

First among white, black, Asian/Pacific Islander, and American Indian/Alaska Native women. Second among Hispanic women.

Breast cancer (21.5)

First among Hispanic women. Second among white, black, Asian/Pacific Islander, and American Indian/Alaska Native women.

Colorectal cancer (12.8)

Third among women of all races and Hispanic origin populations.

Healthy Choices

You can reduce your risk of getting cancer by making healthy choices like keeping a healthy weight, avoiding tobacco, limiting the amount of alcohol you drink, and protecting your skin.

Avoiding Tobacco

Cigarette Smoking

Lung cancer is the leading cause of cancer death, and cigarette smoking causes almost all cases. Compared to non-smokers, men who smoke are about 23 times more likely to develop lung cancer and women who smoke are about 13 times more likely. Smoking causes about 90% of lung cancer deaths in men and almost 80% in women. Smoking also causes cancer of the voice box (larynx), mouth and throat, esophagus, bladder, kidney, pancreas, cervix, and stomach, and causes acute myeloid leukemia.

Secondhand Smoke

Adults who are exposed to secondhand smoke at home or at work increase their risk of developing lung cancer by 20% to 30%. Concentrations of many cancer-causing and toxic chemicals are higher in secondhand smoke than in the smoke inhaled by smokers.

Protecting Your Skin

Skin cancer is the most common kind of cancer in the United States. Exposure to ultraviolet (UV) rays from the sun and tanning beds appears to be the most important environmental factor involved with developing skin cancer. To help prevent skin cancer while still having fun outdoors, protect yourself by seeking shade, applying sunscreen, and wearing sun-protective clothing, a hat, and sunglasses.

Limiting Alcohol Intake

Studies around the world have shown that drinking alcohol regularly increases the risk of getting mouth, voice box, and throat cancers. Daily consumption of around 50g of alcohol doubles or triples the risk for these cancers, compared with the risk in non-drinkers. A large number of studies provide strong evidence that drinking alcohol is a risk factor for primary liver cancer, and more than 100 studies have found an increased risk of breast cancer with increasing alcohol intake. The link between alcohol consumption and colorectal (colon) cancer has been reported in more than 50 studies.

Keeping a Healthy Weight

Research has shown that being overweight or obese substantially raises a person's risk of getting endometrial (uterine), breast, prostate, and colorectal cancers. Overweight is defined as a body mass index (BMI) of 25 to 29, and obesity is defined as a BMI of 30 or higher.

Getting Tested for Hepatitis C

Hepatitis is inflammation of the liver, which is most often caused by a virus. In the United States, the most common type of viral hepatitis is Hepatitis C. Over time, chronic Hepatitis C can lead to serious liver problems including liver damage, cirrhosis, liver failure, or liver cancer. CDC recommends that anyone who was born between 1945 and 1965 get tested for Hepatitis C.

Chapter 3

Cancer Types

Cancer Types

This list of common cancer types includes cancers that are diagnosed with the greatest frequency in the United States, excluding nonmelanoma skin cancers:

- Bladder Cancer
- Breast Cancer
- Colon and Rectal Cancer
- Endometrial Cancer
- Kidney Cancer
- Leukemia
- Lung Cancer
- Melanoma
- Non-Hodgkin Lymphoma
- Pancreatic Cancer
- Prostate Cancer
- Thyroid Cancer

Text in this chapter is excerpted from "Common Cancer Types," National Cancer Institute (NCI), January 26, 2015.

Cancer incidence and mortality statistics reported by the American Cancer Society and other resources were used to create the list. To qualify as a common cancer for the list, the estimated annual incidence for 2015 had to be 40,000 cases or more.

The most common type of cancer on the list is breast cancer, with more than 234,000 new cases expected in the United States in 2015. The next most common cancers are prostate cancer and lung cancer.

Because colon and rectal cancers are often referred to as "colorectal cancers," these two cancer types are combined for the list. For 2015, the estimated number of new cases of colon cancer and rectal cancer are 93,090 and 39,610, respectively, adding to a total of 132,700 new cases of colorectal cancer.

The following table gives the estimated numbers of new cases and deaths for each common cancer type:

Table 3.1. Estimated numbers of new cases and deaths for each common cancer type in US.

Cancer Type	Estimated New Cases	Estimated Deaths
Bladder	74,000	16,000
Breast (Female – Male)	231,840 – 2,350	40,290 – 440
Colon and Rectal (Combined)	132,700	49,700
Endometrial	54,870	10,170
Kidney (Renal Cell and Renal Pelvis) Cancer	61,560	14,080
Leukemia (All Types)	54,270	24,450
Lung (Including Bronchus)	221,200	158,040
Melanoma	73,870	9,940
Non-Hodgkin Lymphoma	71,850	19,790
Pancreatic	48,960	40,560
Prostate	220,800	27,540
Thyroid	62,450	1,950

Chapter 4

Metastatic Cancer

What is metastatic cancer?

Metastatic cancer is cancer that has spread from the place where it first started to another place in the body. A tumor formed by metastatic cancer cells is called a metastatic tumor or a metastasis. The process by which cancer cells spread to other parts of the body is also called metastasis.

Metastatic cancer has the same name and the same type of cancer cells as the original, or primary, cancer. For example, breast cancer that spreads to the lung and forms a metastatic tumor is metastatic breast cancer, not lung cancer.

Under a microscope, metastatic cancer cells generally look the same as cells of the original cancer. Moreover, metastatic cancer cells and cells of the original cancer usually have some molecular features in common, such as the expression of certain proteins or the presence of specific chromosome changes.

Although some types of metastatic cancer can be cured with current treatments, most cannot. Nevertheless, treatments are available for all patients with metastatic cancer. In general, the primary goal of these treatments is to control the growth of the cancer or to relieve symptoms caused by it. In some cases, metastatic cancer treatments may help prolong life. However, most people who die of cancer die of metastatic disease.

Text in this chapter is excerpted from "Metastatic Cancer," National Cancer Institute (NCI), March 28, 2013.

Can any type of cancer form a metastatic tumor?

Virtually all cancers, including cancers of the blood and the lymphatic system (leukemia, multiple myeloma, and lymphoma), can form metastatic tumors. Although rare, the metastasis of blood and lymphatic system cancers to the lung, heart, central nervous system, and other tissues has been reported.

Where does cancer spread?

The most common sites of cancer metastasis are, in alphabetical order, the bone, liver, and lung. Although most cancers have the ability to spread to different parts of the body, they usually spread to one site more often than others. The following table shows the most common sites of metastasis, excluding the lymph nodes, for several types of cancer:

Table 4.1. Common sites of Metastasis

Cancer type	Main sites of Metastasis*
Bladder	Bone, liver, lung
Breast	Bone, brain, liver, lung
Colorectal	Liver, lung, peritoneum
Kidney	Adrenal gland, bone, brain, liver, lung
Lung	Adrenal gland, bone, brain, liver, other lung
Melanoma	Bone, brain, liver, lung, skin/muscle
Ovary	Liver, lung, peritoneum
Pancreas	Liver, lung, peritoneum
Prostate	Adrenal gland, bone, liver, lung
Stomach	Liver, lung, peritoneum
Thyroid	Bone, liver, lung
Uterus	Bone, liver, lung, peritoneum, vagina

In alphabetical order. Brain includes the neural tissue of the brain (parenchyma) and the leptomeninges (the two innermost membranes—arachnoid mater and pia mater—of the three membranes known as the meninges that surround the brain and spinal cord; the space between the arachnoid mater and the pia mater contains cerebrospinal fluid). Lung includes the main part of the lung (parenchyma) as well as the pleura (the membrane that covers the lungs and lines the chest cavity).

How does cancer spread?

Cancer cell metastasis usually involves the following steps:

- **Local invasion:** Cancer cells invade nearby normal tissue.

- **Intravasation:** Cancer cells invade and move through the walls of nearby lymph vessels or blood vessels.

- **Circulation:** Cancer cells move through the lymphatic system and the bloodstream to other parts of the body.

- **Arrest and extravasation:** Cancer cells arrest, or stop moving, in small blood vessels called capillaries at a distant location. They then invade the walls of the capillaries and migrate into the surrounding tissue (extravasation).

- **Proliferation:** Cancer cells multiply at the distant location to form small tumors known as micrometastases.

- **Angiogenesis:** Micrometastases stimulate the growth of new blood vessels to obtain a blood supply. A blood supply is needed to obtain the oxygen and nutrients necessary for continued tumor growth.

Because cancers of the lymphatic system or the blood system are already present inside lymph vessels, lymph nodes, or blood vessels, not all of these steps are needed for their metastasis. Also, the lymphatic system drains into the blood system at two locations in the neck.

The ability of a cancer cell to metastasize successfully depends on its individual properties; the properties of the noncancerous cells, including immune system cells, present at the original location; and the properties of the cells it encounters in the lymphatic system or the bloodstream and at the final destination in another part of the body. Not all cancer cells, by themselves, have the ability to metastasize. In addition, the noncancerous cells at the original location may be able to block cancer cell metastasis. Furthermore, successfully reaching another location in the body does not guarantee that a metastatic tumor will form. Metastatic cancer cells can lie dormant (not grow) at a distant site for many years before they begin to grow again, if at all.

Does metastatic cancer have symptoms?

Some people with metastatic tumors do not have symptoms. Their metastases are found by x-rays or other tests.

When symptoms of metastatic cancer occur, the type and frequency of the symptoms will depend on the size and location of the metastasis. For example, cancer that spreads to the bone is likely to cause pain and can lead to bone fractures. Cancer that spreads to the brain can cause a variety of symptoms, including headaches, seizures, and unsteadiness. Shortness of breath may be a sign of lung metastasis. Abdominal swelling or jaundice (yellowing of the skin) can indicate that cancer has spread to the liver.

Sometimes a person's original cancer is discovered only after a metastatic tumor causes symptoms. For example, a man whose prostate cancer has spread to the bones in his pelvis may have lower back pain (caused by the cancer in his bones) before he experiences any symptoms from the original tumor in his prostate.

Can someone have a metastatic tumor without having a primary cancer?

No. A metastatic tumor is always caused by cancer cells from another part of the body.

In most cases, when a metastatic tumor is found first, the primary cancer can also be found. The search for the primary cancer may involve lab tests, x-rays, computed tomography (CT) scans, magnetic resonance imaging (MRI) scans, positron emission tomography (PET) scans, and other procedures.

However, in some patients, a metastatic tumor is diagnosed but the primary tumor cannot be found, despite extensive tests, because it either is too small or has completely regressed. The pathologist knows that the diagnosed tumor is a metastasis because the cells do not look like those of the organ or tissue in which the tumor was found. Doctors refer to the primary cancer as unknown or occult (hidden), and the patient is said to have cancer of unknown primary origin (CUP).

Because diagnostic techniques are constantly improving, the number of cases of CUP is going down.

If a person who was previously treated for cancer gets diagnosed with cancer a second time, is the new cancer a new primary cancer or metastatic cancer?

The cancer may be a new primary cancer, but, in most cases, it is metastatic cancer.

What treatments are used for metastatic cancer?

Metastatic cancer may be treated with systemic therapy (chemotherapy, biological therapy, targeted therapy, hormonal therapy), local therapy (surgery, radiation therapy), or a combination of these treatments. The choice of treatment generally depends on the type of primary cancer; the size, location, and number of metastatic tumors; the patient's age and general health; and the types of treatment the patient has had in the past. In patients with CUP, it is possible to treat the disease even though the primary cancer has not been found.

Are new treatments for metastatic cancer being developed?

Yes, researchers are studying new ways to kill or stop the growth of primary cancer cells and metastatic cancer cells, including new ways to boost the strength of immune responses against tumors. In addition, researchers are trying to find ways to disrupt individual steps in the metastatic process.

Before any new treatment can be made widely available to patients, it must be studied in clinical trials (research studies) and found to be safe and effective in treating disease. National Cancer Institute (NCI) and many other organizations sponsor clinical trials that take place at hospitals, universities, medical schools, and cancer centers around the country. Clinical trials are a critical step in improving cancer care. The results of previous clinical trials have led to progress not only in the treatment of cancer but also in the detection, diagnosis, and prevention of the disease. Patients interested in taking part in a clinical trial should talk with their doctor.

Chapter 5

Cancer Clusters

What is a cancer cluster?

A cancer cluster is the occurrence of a greater than expected number of cancer cases among a group of people in a defined geographic area over a specific time period. A cancer cluster may be suspected when people report that several family members, friends, neighbors, or co-workers have been diagnosed with the same or related types of cancer. Cancer clusters can help scientists identify cancer-causing substances in the environment. For example, in the early 1970s, a cluster of cases of angiosarcoma of the liver, a rare cancer, was detected among workers in a chemical plant. Further investigation showed that the workers were all exposed to vinyl chloride and that workers in other plants that used vinyl chloride also had an increased rate of angiosarcoma of the liver. Exposure to vinyl chloride is now known to be a major risk factor for angiosarcoma of the liver. However, most suspected cancer clusters turn out, on detailed investigation, not to be true cancer clusters. That is, no cause can be identified, and the clustering of cases turns out to be a random occurrence.

Text in this chapter is excerpted from "Cancer Clusters," National Cancer Institute (NCI), March 18, 2014.

Where can someone report a suspected cancer cluster or find out if one is being investigated?

Concerned individuals can contact their local or state health department to report a suspected cancer cluster or to find out if one is being investigated. Health departments provide the first response to questions about cancer clusters because they, together with state cancer registries, will have the most up-to-date data on cancer incidence in the area. If additional resources are needed to investigate a suspected cancer cluster, the state health department may request assistance from federal agencies, including the Centers for Disease Control and Prevention (CDC) and the Agency for Toxic Substances and Disease Registry (ATSDR), which is part of the CDC. The CDC website provides links to state and local health departments. These agencies may also be listed in the blue pages of government listings in telephone books. Although National Cancer Institute (NCI) does not lead investigations of individual cancer clusters, NCI researchers and staff may provide assistance to other investigative agencies as needed. In addition, scientists at NCI and researchers who are funded by NCI analyze variations in cancer trends, including the frequency, distribution, and patterns of cancer in groups of people. These analyses can detect patterns of cancer in specific populations. For example, NCI's Cancer Mortality Maps website uses data on deaths from the National Center for Health Statistics, which is part of the CDC, and population estimates from the U.S. Census Bureau to provide dynamically generated maps that show geographic patterns of cancer death rates throughout the United States.

How are suspected cancer clusters investigated?

Health departments use established criteria to investigate reports of cancer clusters. The Centers for Disease Control and the Council of State and Territorial Epidemiologists have released updated guidelines for investigating suspected cancer clusters and responding to community concerns.

As a first step, the investigating agency gathers information from the person who reported the suspected cancer cluster. The investigators ask for details about the suspected cluster, such as the types of cancer and number of cases of each type, the age of the people with cancer, and the area and time period over which the cancers were diagnosed. They also ask about specific environmental hazards or concerns in the affected area.

If the review of the findings from this initial investigation suggests the need for further evaluation, investigators then compare information about cases in the suspected cluster with records in the state cancer registry and census data. If the second step reveals a statistically significant excess of cancer cases, the third step is to determine whether an epidemiologic study can be carried out to investigate whether the cluster is associated with risk factors in the local environment. Sometimes, even if there is a clear excess of cancer cases, it is not feasible to carry out further study—for example, if the total number of cases is very small. Finally, if an epidemiologic study is feasible, the fourth step is to determine whether the cluster of cancer cases is associated with a suspect contaminant in the environment. Even if a possible association with an environmental contaminant is found, however, further studies would be needed to confirm that the environmental contaminant did cause the cluster.

What are the challenges in investigating suspected cancer clusters?

Investigators face several challenges when determining whether a greater than expected number of cancer cases represents a cancer cluster.

Understanding the kind of cancers involved

To assess a suspected cancer cluster accurately, investigators must determine whether the type of cancer involved is a primary cancer (a cancer that is located in the original organ or tissue where the cancer started) or a cancer that has metastasized (spread) to another site in the body from the original tissue or organ where the cancer began (also called a secondary cancer). Investigators consider only the primary cancer when they investigate a suspected cancer cluster. A confirmed cancer cluster is more likely if it involves one type of cancer than if it involves multiple different cancer types. This is because most carcinogens in the environment cause only a specific cancer type rather than causing cancer in general.

Ascertaining the number of cancer cases in the suspected cluster

Many reported clusters include too few cancer cases for investigators to determine whether the number of cancer cases is statistically significantly greater than the expected number.

Determining statistical significance

To confirm the existence of a cluster, investigators must show that the number of cancer cases in the cluster is statistically significantly greater than the number of cancer cases expected given the age, sex, and racial distribution of the group of people who developed the disease. If the difference between the actual and expected number of cancer cases is statistically significant, the finding is unlikely to be the result of chance alone. However, it is important to keep in mind that even a statistically significant difference between actual and expected numbers of cases can arise by chance.

Determining the relevant population and geographic area

An important challenge in confirming a cancer cluster is accurately defining the group of people who should be considered potentially at risk of developing the specific cancer (typically the total number of people who live in a specific geographic area). When defining a cancer cluster, there can be a tendency to expand the geographic borders as additional cases of the suspected disease are discovered. However, if investigators define the borders of a cluster based on where they find cancer cases, they may alarm people about cancers that are not related to the suspected cluster. Instead, investigators first define the population and geographic area that is "at risk" and then identify cancer cases within those parameters.

Identifying a cause for a cluster

A confirmed cancer cluster—that is, a finding of a statistically significant excess of cancers—may not be the result of any single external cause or hazard (also called an exposure). A cancer cluster could be the result of chance, an error in the calculation of the expected number of cancer cases, differences in how cancer cases were classified, or a known cause of cancer, such as smoking. Even if a cluster is confirmed, it can be very difficult to identify the cause. People move in and out of a geographic area over time, which can make it difficult for investigators to identify hazards or potential carcinogens to which they may have been exposed and to obtain medical records to confirm the diagnosis of cancer. Also, it typically takes a long time for cancer to develop, and any relevant exposure may have occurred in the past or in a different geographic area from where the cancer was diagnosed.

Where can people get more information about cancer clusters?

In addition to state and local health departments and cancer registries, the following agencies may have more information about cancer clusters.

Agency for Toxic Substances and Disease Registry (ATSDR)

Centers for Disease Control and Prevention
1–800–232–4636 (1–800–CDC–INFO)
http://www.atsdr.cdc.gov

The CDC's ATSDR conducts public health assessments of potentially hazardous waste sites, performs health consultations on specific hazardous substances, designs and conducts health surveillance programs, and provides education and training about hazardous substances. Information about public health assessments conducted by ATSDR can be found on its Public Health Assessments and Health Consultations page. Reports can be searched by state or U.S. territory. Contact information for ATSDR regional offices is available online.

National Center for Environmental Health (NCEH)

Centers for Disease Control and Prevention
1–800–232–4636 (1–800–CDC–INFO)
cdcinfo@cdc.gov
http://www.cdc.gov/nceh/clusters

The CDC's NCEH works to promote healthy and safe environments and prevent harmful exposures. The NCEH website includes general information about cancer clusters, links to resources, and answers to frequently asked questions.

National Institute for Occupational Safety and Health (NIOSH)

Hazard Evaluation and Technical Assistance Branch
Health Hazard Evaluation (HHE) Program
Centers for Disease Control and Prevention
513–841–4382
HHERequestHelp@cdc.gov
http://www.cdc.gov/niosh/hhe

The HHE Program of CDC's NIOSH investigates potentially hazardous working conditions, including suspected cancer clusters. Employees, authorized employee representatives, and employers can request these evaluations. HHE reports are available on the NIOSH website.

Office of Occupational Medicine
Occupational Safety and Health Administration (OSHA)
U.S. Department of Labor
202–693–2323
http://www.osha.gov/dts/oom/index.html

OSHA's Office of Occupational Medicine performs workplace-related case evaluations and cluster investigations, including medical record reviews, employee interviews, and medical screening activities.

Part Two

Cancer Risks and Prevention

Chapter 6

Risk Factors

Risk Factors

Scientists study risk factors and protective factors to find ways to prevent new cancers from starting. Anything that increases your chance of developing cancer is called a cancer risk factor; anything that decreases your chance of developing cancer is called a cancer protective factor.

Some risk factors for cancer can be avoided, but many cannot. For example, both smoking and inheriting certain genes are risk factors for some types of cancer, but only smoking can be avoided. Risk factors that a person can control are called modifiable risk factors.

Many other factors in our environment, diet, and lifestyle may cause or prevent cancer. This chapter reviews only the major cancer risk factors and protective factors that can be controlled or changed to reduce the risk of cancer. Risk factors that are not described in the chapter include certain sexual behaviors, the use of estrogen, and being exposed to certain substances at work or to certain chemicals.

Factors That Are Known to Increase the Risk of Cancer

Cigarette Smoking and Tobacco Use

Tobacco use is strongly linked to an increased risk for many kinds of cancer. Smoking cigarettes is the leading cause of the following types of cancer:

Text in this chapter is excerpted from "Risk Factors (PDQ®)," National Cancer Institute (NCI), July 23, 2015.

- Acute myelogenous leukemia (AML)
- Bladder cancer
- Esophageal cancer
- Kidney cancer
- Lung cancer
- Oral cavity cancer
- Pancreatic cancer
- Stomach cancer

Not smoking or quitting smoking lowers the risk of getting cancer and dying from cancer. Scientists believe that cigarette smoking causes about 30% of all cancer deaths in the United States.

Infections

Certain viruses and bacteria are able to cause cancer. Viruses and other infection-causing agents cause more cases of cancer in the developing world (about 1 in 4 cases of cancer) than in developed nations (less than 1 in 10 cases of cancer). Examples of cancer-causing viruses and bacteria include:

- *Human papilloma virus* (HPV) increases the risk for cancers of the cervix, penis, vagina, anus, and oropharynx.
- *Hepatitis B* and *hepatitis C viruses* increase the risk for liver cancer.
- *Epstein-Barr virus* increases the risk for Burkitt lymphoma.
- *Helicobacter pylori* increases the risk for gastric cancer.

Two vaccines to prevent infection by cancer-causing agents have already been developed and approved by the U.S. Food and Drug Administration (FDA). One is a vaccine to prevent infection with *hepatitis B virus*. The other protects against infection with strains of *human papillomavirus* (HPV) that cause cervical cancer. Scientists continue to work on vaccines against infections that cause cancer.

Radiation

Being exposed to radiation is a known cause of cancer. There are two main types of radiation linked with an increased risk for cancer:

36

- Ultraviolet radiation from sunlight: This is the main cause of nonmelanoma skin cancers.

- Ionizing radiation including:

  - Medical radiation from tests to diagnose cancer such as x-rays, computerized tomography (CT) scans, fluoroscopy, and nuclear medicine scans.

  - Radon gas in our homes.

Scientists believe that ionizing radiation causes leukemia, thyroid cancer, and breast cancer in women. Ionizing radiation may also be linked to myeloma and cancers of the lung, stomach, colon, esophagus, bladder, and ovary. Being exposed to radiation from diagnostic x-rays increases the risk of cancer in patients and x-ray technicians.

The growing use of CT scans over the last 20 years has increased exposure to ionizing radiation. The risk of cancer also increases with the number of CT scans a patient has and the radiation dose used each time.

Immunosuppressive Medicines

Immunosuppressive medicines are linked to an increased risk of cancer. These medicines lower the body's ability to stop cancer from forming. For example, immunosuppressive medicines may be used to keep a patient from rejecting an organ transplant.

Factors That May Affect the Risk of Cancer

Diet

The foods that you eat on a regular basis make up your diet. Diet is being studied as a risk factor for cancer. It is hard to study the effects of diet on cancer because a person's diet includes foods that may protect against cancer and foods that may increase the risk of cancer.

It is also hard for people who take part in the studies to keep track of what they eat over a long period of time. This may explain why studies have different results about how diet affects the risk of cancer.

Some studies show that fruits and non-starchy vegetables may protect against cancers of the mouth, esophagus, and stomach. Fruits may also protect against lung cancer.

Some studies have shown that a diet high in fat, proteins, calories, and red meat increases the risk of colorectal cancer, but other studies have not shown this.

It is not known if a diet low in fat and high in fibre, fruits, and vegetables lowers the risk of colorectal cancer.

Alcohol

Studies have shown that drinking alcohol is linked to an increased risk of the following types of cancers:

- Oral cancer

- Esophageal cancer

- Breast cancer

- Colorectal cancer (in men)

Drinking alcohol may also increase the risk of liver cancer and female colorectal cancer.

Physical Activity

Studies show that people who are physically active have a lower risk of certain cancers than those who are not. It is not known if physical activity itself is the reason for this.

Studies show a strong link between physical activity and a lower risk of colorectal cancer. Some studies show that physical activity protects against postmenopausal breast cancer and endometrial cancer.

Obesity

Studies show that obesity is linked to a higher risk of the following types of cancer:

- Postmenopausal breast cancer

- Colorectal cancer

- Endometrial cancer

- Esophageal cancer

- Kidney cancer

- Pancreatic cancer

Some studies show that obesity is also a risk factor for cancer of the gallbladder.

It is not known if losing weight lowers the risk of cancers that have been linked to obesity.

Environmental Risk Factors

Being exposed to chemicals and other substances in the environment has been linked to some cancers:

- Links between air pollution and cancer risk have been found. These include links between lung cancer and secondhand tobacco smoke, outdoor air pollution, and asbestos.

- Drinking water that contains a large amount of arsenic has been linked to skin, bladder, and lung cancers.

Studies have been done to see if pesticides and other pollutants increase the risk of cancer. The results of those studies have been unclear because other factors can change the results of the studies.

Chapter 7

The Genetics of Cancer

Chapter Contents

Section 7.1

Cancer and Genetics – An Overview

Text in this section is excerpted from "The Genetics of Cancer,"
National Cancer Institute (NCI), April 22, 2015.

Genetic Changes and Cancer

Cancer is a genetic disease—that is, cancer is caused by certain changes to genes that control the way our cells function, especially how they grow and divide. These changes include mutations in the deoxyribonucleic acid (DNA) that makes up our genes.

Genetic changes that increase cancer risk can be inherited from our parents if the changes are present in germ cells, which are the reproductive cells of the body (eggs and sperm). Such changes, called germline changes, are found in every cell of the offspring.

Cancer-causing genetic changes can also be acquired during one's lifetime, as the result of errors that occur as cells divide during a person's lifetime or exposure to substances, such as certain chemicals in tobacco smoke, and radiation, such as ultraviolet rays from the sun, that damage DNA.

Genetic changes that occur after conception are called somatic (or acquired) changes. They can arise at any time during a person's life. The number of cells in the body that carry such changes depends on when the changes occur during a person's lifetime.

In general, cancer cells have more genetic changes than normal cells. But each person's cancer has a unique combination of genetic alterations. Some of these changes may be the result of cancer, rather than the cause. As the cancer continues to grow, additional changes will occur. Even within the same tumor, cancer cells may have different genetic changes.

Hereditary Cancer Syndromes

Inherited genetic mutations play a major role in about 5 to 10 percent of all cancers. Researchers have associated mutations in specific genes with more than 50 hereditary cancer syndromes, which are disorders that may predispose individuals to developing certain cancers.

Genetic tests can tell whether a person from a family that shows signs of such a syndrome has one of these mutations. These tests can also show whether family members without obvious disease have inherited the same mutation as a family member who carries a cancer-associated mutation.

Many experts recommend that genetic testing for cancer risk be considered when someone has a personal or family history that suggests an inherited cancer risk condition, as long as the test results can be adequately interpreted (that is, they can clearly tell whether a specific genetic change is present or absent) and when the results provide information that will help guide a person's future medical care.

Cancers that are not caused by inherited genetic mutations can sometimes appear to "run in families." For example, a shared environment or lifestyle, such as tobacco use, can cause similar cancers to develop among family members. However, certain patterns in a family—such as the types of cancer that develop, other non-cancer conditions that are seen, and the ages at which cancer develops—may suggest the presence of a hereditary cancer syndrome.

Even if a cancer-predisposing mutation is present in a family, not everyone who inherits the mutation will necessarily develop cancer. Several factors influence the outcome in a given person with the mutation, including the pattern of inheritance of the cancer syndrome.

Here are examples of genes that can play a role in hereditary cancer syndromes.

- The most commonly mutated gene in all cancers is TP53, which produces a protein that suppresses the growth of tumors. In addition, germline mutations in this gene can cause Li-Fraumeni syndrome, a rare, inherited disorder that leads to a higher risk of developing certain cancers.

- Inherited mutations in the BRCA1 and BRCA2 genes are associated with hereditary breast and ovarian cancer syndrome, which is a disorder marked by an increased lifetime risk of breast and ovarian cancers in women.

- Another gene that produces a tumor suppressor protein is phosphatase and tensin homolog (PTEN). Mutations in this gene are associated with Cowden syndrome, an inherited disorder that increases the risk of breast, thyroid, endometrial, and other types of cancer.

Genetic Test Results

Genetic tests are usually requested by a person's doctor or other health care provider. Genetic counselling can help people consider the risks, benefits, and limitations of genetic testing in their particular situations.

The results of genetic tests can be positive, negative, or uncertain. A genetic counsellor, doctor, or other health care professional trained in genetics can help an individual or family understand their test results. These professionals can also help explain the incidental findings that a test may yield, such as a genetic risk factor for a disease that is unrelated to the reason for administering the test. And they can clarify the implications of test results for other family members.

Medical test results are normally included in a person's medical records, particularly if a doctor or other health care provider has ordered the test or has been consulted about the test results. Therefore, people considering genetic testing should understand that their results may become known to other people or organizations that have legitimate, legal access to their medical records, such as their insurance company or employer, if their employer provides the patient's health insurance as a benefit.

However, legal protections are in place to prevent genetic discrimination. The Genetic Information Non-discrimination Act of 2008 is a federal law that prohibits discrimination based on genetic information in determining health insurance eligibility or rates and suitability for employment. In addition, because a person's genetic information is considered health information, it is covered by the Privacy Rule of the Health Information Portability and Accountability Act of 1996.

Clinical DNA Sequencing

Until recently, most genetic testing for cancer focused on testing for individual inherited mutations. But, as more efficient and cheaper DNA sequencing technologies have become available, sequencing of an individual's entire genome or the DNA of an individual's tumor is becoming more common.

Clinical DNA sequencing can be useful in detecting many genetic mutations at one time. Targeted multiple-gene panels test for many inherited mutations or somatic mutations at the same time. These panels can include different genes and be tailored to individual tumor types. Targeted gene panels limit the data to be analyzed and include only known genes, which makes the interpretation more straightforward than in broader approaches that assess the whole genome (or tumor genome) or significant parts of it. Multiple-gene panel tests are becoming increasingly common in genetic testing for hereditary cancer syndromes.

Tumor sequencing can identify somatic mutations that may be driving the growth of particular cancers. It can also help doctors sort out which therapies may work best against a particular tumor. For instance, patients whose lung tumors harbor certain mutations may benefit from drugs that target these particular changes.

Testing tumor DNA may reveal a mutation that has not previously been found in that tumor type. But if that mutation occurs in another tumor type and a targeted therapy has been developed for the alteration, the treatment may be effective in the "new" tumor type as well.

Tumor sequencing can also identify germline mutations. Indeed, in some cases, the genetic testing of tumors has shown that a patient's cancer could be associated with a hereditary cancer syndrome that the family was not aware of.

As with testing for specific mutations in hereditary cancer syndromes, clinical DNA sequencing has implications that patients need to consider. For example, they may learn incidentally about the presence of germline mutations that may cause other diseases, in them or in their family members.

Section 7.2

BRCA1 *and BRCA2: Cancer Risk and Genetic Testing*

Text in this section is excerpted from "BRCA1 and BRCA2: Cancer Risk and Genetic Testing," National Cancer Institute (NCI), April 1, 2015.

What are **BRCA1** and **BRCA2?**

BRCA1 and BRCA2 are human genes that produce tumor suppressor proteins. These proteins help repair damaged DNA and, therefore, play a role in ensuring the stability of the cell's genetic material. When either of these genes is mutated, or altered, such that its protein product either is not made or does not function correctly, DNA damage may not be repaired properly. As a result, cells are more likely to develop additional genetic alterations that can lead to cancer.

Specific inherited mutations in BRCA1 and BRCA2 increase the risk of female breast and ovarian cancers, and they have been associated with increased risks of several additional types of cancer. Together, BRCA1 and BRCA2 mutations account for about 20 to 25 percent of hereditary breast cancers and about 5 to 10 percent of all breast cancers. In addition, mutations in BRCA1 and BRCA2 account for around 15 percent of ovarian cancers overall. Breast and ovarian cancers associated with BRCA1 and BRCA2 mutations tend to develop at younger ages than their nonhereditary counterparts.

A harmful BRCA1 or BRCA2 mutation can be inherited from a person's mother or father. Each child of a parent who carries a mutation in one of these genes has a 50 percent chance (or 1 chance in 2) of inheriting the mutation. The effects of mutations in BRCA1 and BRCA2 are seen even when a person's second copy of the gene is normal.

How much does having a **BRCA1** or **BRCA2** gene mutation increase a woman's risk of breast and ovarian cancer?

A woman's lifetime risk of developing breast and/or ovarian cancer is greatly increased if she inherits a harmful mutation in BRCA1 or BRCA2.

Breast cancer: About 12 percent of women in the general population will develop breast cancer sometime during their lives. By contrast, according to the most recent estimates, 55 to 65 percent of women who inherit a harmful BRCA1 mutation and around 45 percent of women who inherit a harmful BRCA2 mutation will develop breast cancer by age 70 years.

Ovarian cancer: About 1.3 percent of women in the general population will develop ovarian cancer sometime during their lives. By contrast, according to the most recent estimates, 39 percent of women who inherit a harmful BRCA1 mutation and 11 to 17 percent of women who inherit a harmful BRCA2 mutation will develop ovarian cancer by age 70 years.

It is important to note that these estimated percentages of lifetime risk are different from those available previously; the estimates have changed as more information has become available, and they may change again with additional research. No long-term general population studies have directly compared cancer risk in women who have and do not have a harmful BRCA1 or BRCA2 mutation.

It is also important to note that other characteristics of a particular woman can make her cancer risk higher or lower than the average risks. These characteristics include her family history of breast, ovarian, and, possibly, other cancers; the specific mutation(s) she has inherited; and other risk factors, such as her reproductive history. However, at this time, based on current data, none of these other factors seems to be as strong as the effect of carrying a harmful BRCA1 or BRCA2 mutation.

What other cancers have been linked to mutations in BRCA1 and BRCA2?

Harmful mutations in BRCA1 and BRCA2 increase the risk of several cancers in addition to breast and ovarian cancer. BRCA1 mutations may increase a woman's risk of developing fallopian tube cancer and peritoneal cancer. Men with BRCA2 mutations, and to a lesser extent BRCA1 mutations, are also at increased risk of breast cancer. Men with harmful BRCA1 or BRCA2 mutations have a higher risk of prostate cancer. Men and women with BRCA1 or BRCA2 mutations may be at increased risk of pancreatic cancer. Mutations in BRCA2 (also known as FANCD1), if they are inherited from both parents, can cause a Fanconi anemia subtype (FA-D1), a syndrome that is associated with childhood solid tumors and development of acute myeloid leukemia. Likewise, mutations in BRCA1 (also known as FANCS), if they are inherited from both parents, can cause another Fanconi anemia subtype.

Are mutations in BRCA1 and BRCA2 more common in certain racial/ethnic populations than others?

Yes. For example, people of Ashkenazi Jewish descent have a higher prevalence of harmful BRCA1 and BRCA2 mutations than people in the general U.S. population. Other ethnic and geographic populations around the world, such as the Norwegian, Dutch, and Icelandic peoples, also have a higher prevalence of specific harmful BRCA1 and BRCA2 mutations.

In addition, limited data indicate that the prevalence of specific harmful BRCA1 and BRCA2 mutations may vary among individual racial and ethnic groups in the United States, including African Americans, Hispanics, Asian Americans, and non-Hispanic Whites.

Are genetic tests available to detect **BRCA1** *and* **BRCA2** *mutations?*

Yes. Several different tests are available, including tests that look for a known mutation in one of the genes (i.e., a mutation that has already been identified in another family member) and tests that check for all possible mutations in both genes. DNA (from a blood or saliva sample) is needed for mutation testing. The sample is sent to a laboratory for analysis. It usually takes about a month to get the test results.

Who should consider genetic testing for **BRCA1** *and* **BRCA2** *mutations?*

Because harmful BRCA1 and BRCA2 gene mutations are relatively rare in the general population, most experts agree that mutation testing of individuals who do not have cancer should be performed only when the person's individual or family history suggests the possible presence of a harmful mutation in BRCA1 or BRCA2.

In December 2013, the United States Preventive Services Task Force recommended that women who have family members with breast, ovarian, fallopian tube, or peritoneal cancer be evaluated to see if they have a family history that is associated with an increased risk of a harmful mutation in one of these genes.

Several screening tools are now available to help health care providers with this evaluation. These tools assess family history factors that are associated with an increased likelihood of having a harmful mutation in BRCA1 or BRCA2, including:

- Breast cancer diagnosed before age 50 years
- Cancer in both breasts in the same woman
- Both breast and ovarian cancers in either the same woman or the same family
- Multiple breast cancers
- Two or more primary types of BRCA1- or BRCA2-related cancers in a single family member
- Ashkenazi Jewish ethnicity

When an individual has a family history that is suggestive of the presence of a BRCA1 or BRCA2 mutation, it may be most informative to first test a family member who has cancer if that person is still alive and willing to be tested. If that person is found to have a harmful BRCA1 or BRCA2 mutation, then other family members may want to consider genetic counseling to learn more about their potential risks and whether genetic testing for mutations in BRCA1 and BRCA2 might be appropriate for them.

If it is not possible to confirm the presence of a harmful BRCA1 or BRCA2 mutation in a family member who has cancer, it is appropriate for both men and women who do not have cancer but have a family medical history that suggests the presence of such a mutation to have genetic counseling for possible testing.

Some individuals—for example, those who were adopted at birth—may not know their family history. In cases where a woman with an unknown family history has an early-onset breast cancer or ovarian cancer or a man with an unknown family history is diagnosed with breast cancer, it may be reasonable for that individual to consider genetic testing for a BRCA1 or BRCA2 mutation. Individuals with an unknown family history who do not have an early-onset cancer are at very low risk of having a harmful BRCA1 or BRCA2 mutation and are unlikely to benefit from routine genetic testing.

Professional societies do not recommend that children, even those with a family history suggestive of a harmful BRCA1 or BRCA2 mutation, undergo genetic testing for BRCA1 or BRCA2. This is because no risk-reduction strategies exist for children, and children's risks of developing a cancer type associated with a BRCA1 or BRCA2 mutation are extremely low. After children with a family history suggestive of a harmful BRCA1 or BRCA2 mutation become adults, however, they may want to obtain genetic counselling about whether or not to undergoing genetic testing.

Should people considering genetic testing for **BRCA1** and **BRCA2** mutations talk with a genetic counsellor?

Genetic counselling is generally recommended before and after any genetic test for an inherited cancer syndrome. This counselling should be performed by a health care professional who is experienced in cancer genetics. Genetic counselling usually covers many aspects of the testing process, including:

- A hereditary cancer risk assessment based on an individual's personal and family medical history

- Discussion of:

  - The appropriateness of genetic testing

- The medical implications of a positive or a negative test result
- The possibility that a test result might not be informative
- The psychological risks and benefits of genetic test results
- The risk of passing a mutation to children
- Explanation of the specific test(s) that might be used and the technical accuracy of the test(s)

How much does **BRCA1** and **BRCA2** mutation testing cost?

The Affordable Care Act considers genetic counseling and BRCA1 and BRCA2 mutation testing for individuals at high risk a covered preventive service. People considering BRCA1 and BRCA2 mutation testing may want to confirm their insurance coverage for genetic tests before having the test.

Some of the genetic testing companies that offer testing for BRCA1 and BRCA2 mutations may offer testing at no charge to patients who lack insurance and meet specific financial and medical criteria.

What does a positive **BRCA1** or **BRCA2** genetic test result mean?

BRCA1 and BRCA2 gene mutation testing can give several possible results: a positive result, a negative result, or an ambiguous or uncertain result.

A positive test result indicates that a person has inherited a known harmful mutation in BRCA1 or BRCA2 and, therefore, has an increased risk of developing certain cancers. However, a positive test result cannot tell whether or when an individual will actually develop cancer. For example, some women who inherit a harmful BRCA1 or BRCA2 mutation will never develop breast or ovarian cancer.

A positive genetic test result may also have important health and social implications for family members, including future generations. Unlike most other medical tests, genetic tests can reveal information not only about the person being tested but also about that person's relatives:

- Both men and women who inherit a harmful BRCA1 or BRCA2 mutation, whether or not they develop cancer themselves, may pass the mutation on to their sons and daughters. Each child has a 50 percent chance of inheriting a parent's mutation.

- If a person learns that he or she has inherited a harmful BRCA1 or BRCA2 mutation, this will mean that each of his or her full siblings has a 50 percent chance of having inherited the mutation as well.

What does a negative BRCA1 or BRCA2 test result mean?

A negative test result can be more difficult to understand than a positive result because what the result means depends in part on an individual's family history of cancer and whether a BRCA1 or BRCA2 mutation has been identified in a blood relative.

If a close (first- or second-degree) relative of the tested person is known to carry a harmful BRCA1 or BRCA2 mutation, a negative test result is clear: it means that person does not carry the harmful mutation that is responsible for the familial cancer, and thus cannot pass it on to their children. Such a test result is called a true negative. A person with such a test result is currently thought to have the same risk of cancer as someone in the general population.

If the tested person has a family history that suggests the possibility of having a harmful mutation in BRCA1 or BRCA2 but complete gene testing identifies no such mutation in the family, a negative result is less clear. The likelihood that genetic testing will miss a known harmful BRCA1 or BRCA2 mutation is very low, but it could happen. Moreover, scientists continue to discover new BRCA1 and BRCA2 mutations and have not yet identified all potentially harmful ones. Therefore, it is possible that a person in this scenario with a "negative" test result actually has an as-yet unknown harmful BRCA1 or BRCA2 mutation that has not been identified.

It is also possible for people to have a mutation in a gene other than BRCA1 or BRCA2 that increases their cancer risk but is not detectable by the test used. People considering genetic testing for BRCA1 and BRCA2 mutations may want to discuss these potential uncertainties with a genetic counselor before undergoing testing.

What does an ambiguous or uncertain BRCA1 or BRCA2 test result mean?

Sometimes, a genetic test finds a change in BRCA1 or BRCA2 that has not been previously associated with cancer. This type of test result may be described as "ambiguous" (often referred to as "a genetic variant of uncertain significance") because it isn't known whether this specific gene change affects a person's risk of developing cancer. One study found that 10 percent of women who underwent BRCA1 and BRCA2 mutation testing had this type of ambiguous result.

As more research is conducted and more people are tested for BRCA1 and BRCA2 mutations, scientists will learn more about these changes and cancer risk. Genetic counseling can help a person understand what an ambiguous change in BRCA1 or BRCA2 may mean in terms of cancer risk. Over time, additional studies of variants of uncertain significance may result in a specific mutation being re-classified as either harmful or clearly not harmful.

How can a person who has a positive test result manage their risk of cancer?

Several options are available for managing cancer risk in individuals who have a known harmful BRCA1 or BRCA2 mutation. These include enhanced screening, prophylactic (risk-reducing) surgery, and chemoprevention.

Enhanced Screening. Some women who test positive for BRCA1 and BRCA2 mutations may choose to start cancer screening at younger ages than the general population or to have more frequent screening. For example, some experts recommend that women who carry a harmful BRCA1 or BRCA2 mutation undergo clinical breast examinations beginning at age 25 to 35 years. And some expert groups recommend that women who carry such a mutation have a mammogram every year, beginning at age 25 to 35 years.

Enhanced screening may increase the chance of detecting breast cancer at an early stage, when it may have a better chance of being treated successfully. Women who have a positive test result should ask their health care provider about the possible harms of diagnostic tests that involve radiation (mammograms or x-rays).

Recent studies have shown that MRI may be more sensitive than mammography for women at high risk of breast cancer. However, mammography can also identify some breast cancers that are not identified by MRI, and MRI may be less specific (i.e., lead to more false-positive results) than mammography. Several organizations, such as the American Cancer Society and the National Comprehensive Cancer Network, now recommend annual screening with mammography and MRI for women who have a high risk of breast cancer.

No effective ovarian cancer screening methods currently exist. Some groups recommend transvaginal ultrasound, blood tests for the antigen CA-125, and clinical examinations for ovarian cancer screening in women with harmful BRCA1 or BRCA2 mutations, but none of these methods appears to detect ovarian tumors at an early enough stage to reduce the risk of dying from ovarian cancer. For a screening method to be considered effective, it must have demonstrated reduced mortality from the disease of interest. This standard has not yet been met for ovarian cancer screening.

The benefits of screening for breast and other cancers in men who carry harmful mutations in BRCA1 or BRCA2 is also not known, but some expert groups recommend that men who are known to carry a harmful mutation undergo regular mammography as well as testing for prostate cancer. The value of these screening strategies remains unproven at present.

Prophylactic (Risk-reducing) Surgery. Prophylactic surgery involves removing as much of the "at-risk" tissue as possible. Women may choose to have both breasts removed (bilateral prophylactic mastectomy) to reduce their risk of breast cancer. Surgery to remove a woman's ovaries and fallopian tubes (bilateral prophylactic salpingo-oophorectomy) can help reduce her risk of ovarian cancer. Removing the ovaries also reduces the risk of breast cancer in premenopausal women by eliminating a source of hormones that can fuel the growth of some types of breast cancer.

No evidence is available regarding the effectiveness of bilateral prophylactic mastectomy in reducing breast cancer risk in men with a harmful BRCA1 or BRCA2 mutation or a family history of breast cancer. Therefore, bilateral prophylactic mastectomy for men at high risk of breast cancer is considered an experimental procedure, and insurance companies will not normally cover it.

Prophylactic surgery does not completely guarantee that cancer will not develop because not all at-risk tissue can be removed by these procedures. Some women have developed breast cancer, ovarian cancer, or primary peritoneal carcinomatosis (a type of cancer similar to ovarian cancer) even after prophylactic surgery. Nevertheless, the mortality reduction associated with this surgery is substantial. Research demonstrates that women who underwent bilateral prophylactic salpingo-oophorectomy had a nearly 80 percent reduction in risk of dying from ovarian cancer, a 56 percent reduction in risk of dying from breast cancer, and a 77 percent reduction in risk of dying from any cause.

Emerging evidence suggests that the amount of protection that removing the ovaries and fallopian tubes provides against the development of breast and ovarian cancer may be similar for carriers of BRCA1 and BRCA2 mutations, in contrast to earlier studies.

Chemoprevention. Chemoprevention is the use of drugs, vitamins, or other agents to try to reduce the risk of, or delay the recurrence of, cancer. Although two chemopreventive drugs (tamoxifen and raloxi-fene) have been approved by the U.S. Food and Drug Administration (FDA) to reduce the risk of breast cancer in women at increased risk, the role of these drugs in women with harmful BRCA1 or BRCA2 mutations is not yet clear.

Data from three studies suggest that tamoxifen may be able to help lower the risk of breast cancer in BRCA1 and BRCA2 mutation carri-ers, including the risk of cancer in the opposite breast among women previously diagnosed with breast cancer. Studies have not examined the effectiveness of raloxifene in BRCA1 and BRCA2 mutation carriers specifically.

Oral contraceptives (birth control pills) are thought to reduce the risk of ovarian cancer by about 50 percent both in the general popula-tion and in women with harmful BRCA1 or BRCA2 mutations.

What are some of the benefits of genetic testing for breast and ovarian cancer risk?

There can be benefits to genetic testing, regardless of whether a person receives a positive or a negative result.

The potential benefits of a true negative result include a sense of relief regarding the future risk of cancer, learning that one's children are not at risk of inheriting the family's cancer susceptibility, and the possibility that special check-ups, tests, or preventive surgeries may not be needed.

A positive test result may bring relief by resolving uncertainty regarding future cancer risk and may allow people to make informed decisions about their future, including taking steps to reduce their cancer risk. In addition, people who have a positive test result may choose to participate in medical research that could, in the long run, help reduce deaths from hereditary breast and ovarian cancer.

What are some of the possible harms of genetic testing for breast and ovarian cancer risk?

The direct medical harms of genetic testing are minimal, but knowl-edge of test results may have harmful effects on a person's emotions, social relationships, finances, and medical choices.

People who receive a positive test result may feel anxious, depressed, or angry. They may have difficulty making choices about whether to have preventive surgery or about which surgery to have.

People who receive a negative test result may experience "survi-vor guilt," caused by the knowledge that they likely do not have an increased risk of developing a disease that affects one or more loved ones.

Because genetic testing can reveal information about more than one family member, the emotions caused by test results can create tension within families. Test results can also affect personal life choices, such as decisions about career, marriage, and childbearing.

Violations of privacy and of the confidentiality of genetic test results are additional potential risks. However, the federal Health Insurance Portability and Accountability Act and various state laws protect the privacy of a person's genetic information. Moreover, the federal Genetic Information Non-discrimination Act, along with many state laws, prohibits discrimination based on genetic information in relation to health insurance and employment, although it does not cover life insurance, disability insurance, or long-term care insurance.

Finally, there is a small chance that test results may not be accurate, leading people to make decisions based on incorrect information. Although inaccurate results are unlikely, people with these concerns should address them during genetic counselling.

What are the implications of having a harmful **BRCA1** or **BRCA2** mutation for breast and ovarian cancer prognosis and treatment?

A number of studies have investigated possible clinical differences between breast and ovarian cancers that are associated with harmful BRCA1 or BRCA2 mutations and cancers that are not associated with these mutations.

There is some evidence that, over the long term, women who carry these mutations are more likely to develop a second cancer in either the same (ipsilateral) breast or the opposite (contralateral) breast than women who do not carry these mutations. Thus, some women with a harmful BRCA1 or BRCA2 mutation who develop breast cancer in one breast opt for a bilateral mastectomy, even if they would otherwise be candidates for breast-conserving surgery. In fact, because of the increased risk of a second breast cancer among BRCA1 and BRCA2 mutation carriers, some doctors recommend that women with early-onset breast cancer and those whose family history is consistent with a mutation in one of these genes have genetic testing when breast cancer is diagnosed.

Breast cancers in women with a harmful BRCA1 mutation are also more likely to be "triple-negative cancers" (i.e., the breast cancer cells do not have estrogen receptors, progesterone receptors, or large amounts of HER2/neu protein), which generally have poorer prognosis than other breast cancers.

Because the products of the BRCA1 and BRCA2 genes are involved in DNA repair, some investigators have suggested that cancer cells with a harmful mutation in either of these genes may be more sensitive to anticancer agents that act by damaging DNA, such as cisplatin. In preclinical studies, drugs called PARP inhibitors, which block the repair of DNA damage, have been found to arrest the growth of cancer cells that have BRCA1 or BRCA2 mutations. These drugs have also shown some activity in cancer patients who carry BRCA1 or BRCA2 mutations, and researchers are continuing to develop and test these drugs.

What research is currently being done to help individuals with harmful **BRCA1** or **BRCA2** mutations?

Research studies are being conducted to find new and better ways of detecting, treating, and preventing cancer in people who carry mutations in BRCA1 and BRCA2. Additional studies are focused on improving genetic counselling methods and outcomes. Our knowledge in these areas is evolving rapidly.

Do inherited mutations in other genes increase the risk of breast and/or ovarian tumors?

Yes. Although harmful mutations in BRCA1 and BRCA2 are responsible for the disease in nearly half of families with multiple cases of breast cancer and up to 90 percent of families with both breast and ovarian cancer, mutations in a number of other genes have been associated with increased risks of breast and/or ovarian cancers. These other genes include several that are associated with the inherited disorders Cowden syndrome, Peutz-Jeghers syndrome, Li-Fraumeni syndrome, and Fanconi anemia, which increase the risk of many cancer types.

Most mutations in these other genes are associated with smaller increases in breast cancer risk than are seen with mutations in BRCA1 and BRCA2. However, researchers recently reported that inherited mutations in the PALB2 gene are associated with a risk of breast cancer nearly as high as that associated with inherited BRCA1 and BRCA2 mutations. They estimated that 33 percent of women who inherit a harmful mutation in PALB2 will develop breast cancer by age 70 years. The estimated risk of breast cancer associated with a harmful PALB2 mutation is even higher for women who have a family history of breast cancer: 58 percent of those women will develop breast cancer by age 70 years.

PALB2, like BRCA1 and BRCA2, is a tumor suppressor gene. The PALB2 gene produces a protein that interacts with the proteins produced by the BRCA1 and BRCA2 genes to help repair breaks in DNA. Harmful mutations in PALB2 (also known as FANCN) are associated with increased risks of ovarian, pancreatic, and prostate cancers in addition to an increased risk of breast cancer. Mutations in PALB2, when inherited from each parent, can cause a Fanconi anemia subtype, FA-N, that is associated with childhood solid tumors.

Although genetic testing for PALB2 mutations is available, expert groups have not yet developed specific guidelines for who should be tested for, or the management of breast cancer risk in individuals with, PALB2 mutations.

Chapter 8

Does Cancer Run in Your Family?

Does Cancer Run in Your Family?

If you have close relatives with breast and/or ovarian cancer, you may be at higher risk for developing these diseases. Learn whether your family health history puts you at higher risk and whether you might benefit from cancer genetic counselling and testing.

Each year, over 200,000 women in the United States are diagnosed with breast cancer and more than 20,000 are diagnosed with ovarian cancer. About 3% of breast cancers (about 6,000 women per year) and 10% of ovarian cancers (about 2,000 women per year) result from inherited mutations (changes) in the BRCA1 and BRCA2 genes that are passed on in families. Knowing your family health history can help you find out if you could be at higher risk of developing breast and/or ovarian cancer. If so, you can take steps to help lower your risk.

Does Your Family Health History Put You At Risk?

You might be at increased risk of having an inherited mutation in the BRCA1 or BRCA2 genes if your family health history includes one or more of the following:

Text in this chapter is excerpted from "Does Breast or Ovarian Cancer Run in Your Family," Centers for Disease Control and Prevention (CDC), September 29, 2014.

- Several close relatives with either breast or ovarian cancer.

- One or more close relatives with breast cancer at a younger age (before age 50).

- A close relative with cancer of both breasts.

- A close relative who had both breast and ovarian cancer.

- A close male relative with breast cancer.

- Ashkenazi Jewish (Eastern European) ancestry plus one or more close relative with breast or ovarian cancer.

- A close relative with a known BRCA1 or BRCA2 mutation.

All women should collect and record their family health history of breast and ovarian cancer. You can inherit BRCA mutations from your mother or your father, so be sure to include information from both sides of your family. Close relatives include your mother, sister(s), daughter(s), grandmothers, aunt(s), niece(s), and granddaughter(s); and similarly for any male relatives with breast cancer.

You can use the Know: BRCA tool to collect your family health history information, assess your risk for BRCA mutations, and share this information with your doctor. Update your family health history on a regular basis and let your doctor know if more cases of breast or ovarian cancer occur.

What Can You Do If You Are Concerned about Your Risk?

If you are concerned that your family health history means that you might have an inherited mutation in your BRCA1 or BRCA2 genes, the first step is to talk to your doctor about your family health history to learn whether genetic counselling might be right for you. Your doctor may refer you to a genetic counsellor or other qualified health care professional to discuss your family health history and to learn about your options for genetic testing.

The genetic counsellor will ask questions about breast and ovarian cancer in your family that may include:

- Which of your close biological relatives had breast or ovarian cancer?

- What age was each of these relatives when the cancer was diagnosed?

- Did any of these relatives have cancer in both breasts, or have both breast and ovarian cancer?

- Have any of your close male relatives had breast cancer?

- Where did your ancestors come from?

The genetic counsellor can use your family health history information to determine your possible cancer risks and whether you might benefit from BRCA genetic testing to find out if you inherited a mutation in your BRCA1 or BRCA2 gene. However, most breast and ovarian cancer is not caused by these genetic mutations, so most women don't need BRCA genetic testing. Genetic testing is most useful if first performed on someone in your family who has had breast or ovarian cancer. If this relative has a BRCA1 or BRCA2 mutation, then her close relatives can be offered testing for that mutation. If she does not have a BRCA1 or BRCA2 mutation, then her relatives may not need to be tested. The genetic counsellor can discuss the pros and cons of testing and what possible test results could mean for you and your family. It is important to note that genetic testing for BRCA mutations will not find all causes of hereditary breast or ovarian cancer. Health insurance often, but not always, covers the cost of genetic counselling and BRCA testing.

Chapter 9

What Women Need to Know about Smoking and Cancer Risk

Chapter Contents

Section 9.1

Health Effects of Cigarette Smoking

Text in this section is excerpted from "Health Effects of Cigarette Smoking," Centers for Disease Control and Prevention (CDC), February 6, 2014.

Overview

Smoking:

- Harms nearly every organ of the body

- Causes many diseases and reduces the health of smokers in general

Quitting smoking lowers your risk for smoking-related diseases and can add years to your life.

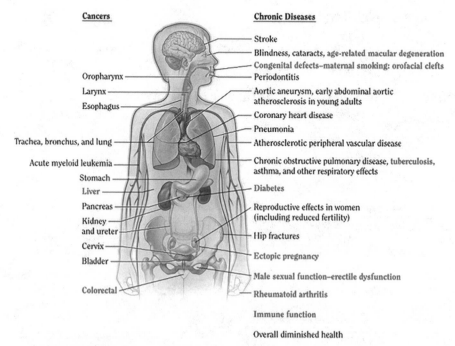

Figure 9.1. Smoking-related disease risks

Smoking and Deaths

- Smoking is the leading preventable cause of death in the United States.

- Cigarette smoking causes more than 480,000 deaths each year in the United States. This is about one in five deaths.

- Smoking causes more deaths each year than all of these combined:

  - *Human immunodeficiency virus* (HIV)

  - Illegal drug use

  - Alcohol use

  - Motor vehicle injuries

  - Firearm-related incidents

- More than 10 times as many U.S. citizens have died prematurely from cigarette smoking than have died in all the wars fought by the United States during its history.

- Smoking causes about 90% (or 9 out of 10) of all lung cancer deaths in men and women. More women die from lung cancer each year than from breast cancer.

- About 80% (or 8 out of 10) of all deaths from chronic obstructive pulmonary disease (COPD) are caused by smoking.

- Cigarette smoking increases risk for death from all causes in men and women.

- The risk of dying from cigarette smoking has increased over the last 50 years in men and women in the United States.

Smoking and Increased Health Risks

Smokers are more likely than non-smokers to develop heart disease, stroke, and lung cancer.

- Smoking is estimated to increase the risk—

  - For coronary heart disease by 2 to 4 times

  - For stroke by 2 to 4 times

  - Of men developing lung cancer by 25 times

  - Of women developing lung cancer by 25.7 times

- Smoking causes diminished overall health, such as self-reported poor health, increased absenteeism from work, and increased health care utilization and cost.

Smoking and Cardiovascular Disease

Smokers are at greater risk for diseases that affect the heart and blood vessels (cardiovascular disease).

- Smoking causes stroke and coronary heart disease—the leading causes of death in the United States.

- Even people who smoke fewer than five cigarettes a day can have early signs of cardiovascular disease.

- Smoking damages blood vessels and can make them thicken and grow narrower. This makes your heart beat faster and your blood pressure go up. Clots can also form.

- A heart attack occurs when a clot blocks the blood flow to your heart. When this happens, your heart cannot get enough oxygen. This damages the heart muscle, and part of the heart muscle can die.

- A stroke occurs when a clot blocks the blood flow to part of your brain or when a blood vessel in or around your brain bursts.

- Blockages caused by smoking can also reduce blood flow to your legs and skin.

Smoking and Respiratory Disease

Smoking can cause lung disease by damaging your airways and the small air sacs (alveoli) found in your lungs.

- Lung diseases caused by smoking include COPD, which includes emphysema and chronic bronchitis.

- Cigarette smoking causes most cases of lung cancer.

- If you have asthma, tobacco smoke can trigger an attack or make an attack worse.

- Smokers are 12 to 13 times more likely to die from COPD than non-smokers.

Smoking and Cancer

Smoking can cause cancer almost anywhere in your body: (See Figure 9.1)

- Bladder
- Blood (acute myeloid leukemia)
- Cervix
- Colon and rectum (colorectal)
- Esophagus
- Kidney and ureter
- Larynx
- Liver
- Oropharynx (includes parts of the throat, tongue, soft palate, and the tonsils)
- Pancreas
- Stomach
- Trachea, bronchus, and lung

If nobody smoked, one of every three cancer deaths in the United States would not happen. Smoking increases the risk of dying from cancer and other diseases in cancer patients and survivors.

Smoking and Other Health Risks

Smoking harms nearly every organ of the body and affects a person's overall health.

- Smoking can make it harder for a woman to become pregnant and can affect her baby's health before and after birth. Smoking increases risks for:
  - Preterm (early) delivery
  - Stillbirth (death of the baby before birth)
  - Low birth weight
  - Sudden infant death syndrome (known as SIDS or crib death)
  - Ectopic pregnancy
  - Orofacial clefts in infants
- Smoking can also affect men's sperm, which can reduce fertility and also increase risks for birth defects and miscarriage (loss of the pregnancy).

- Smoking can affect bone health.

- Women past childbearing years who smoke have lower bone density (weaker bones) than women who never smoked and are at greater risk for broken bones.

- Smoking affects the health of your teeth and gums and can cause tooth loss.

- Smoking can increase your risk for cataracts (clouding of the eye's lens that makes it hard for you to see) and age-related macular degeneration (damage to a small spot near the center of the retina, the part of the eye needed for central vision).

- Smoking is a cause of type 2 diabetes mellitus and can make it harder to control. The risk of developing diabetes is 30–40% higher for active smokers than non-smokers.

- Smoking causes general adverse effects on the body. It can cause inflammation and adverse effects on immune function.

- Smoking is a cause of rheumatoid arthritis.

Quitting and Reduced Risks

- Quitting smoking cuts cardiovascular risks. Just 1 year after quitting smoking, your risk for a heart attack drops sharply.

- Within 2 to 5 years after quitting smoking, your risk for stroke could fall to about the same as a non-smoker's.

- If you quit smoking, your risks for cancers of the mouth, throat, esophagus, and bladder drop by half within 5 years.

- Ten years after you quit smoking, your risk for lung cancer drops by half.

Section 9.2

Smoking and Cancer

Text in this section is excerpted from "Harms of Cigarette Smoking and Health Benefits of Quitting," National Cancer Institute (NCI), December 3, 2014.

Does tobacco smoke contain harmful chemicals?

Yes. Tobacco smoke contains many chemicals that are harmful to both smokers and non-smokers. Breathing even a little tobacco smoke can be harmful.

Of the more than 7,000 chemicals in tobacco smoke, at least 250 are known to be harmful, including hydrogen cyanide, carbon monoxide, and ammonia.

Among the 250 known harmful chemicals in tobacco smoke, at least 69 can cause cancer. These cancer-causing chemicals include the following:

- Acetaldehyde
- Aromatic amines
- Arsenic
- Benzene
- Benzo[α]pyrene
- Beryllium (a toxic metal)
- 1,3–Butadiene (a hazardous gas)
- Cadmium (a toxic metal)
- Chromium (a metallic element)
- Cumene
- Ethylene oxide
- Formaldehyde
- Nickel (a metallic element)

- Polonium-210 (a radioactive chemical element)
- Polycyclic aromatic hydrocarbons (PAHs)
- Tobacco-specific nitrosamines
- Vinyl chloride

What are some of the health problems caused by cigarette smoking?

Smoking has been found to harm nearly every bodily organ and organ system in the body and diminishes a person's overall health.

Smoking is a leading cause of cancer and death from cancer. It causes cancers of the lung, esophagus, larynx, mouth, throat, kidney, bladder, liver, pancreas, stomach, cervix, colon, and rectum, as well as acute myeloid leukemia.

Smoking causes heart disease, stroke, aortic aneurysm (a balloon-like bulge in an artery in the chest), chronic obstructive pulmonary disease (COPD) (chronic bronchitis and emphysema), diabetes, osteoporosis, rheumatoid arthritis, age-related macular degeneration, and cataracts, and worsens asthma symptoms in adults. Smokers are at higher risk of developing pneumonia, tuberculosis, and other airway infections. In addition, smoking causes inflammation and impairs immune function.

Since the 1960s, a smoker's risk of developing lung cancer or COPD has actually increased compared with non-smokers, even though the number of cigarettes consumed per smoker has decreased. There have also been changes in the type of lung cancer smokers develop – a decline in squamous cell carcinomas but a dramatic increase in adenocarcinomas. Both of these effects may be due to changes in the formulation of cigarettes.

Smoking makes it harder for a woman to get pregnant. A pregnant smoker is at higher risk of miscarriage, having an ectopic pregnancy, having her baby born too early and with an abnormally low birth weight, and having her baby born with a cleft lip and/or cleft palate. A woman who smokes during or after pregnancy increases her infant's risk of death from Sudden Infant Death Syndrome (SIDS).

Cigarette smoking and exposure to tobacco smoke cause about 480,000 premature deaths each year in the United States. Of these premature deaths, about 36 percent are from cancer, 39 percent are from heart disease and stroke, and 24 percent are from lung disease.

Smoking is the leading cause of premature, preventable death in this country.

Regardless of their age, smokers can substantially reduce their risk of disease, including cancer, by quitting.

What are the risks of tobacco smoke to non-smokers?

Secondhand smoke (also called environmental tobacco smoke, involuntary smoking, and passive smoking) is the combination of "side stream" smoke (the smoke given off by a burning tobacco product) and "mainstream" smoke (the smoke exhaled by a smoker). The U.S. Environmental Protection Agency, the U.S. National Toxicology Program, the U.S. Surgeon General, and the International Agency for Research on Cancer have classified secondhand smoke as a known human carcinogen (cancer-causing agent). Inhaling secondhand smoke causes lung cancer in non-smoking adults. Approximately 7,300 lung cancer deaths occur each year among adult non-smokers in the United States as a result of exposure to secondhand smoke. The U.S. Surgeon General estimates that living with a smoker increases a non-smoker's chances of developing lung cancer by 20 to 30 percent.

Secondhand smoke causes disease and premature death in non-smoking adults and children. Exposure to secondhand smoke may increase the risk of heart disease by an estimated 25 to 30 percent. In the United States, exposure to secondhand smoke is thought to cause about 34,000 deaths from heart disease each year. Exposure to secondhand smoke also increases the risk of stroke by 20 to 30 percent. Pregnant women exposed to secondhand smoke are at risk of having a baby with low birth weight. Children exposed to secondhand smoke are at an increased risk of SIDS, ear infections, colds, pneumonia, and bronchitis. It can also increase the frequency and severity of asthma symptoms among children who have asthma. Being exposed to secondhand smoke slows the growth of children's lungs and can cause them to cough, wheeze, and feel breathless.

Is smoking addictive?

Yes. Nicotine is a drug that is naturally present in the tobacco plant and is primarily responsible for a person's addiction to tobacco products, including cigarettes. The addiction to cigarettes and other tobacco products that nicotine causes is similar to the addiction produced by using drugs such as heroin and cocaine.

How much nicotine is in cigarettes and cigars?

Cigarettes, cigars, and other tobacco products vary widely in their content of nicotine, cancer-causing substances, and other toxicants. In a cigarette (which contains 0.49 to 0.89 gram of tobacco), the nicotine content can vary between 13.79 and 22.68 milligrams per gram of dry tobacco. In a cigar (which can contain as many as 21.5 grams of tobacco), the nicotine content can vary between 6.3 and 15.6 milligrams per gram of tobacco or 5.9 to 335.2 milligrams per cigar.

The way a person smokes a tobacco product is as important as the nicotine content of the product in determining how much nicotine gets into the body. Nicotine is absorbed into the bloodstream through the lining of the mouth and the lungs and travels to the brain in a matter of seconds. Taking more frequent and deeper puffs of tobacco smoke increases the amount of nicotine absorbed by the body.

Are other tobacco products, such as smokeless tobacco or pipe tobacco, harmful and addictive?

Yes. All forms of tobacco are harmful and addictive. There is no safe tobacco product.

In addition to cigarettes and cigars, other forms of tobacco include smokeless tobacco (also called chewing tobacco, snuff, and snus), pipes, hookahs (waterpipes), bidis, and kreteks.

Pipes: Pipe smoking causes lung cancer and increases the risk of cancers of the mouth, throat, larynx, and esophagus.

Hookahs or waterpipes (other names include argileh, ghelyoon, hubble bubble, shisha, boory, goza, and narghile): A hookah is a device used to smoke tobacco. The smoke passes through a partially filled water bowl before being inhaled by the smoker. Some people think hookah smoking is less harmful and addictive than smoking cigarettes, but research suggests that waterpipe smoke is at least as toxic as cigarette smoke.

Bidis: A bidi is a flavored cigarette made by rolling tobacco in a dried leaf from the tendu tree, which is native to India. Bidi use is associated with heart attacks and cancers of the mouth, throat, larynx, esophagus, and lung.

Kreteks: A kretek is a cigarette made with a mixture of tobacco and cloves. Smoking kreteks is associated with lung cancer and other lung diseases.

What are the immediate benefits of quitting smoking?

The immediate health benefits of quitting smoking are substantial:

- Heart rate and blood pressure, which are abnormally high while smoking, begin to return to normal.

- Within a few hours, the level of carbon monoxide in the blood begins to decline. (Carbon monoxide reduces the blood's ability to carry oxygen.)

- Within a few weeks, people who quit smoking have improved circulation, produce less phlegm, and don't cough or wheeze as often.

- Within several months of quitting, people can expect substantial improvements in lung function.

- Within a few years of quitting, people will have lower risks of cancer, heart disease, and other chronic diseases than if they had continued to smoke.

- In addition, people who quit smoking will have an improved sense of smell, and food will taste better.

What are the long-term benefits of quitting smoking?

Quitting smoking reduces the risk of cancer and many other diseases, such as heart disease and COPD, caused by smoking.

Data from the U.S. National Health Interview Survey show that people who quit smoking, regardless of their age, are less likely to die from smoking-related illness than those who continue to smoke. Smokers who quit before age 40 reduced their chance of dying prematurely from smoking-related diseases by about 90 percent, and those who quit by age 45-54 reduced their chance of dying prematurely by about two-thirds.

People who quit smoking, regardless of their age, have substantial gains in life expectancy compared with those who continue to smoke. Those who quit between the ages of 25 and 34 years lived about 10 years longer; those who quit between ages 35 and 44 lived about 9 years longer; those who quit between ages 45 and 54 lived about 6 years longer; and those who quit between ages 55 and 64 lived about 4 years longer.

Does quitting smoking lower the risk of cancer?

Yes. Quitting smoking reduces the risk of developing and dying from cancer. Although it is never too late to get a benefit from quitting, the benefit is strongest among those who quit at a younger age.

The risk of premature death and the chance of developing cancer from smoking depend on many factors, including the number of years a person smokes, the number of cigarettes he or she smokes per day, the age at which he or she began smoking, and whether or not he or she was already ill at the time of quitting. For people who have already developed cancer, quitting smoking reduces the risk of developing a second cancer.

Should someone already diagnosed with cancer bother to quit smoking?

Yes. Cigarette smoking has a profound adverse impact on health outcomes in cancer patients. For patients with some cancers, quitting smoking at the time of diagnosis may reduce the risk of dying by 30 percent to 40 percent. For those having surgery, chemotherapy, or other treatments, quitting smoking helps improve the body's ability to heal and respond to therapy. It also lowers the risk of pneumonia and respiratory failure. Moreover, quitting smoking may lower the risk of the cancer returning, of dying from the cancer, of a second cancer developing, and of dying from other causes.

Section 9.3

Questions and Answers about Women and Smoking

Text in this section is excerpted from "Smoking and How It Affects Women," Office On Women's Health (OWH), November 21, 2013.

What is the Great American Smokeout?

The Great American Smokeout, sponsored by the American Cancer Society, takes place every year on the third Thursday of November. It encourages smokers to go one day without cigarettes and to make plans to quit smoking for good on the days that follow.

Why is smoking still such an issue?

Smoking is still the single largest preventable cause of disease, disability, and premature death in the United States. Each year, an estimated people die prematurely from smoking or exposure to secondhand smoke and another 8.6 million live with a serious illness caused by smoking.

How does smoking affect women?

About one in six American women is a current smoker. Smoking is directly responsible for 80 percent of lung cancer deaths in American women each year. In fact, lung cancer kills many more women than breast cancer in the United States.

Why shouldn't women smoke during pregnancy?

Smoking during pregnancy increases the risk of pregnancy complications, premature delivery, low birth weight, stillbirth, and sudden infant death syndrome (SIDS). Also, the lungs of babies and children who breathe secondhand smoke don't work as well as the lungs of those who are not exposed to smoke. Quitting smoking is one of the best things you can do for your health and the health of your baby.

Why is it so difficult to quit smoking?

Nicotine, a chemical that is in all tobacco products, is very addictive. More people in the United States are addicted to nicotine than to any other chemical. Because nicotine is so addictive, people can find it hard to quit smoking. They may feel irritable or anxious, have trouble concentrating, and feel hungry when they try to quit.

Most smokers try to quit several times, but many, many succeed. In fact, the number of former U.S. smokers now exceeds the number of current smokers. Smokers can learn from their previous quit attempts and be better prepared to overcome the specific challenges (sometimes called triggers) that make them want to smoke again. With continued encouragement and support, many people finally succeed in quitting for good.

If a woman quits smoking will she see improvements to her health?

Quitting at any time has benefits, no matter how long you've smoked. If a woman quits smoking now:

- 20 minutes after quitting, her heart rate drops.

- 12 hours after quitting, the carbon monoxide level in her blood drops to normal.

- 2 weeks to 3 months after quitting, her heart attack risk begins to drop and her lung function improves.

- 3 weeks after quitting, physical nicotine addiction ends.

- 1 to 9 months after quitting, coughing and shortness of breath decrease.

- 1 year after quitting, her risk for heart attack drops sharply.

What resources are available to help smokers quit?

There are many proven services and treatments that can ease withdrawal symptoms and help you quit. Although many people quit without medication, FDA-approved medications combined with counselling can greatly increase the likelihood of quitting successfully. Combining medication and counselling is more effective than either medication or counselling alone.

Chapter 10

Alcohol and Cancer Risk

Chapter Contents

Section 10.1

Alcohol and Risk of Cancer

This section includes excerpts from "Alcohol and Cancer Risk,"
National Cancer Institute (NCI), June 24, 2013; and text from
"Excessive Alcohol Use and Risks to Women's Health," Centers for
Disease Control and Prevention (CDC), November 19, 2014.

What is alcohol?

Alcohol is the common term for ethanol or ethyl alcohol, a chemical
substance found in beer, wine, and liquor, as well as in some medicines,
mouthwashes, household products, and essential oils (scented liquids
taken from plants). Alcohol is produced by the fermentation of sugars
and starches by yeast.

The main types of alcoholic drinks and their alcohol content are
as follows:

- Beers and hard ciders: 3–7 percent alcohol

- Wines, including sake: 9–15 percent alcohol

- Wines fortified with liquors, such as port: 16–20 percent alcohol

- Liquor, or distilled spirits, such as gin, rum, vodka, and whis-
  key, which are produced by distilling the alcohol from fermented
  grains, fruits, or vegetables: usually 35–40 percent alcohol
  (70–80 proof), but can be higher

According to the National Institute on Alcohol Abuse and Alcoholism, a standard alcoholic drink in the United States contains 14.0
grams (0.6 ounces) of pure alcohol. Generally, this amount of pure
alcohol is found in

- 12 ounces of beer

- 8 ounces of malt liquor

- 5 ounces of wine

- 1.5 ounces or a "shot" of 80-proof liquor

What is the evidence that alcohol drinking is a cause of cancer?

Based on extensive reviews of research studies, there is a strong scientific consensus of an association between alcohol drinking and several types of cancer. In its Report on Carcinogens, the National Toxicology Program of the US Department of Health and Human Services lists consumption of alcoholic beverages as a known human carcinogen. The research evidence indicates that the more alcohol a person drinks—particularly the more alcohol a person drinks regularly over time—the higher his or her risk of developing an alcohol-associated cancer. Based on data from 2009, an estimated 3.5 percent of all cancer deaths in the United States (about 19,500 deaths) were alcohol related.

Clear patterns have emerged between alcohol consumption and the development of the following types of cancer:

Head and neck cancer: Alcohol consumption is a major risk factor for certain head and neck cancers, particularly cancers of the oral cavity (excluding the lips), pharynx (throat), and larynx (voice box). People who consume 50 or more grams of alcohol per day (approximately 3.5 or more drinks per day) have at least a two to three times greater risk of developing these cancers than non-drinkers. Moreover, the risks of these cancers are substantially higher among persons who consume this amount of alcohol and also use tobacco.

Esophageal cancer: Alcohol consumption is a major risk factor for a particular type of esophageal cancer called esophageal squamous cell carcinoma. In addition, people who inherit a deficiency in an enzyme that metabolizes alcohol have been found to have substantially increased risks of alcohol-related esophageal squamous cell carcinoma.

Liver cancer: Alcohol consumption is an independent risk factor for, and a primary cause of, liver cancer (hepatocellular carcinoma). (Chronic infection with *hepatitis B virus* and *hepatitis C virus* are the other major causes of liver cancer.)

Breast cancer: More than 100 epidemiologic studies have looked at the association between alcohol consumption and the risk of breast cancer in women. These studies have consistently found an increased risk of breast cancer associated with increasing alcohol intake. A meta-analysis of 53 of these studies (which included a total of 58,000 women with breast cancer) showed that women who drank more than 45 grams of alcohol per day (approximately three drinks) had 1.5 times the risk of developing breast cancer as non-drinkers (a modestly increased risk). The risk of breast cancer was higher across all levels of alcohol intake: for every 10 grams of alcohol consumed per day (slightly less than one drink), researchers observed a small (7 percent) increase in the risk of breast cancer.

The Million Women Study in the United Kingdom (which included more than 28,000 women with breast cancer) provided a more recent, and slightly higher, estimate of breast cancer risk at low to moderate levels of alcohol consumption: every 10 grams of alcohol consumed per day was associated with a 12 percent increase in the risk of breast cancer.

Colorectal cancer: Alcohol consumption is associated with a modestly increased risk of cancers of the colon and rectum. A meta-analysis of 57 cohort and case-control studies that examined the association between alcohol consumption and colorectal cancer risk showed that people who regularly drank 50 or more grams of alcohol per day (approximately 3.5 drinks) had 1.5 times the risk of developing colorectal cancer as non-drinkers or occasional drinkers. For every 10 grams of alcohol consumed per day, there was a small (7 percent) increase in the risk of colorectal cancer.

Research on alcohol consumption and other cancers:

Numerous studies have examined the association between alcohol consumption and the risk of other cancers, including cancers of the pancreas, ovary, prostate, stomach, uterus, and bladder. For these cancers, either no association with alcohol use has been found or the evidence for an association is inconsistent.

However, for two cancers—renal cell (kidney) cancer and non-Hodgkin lymphoma (NHL)—multiple studies have shown that increased alcohol consumption is associated with a decreased risk of cancer. A meta-analysis of the NHL studies (which included 18,759 people with NHL) found a 15 percent lower risk of NHL among alcohol drinkers compared with non-drinkers. The mechanisms by which alcohol consumption would decrease the risks of either renal cell cancer or NHL are not understood.

How does alcohol increase the risk of cancer?

Researchers have identified multiple ways that alcohol may increase the risk of cancer, including:

- metabolizing (breaking down) ethanol in alcoholic drinks to acetaldehyde, which is a toxic chemical and a probable human carcinogen; acetaldehyde can damage both DNA (the genetic material that makes up genes) and proteins

- generating reactive oxygen species (chemically reactive molecules that contain oxygen), which can damage DNA, proteins, and lipids (fats) through a process called oxidation

- impairing the body's ability to break down and absorb a variety of nutrients that may be associated with cancer risk, including vitamin A; nutrients in the vitamin B complex, such as folate; vitamin C; vitamin D; vitamin E; and carotenoids

- increasing blood levels of estrogen, a sex hormone linked to the risk of breast cancer

Alcoholic beverages may also contain a variety of carcinogenic contaminants that are introduced during fermentation and production, such as nitrosamines, asbestos fibres, phenols, and hydrocarbons.

How does the combination of alcohol and tobacco affect cancer risk?

Epidemiologic research shows that people who use both alcohol and tobacco have much greater risks of developing cancers of the oral cavity, pharynx (throat), larynx, and esophagus than people who use either alcohol or tobacco alone. In fact, for oral and pharyngeal cancers, the risks associated with using both alcohol and tobacco are multiplicative; that is, they are greater than would be expected from adding the individual risks associated with alcohol and tobacco together.

Can a person's genes affect their risk of alcohol-related cancers?

A person's risk of alcohol-related cancers is influenced by their genes, specifically the genes that encode enzymes involved in metabolizing (breaking down) alcohol.

For example, one way the body metabolizes alcohol is through the activity of an enzyme called alcohol dehydrogenase, or ADH. Many individuals of Chinese, Korean, and especially Japanese descent carry a version of the gene for ADH that codes for a "superactive" form of the enzyme. This superactive ADH enzyme speeds the conversion of alcohol (ethanol) to toxic acetaldehyde. As a result, when people who have the superactive enzyme drink alcohol, acetaldehyde builds up. Among people of Japanese descent, those who have this superactive

ADH have a higher risk of pancreatic cancer than those with the more common form of ADH.

Another enzyme, called aldehyde dehydrogenase 2 (ALDH2), metabolizes toxic acetaldehyde to non-toxic substances. Some people, particularly those of East Asian descent, carry a variant of the gene for ALDH2 that codes for a defective form of the enzyme. In people who have the defective enzyme, acetaldehyde builds up when they drink alcohol. The accumulation of acetaldehyde has such unpleasant effects (including facial flushing and heart palpitations) that most people who have inherited the ALDH2 variant are unable to consume large amounts of alcohol. Therefore, most people with the defective form of ALDH2 have a low risk of developing alcohol-related cancers.

However, some individuals with the defective form of ALDH2 can become tolerant to the unpleasant effects of acetaldehyde and consume large amounts of alcohol. Epidemiologic studies have shown that such individuals have a higher risk of alcohol-related esophageal cancer, as well as of head and neck cancers, than individuals with the fully active enzyme who drink comparable amounts of alcohol. These increased risks are seen only among people who carry the ALDH2 variant and drink alcohol—they are not observed in people who carry the variant but do not drink alcohol.

Can drinking red wine help prevent cancer?

Researchers conducting studies using purified proteins, human cells, and laboratory animals have found that certain substances in red wine, such as resveratrol, have anticancer properties. Grapes, raspberries, peanuts, and some other plants also contain resveratrol. However, clinical trials in humans have not provided evidence that resveratrol is effective in preventing or treating cancer. Few epidemiologic studies have looked specifically at the association between red wine consumption and cancer risk in humans.

What happens to cancer risk after a person stops drinking alcohol?

Most of the studies that have examined whether cancer risk declines after a person stops drinking alcohol have focused on head and neck cancers and on esophageal cancer. In general, these studies have found that stopping alcohol consumption is not associated with immediate reductions in cancer risk; instead, it may take years for the risks of cancer to return to those of never drinkers.

For example, a pooled analysis of 13 case-control studies of cancer of the oral cavity and pharynx combined found that alcohol-associated cancer risk did not begin to decrease until at least 10 years after stopping alcohol drinking. Even 16 years after they stopped drinking alcohol, the risk of cancer was still higher for ex-drinkers than for never drinkers.

In several studies, the risk of esophageal cancer was also found to decrease slowly with increasing time since stopping alcohol drinking. A pooled analysis of five case–control studies found that the risk of esophageal cancer did not approach that of never drinkers for at least 15 years after stopping alcohol drinking.

Is it safe for someone to drink alcohol while undergoing cancer chemotherapy?

As with most questions related to a specific individual's cancer treatment, it is best for a patient to check with their health care team about whether or not it is safe to drink alcohol during or immediately following chemotherapy treatment. The doctors and nurses administering the treatment will be able to give specific advice about whether drinking alcohol is safe with particular chemotherapy drugs and/or other medications prescribed along with chemotherapy.

Excessive Alcohol Use and Risks to Women's Health

Although men are more likely to drink alcohol and drink in larger amounts, gender differences in body structure and chemistry cause women to absorb more alcohol, and take longer to break it down and remove it from their bodies (i.e., to metabolize it). In other words, upon drinking equal amounts, women have higher alcohol levels in their blood than men, and the immediate effects occur more quickly and last longer. These differences also make women more vulnerable to alcohol's long-term effects on their health.

Reproductive Health

- National surveys show that about 1 in 2 women of child-bearing age (i.e., aged 18–44 years) use alcohol, and 15% of women who drink alcohol in this age group binge drink.

- About 7.6% of pregnant women used alcohol.

- Excessive drinking may disrupt menstrual cycling and increase the risk of infertility, miscarriage, stillbirth, and premature delivery.

- Women who binge drink are more likely to have unprotected sex and multiple sex partners. These activities increase the risks of unintended pregnancy and sexually transmitted diseases.

Alcohol and Pregnancy

- Women who drink alcohol while pregnant increase their risk of having a baby with Fetal Alcohol Spectrum Disorders (FASD). The most severe form is Fetal Alcohol Syndrome (FAS), which causes mental retardation and birth defects.

- FASD are completely preventable if a woman does not drink while pregnant or while she may become pregnant.

- Studies have shown that about 1 of 20 pregnant women drank excessively before finding out they were pregnant. No amount of alcohol is safe to drink during pregnancy. For women who drink during pregnancy, stopping as soon as possible may lower the risk of having a child with physical, mental, or emotional problems.

- Research suggests that women who drink alcohol while pregnant are more likely to have a baby die from Sudden Infant Death Syndrome (SIDS). This risk substantially increases if a woman binge drinks during her first trimester of pregnancy.

- The risk of miscarriage is also increased if a woman drinks excessively during her first trimester of pregnancy.

Other Health Concerns

- **Liver Disease:** The risk of cirrhosis and other alcohol-related liver diseases is higher for women than for men.

- **Impact on the Brain:** Excessive drinking may result in memory loss and shrinkage of the brain. Research suggests that women are more vulnerable than men to the brain damaging effects of excessive alcohol use, and the damage tends to appear with shorter periods of excessive drinking for women than for men.

- **Impact on the Heart:** Studies have shown that women who drink excessively are at increased risk for damage to the heart muscle than men even for women drinking at lower levels.

- **Cancer:** Alcohol consumption increases the risk of cancer of the mouth, throat, esophagus, liver, colon, and breast among women. The risk of breast cancer increases as alcohol use increases.

• **Sexual Assault:** Binge drinking is a risk factor for sexual assault, especially among young women in college settings. Each year, about 1 in 20 college women are sexually assaulted. Research suggests that there is an increase in the risk of rape or sexual assault when both the attacker and victim have used alcohol prior to the attack.

Section 10.2

Women and Alcohol Use

Text in this section is excerpted from "Women and Alcohol," National Institute on Alcohol Abuse and Alcoholism (NIAAA), August 2013.

Women and Alcohol Use

Women's drinking patterns are different from men's—especially when it comes to the type of beverage, amounts, and frequency. Women's bodies also react differently to alcohol than men's bodies. As a result, women face particular health risks and realities.

Women should be aware of the health risks associated with drinking alcohol, especially because most women drink at least occasionally, and many women drink a lot.

Why Do Women Face Higher Risk?

Research shows that women start to have alcohol-related problems at lower drinking levels than men do. One reason is that, on average, women weigh less than men. In addition, alcohol resides predominantly in body water, and pound for pound, women have less water in their bodies than men do. So after a man and woman of the same weight drink the same amount of alcohol, the woman's blood alcohol concentration will tend to be higher, putting her at greater risk for harm. Other biological differences, including hormones, may contribute as well.

What Are the Health Risks?

Liver Damage: Women who drink are more likely to develop alcoholic hepatitis (liver inflammation) than men who drink the same amount of alcohol. Alcoholic hepatitis can lead to cirrhosis.

Heart Disease: Chronic heavy drinking is a leading cause of heart disease. Among heavy drinkers, women are more susceptible to alcohol-related heart disease than men, even though women drink less alcohol over a lifetime than men.

Breast Cancer: There is an association between drinking alcohol and developing breast cancer. Women who consume about one drink per day have a 10 percent higher chance of developing breast cancer than women who do not drink at all. That risk rises another 10 percent for every extra drink they have per day.

Pregnancy: Any drinking during pregnancy is risky. A pregnant woman who drinks heavily puts her fetus at risk for learning and behavioral problems and abnormal facial features. Even moderate drinking during pregnancy can cause problems. Drinking during pregnancy also may increase the risk for preterm labor.

Some women should never drink at all, including:

- Anyone under age 21

- Anyone who takes medications that can interact negatively with alcohol

- Anyone who is pregnant or trying to conceive

How Much Is Too Much?

A standard drink is roughly 14 grams of pure alcohol, which is found in:

- 12 ounces of beer
- 5 ounces of wine
- 1.5 ounces of distilled spirits

The USDA defines moderate drinking as:

- Up to 1 drink per day for women
- Up to 2 drinks per day for men

Selected consumption statistics for women and men: U.S. adults 18 years of age and older

Women Men

% who had at least 1 drink in the past year 60.5 70.4

% who had at least 1 drink in their lifetime, but not in the past year 14.1 14.5

% who had at least 1 drink in their lifetime 74.6 84.9

% total lifetime abstainers (not even 1 drink) 25.2 14.6

% of past-year drinkers, by usual number of drinks consumed

per drinking day:

1 48.2 28.7

2 29.9 29.0

3+ 21.9 42.3

% of past-year drinkers who drank 4+/5+ drinks on an occasion:

Never in past year 71.2 56.9

Ever in past year 28.8 43.1

1 to 11 times in past year (<monthly) 14.2 15.3

12+ times in past year (monthly or more often) 14.6 27.8

% who drank 12+ drinks over the course of the past year 43.8 60.2

% who drank 12+ drinks over the course of some year, but not the past year 4.4 6.9

% who never drank 12+ drinks over the course of any year 34.9 22.2

% of women who had a past-year pregnancy by drinking status:

Did not drink at all in the past year 41.0

Drank during the past year, but not at all during pregnancy 49.3

Drank but in reduced quantities during pregnancy 8.1

Drank and did not reduce consumption during pregnancy 1.5

At Risk

NIAAA also defines how much drinking may put people at risk for developing alcohol dependence.

Low-risk drinking limits are:

Women: No more than 7 drinks per week and no more than 3 drinks on any single day

Men: No more than 14 drinks per week and no more than 4 drinks on any single day

To stay low risk, you must keep within both the single-day and weekly limits.

Low risk does not mean no risk. Even within these limits, you can have problems if you drink too quickly or have other health issues. Drinking slowly, and making sure you eat enough while drinking, can help minimize alcohol's effects.

Chapter 11

Facts about Human Papillomavirus (HPV) and Cancer Risk

Chapter Contents

Section 11.1

HPV Facts

This section includes excerpts from "HPV and Cancer," National Cancer Institute (NCI), February 19, 2015; and text from "Genital HPV Infection - Fact Sheet," Centers of Disease Control and Prevention (CDC), February 23, 2015.

What are **human papillomaviruses** *(HPVs)?*

Human papillomaviruses (HPVs) are a group of more than 200 related viruses. More than 40 HPV types can be easily spread through direct sexual contact, from the skin and mucous membranes of infected people to the skin and mucous membranes of their partners. They can be spread by vaginal, anal, and oral sex. Other HPV types are responsible for non-genital warts, which are not sexually transmitted.

Sexually transmitted HPV types fall into two categories:

- Low-risk HPVs, which do not cause cancer but can cause skin warts (technically known as condylomata acuminata) on or around the genitals, anus, mouth, or throat. For example, HPV types 6 and 11 cause 90 percent of all genital warts. HPV types 6 and 11 also cause recurrent respiratory papillomatosis, a less common disease in which benign tumors grow in the air passages leading from the nose and mouth into the lungs.

- High-risk HPVs, which can cause cancer. About a dozen high-risk HPV types have been identified. Two of these, HPV types 16 and 18, are responsible for most HPV-caused cancers.

HPV infections are the most common sexually transmitted infections in the United States. About 14 million new genital HPV infections occur each year. In fact, the Centers for Disease Control and Prevention (CDC) estimates that more than 90 percent and 80 percent, respectively, of sexually active men and women will be infected with at least one type of HPV at some point in their lives. Around one-half of these infections are with a high-risk HPV type.

Most high-risk HPV infections occur without any symptoms, go away within 1 to 2 years, and do not cause cancer. Some HPV infections, however, can persist for many years. Persistent infections with high-risk HPV types can lead to cell changes that, if untreated, may progress to cancer.

Which cancers are caused by HPV?

High-risk HPVs cause several types of cancer.

Cervical cancer: Virtually all cases of cervical cancer are caused by HPV, and just two HPV types, 16 and 18, are responsible for about 70 percent of all cases.

Anal cancer: About 95 percent of anal cancers are caused by HPV. Most of these are caused by HPV type 16.

Oropharyngeal cancers (cancers of the middle part of the throat, including the soft palate, the base of the tongue, and the tonsils): About 70 percent of oropharyngeal cancers are caused by HPV. In the United States, more than half of cancers diagnosed in the oropharynx are linked to HPV type 16.

Rarer cancers: HPV causes about 65 percent of vaginal cancers, 50 percent of vulvar cancers, and 35 percent of penile cancers. Most of these are caused by HPV type 16.

High-risk HPV types cause approximately 5 percent of all cancers worldwide. In the United States, high-risk HPV types cause approximately 3 percent of all cancer cases among women and 2 percent of all cancer cases among men.

Who gets HPV infections?

Anyone who has ever been sexually active (that is, engaged in skin-to-skin sexual conduct, including vaginal, anal, or oral sex) can get HPV. HPV is easily passed between partners through sexual contact. HPV infections are more likely in those who have many sex partners or have sex with someone who has had many partners. Because the infection is so common, most people get HPV infections shortly after becoming sexually active for the first time. A person who has had only one partner can get HPV.

Someone can have an HPV infection even if they have no symptoms and their only sexual contact with an HPV-infected person happened many years ago.

Can HPV infections be prevented?

People who are not sexually active almost never develop genital HPV infections. In addition, HPV vaccination before sexual activity can reduce the risk of infection by the HPV types targeted by the vaccine.

The Food and Drug Administration (FDA) has approved three vaccines to prevent HPV infection: Gardasil®, Gardasil® 9, and Cervarix®. These vaccines provide strong protection against new HPV infections, but they are not effective at treating established HPV infections or disease caused by HPV.

Correct and consistent condom use is associated with reduced HPV transmission between sexual partners, but less frequent condom use is not. However, because areas not covered by a condom can be infected by the virus, condoms are unlikely to provide complete protection against the infection.

Can HPV infections be detected?

HPV infections can be detected by testing a sample of cells to see if they contain viral DNA or RNA.

Several HPV tests are currently approved by the FDA for three cervical screening indications: for follow-up testing of women who seem to have abnormal Pap test results, for cervical cancer screening in combination with a Pap test among women over age 30, and for use alone as a first-line primary cervical cancer screening test for women ages 25 and older.

The most common HPV test detects DNA from several high-risk HPV types in a group, but it cannot identify the specific type(s) that are present. Other tests do tell in addition whether there is DNA or RNA from HPV types 16 and 18, the two types that cause most HPV-associated cancers. These tests can detect HPV infections before abnormal cell changes are evident, and before any treatment for cell changes is needed.

There are no FDA-approved tests to detect HPV infections in men. There are also no currently recommended screening methods similar to a Pap test for detecting cell changes caused by HPV infection in anal, vulvar, vaginal, penile, or oropharyngeal tissues. However, this is an area of ongoing research.

What are treatment options for HPV-infected individuals?

There is currently no medical treatment for persistent HPV infections that are not associated with abnormal cell changes. However, the genital warts, benign respiratory tract tumors, precancerous changes at the cervix, and cancers resulting from HPV infections can be treated.

Methods commonly used to treat precancerous cervical changes include cryosurgery (freezing that destroys tissue), LEEP (loop electrosurgical excision procedure, or the removal of cervical tissue using a hot wire loop), surgical conization (surgery with a scalpel, a laser, or both to remove a cone-shaped piece of tissue from the cervix and cervical canal), and laser vaporization conization (use of a laser to destroy cervical tissue).

Treatments for other types of benign respiratory tract tumors and precancerous changes caused by HPV (vaginal, vulvar, penile, and anal lesions) and genital warts include topical chemicals or drugs, excisional surgery, cryosurgery, electrosurgery, and laser surgery. Treatment approaches are being tested in clinical trials, including a randomized controlled trial that will determine whether treating anal precancerous lesions will reduce the risk of anal cancer in people who are infected with HIV.

HPV-infected individuals who develop cancer generally receive the same treatment as patients whose tumors do not harbor HPV infections, according to the type and stage of their tumors. However, people who are diagnosed with HPV-positive oropharyngeal cancer may be treated differently than people with oropharyngeal cancers that are HPV-negative. Recent research has shown that patients with HPV-positive oropharyngeal tumors have a better prognosis and may do just as well on less intense treatment. Ongoing clinical trials are investigating this question.

How does high-risk HPV cause cancer?

HPV infects epithelial cells. These cells, which are organized in layers, cover the inside and outside surfaces of the body, including the skin, the throat, the genital tract, and the anus.

Once HPV enters an epithelial cell, the virus begins to make the proteins it encodes. Two of the proteins made by high-risk HPVs (E6 and E7) interfere with cell functions that normally prevent excessive growth, helping the cell to grow in an uncontrolled manner and to avoid cell death.

Many times these infected cells are recognized by the immune system and eliminated. Sometimes, however, these infected cells are not destroyed, and a persistent infection results. As the persistently infected cells continue to grow, they may develop mutations in cellular genes that promote even more abnormal cell growth, leading to the formation of an area of precancerous cells and, ultimately, a cancerous tumor.

Other factors may increase the risk that an infection with a high-risk HPV type will persist and possibly develop into cancer. These include:

- Smoking or chewing tobacco (for increased risk of oropharyngeal cancer)

- Having a weakened immune system

- Having many children (for increased risk of cervical cancer)

- Long-term oral contraceptive use (for increased risk of cervical cancer)

- Poor oral hygiene (for increased risk of oropharyngeal cancer)

- Chronic inflammation

Researchers believe that it can take between 10 and 30 years from the time of an initial HPV infection until a tumor forms. However, even when severely abnormal cells are seen on the cervix (a condition called cervical intraepithelial neoplasia 3, or CIN3), these do not always lead to cancer. The percentage of CIN3 lesions that progress to invasive cervical cancer has been estimated to be 50 percent or less.

How can I avoid HPV and the health problems it can cause?

You can do several things to lower your chances of getting HPV.

Get vaccinated. HPV vaccines are safe and effective. They can protect individuals against diseases (including cancers) caused by HPV when given in the recommended age groups (see "Who should get vaccinated?" below). HPV vaccines are given in three shots over six months; it is important to get all three doses.

Get screened for cervical cancer. Routine screening for women aged 21 to 65 years old can prevent cervical cancer.

If you are sexually active:

- Use latex condoms the right way every time you have sex. This can lower your chances of getting HPV. But HPV can infect areas that are not covered by a condom – so condoms may not give full protection against getting HPV;

- Be in a mutually monogamous relationship – or have sex only with someone who only has sex with you.

Who should get vaccinated?

All boys and girls ages 11 or 12 years should get vaccinated.

Catch-up vaccines are recommended for males through age 21 and for females through age 26, if they did not get vaccinated when they were younger.

The vaccine is also recommended for gay and bisexual men (or any man who has sex with a man) through age 26. It is also recommended for men and women with compromised immune systems (including people living with HIV/AIDS) through age 26, if they did not get fully vaccinated when they were younger.

How do I know if I have HPV?

There is no test to find out a person's "HPV status." Also, there is no approved HPV test to find HPV in the mouth or throat.

There are HPV tests that can be used to screen for cervical cancer. These tests are recommended for screening only in women aged 30 years and older. They are not recommended to screen men, adolescents, or women under the age of 30 years.

Most people with HPV do not know they are infected and never develop symptoms or health problems from it. Some people find out they have HPV when they get genital warts. Women may find out they have HPV when they get an abnormal Pap test result (during cervical cancer screening). Others may only find out once they've developed more serious problems from HPV, such as cancers.

How common is HPV and the health problems caused by HPV?

HPV (the virus): About 79 million Americans are currently infected with HPV. About 14 million people become newly infected each year. HPV is so common that most sexually-active men and women will get at least one type of HPV at some point in their lives.

Health problems related to HPV include genital warts and cervical cancer.

Genital warts: About 360,000 people in the United States get genital warts each year.

Cervical cancer: More than 11,000 women in the United States get cervical cancer each year.

There are other conditions and cancers caused by HPV that occur in persons living in the United States.

I'm pregnant. Will having HPV affect my pregnancy?

If you are pregnant and have HPV, you can get genital warts or develop abnormal cell changes on your cervix. Abnormal cell changes can be found with routine cervical cancer screening. You should get routine cervical cancer screening even when you are pregnant.

Can I be treated for HPV or health problems caused by HPV?

There is no treatment for the virus itself. However, there are treatments for the health problems that HPV can cause:

- Genital warts can be treated by you or your physician. If left untreated, genital warts may go away, stay the same, or grow in size or number.

- Cervical precancer can be treated. Women who get routine Pap tests and follow up as needed can identify problems before cancer develops. Prevention is always better than treatment.

- Other HPV-related cancers are also more treatable when diagnosed and treated early.

How can people learn more about HPV?

The following federal agency can provide more information about HPV:

Organization:
Centers for Disease Control and Prevention

Address:
1600 Clifton Road
Atlanta, GA 30333
Telephone:
1–800–CDC–INFO (1–800–232–4636)
8:00 a.m. to 8:00 p.m. (ET), Monday to Friday

TTY:
1–888–232–6348

Website:
http://www.cdc.gov/std
http://www.cdc.gov/hpv/
E-mail:cdcinfo@cdc.gov

Section 11.2

HPV Prevalence in US Women

Text in this section is excerpted from "HPV Vaccine Information For Young Women," Centers for Disease Control and Prevention(CDC), March 26, 2015.

HPV Prevalence in US Women

Three vaccines are available to prevent the *human papillomavirus* (HPV) types that cause most cervical cancers as well as some cancers of the anus, vulva (area around the opening of the vagina), vagina, and oropharynx (back of throat including base of tongue and tonsils). Two of these vaccines also prevent HPV types that cause most genital warts. HPV vaccines are given in 3 shots over 6 months.

Why is the HPV vaccine important?

Genital HPV is a common virus that is passed from one person to another through direct skin-to-skin contact during sexual activity. Most sexually active people will get HPV at some time in their lives, though most will never even know it. HPV infection is most common in people in their late teens and early 20s. There are about 40 types of HPV that can infect the genital areas of men and women. Most HPV types cause no symptoms and go away on their own. But some types can cause cervical cancer in women and other less common cancers — like cancers of the anus, penis, vagina, and vulva and oropharynx. Other types of HPV can cause warts in the genital areas of men and women, called genital warts. Genital warts are not life-threatening. But they can cause emotional stress and their treatment can be very uncomfortable. Every year, about 12,000 women are diagnosed with cervical cancer and 4,000 women die from this disease in the U.S. About 1% of sexually active adults in the U.S. have visible genital warts at any point in time.

Which girls/women should receive HPV vaccination?

HPV vaccination is recommended for 11 and 12 year-old girls. It is also recommended for girls and women age 13 through 26 years of age who have not yet been vaccinated or completed the vaccine series; HPV vaccine can also be given to girls beginning at age 9 years.

Will sexually active females benefit from the vaccine?

Ideally females should get the vaccine before they become sexually active and exposed to HPV. Females who are sexually active may also benefit from vaccination, but they may get less benefit. This is because they may have already been exposed to one or more of the HPV types targeted by the vaccines. However, few sexually active young women are infected with all HPV types prevented by the vaccines, so most young women could still get protection by getting vaccinated.

Can pregnant women get the vaccine?

The vaccines are not recommended for pregnant women. Studies show that HPV vaccines do not cause problems for babies born to women who were vaccinated while pregnant, but more research is still needed. A pregnant woman should not get any doses of either HPV vaccine until her pregnancy is completed.

Getting the HPV vaccine when pregnant is not a reason to consider ending a pregnancy. If a woman realizes that she got one or more shots of an HPV vaccine while pregnant, she should do two things:

- Wait until after her pregnancy to finish the remaining HPV vaccine doses.

- Call the pregnancy registry [877-888-4231 for Gardasil, 800-986-8999 for Gardasil 9, or 888-825-5249 for Cervarix].

Should girls and women be screened for cervical cancer before getting vaccinated?

Girls and women do not need to get an HPV test or Pap test to find out if they should get the vaccine. However it is important that women continue to be screened for cervical cancer, even after getting all 3 shots of either HPV vaccine. This is because neither vaccine protects against ALL types of cervical cancer.

How effective are the HPV vaccines?

All HPV vaccines target the HPV types that most commonly cause cervical cancer and can cause some cancers of the vulva, vagina, anus, and oropharynx. Two of the vaccines also protect against the HPV types that cause most genital warts. HPV vaccines are highly effective in preventing the targeted HPV types, as well as the most common health problems caused by them.

The vaccines are less effective in preventing HPV-related disease in young women who have already been exposed to one or more HPV types. That is because the vaccines prevent HPV before a person is exposed to it. HPV vaccines do not treat existing HPV infections or HPV-associated diseases.

How long does vaccine protection last?

Research suggests that vaccine protection is long-lasting. Current studies have followed vaccinated individuals for ten years, and show that there is no evidence of weakened protection over time.

What does the vaccine not protect against?

The vaccines do not protect against all HPV types— so they will not prevent all cases of cervical cancer. Since some cervical cancers will not be prevented by the vaccines, it will be important for women to continue getting screened for cervical cancer. Also, the vaccines do not prevent other sexually transmitted infections (STIs). So it will still be important for sexually active persons to lower their risk for other STIs.

Will girls and women be protected against HPV and related diseases, even if they don't get all 3 doses?

It is not yet known how much protection girls and women get from receiving only one or two doses of an HPV vaccine. So it is important that girls and women get all 3 doses.

How safe are the HPV vaccines?

All three HPV vaccines have been licensed by the Food and Drug Administration (FDA). The CDC has approved these vaccines as safe and effective. The vaccines were studied in thousands of people around the world, and these studies showed no serious safety concerns. Side effects reported in these studies were mild, including pain where the shot was given, fever, dizziness, and nausea. Vaccine safety continues to be monitored by CDC and the FDA. More than 60 million doses of HPV vaccine have been distributed in the United States as of March 2014.

Fainting, which can occur after any medical procedure, has also been noted after HPV vaccination. Fainting after any vaccination is more common in adolescents. Because fainting can cause falls and injuries, adolescents and adults should be seated or lying down during HPV vaccination. Sitting or lying down for about 15 minutes after a vaccination can help prevent fainting and injuries.

Why HPV vaccination is only recommended for women through age 26?

HPV vaccination is not currently recommended for women over age 26 years. Clinical trials showed that, overall, HPV vaccination offered women limited or no protection against HPV-related diseases. For women over age 26 years, the best way to prevent cervical cancer is to get routine cervical cancer screening, as recommended.

Is HPV vaccine covered by insurance plans?

Health insurance plans cover the cost of HPV vaccines. If you don't have insurance, the Vaccines for Children (VFC) program may be able to help.

How can I get help paying for HPV vaccine?

The Vaccines for Children (VFC) program helps families of eligible children who might not otherwise have access to vaccines. The program provides vaccines at no cost to doctors who serve eligible children. Children younger than 19 years of age are eligible for VFC vaccines if they are Medicaid-eligible, American Indian, or Alaska Native or have no health insurance. "Underinsured" children who have health insurance that does not cover vaccination can receive VFC vaccines through Federally Qualified Health Centers or Rural Health Centers. Parents of uninsured or underinsured children who receive vaccines at no cost through the VFC Program should check with their healthcare providers about possible administration fees that might apply. These fees help providers cover the costs that result from important services like storing the vaccines and paying staff members to give vaccines to patients. However, VFC vaccines cannot be denied to an eligible child if a family can't afford the fee.

What vaccinated girls/women need to know: will girls/women who have been vaccinated still need cervical cancer screening?

Yes, vaccinated women will still need regular cervical cancer screening because the vaccines protect against most but not all HPV types that cause cervical cancer. Also, women who got the vaccine after becoming sexually active may not get the full benefit of the vaccine if they had already been exposed to HPV.

Are there other ways to prevent cervical cancer?

Regular cervical cancer screening (Pap and HPV tests) and follow-up can prevent most cases of cervical cancer. The Pap test can detect cell changes in the cervix before they turn into cancer. The HPV test looks for the virus that can cause these cell changes. Screening can detect most, but not all, cervical cancers at an early, treatable stage. Most women diagnosed with cervical cancer in the U.S. have either never been screened, or have not been screened in the last 5 years.

Are there other ways to prevent HPV?

For those who are sexually active, condoms may lower the chances of getting HPV, if used with every sex act, from start to finish. Condoms may also lower the risk of developing HPV-related diseases (genital warts and cervical cancer). But HPV can infect areas that are not covered by a condom—so condoms may not fully protect against HPV.

People can also lower their chances of getting HPV by being in a faithful relationship with one partner; limiting their number of sex partners; and choosing a partner who has had no or few prior sex partners. But even people with only one lifetime sex partner can get HPV. And it may not be possible to determine if a partner who has been sexually active in the past is currently infected. That's why the only sure way to prevent HPV is to avoid all sexual activity.

Section 11.3

Questions and Answers about the HPV Vaccine

Text in this section is excerpted from "HPV (*human papillomavirus*),"
Food and Drug Administration (FDA), March 13, 2015.

Questions and Answers about the HPV Vaccine

HPV (*human papillomavirus*) is a sexually transmitted virus. It is passed on through genital contact (such as vaginal and anal sex). It is also passed on by skin-to-skin contact. At least 50% of people who have had sex will have HPV at some time in their lives. HPV is not a new virus. But many people don't **know about it. Most people don't have any signs. HPV may go away on its own** without causing any health problems.

Who can get HPV?

Anyone who has ever had genital contact with another person may have HPV. Both men and women may get it and pass it on without knowing it. Since there might not be any signs, a person may have HPV even if years have passed since he or she had sex.

You are more likely to get HPV if you have:

• sex at an early age,

• many sex partners, or

• a sex partner who has had many partners.

If there are no signs, why do I need to worry about HPV?

There are over 100 different kinds of HPV and not all of them cause health problems. Some kinds of HPV may cause problems like genital warts. Some kinds of HPV can also cause cancer of the cervix, vagina, vulva, or anus. Most of these problems are caused by types 6, 11, 16, or 18.

Is there a test for HPV?

Yes. It tests for the kinds of HPV that may lead to cervical cancer. The FDA approved the HPV test to be used for women over 30 years old. It may find HPV even before there are changes to the cervix. Women who have the HPV test still need to get the Pap test.

Can I prevent HPV?

FDA has approved vaccines that prevent certain diseases, including cervical cancer, caused by some types of HPV. Ask your doctor if you should get the HPV Vaccine.

What else can I do to lower my chances of getting HPV?

- You can choose not to have sex (abstinence).

- If you have sex, you can limit the number of partners you have.

- Choose a partner who has had no or few sex partners. The fewer partners your partner has had the less likely he or she is to have HPV.

- It is not known how much condoms protect against HPV. Areas not covered by a condom can be exposed to the virus.

Is there a cure for HPV?

There is no cure for the virus (HPV) itself. There are treatments for the health problems that HPV can cause, such as genital warts, cervical changes, and cervical cancer.

What should I know about genital warts?

There are many treatment choices for genital warts. But even after the warts are treated, the virus might still be there and may be passed on to others. If genital warts are not treated they may go away, stay the same, or increase in size or number, but they will not turn into cancer.

What should I know about cervical cancer?

All women should get regular Pap tests. The Pap test looks for cell changes caused by HPV. The test finds cell changes early – so the cervix can be treated before the cells turn into cancer. This test can also find cancer in its early stages so it can be treated before it becomes too serious. It is rare to die from cervical cancer if the disease is caught early.

What should I know about vaginal or vulvar cancer?

Vaginal cancer is cancer of the vagina (birth canal). Vulvar cancer is cancer of the clitoris, vaginal lips, and opening to the vagina. Both of these kinds of cancer are very rare. Not all vaginal or vulvar cancer is caused by HPV.

What should I know about anal cancer?

Anal cancer is cancer that forms in tissues of the anus. The anus is the opening of the rectum (last part of the large intestine) to the outside of the body.

Chapter 12

Cancer Risks Associated with Hormonal Medications

What about hormones?

Symptoms such as hot flashes might result from the changing hormone levels during the menopause transition. After a woman's last menstrual period, when her ovaries make much less estrogen and progesterone, some symptoms of menopause might disappear, but others may continue or get worse.

To help relieve these symptoms, some women use hormones. This is called menopausal hormone therapy (MHT). This approach used to be called hormone replacement therapy or HRT. MHT is a more current, umbrella term that describes several different hormone combinations available in a variety of forms and doses.

How would I use menopausal hormone therapy?

Estrogen is a hormone used to relieve the symptoms of menopause. A woman whose uterus has been removed can use estrogen only (E). But a woman who still has a uterus must add progesterone or a progestin (synthetic progesterone) along with the estrogen (E+P). This combination lowers the chance of an unwanted thickening of the lining

Text in this chapter is excerpted from "Hormones and Menopause," National Institute of Aging (NIA), July 20, 2015.

of the uterus and reduces the risk of cancer of the uterus, an uncommon, but possible result of using estrogen alone

Estrogen comes in many forms. A woman could use a skin patch, vaginal tablet, or cream; take a pill; or get an implant, shot, or vaginal ring insert. She could even apply a gel or spray. There are also different types of estrogen (such as estradiol and conjugated estrogens). Estradiol is the most important type of estrogen in a woman's body before menopause. Other hormones, progesterone or progestin, can be taken as a pill, sometimes in the same pill as the estrogen, as well as a patch (combined with estrogen), shot, IUD (intrauterine device), gel, or vaginal suppository.

The form of MHT your doctor suggests may depend on your symptoms. For example, an estrogen patch (also called transdermal estrogen) or pill (oral estrogen) can relieve hot flashes, night sweats (hot flashes that bother you at night), and vaginal dryness. Other forms—vaginal creams, tablets, or rings—are used mostly for vaginal dryness alone. The vaginal ring insert might also help some urinary tract symptoms.

The dose can also vary, as can the timing of those doses. Some doctors suggest that estrogen be used every day, but that the progesterone or progestin be used cyclically—for 10 to 14 straight days every 4 weeks. A cyclic schedule is thought to mimic how the body makes estrogen and progesterone before menopause. This approach can cause some spotting or bleeding, like a light period, which might get lighter or go away in time. Alternatively, some women take estrogen and progesterone or progestin continuously—every day of the month.

Is there a downside to taking hormones?

Research has found that, for some women, there are serious risks, including an increased chance of heart disease, stroke, blood clots, and breast cancer, when using MHT. The Women's Health Initiative also found an increased risk of possible dementia in women who started MHT after age 65. These concerns are why every woman needs to think a lot before deciding to use menopausal hormone therapy.

Also, some women develop noticeable side effects from using hormones:

- Breast tenderness
- Spotting or a return of monthly periods
- Cramping
- Bloating

By changing the type or amount of the hormones, the way they are taken, or the timing of the doses, your doctor may be able to help control these side effects. Or, over time, they may go away on their own.

What more should I know about the benefits and risks of hormones?

Over the years, research findings have led to a variety of positive, negative, and sometimes conflicting reports about menopausal hormone therapy. Some of these findings came from randomized clinical trials, the most convincing type of research. Historically, clinical trials often used one type of estrogen called conjugated estrogens. Several other types of estrogen, as well as progesterone and progestins, have also been tested in small trials to see if they have an effect on heart disease, breast cancer, or dementia.

Let's look more closely at what we have learned from these small studies.

Hot flashes and night sweats. Estrogen will relieve most women's hot flashes and night sweats. If you stop using estrogen, you may again start having hot flashes. Lifestyle changes and certain prescription medicines also might help some women with hot flashes. For most women, hot flashes and night sweats go away in time.

Vaginal dryness. Estrogen improves vaginal dryness, probably for as long as you continue to use it. If vaginal dryness is your only symptom, your doctor might prescribe a vaginal estrogen. A water-based lubricant, but not petroleum jelly, may also relieve vaginal discomfort.

Cholesterol levels. Estrogen improves cholesterol levels, lowering LDLs (the "bad" kind of cholesterol) and raising HDLs (the "good" kind of cholesterol). The pill form of estrogen can cause the level of triglycerides (a type of fat in the blood) to go up. The estrogen patch does not seem to have this effect, but it also does not improve cholesterol to the same degree as the pill form. But, improving cholesterol levels is not a reason to take estrogen. Other medicines and lifestyle changes will improve cholesterol levels more effectively.

What is the Women's Health Initiative? What have we learned from it?

Before menopause, women generally have a lower risk of heart disease than men. This led experts to wonder whether giving women estrogen after menopause might help prevent heart disease. In 1992, the National Institutes of Health (NIH), the nation's premier medical research agency, began the Women's Health Initiative (WHI) to explore ways postmenopausal women might prevent heart disease, as well as osteoporosis and cancer. One part of the WHI, the Hormone Trial, looked at oral conjugated estrogens used alone (E therapy or ET) or with a particular progestin (EPT) to see if, in postmenopausal women, estrogen could prevent heart disease without increasing the chance of breast cancer.

In July 2002, the EPT part of the WHI Hormone Trial was stopped early because it became clear to the researchers that the overall risk of taking E+P outweighed the benefits:

Benefits
Fewer fractures
Less chance of cancer in the colon and/or rectum

Risks
More strokes
More serious blood clots
More heart attacks
More breast cancers

In April 2004, the rest of the Hormone Trial, the E alone or ET trial, was also halted because using estrogen alone increased the risk of stroke, and it was not likely that there would be a positive effect on heart attacks. Unlike using estrogen plus progestin, using estrogen alone did not increase the risk of heart attacks or breast cancer, but like the EPT trial, there were fewer fractures.

During the first 3 years after stopping the WHI EPT trial, women were no longer at greater risk of heart disease, stroke, or serious blood clots than women who had not used MHT. On the other hand, they also no longer had greater protection from fractures. The women still had an increased risk of breast cancer, but their risk was smaller than it was while they were using hormones. During the first 4 years after stopping the WHI ET trial, the increased risk of stroke disappeared, there was no effect on risk of heart attack, but the slightly lower risk of breast cancer continued.

It appears from the WHI that women should not begin using MHT to protect their health—it does not appear to prevent heart disease or dementia when started several years after menopause. In fact, older women in the study using MHT were at increased risk of certain diseases. Women who were less than age 60 did not appear to be at increased risk of heart disease but were at increased risk of stroke. For these women, the overall risks and benefits appeared to be balanced, but there is no strong evidence to support women under age 60 using MHT to prevent chronic diseases of aging, such as heart disease and dementia.

It is important to remember that the WHI findings are based on the specific oral form (rather than patch, gel, etc.), dose, and type of estrogen and progestin studied in the WHI. Which hormones and dose you use and the way you take them might change these benefits and risks. We don't know how the WHI findings apply to these other types, forms, and doses of estrogen and progesterone or progestin.

What are some other options?

Women now have more options than when the WHI study was first planned. More types of estrogens are available, and some of them come in a variety of forms. For example, synthetic estradiol, now available in several forms (pill, patch, cream, gel, etc.), is chemically identical to the estrogen most active in women's bodies before menopause. If it is not taken by mouth, but rather applied to the skin or taken as a shot, estradiol appears to work the same way as estradiol made in the body. Lower doses of estrogen are available. Investigators are now studying a low-dose estradiol patch (transdermal estradiol) compared to a low-dose conjugated-estrogens pill to see whether one or both slow hardening of the arteries in women around the age of menopause and whether the estradiol patch is as effective and, perhaps, safer than the conjugated estrogens pill. These alternatives are creating more choices for women seeking relief from their menopausal symptoms, as well as a variety of new opportunities for research.

Besides a pill, some estrogens come in different and sometimes new forms—skin patch, gel, emulsion, spray, and vaginal ring, cream, and tablet. These forms work in the body somewhat differently than a pill by entering your body directly through the skin or walls of the vagina. Oral estrogen (a pill) is chemically changed in the liver before reaching your tissues. Some studies suggest that if estrogen enters through the skin and bypasses the liver, the risk of serious blood clots might be lower. Others suggest a lower risk of gallbladder disease. This may also allow a change in dosage—further testing may show that the same benefits might come from lower doses than are needed with a pill.

What questions remain unanswered?

Experts now know more about menopause and have a better understanding of what the WHI results mean. But, they have new questions also.

- The average age of women participating in the trial was 63, more than 10 years older than the average age of menopause, and the WHI was looking at reducing the risk of chronic diseases of growing older like heart disease and osteoporosis. Do the WHI results apply to younger women choosing MHT to relieve symptoms around the time of menopause or to women who have early surgical menopause (surgery to remove both ovaries or the uterus)?

- Other studies show that lower doses of estrogen than were studied in the WHI provide relief from symptoms of menopause for some women and still help women maintain bone density. What are the long-term benefits and risks of lower doses of estrogen?

- In the WHI, women using E alone did not seem to have a greater risk of heart disease than women not using hormones. Does this mean that healthy women in their 50s who start using estrogen alone are not at higher eventual risk for heart disease than women who don't use estrogen?

- Would using progesterone or a different progestin than the one used in the WHI be less risky to a woman's heart, blood vessels, and breasts?

- The combination menopausal hormone therapy used in the WHI makes it somewhat more likely that a woman could develop breast cancer, especially with long-term use. Is using a different type of estrogen, a smaller dose of estrogen or progesterone, or a different progestin (instead of medroxyprogesterone acetate) safer?

- Does using estrogen around the time of menopause increase the risk of possible dementia in later life, as starting it after age 65 did in the WHI Memory Study (WHIMS)? Or does it decrease the risk of dementia later in life?

The National Institute on Aging and other parts of the National Institutes of Health, along with other medical research centers, continue to explore questions such as these. They hope that in the future these studies will give women additional facts needed to make informed decisions about relieving menopausal symptoms.

What are "natural hormones"?

The "natural hormones" women generally use are estrogen and progesterone made from plants such as soy or yams. Some people also call them bio identical hormones because they are supposed to be chemically the same as the hormones naturally made by a woman's body. These so-called natural hormones are put together (compounded) by a compounding pharmacist. This pharmacist follows a formula decided on by a doctor familiar with this approach. Compounded hormones are not regulated or approved by the FDA. So, we don't know much about how safe or effective they are or how the quality and quantity vary from batch to batch.

Some drug companies also make estrogens and progesterone from plants like soy and yams. Some of these are also chemically identical to the hormones made by your body. These other forms of MHT are available by prescription. Importantly, these estrogens and progesterone made by drug companies are regulated and approved by the FDA

There are also "natural" treatments for the symptoms of menopause that are available over-the-counter, without a prescription. Black cohosh is one that women use, but a couple of clinical trials have shown that it did not relieve hot flashes in postmenopausal women or those approaching menopause. Because of rare reports of serious liver disease, scientists are concerned about the possible effects of black cohosh on the liver. Other "natural" treatments are made from soy or yams. None of these are regulated or approved by the FDA.

What's right for me?

There is no single answer for all women who are trying to decide whether to use MHT. You have to look at your own needs and weigh your own risks. Here are some questions you can ask yourself and talk to your doctor about:

- Do menopausal symptoms such as hot flashes or vaginal dryness bother me a lot? Like many women, your hot flashes or night sweats will likely go away over time, but vaginal dryness may not. MHT can help with troubling symptoms.

- Am I at risk for developing osteoporosis? Estrogen might protect bone mass while you use it. However, there are other drugs that can protect your bones without MHT's risks. Talk to your doctor about the risks and benefits of those medicines for you.

- Do I have a history of heart disease or risk factors such as high blood cholesterol? If so, using estrogen and progestin can increase that risk even more.

- Do I have a family history of breast cancer? If you have a family history of breast cancer, check with your doctor about your risk.

- I have high levels of triglycerides and a family history of gallbladder disease. Can I use MHT? The safety of any kind of MHT in women with high levels of triglycerides or a family history of gallbladder disease is not known. But some experts think that using a patch will not raise your triglyceride level or increase your chance of gallbladder problems. Using an oral estrogen pill might.

- Do I have liver disease or a history of stroke or blood clots in my veins? MHT, especially taken by mouth, might not be safe for you to use.

In all cases, talk to your doctor about how best to treat or prevent your menopause symptoms or diseases for which you are at risk.

If you are already using menopausal hormone therapy and think you would like to stop, first ask your doctor how to do that. Some doctors suggest tapering off slowly.

Whatever decision you make now about using MHT is not final. You can start or end the treatment at any time, although, as we learned from the WHI, it appears that it is best not to start MHT many years after menopause. If you stop, some of your risks will lessen over time, but so will the benefits. Discuss your decision about menopausal hormone therapy with your doctor at your annual check-up.

MHT is not one size fits all

Each woman is different, and the decision for each one about menopausal hormone therapy will probably also be different.

Chapter 13

Radiation and Cancer Risk

Chapter Contents

Section 13.1

Radon and Cancer Risk

Text in this section is excerpted from "Radon," National Cancer
Institute (NCI), March 20, 2015.

What is radon?

Radon is a radioactive gas that is released from the normal decay
of the elements uranium, thorium, and radium in rocks and soil. The
invisible, odorless gas seeps up through the ground and diffuses into
the air. In a few areas, depending on local geology, radon dissolves
into ground water and can be released into the air when the water
is used. Radon gas usually exists at very low levels outdoors, but the
gas can accumulate in areas without adequate ventilation, such as
underground mines.

How are people exposed to radon?

Radon is present in nearly all air, so everyone breathes in radon
every day, usually at very low levels. Radon can enter homes through
cracks in floors, walls, or foundations, and collect indoors. It can also
be released from building materials, or from water obtained from wells
that contain radon. Radon levels may be higher in homes that are
well insulated, tightly sealed, and/or built on soil rich in the elements
uranium, thorium, and radium. Basements and first floors typically
have the highest radon levels because of their closeness to the ground.

Workers employed in uranium, hard rock, and phosphate mining
potentially are exposed to radon at high concentrations. Uranium
miners generally are believed to have the highest exposures.

Which cancers are associated with exposure to radon?

Radon was identified as a health problem when scientists noted
that underground uranium miners who were exposed to it died of lung
cancer at high rates. Experimental studies in animals confirmed the
results of the miner studies by showing higher rates of lung tumors
among rodents exposed to high levels of radon. There has been a

suggestion of an increased risk of leukemia associated with radon exposure in adults and children; the evidence, however, is not conclusive.

How can exposures be reduced?

Check the radon levels in your home regularly. The U.S. Environmental Protection Agency has more information about residential radon exposure and what people can do about it in its Consumer's Guide to Radon Reduction.

Section 13.2

Cell Phones and Cancer Risk

Text in this section is excerpted from "Cell Phones and Cancer Risk,"
National Cancer Institute (NCI), June 24, 2013.

Why is there concern that cell phones may cause cancer or other health problems?

There are three main reasons why people are concerned that cell phones (also known as "wireless" or "mobile" telephones) might have the potential to cause certain types of cancer or other health problems:

- Cell phones emit radiofrequency energy (radio waves), a form of non-ionizing radiation. Tissues nearest to where the phone is held can absorb this energy.

- The number of cell phone users has increased rapidly. As of 2010, there were more than 303 million subscribers to cell phone service in the United States, according to the Cellular Telecommunications and Internet Association. This is a nearly threefold increase from the 110 million users in 2000. Globally, the number of cell phone subscriptions is estimated by the International Telecommunications Union to be 5 billion.

- Over time, the number of cell phone calls per day, the length of each call, and the amount of time people use cell phones have increased. Cell phone technology has also undergone substantial changes.

What is radiofrequency energy and how does it affect the body?

Radiofrequency energy is a form of electromagnetic radiation. Electromagnetic radiation can be categorized into two types: ionizing (e.g., x-rays, radon, and cosmic rays) and non-ionizing (e.g., radiofrequency and extremely low-frequency or power frequency).

Exposure to ionizing radiation, such as from radiation therapy, is known to increase the risk of cancer. However, although many studies have examined the potential health effects of non-ionizing radiation from radar, microwave ovens, and other sources, there is currently no consistent evidence that non-ionizing radiation increases cancer risk.

The only known biological effect of radiofrequency energy is heating. The ability of microwave ovens to heat food is one example of this effect of radiofrequency energy. Radiofrequency exposure from cell phone use does cause heating; however, it is not sufficient to measurably increase body temperature.

A recent study showed that when people used a cell phone for 50 minutes, brain tissues on the same side of the head as the phone's antenna metabolized more glucose than did tissues on the opposite side of the brain. The researchers noted that the results are preliminary, and possible health outcomes from this increase in glucose metabolism are still unknown.

How is radiofrequency energy exposure measured in epidemiologic studies?

Levels of radiofrequency exposure are indirectly estimated using information from interviews or questionnaires. These measures include the following:

- How "regularly" study participants use cell phones (the minimum number of calls per week or month)

- The age and the year when study participants first used a cell phone and the age and the year of last use (allows calculation of the duration of use and time since the start of use)

- The average number of cell phone calls per day, week, or month (frequency)

- The average length of a typical cell phone call

- The total hours of lifetime use, calculated from the length of typical call times, the frequency of use, and the duration of use.

What has research shown about the possible cancer-causing effects of radiofrequency energy?

Although there have been some concerns that radiofrequency energy from cell phones held closely to the head may affect the brain and other tissues, to date there is no evidence from studies of cells, animals, or humans that radiofrequency energy can cause cancer.

It is generally accepted that damage to DNA is necessary for cancer to develop. However, radiofrequency energy, unlike ionizing radiation, does not cause DNA damage in cells, and it has not been found to cause cancer in animals or to enhance the cancer-causing effects of known chemical carcinogens in animals.

Researchers have carried out several types of epidemiologic studies to investigate the possibility of a relationship between cell phone use and the risk of malignant (cancerous) brain tumors, such as gliomas, as well as benign (noncancerous) tumors, such as acoustic neuromas (tumors in the cells of the nerve responsible for hearing), most meningiomas (tumors in the meninges, membranes that cover and protect the brain and spinal cord), and parotid gland tumors (tumors in the salivary glands).

In one type of study, called a case-control study, cell phone use is compared between people with these types of tumors and people without them. In another type of study, called a cohort study, a large group of people is followed over time and the rate of these tumors in people who did and didn't use cell phones is compared. Cancer incidence data can also be analyzed over time to see if the rates of cancer changed in large populations during the time that cell phone use increased dramatically. The results of these studies have generally not provided clear evidence of a relationship between cell phone use and cancer, but there have been some statistically significant findings in certain subgroups of people.

Findings from specific research studies are summarized below:

- The Interphone Study, conducted by a consortium of researchers from 13 countries, is the largest health-related case-control study of use of cell phones and head and neck tumors. Most published analyses from this study have shown no statistically significant increases in brain or central nervous system cancers related to higher amounts of cell phone use. One recent analysis showed a statistically significant, albeit modest, increase in the risk of glioma among the small proportion of study participants who spent the most total time on cell phone calls. However, the researchers considered this finding inconclusive because they felt that the amount of use reported by some respondents was unlikely and because the participants who reported lower levels of use appeared to have a slightly reduced risk of brain cancer compared with people who did not use cell phones regularly. Another recent study from the group found no relationship between brain tumor locations and regions of the brain that were exposed to the highest level of radiofrequency energy from cell phones.

- A cohort study in Denmark linked billing information from more than 358,000 cell phone subscribers with brain tumor incidence data from the Danish Cancer Registry. The analyses found no association between cell phone use and the incidence of glioma, meningioma, or acoustic neuroma, even among people who had been cell phone subscribers for 13 or more years.

- The prospective Million Women Study in the United Kingdom found that self-reported cell phone use was not associated with an increased risk of glioma, meningioma, or non-central nervous system tumors. The researchers did find that the use of cell phones for more than 5 years was associated with an increased risk of acoustic neuroma, and that the risk of acoustic neuroma increased with increasing duration of cell phone use. However, the incidence of these tumors among men and women in the United Kingdom did not increase during 1998 to 2008, even though cell phone use increased dramatically over that decade.

- An early case-control study in the United States was unable to demonstrate a relationship between cell phone use and glioma or meningioma.

- Some case-control studies in Sweden found statistically significant trends of increasing brain cancer risk for the total amount of cell phone use and the years of use among people who began using cell phones before age 20. However, another large, case-control study in Sweden did not find an increased risk of brain cancer among people between the ages of 20 and 69. In addition, the international CEFALO study, which compared children who were diagnosed with brain cancer between ages 7 and 19 with similar children who were not, found no relationship between their cell phone use and risk for brain cancer.

- NCI's Surveillance, Epidemiology, and End Results (SEER) Program, which tracks cancer incidence in the United States over time, found no increase in the incidence of brain or other central nervous system cancers between 1987 and 2007, despite the dramatic increase in cell phone use in this country during that time. Similarly, incidence data from Denmark, Finland, Norway, and Sweden for the period 1974–2008 revealed no increase in age-adjusted incidence of brain tumors. A 2012 study by NCI researchers, which compared observed glioma incidence rates in SEER with projected rates based on risks observed in the Interphone study, found that the projected rates were consistent with observed U.S. rates. The researchers also compared the SEER rates with projected rates based on a Swedish study published in 2011. They determined that the projected rates were at least 40 percent higher than, and incompatible with, the actual U.S. rates.

- Studies of workers exposed to radiofrequency energy have shown no evidence of increased risk of brain tumors among U.S. Navy electronics technicians, aviation technicians, or fire control technicians, those working in an electromagnetic pulse test program, plastic-ware workers, cellular phone manufacturing workers, or Navy personnel with a high probability of exposure to radar.

Why are the findings from different studies of cell phone use and cancer risk inconsistent?

A limited number of studies have shown some evidence of statistical association of cell phone use and brain tumor risks, but most studies have found no association. Reasons for these discrepancies include the following:

- **Recall bias,** which may happen when a study collects data about prior habits and exposures using questionnaires administered after disease has been diagnosed in some of the study participants. It is possible that study participants who have brain tumors may remember their cell phone use differently than individuals without brain tumors. Many epidemiologic studies of cell phone use and brain cancer risk lack verifiable data about the total amount of cell phone use over time. In addition, people who develop a brain tumor may have a tendency to recall using their cell phone mostly on the same side of their head where the tumor was found, regardless of whether they actually used their phone on that side of their head a lot or only a little.

- **Inaccurate reporting,** which may happen when people say that something has happened more or less often than it actually did. People may not remember how much they used cell phones in a given time period.

- **Morbidity and mortality** among study participants who have brain cancer. Gliomas are particularly difficult to study, for example, because of their high death rate and the short survival of people who develop these tumors. Patients who survive initial treatment are often impaired, which may affect their responses to questions. Furthermore, for people who have died, next-of-kin are often less familiar with the cell phone use patterns of their deceased family member and may not accurately describe their patterns of use to an interviewer.

- **Participation bias,** which can happen when people who are diagnosed with brain tumors are more likely than healthy people (known as controls) to enrol in a research study. Also, controls who did not or rarely used cell phones were less likely to participate in the Interphone study than controls who used cell phones regularly. For example, the Interphone study reported participation rates of 78 percent for meningioma patients (range 56–92 percent for the individual studies), 64 percent for the glioma patients (range 36–92 percent), and 53 percent for control subjects (range 42–74 percent). One series of Swedish studies reported participation rates of 85 percent in people with brain cancer and 84 percent in control subjects.

- **Changing technology and methods of use.** Older studies evaluated radiofrequency energy exposure from analog cell phones. However, most cell phones today use digital technology, which operates at a different frequency and a lower power level than analog phones. Digital cell phones have been in use for more than a decade in the United States, and cellular technology continues to change. Texting, for example, has become a popular way of using a cell phone to communicate that does not require bringing the phone close to the head. Furthermore, the use of hands-free technology, such as wired and wireless headsets, is increasing and may decrease radiofrequency energy exposure to the head and brain.

What do expert organizations conclude?

The International Agency for Research on Cancer Exit Disclaimer (IARC), a component of the World Health Organization, has recently classified radiofrequency fields as "possibly carcinogenic to humans," based on limited evidence from human studies, limited evidence from studies of radiofrequency energy and cancer in rodents, and weak mechanistic evidence (from studies of genotoxicity, effects on immune system function, gene and protein expression, cell signalling, oxidative stress, and apoptosis, along with studies of the possible effects of radiofrequency energy on the blood-brain barrier).

The American Cancer Society Exit Disclaimer (ACS) states that the IARC classification means that there could be some risk associated with cancer, but the evidence is not strong enough to be considered causal and needs to be investigated further. Individuals who are concerned about radiofrequency exposure can limit their exposure, including using an ear piece and limiting cell phone use, particularly among children.

The National Institute of Environmental Health Sciences (NIEHS) states that the weight of the current scientific evidence has not conclusively linked cell phone use with any adverse health problems, but more research is needed.

The U.S. Food and Drug Administration (FDA), which is responsible for regulating the safety of machines and devices that emit radiation (including cell phones), notes that studies reporting biological changes associated with radiofrequency energy have failed to be replicated and that the majority of human epidemiologic studies have failed to show a relationship between exposure to radiofrequency energy from cell phones and health problems.

The U.S. Centers for Disease Control and Prevention (CDC) states that, although some studies have raised concerns about the possible risks of cell phone use, scientific research as a whole does not support a statistically significant association between cell phone use and health effects.

The Federal Communications Commission (FCC) concludes that there is no scientific evidence that proves that wireless phone use can lead to cancer or to other health problems, including headaches, dizziness, or memory loss.

121

What studies are under way that will help further our understanding of the health effects of cell phone use?

A large prospective cohort study of cell phone use and its possible long-term health effects was launched in Europe in March 2010. This study, known as COSMOS Exit Disclaimer, has enrolled approximately 290,000 cell phone users aged 18 years or older to date and will follow them for 20 to 30 years.

Participants in COSMOS will complete a questionnaire about their health, lifestyle, and current and past cell phone use. This information will be supplemented with information from health records and cell phone records.

The challenge of this ambitious study is to continue following the participants for a range of health effects over many decades. Researchers will need to determine whether participants who leave are somehow different from those who remain throughout the follow-up period.

Another study already under way is a case-control study called Mobi-Kids Exit Disclaimer, which will include 2000 young people (aged 10-24 years) with newly diagnosed brain tumors and 4000 healthy young people. The goal of the study is to learn more about risk factors for childhood brain tumors. Results are expected in 2016.

Although recall bias is minimized in studies that link participants to their cell phone records, such studies face other problems. For example, it is impossible to know who is using the listed cell phone or whether that individual also places calls using other cell phones. To a lesser extent, it is not clear whether multiple users of a single phone will be represented on a single phone company account.

The NIEHS, which is part of the National Institutes of Health, is carrying out a study of risks related to exposure to radiofrequency energy (the type used in cell phones) in highly specialized labs that can specify and control sources of radiation and measure their effects on rodents.

What can cell phone users do to reduce their exposure to radiofrequency energy?

The FDA and FCC have suggested some steps that concerned cell phone users can take to reduce their exposure to radiofrequency energy:

- Reserve the use of cell phones for shorter conversations or for times when a landline phone is not available.

- Use a hands-free device, which places more distance between the phone and the head of the user.

Hands-free kits reduce the amount of radiofrequency energy exposure to the head because the antenna, which is the source of energy, is not placed against the head.

Where can I find more information about radiofrequency energy from my cell phone?

The FCC provides information about the specific absorption rate (SAR) of cell phones produced and marketed within the last 1 to 2 years. The SAR corresponds with the relative amount of radiofrequency energy absorbed by the head of a cell phone user.

What are other sources of radiofrequency energy?

The most common exposures to radiofrequency energy are from telecommunications devices and equipment. In the United States, cell phones currently operate in a frequency range of about 1,800 to 2,200 megahertz (MHz). In this range, the electromagnetic radiation produced is in the form of non-ionizing radiofrequency energy.

Cordless phones (phones that have a base unit connected to the telephone wiring in a house) often operate at radio frequencies similar to those of cell phones; however, since cordless phones have a limited range and require a nearby base, their signals are generally much less powerful than those of cell phones.

Among other radiofrequency energy sources, AM/FM radios and VHF/UHF televisions operate at lower radio frequencies than cell phones, whereas sources such as radar, satellite stations, magnetic resonance imaging (MRI) devices, industrial equipment, and microwave ovens operate at somewhat higher radio frequencies.

How common is brain cancer? Has the incidence of brain cancer changed over time?

Brain cancer incidence and mortality (death) rates have changed little in the past decade. In the United States, 23,130 new diagnoses and 14,080 deaths from brain cancer were estimated for 2013.

The 5-year relative survival for brain cancers diagnosed from 2003 through 2009 was 35 percent. This is the percentage of people diagnosed with brain cancer who will still be alive 5 years after diagnosis compared with the survival of a person of the same age and sex who does not have cancer.

The risk of developing brain cancer increases with age. From 2006 through 2010, there were fewer than 5 brain cancer cases for every 100,000 people in the United States under age 65, compared with approximately 19 cases for every 100,000 people in the United States who were ages 65 or older.

Section 13.3

Magnetic Field Exposure and Cancer Risk

Text in this section is excerpted from "Magnetic Field Exposure and Cancer," National Cancer Institute (NCI), November 3, 2014.

What are electric and magnetic fields?

Electric and magnetic fields are invisible areas of energy that are produced by electricity, which is the movement of electrons, or current, through a wire.

An electric field is produced by voltage, which is the pressure used to push the electrons through the wire, much like water being pushed through a pipe. As the voltage increases, the electric field increases in strength.

A magnetic field results from the flow of current through wires or electrical devices and increases in strength as the current increases. The strength of a magnetic field decreases rapidly with increased distance from its source.

Electric fields are produced whether or not a device is turned on, but magnetic fields are produced only when current is flowing, which usually requires a device to be turned on. Power lines produce magnetic fields continuously because current is always flowing through them.

Electric and magnetic fields together are referred to as electromagnetic fields, or EMFs. There are both natural and human-made sources of EMFs. The earth's magnetic field, which causes a compass to point north, is an example of a naturally occurring EMF. Power lines, wiring, and electrical appliances, such as electric shavers, hair dryers, computers, televisions, and electric blankets produce what are called extremely low frequency (ELF) EMFs. ELF-EMFs have frequencies of up to 300 cycles per second, or Hertz (Hz); for example, the frequency of alternating current in power lines is 50 or 60 Hz. Cell phones produce radiofrequency EMFs above the ELF range.

Electric fields are easily shielded or weakened by walls and other objects, whereas magnetic fields can pass through buildings, living things, and most other materials. Consequently, magnetic fields are the component of ELF-EMFs that are usually studied in relation to their possible health effects.

Why are ELF-EMFs studied in relation to cancer?

Any possible health effects of ELF-EMFs would be of concern because power lines and electrical appliances are present everywhere in modern life, and people are constantly encountering these fields, both in their homes and in certain workplaces. Also, the presence of ELF-EMFs in homes means that children are exposed. Even if ELF-EMFs were to increase an individual's risk of disease only slightly, widespread exposure to ELF-EMFs could translate to meaningful increased risks at the population level.

Several early epidemiologic studies raised the possibility of an association between certain cancers, especially childhood cancers, and ELF-EMFs. Most subsequent studies have not shown such an association, but scientists have continued to investigate the possibility that one exists.

No mechanism by which ELF-EMFs could cause cancer has been identified. Unlike high-energy (ionizing) radiation, ELF-EMFs are low energy and non-ionizing and cannot damage DNA or cells directly. Some scientists have speculated that ELF-EMFs could cause cancer through other mechanisms, such as by reducing levels of the hormone melatonin. (There is some evidence that melatonin may suppress the development of certain tumors.) However, studies of animals exposed to ELF-EMFs have not provided any indications that ELF-EMF exposure is associated with cancer.

What is the evidence for an association between magnetic field exposure and cancer in children?

Numerous epidemiologic studies and comprehensive reviews of the scientific literature have evaluated possible associations between exposure to ELF magnetic fields and risk of cancer in children. Most of the research has focused on leukemia and brain tumors, the two most common cancers in children. Studies have examined associations of these cancers with living near power lines, with magnetic fields in the home, and with exposure of parents to high levels of magnetic fields in the workplace.

Exposure from power lines

Although a study in 1979 pointed to a possible association between living near electric power lines and childhood leukemia, more recent studies have had mixed findings. Currently, researchers conclude that there is little evidence that exposure to ELF-EMFs from power lines causes leukemia, brain tumors, or any other cancers in children.

Exposure in homes

Many studies have also looked for possible associations between magnetic fields measured in homes and residences and the risk of childhood cancers, especially leukemia. Individual studies have had varying results, but most have not found an association or have found it only for those children who lived in homes with very high levels of magnetic fields, which are present in few residences.

To develop the most accurate estimates of the risks of leukemia in children from magnetic fields in the home, researchers have analyzed the combined data from many studies. In one such analysis that combined data from nine studies done in several countries, leukemia risk was increased only in those children with the highest exposure (a category that included less than 1 percent of the children); these children had a twofold excess risk of childhood leukemia. In another analysis that combined data from 15 individual studies, a similar increase in risk was seen in children with the highest exposure level. A more recent analysis of seven studies published after 2000 found a similar trend, but the increase was not statistically significant.

Overall, these analyses suggest that if there is any increase in leukemia risk from magnetic fields, it is restricted to children with the very highest exposure levels. But it is possible that this increase is not real, because if magnetic fields caused childhood leukemia, certain patterns would have been found, such as increasing risk with increasing levels of magnetic field exposure. Such patterns were not seen.

Another way that people can be exposed to magnetic fields in the home is from household electrical appliances. Although magnetic fields near many electrical appliances are higher than those near power lines, appliances contribute less to a person's total exposure to magnetic fields because most appliances are used only for short periods of time. Again, studies have not found consistent evidence for an association between the use of household electrical appliances and risk of childhood leukemia.

Parental exposure and risk in children

Several studies have examined possible associations between maternal or paternal exposure to high levels of magnetic fields before conception and/or during pregnancy and the risk of cancer in their future children. The results to date have been inconsistent. Studies are ongoing to evaluate this question.

Exposure and cancer survival

A few studies have investigated whether magnetic field exposure is associated with prognosis or survival of children with leukemia. Several small retrospective studies of this question have yielded inconsistent results. An analysis that combined prospective data for more than 3000 children with acute lymphoid leukemia from eight countries showed that ELF magnetic field exposure was not associated with their survival or risk of relapse.

What is the evidence that magnetic field exposure is linked to cancer in adults?

Although some studies have reported associations between ELF-EMF exposure and cancer in adults, other studies have not found evidence for such associations.

The majority of epidemiologic studies have shown no relationship between breast cancer in women and exposure to ELF-EMFs in the home, although several individual studies have shown hints of an association.

Several studies conducted in the 1980s and early 1990s reported that people who worked in some electrical occupations (such as power station operators and phone line workers) had higher-than-expected rates of some types of cancer, particularly leukemia, brain tumors, and male breast cancer. Some occupational studies showed very small increases in the risks of leukemia and brain cancer, but these results were based on participants' job titles and not on actual measurements of their exposures. More recent studies, including some that considered the participant's job title as well as measurements of their exposures, have not shown consistent findings of an increasing risk of leukemia, brain tumors, or female breast cancer with increasing exposure to magnetic fields at work.

Section 13.4

What Are the Radiation Risks from Computed Tomography (CT)?

Text in this section is excerpted from "Medical X-ray Imaging," Food and Drug Administration (FDA), February 10, 2015.

What are the Radiation Risks from Computed Tomography (CT)?

As in many aspects of medicine, there are both benefits and risks associated with the use of Computed Tomography (CT). The main risks are those associated with

- abnormal test results, for a benign or incidental finding, leading to unneeded, possibly invasive, follow-up tests that may present additional risks and

- the increased possibility of cancer induction from x-ray radiation exposure.

The probability for absorbed x-rays to induce cancer or heritable mutations leading to genetically associated diseases in offspring is thought to be very small for radiation doses of the magnitude that are associated with CT procedures. Such estimates of cancer and genetically heritable risk from x-ray exposure have a broad range of statistical uncertainty, and there is some scientific controversy regarding the effects from very low doses and dose rates as discussed below. Under some rare circumstances of prolonged, high-dose exposure, x-rays can cause other adverse health effects, such as skin erythema (reddening), skin tissue injury, and birth defects following in-utero exposure. But at the exposure levels associated with most medical imaging procedures, including most CT procedures, these other adverse effects would not occur.

Because of the rapidly growing use of paediatric CT and the potential for increased radiation exposure to children undergoing these scans, special considerations should be applied when using pediatric CT. Doses from a single pediatric CT scan can range from about 5 mSv to 60 mSv. Among children who have undergone CT scans, approximately one-third have had at least three scans.

Risk Estimates

In the field of radiation protection, it is commonly assumed that the risk for adverse health effects from cancer is proportional to the amount of radiation dose absorbed and the amount of dose depends on the type of x-ray examination. A CT examination with an effective dose of 10 millisieverts (abbreviated mSv; 1 mSv = 1 mGy in the case of x-rays.) may be associated with an increase in the possibility of fatal cancer of approximately 1 chance in 2000. This increase in the possibility of a fatal cancer from radiation can be compared to the natural incidence of fatal cancer in the U.S. population, about 1 chance in 5. In other words, for any one person the risk of radiation-induced cancer is much smaller than the natural risk of cancer. Nevertheless, this small increase in radiation-associated cancer risk for an individual can become a public health concern if large numbers of the population undergo increased numbers of CT screening procedures of uncertain benefit.

It must be noted that there is uncertainty regarding the risk estimates for low levels of radiation exposure as commonly experienced in diagnostic radiology procedures. There are some that question whether there is adequate evidence for a risk of cancer induction at low doses. However, this position has not been adopted by most authoritative bodies in the radiation protection and medical arenas.

Radiation Dose

The effective doses from diagnostic CT procedures are typically estimated to be in the range of 1 to 10 mSv. This range is not much less than the lowest doses of 5 to 20 mSv received by some of the Japanese survivors of the atomic bombs. These survivors, who are estimated to have experienced doses only slightly larger than those encountered in CT, have demonstrated a small but increased radiation-related excess relative risk for cancer mortality.

Radiation dose from CT procedures varies from patient to patient. A particular radiation dose will depend on the size of the body part examined, the type of procedure, and the type of CT equipment and its operation. Typical values cited for radiation dose should be considered as estimates that cannot be precisely associated with any individual patient, examination, or type of CT system. The actual dose from a procedure could be two or three times larger or smaller than the estimates. Facilities performing "screening" procedures may adjust the radiation dose used to levels less (by factors such as 1/2 to 1/5 for so called "low dose CT scans") than those typically used for diagnostic CT procedures. However, no comprehensive data is available to permit estimation of the extent of this practice and reducing the dose can have an adverse impact on the image quality produced. Such reduced image quality may be acceptable in certain imaging applications.

The quantity most relevant for assessing the risk of cancer detriment from a CT procedure is the "effective dose". Effective dose is evaluated in units of millisieverts (abbreviated mSv; 1 mSv = 1 mGy in the case of x-rays.) Using the concept of effective dose allows comparison of the risk estimates associated with partial or whole-body radiation exposures. This quantity also incorporates the different radiation sensitivities of the various organs in the body.

Estimates of the effective dose from a diagnostic CT procedure can vary by a factor of 10 or more depending on the type of CT procedure, patient size and the CT system and its operating technique.

A list of representative diagnostic procedures and associated doses are given in Table 13.1.

Table No: 13.1. Radiation Dose Comparison

Diagnostic Procedure	Typical Effective Dose (mSv)[1]	Number of Chest X-rays (PA film) for Equivalent Effective Dose[2]	Time Period for Equivalent Effective Dose from Natural Background Radiation[3]
Chest x-ray (PA film)	0.02	1	2.4 days
Skull x ray	0.1	5	12 days
Lumbar spine	1.5	75	182 days
I.V. urogram	3	150	1.0 years
Upper G.I. exam	6	300	2.0 years
Barium enema	8	400	2.7 years
CT head	2	100<	243 days
CT abdomen	8	400	2.7 years

1. *Average effective dose in millisieverts (mSv) as compiled by Fred A. Mettler, Jr., et al., "Effective Doses in Radiology and Diagnostic Nuclear Medicine: A Catalog," Radiology Vol. 248, No. 1, pp. 254-263, July 2008.*

2. *Based on the assumption of an average "effective dose" from chest x-ray (PA film) of 0.02 mSv.*

3. *Based on the assumption of an average "effective dose" from natural background radiation of 3 mSv per year in the United States.*

Chapter 14

Environment and Cancer Risk

Cancer-Causing Substances in the Environment

Cancer is caused by changes to certain genes that alter the way our cells function. Some of these genetic changes occur naturally when DNA is replicated during the process of cell division. But others are the result of environmental exposures that damage DNA. These exposures may include substances, such as the chemicals in tobacco smoke, or radiation, such as ultraviolet rays from the sun.

People can avoid some cancer-causing exposures, such as tobacco smoke and the sun's rays. But others are harder to avoid, especially if they are in the air we breathe, the water we drink, the food we eat, or the materials we use to do our jobs. Scientists are studying which exposures may cause or contribute to the development of cancer. Understanding which exposures are harmful, and where they are found, may help people to avoid them.

The substances listed below are among the most likely carcinogens to affect human health. Simply because a substance has been designated as a carcinogen, however, does not mean that the substance will necessarily cause cancer. Many factors influence whether a person exposed to a carcinogen will develop cancer, including the amount and duration of the exposure and the individual's genetic

This chapter includes excerpts from "Cancer-Causing Substances in the Environment," National Cancer Institute (NCI), March 18, 2015; and text from "Environmental Carcinogens and Cancer Risk," National Cancer Institute (NCI), March 20, 2015.

131

background. Environmental Carcinogens that cause Cancer Risks includes:

- Aflatoxins
- Aristolochic Acids
- Arsenic
- Asbestos
- Benzene
- Benzidine
- Beryllium
- 1,3-Butadiene
- Cadmium
- Coal Tar and Coal-Tar Pitch
- Coke-Oven Emissions
- Crystalline Silica (respirable size)
- Erionite
- Ethylene Oxide
- Formaldehyde
- Hexavalent Chromium Compounds
- Indoor Emissions from the Household Combustion of Coal
- Mineral Oils: Untreated and Mildly Treated
- Nickel Compounds
- Radon
- Secondhand Tobacco Smoke (Environmental Tobacco Smoke)
- Soot
- Strong Inorganic Acid Mists Containing Sulfuric Acid
- Thorium
- Vinyl Chloride
- Wood Dust

Environmental Carcinogens and Cancer Risk

Does any exposure to a known carcinogen always result in cancer?

Any substance that causes cancer is known as a carcinogen. But simply because a substance has been designated as a carcinogen does not mean that the substance will necessarily cause cancer. Many factors influence whether a person exposed to a carcinogen will develop cancer, including the amount and duration of the exposure and the individual's genetic background. Cancers caused by involuntary exposures to environmental carcinogens are most likely to occur in subgroups of the population, such as workers in certain industries who may be exposed to carcinogens on the job.

How can exposures to carcinogens be limited?

In the United States, regulations have been put in place to reduce exposures to known carcinogens in the workplace. Outside of the workplace, people can also take steps to limit their exposure to known carcinogens, such as testing their basement for radon, quitting smoking, limiting sun exposure, or maintaining a healthy weight.

How many cancers are caused by involuntary exposure to carcinogens in the environment?

This question cannot be answered with certainty because the precise causes of most cancers are not known. Some researchers have suggested that, in most populations, environmental exposures are responsible for a relatively small proportion of total cancers (less than 4 percent), whereas other researchers attribute a higher proportion (19 percent) to environmental exposures.

Who decides which environmental exposures cause cancer in humans?

Two organizations—the National Toxicology Program (NTP), an interagency program of the U.S. Department of Health and Human Services (HHS), and the International Agency for Research on Cancer (IARC), the cancer agency of the World Health Organization—have developed lists of substances that, based on the available scientific evidence, are known or are reasonably anticipated to be human carcinogens.

Specifically, the NTP publishes the Report on Carcinogens every few years. This congressionally mandated publication identifies agents, substances, mixtures, or exposures (collectively called "substances") in the environment that may cause cancer in humans. The 2014 edition lists 56 known human carcinogens and includes descriptions of the process for preparing the science-based report and the criteria used to list a substance as a carcinogen.

IARC also produces science-based reports on substances that can increase the risk of cancer in humans. Since 1971, the agency has evaluated more than 900 agents, including chemicals, complex mixtures, occupational exposures, physical agents, biological agents, and lifestyle factors. Of these, more than 400 have been identified as carcinogenic, probably carcinogenic, or possibly carcinogenic to humans.

IARC convenes expert scientists to evaluate the evidence that an agent can increase the risk of cancer. The agency describes the principles, procedures, and scientific criteria that guide the evaluationsExit Disclaimer. For instance, agents are selected for review based on two main criteria: (a) there is evidence of human exposure and (b) there is some evidence or suspicion of carcinogenicity.

How does the NTP decide whether to include a substance on its list of known human carcinogens?

As new potential carcinogens are identified, they are evaluated scientifically by the NTP's Board of Scientific Counselors and the NTP Director. Next, a draft Report on Carcinogens Monograph is prepared, which is reviewed by other scientific experts as needed, the public, and other federal agencies. The draft monograph is then revised as necessary and released for additional public comment and peer review by a dedicated panel of experts. Lastly, a finalized monograph and recommendation for listing is sent to the HHS Secretary for approval.

Chapter 15

Helicobacter Pylori *and Cancer*

What is Helicobacter pylori?

Helicobacter pylori, or *H. pylori*, is a spiral-shaped bacterium that grows in the mucus layer that coats the inside of the human stomach.

To survive in the harsh, acidic environment of the stomach, *H. pylori* secretes an enzyme called urease, which converts the chemical urea to ammonia. The production of ammonia around *H. pylori* neutralizes the acidity of the stomach, making it more hospitable for the bacterium. In addition, the helical shape of *H. pylori* allows it to burrow into the mucus layer, which is less acidic than the inside space, or lumen, of the stomach. *H. pylori* can also attach to the cells that line the inner surface of the stomach.

Although immune cells that normally recognize and attack invading bacteria accumulate near sites of *H. pylori* infection, they are unable to reach the stomach lining. In addition, *H. pylori* has developed ways of interfering with local immune responses, making them ineffective in eliminating this bacterium.

H. pylori has coexisted with humans for many thousands of years, and infection with this bacterium is common. The Centers for Disease Control and Prevention (CDC) estimates that approximately two-thirds

---

Text in this chapter is excerpted from "*Helicobacter pylori* and Cancer," National Cancer Institute (NCI), September 5, 2013.

of the world's population harbors the bacterium, with infection rates much higher in developing countries than in developed nations.

Although *H. pylori* infection does not cause illness in most infected people, it is a major risk factor for peptic ulcer disease and is responsible for the majority of ulcers of the stomach and upper small intestine.

In 1994, the International Agency for Research on Cancer classified *H. pylori* as a carcinogen, or cancer-causing agent, in humans, despite conflicting results at the time. Since then, it has been increasingly accepted that colonization of the stomach with *H. pylori* is an important cause of gastric cancer and of gastric mucosa-associated lymphoid tissue (MALT) lymphoma. Infection with *H. pylori* is also associated with a reduced risk of esophageal adenocarcinoma.

H. pylori is thought to spread through contaminated food and water and through direct mouth-to-mouth contact. In most populations, the bacterium is first acquired during childhood. Infection is more likely in children living in poverty, in crowded conditions, and in areas with poor sanitation.

What is gastric cancer?

Gastric cancer, or cancer of the stomach, was once considered a single entity. Now, scientists divide this cancer into two main classes: gastric cardia cancer (cancer of the top inch of the stomach, where it meets the esophagus) and non-cardia gastric cancer (cancer in all other areas of the stomach).

According to NCI's Surveillance, Epidemiology, and End Results (SEER) Program, an estimated 21,600 people in the United States will be diagnosed with gastric cancer and 10,990 people will die of this cancer during 2013. Gastric cancer is the second most common cause of cancer-related deaths in the world, killing approximately 738,000 people in 2008. Gastric cancer is less common in the United States and other Western countries than in countries in Asia and South America.

Overall gastric cancer incidence is decreasing. However, this decline is mainly in the rates of non-cardia gastric cancer. Gastric cardia cancer, which was once very uncommon, has risen in incidence in recent decades.

Infection with *H. pylori* is the primary identified cause of gastric cancer. Other risk factors for gastric cancer include chronic gastritis; older age; a diet high in salted, smoked, or poorly preserved foods and low in fruits and vegetables; tobacco smoking; pernicious anemia; a history of stomach surgery for benign conditions; and a family history of stomach cancer.

H. pylori has different associations with the two main classes of gastric cancer. Whereas people infected with *H. pylori* have an increased risk of non-cardia gastric cancer, their risk of gastric cardia cancer is not increased and may even be decreased.

What evidence shows that H. pylori *infection causes non-cardia gastric cancer?*

Epidemiologic studies have shown that individuals infected with *H. pylori* have an increased risk of gastric adenocarcinoma. The risk increase appears to be restricted to non-cardia gastric cancer. For example, a 2001 combined analysis of 12 case–control studies of *H. pylori* and gastric cancer estimated that the risk of non-cardia gastric cancer was nearly six times higher for *H. pylori*-infected people than for uninfected people.

Additional evidence for an association between *H. pylori* infection and the risk of non-cardia gastric cancer comes from prospective cohort studies such as the Alpha-Tocopherol, Beta-Carotene (ATBC) Cancer Prevention Study in Finland. Comparing subjects who developed non-cardia gastric cancer with cancer-free control subjects, the researchers found that *H. pylori*-infected individuals had a nearly eightfold increased risk for non-cardia gastric cancer.

What is the evidence that H. pylori *infection may reduce the risk of some cancers?*

Several studies have detected an inverse relationship between *H. pylori* infection and gastric cardia cancer, although the evidence is not entirely consistent. The possibility of an inverse relationship between the bacterium and gastric cardia cancer is supported by the corresponding decrease in *H. pylori* infection rates in Western countries during the past century—the result of improved hygiene and widespread antibiotic use—and the increase in rates of gastric cardia cancer in these same regions.

Similar epidemiologic evidence suggests that *H. pylori* infection may be associated with a lower risk of esophageal adenocarcinoma. For example, a large case–control study in Sweden showed that the risk of esophageal adenocarcinoma in *H. pylori*-infected individuals was one-third that of uninfected individuals. A meta-analysis of 13 studies, including the Swedish study, found a 45 percent reduction in risk of esophageal adenocarcinoma with *H. pylori* infection. Moreover, as with gastric cardia cancer, dramatic increases in esophageal adenocarcinoma rates in several Western countries parallel the declines in *H. pylori* infection rates.

How might H. pylori *infection decrease the risk of some cancers but increase the risk of other cancers?*

Although it is not known for certain how *H. pylori* infection increases the risk of non-cardia gastric cancer, some researchers speculate that the long-term presence of an inflammatory response predisposes cells in the stomach lining to become cancerous. This idea is supported by the finding that increased expression of a single cytokine (interleukin-1-beta) in the stomach of transgenic mice causes sporadic gastric inflammation and cancer. The increased cell turnover resulting from ongoing cellular damage could increase the likelihood that cells will develop harmful mutations.

One hypothesis that may explain reduced risks of gastric cardia cancer and esophageal adenocarcinoma in *H. pylori*-infected individuals relates to the decline in stomach acidity that is often seen after decades of *H. pylori* colonization. This decline would reduce acid reflux into the esophagus, a major risk factor for adenocarcinomas affecting the upper stomach and esophagus.

What is cagA-positive H. pylori *and how does it affect the risk of gastric and esophageal cancers?*

Some *H. pylori* bacteria use a needle-like appendage to inject a toxin produced by a gene called cytotoxin-associated gene A (cagA) into the junctions where cells of the stomach lining meet. This toxin (known as cagA) alters the structure of stomach cells and allows the bacteria to attach to them more easily. Long-term exposure to the toxin causes chronic inflammation. However, not all strains of *H. pylori* carry the cagA gene; those that do are classified as cagA-positive.

Epidemiologic evidence suggests that infection with cagA-positive strains is especially associated with an increased risk of non-cardia gastric cancer and with reduced risks of gastric cardia cancer and esophageal adenocarcinoma. For example, a meta-analysis of 16 case–control studies conducted around the world showed that individuals infected with cagA-positive *H. pylori* had twice the risk of non-cardia gastric cancer than individuals infected with cagA-negative *H. pylori*. Conversely, a case–control study conducted in Sweden found that people infected with cagA-positive *H. pylori* had a statistically significantly reduced risk of esophageal adenocarcinoma. Similarly, another case–control study conducted in the United States found that infection with cagA-positive *H. pylori* was associated with a reduced risk of esophageal adenocarcinoma and gastric cardia cancer combined, but that infection with cagA-negative strains was not associated with risk.

Recent research has suggested a potential mechanism by which cagA could contribute to gastric carcinogenesis. In three studies, infection with cagA-positive *H. pylori* was associated with inactivation of tumor suppressor proteins, including p53.

What is gastric mucosa-associated lymphoid tissue (MALT) lymphoma, and what is the evidence that it can be caused by **H. pylori** *infection?*

Gastric MALT lymphoma is a rare type of non-Hodgkin lymphoma that is characterized by the slow multiplication of B lymphocytes, a type of immune cell, in the stomach lining. This cancer represents approximately 12 percent of the extranodal (outside of lymph nodes) non-Hodgkin lymphoma that occurs among men and approximately 18 percent of extranodal non-Hodgkin lymphoma among women. During the period 1999–2003, the annual incidence of gastric MALT lymphoma in the United States was about one case for every 100,000 persons in the population.

Normally, the lining of the stomach lacks lymphoid (immune system) tissue, but development of this tissue is often stimulated in response to colonization of the lining by *H. pylori*. Only in rare cases does this tissue give rise to MALT lymphoma. However, nearly all patients with gastric MALT lymphoma show signs of *H. pylori* infection, and the risk of developing this tumor is more than six times higher in infected people than in uninfected people.

Is **H. pylori** *infection associated with any other cancer?*

Whether *H. pylori* infection is associated with risk of other cancers remains unclear. Some studies have found a possible association between *H. pylori* infection and pancreatic cancer, but the evidence is conflicting. Studies investigating the possibility that *H. pylori* is a risk factor for colorectal adenocarcinoma or lung cancer have found no evidence that it is associated with the risk of either type of cancer.

Can treatment to eradicate **H. pylori** *infection reduce gastric cancer rates?*

Long-term follow-up of data from a randomized clinical trial carried out in Shandong, China—an area where rates of gastric cancer are

very high—found that short-term treatment with antibiotics to eradicate *H. pylori* reduced the incidence of gastric cancer. During a nearly
15-year period after treatment, gastric cancer incidence was reduced
by almost 40 percent. When the results of this trial were pooled with
those of several smaller trials examining the effects on gastric cancer
incidence of antimicrobial treatment to eradicate *H. pylori*, a similar
reduction was seen.

Who should seek diagnosis and treatment of an H. pylori infection?

According to the Centers for Disease Control and Prevention (CDC),
people who have active gastric or duodenal ulcers or a documented
history of ulcers should be tested for *H. pylori*, and, if they are infected,
should be treated. Testing for and treating *H. pylori* infection is also
recommended after resection of early gastric cancer and for low-grade
gastric MALT lymphoma. However, most experts agree that the available evidence does not support widespread testing for and eradication
of *H. pylori* infection.

Chapter 16

Cancer Prevention

Chapter Contents

Section 16.1

An Overview on Cancer Prevention

Text in this section is excerpted from "Cancer Prevention Overview
(PDQ®)," National Cancer Institute (NCI), July 23, 2015.

What is Cancer Prevention?

Cancer prevention is action taken to lower the chance of getting cancer. In 2014, about 1.6 million people will be diagnosed with cancer in the United States. In addition to the physical problems and emotional distress caused by cancer, the high costs of care are also a burden to patients, their families, and to the public. By preventing cancer, the number of new cases of cancer is lowered. Hopefully, this will reduce the burden of cancer and lower the number of deaths caused by cancer.

Cancer is not a single disease but a group of related diseases. Many things in our genes, our lifestyle, and the environment around us may increase or decrease our risk of getting cancer.

Scientists are studying many different ways to help prevent cancer, including the following:

- Ways to avoid or control things known to cause cancer.

- Changes in diet and lifestyle.

- Finding precancerous conditions early. Precancerous conditions are conditions that may become cancer.

- Chemoprevention (medicines to treat a precancerous condition or to keep cancer from starting).

Carcinogenesis

Carcinogenesis is the process in which normal cells turn into cancer cells.

Carcinogenesis is the series of steps that take place as a normal cell becomes a cancer cell. Cells are the smallest units of the body and they make up the body's tissues. Each cell contains genes that guide the way the body grows, develops, and repairs itself. There are many genes that control whether a cell lives or dies, divides (multiplies), or takes on special functions, such as becoming a nerve cell or a muscle cell.

Changes (mutations) in genes occur during carcinogenesis.

Changes (mutations) in genes can cause normal controls in cells to break down. When this happens, cells do not die when they should and new cells are produced when the body does not need them. The buildup of extra cells may cause a mass (tumor) to form.

Tumors can be benign or malignant (cancerous). Malignant tumor cells invade nearby tissues and spread to other parts of the body. Benign tumor cells do not invade nearby tissues or spread.

Risk Factors

Scientists study risk factors and protective factors to find ways to prevent new cancers from starting. Anything that increases your chance of developing cancer is called a cancer risk factor; anything that decreases your chance of developing cancer is called a cancer protective factor.

Some risk factors for cancer can be avoided, but many cannot. For example, both smoking and inheriting certain genes are risk factors for some types of cancer, but only smoking can be avoided. Risk factors that a person can control are called modifiable risk factors.

Many other factors in our environment, diet, and lifestyle may cause or prevent cancer. This section reviews only the major cancer risk factors and protective factors that can be controlled or changed to reduce the risk of cancer. Risk factors that are not described in the section include certain sexual behaviors, the use of estrogen, and being exposed to certain substances at work or to certain chemicals.

Factors That Are Known to Increase the Risk of Cancer

Cigarette Smoking and Tobacco Use

Tobacco use is strongly linked to an increased risk for many kinds of cancer. Smoking cigarettes is the leading cause of the following types of cancer:

- Acute myelogenous leukemia (AML).
- Bladder cancer.
- Esophageal cancer.

- Kidney cancer.
- Lung cancer.
- Oral cavity cancer.
- Pancreatic cancer.
- Stomach cancer.

Not smoking or quitting smoking lowers the risk of getting cancer and dying from cancer. Scientists believe that cigarette smoking causes about 30% of all cancer deaths in the United States.

Infections

Certain viruses and bacteria are able to cause cancer. Viruses and other infection-causing agents cause more cases of cancer in the developing world (about 1 in 4 cases of cancer) than in developed nations (less than 1 in 10 cases of cancer). Examples of cancer-causing viruses and bacteria include:

- *Human papillomavirus* (HPV) increases the risk for cancers of the cervix, penis, vagina, anus, and oropharynx.
- *Hepatitis B* and *hepatitis C viruses* increase the risk for liver cancer.
- *Epstein-Barr virus* increases the risk for Burkitt lymphoma.
- *Helicobacter pylori* increases the risk for gastric cancer.

Two vaccines to prevent infection by cancer-causing agents have already been developed and approved by the U.S. Food and Drug Administration (FDA). One is a vaccine to prevent infection with *hepatitis B virus*. The other protects against infection with strains of *human papillomavirus* (HPV) that cause cervical cancer. Scientists continue to work on vaccines against infections that cause cancer.

Radiation

Being exposed to radiation is a known cause of cancer. There are two main types of radiation linked with an increased risk for cancer:

- Ultraviolet radiation from sunlight: This is the main cause of nonmelanoma skin cancers.

- Ionizing radiation including:
  - Medical radiation from tests to diagnose cancer such as x-rays, CT scans, fluoroscopy, and nuclear medicine scans.
  - Radon gas in our homes.

Scientists believe that ionizing radiation causes leukemia, thyroid cancer, and breast cancer in women. Ionizing radiation may also be linked to myeloma and cancers of the lung, stomach, colon, esophagus, bladder, and ovary. Being exposed to radiation from diagnostic x-rays increases the risk of cancer in patients and x-ray technicians.

The growing use of CT scans over the last 20 years has increased exposure to ionizing radiation. The risk of cancer also increases with the number of CT scans a patient has and the radiation dose used each time.

Immunosuppressive Medicines

Immunosuppressive medicines are linked to an increased risk of cancer. These medicines lower the body's ability to stop cancer from forming. For example, immunosuppressive medicines may be used to keep a patient from rejecting an organ transplant.

Factors That May Affect the Risk of Cancer

Diet

The foods that you eat on a regular basis make up your diet. Diet is being studied as a risk factor for cancer. It is hard to study the effects of diet on cancer because a person's diet includes foods that may protect against cancer and foods that may increase the risk of cancer.

It is also hard for people who take part in the studies to keep track of what they eat over a long period of time. This may explain why studies have different results about how diet affects the risk of cancer.

Some studies show that fruits and nonstarchy vegetables may protect against cancers of the mouth, esophagus, and stomach. Fruits may also protect against lung cancer.

Some studies have shown that a diet high in fat, proteins, calories, and red meat increases the risk of colorectal cancer, but other studies have not shown this.

It is not known if a diet low in fat and high in fiber, fruits, and vegetables lowers the risk of colorectal cancer.

Alcohol

Studies have shown that drinking alcohol is linked to an increased risk of the following types of cancers:

- Oral cancer.

- Esophageal cancer.

- Breast cancer.

Drinking alcohol may also increase the risk of liver cancer and female colorectal cancer.

Physical Activity

Studies show that people who are physically active have a lower risk of certain cancers than those who are not. It is not known if physical activity itself is the reason for this.

Studies show a strong link between physical activity and a lower risk of colorectal cancer. Some studies show that physical activity protects against postmenopausal breast cancer and endometrial cancer.

Obesity

Studies show that obesity is linked to a higher risk of the following types of cancer:

- Postmenopausal breast cancer.

- Colorectal cancer.

- Endometrial cancer.

- Esophageal cancer.

- Kidney cancer.

- Pancreatic cancer.

Some studies show that obesity is also a risk factor for cancer of the gallbladder.

It is not known if losing weight lowers the risk of cancers that have been linked to obesity.

Environmental Risk Factors

Being exposed to chemicals and other substances in the environment has been linked to some cancers:

- Links between air pollution and cancer risk have been found. These include links between lung cancer and secondhand tobacco smoke, outdoor air pollution, and asbestos.

- Drinking water that contains a large amount of arsenic has been linked to skin, bladder, and lung cancers.

Studies have been done to see if pesticides and other pollutants increase the risk of cancer. The results of those studies have been unclear because other factors can change the results of the studies.

Interventions That Are Known to Lower Cancer Risk

An intervention is a treatment or action taken to prevent or treat disease, or improve health in other ways. Many studies are being done to find ways to keep cancer from starting or recurring (coming back).

Chemoprevention is being studied in patients who have a high risk of developing cancer.

Chemoprevention is the use of substances to lower the risk of cancer, or keep it from recurring. The substances may be natural or made in the laboratory. Some chemopreventive agents are tested in people who are at high risk for a certain type of cancer. The risk may be because of a precancerous condition, family history, or lifestyle factors.

Some chemoprevention studies have shown good results. For example, selective estrogen receptor modulators (SERMS) such as tamoxifen or raloxifene have been shown to reduce the risk of breast cancer in women at high risk. Finasteride and dutasteride have been shown to reduce the risk of prostate cancer.

New ways to prevent cancer are being studied in clinical trials.

Chemoprevention agents that are being studied in clinical trials include COX-2 inhibitors. They are being studied for the prevention of colorectal and breast cancer. Aspirin is being studied for the prevention of colorectal cancer.

Interventions That Are Not Known to Lower Cancer Risk

Vitamin and dietary supplements have not been shown to prevent cancer.

An intervention is a treatment or action taken to prevent or treat disease, or improve health in other ways.

There is not enough proof that taking multivitamin and mineral supplements or single vitamins or minerals can prevent cancer. The following vitamins and mineral supplements have been studied, but have not been shown to lower the risk of cancer:

- Vitamin B6.
- Vitamin B12.
- Vitamin E.
- Vitamin C.
- Beta carotene.
- Folic acid.
- Selenium.
- Vitamin D.

The Selenium and Vitamin E Cancer Prevention Trial (SELECT) found that vitamin E taken alone increased the risk of prostate cancer. The risk continued even after the men stopped taking vitamin E. Taking selenium with vitamin E or taking selenium alone did not increase the risk of prostate cancer.

Vitamin D has also been studied to see if it has anticancer effects. Skin exposed to sunshine can make vitamin D. Vitamin D can also be consumed in the diet and in dietary supplements. Taking vitamin D in doses from 400-1100 IU / day has not been shown to lower the risk of cancer.

The VITamin D and OmegA-3 TriaL (VITAL) is under way to study whether taking vitamin D (2000 IU/ day) and omega-3 fatty acids from marine (oily fish) sources lowers the risk of cancer.

The Physicians' Health Study found that men who have had cancer in the past and take a multivitamin daily may have a slightly lower risk of having a second cancer.

Section 16.2

Antioxidants and Cancer Prevention

Text in this section is excerpted from "Antioxidants and Cancer Prevention," National Cancer Institute (NCI), January 16, 2014.

What are free radicals, and do they play a role in cancer development?

Free radicals are highly reactive chemicals that have the potential to harm cells. They are created when an atom or a molecule (a chemical that has two or more atoms) either gains or loses an electron (a small negatively charged particle found in atoms). Free radicals are formed naturally in the body and play an important role in many normal cellular processes. At high concentrations, however, free radicals can be hazardous to the body and damage all major components of cells, including DNA, proteins, and cell membranes. The damage to cells caused by free radicals, especially the damage to DNA, may play a role in the development of cancer and other health conditions.

Abnormally high concentrations of free radicals in the body can be caused by exposure to ionizing radiation and other environmental toxins. When ionizing radiation hits an atom or a molecule in a cell, an electron may be lost, leading to the formation of a free radical. The production of abnormally high levels of free radicals is the mechanism by which ionizing radiation kills cells. Moreover, some environmental toxins, such as cigarette smoke, some metals, and high-oxygen atmospheres, may contain large amounts of free radicals or stimulate the body's cells to produce more free radicals.

Free radicals that contain the element oxygen are the most common type of free radicals produced in living tissue. Another name for them is "reactive oxygen species," or "ROS."

What are antioxidants?

Antioxidants are chemicals that interact with and neutralize free radicals, thus preventing them from causing damage. Antioxidants are also known as "free radical scavengers."

The body makes some of the antioxidants it uses to neutralize free radicals. These antioxidants are called endogenous antioxidants. However, the body relies on external (exogenous) sources, primarily the diet, to obtain the rest of the antioxidants it needs. These exogenous antioxidants are commonly called dietary antioxidants. Fruits, vegetables, and grains are rich sources of dietary antioxidants. Some dietary antioxidants are also available as dietary supplements.

Examples of dietary antioxidants include beta-carotene, lycopene, and vitamins A, C, and E (alpha-tocopherol). The mineral element selenium is often thought to be a dietary antioxidant, but the antioxidant effects of selenium are most likely due to the antioxidant activity of proteins that have this element as an essential component (i.e., selenium-containing proteins), and not to selenium itself.

Can antioxidant supplements help prevent cancer?

In laboratory and animal studies, the presence of increased levels of exogenous antioxidants has been shown to prevent the types of free radical damage that have been associated with cancer development. Therefore, researchers have investigated whether taking dietary antioxidant supplements can help lower the risk of developing or dying from cancer in humans.

Many observational studies, including case–control studies and cohort studies, have been conducted to investigate whether the use of dietary antioxidant supplements is associated with reduced risks of cancer in humans. Overall, these studies have yielded mixed results. Because observational studies cannot adequately control for biases that might influence study outcomes, the results of any individual observational study must be viewed with caution.

Randomized controlled clinical trials, however, lack most of the biases that limit the reliability of observational studies. Therefore, randomized trials are considered to provide the strongest and most reliable evidence of the benefit and/or harm of a health-related intervention. To date, nine randomized controlled trials of dietary antioxidant supplements for cancer prevention have been conducted worldwide. Many of the trials were sponsored by the National Cancer Institute (NCI). The results of these nine trials are summarized below.

- **Linxian General Population Nutrition Intervention Trial:** This trial was the first large-scale randomized trial to investigate the effects of antioxidant supplements on cancer risk. In the trial, healthy Chinese men and women at increased risk of developing esophageal cancer and gastric cancer were randomly

assigned to take a combination of 15 milligrams (mg) beta-carotene, 30 mg alpha-tocopherol, and 50 micrograms (µg) selenium
daily for 5 years or to take no antioxidant supplements. The initial results of the trial showed that people who took antioxidant
supplements had a lower risk of death from gastric cancer but
not from esophageal cancer. However, their risks of developing
gastric cancer and/or esophageal cancer were not affected by
antioxidant supplementation. In 2009, 15-year results from this
trial were reported (10 years after antioxidant supplementation
ended). In the updated results, a reduced risk of death from gastric cancer was no longer found for those who took antioxidant
supplements compared with those who did not.

- **Alpha-Tocopherol/Beta-Carotene Cancer Prevention
  Study (ATBC):** This trial investigated whether the use of
  alpha-tocopherol and/or beta-carotene supplements for 5 to 8
  years could help reduce the incidence of lung and other cancers
  in middle-aged male smokers in Finland. Initial results of the
  trial, reported in 1994, showed an increase in the incidence of
  lung cancer among the participants who took beta-carotene
  supplements (20 mg per day); in contrast, alpha-tocopherol
  supplementation (50 mg per day) had no effect on lung cancer
  incidence. Later results showed no effect of beta-carotene or
  alpha-tocopherol supplementation on the incidence of urothelial
  (bladder, ureter, or renal pelvis), pancreatic, colorectal, renal cell
  (kidney), or upper aerodigestive tract (oral/pharyngeal, esophageal, or laryngeal) cancers.

- **Carotene and Retinol Efficacy Trial (CARET):** This
  U.S. trial examined the effects of daily supplementation with
  beta-carotene and retinol (vitamin A) on the incidence of lung
  cancer, other cancers, and death among people who were at high
  risk of lung cancer because of a history of smoking or exposure
  to asbestos. The trial began in 1983 and ended in late 1995, 2
  years earlier than originally planned. Results reported in 1996
  showed that daily supplementation with both 15 mg beta-carotene and 25,000 International Units (IU) retinol was associated with increased lung cancer and increased death from all
  causes (all-cause mortality). A 2004 report showed that these
  adverse effects persisted up to 6 years after supplementation
  ended, although the elevated risks of lung cancer and all-cause
  mortality were no longer statistically significant. Additional
  results, reported in 2009, showed that beta-carotene and retinol

supplementation had no effect on the incidence of prostate cancer.

- **Physicians' Health Study I (PHS I):** This trial examined the effects of long-term beta-carotene supplementation on cancer incidence, cancer mortality, and all-cause mortality among U.S. male physicians. The results of the study, reported in 1996, showed that beta-carotene supplementation (50 mg every other day for 12 years) had no effect on any of these outcomes in smokers or nonsmokers.

- **Women's Health Study (WHS):** This trial investigated the effects of beta-carotene supplementation (50 mg every other day), vitamin E supplementation (600 IU every other day), and aspirin (100 mg every other day) on the incidence of cancer and cardiovascular disease in U.S. women ages 45 and older. The results, reported in 1999, showed no benefit or harm associated with 2 years of beta-carotene supplementation. In 2005, similar results were reported for vitamin E supplementation.

- **Supplémentation en Vitamines et Minéraux Antioxydants (SU.VI.MAX) Study:** This trial investigated the effects of daily supplementation with a combination of antioxidants and minerals on the incidence of cancer and cardiovascular disease in French men and women. The initial results of the study, reported in 2004, showed that daily supplementation with vitamin C (120 mg), vitamin E (30 mg), beta-carotene (6 mg), and the minerals selenium (100 μg) and zinc (20 mg) for a median of 7.5 years had no effect on the incidence of cancer or cardiovascular disease or on all-cause mortality. However, when the data for men and women were analyzed separately, antioxidant and mineral supplementation was associated with lower total cancer incidence and all-cause mortality among men but not among women, and with an increase in skin cancer incidence, including melanoma, among women but not among men. The beneficial effects of the supplements for men disappeared within 5 years of ending supplementation, as did the increased risk of skin cancer among women.

- **Heart Outcomes Prevention Evaluation–The Ongoing Outcomes (HOPE–TOO) Study:** This international trial examined the effects of alpha-tocopherol supplementation on cancer incidence, death from cancer, and the incidence of major cardiovascular events (heart attack, stroke, or death from heart disease) in people diagnosed with cardiovascular disease or diabetes. The results, reported in 2005, showed no effect of daily supplementation with alpha-tocopherol (400 IU) for a median of 7 years on any of the outcomes.

- **Selenium and Vitamin E Cancer Prevention Trial (SELECT):** This U.S. trial investigated whether daily supplementation with selenium (200 μg), vitamin E (400 IU), or both would reduce the incidence of prostate cancer in men ages 50 and older. The study began in 2001 and was stopped in 2008, approximately 5 years earlier than originally planned. Results reported in late 2008 showed that the use of these supplements for a median duration of 5.5 years did not reduce the incidence of prostate or other cancers. Updated findings from the study, reported in 2011, showed that, after an average of 7 years (5.5 years on supplements and 1.5 years off supplements), there were 17 percent more cases of prostate cancer among men taking vitamin E alone than among men taking a placebo. No increase in prostate risk was observed for men assigned to take selenium alone or vitamin E plus selenium compared with men assigned to take a placebo.

- **Physicians' Health Study II (PHS II):** This trial examined whether supplementation with vitamin E, vitamin C, or both would reduce the incidence of cancer in male U.S. physicians ages 50 years and older. The results, reported in 2009, showed that the use of these supplements (400 IU vitamin E every other day, 500 mg vitamin C every day, or a combination of the two) for a median of 7.6 years did not reduce the incidence of prostate cancer or other cancers, including lymphoma, leukemia, melanoma, and cancers of the lung, bladder, pancreas, and colon and rectum.

Overall, these nine randomized controlled clinical trials did not provide evidence that dietary antioxidant supplements are beneficial in primary cancer prevention. In addition, a systematic review of the available evidence regarding the use of vitamin and mineral supplements for the prevention of chronic diseases, including cancer, conducted for the United States Preventive Services Task Force (USPSTF) likewise found no clear evidence of benefit in preventing cancer.

It is possible, however, that the lack of benefit in clinical studies can be explained by differences in the effects of the tested antioxidants when they are consumed as purified chemicals as opposed to when they are consumed in foods, which contain complex mixtures of antioxidants, vitamins, and minerals. Therefore, acquiring a more complete understanding of the antioxidant content of individual foods, how the various antioxidants and other substances in foods interact with one another, and factors that influence the uptake and distribution of food-derived antioxidants in the body are active areas of ongoing cancer prevention research.

Should people already diagnosed with cancer take antioxidant supplements?

Several randomized controlled trials, some including only small numbers of patients, have investigated whether taking antioxidant supplements during cancer treatment alters the effectiveness or reduces the toxicity of specific therapies. Although these trials had mixed results, some found that people who took antioxidant supplements during cancer therapy had worse outcomes, especially if they were smokers.

Additional large randomized controlled trials are needed to provide clear scientific evidence about the potential benefits or harms of taking antioxidant supplements during cancer treatment. Until more is known about the effects of antioxidant supplements in cancer patients, these supplements should be used with caution. Cancer patients should inform their doctors about their use of any dietary supplement.

Section 16.3

Vitamin D and Cancer Prevention

Text in this section is excerpted from "Vitamin D and Cancer Prevention," National Cancer Institute (NCI), October 21, 2013.

What is vitamin D?

Vitamin D is the name given to a group of fat-soluble prohormones (substances that usually have little hormonal activity by themselves but that the body can turn into hormones). Vitamin D helps the body use calcium and phosphorus to make strong bones and teeth. Skin exposed to sunshine can make vitamin D, and vitamin D can also be obtained from certain foods. Vitamin D deficiency can cause a weakening of the bones that is called rickets in children and osteomalacia in adults.

Two major forms of vitamin D that are important to humans are vitamin D2, or ergocalciferol, and vitamin D3, or cholecalciferol. Vitamin D2 is made naturally by plants, and vitamin D3 is made naturally by the body when skin is exposed to ultraviolet radiation in sunlight. Both forms are converted to 25-hydroxyvitamin D in the liver. 25-Hydroxyvitamin D then travels through the blood to the kidneys, where it is further modified to 1,25-dihydroxyvitamin D, or calcitriol, the active form of vitamin D in the body. The most accurate method of evaluating a person's vitamin D status is to measure the level of 25-hydroxyvitamin D in the blood.

Most people get at least some of the vitamin D they need through sunlight exposure. Dietary sources include a few foods that naturally contain vitamin D, such as fatty fish, fish liver oil, and eggs. However, most dietary vitamin D comes from foods fortified with vitamin D, such as milk, juices, and breakfast cereals. Vitamin D can also be obtained through dietary supplements.

The Institute of Medicine (IOM) of the National Academies has developed the following recommended daily intakes of vitamin D, assuming minimal sun exposure:

- For those between 1 and 70 years of age, including women who are pregnant or lactating, the recommended dietary allowance (RDA) is 15 micrograms (μg) per day. Because 1 μg is equal to 40 International Units (IU), this RDA can also be expressed as 600 IU per day.

- For those 71 years or older, the RDA is 20 μg per day (800 IU per day).

- For infants, the IOM could not determine an RDA due to a lack of data. However, the IOM set an Adequate Intake level of 10 μg per day (400 IU per day), which should provide sufficient vitamin D.

Although the average dietary intakes of vitamin D in the United States are below guideline levels, data from the National Health and Nutrition Examination Survey revealed that more than 80 percent of Americans had adequate vitamin D levels in their blood.

Even though most people are unlikely to have high vitamin D intakes, it is important to remember that excessive intake of any nutrient, including vitamin D, can cause toxic effects. Too much vitamin D can be harmful because it increases calcium levels, which can lead to calcinosis (the deposit of calcium salts in soft tissues, such as the kidneys, heart, or lungs) and hypercalcemia (high blood levels of calcium). The safe upper intake level of vitamin D for adults and children older than 8 years of age is 100 μg per day (4000 IU per day). Toxicity from too much vitamin D is more likely to occur from high intakes of dietary supplements than from high intakes of foods that contain vitamin D. Excessive sun exposure does not cause vitamin D toxicity. However, the IOM states that people should not try to increase vitamin D production by increasing their exposure to sunlight because this will also increase their risk of skin cancer.

Why are cancer researchers studying a possible connection between vitamin D and cancer risk?

Early epidemiologic research showed that incidence and death rates for certain cancers were lower among individuals living in southern latitudes, where levels of sunlight exposure are relatively high, than among those living at northern latitudes. Because exposure to ultraviolet light from sunlight leads to the production of vitamin D, researchers hypothesized that variation in vitamin D levels might account for this association. However, additional research based on stronger study designs is required to determine whether higher vitamin D levels are related to lower cancer incidence or death rates.

Experimental evidence has also suggested a possible association between vitamin D and cancer risk. In studies of cancer cells and of tumors in mice, vitamin D has been found to have several activities that might slow or prevent the development of cancer, including promoting cellular differentiation, decreasing cancer cell growth, stimulating cell death (apoptosis), and reducing tumor blood vessel formation (angiogenesis).

What is the evidence that vitamin D can help reduce the risk of cancer in people?

A number of epidemiologic studies have investigated whether people with higher vitamin D intakes or higher blood levels of vitamin D have lower risks of specific cancers. The results of these studies have been inconsistent, possibly because of the challenges in carrying out such studies. For example, dietary studies do not account for vitamin D made in the skin from sunlight exposure, and the level of vitamin D measured in the blood at a single point in time (as in most studies) may not reflect a person's true vitamin D status. Also, it is possible that people with higher vitamin D intakes or blood levels are more likely to have other healthy behaviors. It may be one of these other behaviors, rather than vitamin D intake, that influences cancer risk.

Several randomized trials of vitamin D intake have been carried out, but these were designed to assess bone health or other non-cancer outcomes. Although some of these trials have yielded information on cancer incidence and mortality, the results need to be confirmed by additional research because the trials were not designed to study cancer specifically.

The cancers for which the most human data are available are colorectal, breast, prostate, and pancreatic cancer. Numerous epidemiologic studies have shown that higher intake or blood levels of vitamin D are associated with a reduced risk of colorectal cancer. In contrast, the Women's Health Initiative randomized trial found that healthy women who took vitamin D and calcium supplements for an average of 7 years did not have a reduced incidence of colorectal cancer. Some scientists have pointed out that the relatively low level of vitamin D supplementation (10 μg, or 400 IU, once a day), the ability of participants to take additional vitamin D on their own, and the short duration of participant follow-up in this trial might explain why no reduction in colorectal cancer risk was found. Evidence on the association between vitamin D and the risks of all other malignancies studied is inconclusive.

How is vitamin D being studied now in clinical cancer research?

Taken together, the available data are not comprehensive enough to establish whether taking vitamin D can prevent cancer. To fully understand the effects of vitamin D on cancer and other health outcomes, new randomized trials need to be conducted. However, the appropriate dose of vitamin D to use in such trials is still not clear. Other remaining questions include when to start taking vitamin D, and for how long, to potentially see a benefit.

To begin addressing these issues, researchers are conducting two phase I trials to determine what dose of vitamin D may be useful for chemoprevention of prostate, colorectal, and lung cancers (trial descriptions here and here). In addition, larger randomized trials have been initiated to examine the potential role of vitamin D in the prevention of cancer. The Vitamin D/Calcium Polyp Prevention Study, which has finished recruiting approximately 2,200 participants, is testing whether vitamin D supplements, given alone or with calcium, can prevent the development of colorectal adenomas (precancerous growths) in patients who previously had an adenoma removed. The study's estimated completion date is December 2017. The Vitamin D and Omega-3 Trial (VITAL) will examine whether vitamin D supplements can prevent the development of a variety of cancer types in healthy older men and women. The organizers of VITAL expect to recruit 20,000 participants and complete the trial by June 2016.

Researchers are also beginning to study vitamin D analogs–chemicals with structures similar to that of vitamin D–which may have the anticancer activity of vitamin D but not its ability to increase calcium levels.

Part Three

Breast Cancer

Chapter 17

Breast Cancer – An Overview

Chapter Contents

Section 17.1

General Information about Breast Cancer

This section includes excerpts from "Breast Cancer Treatment (PDQ®)," National Cancer Institute (NCI), July 23, 2015; text from "Changing patterns in survival for U.S. women with invasive breast cancer," National Cancer Institute (NCI), July 20, 2015; and text from "Breast Cancer: Know the Risks Infographic," Centers for Disease Control and Prevention (CDC), December 10, 2013.

Breast cancer is a disease in which malignant (cancer) cells form in the tissues of the breast.

The breast is made up of lobes and ducts. Each breast has 15 to 20 sections called lobes. Each lobe has many smaller sections called lobules. Lobules end in dozens of tiny bulbs that can make milk. The lobes, lobules, and bulbs are linked by thin tubes called ducts.

Each breast also has blood vessels and lymph vessels. The lymph vessels carry an almost colorless fluid called lymph. Lymph vessels carry lymph between lymph nodes. Lymph nodes are small bean-shaped structures that are found throughout the body. They filter substances in lymph and help fight infection and disease. Clusters of lymph nodes are found near the breast in the axilla (under the arm), above the collarbone, and in the chest.

The most common type of breast cancer is ductal carcinoma, which begins in the cells of the ducts. Cancer that begins in the lobes or lobules is called lobular carcinoma and is more often found in both breasts than are other types of breast cancer. Inflammatory breast cancer is an uncommon type of breast cancer in which the breast is warm, red, and swollen.

Having a family history of breast cancer and other factors increase the risk of breast cancer.

Anything that increases your chance of getting a disease is called a risk factor. Having a risk factor does not mean that you will get cancer; not having risk factors does not mean that you will not get cancer. Talk with your doctor if you think you may be at risk.

Older age is the main risk factor for most cancers. The chance of getting cancer increases as you get older. Other risk factors for breast cancer include:

- A family history of breast cancer in a first-degree relative (mother, daughter, or sister).

- Inherited changes in the BRCA1 and BRCA2 genes or in other genes that increase the risk of breast cancer.

- Drinking alcoholic beverages.

- Breast tissue that is dense on a mammogram.

- Exposure of breast tissue to estrogen made by the body:

  - Menstruating at an early age.

  - Older age at first birth or never having given birth.

  - Starting menopause at a later age.

- Taking hormones such as estrogen combined with progestin for symptoms of menopause.

- Obesity.

- A personal history of invasive breast cancer, ductal carcinoma in situ (DCIS), or lobular carcinoma in situ (LCIS).

- A personal history of benign (non-cancer) breast disease.

- Being White.

- Treatment with radiation therapy to the breast/chest.

Breast cancer is sometimes caused by inherited gene mutations (changes).

The genes in cells carry the hereditary information that is received from a person's parents. Hereditary breast cancer makes up about 5% to 10% of all breast cancer. Some mutated genes related to breast cancer are more common in certain ethnic groups.

Women who have certain gene mutations, such as a BRCA1 or BRCA2 mutation, have an increased risk of breast cancer. These women also have an increased risk of ovarian cancer, and may have an increased risk of other cancers. Men who have a mutated gene related to breast cancer also have an increased risk of breast cancer.

There are tests that can detect (find) mutated genes. These genetic tests are sometimes done for members of families with a high risk of cancer.

Decreasing the length of time a woman's breast tissue is exposed to estrogen decreases the risk of breast cancer.

Anything that decreases your chance of getting a disease is called a protective factor.

Protective factors for breast cancer include the following:

- Taking any of the following:
  - Estrogen-only hormone therapy after a hysterectomy.
  - Selective estrogen receptor modulators (SERMs).
  - Aromatase inhibitors.
- Less exposure of breast tissue to estrogen made by the body:
  - Early pregnancy.
  - Breastfeeding.
- Getting enough exercise.
- Having any of the following procedures:
  - Risk-reducing mastectomy.
  - Risk-reducing oophorectomy.
  - Ovarian ablation.

Signs of breast cancer include a lump or change in the breast.

These and other signs may be caused by breast cancer or by other conditions. Check with your doctor if you have any of the following:

- A lump or thickening in or near the breast or in the underarm area.
- A change in the size or shape of the breast.
- A dimple or puckering in the skin of the breast.
- A nipple turned inward into the breast.
- Fluid, other than breast milk, from the nipple, especially if it's bloody.

- Scaly, red, or swollen skin on the breast, nipple, or areola (the dark area of skin around the nipple).

- Dimples in the breast that look like the skin of an orange, called peau d'orange.

Tests that examine the breasts are used to detect (find) and diagnose breast cancer.

Check with your doctor if you notice any changes in your breasts. The following tests and procedures may be used:

Physical exam and history: An exam of the body to check general signs of health, including checking for signs of disease, such as lumps or anything else that seems unusual. A history of the patient's health habits and past illnesses and treatments will also be taken.

Clinical breast exam (CBE): An exam of the breast by a doctor or other health professional. The doctor will carefully feel the breasts and under the arms for lumps or anything else that seems unusual.

Mammogram: An x-ray of the breast.

Ultrasound exam: A procedure in which high-energy sound waves (ultrasound) are bounced off internal tissues or organs and make echoes. The echoes form a picture of body tissues called a sonogram. The picture can be printed to be looked at later.

MRI (magnetic resonance imaging): A procedure that uses a magnet, radio waves, and a computer to make a series of detailed pictures of both breasts. This procedure is also called nuclear magnetic resonance imaging (NMRI).

Blood chemistry studies: A procedure in which a blood sample is checked to measure the amounts of certain substances released into the blood by organs and tissues in the body. An unusual (higher or lower than normal) amount of a substance can be a sign of disease.

Biopsy: The removal of cells or tissues so they can be viewed under a microscope by a pathologist to check for signs of cancer. If a lump in the breast is found, a biopsy may be done.

There are four types of biopsy used to check for breast cancer:

- **Excisional biopsy:** The removal of an entire lump of tissue.

165

- **Incisional biopsy:** The removal of part of a lump or a sample of tissue.

- **Core biopsy:** The removal of tissue using a wide needle.

- **Fine-needle aspiration (FNA) biopsy:** The removal of tissue or fluid, using a thin needle.

If cancer is found, tests are done to study the cancer cells.

Decisions about the best treatment are based on the results of these tests. The tests give information about:

- how quickly the cancer may grow.

- how likely it is that the cancer will spread through the body.

- how well certain treatments might work.

- how likely the cancer is to recur (come back).

Tests include the following:

- **Estrogen and progesterone receptor test:** A test to measure the amount of estrogen and progesterone (hormones) receptors in cancer tissue. If there are more estrogen and progesterone receptors than normal, the cancer is called estrogen and/or progesterone receptor positive. This type of breast cancer may grow more quickly. The test results show whether treatment to block estrogen and progesterone may stop the cancer from growing.

- **Human epidermal growth factor type 2 receptor (HER2/neu) test:** A laboratory test to measure how many HER2/neu genes there are and how much HER2/neu protein is made in a sample of tissue. If there are more HER2/neu genes or higher levels of HER2/neu protein than normal, the cancer is called HER2/neu positive. This type of breast cancer may grow more quickly and is more likely to spread to other parts of the body. The cancer may be treated with drugs that target the HER2/neu protein, such as trastuzumab and pertuzumab.

- **Multigene tests:** Tests in which samples of tissue are studied to look at the activity of many genes at the same time. These tests may help predict whether cancer will spread to other parts of the body or recur (come back).

  - **Oncotype DX:** This test helps predict whether stage I or stage II breast cancer that is estrogen receptor positive and node negative will spread to other parts of the body. If the risk that the cancer will spread is high, chemotherapy may be given to lower the risk.

- **MammaPrint:** This test helps predict whether stage I or stage II breast cancer that is node negative will spread to other parts of the body. If the risk that the cancer will spread is high, chemotherapy may be given to lower the risk.

Based on these tests, breast cancer is described as:

- Hormone receptor positive (estrogen and/or progesterone receptor positive) or hormone receptor negative (estrogen and/or progesterone receptor negative).
- HER2/neu positive or HER2/neu negative.
- Triple negative (estrogen receptor, progesterone receptor, and HER2/neu negative).

Certain factors affect prognosis (chance of recovery) and treatment options.

Breast cancer mortality rates have been declining among women in many western countries since the 1970s. Overall, breast cancer survival rates following diagnosis have improved for all women diagnosed with local and regional (area around the tumor) disease. Women diagnosed before age 70 have experienced lower short-term (less than 5 years) death rates, even for metastatic disease. And the long-term death rates (survival beyond the first 5 years) have improved among those with local and regional disease in all age groups.

Tumor size at diagnosis has shrunk since the 1980s, but new evidence shows that changes in tumor size within each stage at diagnosis explain only a small proportion of the improvement in breast cancer mortality in women under the age of 70. However, changes in tumor size account for about half of the improvements for women diagnosed with local or regional breast cancer at age 70 and older.

This conclusion comes from an analysis of data from National Cancer Institute's (NCI) Surveillance, Epidemiology, and End Results (SEER) database. The study also found that changes in estrogen receptor (ER) status explain little of the improvement after adjustment for tumor size, except for women age 70 and older within 5 years after diagnosis. Results of this study, by Mitchell H. Gail, M.D., Ph.D., and William F. Anderson, M.D., both with the NCI Division of Cancer Epidemiology and Genetics, and their colleague, Ju-Hyun Park, Ph.D., Dongguk University-Seoul, appeared online July 20, 2015, in the Journal of Clinical Oncology.

The investigative team analyzed data that included: age at breast cancer diagnosis; year of diagnosis; tumor size; lymph node status (negative or positive); stage of breast cancer (localized, regional, or metastasized); and ER status (positive, negative, unknown). These data revealed the pattern of changes in survival following diagnosis, and allowed the researchers to determine the contribution of tumor size and ER status to improvements in individual survival outcomes among women with a first primary invasive breast cancer. Their analysis showed that the hazard of breast-cancer-specific death declined over the period from 1973–2010, not only in the first five years following diagnosis, but also thereafter. They found that smaller tumor size within each stage explained less than 17 percent of these positive trends, except for women over age 70.

In the older women with local disease, smaller tumor size explained 49 percent of improvement; for those with regional disease it explained 38 percent of improvement. They also found that tumor size usually accounted for more of the improvement in the first five years after diagnosis than in later years, regardless of age. While treatments seem to account for much of the improvement in breast cancer survival after diagnosis, more favorable tumor biology may also have an influence on trends.

Experts have established that rates of harder-to-treat estrogen receptor-negative tumors have been declining since 1990. Some of the stage-specific survival improvements may also be due to changes in diagnostic procedures over time that tend to increase the proportion of women with more favorable prognoses within each stage. Findings from this large-scale study help clarify factors associated with breast cancer survival in women of all ages, according to the investigators.

Breast Cancer: Know the Risks

Many things can increase the chance that you'll get breast cancer. They're called risk factors. Some things you can change. Others you can't.

Menstruation

- Starting your period before age 12.

- Starting menopause (the "change of life") after age 55.

Motherhood

- Having children after age 35 or never having children.

- Not breastfeeding your babies.

Hormones

- If you're taking hormone replacement therapy (HRT), ask your doctor if you need it.

- Some types of HRT increase your risk for breast cancer and can cause "dense breasts" (more breast tissue than fat tissue). Dense breasts increase your risk for breast cancer and make it harder for a mammogram to find cancer.

Lifestyle

- Get at least 4 hours of exercise each week.

- Keep a healthy weight, especially after menopause.

- Limit alcoholic drinks to one per day.

Family History and Genetics

- Relatives with breast cancer or ovarian cancer at a young age.

- Changes in the BRCA1 or BRCA2 genes related to breast cancer.

Other Risk Factors

- Getting older.

- Radiation treatment to the chest area.

- Breast cancer or certain other breast problems in the past.

Having one or more of these risks doesn't mean you'll get breast cancer. Also, some women have breast cancer even when they don't have any of these risks. So, talk to your doctor about what you can do to lower your risk, and the right screening for you.

Section 17.2

Stages of Breast Cancer

Text in this section is excerpted from "Breast Cancer Treatment (PDQ®)," National Cancer Institute (NCI), July 23, 2015.

After breast cancer has been diagnosed, tests are done to find out if cancer cells have spread within the breast or to other parts of the body.

The process used to find out whether the cancer has spread within the breast or to other parts of the body is called staging. The information gathered from the staging process determines the stage of the disease. It is important to know the stage in order to plan treatment.

The following tests and procedures may be used in the staging process:

Sentinel lymph node biopsy: The removal of the sentinel lymph node during surgery. The sentinel lymph node is the first lymph node to receive lymphatic drainage from a tumor. It is the first lymph node the cancer is likely to spread to from the tumor. A radioactive substance and/or blue dye is injected near the tumor. The substance or dye flows through the lymph ducts to the lymph nodes. The first lymph node to receive the substance or dye is removed. A pathologist views the tissue under a microscope to look for cancer cells. If cancer cells are not found, it may not be necessary to remove more lymph nodes.

Chest x-ray: An x-ray of the organs and bones inside the chest. An x-ray is a type of energy beam that can go through the body and onto film, making a picture of areas inside the body.

CT scan (CAT scan): A procedure that makes a series of detailed pictures of areas inside the body, taken from different angles. The pictures are made by a computer linked to an x-ray machine. A dye may be injected into a vein or swallowed to help the organs or tissues show up more clearly. This procedure is also called computed tomography, computerized tomography, or computerized axial tomography.

Bone scan: A procedure to check if there are rapidly dividing cells, such as cancer cells, in the bone. A very small amount of radioactive material is injected into a vein and travels through the bloodstream. The radioactive material collects in the bones and is detected by a scanner.

PET scan (positron emission tomography scan): A procedure to find malignant tumor cells in the body. A small amount of radioactive glucose (sugar) is injected into a vein. The PET scanner rotates around the body and makes a picture of where glucose is being used in the body. Malignant tumor cells show up brighter in the picture because they are more active and take up more glucose than normal cells do.

There are three ways that cancer spreads in the body.

Cancer can spread through tissue, the lymph system, and the blood:

- Tissue. The cancer spreads from where it began by growing into nearby areas.
- Lymph system. The cancer spreads from where it began by getting into the lymph system. The cancer travels through the lymph vessels to other parts of the body.
- Blood. The cancer spreads from where it began by getting into the blood. The cancer travels through the blood vessels to other parts of the body.

Cancer may spread from where it began to other parts of the body.

When cancer spreads to another part of the body, it is called metastasis. Cancer cells break away from where they began (the primary tumor) and travel through the lymph system or blood.

- Lymph system. The cancer gets into the lymph system, travels through the lymph vessels, and forms a tumor (metastatic tumor) in another part of the body.
- Blood. The cancer gets into the blood, travels through the blood vessels, and forms a tumor (metastatic tumor) in another part of the body.

The metastatic tumor is the same type of cancer as the primary tumor. For example, if breast cancer spreads to the bone, the cancer cells in the bone are actually breast cancer cells. The disease is metastatic breast cancer, not bone cancer.

The following stages are used for breast cancer:

This section describes the stages of breast cancer. The breast cancer stage is based on the results of testing that is done on the tumor and lymph nodes removed during surgery and other tests.

Stage 0 (carcinoma in situ)

There are 3 types of breast carcinoma in situ:

- Ductal carcinoma in situ (DCIS) is a noninvasive condition in which abnormal cells are found in the lining of a breast duct. The abnormal cells have not spread outside the duct to other tissues in the breast. In some cases, DCIS may become invasive cancer and spread to other tissues. At this time, there is no way to know which lesions could become invasive.

- Lobular carcinoma in situ (LCIS) is a condition in which abnormal cells are found in the lobules of the breast. This condition seldom becomes invasive cancer.

- Paget disease of the nipple is a condition in which abnormal cells are found in the nipple only.

Stage I

In stage I, cancer has formed. Stage I is divided into stages IA and IB.

- In stage IA, the tumor is 2 centimeters or smaller. Cancer has not spread outside the breast.

- In stage IB, small clusters of breast cancer cells (larger than 0.2 millimeter but not larger than 2 millimeters) are found in the lymph nodes and either:

  - no tumor is found in the breast; or

  - the tumor is 2 centimeters or smaller.

Stage II

Stage II is divided into stages IIA and IIB.

- In stage IIA:

- no tumor is found in the breast or the tumor is 2 centimeters or smaller. Cancer (larger than 2 millimeters) is found in 1 to 3 axillary lymph nodes or in the lymph nodes near the breastbone (found during a sentinel lymph node biopsy); or

- the tumor is larger than 2 centimeters but not larger than 5 centimeters. Cancer has not spread to the lymph nodes.

In stage IIB, the tumor is:

- larger than 2 centimeters but not larger than 5 centimeters. Small clusters of breast cancer cells (larger than 0.2 millimeter but not larger than 2 millimeters) are found in the lymph nodes; or

- larger than 2 centimeters but not larger than 5 centimeters. Cancer has spread to 1 to 3 axillary lymph nodes or to the lymph nodes near the breastbone (found during a sentinel lymph node biopsy); or

- larger than 5 centimeters. Cancer has not spread to the lymph nodes.

Stage IIIA

In stage IIIA:

- no tumor is found in the breast or the tumor may be any size. Cancer is found in 4 to 9 axillary lymph nodes or in the lymph nodes near the breastbone (found during imaging tests or a physical exam); or

- the tumor is larger than 5 centimeters. Small clusters of breast cancer cells (larger than 0.2 millimeter but not larger than 2 millimeters) are found in the lymph nodes; or

- the tumor is larger than 5 centimeters. Cancer has spread to 1 to 3 axillary lymph nodes or to the lymph nodes near the breastbone (found during a sentinel lymph node biopsy).

Stage IIIB

In stage IIIB, the tumor may be any size and cancer has spread to the chest wall and/or to the skin of the breast and caused swelling or an ulcer. Also, cancer may have spread to:

- up to 9 axillary lymph nodes; or

- the lymph nodes near the breastbone.

Cancer that has spread to the skin of the breast may also be inflammatory breast cancer.

Stage IIIC

In stage IIIC, no tumor is found in the breast or the tumor may be any size. Cancer may have spread to the skin of the breast and caused swelling or an ulcer and/or has spread to the chest wall. Also, cancer has spread to:

- 10 or more axillary lymph nodes; or

- lymph nodes above or below the collarbone; or

- axillary lymph nodes and lymph nodes near the breastbone.

Cancer that has spread to the skin of the breast may also be inflammatory breast cancer.

For treatment, stage IIIC breast cancer is divided into operable and inoperable stage IIIC.

Stage IV

In stage IV, cancer has spread to other organs of the body, most often the bones, lungs, liver, or brain.

Section 17.3

Inflammatory Breast Cancer

Text in this section is excerpted from "Breast Cancer Treatment (PDQ®)," National Cancer Institute (NCI), July 23, 2015.

What is inflammatory breast cancer?

Inflammatory breast cancer (IBC) is a rare and very aggressive disease in which cancer cells block lymph vessels in the skin of the breast. This type of breast cancer is called "inflammatory" because the breast often looks swollen and red, or "inflamed."

Inflammatory breast cancer accounts for 1 to 5 percent of all breast cancers diagnosed in the United States. Most inflammatory breast cancers are invasive ductal carcinomas, which means they developed from cells that line the milk ducts of the breast and then spread beyond the ducts.

Inflammatory breast cancer progresses rapidly, often in a matter of weeks or months. Inflammatory breast cancer is either stage III or IV at diagnosis, depending on whether cancer cells have spread only to nearby lymph nodes or to other tissues as well.

Additional features of inflammatory breast cancer include the following:

- Compared with other types of breast cancer, inflammatory breast cancer tends to be diagnosed at younger ages (median age of 57 years, compared with a median age of 62 years for other types of breast cancer).

- It is more common and diagnosed at younger ages in African American women than in white women. The median age at diagnosis in African American women is 54 years, compared with a median age of 58 years in white women.

- Inflammatory breast tumors are frequently hormone receptor negative, which means that hormone therapies, such as tamoxifen, that interfere with the growth of cancer cells fuelled by estrogen may not be effective against these tumors.

- Inflammatory breast cancer is more common in obese women than in women of normal weight.

Like other types of breast cancer, inflammatory breast cancer can occur in men, but usually at an older age (median age at diagnosis of 66.5 years) than in women.

What are the symptoms of inflammatory breast cancer?

Symptoms of inflammatory breast cancer include swelling (edema) and redness (erythema) that affect a third or more of the breast. The skin of the breast may also appear pink, reddish purple, or bruised. In addition, the skin may have ridges or appear pitted, like the skin of an orange (called peau d'orange). These symptoms are caused by the build-up of fluid (lymph) in the skin of the breast. This fluid build-up occurs because cancer cells have blocked lymph vessels in the skin, preventing the normal flow of lymph through the tissue. Sometimes, the breast may contain a solid tumor that can be felt during a physical exam, but, more often, a tumor cannot be felt.

Other symptoms of inflammatory breast cancer include a rapid increase in breast size; sensations of heaviness, burning, or tenderness in the breast; or a nipple that is inverted (facing inward). Swollen lymph nodes may also be present under the arm, near the collarbone, or in both places.

It is important to note that these symptoms may also be signs of other diseases or conditions, such as an infection, injury, or another type of breast cancer that is locally advanced. For this reason, women with inflammatory breast cancer often have a delayed diagnosis of their disease.

How is inflammatory breast cancer diagnosed?

Inflammatory breast cancer can be difficult to diagnose. Often, there is no lump that can be felt during a physical exam or seen in a screening mammogram. In addition, most women diagnosed with inflammatory breast cancer have non-fatty (dense) breast tissue, which makes cancer detection in a screening mammogram more difficult. Also, because inflammatory breast cancer is so aggressive, it can arise between scheduled screening mammograms and progress quickly. The symptoms of inflammatory breast cancer may be mistaken for those of mastitis, which is an infection of the breast, or another form of locally advanced breast cancer.

To help prevent delays in diagnosis and in choosing the best course of treatment, an international panel of experts published guidelines on how doctors can diagnose and stage inflammatory breast cancer correctly. Their recommendations are summarized below.

Minimum criteria for a diagnosis of inflammatory breast cancer include the following:

- A rapid onset of erythema (redness), edema (swelling), and a peau d'orange appearance and/or abnormal breast warmth, with or without a lump that can be felt.

- The above-mentioned symptoms have been present for less than 6 months.

- The erythema covers at least a third of the breast.

- Initial biopsy samples from the affected breast show invasive carcinoma.

Further examination of tissue from the affected breast should include testing to see if the cancer cells have hormone receptors (estrogen and progesterone receptors) or if they have greater than normal amounts of the HER2 gene and/or the HER2 protein (HER2-positive breast cancer).

Imaging and staging tests should include the following:

- A diagnostic mammogram and an ultrasound of the breast and regional (nearby) lymph nodes.

- A PET scan or a CT scan and a bone scan to see if the cancer has spread to other parts of the body.

Proper diagnosis and staging of cancer helps doctors develop the best treatment plan and estimate the likely outcome of the disease, including the chances for recurrence and survival.

How is inflammatory breast cancer treated?

Inflammatory breast cancer is treated first with systemic chemotherapy to help shrink the tumor, then with surgery to remove the tumor, followed by radiation therapy. This approach to treatment is called a multimodal approach. Studies have found that women with inflammatory breast cancer who are treated with a multi-modal approach have better responses to therapy and longer survival. Treatments used in a multimodal approach may include those described below.

- Neoadjuvant chemotherapy: This type of chemotherapy is given before surgery and usually includes both anthracycline and taxane drugs. At least six cycles of neoadjuvant chemotherapy given over the course of 4 to 6 months before attempting to remove the tumor has been recommended, unless the disease continues to progress during this time and doctors decide that surgery should not be delayed.

- Targeted therapy: This type of treatment may be used if a woman's biopsy samples show that her cancer cells have a tumor marker that can be targeted with specific drugs. For example, inflammatory breast cancers often produce greater than normal amounts of the HER2 protein, which means they may respond positively to drugs, such as trastuzumab (Herceptin), that target this protein. Anti-HER2 therapy can be given as part of neoadjuvant therapy and after surgery (adjuvant therapy). Studies have shown that women with inflammatory breast cancer who received trastuzumab in addition to chemotherapy have better responses to treatment and better survival.

- Hormone therapy: If a woman's biopsy samples show that her cancer cells contain hormone receptors, hormone therapy is another treatment option. For example, breast cancer cells that have estrogen receptors depend on the female hormone estrogen to promote their growth. Drugs such as tamoxifen, which prevent estrogen from binding to its receptor, and aromatase inhibitors such as letrozole, which block the body's ability to make estrogen, can cause estrogen-dependent cancer cells to stop growing and die.

- Surgery: The standard surgery for inflammatory breast cancer is a modified radical mastectomy. This surgery involves removal of the entire affected breast and most or all of the lymph nodes under the adjacent arm. Often, the lining over the underlying chest muscles is also removed, but the chest muscles are preserved. Sometimes, however, the smaller chest muscle (pectoralis minor) may be removed, too.

- Radiation therapy: Post-mastectomy radiation therapy to the chest wall under the breast that was removed is a standard part of multi-modal therapy for inflammatory breast cancer. If a woman received trastuzumab before surgery, she may continue to receive it during postoperative radiation therapy. Breast reconstruction can be performed in women with inflammatory breast cancer. However, because of the importance of radiation therapy in treating this disease, experts generally recommend delayed reconstruction.

- Adjuvant therapy: Adjuvant systemic therapy may be given after surgery to reduce the chance of cancer recurrence. This therapy may include additional chemotherapy, antihormonal therapy, targeted therapy (such as trastuzumab), or some combination of these treatments.

- Supportive/palliative care: The goal of supportive/palliative care is to improve the quality of life of patients who have a serious or life-threatening disease, such as cancer, and to provide support to their loved ones.

What is the prognosis of patients with inflammatory breast cancer?

The prognosis, or likely outcome, for a patient diagnosed with cancer is often viewed as the chance that the cancer will be treated successfully and that the patient will recover completely. Many factors can influence a cancer patient's prognosis, including the type and location of the cancer, the stage of the disease, the patient's age and overall general health, and the extent to which the patient's disease responds to treatment.

Because inflammatory breast cancer usually develops quickly and spreads aggressively to other parts of the body, women diagnosed with this disease, in general, do not survive as long as women diagnosed with other types of breast cancer. According to statistics from National Cancer Institute's (NCI) Surveillance, Epidemiology, and End Results (SEER) program, the 5-year relative survival for women diagnosed with inflammatory breast cancer during the period from 1988 through 2001 was 34 percent, compared with a 5-year relative survival of up to 87 percent among women diagnosed with other stages of invasive breast cancers.

It is important to keep in mind, however, that these survival statistics are based on large numbers of patients and that an individual woman's prognosis could be better or worse, depending on her tumor characteristics and medical history. Women who have inflammatory breast cancer are encouraged to talk with their doctor about their prognosis, given their particular situation.

Research has shown that the following factors are associated with a better prognosis for women with inflammatory breast cancer:

- Stage of disease: Women with stage III disease have a better prognosis than women with stage IV disease. Among women who have stage III inflammatory breast cancer, about 40 percent survive at least 5 years after their diagnosis, whereas among women with stage IV inflammatory breast cancer, only about 11 percent survive for at least 5 years after their diagnosis.

- Tumor grade: Women with grade I or grade II tumors have a better prognosis than those with grade III tumors. Tumor grade is a term that describes what cancer cells look like under a microscope, with a higher grade indicating a more abnormal appearance and a more aggressive cancer that is likely to grow and spread. Among women who are diagnosed with grade I or grade II inflammatory breast cancer, 77 percent survived at least 2 years after their diagnosis, whereas among women who were diagnosed with grade III inflammatory breast cancer, 65 percent survived at least 2 years after their diagnosis.

- Ethnicity: African American women who have inflammatory breast cancer generally have a worse prognosis than women of other racial and ethnic groups. Studies have found that around 53 percent of African American women who are diagnosed with inflammatory breast cancer survive at least 2 years after diagnosis, whereas 69 percent of women from other racial and ethnic groups survive at least 2 years after diagnosis.

- Estrogen receptor status: Women with inflammatory breast whose cancer cells have estrogen receptors have a better prognosis than those whose cancer cells are estrogen receptor negative. The median survival for women with estrogen-receptor negative inflammatory breast cancer is 2 years, whereas the median survival for those with estrogen receptor-positive inflammatory breast cancer is 4 years.

- Type of treatment: Multimodal treatment of inflammatory breast cancer improves a woman's prognosis. Historically, among women who had only surgery, radiation therapy, or surgery and radiation therapy, fewer than 5 percent survived longer than 5 years. However, when women are treated with neoadjuvant chemotherapy, mastectomy, adjuvant chemotherapy, and radiation therapy, their 5-year disease-free survival ranges from 24 to 49 percent. One long-term study found that 28 percent of women with inflammatory breast cancer survived 15 years or longer after they were treated with multimodal therapy.

Ongoing research, especially at the molecular level, will increase our understanding of how inflammatory breast cancer begins and progresses. This knowledge should enable the development of new treatments and more accurate prognoses for women diagnosed with this disease. It is important, therefore, that women who are diagnosed with inflammatory breast cancer talk with their doctor about the option of participating in a clinical trial.

What clinical trials are available for women with inflammatory breast cancer?

NCI sponsors clinical trials of new treatments for all types of cancer, as well as trials that test better ways to use existing treatments. Participation in clinical trials is a treatment option for many patients with inflammatory breast cancer, and all patients with this disease are encouraged to consider treatment in a clinical trial.

Section 17.4

Breast Cancer and Pregnancy

Text in this section is excerpted from "Breast Cancer Treatment (PDQ®) and Pregnancy," National Cancer Institute (NCI), May 23, 2014.

Breast cancer is a disease in which malignant (cancer) cells form in the tissues of the breast.

The breast is made up of lobes and ducts. Each breast has 15 to 20 sections called lobes. Each lobe has many smaller sections called lobules. Lobules end in dozens of tiny bulbs that can make milk. The lobes, lobules, and bulbs are linked by thin tubes called ducts.

Each breast also has blood vessels and lymph vessels. The lymph vessels carry an almost colorless fluid called lymph. Lymph vessels carry lymph between lymph nodes. Lymph nodes are small bean-shaped structures that are found throughout the body. They filter substances in lymph and help fight infection and disease. Clusters of lymph nodes are found near the breast in the axilla (under the arm), above the collarbone, and in the chest.

Breast cancer is sometimes detected (found) in women who are pregnant or have just given birth.

In women who are pregnant or who have just given birth, breast cancer occurs most often between the ages of 32 and 38. Breast cancer occurs about once in every 3,000 pregnancies.

Signs of breast cancer include a lump or change in the breast.

These and other signs may be caused by breast cancer or by other conditions. Check with your doctor if you have any of the following:

- A lump or thickening in or near the breast or in the underarm area.

- A change in the size or shape of the breast.

- A dimple or puckering in the skin of the breast.

- A nipple turned inward into the breast.
- Fluid, other than breast milk, from the nipple, especially if it's bloody.
- Scaly, red, or swollen skin on the breast, nipple, or areola (the dark area of skin that is around the nipple).
- Dimples in the breast that look like the skin of an orange, called peau d'orange.

It may be difficult to detect (find) breast cancer early in pregnant or nursing women, whose breasts are often tender and swollen.

Women who are pregnant, nursing, or have just given birth usually have tender, swollen breasts. This can make small lumps difficult to detect and may lead to delays in diagnosing breast cancer. Because of these delays, cancers are often found at a later stage in these women.

Breast examination should be part of prenatal and postnatal care.

To detect breast cancer, pregnant and nursing women should examine their breasts themselves. Women should also receive clinical breast examinations during their routine prenatal and postnatal examinations.

Tests that examine the breasts are used to detect (find) and diagnose breast cancer.

Check with your doctor if you notice any changes in your breasts. The following tests and procedures may be used:

Physical exam and history: An exam of the body to check general signs of health, including checking for signs of disease, such as lumps or anything else that seems unusual. A history of the patient's health habits and past illnesses and treatments will also be taken.

Clinical breast exam (CBE): An exam of the breast by a doctor or other health professional. The doctor will carefully feel the breasts and under the arms for lumps or anything else that seems unusual.

Mammogram: An x-ray of the breast.

Ultrasound exam: A procedure in which high-energy sound waves (ultrasound) are bounced off internal tissues or organs and make echoes. The echoes form a picture of body tissues called a sonogram. The picture can be printed to be looked at later.

MRI (magnetic resonance imaging): A procedure that uses a magnet, radio waves, and a computer to make a series of detailed pictures of both breasts. This procedure is also called nuclear magnetic resonance imaging (NMRI).

Blood chemistry studies: A procedure in which a blood sample is checked to measure the amounts of certain substances released into the blood by organs and tissues in the body. An unusual (higher or lower than normal) amount of a substance can be a sign of disease.

Biopsy: The removal of cells or tissues so they can be viewed under a microscope by a pathologist to check for signs of cancer. If a lump in the breast is found, a biopsy may be done.

There are four types of biopsy used to check for breast cancer:

- **Excisional biopsy:** The removal of an entire lump of tissue.

- **Incisional biopsy:** The removal of part of a lump or a sample of tissue.

- **Core biopsy:** The removal of tissue using a wide needle.

- **Fine-needle aspiration (FNA) biopsy:** The removal of tissue or fluid, using a thin needle.

Certain factors affect prognosis (chance of recovery) and treatment options.

The prognosis (chance of recovery) and treatment options depend on the following:

- The stage of the cancer (the size of the tumor and whether it is in the breast only or has spread to lymph nodes or other places in the body).

- The type of breast cancer.

- Estrogen receptor and progesterone receptor levels in the tumor tissue.

- Human epidermal growth factor type 2 receptor (HER2/neu) levels in the tumor tissue.

- Whether the tumor tissue is triple negative (cells that do not have estrogen receptors, progesterone receptors, or high levels of HER2/neu).

- How fast the tumor is growing.

- How likely the tumor is to recur (come back).

- A woman's age, general health, and menopausal status (whether a woman is still having menstrual periods).

- Whether the cancer has just been diagnosed or has recurred (come back).

Chapter 18

Breast Cancer Prevention and Diagnosis

Chapter Contents

Section 18.1

Breast Cancer Prevention

Text in this section is excerpted from "Breast Cancer Prevention (PDQ®)," National Cancer Institute (NCI), July 21, 2015.

Avoiding risk factors and increasing protective factors may help prevent cancer.

Avoiding cancer risk factors may help prevent certain cancers. Risk factors include smoking, being overweight, and not getting enough exercise. Increasing protective factors such as quitting smoking, eating a healthy diet, and exercising may also help prevent some cancers. Talk to your doctor or other health care professional about how you might lower your risk of cancer.

NCI's Breast Cancer Risk Assessment Tool uses a woman's risk factors to estimate her risk for breast cancer during the next five years and up to age 90. This online tool is meant to be used by a health care provider.

The following are risk factors for breast cancer:

Older age

Older age is the main risk factor for most cancers. The chance of getting cancer increases as you get older.

A personal history of breast cancer or benign (noncancer) breast disease

Women with any of the following have an increased risk of breast cancer:

- A personal history of invasive breast cancer, ductal carcinoma in situ (DCIS), or lobular carcinoma in situ (LCIS).

- A personal history of benign (noncancer) breast disease.

A family history of breast cancer

Women with a family history of breast cancer in a first-degree relative (mother, sister, or daughter) have an increased risk of breast cancer.

Inherited gene changes

Women who have inherited changes in the BRCA1 and BRCA2 genes or in certain other genes have a higher risk of breast cancer, ovarian cancer, and maybe colon cancer. The risk of breast cancer caused by inherited gene changes depends on the type of gene mutation, family history of cancer, and other factors.

Men who have inherited certain changes in the BRCA2 gene have a higher risk of breast, prostate, and pancreatic cancers, and lymphoma.

Dense breasts

Having breast tissue that is dense on a mammogram is a factor in breast cancer risk. The level of risk depends on how dense the breast tissue is. Women with very dense breasts have a higher risk of breast cancer than women with low breast density.

Increased breast density is often an inherited trait, but it may also occur in women who have not had children, have a first pregnancy late in life, take postmenopausal hormones, or drink alcohol.

Exposure of breast tissue to estrogen made in the body

Estrogen is a hormone made by the body. It helps the body develop and maintain female sex characteristics. Being exposed to estrogen over a long time may increase the risk of breast cancer. Estrogen levels are highest during the years a woman is menstruating.

A woman's exposure to estrogen is increased in the following ways:

Early menstruation: Beginning to have menstrual periods at age 11 or younger increases the number of years the breast tissue is exposed to estrogen.

Starting menopause at a later age: The more years a woman menstruates, the longer her breast tissue is exposed to estrogen.

Older age at first birth or never having given birth: Because estrogen levels are lower during pregnancy, breast tissue is exposed to more estrogen in women who become pregnant for the first time after age 35 or who never become pregnant.

Taking hormone therapy for symptoms of menopause

Hormones, such as estrogen and progesterone, can be made into a pill form in a laboratory. Estrogen, progestin, or both may be given to replace the estrogen no longer made by the ovaries in postmenopausal women or women who have had their ovaries removed. This is called hormone replacement therapy (HRT) or hormone therapy (HT). Combination HRT/HT is estrogen combined with progestin. This type of HRT/HT increases the risk of breast cancer. Studies show that when women stop taking estrogen combined with progestin, the risk of breast cancer decreases.

Radiation therapy to the breast or chest

Radiation therapy to the chest for the treatment of cancer increases the risk of breast cancer, starting 10 years after treatment. The risk of breast cancer depends on the dose of radiation and the age at which it is given. The risk is highest if radiation treatment was used during puberty, when breasts are forming.

Radiation therapy to treat cancer in one breast does not appear to increase the risk of cancer in the other breast.

For women who have inherited changes in the BRCA1 and BRCA2 genes, exposure to radiation, such as that from chest x-rays, may further increase the risk of breast cancer, especially in women who were x-rayed before 20 years of age.

Obesity

Obesity increases the risk of breast cancer, especially in postmenopausal women who have not used hormone replacement therapy.

Drinking alcohol

Drinking alcohol increases the risk of breast cancer. The level of risk rises as the amount of alcohol consumed rises.

Being White

White women have an increased risk of breast cancer.

The following are protective factors for breast cancer:

Less exposure of breast tissue to estrogen made by the body

Decreasing the length of time a woman's breast tissue is exposed to estrogen may help prevent breast cancer. Exposure to estrogen is reduced in the following ways:

- **Early pregnancy:** Estrogen levels are lower during pregnancy. Women who have a full-term pregnancy before age 20 have a lower risk of breast cancer than women who have not had children or who give birth to their first child after age 35.

- **Breast-feeding:** Estrogen levels may remain lower while a woman is breast-feeding. Women who breastfed have a lower risk of breast cancer than women who have had children but did not breastfeed.

Taking estrogen-only hormone therapy after hysterectomy, selective estrogen receptor modulators, or aromatase inhibitors and inactivators

Estrogen-only hormone therapy after hysterectomy

Hormone therapy with estrogen only may be given to women who have had a hysterectomy. In these women, estrogen-only therapy after menopause may decrease the risk of breast cancer. There is an increased risk of stroke and heart and blood vessel disease in postmenopausal women who take estrogen after a hysterectomy.

Selective estrogen receptor modulators

Tamoxifen and raloxifene belong to the family of drugs called selective estrogen receptor modulators (SERMs). SERMs act like estrogen on some tissues in the body, but block the effect of estrogen on other tissues.

Treatment with tamoxifen or raloxifene lowers the risk of breast cancer in postmenopausal women. Tamoxifen also lowers the risk of breast cancer in high-risk premenopausal women. With either drug, the reduced risk lasts for several years after treatment is stopped. Lower rates of broken bones have been noted in patients taking raloxifene.

Taking tamoxifen increases the risk of hot flashes, endometrial cancer, stroke, cataracts, and blood clots (especially in the lungs and legs). The risk of having these problems increases with age. Women younger than 50 years who have a high risk of breast cancer may benefit the most from taking tamoxifen. The risk of having these problems decreases after tamoxifen is stopped. Talk with your doctor about the risks and benefits of taking this drug.

Taking raloxifene increases the risk of blood clots in the lungs and legs, but does not appear to increase the risk of endometrial cancer. In postmenopausal women with osteoporosis (decreased bone density), raloxifene lowers the risk of breast cancer for women who have a high or low risk of breast cancer. It is not known if raloxifene would have

189

the same effect in women who do not have osteoporosis. Talk with your doctor about the risks and benefits of taking this drug.

Aromatase inhibitors and inactivators

Aromatase inhibitors (anastrozole, letrozole) and inactivators (exemestane) lower the risk of a new breast cancer in women who have a history of breast cancer. Aromatase inhibitors also decrease the risk of breast cancer in women with the following conditions:

- Postmenopausal women with a personal history of breast cancer.

- Women with no personal history of breast cancer who are 60 years and older, have a history of ductal carcinoma in situ with mastectomy, or have a high risk of breast cancer based on the Gail model tool (a tool used to estimate the risk of breast cancer).

In women with an increased risk of breast cancer, taking aromatase inhibitors decreases the amount of estrogen made by the body. Before menopause, estrogen is made by the ovaries and other tissues in a woman's body, including the brain, fat tissue, and skin. After menopause, the ovaries stop making estrogen, but the other tissues do not. Aromatase inhibitors block the action of an enzyme called aromatase, which is used to make all of the body's estrogen. Aromatase inactivators stop the enzyme from working.

Possible harms from taking aromatase inhibitors include muscle and joint pain, osteoporosis, hot flashes, and feeling very tired.

Risk-reducing mastectomy

Some women who have a high risk of breast cancer may choose to have a risk-reducing mastectomy (the removal of both breasts when there are no signs of cancer). The risk of breast cancer is much lower in these women and most feel less anxious about their risk of breast cancer. However, it is very important to have a cancer risk assessment and counseling about the different ways to prevent breast cancer before making this decision.

Ovarian ablation

The ovaries make most of the estrogen that is made by the body. Treatments that stop or lower the amount of estrogen made by the ovaries include surgery to remove the ovaries, radiation therapy, or taking certain drugs. This is called ovarian ablation.

Premenopausal women who have a high risk of breast cancer due to certain changes in the BRCA1 and BRCA2 genes may choose to have a risk-reducing oophorectomy (the removal of both ovaries when there are no signs of cancer). This decreases the amount of estrogen made by the body and lowers the risk of breast cancer.

Risk-reducing oophorectomy also lowers the risk of breast cancer in normal premenopausal women and in women with an increased risk of breast cancer due to radiation to the chest. However, it is very important to have a cancer risk assessment and counseling before making this decision. The sudden drop in estrogen levels may cause the symptoms of menopause to begin. These include hot flashes, trouble sleeping, anxiety, and depression. Long-term effects include decreased sex drive, vaginal dryness, and decreased bone density.

Getting enough exercise

Women who exercise four or more hours a week have a lower risk of breast cancer. The effect of exercise on breast cancer risk may be greatest in premenopausal women who have normal or low body weight.

It is not clear whether the following affect the risk of breast cancer:

Oral contraceptives

Certain oral contraceptives contain estrogen. Some studies have shown that taking oral contraceptives ("the pill") may slightly increase the risk of breast cancer in current users. This risk decreases over time. Other studies have not shown an increased risk of breast cancer in women who take oral contraceptives.

Progestin-only contraceptives that are injected or implanted do not appear to increase the risk of breast cancer. More studies are needed to know whether progestin-only oral contraceptives increase the risk of breast cancer.

Environment

Studies have not proven that being exposed to certain substances in the environment, such as chemicals, increases the risk of breast cancer.

The following do not affect the risk of breast cancer:

- Having an abortion.
- Making diet changes such as eating less fat or more fruits and vegetables.
- Taking vitamins, including fenretinide (a type of vitamin A).

- Cigarette smoking, both active and passive (inhaling second-hand smoke).

- Using underarm deodorant or antiperspirant.

- Taking statins (cholesterol -lowering drugs).

- Taking bisphosphonates (drugs used to treat osteoporosis and hypercalcemia) by mouth or by intravenous infusion.

Cancer prevention clinical trials are used to study ways to prevent cancer.

Cancer prevention clinical trials are used to study ways to lower the risk of developing certain types of cancer. Some cancer prevention trials are conducted with healthy people who have not had cancer but who have an increased risk for cancer. Other prevention trials are conducted with people who have had cancer and are trying to prevent another cancer of the same type or to lower their chance of developing a new type of cancer. Other trials are done with healthy volunteers who are not known to have any risk factors for cancer.

The purpose of some cancer prevention clinical trials is to find out whether actions people take can prevent cancer. These may include exercising more or quitting smoking or taking certain medicines, vitamins, minerals, or food supplements.

Section 18.2

Breast Cancer Screening

Text in this section is excerpted from "Breast Cancer Screening (PDQ®)," National Cancer Institute (NCI), April 13, 2015.

Tests are used to screen for different types of cancer.

Some screening tests are used because they have been shown to be helpful both in finding cancers early and in decreasing the chance of dying from these cancers. Other tests are used because they have been shown to find cancer in some people; however, it has not been proven in clinical trials that use of these tests will decrease the risk of dying from cancer.

Scientists study screening tests to find those with the fewest risks and most benefits. Cancer screening trials also are meant to show whether early detection (finding cancer before it causes symptoms) decreases a person's chance of dying from the disease. For some types of cancer, the chance of recovery is better if the disease is found and treated at an early stage.

Clinical trials that study cancer screening methods are taking place in many parts of the country.

Three tests are used by health care providers to screen for breast cancer:

Mammogram

Mammography is the most common screening test for breast cancer. A mammogram is an x-ray of the breast. This test may find tumors that are too small to feel. A mammogram may also find ductal carcinoma in situ (DCIS). In DCIS, there are abnormal cells in the lining of a breast duct, which may become invasive cancer in some women.

Mammograms are less likely to find breast tumors in women younger than 50 years than in older women. This may be because younger women have denser breast tissue that appears white on a mammogram. Because tumors also appear white on a mammogram, they can be harder to find when there is dense breast tissue.

The following may affect whether a mammogram is able to detect (find) breast cancer:

- The size of the tumor.

- How dense the breast tissue is.

- The skill of the radiologist.

Women aged 40 to 74 years who have screening mammograms have a lower chance of dying from breast cancer than women who do not have screening mammograms.

Clinical breast exam (CBE)

A clinical breast exam is an exam of the breast by a doctor or other health professional. The doctor will carefully feel the breasts and under the arms for lumps or anything else that seems unusual. It is not known if having clinical breast exams decreases the chance of dying from breast cancer.

Breast self-exams may be done by women or men to check their breasts for lumps or other changes. It is important to know how your breasts usually look and feel. If you feel any lumps or notice any other changes, talk to your doctor. Doing breast self-exams has not been shown to decrease the chance of dying from breast cancer.

MRI (magnetic resonance imaging) in women with a high risk of breast cancer

MRI is a procedure that uses a magnet, radio waves, and a computer to make a series of detailed pictures of areas inside the body. This procedure is also called nuclear magnetic resonance imaging (NMRI). MRI does not use any x-rays.

MRI is used as a screening test for women who have one or more of the following:

- Certain gene changes, such as in the BRCA1 or BRCA2 genes.

- A family history (first degree relative, such as a mother, daughter or sister) with breast cancer.

- Certain genetic syndromes, such as Li-Fraumeni or Cowden syndrome.

MRIs find breast cancer more often than mammograms do, but it is common for MRI results to appear abnormal even when there isn't any cancer.

Other screening tests are being studied in clinical trials.

Thermography

Thermography is a procedure in which a special camera that senses heat is used to record the temperature of the skin that covers the breasts. A computer makes a map of the breast showing the changes in temperature. Tumors can cause temperature changes that may show up on the thermogram.

There have been no clinical trials of thermography to find out how well it detects breast cancer or if having the procedure decreases the risk of dying from breast cancer.

Tissue sampling

Breast tissue sampling is taking cells from breast tissue to check under a microscope. Abnormal cells in breast fluid have been linked to an increased risk of breast cancer in some studies. Scientists are studying whether breast tissue sampling can be used to find breast cancer at an early stage or predict the risk of developing breast cancer. Three ways of taking tissue samples are being studied:

- Fine-needle aspiration: A thin needle is inserted into the breast tissue around the areola (darkened area around the nipple) to take out a sample of cells and fluid.

- Nipple aspiration: The use of gentle suction to collect fluid through the nipple. This is done with a device similar to the breast pumps used by women who are breast-feeding.

- Ductal lavage: A hair-size catheter (tube) is inserted into the nipple and a small amount of salt water is released into the duct. The water picks up breast cells and is removed.

Screening clinical trials are taking place in many parts of the country.

Section 18.3

Risks of Breast Cancer Screening

Text in this section is excerpted from "Breast Cancer Screening (PDQ®)," National Cancer Institute (NCI), April 13, 2015.

Screening tests have risks.

Decisions about screening tests can be difficult. Not all screening tests are helpful and most have risks. Before having any screening test, you may want to discuss the test with your doctor. It is important to know the risks of the test and whether it has been proven to reduce the risk of dying from cancer.

The risks of breast cancer screening tests include the following:

Finding breast cancer may not improve health or help a woman live longer.

Screening may not help you if you have fast-growing breast cancer or if it has already spread to other places in your body. Also, some breast cancers found on a screening mammogram may never cause symptoms or become life-threatening. Finding these cancers is called overdiagnosis. When such cancers are found, treatment would not help you live longer and may instead cause serious side effects. At this time, it is not possible to be sure which breast cancers found by screening will cause problems and which ones will not.

False-negative test results can occur.

Screening test results may appear to be normal even though breast cancer is present. A woman who receives a false-negative test result (one that shows there is no cancer when there really is) may delay seeking medical care even if she has symptoms.

One in 5 cancers may be missed by mammography. False-negative results occur more often in younger women than in older women because the breast tissue of younger women is more dense. The chance of a false-negative result is also affected by the following:

- The size of the tumor.

- The rate of tumor growth.

- The level of hormones, such as estrogen and progesterone, in the woman's body.

- The skill of the radiologist.

False-positive test results can occur.

Screening test results may appear to be abnormal even though no cancer is present. A false-positive test result (one that shows there is cancer when there really isn't) is usually followed by more tests (such as biopsy), which also have risks.

Most abnormal test results turn out not to be cancer. False-positive results are more common in the following:

- Younger women.

- Women who have had previous breast biopsies.

- Women with a family history of breast cancer.

- Women who take hormones, such as estrogen and progestin.

The skill of the radiologist also can affect the chance of a false-positive result.

Anxiety from additional testing may result from false positive results.

False-positive results from screening mammograms are usually followed by more testing that can lead to anxiety. In one study, women who had a false-positive screening mammogram followed by more testing reported feeling anxiety 3 months later, even though cancer was not diagnosed. However, several studies show that women who feel anxiety after false-positive test results are more likely to schedule regular breast screening exams in the future.

Mammograms expose the breast to radiation.

Being exposed to radiation is a risk factor for breast cancer. The risk of breast cancer from radiation exposure is higher in women who received radiation before age 30 and at high doses. For women older than 40 years, the benefits of an annual screening mammogram may be greater than the risks from radiation exposure.

There may be pain or discomfort during a mammogram.

During a mammogram, the breast is placed between 2 plates that are pressed together. Pressing the breast helps to get a better x-ray of the breast. Some women have pain or discomfort during a mammogram.

The risks and benefits of screening for breast cancer may be different in different age groups.

The benefits of breast cancer screening may vary among age groups:

- In women who are expected to live 5 years or fewer, finding and treating early stage breast cancer may reduce their quality of life without helping them live longer.

- As with other women, in women older than 65 years, the results of a screening test may lead to more diagnostic tests and anxiety while waiting for the test results. Also, the breast cancers found are usually not life-threatening.

- It has not been shown that women with an average risk of developing breast cancer benefit from starting screening mammography before age 40.

Women who have had radiation treatment to the chest, especially at a young age, are advised to have routine breast cancer screening.

Yearly MRI screening may begin 8 years after treatment or by age 25 years, whichever is later. The benefits and risks of mammograms and MRIs for these women have not been studied.

There is no information on the benefits or risks of breast cancer screening in men.

No matter how old you are, if you have risk factors for breast cancer you should ask for medical advice about when to begin having breast cancer screening tests and how often to have them.

Chapter 19

Breast Cancer Treatment

Chapter Contents

Section 19.1

Treatment Options for Breast Cancer

Text in this section is excerpted from "Breast Cancer Treatment
(PDQ®)," National Cancer Institute (NCI), July 23, 2015.

There are different types of treatment for patients with breast cancer.

Different types of treatment are available for patients with breast
cancer. Some treatments are standard (the currently used treatment),
and some are being tested in clinical trials. A treatment clinical trial is
a research study meant to help improve current treatments or obtain
information on new treatments for patients with cancer. When clinical trials show that a new treatment is better than the standard
treatment, the new treatment may become the standard treatment.
Patients may want to think about taking part in a clinical trial. Some
clinical trials are open only to patients who have not started treatment.

Five types of standard treatment are used:

Surgery

Most patients with breast cancer have surgery to remove the cancer.

Sentinel lymph node biopsy is the removal of the sentinel lymph
node during surgery. The sentinel lymph node is the first lymph node to
receive lymphatic drainage from a tumor. It is the first lymph node where
the cancer is likely to spread. A radioactive substance and/or blue dye is
injected near the tumor. The substance or dye flows through the lymph
ducts to the lymph nodes. The first lymph node to receive the substance
or dye is removed. A pathologist views the tissue under a microscope to
look for cancer cells. After the sentinel lymph node biopsy, the surgeon
removes the tumor using breast-conserving surgery or mastectomy.
If cancer cells are not found, it may not be necessary to remove more
lymph nodes. If cancer cells are found, more lymph nodes will be removed
through a separate incision. This is called a lymph node dissection.

Types of surgery include the following:

- Breast-conserving surgery is an operation to remove the cancer and some normal tissue around it, but not the breast itself. Part of the chest wall lining may also be removed if the cancer is near it. This type of surgery may also be called lumpectomy, partial mastectomy, segmental mastectomy, quadrantectomy, or breast-sparing surgery.

- Total mastectomy: Surgery to remove the whole breast that has cancer. This procedure is also called a simple mastectomy. Some of the lymph nodes under the arm may be removed and checked for cancer. This may be done at the same time as the breast surgery or after. This is done through a separate incision.

- Modified radical mastectomy: Surgery to remove the whole breast that has cancer, many of the lymph nodes under the arm, the lining over the chest muscles, and sometimes, part of the chest wall muscles.

Chemotherapy may be given before surgery to remove the tumor. When given before surgery, chemotherapy will shrink the tumor and reduce the amount of tissue that needs to be removed during surgery. Treatment given before surgery is called preoperative therapy or neoadjuvant therapy.

Even if the doctor removes all the cancer that can be seen at the time of the surgery, some patients may be given radiation therapy, chemotherapy, or hormone therapy after surgery, to kill any cancer cells that are left. Treatment given after the surgery, to lower the risk that the cancer will come back, is called postoperative therapy or adjuvant therapy.

If a patient is going to have a mastectomy, breast reconstruction (surgery to rebuild a breast's shape after a mastectomy) may be considered. Breast reconstruction may be done at the time of the mastectomy or at some time after. The reconstructed breast may be made with the patient's own (nonbreast) tissue or by using implants filled with saline or silicone gel.

Radiation therapy

Radiation therapy is a cancer treatment that uses high-energy x-rays or other types of radiation to kill cancer cells or keep them from growing. There are two types of radiation therapy. External radiation therapy uses a machine outside the body to send radiation toward the cancer. Internal radiation therapy uses a radioactive substance sealed in needles, seeds, wires, or catheters that are placed directly into or near the cancer.

The way the radiation therapy is given depends on the type and stage of the cancer being treated. External radiation therapy is used to treat breast cancer.

Chemotherapy

Chemotherapy is a cancer treatment that uses drugs to stop the growth of cancer cells, either by killing the cells or by stopping them from dividing. When chemotherapy is taken by mouth or injected into a vein or muscle, the drugs enter the bloodstream and can reach cancer cells throughout the body (systemic chemotherapy). When chemotherapy is placed directly into the cerebrospinal fluid, an organ, or a body cavity such as the abdomen, the drugs mainly affect cancer cells in those areas (regional chemotherapy).

The way the chemotherapy is given depends on the type and stage of the cancer being treated. Systemic chemotherapy is used in the treatment of breast cancer.

Hormone therapy

Hormone therapy is a cancer treatment that removes hormones or blocks their action and stops cancer cells from growing. Hormones are substances made by glands in the body and circulated in the bloodstream. Some hormones can cause certain cancers to grow. If tests show that the cancer cells have places where hormones can attach (receptors), drugs, surgery, or radiation therapy is used to reduce the production of hormones or block them from working. The hormone estrogen, which makes some breast cancers grow, is made mainly by the ovaries. Treatment to stop the ovaries from making estrogen is called ovarian ablation.

Hormone therapy with tamoxifen is often given to patients with early localized breast cancer that can be removed by surgery and those with metastatic breast cancer (cancer that has spread to other parts of the body). Hormone therapy with tamoxifen or estrogens can act on cells all over the body and may increase the chance of developing endometrial cancer. Women taking tamoxifen should have a pelvic exam every year to look for any signs of cancer. Any vaginal bleeding, other than menstrual bleeding, should be reported to a doctor as soon as possible.

Hormone therapy with an aromatase inhibitor is given to some postmenopausal women who have hormone receptor–positive breast cancer. Aromatase inhibitors decrease the body's estrogen by blocking an enzyme called aromatase from turning androgen into estrogen. Anastrozole and letrozole are two types of aromatase inhibitors.

For the treatment of early localized breast cancer that can be removed by surgery, certain aromatase inhibitors may be used as adjuvant therapy instead of tamoxifen or after 2 to 3 years of tamoxifen use. For the treatment of metastatic breast cancer, aromatase inhibitors are being tested in clinical trials to compare them to hormone therapy with tamoxifen.

Targeted therapy

Targeted therapy is a type of treatment that uses drugs or other substances to identify and attack specific cancer cells without harming normal cells. Monoclonal antibodies, tyrosine kinase inhibitors, and cyclin-dependent kinase inhibitors are types of targeted therapies used in the treatment of breast cancer.

Monoclonal antibody therapy is a cancer treatment that uses antibodies made in the laboratory, from a single type of immune system cell. These antibodies can identify substances on cancer cells or normal substances that may help cancer cells grow. The antibodies attach to the substances and kill the cancer cells, block their growth, or keep them from spreading. Monoclonal antibodies are given by infusion. They may be used alone or to carry drugs, toxins, or radioactive material directly to cancer cells. Monoclonal antibodies may be used in combination with chemotherapy as adjuvant therapy.

Types of monoclonal antibody therapy include the following:

- Trastuzumab is a monoclonal antibody that blocks the effects of the growth factor protein HER2, which sends growth signals to breast cancer cells. About one-fourth of patients with breast cancer have tumors that may be treated with trastuzumab combined with chemotherapy.

- Pertuzumab is a monoclonal antibody that may be combined with trastuzumab and chemotherapy to treat breast cancer. It may be used to treat certain patients with HER2 positive breast cancer that has metastasized (spread to other parts of the body). It may also be used as neoadjuvant therapy in certain patients with early stage HER2 positive breast cancer.

- Ado-trastuzumab emtansine is a monoclonal antibody linked to an anticancer drug. This is called an antibody-drug conjugate. It is used to treat HER2 positive breast cancer that has spread to other parts of the body or recurred (come back).

Tyrosine kinase inhibitors are targeted therapy drugs that block signals needed for tumors to grow. Tyrosine kinase inhibitors may be used with other anticancer drugs as adjuvant therapy. Tyrosine kinase inhibitors include the following:

- Lapatinib is a tyrosine kinase inhibitor that blocks the effects of the HER2 protein and other proteins inside tumor cells. It may be used with other drugs to treat patients with HER2 positive breast cancer that has progressed after treatment with trastuzumab.

Cyclin-dependent kinase inhibitors are targeted therapy drugs that block proteins called cyclin-dependent kinases, which cause the growth of cancer cells. Cyclin-dependent kinase inhibitors include the following:

- Palbociclib is a cyclin-dependent kinase inhibitor used with the drug letrozole to treat breast cancer that is estrogen receptor positive and HER2 negative and has spread to other parts of the body. It is used in postmenopausal women whose cancer has not been treated with hormone therapy.

PARP inhibitors are a type of targeted therapy that block DNA repair and may cause cancer cells to die. PARP inhibitor therapy is being studied for the treatment of patients with triple negative breast cancer or tumors with BRCA1 or BRCA2 mutations.

Some treatments for breast cancer may cause side effects months or years after treatment has ended.

Some treatments for breast cancer may cause side effects that continue or appear months or years after treatment has ended. These are called late effects.

Late effects of radiation therapy are not common, but may include:

- Inflammation of the lung after radiation therapy to the breast, especially when chemotherapy is given at the same time.

- Arm lymphedema, especially when radiation therapy is given after lymph node dissection.

- In women younger than 45 years who receive radiation therapy to the chest wall after mastectomy, there may be a higher risk of developing breast cancer in the other breast.

Late effects of chemotherapy depend on the drugs used, but may include:

- Heart failure.
- Blood clots.
- Premature menopause.
- Second cancer, such as leukemia.

Late effects of targeted therapy with trastuzumab may include:

- Heart problems such as heart failure.

New types of treatment are being tested in clinical trials.

High-dose chemotherapy with stem cell transplant

High-dose chemotherapy with stem cell transplant is a way of giving high doses of chemotherapy and replacing blood-forming cells destroyed by the cancer treatment. Stem cells (immature blood cells) are removed from the blood or bone marrow of the patient or a donor and are frozen and stored. After the chemotherapy is completed, the stored stem cells are thawed and given back to the patient through an infusion. These reinfused stem cells grow into (and restore) the body's blood cells.

Studies have shown that high-dose chemotherapy followed by stem cell transplant does not work better than standard chemotherapy in the treatment of breast cancer. Doctors have decided that, for now, high-dose chemotherapy should be tested only in clinical trials. Before taking part in such a trial, women should talk with their doctors about the serious side effects, including death, that may be caused by high-dose chemotherapy.

Patients may want to think about taking part in a clinical trial.

For some patients, taking part in a clinical trial may be the best treatment choice. Clinical trials are part of the cancer research process. Clinical trials are done to find out if new cancer treatments are safe and effective or better than the standard treatment.

Many of today's standard treatments for cancer are based on earlier clinical trials. Patients who take part in a clinical trial may receive the standard treatment or be among the first to receive a new treatment.

Patients who take part in clinical trials also help improve the way cancer will be treated in the future. Even when clinical trials do not lead to effective new treatments, they often answer important questions and help move research forward.

Patients can enter clinical trials before, during, or after starting their cancer treatment.

Some clinical trials only include patients who have not yet received treatment. Other trials test treatments for patients whose cancer has not gotten better. There are also clinical trials that test new ways to stop cancer from recurring (coming back) or reduce the side effects of cancer treatment.

Clinical trials are taking place in many parts of the country.

Follow-up tests may be needed.

Some of the tests that were done to diagnose the cancer or to find out the stage of the cancer may be repeated. Some tests will be repeated in order to see how well the treatment is working. Decisions about whether to continue, change, or stop treatment may be based on the results of these tests.

Some of the tests will continue to be done from time to time after treatment has ended. The results of these tests can show if your condition has changed or if the cancer has recurred (come back). These tests are sometimes called follow-up tests or check-ups.

Section 19.2

Surgery Choices for Women with DCIS or Breast Cancer

Text in this section is excerpted from "Surgery Choices for Women
with DCIS or Breast Cancer (PDQ®)," National Cancer Institute
(NCI), January 19, 2015.

Are You Facing a Decision about Surgery for DCIS or Breast Cancer?

Do you have ductal carcinoma in situ (DCIS) or breast cancer that
can be removed with surgery? If so, you may be able to choose which type
of breast surgery to have. Often, your choice is between breast-sparing
surgery (surgery that takes out the cancer and leaves most of the breast)
and a mastectomy (surgery that removes the whole breast).

Once you are diagnosed, treatment will usually not begin right
away. There should be enough time for you to meet with breast cancer
surgeons, learn the facts about your surgery choices, and think about
what is important to you. Learning all you can will help you make a
choice you can feel good about.

Talk with Your Doctor

Talk with a breast cancer surgeon about your choices. Find out:

- what happens during surgery
- the types of problems that sometimes occur
- any treatment you might need after surgery

Be sure to ask a lot of questions and learn as much as you can. You
may also wish to talk with family members, friends, or others who
have had surgery.

Get a Second Opinion

After talking with a surgeon, think about getting a second opinion.
A second opinion means getting the advice of another surgeon. This
surgeon might tell you about other treatment options. Or, he or she

may agree with the advice you got from the first doctor.Some people worry about hurting their surgeon's feelings if they get a second opinion. But, it is very common and good surgeons don't mind. Also, some insurance companies require it. It is better to get a second opinion than worry that you made the wrong choice.If you think you might have a mastectomy, this is also a good time to learn about breast reconstruction. Think about meeting with a reconstructive plastic surgeon to learn about this surgery and if it seems like a good option for you.

Check with Your Insurance Company

Each insurance plan is different. Knowing how much your plan will pay for each type of surgery, including reconstruction, special bras, prostheses, and other needed treatments can help you decide which surgery is best for you.

Learn about the Types of Surgery

Most women with DCIS or breast cancer that can be treated with surgery have three surgery choices.

Breast-Sparing Surgery

Breast-sparing surgery means the surgeon removes only the DCIS or cancer and some normal tissue around it. If you have cancer, the surgeon will also remove one or more lymph nodes from under your arm. Breast-sparing surgery usually keeps your breast looking much like it did before surgery.

Other words for breast-sparing surgery include:

- Lumpectomy
- Partial mastectomy
- Breast-conserving surgery
- Segmental mastectomy

After breast-sparing surgery, most women also receive radiation therapy. The main goal of this treatment is to keep cancer from coming back in the same breast. Some women will also need chemotherapy, hormone therapy, and/or targeted therapy.

Mastectomy

In a mastectomy, the surgeon removes the whole breast that contains the DCIS or cancer. There are two main types of mastectomy. They are:

- Total (simple) mastectomy. The surgeon removes your whole breast. Sometimes, the surgeon also takes out one or more of the lymph nodes under your arm.

- Modified radical mastectomy. The surgeon removes your whole breast, many of the lymph nodes under your arm, and the lining over your chest muscles.

Some women will also need radiation therapy, chemotherapy, hormone therapy, and/or targeted therapy.

If you have a mastectomy, you may choose to wear a prosthesis (breast-like form) in your bra or have breast reconstruction surgery.

Breast Reconstruction Surgery

You can have breast reconstruction at the same time as the mastectomy, or anytime after. This type of surgery is done by a plastic surgeon with experience in reconstruction surgery. The surgeon uses an implant or tissue from another part of your body to create a breast-like shape that replaces the breast that was removed. The surgeon may also make the form of a nipple and add a tattoo that looks like the areola (the dark area around your nipple).

There are two main types of breast reconstruction surgery:

Breast Implant

Breast reconstruction with an implant is often done in steps. The first step is called tissue expansion. This is when the plastic surgeon places a balloon expander under the chest muscle. Over many weeks, saline (salt water) will be added to the expander to stretch the chest muscle and the skin on top of it. This process makes a pocket for the implant.

Once the pocket is the correct size, the surgeon will remove the expander and place an implant (filled with saline or silicone gel) into the pocket. This creates a new breast-like shape. Although this shape looks like a breast, you will not have the same feeling in it because nerves were cut during your mastectomy.

Breast implants do not last a lifetime. If you choose to have an implant, chances are you will need more surgery later on to remove or replace it. Implants can cause problems such as breast hardness, pain, and infection. The implant may also break, move, or shift. These problems can happen soon after surgery or years later.

209

Tissue Flap

In tissue flap surgery, a reconstructive plastic surgeon builds a new breast-like shape from muscle, fat, and skin taken from other parts of your body (usually your belly, back, or buttock). This new breast-like shape should last the rest of your life. Women who are very thin or obese, smoke, or have serious health problems often cannot have tissue flap surgery.

Healing after tissue flap surgery often takes longer than healing after breast implant surgery. You may have other problems, as well. For example, if you have a muscle removed, you might lose strength in the area from which it was taken. Or, you may get an infection or have trouble healing. Tissue flap surgery is best done by a reconstructive plastic surgeon who has special training in this type of surgery and has done it many times before.

Compare the Types of Surgery

The charts in this section can help you compare the different surgeries with each other. See how the surgeries are alike and how they are different.

Before Surgery

Is this surgery right for me?

Breast-Sparing Surgery	Most women with DCIS or breast cancer can choose to have breast-sparing surgery, usually followed by radiation therapy.
Mastectomy	Most women with DCIS or breast cancer can choose to have a mastectomy. A mastectomy may be a better choice for you if: • You have small breasts and a large area of DCIS or cancer. • ou have DCIS or cancer in more than one part of your breast. • The DCIS or cancer is under the nipple. • You are not able to receive radiation therapy.
Mastectomy with Reconstruction	If you have a mastectomy, you might also want breast reconstruction surgery. You can choose to have reconstruction surgery at the same time as your mastectomy or wait and have it later.

Recovering from Surgery

Will I have pain?

Most people have some pain after surgery.

Talk with your doctor or nurse before surgery about ways to control pain after surgery. Also, tell them if your pain control is not working.

How long before I can return to normal activities?

Breast-Sparing Surgery	Most women are ready to return to most of their usual activities within 5 to 10 days.
Mastectomy	It may take 3 to 4 weeks to feel mostly normal after a mastectomy.
Mastectomy with Reconstruction	Your recovery will depend on the type of reconstruction you have. It can take 6 to 8 weeks or longer to fully recover from breast reconstruction.

What other problems might I have?

Breast-Sparing Surgery	You may feel very tired and have skin changes from radiation therapy.
Mastectomy	You may feel out of balance if you had large breasts and do not have reconstruction surgery. This may also lead to neck and shoulder pain.
Mastectomy with Reconstruction	You may not like how your breast-like shape looks. If you have an implant: • Your breast may harden and can become painful. • You will likely need more surgery if your implant breaks or leaks. If you have flap surgery, you may lose strength in the part of your body where a muscle was removed.

What other types of treatment might I need?

If you chose to have breast sparing surgery, you will usually need radiation therapy. Radiation treatments are usually given 5 days a week for 5 to 8 weeks.

If you have a mastectomy, you may still need radiation therapy.

No matter which surgery you choose, you might need:

- Chemotherapy
- Hormone therapy
- Targeted therapy

Life After Surgery

What will my breast look like?

Breast-Sparing Surgery	Your breast should look a lot like it did before surgery.
	But if your tumor is large, your breast may look different or smaller after breast-sparing surgery.
	You will have a small scar where the surgeon cut to remove the DCIS or cancer. The length of the scar will depend on how large an incision the surgeon needed to make.
Mastectomy	Your breast and nipple will be removed. You will have a flat chest on the side of your body where the breast was removed.
	You will have a scar over the place where your breast was removed. The length of the scar will depend on the size of your breast. If you have smaller breasts, your scar is likely to be smaller than if you have larger breasts. • You will have a breast-like shape, but your breast will not look or feel like it did before surgery. And, it will not look or feel like your other breast.
Mastectomy with Reconstruction	You will have scars where the surgeon stitched skin together to make the new breast-like shape.
	If you have tissue flap reconstruction, you will have scars around the new breast, as well as the area where the surgeon removed the muscle, fat, and skin to make the new breast-like shape.

To get a better idea of what to expect, ask your surgeon if you can see before and after pictures of other women who have had different types of surgery.

Remember, even though surgery leaves scars where the surgeon cut the skin and stitched it back together, they tend to fade over time.

Will my breast have feeling?

Breast-Sparing Surgery	Yes. You should still have feeling in your breast, nipple, and areola (the dark area around your nipple).
Mastectomy	Maybe. After surgery, the skin around where the surgeon cut and maybe the area under your arm will be numb (have no feeling).
	This numb feeling may improve over 1 to 2 years, but it will never feel like it once did. Also, the skin where your breast was may feel tight.
Mastectomy with Reconstruction	No. The area around your breast will not have feeling.

Will I need more surgery?

Breast-Sparing Surgery	If the surgeon does not remove all the DCIS or cancer the first time, you may need more surgery.
Mastectomy	If you have problems after your mastectomy, you may need more surgery.
Mastectomy with Reconstruction	You will need more than one surgery to build a new breast-like shape. The number of surgeries you need will depend on the type of reconstruction you have and if you choose to have a nipple or areola added.
	Some women may also decide to have surgery on the opposite breast to help it match the new breast-like shape better.
	If you have an implant, you are likely to need surgery many years later to remove or replace it.

With all three surgeries, you may need more surgery to remove lymph nodes from under your arm. Having your lymph nodes removed can cause lymphedema.

Will the type of surgery I have affect how long I live?

No. Research has shown that women who have breast-sparing surgery live as long as women who have a mastectomy. This does not change if you also have reconstruction.

213

What are the chances that my cancer will return in the same area?

Breast-Sparing Surgery	There is a chance that your cancer will come back in the same breast. But if it does, it is not likely to affect how long you live. About 10% of women (1 out of every 10) who have breast-sparing surgery along with radiation therapy get cancer in the same breast within 12 years. If this happens, you can be effectively treated with a mastectomy.
Mastectomy	There is a smaller chance that your cancer will return in the same area than if you have breast-sparing surgery. About 5% of women (1 out of every 20) who have a mastectomy will get cancer on the same side of their chest within 12 years.
Mastectomy with Reconstruction	Your chances are the same as mastectomy, since breast reconstruction surgery does not affect the chances of the cancer returning.

Think about What Is Important to You

After you have talked with a breast cancer surgeon and learned the facts, you may also want to talk with your spouse or partner, family, friends, or other women who have had breast cancer surgery.

Then, think about what is important to you. Thinking about these questions and talking them over with others might help:

About Surgery Choices

- If I have breast-sparing surgery, am I willing and able to have radiation therapy 5 days a week for 5 to 8 weeks?

- If I have a mastectomy, do I also want breast reconstruction surgery?

- If I have breast reconstruction surgery, do I want it at the same time as my mastectomy?

- What treatment does my insurance cover? What do I have to pay for?

Life after Surgery

- How important is it to me how my breast looks after cancer surgery?

- How important is it to me how my breast feels after cancer surgery?

- If I have a mastectomy and do not have reconstruction, will my insurance cover my prostheses and special bras?

- Where can I find breast prostheses and special bras?

Section 19.3

Advanced Breast Cancer Treatment through Palbociclib

Text in this section is excerpted from "Palbociclib Improves Survival in Women with Hormone Receptor-Positive Metastatic Breast Cancer," National Cancer Institute (NCI), July 24, 2015.

Summary

Interim results from a randomized phase III clinical trial show that women with estrogen receptor (ER)-positive and human epidermal growth factor receptor 2 (HER2)-negative metastatic breast cancer that progressed during prior hormone therapy lived longer without their disease progressing if they received palbociclib (Ibrance®) plus fulvestrant (Faslodex®) than if they received a placebo plus fulvestrant.

Background

A mainstay of treatment for ER-positive, HER2-negative early breast cancer is hormone therapy. Although this treatment reduces relapse rates, some women do relapse and subsequently their cancers are difficult to treat. One promising treatment may be to use drugs that target cyclin-dependent kinases (CDK4 and CDK6), which appear to promote tumor cell proliferation in hormone-receptor positive breast cancer.

Palbociclib is an oral agent that inhibits CDK4 and CDK6. This drug received accelerated approval from the Food and Drug Administration (FDA) to be used together with the hormone therapy letrozole (Femara®) as a first-line (initial) treatment for postmenopausal women with ER-positive, HER2-negative metastatic breast cancer, based on the improvement in progression-free survival seen in a trial called PALOMA1.

Fulvestrant, like letrozole, is a hormone therapy. However, the two work in different ways. Letrozole is an aromatase inhibitor, which stops production of estrogen in the ovaries and other tissues, whereas fulvestrant is an antiestrogen that binds to the estrogen receptor and leads to its destruction.

The PALOMA3 phase III trial was designed to test whether adding palbociclib to fulvestrant results in longer progression-free survival than fulvestrant alone in women with advanced ER-positive, HER2-negative breast cancer that had progressed during prior hormone therapy.

The Study

More than 520 women with ER-positive, HER2-negative breast cancer that had relapsed or progressed during prior hormone therapy were enrolled in the PALOMA3 trial. These patients were recruited into the study from more than 140 sites in 17 countries. They were randomly assigned, in a two-to-one ratio, to receive palbociclib and fulvestrant (347 patients) or a placebo and fulvestrant (174 patients).

The patients were permitted to have had one line of chemotherapy for metastatic disease before trial enrollment. Twenty percent of those enrolled in each arm of the trial were premenopausal or perimenopausal and received the drug goserelin to suppress ovarian function.

The trial's primary endpoint was progression-free survival. The secondary endpoints included overall survival, objective response, rate of clinical benefit, patient-reported outcomes, and safety.

Nicolas Turner, M.D., Ph.D., of the Royal Marsden Hospital and Institute of Cancer Research in London, led the study, which was sponsored by Pfizer, the maker of palbociclib.

Results

This paper reported a prespecified interim analysis. At the time of the analysis, the median progression-free survival for women in the palbociclib-plus-fulvestrant group was 9.2 months, compared with 3.8 months for women who received a placebo plus fulvestrant. An analysis by menopausal status showed that the addition of palbociclib to fulvestrant improved progression-free survival in both premenopausal/perimenopausal and postmenopausal women.

Rates of overall objective (measurable) response were 10.4 percent in the palbociclib group and 6.3 percent in the placebo group. The rate of clinical benefit (the response of prolonged stable disease) at the interim analysis was 34 percent in the palbociclib group and 19 percent in the placebo group.

Serious adverse events (any cause) occurred in 9.6 percent of the patients in the palbociclib group and 14.0 percent of the patients in the placebo group. Hematologic side effects were more frequent in the palbociclib group.

Treatment was discontinued due to adverse events in 2.6 percent of patients in the palbociclib group and 1.7 percent in the placebo group. The adverse events included disorders of the blood such as neutropenia, leukopenia, anemia, and thrombocytopenia, most of which were treatable. The adverse events reported in the PALOMA3 study were consistent with those identified in the PALOMA1 study.

Women who received palbociclib plus fulvestrant maintained their global quality of life, whereas quality of life declined in women who received a placebo plus fulvestrant.

At the time of this analysis, overall survival data were still immature.

Limitations

"The data are based on a prespecified interim analysis that showed the study had met the primary endpoint of improved progression-free survival," said Stan Lipkowitz, M.D., Ph.D., of NCI's Center for Cancer Research. "However, the median follow up was short—5.6 months—and the overall survival data were not mature.

"An issue not addressed is the use of palbociclib with fulvestrant after it has already been given as a first-line treatment in combination with letrozole. Based on the PALOMA1 data, and the accelerated FDA approval, many patients will likely receive palbociclib and letrozole in the first-line setting. Such patients who received palbociclib and letrozole would not have met the entry criteria for the PALOMA3 study," Dr. Lipkowitz added. "It will increasingly be the case that patients will have received palbociclib with letrozole as first-line therapy. Thus, this study does not provide guidance for whether patients who have had palbociclib and letrozole in the first-line will still benefit by adding palbociclib to fulvestrant in second-line treatment."

Section 19.4

Breast Reconstruction after Mastectomy

Text in this section is excerpted from "Breast Reconstruction After Mastectomy," National Cancer Institute (NCI), Febuary 12, 2013.

What is breast reconstruction?

Many women who have a mastectomy—surgery to remove an entire breast to treat or prevent breast cancer—have the option of having more surgery to rebuild the shape of the removed breast.

Breast reconstruction surgery can be either immediate or delayed. With immediate reconstruction, a surgeon performs the first stage to rebuild the breast during the same operation as the mastectomy. A method called skin-sparing mastectomy may be used to save enough breast skin to cover the reconstruction.

With delayed reconstruction, the surgeon performs the first stage to rebuild the breast after the chest has healed from the mastectomy and after the woman has completed adjuvant therapy.

A third option is immediate-delayed reconstruction. With this method, a tissue expander is placed under the skin during the mastectomy to preserve space for an implant while the tissue that was removed is examined. If the surgical team decides that the woman does not need radiation therapy, an implant can be placed where the tissue expander was without further delay. However, if the woman will need to have radiation therapy after mastectomy, her breast reconstruction can be delayed until after radiation therapy is complete.

Breasts can be rebuilt using implants (saline or silicone) or autologous tissue (that is, tissue from elsewhere in the body). Most breast reconstructions performed today are immediate reconstructions with implants.

How do surgeons use implants to reconstruct a woman's breast?

Implants can be inserted underneath the skin and chest muscle that remain after a mastectomy, usually as part of a two-stage procedure.

In the first stage, the surgeon places a device called an expander under the chest muscle. The expander is slowly filled with saline during visits to the doctor after surgery. In the second stage, after the chest tissue has relaxed and healed enough, the expander is removed and replaced with an implant. The chest tissue is usually ready for the implant 6 weeks to 6 months after mastectomy.

Expanders can be placed as part of either immediate or delayed reconstructions. An optional third stage of breast reconstruction involves recreating a nipple on the reconstructed breast.

How do surgeons use tissue from a woman's own body to reconstruct the breast?

In autologous tissue reconstruction, a piece of tissue containing skin, fat, blood vessels, and sometimes muscle is taken from elsewhere in a woman's body and used to rebuild the breast. This piece of tissue is called a flap. Different sites in the body can provide flaps for breast reconstruction.

- TRAM flap: Tissue, including muscle, that comes from the lower abdomen. This is the most common type of tissue used in breast reconstruction.
- DIEP flap: Tissue that comes from the abdomen as in a TRAM flap, but only contains skin and fat.
- Latissimus dorsi flap: Tissue that comes from the middle and side of the back.

More rarely, flaps are taken from the thigh or buttocks.

Wherever the flaps come from, they can either be pedicled or free. With a pedicled flap, the tissue and attached blood vessels are moved together through the body to the breast area. With a free flap, the tissue is cut free from its blood supply and attached to new blood vessels in the breast area.

Rarely, an implant and autologous tissue will be used together. They might be used together when there isn't enough skin and muscle left after mastectomy to allow for expansion and use of an implant. In these cases, the autologous tissue is used to cover the implant.

How do surgeons reconstruct the nipple and areola?

After the chest heals from reconstruction surgery and the woman has completed adjuvant therapy, a surgeon can reconstruct the nipple and areola. Usually, the new nipple is created by cutting and moving small pieces of skin from the reconstructed breast to the nipple site and shaping them into a new nipple. A few months after nipple reconstruction, the surgeon can recreate the areola. This is usually done using tattoo ink. However, in some cases, skin grafts may be taken from the groin or abdomen and attached to the breast to create an areola.

Skin-sparing mastectomy that preserves a woman's own nipple and areola (called nipple-sparing mastectomy) is performed by some surgeons on select women who are at low risk of cancer recurrence.

What factors can affect the choice of breast reconstruction method?

Most women can choose their type of breast reconstruction method based on what is important to them. However, some treatment issues are important to think about. For example, radiation therapy can damage a reconstructed breast, especially if it contains an implant. Therefore, if a woman knows she needs radiation therapy after mastectomy, that information may affect her decision.

Sometimes, a woman may not know whether she needs radiation therapy until after her mastectomy. This can make planning ahead for an immediate reconstruction difficult. In this case, it may be helpful for the woman to talk with a reconstructive surgeon in addition to her breast surgeon or oncologist before choosing the type of reconstructive surgery.

Other factors that can influence the type of reconstructive surgery a woman chooses include the size and shape of the breast that is being replaced, the woman's age and health, the availability of autologous tissue, and the location of the breast tumor.

Each type of reconstruction has factors that a woman should think about before making a decision. Some of the more common concerns are listed below.

Reconstruction with implants

Surgery and recovery

- Enough skin and muscle must remain after mastectomy to cover the implant

- Shorter surgical procedure than for reconstruction with autologous tissue; little blood loss

- Recovery period may be shorter

- Many follow-up visits may be needed to inflate the expander and insert the implant

Possible complications

- Infection
- Pooling of blood (hematoma) within the reconstructed breast
- Extrusion of the implant (the implant breaks through the skin)
- Implant rupture (the implant breaks open and saline or silicone leaks into the surrounding tissue)
- Formation of hard scar tissue around the implant (known as a contracture)

Other considerations

- Can be damaged by radiation therapy
- May not be adequate for women with very large breasts
- Will not last a lifetime; the longer a woman has implants, the more likely she is to have complications and to need to have her implants removed or replaced
- Silicone implants may provide a more natural-looking breast shape than saline
- The Food and Drug Administration (FDA) recommends that women with silicone implants undergo periodic MRI screenings to detect possible "silent" rupture of the implants

Reconstruction with autologous tissue

Surgery and recovery

- Longer surgical procedure than for implants; more blood loss
- Recovery period may be longer
- Pedicled flap reconstruction is a shorter operation than free flap but requires more donor tissue
- Free flap reconstruction uses less donor tissue than pedicled flap reconstruction but is a longer, highly technical operation requiring a surgeon with experience re-attaching blood vessels

Possible complications

- Necrosis (death) of the transferred tissue
- Blood clots

- Pain and weakness at the site from which the donor tissue was taken
- Obesity, diabetes, and smoking may increase the rate of complications

Other considerations

- May provide a more natural breast shape than implants
- Less likely to be damaged by radiation therapy than implants
- Leaves a scar at the site from which the donor tissue was taken

Any type of breast reconstruction can fail if healing does not occur properly. In these cases, the implant or flap will have to be removed. If an implant reconstruction fails, a woman can sometimes have a second reconstruction using autologous tissue. If an autologous tissue reconstruction fails, a second flap cannot be moved to the breast area, and an implant cannot be used for another reconstruction attempt due to the lack of chest tissue available to cover the implant.

What type of follow-up care and rehabilitation is needed after breast reconstruction?

Any type of reconstruction increases the number of side effects a woman may experience compared with those after a mastectomy alone. A woman's medical team will watch her closely after surgery for complications, some of which can occur months or even years later.

Women who have autologous tissue reconstruction may need physical therapy to help them make up for weakness experienced at the site from which the donor tissue was taken, such as abdominal weakness. A physical therapist can help a woman use exercises to regain strength, adjust to new physical limitations, and figure out the safest ways to perform everyday activities.

Will health insurance pay for breast reconstruction?

Since 1999, the Women's Health and Cancer Rights Act (WHCRA) has required group health plans, insurance companies, and HMOs that offer mastectomy coverage to also pay for reconstructive surgery after mastectomy. This coverage must include reconstruction of the other breast to give a more balanced look, breast prostheses, and treatment of all physical complications of the mastectomy, including lymphedema.

WHCRA does not apply to Medicare and Medicaid recipients. Some health plans sponsored by religious organizations and some government health plans may also be exempt from WHCRA. More information about WHCRA can be found through the Department of Labor.

A woman considering breast reconstruction may want to discuss costs and health insurance coverage with her doctor and insurance company before choosing to have the surgery. Some insurance companies require a second opinion before they will agree to pay for a surgery.

Does breast reconstruction affect the ability to check for breast cancer recurrence?

Studies have shown that breast reconstruction does not increase the chances of breast cancer coming back or make it harder to check for recurrence with mammography.

Women who have one breast removed by mastectomy will still have mammograms of the other breast. Women who have had a skin-sparing mastectomy or who are at high risk of breast cancer recurrence may have mammograms of the reconstructed breast if it was reconstructed using autologous tissue. However, mammograms are generally not performed on breasts that are reconstructed with an implant after mastectomy.

A woman with a breast implant should tell the radiology technician about her implant before she has a mammogram. Special procedures may be necessary to improve the accuracy of the mammogram and to avoid damaging the implant.

Chapter 20

Drugs Approved for Breast Cancer

Drugs Approved for Breast Cancer

This chapter lists cancer drugs approved by the Food and Drug Administration (FDA) for breast cancer. The list includes generic and brand names. This chapter also lists common drug combinations used in breast cancer. The individual drugs in the combinations are FDA-approved. However, the drug combinations themselves usually are not approved, although they are widely used.

There may be drugs used in breast cancer that are not listed here.

Drugs Used to Prevent Breast Cancer

Evista (Raloxifene Hydrochloride)

Raloxifene hydrochloride is approved to prevent:

Breast cancer. It is used to decrease the chance of invasive breast cancer in postmenopausal women who have a high risk for developing the disease or who have osteoporosis.

Raloxifene hydrochloride is also approved to prevent and treat:

- **Osteoporosis** in postmenopausal women.

Text in this chapter is excerpted from "Drugs Approved for Breast Cancer," National Cancer Institute (NCI), November 25, 2014.

Raloxifene hydrochloride is also being studied in the treatment of other types of cancer.

Keoxifene (Raloxifene Hydrochloride)

Raloxifene hydrochloride is approved to prevent:

- **Breast cancer.** It is used to decrease the chance of invasive breast cancer in postmenopausal women who have a high risk for developing the disease or who have osteoporosis.

Raloxifene hydrochloride is also approved to prevent and treat:

- **Osteoporosis** in postmenopausal women.

Raloxifene hydrochloride is also being studied in the treatment of other types of cancer.

Nolvadex (Tamoxifen Citrate)

Tamoxifen citrate is approved to treat:

- **Breast cancer** in women and men.

Tamoxifen citrate is also approved to prevent:

- **Breast cancer** in women who are at high risk for the disease.

Tamoxifen citrate is also being studied in the treatment of other types of cancer.

Raloxifene Hydrochloride

Raloxifene hydrochloride is approved to prevent:

- **Breast cancer.** It is used to decrease the chance of invasive breast cancer in postmenopausal women who have a high risk for developing the disease or who have osteoporosis.

Raloxifene hydrochloride is also approved to prevent and treat:

- **Osteoporosis** in postmenopausal women.

Raloxifene hydrochloride is also being studied in the treatment of other types of cancer.

Tamoxifen Citrate

Tamoxifen citrate is approved to treat:

- **Breast cancer** in women and men.

Tamoxifen citrate is also approved to prevent:

- **Breast cancer** in women who are at high risk for the disease.

Tamoxifen citrate is also being studied in the treatment of other types of cancer.

Drugs Used to Treat Breast Cancer

Abitrexate (Methotrexate)

Methotrexate is approved to be used alone or with other drugs to treat:

- **Acute lymphoblastic leukemia** that has spread to the central nervous system, or to prevent it from spreading there.

- **Breast cancer.**

- **Gestational trophoblastic disease.**

- **Head and neck cancer** (certain types).

- **Lung cancer.**

- **Mycosis fungoides** (a type of cutaneous T-cell lymphoma) that is advanced.

- **Non-Hodgkin lymphoma** that is advanced.

- **Osteosarcoma** that has not spread to other parts of the body. It is used following surgery to remove the primary tumor.

Methotrexate is also being studied in the treatment of other types of cancer.

Abraxane (Paclitaxel Albumin-stabilized Nanoparticle Formulation)

Paclitaxel albumin-stabilized nanoparticle formulation is approved to be used alone or with other drugs to treat:

- **Breast cancer** that has recurred (come back) or metastasized (spread to other parts of the body).

- **Non-small cell lung cancer** that is locally advanced or has metastasized and cannot be treated with surgery or radiation therapy. It is used with carboplatin.

- **Pancreatic cancer** that has metastasized. It is used with gemcitabine hydrochloride.

Paclitaxel albumin-stabilized nanoparticle formulation is also being studied in the treatment of other types of cancer.

Paclitaxel albumin-stabilized nanoparticle formulation is a form of paclitaxel contained in nanoparticles (very tiny particles of protein). The drug is also called nanoparticle paclitaxel and protein-bound paclitaxel. This form may work better than other forms of paclitaxel and have fewer side effects.

Ado-Trastuzumab Emtansine

Ado-trastuzumab emtansine is approved to treat:

- **Breast cancer** that is HER2 positive and has metastasized (spread to other parts of the body). It is used in patients who have already been treated with trastuzumab and a taxane. It is also used in these patients if the cancer recurs (comes back) after adjuvant therapy.

Ado-trastuzumab emtansine is also being studied in the treatment of other types of cancer.

Adrucil (Fluorouracil)

Fluorouracil is approved to be used alone or with other drugs to treat:

- **Actinic keratosis.**

- **Basal cell carcinoma** that is superficial and cannot be removed by surgery.

- **Breast cancer.**

- **Colorectal cancer** that is advanced, has recurred (come back), or has not gotten better with other chemotherapy.

- **Gastric (stomach) adenocarcinoma.**

- **Pancreatic cancer.**

- **Squamous cell carcinoma of the head and neck** that is locally advanced and cannot be treated with surgery.

Fluorouracil is also called 5-FU. Fluorouracil is also being studied in the treatment of other conditions and types of cancer.

Afinitor (Everolimus)

Everolimus is approved to treat:

- **Breast cancer.** It is used in combination with exemestane in postmenopausal women with advanced hormone receptor positive (HR+) breast cancer that is also HER2 negative (HER2-) and has not gotten better with other chemotherapy.

- **Pancreatic cancer.** It is used in adults with progressive neuroendocrine tumors that cannot be removed by surgery, are locally advanced, or have metastasized (spread to other parts of the body).

- **Renal cell carcinoma** (a type of kidney cancer) that is advanced, in adults who have not gotten better with other chemotherapy.

- **Subependymal giant cell astrocytoma** in adults and children who have tuberous sclerosis and are not able to have surgery. Everolimus is available as tablets (Afinitor) or tablets for oral suspension (Afinitor Disperz). Only Afinitor Disperz is used in children.

Everolimus is also being studied in the treatment of other types of cancer.

Anastrozole

Anastrozole is approved to be used alone or with other treatments to treat:

- **Breast cancer** in postmenopausal women.

Anastrozole is also being studied in the treatment of other types of cancer.

Aredia (Pamidronate Disodium)

Pamidronate disodium is approved to be given with chemotherapy to treat bone damage caused by:

- **Breast cancer** that has metastasized (spread) to bone.

- **Multiple myeloma** that has metastasized to bone.

Pamidronate disodium is also approved to treat:

- **Hypercalcemia** (high blood levels of calcium) caused by malignant tumors.

Pamidronate disodium is also being studied in the treatment of other types of cancer.

Arimidex (Anastrozole)

Anastrozole is approved to be used alone or with other treatments to treat:

- **Breast cancer** in postmenopausal women.

Anastrozole is also being studied in the treatment of other types of cancer.

Aromasin (Exemestane)

Exemestane is approved to treat:

- **Breast cancer** that is advanced.

- **Breast cancer** that is early-stage and estrogen receptor positive.

Exemestane is used in postmenopausal women who have already been treated with tamoxifen citrate.
Exemestane is also being studied in the treatment of other types of cancer.

Capecitabine

Capecitabine is approved to be used alone or with other drugs to treat:

- **Breast cancer** that has metastasized (spread to other parts of the body) in patients whose disease has not gotten better with other chemotherapy.

- **Colorectal cancer.** It is used to treat stage III colorectal cancer in patients who have had surgery to remove the cancer. It is also used as first-line treatment of patients with metastatic colorectal cancer.

Capecitabine is also being studied in the treatment of other types of cancer.

Clafen (Cyclophosphamide)

Cyclophosphamide is approved to be used alone or with other drugs to treat:

- **Acute lymphoblastic leukemia** (ALL) in children.
- **Acute myeloid leukemia** (AML).
- **Breast cancer.**
- **Chronic lymphocytic leukemia** (CLL).
- **Chronic myelogenous leukemia** (CML).
- **Hodgkin lymphoma.**
- **Multiple myeloma.**
- **Mycosis fungoides.**
- **Neuroblastoma.**
- **Non-Hodgkin lymphoma** (NHL).
- **Ovarian cancer.**
- **Retinoblastoma.**

Cyclophosphamide is also being studied in the treatment of other types of cancer.

Cyclophosphamide

- Cyclophosphamide is approved to be used alone or with other drugs to treat:
- **Acute lymphoblastic leukemia** (ALL) in children.
- **Acute myeloid leukemia** (AML).
- **Breast cancer.**
- **Chronic lymphocytic leukemia** (CLL).
- **Chronic myelogenous leukemia** (CML).
- **Hodgkin lymphoma.**
- **Multiple myeloma.**
- **Mycosis fungoides.**
- **Neuroblastoma.**

- **Non-Hodgkin lymphoma** (NHL).
- **Ovarian cancer.**
- **Retinoblastoma.**

Cyclophosphamide is also being studied in the treatment of other types of cancer.

Cytoxan (Cyclophosphamide)

Cyclophosphamide is approved to be used alone or with other drugs to treat:

- **Acute lymphoblastic leukemia** (ALL) in children.
- **Acute myeloid leukemia** (AML).
- **Breast cancer.**
- **Chronic lymphocytic leukemia** (CLL).
- **Chronic myelogenous leukemia** (CML).
- **Hodgkin lymphoma.**
- **Multiple myeloma.**
- **Mycosis fungoides.**
- **Neuroblastoma.**
- **Non-Hodgkin lymphoma** (NHL).
- **Ovarian cancer.**
- **Retinoblastoma.**

Cyclophosphamide is also being studied in the treatment of other types of cancer.

Docetaxel

Docetaxel is approved to be used alone or with other drugs to treat:

- **Breast cancer** that is locally advanced or has metastasized (spread to other parts of the body) and has not gotten better with other chemotherapy. It is also used to treat breast cancer that is node-positive and can be removed by surgery.

- **Adenocarcinoma** of the stomach or gastroesophageal junction that is advanced. It is used in patients who have not been treated with chemotherapy for advanced disease.

- **Non-small cell lung cancer** in certain patients whose cancer is locally advanced or has metastasized.

- **Prostate cancer** that has metastasized in men whose cancer is hormone-refractory (does not respond to hormone treatment).

- **Squamous cell carcinoma** of the head and neck that is locally advanced and cannot be treated with surgery.

Docetaxel is also being studied in the treatment of other types of cancer.

Doxorubicin Hydrochloride

Doxorubicin hydrochloride is approved to be used alone or with other drugs to treat:

- **Acute lymphoblastic leukemia** (ALL).
- **Acute myeloid leukemia** (AML).
- **Breast cancer.** It is also used as adjuvant therapy for breast cancer that has spread to the lymph nodes after surgery.
- **Gastric (stomach) cancer.**
- **Hodgkin lymphoma.**
- **Neuroblastoma.**
- **Non-Hodgkin lymphoma.**
- **Ovarian cancer.**
- **Small cell lung cancer.**
- **Soft tissue and bone sarcomas.**
- **Thyroid cancer.**
- **Transitional cell bladder cancer.**
- **Wilms tumor.**

Doxorubicin hydrochloride is also being studied in the treatment of other types of cancer.

Efudex (Fluorouracil)

Fluorouracil is approved to be used alone or with other drugs to treat:

- **Actinic keratosis.**

- **Basal cell carcinoma** that is superficial and cannot be removed by surgery.

- **Breast cancer.**

- **Colorectal cancer** that is advanced, has recurred (come back), or has not gotten better with other chemotherapy.

- **Gastric (stomach) adenocarcinoma.**

- **Pancreatic cancer.**

- **Squamous cell carcinoma** of the head and neck that is locally advanced and cannot be treated with surgery.

Fluorouracil is also called 5-FU. Fluorouracil is also being studied in the treatment of other conditions and types of cancer.

Ellence (Epirubicin Hydrochloride)

Epirubicin hydrochloride is approved to be used with other drugs to treat:

- **Breast cancer.** It is used after surgery in patients with early-stage breast cancer that has spread to the lymph nodes under the arm.

Epirubicin hydrochloride is also being studied in the treatment of other types of cancer.

Epirubicin Hydrochloride

Epirubicin hydrochloride is approved to be used with other drugs to treat:

- **Breast cancer.** It is used after surgery in patients with early-stage breast cancer that has spread to the lymph nodes under the arm.

Epirubicin hydrochloride is also being studied in the treatment of other types of cancer.

Eribulin Mesylate

Eribulin mesylate is approved to treat:

- **Breast cancer** that has metastasized (spread to other parts of the body) in patients who have already been treated with other chemotherapy.

Eribulin mesylate is also being studied in the treatment of other types of cancer.

Everolimus

Everolimus is approved to treat:

- **Breast cancer.** It is used in combination with exemestane in postmenopausal women with advanced hormone receptor positive (HR+) breast cancer that is also HER2 negative (HER2-) and has not gotten better with other chemotherapy.

- **Pancreatic cancer.** It is used in adults with progressive neuroendocrine tumors that cannot be removed by surgery, are locally advanced, or have metastasized (spread to other parts of the body).

- **Renal cell carcinoma** (a type of kidney cancer) that is advanced, in adults who have not gotten better with other chemotherapy.

- **Subependymal giant cell astrocytoma** in adults and children who have tuberous sclerosis and are not able to have surgery. Everolimus is available as tablets (Afinitor) or tablets for oral suspension (Afinitor Disperz). Only Afinitor Disperz is used in children.

Everolimus is also being studied in the treatment of other types of cancer.

Exemestane

Exemestane is approved to treat:

- **Breast cancer** that is advanced.

- **Breast cancer** that is early-stage and estrogen receptor positive.

Exemestane is used in postmenopausal women who have already been treated with tamoxifen citrate.

Exemestane is also being studied in the treatment of other types of cancer.

Fareston (Toremifene)

Toremifene is approved to treat:

- **Breast cancer** that has metastasized (spread to other parts of the body). It is used in postmenopausal women whose cancer is estrogen receptor positive (ER+) or when it is not known if the cancer is ER+ or estrogen receptor negative (ER-).

Faslodex (Fulvestrant)

Fulvestrant is approved to treat:

- **Breast cancer** in postmenopausal women. It is used in patients with estrogen receptor positive breast cancer that has metastasized (spread to other parts of the body) after treatment with other antiestrogens.

Fulvestrant is also being studied in the treatment of other types of cancer.

Femara (Letrozole)

Letrozole is approved to be used alone or with other drugs to treat:

- **Breast cancer** in postmenopausal women who have any of the following types of breast cancer–

  - Early-stage, hormone receptor positive (HR+) breast cancer in women who have already received other treatment.

  - Early-stage breast cancer that has been treated with tamoxifen citrate for at least five years.

  - Breast cancer that is locally advanced or has metastasized (spread to other parts of the body), is HER2 positive (HER2+) and HR+.

  - Breast cancer that is locally advanced or has metastasized and it is not known whether the cancer is HR+ or hormone receptor negative (HR-).

  - Advanced breast cancer that has gotten worse after anti-estrogen therapy.

Letrozole is also being studied in the treatment of other types of cancer.

Fluoroplex (Fluorouracil)

Fluorouracil is approved to be used alone or with other drugs to treat:

- **Actinic keratosis.**

- **Basal cell carcinoma** that is superficial and cannot be removed by surgery.

- **Breast cancer.**

- **Colorectal cancer** that is advanced, has recurred (come back), or has not gotten better with other chemotherapy.

- **Gastric (stomach) adenocarcinoma.**

- **Pancreatic cancer.**

- **Squamous cell carcinoma** of the head and neck that is locally advanced and cannot be treated with surgery.

Fluorouracil is also called 5-FU. Fluorouracil is also being studied in the treatment of other conditions and types of cancer.

Fluorouracil

Fluorouracil is approved to be used alone or with other drugs to treat:

- **Actinic keratosis.**

- **Basal cell carcinoma** that is superficial and cannot be removed by surgery.

- **Breast cancer.**

- **Colorectal cancer** that is advanced, has recurred (come back), or has not gotten better with other chemotherapy.

- **Gastric (stomach) adenocarcinoma.**

- **Pancreatic cancer.**

- **Squamous cell carcinoma** of the head and neck that is locally advanced and cannot be treated with surgery.

Fluorouracil is also called 5-FU. Fluorouracil is also being studied in the treatment of other conditions and types of cancer.

Folex (Methotrexate)

Methotrexate is approved to be used alone or with other drugs to treat:

- **Acute lymphoblastic leukemia** that has spread to the central nervous system, or to prevent it from spreading there.

- **Breast cancer.**
- **Gestational trophoblastic disease.**
- **Head and neck cancer** (certain types).
- **Lung cancer.**
- **Mycosis fungoides** (a type of cutaneous T-cell lymphoma) that is advanced.
- **Non-Hodgkin lymphoma that is advanced.**
- **Osteosarcoma** that has not spread to other parts of the body. It is used following surgery to remove the primary tumor.

Methotrexate is also being studied in the treatment of other types of cancer.

Folex PFS (Methotrexate)

Methotrexate is approved to be used alone or with other drugs to treat:

- **Acute lymphoblastic leukemia** that has spread to the central nervous system, or to prevent it from spreading there.
- **Breast cancer.**
- **Gestational trophoblastic disease.**
- **Head and neck cancer** (certain types).
- **Lung cancer.**
- **Mycosis fungoides** (a type of cutaneous T-cell lymphoma) that is advanced.
- **Non-Hodgkin lymphoma** that is advanced.
- **Osteosarcoma** that has not spread to other parts of the body. It is used following surgery to remove the primary tumor.

Methotrexate is also being studied in the treatment of other types of cancer.

Fulvestrant

Fulvestrant is approved to treat:

- **Breast cancer** in postmenopausal women. It is used in patients with estrogen receptor positive breast cancer that has metastasized (spread to other parts of the body) after treatment with other antiestrogens.

Fulvestrant is also being studied in the treatment of other types of cancer.

Gemcitabine Hydrochloride

Gemcitabine hydrochloride is approved to be used alone or with other drugs to treat:

- **Breast cancer** that has metastasized (spread to other parts of the body) and has not gotten better with other chemotherapy. It is used with paclitaxel.

- **Non-small cell lung cancer** that is advanced or has metastasized. It is used in patients whose disease cannot be removed by surgery. It is used with cisplatin.

- **Ovarian cancer** that is advanced and has not gotten better with other chemotherapy. It is used with carboplatin.

- **Pancreatic cancer** that is advanced or has metastatsized. It is used in patients whose disease cannot be removed by surgery and who have already been treated with other chemotherapy. It is used with paclitaxel albumin-stabilized nanoparticle formulation.

Gemcitabine hydrochloride is also being studied in the treatment of other types of cancer.

Gemzar (Gemcitabine Hydrochloride)

Gemcitabine hydrochloride is approved to be used alone or with other drugs to treat:

- **Breast cancer** that has metastasized (spread to other parts of the body) and has not gotten better with other chemotherapy. It is used with paclitaxel.

- **Non-small cell lung cancer** that is advanced or has metastasized. It is used in patients whose disease cannot be removed by surgery. It is used with cisplatin.

- **Ovarian cancer** that is advanced and has not gotten better with other chemotherapy. It is used with carboplatin.

- **Pancreatic cancer** that is advanced or has metastatsized. It is used in patients whose disease cannot be removed by surgery and who have already been treated with other chemotherapy. It is used with paclitaxel albumin-stabilized nanoparticle formulation.

Gemcitabine hydrochloride is also being studied in the treatment of other types of cancer.

Goserelin Acetate

Goserelin acetate is approved to treat:

- **Breast cancer** that is advanced. It is used as palliative treatment in premenopausal and perimenopausal women.

- **Prostate cancer.** It is used with flutamide and radiation therapy in localized prostate cancer. It is also used as palliative treatment in advanced prostate cancer.

Goserelin acetate is also being studied in conditions related to cancer.

Halaven (Eribulin Mesylate)

Eribulin mesylate is approved to treat:

- **Breast cancer** that has metastasized (spread to other parts of the body) in patients who have already been treated with other chemotherapy.

Eribulin mesylate is also being studied in the treatment of other types of cancer.

Herceptin (Trastuzumab)

Trastuzumab is approved to be used alone or with other drugs to treat:

- **Adenocarcinoma** of the stomach or gastroesophageal junction. It is used for HER2 positive (HER2+) disease that has metastasized (spread to other parts of the body) in patients who have not already been treated for metastatic cancer.

- **Breast cancer** that is HER2+.

Trastuzumab is also being studied in the treatment of other types of cancer.

Ibrance (Palbociclib)

Palbociclib is approved to be used with letrozole to treat:

- **Breast cancer** that is estrogen receptor positive (ER+) and HER2 negative (HER2-) and has metastasized (spread to other parts of the body). It is used in postmenopausal women who have not been treated with hormone therapy.

Palbociclib is also being studied in the treatment of other types of cancer.

Ixabepilone

Ixabepilone is approved to be used alone or with capecitabine to treat:

- **Breast cancer** that is locally advanced or has metastasized (spread to other parts of the body). It is used in patients who have not gotten better with other chemotherapy.

Ixabepilone is also being studied in the treatment of other types of cancer.

Ixempra (Ixabepilone)

Ixabepilone is approved to be used alone or with capecitabine to treat:

- **Breast cancer** that is locally advanced or has metastasized (spread to other parts of the body). It is used in patients who have not gotten better with other chemotherapy.

Ixabepilone is also being studied in the treatment of other types of cancer.

Kadcyla (Ado-Trastuzumab Emtansine)

Ado-trastuzumab emtansine is approved to treat:

- **Breast cancer** that is HER2 positive and has metastasized (spread to other parts of the body). It is used in patients who have already been treated with trastuzumab and a taxane. It is also used in these patients if the cancer recurs (comes back) after adjuvant therapy.

Ado-trastuzumab emtansine is also being studied in the treatment of other types of cancer.

Lapatinib Ditosylate

Lapatinib ditosylate is approved to be used with other drugs to treat:

- **Breast cancer** that is advanced or has metastasized (spread to other parts of the body). It is used with:

- Capecitabine in women with HER2 positive (HER2+) breast cancer whose disease has not gotten better with other chemotherapy.

- Letrozole in postmenopausal women with HER2+ and hormone receptor positive breast cancer who need hormone therapy.

Lapatinib ditosylate is also being studied in the treatment of other types of cancer.

Letrozole

Letrozole is approved to be used alone or with other drugs to treat:

- **Breast cancer** in postmenopausal women who have any of the following types of breast cancer–

    - Early-stage, hormone receptor positive (HR+) breast cancer in women who have already received other treatment.

    - Early-stage breast cancer that has been treated with tamoxifen citrate for at least five years.

    - Breast cancer that is locally advanced or has metastasized (spread to other parts of the body), is HER2 positive (HER2+) and HR+.

    - Breast cancer that is locally advanced or has metastasized and it is not known whether the cancer is HR+ or hormone receptor negative (HR-).

    - Advanced breast cancer that has gotten worse after anti-estrogen therapy.

Letrozole is also being studied in the treatment of other types of cancer.

Megace (Megestrol Acetate)

Megestrol acetate in tablet form is approved for palliative treatment of advanced disease in:

- **Breast cancer.**

- **Endometrial cancer.**

Megestrol acetate in liquid suspension form is approved to treat the following conditions in patients with AIDS:

- **Anorexia** (loss of appetite).

- **Cachexia** (weakness and loss of weight and muscle).

Megestrol acetate is also being studied in the treatment of anorexia and cachexia in cancer and other conditions.

Megestrol Acetate

Megestrol acetate in tablet form is approved for palliative treatment of advanced disease in:

- **Breast cancer.**

- **Endometrial cancer.**

Megestrol acetate in liquid suspension form is approved to treat the following conditions in patients with AIDS:

- **Anorexia (loss of appetite).**

- **Cachexia (weakness and loss of weight and muscle).**

Megestrol acetate is also being studied in the treatment of anorexia and cachexia in cancer and other conditions.

Methotrexate

Methotrexate is approved to be used alone or with other drugs to treat:

- **Acute lymphoblastic leukemia** that has spread to the central nervous system, or to prevent it from spreading there.

- **Breast cancer.**

- **Gestational trophoblastic disease.**

- **Head and neck cancer** (certain types).

- **Lung cancer.**

- **Mycosis fungoides** (a type of cutaneous T-cell lymphoma) that is advanced.

- **Non-Hodgkin lymphoma** that is advanced.

- **Osteosarcoma** that has not spread to other parts of the body. It is used following surgery to remove the primary tumor.

Methotrexate is also being studied in the treatment of other types of cancer.

Methotrexate LPF (Methotrexate)

Methotrexate is approved to be used alone or with other drugs to treat:

- **Acute lymphoblastic leukemia** that has spread to the central nervous system, or to prevent it from spreading there.

- **Breast cancer**.

- **Gestational trophoblastic disease.**

- **Head and neck cancer** (certain types).

- **Lung cancer.**

- **Mycosis fungoides** (a type of cutaneous T-cell lymphoma) that is advanced.

- **Non-Hodgkin lymphoma** that is advanced.

- **Osteosarcoma** that has not spread to other parts of the body. It is used following surgery to remove the primary tumor.

Methotrexate is also being studied in the treatment of other types of cancer.

Mexate (Methotrexate)

Methotrexate is approved to be used alone or with other drugs to treat:

- **Acute lymphoblastic leukemia** that has spread to the central nervous system, or to prevent it from spreading there.

- **Breast cancer**.

- **Gestational trophoblastic disease.**

- **Head and neck cancer** (certain types).

- **Lung cancer.**

- **Mycosis fungoides** (a type of cutaneous T-cell lymphoma) that is advanced.

- **Non-Hodgkin lymphoma** that is advanced.

- **Osteosarcoma** that has not spread to other parts of the body. It is used following surgery to remove the primary tumor.

Methotrexate is also being studied in the treatment of other types of cancer.

Mexate-AQ (Methotrexate)

Methotrexate is approved to be used alone or with other drugs to treat:

- **Acute lymphoblastic leukemia** that has spread to the central nervous system, or to prevent it from spreading there.

- **Breast cancer**.

- **Gestational trophoblastic disease.**

- **Head and neck cancer** (certain types).

- **Lung cancer.**

- **Mycosis fungoides** (a type of cutaneous T-cell lymphoma) that is advanced.

- **Non-Hodgkin lymphoma** that is advanced.

- **Osteosarcoma** that has not spread to other parts of the body. It is used following surgery to remove the primary tumor.

Methotrexate is also being studied in the treatment of other types of cancer.

Neosar (Cyclophosphamide)

Cyclophosphamide is approved to be used alone or with other drugs to treat:

- **Acute lymphoblastic leukemia** (ALL) in children.

- **Acute myeloid leukemia** (AML).

- **Breast cancer.**

- **Chronic lymphocytic leukemia** (CLL).

- **Chronic myelogenous leukemia** (CML).

- **Hodgkin lymphoma.**

- **Multiple myeloma.**

- **Mycosis fungoides.**
- **Neuroblastoma.**
- **Non-Hodgkin lymphoma** (NHL).
- **Ovarian cancer.**
- **Retinoblastoma.**

Cyclophosphamide is also being studied in the treatment of other types of cancer.

Nolvadex (Tamoxifen Citrate)

Tamoxifen citrate is approved to treat:

- **Breast cancer** in women and men.

Tamoxifen citrate is also approved to prevent:

- **Breast cancer** in women who are at high risk for the disease.

Tamoxifen citrate is also being studied in the treatment of other types of cancer.

Paclitaxel

Paclitaxel is approved to be used alone or with other drugs to treat:

- **AIDS-related Kaposi sarcoma.**
- **Breast cancer.**
- **Non-small cell lung cancer.**
- **Ovarian cancer.**

Paclitaxel is also being studied in the treatment of other types of cancer.

Paclitaxel is also available in a different form called paclitaxel albumin-stabilized nanoparticle formulation.

Paclitaxel Albumin-stabilized Nanoparticle Formulation

Paclitaxel albumin-stabilized nanoparticle formulation is approved to be used alone or with other drugs to treat:

- **Breast cancer** that has recurred (come back) or metastasized (spread to other parts of the body).

- **Non-small cell lung cancer** that is locally advanced or has metastasized and cannot be treated with surgery or radiation therapy. It is used with carboplatin.

- **Pancreatic cancer** that has metastasized. It is used with gemcitabine hydrochloride.

Paclitaxel albumin-stabilized nanoparticle formulation is also being studied in the treatment of other types of cancer.

Paclitaxel albumin-stabilized nanoparticle formulation is a form of paclitaxel contained in nanoparticles (very tiny particles of protein). The drug is also called nanoparticle paclitaxel and protein-bound paclitaxel. This form may work better than other forms of paclitaxel and have fewer side effects.

Palbociclib

Palbociclib is approved to be used with letrozole to treat:

- **Breast cancer** that is estrogen receptor positive (ER+) and HER2 negative (HER2-) and has metastasized (spread to other parts of the body). It is used in postmenopausal women who have not been treated with hormone therapy.

Palbociclib is also being studied in the treatment of other types of cancer.

Pamidronate Disodium

Pamidronate disodium is approved to be given with chemotherapy to treat bone damage caused by:

- **Breast cancer** that has metastasized (spread) to bone.
- **Multiple myeloma** that has metastasized to bone.

Pamidronate disodium is also approved to treat:

- **Hypercalcemia** (high blood levels of calcium) caused by malignant tumors.

Pamidronate disodium is also being studied in the treatment of other types of cancer.

Perjeta (Pertuzumab)

Pertuzumab is approved to be used with trastuzumab and docetaxel to treat:

- **Breast cancer** that is HER2 positive (HER2+) and has metastasized (spread to other parts of the body). It is used in patients who have not been treated with anticancer drugs for metastatic disease.

- **Breast cancer** that is HER2+ and is locally advanced, inflammatory, or early-stage. It is used in patients who have a high risk that the cancer will metastasize or recur (come back). It is given as neoadjuvant therapy (to shrink the tumor before surgery).

Pertuzumab is also being studied in the treatment of other types of cancer.

Pertuzumab

Pertuzumab is approved to be used with trastuzumab and docetaxel to treat:

- **Breast cancer** that is HER2 positive (HER2+) and has metastasized (spread to other parts of the body). It is used in patients who have not been treated with anticancer drugs for metastatic disease.

- **Breast cancer** that is HER2+ and is locally advanced, inflammatory, or early-stage. It is used in patients who have a high risk that the cancer will metastasize or recur (come back). It is given as neoadjuvant therapy (to shrink the tumor before surgery).

Pertuzumab is also being studied in the treatment of other types of cancer.

Tamoxifen Citrate

Tamoxifen citrate is approved to treat:

- **Breast cancer** in women and men.

Tamoxifen citrate is also approved to prevent:

- **Breast cancer** in women who are at high risk for the disease.

Tamoxifen citrate is also being studied in the treatment of other types of cancer.

Taxol (Paclitaxel)

Paclitaxel is approved to be used alone or with other drugs to treat:

- **AIDS-related Kaposi sarcoma.**
- **Breast cancer.**
- **Non-small cell lung cancer.**
- **Ovarian cancer.**

Paclitaxel is also being studied in the treatment of other types of cancer.

Paclitaxel is also available in a different form called paclitaxel albumin-stabilized nanoparticle formulation.

Taxotere (Docetaxel)

Docetaxel is approved to be used alone or with other drugs to treat:

- **Breast cancer** that is locally advanced or has metastasized (spread to other parts of the body) and has not gotten better with other chemotherapy. It is also used to treat breast cancer that is node-positive and can be removed by surgery.

- **Adenocarcinoma** of the stomach or gastroesophageal junction that is advanced. It is used in patients who have not been treated with chemotherapy for advanced disease.

- **Non-small cell lung cancer** in certain patients whose cancer is locally advanced or has metastasized.

- **Prostate cancer** that has metastasized in men whose cancer is hormone-refractory (does not respond to hormone treatment).

- **Squamous cell carcinoma** of the head and neck that is locally advanced and cannot be treated with surgery.

Docetaxel is also being studied in the treatment of other types of cancer.

Thiotepa

Thiotepa is approved to treat:

- **Bladder cancer.**
- **Breast cancer.**

249

- **Malignant pleural effusion, malignant pericardial effusion,** and **malignant peritoneal effusion.**

- **Ovarian cancer.**

Thiotepa is also being studied in the treatment of other types of cancer and as part of a regimen to prepare patients for bone marrow and stem cell transplants.

Toremifene

Toremifene is approved to treat:

- **Breast cancer** that has metastasized (spread to other parts of the body). It is used in postmenopausal women whose cancer is estrogen receptor positive (ER+) or when it is not known if the cancer is ER+ or estrogen receptor negative (ER-).

Trastuzumab

Trastuzumab is approved to be used alone or with other drugs to treat:

- **Adenocarcinoma** of the stomach or gastroesophageal junction. It is used for HER2 positive (HER2+) disease that has metastasized (spread to other parts of the body) in patients who have not already been treated for metastatic cancer.

- **Breast cancer** that is HER2+.

Trastuzumab is also being studied in the treatment of other types of cancer.

Tykerb (Lapatinib Ditosylate)

Lapatinib ditosylate is approved to be used with other drugs to treat:

- **Breast cancer** that is advanced or has metastasized (spread to other parts of the body). It is used with:

- Capecitabine in women with HER2 positive (HER2+) breast cancer whose disease has not gotten better with other chemotherapy.

- Letrozole in postmenopausal women with HER2+ and hormone receptor positive breast cancer who need hormone therapy.

Lapatinib ditosylate is also being studied in the treatment of other types of cancer.

Velban (Vinblastine Sulfate)

Vinblastine sulfate is approved to treat:

- **Breast cancer** that has not gotten better with other treatment.
- **Choriocarcinoma** that has not gotten better with other chemotherapy. Choriocarcinoma is a type of gestational trophoblastic disease.
- **Hodgkin lymphoma.**
- **Kaposi sarcoma.**
- **Mycosis fungoides.**
- **Non-Hodgkin lymphoma (NHL).**
- **Testicular cancer.**

Velsar (Vinblastine Sulfate)

Vinblastine sulfate is approved to treat:

- **Breast cancer** that has not gotten better with other treatment.
- **Choriocarcinoma** that has not gotten better with other chemotherapy. Choriocarcinoma is a type of gestational trophoblastic disease.
- **Hodgkin lymphoma.**
- **Kaposi sarcoma.**
- **Mycosis fungoides.**
- **Non-Hodgkin lymphoma (NHL).**
- **Testicular cancer.**

Vinblastine Sulfate

Vinblastine sulfate is approved to treat:

- **Breast cancer** that has not gotten better with other treatment.
- **Choriocarcinoma** that has not gotten better with other chemotherapy. Choriocarcinoma is a type of gestational trophoblastic disease.

- **Hodgkin lymphoma.**

- **Kaposi sarcoma.**

- **Mycosis fungoides.**

- **Non-Hodgkin lymphoma (NHL).**

- **Testicular cancer.**

Xeloda (Capecitabine)

Capecitabine is approved to be used alone or with other drugs to treat:

- **Breast cancer** that has metastasized (spread to other parts of the body) in patients whose disease has not gotten better with other chemotherapy.

- **Colorectal cancer.** It is used to treat stage III colorectal cancer in patients who have had surgery to remove the cancer. It is also used as first-line treatment of patients with metastatic colorectal cancer.

Capecitabine is also being studied in the treatment of other types of cancer.

Zoladex (Goserelin Acetate)

Goserelin acetate is approved to treat:

- **Breast cancer** that is advanced. It is used as palliative treatment in premenopausal and perimenopausal women.

- **Prostate cancer.** It is used with flutamide and radiation therapy in localized prostate cancer. It is also used as palliative treatment in advanced prostate cancer.

Goserelin acetate is also being studied in conditions related to cancer.

Drug Combinations Used in Breast Cancer

AC

AC is used to treat:

- **Breast cancer.**

This combination may also be used with other drugs or treatments or to treat other types of cancer.

AC-T

AC-T is used to treat:

- **Breast cancer.**

This combination may also be used with other drugs or treatments or to treat other types of cancer.

CAF

CAF is used to treat:

- **Breast cancer.**

This combination may also be used with other drugs or treatments or to treat other types of cancer.

CMF

CMF is used to treat:

- **Breast cancer.**

This combination may also be used with other drugs or treatments or to treat other types of cancer.

FEC

FEC is used to treat:

- **Breast cancer.**

FEC is also known as CEF. This combination may also be used with other drugs or treatments or to treat other types of cancer.

TAC

TAC is used to treat:

- **Breast cancer.** It is often used as adjuvant therapy.

This combination may also be used with other drugs or treatments or to treat other types of cancer.

Part Four

Gynecological Cancer

Chapter 21

Frequently Asked Questions about Gynecological Cancer

What Is Gynecologic Cancer?

Gynecologic cancer is any cancer that starts in a woman's reproductive organs. Cancer is always named for the part of the body where it starts. Gynecologic cancers begin in different places within a woman's pelvis, which is the area below the stomach and in between the hip bones.

- **Cervical cancer** begins in the cervix, which is the lower, narrow end of the uterus. (The uterus is also called the womb.)

- **Ovarian cancer** begins in the ovaries, which are located on each side of the uterus.

- **Uterine cancer** begins in the uterus, the pear-shaped organ in a woman's pelvis where the baby grows when a woman is pregnant.

- **Vaginal cancer** begins in the vagina, which is the hollow, tube-like channel between the bottom of the uterus and the outside of the body.

- **Vulvar cancer** begins in the vulva, the outer part of the female genital organs.

Text in this chapter is excerpted from "Gynecologic Cancers," National Cancer Institute (NCI), July 28, 2015.

Each gynecologic cancer is unique, with different signs and symptoms, different risk factors (things that may increase your chance of getting a disease), and different prevention strategies. All women are at risk for gynecologic cancers, and risk increases with age. When gynecologic cancers are found early, treatment is most effective.

What Are the Symptoms?

There is no way to know for sure if you will get a gynecologic cancer. That's why it is important to pay attention to your body and know what is normal for you, so you can recognize the warning signs or symptoms of gynecologic cancer.

If you have vaginal bleeding that is unusual for you, talk to a doctor right away. You should also see a doctor if you have any other warning signs that last for two weeks or longer and are not normal for you. Symptoms may be caused by something other than cancer, but the only way to know is to see a doctor.

Signs and symptoms are not the same for everyone and each gynecologic cancer (cervical, ovarian, uterine, vaginal, and vulvar cancers) has its own signs and symptoms.

Gynecologic Cancer Symptoms

Symptoms	Cervical Cancer	Ovarian Cancer	Uterine Cancer	Vaginal Cancer	Vulvar Cancer
Abnormal vaginal bleeding or discharge	●	●	●	●	
Pelvic pain or pressure		●	●		●
Abdominal or back pain		●			
Bloating		●			
Changes in bathroom habits		●		●	
Itching or burning of the vulva					●
Changes in vulva color or skin, such as a rash, sores, or warts					●

Figure 21.1. Gynecologic Cancer Symptoms

What Can I Do to Reduce My Risk?

HPV Vaccine

Some gynecologic cancers are caused by the *human papillomavirus* (HPV), a very common sexually transmitted infection. Vaccines protect against the HPV types that most often cause cervical, vaginal, and vulvar cancers. It is recommended for 11- and 12-year-old girls and boys. (Note: The vaccine can be given beginning at age 9.) It also can be given to females or males who are 13–26 who did not get any or all of the shots when they were younger. Ideally, girls and boys should get three doses of this vaccine before their first sexual contact. If you or someone you care about is in this age range, talk with a doctor about it.

Screening Tests

Screening is when a test is used to look for a disease before there are any symptoms. Cancer screening tests are effective when they can find disease early, which can lead to more effective treatment. (Diagnostic tests are used when a person has symptoms. The purpose of diagnostic tests is to find out, or diagnose, what is causing the symptoms. Diagnostic tests also may be used to check a person who is considered at high risk for cancer.)

Of all the gynecologic cancers, only cervical cancer has a screening test—the Pap test—that can find this cancer early, when treatment works best. The Pap test also helps prevent cervical cancer by finding precancerous cell changes on the cervix that might become cervical cancer if they are not treated appropriately. In addition to the Pap test, which is the main screening test for cervical cancer, a test called the HPV test looks for HPV infection. It can be used along with the Pap test for screening women aged 30 years and older. It also is used to provide more information when Pap test results are unclear for women aged 21 and older.

Since there is no simple and reliable way to screen for any gynecologic cancers except cervical cancer, it is especially important to recognize warning signs and learn if there are things you can do to reduce your risk. Talk with your doctor if you believe that you are at increased risk for gynecologic cancer. Ask what you might do to lower your risk and whether there are tests that you should have.

How Are Gynecologic Cancers Treated?

If your doctor says that you have a gynecologic cancer, ask to be referred to a gynecologic oncologist—a doctor who has been trained to treat cancers of a woman's reproductive system. This doctor will work with you to create a treatment plan.

Types of Treatment

Gynecologic cancers are treated in several ways. It depends on the kind of cancer and how far it has spread. Treatments include surgery, chemotherapy, and radiation. Women with a gynecologic cancer often get more than one kind of treatment.

- **Surgery:** Doctors remove cancer tissue in an operation.
- **Chemotherapy:** Using special medicines to shrink or kill the cancer. The drugs can be pills you take or medicines given in your veins, or sometimes both.
- **Radiation:** Using high-energy rays (similar to X-rays) to kill the cancer.

Different treatments may be provided by different doctors on your medical team.

- Gynecologic oncologists are doctors who have been trained to treat cancers of a woman's reproductive system.
- Surgeons are doctors who perform operations.
- Medical oncologists are doctors who treat cancer with medicine.
- Radiation oncologists are doctors who treat cancer with radiation.

Clinical Trials

Clinical trials use new treatment options to see if they are safe and effective. If you have cancer, you may want to take part. Visit the sites listed below for more information.

- NIH Clinical Research Trials and You (National Institutes of Health)
- Learn About Clinical Trials (National Cancer Institute)
- Search for Clinical Trials (National Cancer Institute)
- ClinicalTrials.gov (National Institutes of Health)

Complementary and Alternative Medicine

Complementary and alternative medicine are medicines and health practices that are not standard cancer treatments. Complementary medicine is used in addition to standard treatments, and alternative medicine is used instead of standard treatments. Meditation, yoga, and supplements like vitamins and herbs are some examples.

Many kinds of complementary and alternative medicine have not been tested scientifically and may not be safe. Talk to your doctor before you start any kind of complementary or alternative medicine.

Which Treatment Is Right for Me?

Choosing the treatment that is right for you may be hard. Talk to your cancer doctor about the treatment options available for your type and stage of cancer. Your doctor can explain the risks and benefits of each treatment and their side effects.

Sometimes people get an opinion from more than one cancer doctor. This is called a "second opinion." Getting a second opinion may help you choose the treatment that is right for you.

Chapter 22

Cervical Cancer

Chapter Contents

Section 22.1

General Information about Cervical Cancer

Text in this section is excerpted from "Cervical Cancer Treatment (PDQ®)," National Cancer Institute (NCI), June 12, 2015.

Cervical cancer is a disease in which malignant (cancer) cells form in the tissues of the cervix.

The cervix is the lower, narrow end of the uterus (the hollow, pear-shaped organ where a fetus grows). The cervix leads from the uterus to the vagina (birth canal).

Cervical cancer usually develops slowly over time. Before cancer appears in the cervix, the cells of the cervix go through changes known as dysplasia, in which abnormal cells begin to appear in the cervical tissue. Over time, the abnormal cells may become cancer cells and start to grow and spread more deeply into the cervix and to surrounding areas.

Cervical cancer in children is rare.

Human papillomavirus *(HPV) infection is the major risk factor for cervical cancer.*

Anything that increases your risk of getting a disease is called a risk factor. Having a risk factor does not mean that you will get cancer; not having risk factors doesn't mean that you will not get cancer. Talk with your doctor if you think you may be at risk.

Infection of the cervix with *human papillomavirus* (HPV) is almost always the cause of cervical cancer. Not all women with HPV infection, however, will develop cervical cancer. Women who do not regularly have tests to detect HPV or abnormal cells in the cervix are at increased risk of cervical cancer. There are two vaccines to prevent HPV in girls and young women who do not have HPV.

Other possible risk factors include the following:

- Giving birth to many children.

- Having many sexual partners.

- Having first sexual intercourse at a young age.

- Smoking cigarettes.

- Using oral contraceptives ("the Pill").

There are usually no signs or symptoms of early cervical cancer but it can be detected early with regular check-ups.

Early cervical cancer may not cause signs or symptoms. Women should have regular check-ups, including tests to check for HPV or abnormal cells in the cervix. The prognosis (chance of recovery) is better when the cancer is found early.

Tests that examine the cervix are used to detect (find) and diagnose cervical cancer.

The following procedures may be used:

- **Physical exam and history:** An exam of the body to check general signs of health, including checking for signs of disease, such as lumps or anything else that seems unusual. A history of the patient's health habits and past illnesses and treatments will also be taken.

- **Pelvic exam:** An exam of the vagina, cervix, uterus, fallopian tubes, ovaries, and rectum. A speculum is inserted into the vagina and the doctor or nurse looks at the vagina and cervix for signs of disease. A Pap test of the cervix is usually done. The doctor or nurse also inserts one or two lubricated, gloved fingers of one hand into the vagina and places the other hand over the lower abdomen to feel the size, shape, and position of the uterus and ovaries. The doctor or nurse also inserts a lubricated, gloved finger into the rectum to feel for lumps or abnormal areas.

- **Pap test:** A procedure to collect cells from the surface of the cervix and vagina. A piece of cotton, a brush, or a small wooden stick is used to gently scrape cells from the cervix and vagina. The cells are viewed under a microscope to find out if they are abnormal. This procedure is also called a Pap smear.

- *Human papillomavirus* **(HPV) test:** A laboratory test used to check DNA or RNA for certain types of HPV infection. Cells are collected from the cervix and DNA or RNA from the cells is checked to find out if an infection is caused by a type of HPV that is linked to cervical cancer. This test may be done using the sample of cells removed during a Pap test. This test may also be done if the results of a Pap test show certain abnormal cervical cells.

- **Endocervical curettage:** A procedure to collect cells or tissue from the cervical canal using a curette (spoon-shaped instrument). Tissue samples are taken and checked under a microscope for signs of cancer. This procedure is sometimes done at the same time as a colposcopy.

- **Colposcopy:** A procedure in which a colposcope (a lighted, magnifying instrument) is used to check the vagina and cervix for abnormal areas. Tissue samples may be taken using a curette (spoon-shaped instrument) or a brush and checked under a microscope for signs of disease.

- **Biopsy:** If abnormal cells are found in a Pap test, the doctor may do a biopsy. A sample of tissue is cut from the cervix and viewed under a microscope by a pathologist to check for signs of cancer. A biopsy that removes only a small amount of tissue is usually done in the doctor's office. A woman may need to go to a hospital for a cervical cone biopsy (removal of a larger, cone-shaped sample of cervical tissue).

Certain factors affect prognosis (chance of recovery) and treatment options.

The prognosis (chance of recovery) depends on the following:

- The stage of the cancer (the size of the tumor and whether it affects part of the cervix or the whole cervix, or has spread to the lymph nodes or other places in the body).

- The type of cervical cancer.

- The patient's age and general health.

- Whether the patient has a certain type of *human papillomavirus* (HPV).

- Whether the patient has *human immunodeficiency virus* (HIV).

- Whether the cancer has just been diagnosed or has recurred (come back).

Treatment options depend on the following:

- The stage of the cancer.

- The type of cervical cancer.

- The patient's desire to have children.

- The patient's age.

Treatment of cervical cancer during pregnancy depends on the stage of the cancer and the stage of the pregnancy. For cervical cancer found early or for cancer found during the last trimester of pregnancy, treatment may be delayed until after the baby is born.

Section 22.2

Stages of Cervical Cancer

Text in this section is excerpted from "Cervical Cancer Treatment (PDQ®)," National Cancer Institute (NCI), June 12, 2015.

After cervical cancer has been diagnosed, tests are done to find out if cancer cells have spread within the cervix or to other parts of the body.

The process used to find out if cancer has spread within the cervix or to other parts of the body is called staging. The information gathered from the staging process determines the stage of the disease. It is important to know the stage in order to plan treatment.

The following tests and procedures may be used in the staging process:

- **CT scan (CAT scan):** A procedure that makes a series of detailed pictures of areas inside the body, taken from different angles. The pictures are made by a computer linked to an x-ray machine. A dye may be injected into a vein or swallowed to help the organs or tissues show up more clearly. This procedure is also called computed tomography, computerized tomography, or computerized axial tomography.

- **PET scan (positron emission tomography scan):** A procedure to find malignant tumor cells in the body. A small amount of radioactive glucose (sugar) is injected into a vein. The PET scanner rotates around the body and makes a picture of where glucose is being used in the body. Malignant tumor cells show up brighter in the picture because they are more active and take up more glucose than normal cells do.

- **MRI (magnetic resonance imaging):** A procedure that uses a magnet, radio waves, and a computer to make a series of detailed pictures of areas inside the body. This procedure is also called nuclear magnetic resonance imaging (NMRI).

- **Ultrasound exam:** A procedure in which high-energy sound waves (ultrasound) are bounced off internal tissues or organs and make echoes. The echoes form a picture of body tissues called a sonogram. This picture can be printed to be looked at later.

- **Chest x-ray:** An x-ray of the organs and bones inside the chest. An x-ray is a type of energy beam that can go through the body and onto film, making a picture of areas inside the body.

- **Cystoscopy:** A procedure to look inside the bladder and urethra to check for abnormal areas. A cystoscope is inserted through the urethra into the bladder. A cystoscope is a thin, tube-like instrument with a light and a lens for viewing. It may also have a tool to remove tissue samples, which are checked under a microscope for signs of cancer.

- **Laparoscopy:** A surgical procedure to look at the organs inside the abdomen to check for signs of disease. Small incisions (cuts) are made in the wall of the abdomen and a laparoscope (a thin, lighted tube) is inserted into one of the incisions. Other instruments may be inserted through the same or other incisions to perform procedures such as removing organs or taking tissue samples to be checked under a microscope for signs of disease.

- **Pretreatment surgical staging:** Surgery (an operation) is done to find out if the cancer has spread within the cervix or to other parts of the body. In some cases, the cervical cancer can be removed at the same time. Pretreatment surgical staging is usually done only as part of a clinical trial.

The results of these tests are viewed together with the results of the original tumor biopsy to determine the cervical cancer stage.

There are three ways that cancer spreads in the body.

Cancer can spread through tissue, the lymph system, and the blood:

- **Tissue.** The cancer spreads from where it began by growing into nearby areas.

- **Lymph system.** The cancer spreads from where it began by getting into the lymph system. The cancer travels through the lymph vessels to other parts of the body.

- **Blood.** The cancer spreads from where it began by getting into the blood. The cancer travels through the blood vessels to other parts of the body.

Cancer may spread from where it began to other parts of the body.

When cancer spreads to another part of the body, it is called metastasis. Cancer cells break away from where they began (the primary tumor) and travel through the lymph system or blood.

- Lymph system. The cancer gets into the lymph system, travels through the lymph vessels, and forms a tumor (metastatic tumor) in another part of the body.

- Blood. The cancer gets into the blood, travels through the blood vessels, and forms a tumor (metastatic tumor) in another part of the body.

The metastatic tumor is the same type of cancer as the primary tumor. For example, if cervical cancer spreads to the lung, the cancer cells in the lung are actually cervical cancer cells. The disease is metastatic cervical cancer, not lung cancer.

The following stages are used for cervical cancer:

Carcinoma in Situ (Stage 0)

In carcinoma in situ (stage 0), abnormal cells are found in the innermost lining of the cervix. These abnormal cells may become cancer and spread into nearby normal tissue.

Stage I

In stage I, cancer is found in the cervix only.

Stage I is divided into stages IA and IB, based on the amount of cancer that is found.

Stage IA:

A very small amount of cancer that can only be seen with a microscope is found in the tissues of the cervix.

Stage IA is divided into stages IA1 and IA2, based on the size of the tumor.

- In stage IA1, the cancer is not more than 3 millimeters deep and not more than 7 millimeters wide.

- In stage IA2, the cancer is more than 3 but not more than 5 millimeters deep, and not more than 7 millimeters wide.

- Stage IB

Stage IB is divided into stages IB1 and IB2, based on the size of the tumor.

- In stage IB1:

- the cancer can only be seen with a microscope and is more than 5 millimeters deep and more than 7 millimeters wide; or

- the cancer can be seen without a microscope and is not more than 4 centimeters.

- In stage IB2, the cancer can be seen without a microscope and is more than 4 centimeters.

Stage II

In stage II, cancer has spread beyond the uterus but not onto the pelvic wall (the tissues that line the part of the body between the hips) or to the lower third of the vagina.

Stage II is divided into stages IIA and IIB, based on how far the cancer has spread.

- Stage IIA: Cancer has spread beyond the cervix to the upper two thirds of the vagina but not to tissues around the uterus. Stage IIA is divided into stages IIA1 and IIA2, based on the size of the tumor.

- In stage IIA1, the tumor can be seen without a microscope and is not more than 4 centimeters.

- In stage IIA2, the tumor can be seen without a microscope and is more than 4 centimeters.

- Stage IIB: Cancer has spread beyond the cervix to the tissues around the uterus but not onto the pelvic wall.

Stage III

In stage III, cancer has spread to the lower third of the vagina, and/or onto the pelvic wall, and/or has caused kidney problems.

Stage III is divided into stages IIIA and IIIB, based on how far the cancer has spread.

Stage IIIA:

Cancer has spread to the lower third of the vagina but not onto the pelvic wall.

- Stage IIIB:

- Cancer has spread onto the pelvic wall; or

- the tumor has become large enough to block one or both ureters (tubes that connect the kidneys to the bladder) and has caused one or both kidneys to get bigger or stop working.

Stage IV

In stage IV, cancer has spread beyond the pelvis, or can be seen in the lining of the bladder and/or rectum, or has spread to other parts of the body.

Stage IV is divided into stages IVA and IVB, based on where the cancer has spread.

- Stage IVA:

Cancer has spread to nearby organs, such as the bladder or rectum.

- Stage IVB:

Cancer has spread to other parts of the body, such as the liver, lungs, bones, or distant lymph nodes.

Section 22.3

Cervical Cancer Prevention

Text in this section is excerpted from "Cervical Cancer Prevention
(PDQ®)," National Cancer Institute (NCI), April 9, 2015.

Avoiding risk factors and increasing protective factors may help prevent cancer.

Avoiding cancer risk factors may help prevent certain cancers. Risk
factors include smoking, being overweight, and not getting enough
exercise. Increasing protective factors such as quitting smoking, eating
a healthy diet, and exercising may also help prevent some cancers.
Talk to your doctor or other health care professional about how you
might lower your risk of cancer.

The following risk factors increase the risk of cervical cancer:

HPV Infection

The most common cause of cervical cancer is infection of the cervix
with *human papillomavirus* (HPV). There are more than 80 types
of *human papillomavirus*. About 30 types can infect the cervix and
about half of them have been linked to cervical cancer. HPV infection
is common but only a very small number of women infected with HPV
develop cervical cancer.

HPV infections that cause cervical cancer are spread mainly through
sexual contact. Women who become sexually active at a young age and
who have many sexual partners are at a greater risk of HPV infection
and developing cervical cancer.

Smoking

Smoking cigarettes and breathing in second hand smoke increase
the risk of cervical cancer. The risk increases with the number of
cigarettes smoked per day and the younger the age when smoking
began. Among women infected with HPV, cervical dysplasia and
invasive cancer occur 2 to 3 times more often in current and former
smokers.

DES Exposure

Being exposed to diethylstilbestrol (DES) while in the mother's womb increases the risk of cervical dysplasia and cervical cancer. Between 1940 and 1971, the drug DES was given to some pregnant women in the United States to prevent miscarriage (premature birth of a fetus that cannot survive) and premature labor.

The following risk factors may increase the risk of cervical cancer:

High number of full-term pregnancies

Women who have had 7 or more full-term pregnancies may have an increased risk of cervical cancer.

Long-term use of oral contraceptives

Women who have used oral contraceptives ("the Pill") for 5 years or more have a greater risk of cervical cancer than women who have never used oral contraceptives. The risk is higher after 10 years of use.

The following protective factors may decrease the risk of cervical cancer:

Preventing HPV infection

HPV may be prevented by the following:

- Avoiding sexual activity: HPV infection of the cervix is the most common cause of cervical cancer. Avoiding sexual activity decreases the risk of HPV infection.

- Using barrier protection or spermicidal gels: Some methods used to prevent sexually transmitted diseases (STDs) decrease the risk of HPV infection. The use of barrier methods of birth control (such as a condom or gel that kills sperm) help protect against HPV infection.

- Getting an HPV Vaccine: Two HPV vaccines have been approved by the U.S. Food and Drug Administration (FDA). The HPV vaccines have been shown to prevent infection with the two types of HPV that cause most cervical cancers. The vaccines protect against infection with these types of HPV for 6 to 8 years. It is not known if the protection lasts longer. The vaccines do not protect women who are already infected with HPV.

Screening

Regular pelvic exams and Pap tests help find abnormal cells in the cervix before cancer develops. However, test and procedures that may be used after an abnormal pelvic exam or Pap test result have risks. For example, the treatment of low-grade lesions may affect a woman's ability to become pregnant or carry a baby to full term. In women younger than 25 years, screening with the Pap test has more risks than benefits. Screening with the Pap test is not helpful in women older than 60 years who have had recent negative Pap tests.

Cancer prevention clinical trials are used to study ways to prevent cancer.

Cancer prevention clinical trials are used to study ways to lower the risk of developing certain types of cancer. Some cancer prevention trials are conducted with healthy people who have not had cancer but who have an increased risk for cancer. Other prevention trials are conducted with people who have had cancer and are trying to prevent another cancer of the same type or to lower their chance of developing a new type of cancer. Other trials are done with healthy volunteers who are not known to have any risk factors for cancer.

The purpose of some cancer prevention clinical trials is to find out whether actions people take can prevent cancer. These may include eating fruits and vegetables, exercising, quitting smoking, or taking certain medicines, vitamins, minerals, or food supplements.

Section 22.4

Cervical Cancer Screening

Text in this section is excerpted from "Cervical Cancer Screening (PDQ®)," National Cancer Institute (NCI), January 21, 2015.

Tests are used to screen for different types of cancer.

Some screening tests are used because they have been shown to be helpful both in finding cancers early and in decreasing the chance of dying from these cancers. Other tests are used because they have been shown to find cancer in some people; however, it has not been proven in clinical trials that use of these tests will decrease the risk of dying from cancer.

Scientists study screening tests to find those with the fewest risks and most benefits. Cancer screening trials also are meant to show whether early detection (finding cancer before it causes symptoms) decreases a person's chance of dying from the disease. For some types of cancer, the chance of recovery is better if the disease is found and treated at an early stage.

Studies show that screening for cervical cancer helps decrease the number of deaths from the disease.

Regular screening of women between the ages of 21 and 65 years with the Pap test decreases their chance of dying from cervical cancer.

A Pap test is commonly used to screen for cervical cancer.

A Pap test is a procedure to collect cells from the surface of the cervix and vagina. A piece of cotton, a brush, or a small wooden stick is used to gently scrape cells from the cervix and vagina. The cells are viewed under a microscope to find out if they are abnormal. This procedure is also called a Pap smear. A new method of collecting and viewing cells has been developed, in which the cells are placed into a liquid before being placed on a slide. It is not known if the new method will work better than the standard method to reduce the number of deaths from cervical cancer.

An HPV test may be done with or without a Pap test to screen for cervical cancer.

Screening women aged 30 and older with both the Pap test and the HPV test every 5 years finds more cervical changes that can lead to cancer than screening with the Pap test alone. Screening with both the Pap test and the HPV test lowers the number of cases of cervical cancer.

An HPV DNA test may be used without a Pap test for cervical cancer screening in women aged 25 years and older.

Section 22.5

Risks of Cervical Cancer Screening

Text in this section is excerpted from "Cervical Cancer Screening
(PDQ®)," National Cancer Institute (NCI), January 21, 2015.

Screening tests have risks.

Decisions about screening tests can be difficult. Not all screening
tests are helpful and most have risks. Before having any screening test,
you may want to discuss the test with your doctor. It is important to
know the risks of the test and whether it has been proven to reduce
the risk of dying from cancer.

The risks of cervical cancer screening include the following:

Unnecessary follow-up tests may be done.

In women younger than 21 years, screening with the Pap test may
show changes in the cells of the cervix that are not cancer. This may
lead to unnecessary follow-up tests and possibly treatment. Women in
this age group have a very low risk of cervical cancer and it is likely
that any abnormal cells will go away on their own.

False-negative test results can occur.

Screening test results may appear to be normal even though cervical cancer is present. A woman who receives a false-negative test
result (one that shows there is no cancer when there really is) may
delay seeking medical care even if she has symptoms.

False-positive test results can occur.

Screening test results may appear to be abnormal even though
no cancer is present. Also, some abnormal cells in the cervix never
become cancer. When a Pap test shows a false-positive result (one
that shows there is cancer when there really isn't), it can cause
anxiety and is usually followed by more tests and procedures (such
as colposcopy, cryotherapy, or LEEP), which also have risks. The
long-term effects of these procedures on fertility and pregnancy are
not known.

The HPV test finds many infections that will not lead to cervical dysplasia or cervical cancer, especially in women younger than 30 years.

When both the Pap test and the HPV test are done, false-positive test results are more common.

Your doctor can advise you about your risk for cervical cancer and your need for screening tests.

Your doctor can advise you about your risk for cervical cancer and your need for screening tests.

Studies show that the number of cases of cervical cancer and deaths from cervical cancer are greatly reduced by screening with Pap tests. Many doctors recommend a Pap test be done every year. New studies have shown that after a woman has a Pap test and the results show no sign of abnormal cells, the Pap test can be repeated every 2 to 3 years.

The Pap test is not a helpful screening test for cervical cancer in the following groups of women:

- Women who are younger than 21 years.

- Women who have had a total hysterectomy (surgery to remove the uterus and cervix) for a condition that is not cancer.

- Women who are aged 65 years or older and have a Pap test result that shows no abnormal cells. These women are very unlikely to have abnormal Pap test results in the future.

The decision about how often to have a Pap test is best made by you and your doctor.

Section 22.6

Treatment Options for Cervical Cancer

Text in this section is excerpted from "Cervical Cancer Treatment
(PDQ®)," National Cancer Institute (NCI), June 12, 2015.

There are different types of treatment for patients with cervical cancer.

Different types of treatment are available for patients with cervical cancer. Some treatments are standard (the currently used treatment), and some are being tested in clinical trials. A treatment clinical trial is a research study meant to help improve current treatments or obtain information on new treatments for patients with cancer. When clinical trials show that a new treatment is better than the standard treatment, the new treatment may become the standard treatment. Patients may want to think about taking part in a clinical trial. Some clinical trials are open only to patients who have not started treatment.

Four types of standard treatment are used:

Surgery
Surgery (removing the cancer in an operation) is sometimes used to treat cervical cancer. The following surgical procedures may be used:

- Conization: A procedure to remove a cone-shaped piece of tissue from the cervix and cervical canal. A pathologist views the tissue under a microscope to look for cancer cells. Conization may be used to diagnose or treat a cervical condition. This procedure is also called a cone biopsy.

Conization may be done using one of the following procedures:

- Cold-knife conization: A surgical procedure that uses a scalpel (sharp knife) to remove abnormal tissue or cancer.

- Loop electrosurgical excision procedure (LEEP): A surgical procedure that uses electrical current passed through a thin wire loop as a knife to remove abnormal tissue or cancer.

- Laser surgery: A surgical procedure that uses a laser beam (a narrow beam of intense light) as a knife to make bloodless cuts in tissue or to remove a surface lesion such as a tumor.

The type of conization procedure used depends on where the cancer cells are in the cervix and the type of cervical cancer.

- Total hysterectomy: Surgery to remove the uterus, including the cervix. If the uterus and cervix are taken out through the vagina, the operation is called a vaginal hysterectomy. If the uterus and cervix are taken out through a large incision (cut) in the abdomen, the operation is called a total abdominal hysterectomy. If the uterus and cervix are taken out through a small incision in the abdomen using a laparoscope, the operation is called a total laparoscopic hysterectomy.

- Radical hysterectomy: Surgery to remove the uterus, cervix, part of the vagina, and a wide area of ligaments and tissues around these organs. The ovaries, fallopian tubes, or nearby lymph nodes may also be removed.

- Modified radical hysterectomy: Surgery to remove the uterus, cervix, upper part of the vagina, and ligaments and tissues that closely surround these organs. Nearby lymph nodes may also be removed. In this type of surgery, not as many tissues and/or organs are removed as in a radical hysterectomy.

- Radical trachelectomy: Surgery to remove the cervix, nearby tissue and lymph nodes, and the upper part of the vagina. The uterus and ovaries are not removed.

- Bilateral salpingo-oophorectomy: Surgery to remove both ovaries and both fallopian tubes.

- Pelvic exenteration: Surgery to remove the lower colon, rectum, and bladder. The cervix, vagina, ovaries, and nearby lymph nodes are also removed. Artificial openings (stoma) are made for urine and stool to flow from the body to a collection bag. Plastic surgery may be needed to make an artificial vagina after this operation.

Radiation therapy

Radiation therapy is a cancer treatment that uses high-energy x-rays or other types of radiation to kill cancer cells or keep them from growing. There are two types of radiation therapy. External radiation therapy uses a machine outside the body to send radiation toward the cancer. Internal radiation therapy uses a radioactive substance sealed in needles, seeds, wires, or catheters that are placed directly into or near the cancer. The way the radiation therapy is given depends on the type and stage of the cancer being treated.

Intensity-modulated radiation therapy (IMRT) is a type of 3-dimensional (3-D) radiation therapy that uses a computer to make pictures of the size and shape of the tumor. Thin beams of radiation of different intensities (strengths) are aimed at the tumor from many angles. This type of radiation therapy causes less damage to healthy tissue near the tumor.

Chemotherapy

Chemotherapy is a cancer treatment that uses drugs to stop the growth of cancer cells, either by killing the cells or by stopping them from dividing. When chemotherapy is taken by mouth or injected into a vein or muscle, the drugs enter the bloodstream and can reach cancer cells throughout the body (systemic chemotherapy). When chemotherapy is placed directly into the cerebrospinal fluid, an organ, or a body cavity such as the abdomen, the drugs mainly affect cancer cells in those areas (regional chemotherapy). The way the chemotherapy is given depends on the type and stage of the cancer being treated.

Targeted therapy

Targeted therapy is a type of treatment that uses drugs or other substances to identify and attack specific cancer cells without harming normal cells.

Monoclonal antibody therapy is a type of targeted therapy that uses antibodies made in the laboratory from a single type of immune system cell. These antibodies can identify substances on cancer cells or normal substances that may help cancer cells grow. The antibodies attach to the substances and kill the cancer cells, block their growth, or keep them from spreading. Monoclonal antibodies are given by infusion. They may be used alone or to carry drugs, toxins, or radioactive material directly to cancer cells.

Bevacizumab is a monoclonal antibody that binds to a protein called vascular endothelial growth factor (VEGF) and may prevent the growth of new blood vessels that tumors need to grow. Bevacizumab is used to treat cervical cancer that has metastasized (spread to other parts of the body) and recurrent cervical cancer.

Patients may want to think about taking part in a clinical trial.

For some patients, taking part in a clinical trial may be the best treatment choice. Clinical trials are part of the cancer research process. Clinical trials are done to find out if new cancer treatments are safe and effective or better than the standard treatment.

Many of today's standard treatments for cancer are based on earlier clinical trials. Patients who take part in a clinical trial may receive the standard treatment or be among the first to receive a new treatment.

Patients who take part in clinical trials also help improve the way cancer will be treated in the future. Even when clinical trials do not lead to effective new treatments, they often answer important questions and help move research forward.

Patients can enter clinical trials before, during, or after starting their cancer treatment.

Some clinical trials only include patients who have not yet received treatment. Other trials test treatments for patients whose cancer has not gotten better. There are also clinical trials that test new ways to stop cancer from recurring (coming back) or reduce the side effects of cancer treatment.

Clinical trials are taking place in many parts of the country. See the Treatment Options section that follows for links to current treatment clinical trials. These have been retrieved from NCI's listing of clinical trials.

Follow-up tests may be needed.

Some of the tests that were done to diagnose the cancer or to find out the stage of the cancer may be repeated. Some tests will be repeated in order to see how well the treatment is working. Decisions about whether to continue, change, or stop treatment may be based on the results of these tests.

Some of the tests will continue to be done from time to time after treatment has ended. The results of these tests can show if your condition has changed or if the cancer has recurred (come back). These tests are sometimes called follow-up tests or check-ups.

Your doctor will ask if you have any of the following signs or symptoms, which may mean the cancer has come back:

- Pain in the abdomen, back, or leg.

- Swelling in the leg.

- Trouble urinating.

- Cough.

- Feeling tired.

For cervical cancer, follow-up tests are usually done every 3 to 4 months for the first 2 years, followed by check-ups every 6 months. The check-up includes a current health history and exam of the body to check for signs and symptoms of recurrent cervical cancer and for late effects of treatment.

Chapter 23

Endometrial Cancer

Chapter Contents

Section 23.1

General Information about Endometrial Cancer

Text in this section is excerpted from "Endometrial Cancer Treatment (PDQ®)," National Cancer Institute (NCI), August 12, 2015.

Endometrial cancer is a disease in which malignant (cancer) cells form in the tissues of the endometrium.

The endometrium is the lining of the uterus, a hollow, muscular organ in a woman's pelvis. The uterus is where a fetus grows. In most nonpregnant women, the uterus is about 3 inches long. The lower, narrow end of the uterus is the cervix, which leads to the vagina.

Cancer of the endometrium is different from cancer of the muscle of the uterus, which is called sarcoma of the uterus.

Obesity, high blood pressure, and diabetes mellitus may increase the risk of endometrial cancer.

Anything that increases your risk of getting a disease is called a risk factor. Having a risk factor does not mean that you will get cancer; not having risk factors doesn't mean that you will not get cancer. Talk with your doctor if you think you may be at risk. Risk factors for endometrial cancer include the following:

- Being obese.

- Having high blood pressure.

- Having diabetes mellitus.

Taking tamoxifen for breast cancer or taking estrogen alone (without progesterone) can increase the risk of endometrial cancer.

Endometrial cancer may develop in breast cancer patients who have been treated with tamoxifen. A patient taking this drug should have a pelvic exam every year and report any vaginal bleeding (other than menstrual bleeding) as soon as possible. Women taking estrogen (a hormone that can affect the growth of some cancers) alone have an increased risk of endometrial cancer. Taking estrogen combined with progesterone (another hormone) does not increase a woman's risk of this cancer.

Signs and symptoms of endometrial cancer include unusual vaginal discharge or pain in the pelvis.

These and other signs and symptoms may be caused by endometrial cancer or by other conditions. Check with your doctor if you have any of the following:

- Bleeding or discharge not related to menstruation (periods).
- Difficult or painful urination.
- Pain during sexual intercourse.
- Pain in the pelvic area.

Tests that examine the endometrium are used to detect (find) and diagnose endometrial cancer.

Because endometrial cancer begins inside the uterus, it does not usually show up in the results of a Pap test. For this reason, a sample of endometrial tissue must be removed and checked under a microscope to look for cancer cells. One of the following procedures may be used:

- **Endometrial biopsy :** The removal of tissue from the endometrium (inner lining of the uterus) by inserting a thin, flexible tube through the cervix and into the uterus. The tube is used to gently scrape a small amount of tissue from the endometrium and then remove the tissue samples. A pathologist views the tissue under a microscope to look for cancer cells.

- **Dilatation and curettage :** A procedure to remove samples of tissue from the inner lining of the uterus. The cervix is dilated and a curette (spoon-shaped instrument) is inserted into the uterus to remove tissue. The tissue samples are checked under a microscope for signs of disease. This procedure is also called a D&C.

Other tests and procedures used to diagnose endometrial cancer include the following:

- **Physical exam and history :** An exam of the body to check general signs of health, including checking for signs of disease,

285

such as lumps or anything else that seems unusual. A history of the patient's health habits and past illnesses and treatments will also be taken.

- **Transvaginal ultrasound exam:** A procedure used to examine the vagina, uterus, fallopian tubes, and bladder. An ultrasound transducer (probe) is inserted into the vagina and used to bounce high-energy sound waves (ultrasound) off internal tissues or organs and make echoes. The echoes form a picture of body tissues called a sonogram. The doctor can identify tumors by looking at the sonogram.

- **CT scan (CAT scan):** A procedure that makes a series of detailed pictures of areas inside the body, taken from different angles. The pictures are made by a computer linked to an x-ray machine. A dye may be injected into a vein or swallowed to help the organs or tissues show up more clearly. This procedure is also called computed tomography, computerized tomography, or computerized axial tomography.

Certain factors affect prognosis (chance of recovery) and treatment options.

The prognosis (chance of recovery) and treatment options depend on the following:

- The stage of the cancer (whether it is in the endometrium only, involves the whole uterus, or has spread to other places in the body).

- How the cancer cells look under a microscope.

- Whether the cancer cells are affected by progesterone.

Endometrial cancer is highly curable.

Section 23.2

Stages of Endometrial Cancer

Text in this section is excerpted from "Endometrial Cancer Treatment
(PDQ®)," National Cancer Institute (NCI), August 12, 2015.

*After endometrial cancer has been diagnosed, tests are done
to find out if cancer cells have spread within the uterus or to
other parts of the body.*

The process used to find out whether the cancer has spread within
the uterus or to other parts of the body is called staging. The information gathered from the staging process determines the stage of the
disease. It is important to know the stage in order to plan treatment.
Certain tests and procedures are used in the staging process. A hysterectomy (an operation in which the uterus is removed) will usually
be done to help find out how far the cancer has spread.

The following procedures may be used in the staging process:

- **Pelvic exam :** An exam of the vagina, cervix, uterus, fallopian
  tubes, ovaries, and rectum. A speculum is inserted into the
  vagina and the doctor or nurse looks at the vagina and cervix
  for signs of disease. A Pap test of the cervix is usually done. The
  doctor or nurse also inserts one or two lubricated, gloved fingers
  of one hand into the vagina and places the other hand over the
  lower abdomen to feel the size, shape, and position of the uterus
  and ovaries. The doctor or nurse also inserts a lubricated, gloved
  finger into the rectum to feel for lumps or abnormal areas.

- **Chest x-ray :** An x-ray of the organs and bones inside the chest.
  An x-ray is a type of energy beam that can go through the body
  and onto film, making a picture of areas inside the body.

- **MRI (magnetic resonance imaging):** A procedure that uses
  a magnet, radio waves, and a computer to make a series of
  detailed pictures of areas inside the body. This procedure is also
  called nuclear magnetic resonance imaging (NMRI).

- **PET scan (positron emission tomography scan):** A procedure to find malignant tumor cells in the body. A small amount

of radioactive glucose (sugar) is injected into a vein. The PET scanner rotates around the body and makes a picture of where glucose is being used in the body. Malignant tumor cells show up brighter in the picture because they are more active and take up more glucose than normal cells do.

There are three ways that cancer spreads in the body.

Cancer can spread through tissue, the lymph system, and the blood:

- Tissue. The cancer spreads from where it began by growing into nearby areas.

- Lymph system. The cancer spreads from where it began by getting into the lymph system. The cancer travels through the lymph vessels to other parts of the body.

- Blood. The cancer spreads from where it began by getting into the blood. The cancer travels through the blood vessels to other parts of the body.

Cancer may spread from where it began to other parts of the body.

When cancer spreads to another part of the body, it is called metastasis. Cancer cells break away from where they began (the primary tumor) and travel through the lymph system or blood.

- Lymph system. The cancer gets into the lymph system, travels through the lymph vessels, and forms a tumor (metastatic tumor) in another part of the body.

- Blood. The cancer gets into the blood, travels through the blood vessels, and forms a tumor (metastatic tumor) in another part of the body.

The metastatic tumor is the same type of cancer as the primary tumor. For example, if endometrial cancer spreads to the lung, the cancer cells in the lung are actually endometrial cancer cells. The disease is metastatic endometrial cancer, not lung cancer.

The following stages are used for endometrial cancer:

Stage I

In stage I, cancer is found in the uterus only. Stage I is divided into stages IA and IB, based on how far the cancer has spread.

- Stage IA: Cancer is in the endometrium only or less than half-way through the myometrium (muscle layer of the uterus).

- Stage IB: Cancer has spread halfway or more into the myometrium.

Stage II

In stage II, cancer has spread into connective tissue of the cervix, but has not spread outside the uterus.

Stage III

In stage III, cancer has spread beyond the uterus and cervix, but has not spread beyond the pelvis. Stage III is divided into stages IIIA, IIIB, and IIIC, based on how far the cancer has spread within the pelvis.

- Stage IIIA: Cancer has spread to the outer layer of the uterus and/or to the fallopian tubes, ovaries, and ligaments of the uterus.

- Stage IIIB: Cancer has spread to the vagina and/or to the parametrium (connective tissue and fat around the uterus).

- Stage IIIC: Cancer has spread to lymph nodes in the pelvis and/or around the aorta (largest artery in the body, which carries blood away from the heart).

Stage IV

In stage IV, cancer has spread beyond the pelvis. Stage IV is divided into stages IVA and IVB, based on how far the cancer has spread.

- Stage IVA: Cancer has spread to the bladder and/or bowel wall.

- Stage IVB: Cancer has spread to other parts of the body beyond the pelvis, including the abdomen and/or lymph nodes in the groin.

Section 23.3

Endometrial Cancer Prevention

Text in this section is excerpted from "Endometrial Cancer
Prevention (PDQ®)," National Cancer Institute (NCI), July 13, 2015.

Avoiding risk factors and increasing protective factors may help prevent cancer.

Avoiding cancer risk factors may help prevent certain cancers. Risk
factors include smoking, being overweight, and not getting enough
exercise. Increasing protective factors such as quitting smoking, eating
a healthy diet, and exercising may also help prevent some cancers.
Talk to your doctor or other health care professional about how you
might lower your risk of cancer.

The following risk factors may increase the risk of endometrial cancer:

Estrogen

Estrogen is a hormone made by the body. It helps the body develop
and maintain female sex characteristics. Estrogen can affect the
growth of some cancers, including endometrial cancer. A woman's
risk of developing endometrial cancer is increased by being exposed
to estrogen in the following ways:

- Estrogen-only hormone replacement therapy: Estrogen may be
  given to replace the estrogen no longer produced by the ovaries
  in postmenopausal women or women whose ovaries have been
  removed. This is called hormone replacement therapy (HRT), or
  hormone therapy (HT). The use of hormone replacement therapy
  that contains only estrogen increases the risk of endometrial
  hyperplasia in postmenopausal women. Endometrial hyperplasia is an abnormal thickening of the endometrium (lining of the
  uterus). It is not cancer, but in some cases, it may lead to endometrial cancer. For this reason, estrogen therapy alone is usually prescribed only for women who do not have a uterus.

When estrogen is combined with progestin (another hormone), it is called combination estrogen-progestin replacement therapy. For postmenopausal women, taking estrogen in combination with progestin does not increase the risk of endometrial cancer, but it does increase the risk of breast cancer, heart disease, stroke, and blood clots.

- Early menstruation: Beginning to have menstrual periods at an early age increases the number of years the body is exposed to estrogen and increases a woman's risk of endometrial cancer.

- Late menopause: Women who reach menopause at an older age are exposed to estrogen for a longer time and have an increased risk of endometrial cancer.

- Never being pregnant: Because estrogen levels are lower during pregnancy, women who have never been pregnant are exposed to estrogen for a longer time than women who have been pregnant. This increases the risk of endometrial cancer.

Tamoxifen

Tamoxifen is one of a group of drugs called selective estrogen receptor modulators, or SERMs. Tamoxifen acts like estrogen on some tissues in the body, such as the uterus, but blocks the effects of estrogen on other tissues, such as the breast. Tamoxifen is used to prevent breast cancer in women who are at high risk for the disease. However, using tamoxifen for more than 2 years increases the risk of endometrial cancer. This risk is greater in postmenopausal women.

Raloxifene is a SERM that is used to prevent bone weakness in postmenopausal women. It does not have estrogen-like effects on the uterus and has not been shown to increase the risk of endometrial cancer. Other SERMs are being studied in clinical trials.

Hereditary nonpolyposis colon cancer syndrome

Hereditary nonpolyposis colon cancer (HNPCC) syndrome (also known as Lynch Syndrome) is an inherited disorder caused by changes in certain genes. Women who have HNPCC syndrome have a much higher risk of developing endometrial cancer than women who do not have HNPCC syndrome.

Other inherited conditions

Polycystic ovary syndrome (a disorder of the hormones made by the ovaries), and Cowden syndrome are inherited conditions that are linked to an increased risk of endometrial cancer.

Family history of endometrial cancer

Women with a family history of endometrial cancer in a first-degree relative (mother, sister, or daughter) may also be at increased risk of endometrial cancer.

Body fat

Obesity increases the risk of endometrial cancer. This may be because obesity is related to other risk factors such as estrogen levels, polycystic ovary syndrome, and lack of physical activity.

It is not known if losing weight decreases the risk of endometrial cancer.

The following protective factors may decrease the risk of endometrial cancer:

Cancer prevention clinical trials are used to study ways to prevent cancer.

Cancer prevention clinical trials are used to study ways to lower the risk of developing certain types of cancer. Some cancer prevention trials are conducted with healthy people who have not had cancer but who have an increased risk for cancer. Other prevention trials are conducted with people who have had cancer and are trying to prevent another cancer of the same type or to lower their chance of developing a new type of cancer. Other trials are done with healthy volunteers who are not known to have any risk factors for cancer.

The purpose of some cancer prevention clinical trials is to find out whether actions people take can prevent cancer. These may include eating fruits and vegetables, exercising, quitting smoking, or taking certain medicines, vitamins, minerals, or food supplements.

Section 23.4

Endometrial Cancer Screening

Text in this section is excerpted from "Endometrial Cancer Screening (PDQ®)," National Cancer Institute (NCI), July 23, 2015.

Tests are used to screen for different types of cancer.

Some screening tests are used because they have been shown to be helpful both in finding cancers early and decreasing the chance of dying from these cancers. Other tests are used because they have been shown to find cancer in some people; however, it has not been proven in clinical trials that use of these tests will decrease the risk of dying from cancer.

Scientists study screening tests to find those with the fewest risks and most benefits. Cancer screening trials also are meant to show whether early detection (finding cancer before it causes symptoms) decreases a person's chance of dying from the disease. For some types of cancer, finding and treating the disease at an early stage may result in a better chance of recovery.

Endometrial cancer is usually found early.

Endometrial cancer usually causes symptoms (such as vaginal bleeding) and is found at an early stage, when there is a good chance of recovery.

There is no standard or routine screening test for endometrial cancer.

Screening for endometrial cancer is under study and there are screening clinical trials taking place in many parts of the country.

Tests that may detect (find) endometrial cancer are being studied:

Pap test

A Pap test is a procedure to collect cells from the surface of the cervix and vagina. A piece of cotton, a brush, or a small wooden stick is used to gently scrape cells from the cervix and vagina. The cells are viewed under a microscope to find out if they are abnormal. This procedure is also called a Pap smear.

Pap tests are not used to screen for endometrial cancer; however, Pap test results sometimes show signs of an abnormal endometrium (lining of the uterus). Follow-up tests may detect endometrial cancer.

Transvaginal ultrasound

No studies have shown that screening by transvaginal ultrasound (TVU) lowers the number of deaths caused by endometrial cancer.

Transvaginal ultrasound (TVU) is a procedure used to examine the vagina, uterus, fallopian tubes, and bladder. It is also called endovaginal ultrasound. An ultrasound transducer (probe) is inserted into the vagina and used to bounce high-energy sound waves (ultrasound) off internal tissues or organs and make echoes. The echoes form a picture of body tissues called a sonogram. The doctor can identify tumors by looking at the sonogram.

TVU is commonly used to examine women who have abnormal vaginal bleeding. For women who have or are at risk for hereditary non-polyposis colon cancer, experts suggest yearly screening with transvaginal ultrasound, beginning as early as age 25.

The use of tamoxifen to treat or prevent breast cancer increases the risk of endometrial cancer. TVU is not useful in screening for endometrial cancer in women who take tamoxifen but do not have any symptoms of endometrial cancer. In women taking tamoxifen, TVU should be used in those who have vaginal bleeding.

Endometrial sampling

It has not been proven that screening by endometrial sampling (biopsy) lowers the number of deaths caused by endometrial cancer.

Endometrial sampling is the removal of tissue from the endometrium by inserting a brush, curette, or thin, flexible tube through the cervix and into the uterus. The tool is used to gently scrape a small amount of tissue from the endometrium and then remove the tissue samples. A pathologist views the tissue under a microscope to look for cancer cells.

Endometrial sampling is commonly used to examine women who have abnormal vaginal bleeding. If you have abnormal vaginal bleeding, check with your doctor.

Section 23.5

Risks of Endometrial Cancer Screening

Text in this section is excerpted from "Endometrial Cancer Screening (PDQ®)," National Cancer Institute (NCI), July 23, 2015.

Screening tests have risks.

Decisions about screening tests can be difficult. Not all screening tests are helpful and most have risks. Before having any screening test, you may want to discuss the test with your doctor. It is important to know the risks of the test and whether it has been proven to reduce the risk of dying from cancer.

The risks of endometrial cancer screening tests include the following:

Finding endometrial cancer may not improve health or help a woman live longer.

Screening may not improve your health or help you live longer if you have advanced endometrial cancer or if it has already spread to other places in your body.

Some cancers never cause symptoms or become life-threatening, but if found by a screening test, the cancer may be treated. It is not known if treatment of these cancers would help you live longer than if no treatment were given, and treatments for cancer may have serious side effects.

False-negative test results can occur.

Screening test results may appear to be normal even though endometrial cancer is present. A woman who receives a false-negative test result (one that shows there is no cancer when there really is) may delay seeking medical care even if she has symptoms.

False-positive test results can occur.

Screening test results may appear to be abnormal even though no cancer is present. A false-positive test result (one that shows there is cancer when there really isn't) can cause anxiety and is usually followed by more tests (such as biopsy), which also have risks.

Side effects may be caused by the test itself.

Side effects that may be caused by screening tests for endometrial cancer include:

- Discomfort.

- Bleeding.

- Infection.

- Puncture of the uterus (rare).

If you have any questions about your risk for endometrial cancer or the need for screening tests, check with your doctor.

Section 23.6

Treatment Options for Endometrial Cancer

Text in this section is excerpted from "Endometrial Cancer Treatment (PDQ®)," National Cancer Institute (NCI), August 12, 2015.

There are different types of treatment for patients with endometrial cancer.

Different types of treatment are available for patients with endometrial cancer. Some treatments are standard (the currently used treatment), and some are being tested in clinical trials. A treatment clinical trial is a research study meant to help improve current treatments or obtain information on new treatments for patients with cancer. When clinical trials show that a new treatment is better than the standard treatment, the new treatment may become the standard treatment. Patients may want to think about taking part in a clinical trial. Some clinical trials are open only to patients who have not started treatment.

Five types of standard treatment are used:

Surgery

Surgery (removing the cancer in an operation) is the most common treatment for endometrial cancer. The following surgical procedures may be used:

- Total hysterectomy: Surgery to remove the uterus, including the cervix. If the uterus and cervix are taken out through the vagina, the operation is called a vaginal hysterectomy. If the uterus and cervix are taken out through a large incision (cut) in the abdomen, the operation is called a total abdominal hysterectomy. If the uterus and cervix are taken out through a small incision (cut) in the abdomen using a laparoscope, the operation is called a total laparoscopic hysterectomy.

- Bilateral salpingo-oophorectomy: Surgery to remove both ovaries and both fallopian tubes.

- Radical hysterectomy: Surgery to remove the uterus, cervix, and part of the vagina. The ovaries, fallopian tubes, or nearby lymph nodes may also be removed.

Even if the doctor removes all the cancer that can be seen at the time of the surgery, some patients may be given radiation therapy or hormone treatment after surgery to kill any cancer cells that are left. Treatment given after the surgery, to lower the risk that the cancer will come back, is called adjuvant therapy.

Radiation therapy

Radiation therapy is a cancer treatment that uses high-energy x-rays or other types of radiation to kill cancer cells or keep them from growing. There are two types of radiation therapy. External radiation therapy uses a machine outside the body to send radiation toward the cancer. Internal radiation therapy uses a radioactive substance sealed in needles, seeds, wires, or catheters that are placed directly into or near the cancer. The way the radiation therapy is given depends on the type and stage of the cancer being treated.

Chemotherapy

Chemotherapy is a cancer treatment that uses drugs to stop the growth of cancer cells, either by killing the cells or by stopping the cells from dividing. When chemotherapy is taken by mouth or injected into a vein or muscle, the drugs enter the bloodstream and can reach cancer cells throughout the body (systemic chemotherapy). When chemotherapy is placed directly into the cerebrospinal fluid, an organ, or a body cavity such as the abdomen, the drugs mainly affect cancer cells in those areas (regional chemotherapy). The way the chemotherapy is given depends on the type and stage of the cancer being treated.

Hormone therapy

Hormone therapy is a cancer treatment that removes hormones or blocks their action and stops cancer cells from growing. Hormones are substances made by glands in the body and circulated in the bloodstream. Some hormones can cause certain cancers to grow. If tests show that the cancer cells have places where hormones can attach (receptors), drugs, surgery, or radiation therapy is used to reduce the production of hormones or block them from working.

Biologic therapy

Biologic therapy is a treatment that uses the patient's immune system to fight cancer. Substances made by the body or made in a laboratory are used to boost, direct, or restore the body's natural defenses against cancer. This type of cancer treatment is also called biotherapy or immunotherapy.

Targeted therapy

Targeted therapy is a type of treatment that uses drugs or other substances to identify and attack specific cancer cells without harming normal cells. Monoclonal antibodies and tyrosine kinase inhibitors are two types of targeted therapy being studied in the treatment of endometrial cancer.

Monoclonal antibody therapy is a cancer treatment that uses antibodies made in the laboratory from a single type of immune system cell. These antibodies can identify substances on cancer cells or normal substances that may help cancer cells grow. The antibodies attach to the substances and kill the cancer cells, block their growth, or keep them from spreading. Monoclonal antibodies are given by infusion. They may be used alone or to carry drugs, toxins, or radioactive material directly to cancer cells.

Tyrosine kinase inhibitors are targeted therapy drugs that block signals needed for tumors to grow. Tyrosine kinase inhibitors may be used with other anticancer drugs as adjuvant therapy.

Patients may want to think about taking part in a clinical trial.

For some patients, taking part in a clinical trial may be the best treatment choice. Clinical trials are part of the cancer research process. Clinical trials are done to find out if new cancer treatments are safe and effective or better than the standard treatment.

Many of today's standard treatments for cancer are based on earlier clinical trials. Patients who take part in a clinical trial may receive the standard treatment or be among the first to receive a new treatment.

Patients who take part in clinical trials also help improve the way cancer will be treated in the future. Even when clinical trials do not lead to effective new treatments, they often answer important questions and help move research forward.

Patients can enter clinical trials before, during, or after starting their cancer treatment.

Some clinical trials only include patients who have not yet received treatment. Other trials test treatments for patients whose cancer has not gotten better. There are also clinical trials that test new ways to stop cancer from recurring (coming back) or reduce the side effects of cancer treatment.

Clinical trials are taking place in many parts of the country.

Follow-up tests may be needed.

Some of the tests that were done to diagnose the cancer or to find out the stage of the cancer may be repeated. Some tests will be repeated in order to see how well the treatment is working. Decisions about whether to continue, change, or stop treatment may be based on the results of these tests.

Some of the tests will continue to be done from time to time after treatment has ended. The results of these tests can show if your condition has changed or if the cancer has recurred (come back). These tests are sometimes called follow-up tests or check-ups.

Chapter 24

Gestational Trophoblastic Disease

Chapter Contents

Section 24.1

General Information about Gestational Trophoblastic Disease

Text in this section is excerpted from "Gestational Trophoblastic Disease Treatment (PDQ®)," National Cancer Institute (NINDS), June 26, 2015.

Gestational trophoblastic disease (GTD) is a group of rare diseases in which abnormal trophoblast cells grow inside the uterus after conception.

In gestational trophoblastic disease (GTD), a tumor develops inside the uterus from tissue that forms after conception (the joining of sperm and egg). This tissue is made of trophoblast cells and normally surrounds the fertilized egg in the uterus. Trophoblast cells help connect the fertilized egg to the wall of the uterus and form part of the placenta (the organ that passes nutrients from the mother to the fetus).

Sometimes there is a problem with the fertilized egg and trophoblast cells. Instead of a healthy fetus developing, a tumor forms. Until there are signs or symptoms of the tumor, the pregnancy will seem like a normal pregnancy.

Most GTD is benign (not cancer) and does not spread, but some types become malignant (cancer) and spread to nearby tissues or distant parts of the body.

Gestational trophoblastic disease (GTD) is a general term that includes different types of disease:

- Hydatidiform Moles (HM)
- Complete HM.
- Partial HM.
- Gestational Trophoblastic Neoplasia (GTN)
- Invasive moles.
- Choriocarcinomas.
- Placental-site trophoblastic tumors (PSTT; very rare).
- Epithelioid trophoblastic tumors (ETT; even more rare).

Hydatidiform mole (HM) is the most common type of GTD.

HMs are slow-growing tumors that look like sacs of fluid. An HM is also called a molar pregnancy. The cause of hydatidiform moles is not known.

HMs may be complete or partial:

- A complete HM forms when sperm fertilizes an egg that does not contain the mother's DNA. The egg has DNA from the father and the cells that were meant to become the placenta are abnormal.

- A partial HM forms when sperm fertilizes a normal egg and there are two sets of DNA from the father in the fertilized egg. Only part of the fetus forms and the cells that were meant to become the placenta are abnormal.

Most hydatidiform moles are benign, but they sometimes become cancer. Having one or more of the following risk factors increases the risk that a hydatidiform mole will become cancer:

- A pregnancy before 20 or after 35 years of age.
- A very high level of beta human chorionic gonadotropin (β-hCG), a hormone made by the body during pregnancy.
- A large tumor in the uterus.
- An ovarian cyst larger than 6 centimeters.
- High blood pressure during pregnancy.
- An overactive thyroid gland (extra thyroid hormone is made).
- Severe nausea and vomiting during pregnancy.
- Trophoblastic cells in the blood, which may block small blood vessels.
- Serious blood clotting problems caused by the HM.

Gestational trophoblastic neoplasia (GTN) is a type of gestational trophoblastic disease (GTD) that is almost always malignant.

Gestational trophoblastic neoplasia (GTN) includes the following:

Invasive moles

Invasive moles are made up of trophoblast cells that grow into the muscle layer of the uterus. Invasive moles are more likely to grow and spread than a hydatidiform mole. Rarely, a complete or partial HM may become an invasive mole. Sometimes an invasive mole will disappear without treatment.

Choriocarcinomas

A choriocarcinoma is a malignant tumor that forms from trophoblast cells and spreads to the muscle layer of the uterus and nearby blood vessels. It may also spread to other parts of the body, such as the brain, lungs, liver, kidney, spleen, intestines, pelvis, or vagina. A choriocarcinoma is more likely to form in women who have had any of the following:

- Molar pregnancy, especially with a complete hydatidiform mole.

- Normal pregnancy.

- Tubal pregnancy (the fertilized egg implants in the fallopian tube rather than the uterus).

- Miscarriage.

Placental-site trophoblastic tumors

A placental-site trophoblastic tumor (PSTT) is a rare type of gestational trophoblastic neoplasia that forms where the placenta attaches to the uterus. The tumor forms from trophoblast cells and spreads into the muscle of the uterus and into blood vessels. It may also spread to the lungs, pelvis, or lymph nodes. A PSTT grows very slowly and signs or symptoms may appear months or years after a normal pregnancy.

Epithelioid trophoblastic tumors

An epithelioid trophoblastic tumor (ETT) is a very rare type of gestational trophoblastic neoplasia that may be benign or malignant. When the tumor is malignant, it may spread to the lungs.

Age and a previous molar pregnancy affect the risk of GTD.

Anything that increases your risk of getting a disease is called a risk factor. Having a risk factor does not mean that you will get cancer; not having risk factors doesn't mean that you will not get cancer. Talk to your doctor if you think you may be at risk. Risk factors for GTD include the following:

- Being pregnant when you are younger than 20 or older than 35 years of age.

- Having a personal history of hydatidiform mole.

Signs of GTD include abnormal vaginal bleeding and a uterus that is larger than normal.

These and other signs and symptoms may be caused by gestational trophoblastic disease or by other conditions. Check with your doctor if you have any of the following:

- Vaginal bleeding not related to menstruation.
- A uterus that is larger than expected during pregnancy.
- Pain or pressure in the pelvis.
- Severe nausea and vomiting during pregnancy.
- High blood pressure with headache and swelling of feet and hands early in the pregnancy.
- Vaginal bleeding that continues for longer than normal after delivery.
- Fatigue, shortness of breath, dizziness, and a fast or irregular heartbeat caused by anemia.

GTD sometimes causes an overactive thyroid. Signs and symptoms of an overactive thyroid include the following:

- Fast or irregular heartbeat.
- Shakiness.
- Sweating.
- Frequent bowel movements.
- Trouble sleeping.
- Feeling anxious or irritable.
- Weight loss.

Tests that examine the uterus are used to detect (find) and diagnose gestational trophoblastic disease.

The following tests and procedures may be used:

- **Physical exam and history:** An exam of the body to check general signs of health, including checking for signs of disease, such as lumps or anything else that seems unusual. A history of the patient's health habits and past illnesses and treatments will also be taken.

- **Pelvic exam:** An exam of the vagina, cervix, uterus, fallopian tubes, ovaries, and rectum. A speculum is inserted into the vagina and the doctor or nurse looks at the vagina and cervix for signs of disease. A Pap test of the cervix is usually done. The doctor or nurse also inserts one or two lubricated, gloved fingers of one hand into the vagina and places the other hand over the lower abdomen to feel the size, shape, and position of the uterus and ovaries. The doctor or nurse also inserts a lubricated, gloved finger into the rectum to feel for lumps or abnormal areas.

- **Ultrasound exam of the pelvis:** A procedure in which high-energy sound waves (ultrasound) are bounced off internal tissues or organs in the pelvis and make echoes. The echoes form a picture of body tissues called a sonogram. Sometimes a transvaginal ultrasound (TVUS) will be done. For TVUS, an ultrasound transducer (probe) is inserted into the vagina to make the sonogram.

- **Blood chemistry studies:** A procedure in which a blood sample is checked to measure the amounts of certain substances released into the blood by organs and tissues in the body. An unusual (higher or lower than normal) amount of a substance can be a sign of disease. Blood is also tested to check the liver, kidney, and bone marrow.

- **Serum tumor marker test:** A procedure in which a sample of blood is checked to measure the amounts of certain substances made by organs, tissues, or tumor cells in the body. Certain substances are linked to specific types of cancer when found in increased levels in the body. These are called tumor markers. For GTD, the blood is checked for the level of beta human chorionic gonadotropin (β-hCG), a hormone that is made by the body during pregnancy. β-hCG in the blood of a woman who is not pregnant may be a sign of GTD.

- **Urinalysis:** A test to check the color of urine and its contents, such as sugar, protein, blood, bacteria, and the level of β-hCG.

Certain factors affect prognosis (chance of recovery) and treatment options.

Gestational trophoblastic disease usually can be cured. Treatment and prognosis depend on the following:

- The type of GTD.

- Whether the tumor has spread to the uterus, lymph nodes, or distant parts of the body.

- The number of tumors and where they are in the body.

- The size of the largest tumor.

- The level of β-hCG in the blood.

- How soon the tumor was diagnosed after the pregnancy began.

- Whether GTD occurred after a molar pregnancy, miscarriage, or normal pregnancy.

- Previous treatment for gestational trophoblastic neoplasia.

Treatment options also depend on whether the woman wishes to become pregnant in the future.

Section 24.2

Stages of Gestational Trophoblastic Tumors and Neoplasia

Text in this section is excerpted from "Gestational Trophoblastic Disease Treatment (PDQ®)," National Cancer Institute (NINDS), June 26, 2015.

After gestational trophoblastic neoplasia has been diagnosed, tests are done to find out if cancer has spread from where it started to other parts of the body.

The process used to find out the extent or spread of cancer is called staging. The information gathered from the staging process helps determine the stage of disease. For GTN, stage is one of the factors used to plan treatment.

The following tests and procedures may be done to help find out the stage of the disease:

- **Chest x-ray:** An x-ray of the organs and bones inside the chest. An x-ray is a type of energy beam that can go through the body onto film, making pictures of areas inside the body.

- **CT scan (CAT scan):** A procedure that makes a series of detailed pictures of areas inside the body, taken from different angles. The pictures are made by a computer linked to an x-ray machine. A dye may be injected into a vein or swallowed to help the organs or tissues show up more clearly. This procedure is also called computed tomography, computerized tomography, or computerized axial tomography.

- **MRI (magnetic resonance imaging) with gadolinium:** A procedure that uses a magnet, radio waves, and a computer to make a series of detailed pictures of areas inside the body, such as brain and spinal cord. A substance called gadolinium is injected into a vein. The gadolinium collects around the cancer cells so they show up brighter in the picture. This procedure is also called nuclear magnetic resonance imaging (NMRI).

- **Lumbar puncture:** A procedure used to collect cerebrospinal fluid (CSF) from the spinal column. This is done by placing a needle between two bones in the spine and into the spinal column. A sample of CSF is removed and checked under a microscope for signs that the cancer has spread to the brain and spinal cord. This procedure is also called an LP or spinal tap.

There are three ways that cancer spreads in the body.

Cancer can spread through tissue, the lymph system, and the blood:

- Tissue. The cancer spreads from where it began by growing into nearby areas.

- Lymph system. The cancer spreads from where it began by getting into the lymph system. The cancer travels through the lymph vessels to other parts of the body.

- Blood. The cancer spreads from where it began by getting into the blood. The cancer travels through the blood vessels to other parts of the body.

Cancer may spread from where it began to other parts of the body.

When cancer spreads to another part of the body, it is called metastasis. Cancer cells break away from where they began (the primary tumor) and travel through the lymph system or blood.

- Lymph system. The cancer gets into the lymph system, travels through the lymph vessels, and forms a tumor (metastatic tumor) in another part of the body.

- Blood. The cancer gets into the blood, travels through the blood vessels, and forms a tumor (metastatic tumor) in another part of the body.

The metastatic tumor is the same type of cancer as the primary tumor. For example, if choriocarcinoma spreads to the lung, the cancer cells in the lung are actually choriocarcinoma cells. The disease is metastatic choriocarcinoma, not lung cancer.

There is no staging system for hydatidiform moles.

Hydatidiform moles (HM) are found in the uterus only and do not spread to other parts of the body.

The following stages are used for GTN:

Stage I
In stage I, the tumor is in the uterus only.

Stage II
In stage II, cancer has spread outside of the uterus to the ovary, fallopian tube, vagina, and/or the ligaments that support the uterus.

Stage III
In stage III, cancer has spread to the lung.

Stage IV
In stage IV, cancer has spread to distant parts of the body other than the lungs.

The treatment of gestational trophoblastic neoplasia is based on the type of disease, stage, or risk group.

Invasive moles and choriocarcinomas are treated based on risk groups. The stage of the invasive mole or choriocarcinoma is one factor used to determine risk group. Other factors include the following:

- The age of the patient when the diagnosis is made.

- Whether the GTN occurred after a molar pregnancy, miscarriage, or normal pregnancy.

- How soon the tumor was diagnosed after the pregnancy began.

- The level of beta human chorionic gonadotropin (β-hCG) in the blood.

- The size of the largest tumor.
- Where the tumor has spread to and the number of tumors in the body.
- How many chemotherapy drugs the tumor has been treated with (for recurrent or resistant tumors).

There are two risk groups for invasive moles and choriocarcinomas: low risk and high risk. Patients with low-risk disease usually receive less aggressive treatment than patients with high-risk disease.

Placental-site trophoblastic tumor (PSTT) and epithelioid tropho-blastic tumor (ETT) treatments depend on the stage of disease.

Section 24.3

Treatment Options for Gestational Trophoblastic Disease

Text in this section is excerpted from "Gestational Trophoblastic Disease Treatment (PDQ®)," National Cancer Institute (NINDS), June 26, 2015.

There are different types of treatment for patients with gestational trophoblastic disease.

Different types of treatment are available for patients with ges-tational trophoblastic disease. Some treatments are standard (the currently used treatment), and some are being tested in clinical trials. Before starting treatment, patients may want to think about taking part in a clinical trial. A treatment clinical trial is a research study meant to help improve current treatments or obtain information on new treatments for patients with cancer. When clinical trials show that a new treatment is better than the standard treatment, the new treatment may become the standard treatment.

Three types of standard treatment are used:

Surgery

The doctor may remove the cancer using one of the following operations:

- Dilatation and curettage (D&C) with suction evacuation: A surgical procedure to remove abnormal tissue and parts of the inner lining of the uterus. The cervix is dilated and the material inside the uterus is removed with a small vacuum-like device. The walls of the uterus are then gently scraped with a curette (spoon-shaped instrument) to remove any material that may remain in the uterus. This procedure may be used for molar pregnancies.

- Hysterectomy: Surgery to remove the uterus, and sometimes the cervix. If the uterus and cervix are taken out through the vagina, the operation is called a vaginal hysterectomy. If the uterus and cervix are taken out through a large incision (cut) in the abdomen, the operation is called a total abdominal hysterectomy. If the uterus and cervix are taken out through a small incision (cut) in the abdomen using a laparoscope, the operation is called a total laparoscopic hysterectomy.

Chemotherapy

Chemotherapy is a cancer treatment that uses drugs to stop the growth of cancer cells, either by killing the cells or by stopping them from dividing. When chemotherapy is taken by mouth or injected into a vein or muscle, the drugs enter the bloodstream and can reach cancer cells throughout the body (systemic chemotherapy). When chemotherapy is placed directly into the cerebrospinal fluid, an organ, or a body cavity such as the abdomen, the drugs mainly affect cancer cells in those areas (regional chemotherapy). The way the chemotherapy is given depends on the type and stage of the cancer being treated, or whether the tumor is low-risk or high-risk.

Combination chemotherapy is treatment using more than one anticancer drug.

Even if the doctor removes all the cancer that can be seen at the time of the surgery, some patients may be given chemotherapy after surgery to kill any tumor cells that are left. Treatment given after the surgery, to lower the risk that the cancer will come back, is called adjuvant therapy.

Radiation therapy

Radiation therapy is a cancer treatment that uses high-energy x-rays or other types of radiation to kill cancer cells or keep them from growing. There are two types of radiation therapy. External radiation therapy uses a machine outside the body to send radiation toward the cancer. Internal radiation therapy uses a radioactive substance sealed in needles, seeds, wires, or catheters that are placed directly into or near the cancer. The way the radiation therapy is given depends on the type of cancer being treated.

Patients may want to think about taking part in a clinical trial.

For some patients, taking part in a clinical trial may be the best treatment choice. Clinical trials are part of the cancer research process. Clinical trials are done to find out if new cancer treatments are safe and effective or better than the standard treatment.

Many of today's standard treatments for cancer are based on earlier clinical trials. Patients who take part in a clinical trial may receive the standard treatment or be among the first to receive a new treatment.

Patients who take part in clinical trials also help improve the way cancer will be treated in the future. Even when clinical trials do not lead to effective new treatments, they often answer important questions and help move research forward.

Patients can enter clinical trials before, during, or after starting their cancer treatment.

Some clinical trials only include patients who have not yet received treatment. Other trials test treatments for patients whose cancer has not gotten better. There are also clinical trials that test new ways to stop cancer from recurring (coming back) or reduce the side effects of cancer treatment.

Clinical trials are taking place in many parts of the country. See the Treatment Options section that follows for links to current treatment clinical trials. These have been retrieved from NCI's listing of clinical trials.

Hydatidiform Moles

Treatment of a hydatidiform mole may include the following:

- Surgery (Dilatation and curettage with suction evacuation) to remove the tumor.

After surgery, beta human chorionic gonadotropin (β-hCG) blood tests are done every week until the β-hCG level returns to normal. Patients also have follow-up doctor visits monthly for up to 6 months. If the level of β-hCG does not return to normal or increases, it may mean the hydatidiform mole was not completely removed and it has become cancer. Pregnancy causes β-hCG levels to increase, so your doctor will ask you not to become pregnant until follow-up is finished.

For disease that remains after surgery, treatment is usually chemotherapy.

Gestational Trophoblastic Neoplasia

Low-risk Gestational Trophoblastic Neoplasia
Treatment of low-risk gestational trophoblastic neoplasia (GTN) (invasive mole or choriocarcinoma) may include the following:

- Chemotherapy with one or more anticancer drugs. Treatment is given until the beta human chorionic gonadotropin (β-hCG) level is normal for at least 3 weeks after treatment ends.

If the level of β-hCG in the blood does not return to normal or the tumor spreads to distant parts of the body, chemotherapy regimens used for high-risk metastatic GTN are given.

High-risk Metastatic Gestational Trophoblastic Neoplasia
Treatment of high-risk metastatic gestational trophoblastic neoplasia (invasive mole or choriocarcinoma) may include the following:

- Combination chemotherapy.

- Intrathecal chemotherapy and radiation therapy to the brain (for cancer that has spread to the lung, to keep it from spreading to the brain).

- High-dose chemotherapy or intrathecal chemotherapy and/or radiation therapy to the brain (for cancer that has spread to the brain).

Placental-Site Gestational Trophoblastic Tumors and Epithelioid Trophoblastic Tumors

Treatment of stage I placental-site gestational trophoblastic tumors and epithelioid trophoblastic tumors may include the following:

- Surgery to remove the uterus.

  Treatment of stage II placental-site gestational trophoblastic tumors and epithelioid trophoblastic tumors may include the following:

- Surgery to remove the tumor, which may be followed by combination chemotherapy.

Treatment of stage III and IV placental-site gestational trophoblastic tumors and epithelioid trophoblastic tumors may include following:

- Combination chemotherapy.

- Surgery to remove cancer that has spread to other places, such as the lung or abdomen.

Recurrent or Resistant Gestational Trophoblastic Neoplasia

Treatment of recurrent or resistant gestational trophoblastic tumor may include the following:

- Chemotherapy with one or more anticancer drugs for tumors previously treated with surgery.

- Combination chemotherapy for tumors previously treated with chemotherapy.

- Surgery for tumors that do not respond to chemotherapy.

Chapter 25

Ovarian, Fallopian Tube, and Primary Peritoneal Cancer

Chapter Contents

Section 25.1

General Information about Ovarian Epithelial, Fallopian Tube, and Primary Peritoneal Cancer

Text in this section is excerpted from "Ovarian Epithelial, Fallopian Tube, and Primary Peritoneal Cancer Treatment (PDQ®)," National Cancer Institute (NCI), July 2, 2015.

Ovarian epithelial cancer, fallopian tube cancer, and primary peritoneal cancer are diseases in which malignant (cancer) cells form in the tissue covering the ovary or lining the fallopian tube or peritoneum.

The ovaries are a pair of organs in the female reproductive system. They are in the pelvis, one on each side of the uterus (the hollow, pear-shaped organ where a fetus grows). Each ovary is about the size and shape of an almond. The ovaries make eggs and female hormones (chemicals that control the way certain cells or organs work).

The fallopian tubes are a pair of long, slender tubes, one on each side of the uterus. Eggs pass from the ovaries, through the fallopian tubes, to the uterus. Cancer sometimes begins at the end of the fallopian tube near the ovary and spreads to the ovary.

The peritoneum is the tissue that lines the abdominal wall and covers organs in the abdomen. Primary peritoneal cancer is cancer that forms in the peritoneum and has not spread there from another part of the body. Cancer sometimes begins in the peritoneum and spreads to the ovary.

Ovarian epithelial cancer is one type of cancer that affects the ovary.

Ovarian epithelial cancer, fallopian tube cancer, and primary peritoneal cancer are treated the same way.

Women who have a family history of ovarian cancer are at an increased risk of ovarian cancer.

Anything that increases your risk of getting a disease is called a risk factor. Having a risk factor does not mean that you will get cancer;

not having risk factors doesn't mean that you will not get cancer. Talk with your doctor if you think you may be at risk.

Women who have one first-degree relative (mother, daughter, or sister) with a history of ovarian cancer have an increased risk of ovarian cancer. This risk is higher in women who have one first-degree relative and one second-degree relative (grandmother or aunt) with a history of ovarian cancer. This risk is even higher in women who have two or more first-degree relatives with a history of ovarian cancer.

Some ovarian, fallopian tube, and primary peritoneal cancers are caused by inherited gene mutations (changes).

The genes in cells carry the hereditary information that is received from a person's parents. Hereditary ovarian cancer makes up about 5% to 10% of all cases of ovarian cancer. Three hereditary patterns have been identified: ovarian cancer alone, ovarian and breast cancers, and ovarian and colon cancers.

Fallopian tube cancer and peritoneal cancer may also be caused by certain inherited gene mutations.

There are tests that can detect mutated genes. These genetic tests are sometimes done for members of families with a high risk of cancer.

Women with an increased risk of ovarian cancer may consider surgery to lessen the risk.

Some women who have an increased risk of ovarian cancer may choose to have a risk-reducing oophorectomy (the removal of healthy ovaries so that cancer cannot grow in them). In high-risk women, this procedure has been shown to greatly decrease the risk of ovarian cancer.

Signs and symptoms of ovarian, fallopian tube, or peritoneal cancer include pain or swelling in the abdomen.

Ovarian, fallopian tube, or peritoneal cancer may not cause early signs or symptoms. When signs or symptoms do appear, the cancer is often advanced. Signs and symptoms may include the following:

- Pain, swelling, or a feeling of pressure in the abdomen or pelvis.

- Vaginal bleeding that is heavy or irregular, especially after menopause.

- Vaginal discharge that is clear, white, or colored with blood.

317

- A lump in the pelvic area.

- Gastrointestinal problems, such as gas, bloating, or constipation.

These signs and symptoms also may be caused by other conditions and not by ovarian, fallopian tube, or peritoneal cancer. If the signs or symptoms get worse or do not go away on their own, check with your doctor so that any problem can be diagnosed and treated as early as possible.

Tests that examine the ovaries and pelvic area are used to detect (find) and diagnose ovarian, fallopian tube, and peritoneal cancer.

The following tests and procedures may be used:

- **Physical exam and history:** An exam of the body to check general signs of health, including checking for signs of disease, such as lumps or anything else that seems unusual. A history of the patient's health habits and past illnesses and treatments will also be taken.

- **Pelvic exam:** An exam of the vagina, cervix, uterus, fallopian tubes, ovaries, and rectum. A speculum is inserted into the vagina and the doctor or nurse looks at the vagina and cervix for signs of disease. A Pap test of the cervix is usually done. The doctor or nurse also inserts one or two lubricated, gloved fingers of one hand into the vagina and places the other hand over the lower abdomen to feel the size, shape, and position of the uterus and ovaries. The doctor or nurse also inserts a lubricated, gloved finger into the rectum to feel for lumps or abnormal areas.

- **Ultrasound exam:** A procedure in which high-energy sound waves (ultrasound) are bounced off internal tissues or organs in the abdomen, and make echoes. The echoes form a picture of body tissues called a sonogram. The picture can be printed to be looked at later.

Some patients may have a transvaginal ultrasound.

- **CA 125 assay:** A test that measures the level of CA 125 in the blood. CA 125 is a substance released by cells into the bloodstream. An increased CA 125 level can be a sign of cancer or another condition such as endometriosis.

- **CT scan (CAT scan):** A procedure that makes a series of detailed pictures of areas inside the body, taken from different angles. The pictures are made by a computer linked to an x-ray machine. A dye may be injected into a vein or swallowed to help the organs or tissues show up more clearly. This procedure is also called computed tomography, computerized tomography, or computerized axial tomography.

- **PET scan (positron emission tomography scan):** A procedure to find malignant tumor cells in the body. A very small amount of radioactive glucose (sugar) is injected into a vein. The PET scanner rotates around the body and makes a picture of where glucose is being used in the body. Malignant tumor cells show up brighter in the picture because they are more active and take up more glucose than normal cells do.

- **MRI (magnetic resonance imaging):** A procedure that uses a magnet, radio waves, and a computer to make a series of detailed pictures of areas inside the body. This procedure is also called nuclear magnetic resonance imaging (NMRI).

- **Chest x-ray:** An x-ray of the organs and bones inside the chest. An x-ray is a type of energy beam that can go through the body and onto film, making a picture of areas inside the body.

- **Biopsy:** The removal of cells or tissues so they can be viewed under a microscope by a pathologist to check for signs of cancer. The tissue is usually removed during surgery to remove the tumor.

Certain factors affect treatment options and prognosis (chance of recovery).

The prognosis (chance of recovery) and treatment options depend on the following:

- The stage and grade of the cancer.

- The type and size of the tumor.

- Whether all of the tumor can be removed by surgery.

- Whether the patient has swelling of the abdomen.

- The patient's age and general health.

- Whether the cancer has just been diagnosed or has recurred (come back).

Section 25.2

Stages of Ovarian Epithelial, Fallopian Tube, and Primary Peritoneal Cancer

Text in this section is excerpted from "Ovarian Epithelial, Fallopian Tube, and Primary Peritoneal Cancer Treatment (PDQ®)," National Cancer Institute (NCI), July 2, 2015.

After ovarian, fallopian tube, or peritoneal cancer has been diagnosed, tests are done to find out if cancer cells have spread within the ovaries or to other parts of the body.

The process used to find out whether cancer has spread within the organ or to other parts of the body is called staging. The information gathered from the staging process determines the stage of the disease. It is important to know the stage in order to plan treatment. The results of the tests used to diagnose cancer are often also used to stage the disease.

There are three ways that cancer spreads in the body.

Cancer can spread through tissue, the lymph system, and the blood:

- Tissue. The cancer spreads from where it began by growing into nearby areas.

- Lymph system. The cancer spreads from where it began by getting into the lymph system. The cancer travels through the lymph vessels to other parts of the body.

- Blood. The cancer spreads from where it began by getting into the blood. The cancer travels through the blood vessels to other parts of the body.

Cancer may spread from where it began to other parts of the body.

When cancer spreads to another part of the body, it is called metastasis. Cancer cells break away from where they began (the primary tumor) and travel through the lymph system or blood.

- Lymph system. The cancer gets into the lymph system, travels through the lymph vessels, and forms a tumor (metastatic tumor) in another part of the body.

- Blood. The cancer gets into the blood, travels through the blood vessels, and forms a tumor (metastatic tumor) in another part of the body.

The metastatic tumor is the same type of cancer as the primary tumor. For example, if ovarian epithelial cancer spreads to the lung, the cancer cells in the lung are actually ovarian epithelial cancer cells. The disease is metastatic ovarian epithelial cancer, not lung cancer.

The following stages are used for ovarian epithelial, fallopian tube, and primary peritoneal cancer:

Stage I
In stage I, cancer is found in one or both ovaries or fallopian tubes. Stage I is divided into stage IA, stage IB, and stage IC.

- Stage IA: Cancer is found inside a single ovary or fallopian tube.

- Stage IB: Cancer is found inside both ovaries and fallopian tubes.

- Stage IC: Cancer is found inside one or both ovaries or fallopian tubes and one of the following is true:

- cancer is also found on the outside surface of one or both ovaries or fallopian tubes; or

- the capsule (outer covering) of the ovary has ruptured (broken open); or

- cancer cells are found in the fluid of the peritoneal cavity (the body cavity that contains most of the organs in the abdomen) or in washings of the peritoneum (tissue lining the peritoneal cavity).

Stage II
In stage II, cancer is found in one or both ovaries or fallopian tubes and has spread into other areas of the pelvis or primary peritoneal cancer is found within the pelvis. Stage II ovarian epithelial and fallopian tube cancers are divided into stage IIA and stage IIB.

- Stage IIA: Cancer has spread from where it first formed to the uterus and/or the fallopian tubes and/or the ovaries.

- Stage IIB: Cancer has spread from the ovary or fallopian tube to organs in the peritoneal cavity (the space that contains the abdominal organs).

Stage III

In stage III, cancer is found in one or both ovaries or fallopian tubes, or is primary peritoneal cancer, and has spread outside the pelvis to other parts of the abdomen and/or to nearby lymph nodes. Stage III is divided into stage IIIA, stage IIIB, and stage IIIC.

- In stage IIIA, one of the following is true:

- Cancer has spread to lymph nodes in the area outside or behind the peritoneum only; or

- Cancer cells that can be seen only with a microscope have spread to the surface of the peritoneum outside the pelvis. Cancer may have spread to nearby lymph nodes.

- Stage IIIB: Cancer has spread to the peritoneum outside the pelvis and the cancer in the peritoneum is 2 centimeters or smaller. Cancer may have spread to lymph nodes behind the peritoneum.

- Stage IIIC: Cancer has spread to the peritoneum outside the pelvis and the cancer in the peritoneum is larger than 2 centimeters. Cancer may have spread to lymph nodes behind the peritoneum or to the surface of the liver or spleen.

Stage IV

In stage IV, cancer has spread beyond the abdomen to other parts of the body. Stage IV is divided into stage IVA and stage IVB.

- Stage IVA: Cancer cells are found in extra fluid that builds up around the lungs.

- Stage IVB: Cancer has spread to organs and tissues outside the abdomen, including lymph nodes in the groin.

Ovarian epithelial, fallopian tube, and primary peritoneal cancers are grouped for treatment as early or advanced cancer.

Stage I ovarian epithelial and fallopian tube cancers are treated as early cancers.

Stages II, III, and IV ovarian epithelial, fallopian tube, and primary peritoneal cancers are treated as advanced cancers.

Section 25.3

Ovarian, Fallopian Tube, and Primary Peritoneal Cancer Prevention

Text in this section is excerpted from "Ovarian, Fallopian Tube, and Primary Peritoneal Cancer Prevention (PDQ®)," National Cancer Institute (NCI), April 9, 2015.

Avoiding risk factors and increasing protective factors may help prevent cancer.

Avoiding cancer risk factors may help prevent certain cancers. Risk factors include smoking, being overweight, and not getting enough exercise. Increasing protective factors such as quitting smoking, eating a healthy diet, and exercising may also help prevent some cancers. Talk to your doctor or other health care professional about how you might lower your risk of cancer.

The following are risk factors for ovarian, fallopian tube, and primary peritoneal cancer:

The following are protective factors for ovarian, fallopian tube, and primary peritoneal cancer:

Oral contraceptives
Taking oral contraceptives ("the pill") lowers the risk of ovarian cancer. The longer oral contraceptives are used, the lower the risk may be. The decrease in risk may last up to 30 years after a woman has stopped taking oral contraceptives.

Taking oral contraceptives increases the risk of blood clots. This risk is higher in women who also smoke.

Tubal ligation
The risk of ovarian cancer is decreased in women who have a tubal ligation (surgery to close both fallopian tubes).

Breastfeeding
Breastfeeding is linked to a decreased risk of ovarian cancer. The longer a woman breastfeeds, the lower her risk of ovarian cancer.

Risk-reducing salpingo-oophorectomy

Some women who have a high risk of ovarian cancer may choose to have a risk-reducing salpingo-oophorectomy (surgery to remove the fallopian tubes and ovaries when there are no signs of cancer). This includes women who have inherited certain changes in the BRCA1 and BRCA2 genes or have an inherited syndrome.

It is very important to have a cancer risk assessment and counselling before making this decision. These and other factors may be discussed:

- Infertility.

- Early menopause: The drop in estrogen levels caused by removing the ovaries can cause early menopause. Symptoms of menopause include the following:

  - Hot flashes.

  - Night sweats.

  - Trouble sleeping.

  - Mood changes.

  - Decreased sex drive.

- Heart disease.

- Vaginal dryness.

- Frequent urination.

- Osteoporosis (decreased bone density).

These symptoms may not be the same in all women. Hormone replacement therapy (HRT) may be used to lessen these symptoms.

- Risk of ovarian cancer in the peritoneum: Women who have had a risk-reducing salpingo-oophorectomy continue to have a small risk of ovarian cancer in the peritoneum (thin layer of tissue that lines the inside of the abdomen). This may occur if ovarian cancer cells had already spread to the peritoneum before the surgery or if some ovarian tissue remains after surgery.

It is not clear whether the following affect the risk of ovarian, fallopian tube, and primary peritoneal cancer:

Diet

Studies of dietary factors including various foods, teas, and nutrients have not found a strong link to ovarian cancer.

Alcohol

Studies have not shown a link between drinking alcohol and the risk of ovarian cancer.

Aspirin and non-steroidal anti-inflammatory drugs

Some studies of aspirin and non-steroidal anti-inflammatory drugs (NSAIDs) have found a decreased risk of ovarian cancer and others have not.

Smoking

Some studies found a very small increased risk of one rare type of ovarian cancer in women who were current smokers compared with women who never smoked.

Talc

Studies of women who used talcum powder (talc) dusted on the perineum (the area between the vagina and the anus) have not found clear evidence of an increased risk of ovarian cancer.

Infertility treatment

Overall, studies in women using fertility drugs have not found clear evidence of an increased risk of ovarian cancer. Risk of ovarian borderline malignant tumors may be higher in women who take fertility drugs. The risk of invasive ovarian cancer may be higher in women who do not get pregnant after taking fertility drugs.

Cancer prevention clinical trials are used to study ways to prevent cancer.

Cancer prevention clinical trials are used to study ways to lower the risk of developing certain types of cancer. Some cancer prevention trials are conducted with healthy people who have not had cancer but who have an increased risk for cancer. Other prevention trials are conducted with people who have had cancer and are trying to prevent another cancer of the same type or to lower their chance of developing a new type of cancer. Other trials are done with healthy volunteers who are not known to have any risk factors for cancer.

The purpose of some cancer prevention clinical trials is to find out whether actions people take can prevent cancer. These may include eating fruits and vegetables, exercising, quitting smoking, or taking certain medicines, vitamins, minerals, or food supplements.

Section 25.4

Ovarian, Fallopian Tube, and Primary Peritoneal Cancer Screening

Text in this section is excerpted from "Ovarian, Fallopian Tube, and Primary Peritoneal Cancer Screening (PDQ®)," National Cancer Institute (NCI), July 2, 2015.

Tests are used to screen for different types of cancer.

Some screening tests are used because they have been shown to be helpful both in finding cancers early and in decreasing the chance of dying from these cancers. Other tests are used because they have been shown to find cancer in some people; however, it has not been proven in clinical trials that use of these tests will decrease the risk of dying from cancer.

Scientists study screening tests to find those with the fewest risks and most benefits. Cancer screening trials also are meant to show whether early detection (finding cancer before it causes symptoms) decreases a person's chance of dying from the disease. For some types of cancer, finding and treating the disease at an early stage may result in a better chance of recovery.

There is no standard or routine screening test for ovarian, fallopian tube, and primary peritoneal cancer.

Screening for ovarian cancer has not been proven to decrease the death rate from the disease.

Screening for ovarian cancer is under study and there are screening clinical trials taking place in many parts of the country.

Tests that may detect (find) ovarian, fallopian tube, and primary peritoneal cancer are being studied:

Pelvic exam

A pelvic exam is an exam of the vagina, cervix, uterus, fallopian tubes, ovaries, and rectum. A speculum is inserted into the vagina and the doctor or nurse looks at the vagina and cervix for signs of disease. The doctor or nurse also inserts one or two lubricated, gloved fingers of one hand into the vagina and places the other hand over the lower abdomen to feel the size, shape, and position of the uterus and ovaries. The doctor or nurse also inserts a lubricated, gloved finger into the rectum to feel for lumps or abnormal areas.

Ovarian cancer is usually advanced when first found by a pelvic exam.

Transvaginal ultrasound

Transvaginal ultrasound (TVU) is a procedure used to examine the vagina, uterus, fallopian tubes, and bladder. An ultrasound transducer (probe) is inserted into the vagina and used to bounce high-energy sound waves (ultrasound) off internal tissues or organs and make echoes. The echoes form a picture of body tissues called a sonogram.

CA-125 assay

A CA 125 assay is a test that measures the level of CA 125 in the blood. CA 125 is a substance released by cells into the bloodstream. An increased CA-125 level is sometimes a sign of certain types of cancer, including ovarian cancer, or other conditions.

Scientists at the National Cancer Institute studied the combination of using TVU and CA-125 levels as a way to screen for and prevent deaths from ovarian cancer. The results of this study showed no decrease in deaths from ovarian cancer.

Section 25.5

Risks of Ovarian, Fallopian Tube, and Primary Peritoneal Cancer Screening

Text in this section is excerpted from "Ovarian, Fallopian Tube, and Primary Peritoneal Cancer Screening (PDQ®)," National Cancer Institute (NCI), July 2, 2015.

Screening tests have risks.

Decisions about screening tests can be difficult. Not all screening tests are helpful and most have risks. Before having any screening test, you may want to talk about the test with your doctor. It is important to know the risks of the test and whether it has been proven to reduce the risk of dying from cancer.

The risks of ovarian, fallopian tube, and primary peritoneal cancer screening tests include the following:

Finding ovarian, fallopian tube, and primary peritoneal cancer may not improve health or help a woman live longer.

Screening may not improve your health or help you live longer if you have advanced ovarian cancer or if it has already spread to other places in your body.

Some cancers never cause symptoms or become life-threatening, but if found by a screening test, the cancer may be treated. It is not known if treatment of these cancers would help you live longer than if no treatment were given, and treatments for cancer may have serious side effects.

False-negative test results can occur.

Screening test results may appear to be normal even though ovarian cancer is present. A woman who receives a false-negative test result (one that shows there is no cancer when there really is) may delay seeking medical care even if she has symptoms.

False-positive test results can occur.

Screening test results may appear to be abnormal even though no cancer is present. A false-positive test result (one that shows there is cancer when there really isn't) can cause anxiety and is usually followed by more tests (such as a laparoscopy or a laparotomy to see if cancer is present), which also have risks. Complications from tests to diagnose ovarian cancer include infection, blood loss, bowel injury, and heart and blood vessel problems. An unnecessary oophorectomy (removal of one or both ovaries) may also result.

Your doctor can advise you about your risk for ovarian cancer and your need for screening tests.

Section 25.6

Treatment Options for Ovarian Epithelial, Fallopian Tube, and Primary Peritoneal Cancer

Text in this section is excerpted from "Ovarian Epithelial, Fallopian Tube, and Primary Peritoneal Cancer Treatment (PDQ®)," National Cancer Institute (NCI), July 2, 2015.

There are different types of treatment for patients with ovarian epithelial cancer.

Different types of treatment are available for patients with ovarian epithelial cancer. Some treatments are standard, and some are being tested in clinical trials. A treatment clinical trial is a research study meant to help improve current treatments or obtain information on new treatments for patients with cancer. When clinical trials show that a new treatment is better than the treatment currently used as standard treatment, the new treatment may become the standard treatment. Patients may want to think about taking part in a clinical trial. Some clinical trials are open only to patients who have not started treatment.

Four kinds of standard treatment are used.

Surgery
Most patients have surgery to remove as much of the tumor as possible. Different types of surgery may include:

- Hysterectomy: Surgery to remove the uterus and, sometimes, the cervix. When only the uterus is removed, it is called a partial hysterectomy. When both the uterus and the cervix are removed, it is called a total hysterectomy. If the uterus and cervix are taken out through the vagina, the operation is called a vaginal hysterectomy. If the uterus and cervix are taken out through a large incision (cut) in the abdomen, the operation is called a total abdominal hysterectomy. If the uterus and cervix are taken out through a small incision (cut) in the abdomen using a laparoscope, the operation is called a total laparoscopic hysterectomy.

- Unilateral salpingo-oophorectomy: A surgical procedure to remove one ovary and one fallopian tube.

- Bilateral salpingo-oophorectomy: A surgical procedure to remove both ovaries and both fallopian tubes.

- Omentectomy: A surgical procedure to remove the omentum (tissue in the peritoneum that contains blood vessels, nerves, lymph vessels, and lymph nodes).

- Lymph node biopsy: The removal of all or part of a lymph node. A pathologist views the tissue under a microscope to look for cancer cells.

Radiation therapy

Radiation therapy is a cancer treatment that uses high-energy x-rays or other types of radiation to kill cancer cells or keep them from growing. There are two types of radiation therapy. External radiation therapy uses a machine outside the body to send radiation toward the cancer. Internal radiation therapy uses a radioactive substance sealed in needles, seeds, wires, or catheters that are placed directly into or near the cancer. The way the radiation therapy is given depends on the type and stage of the cancer being treated.

Some women receive a treatment called intraperitoneal radiation therapy, in which radioactive liquid is put directly in the abdomen through a catheter.

Chemotherapy

Chemotherapy is a cancer treatment that uses drugs to stop the growth of cancer cells, either by killing the cells or by stopping them from dividing. When chemotherapy is taken by mouth or injected into a vein or muscle, the drugs enter the bloodstream and can reach cancer cells throughout the body (systemic chemotherapy). When chemotherapy is placed directly into the cerebrospinal fluid, an organ, or a body cavity such as the abdomen, the drugs mainly affect cancer cells in those areas (regional chemotherapy).

A type of regional chemotherapy used to treat ovarian cancer is intraperitoneal (IP) chemotherapy. In IP chemotherapy, the anticancer drugs are carried directly into the peritoneal cavity (the space that contains the abdominal organs) through a thin tube.

Treatment with more than one anticancer drug is called combination chemotherapy.

The way the chemotherapy is given depends on the type and stage of the cancer being treated.

Targeted therapy

Targeted therapy is a type of treatment that uses drugs or other substances to identify and attack specific cancer cells without harming normal cells.

Monoclonal antibody therapy is a type of targeted therapy that uses antibodies made in the laboratory, from a single type of immune system cell. These antibodies can identify substances on cancer cells or normal substances that may help cancer cells grow. The antibodies attach to the substances and kill the cancer cells, block their growth, or keep them from spreading. Monoclonal antibodies are given by infusion. They may be used alone or to carry drugs, toxins, or radioactive material directly to cancer cells.

Bevacizumab is a monoclonal antibody that may be used with chemotherapy to treat ovarian epithelial cancer, fallopian tube cancer, or primary peritoneal cancer that has recurred (come back).

Other types of targeted therapy are being studied in the treatment of ovarian epithelial cancer. PARP inhibitors are targeted therapy drugs that block DNA repair and may cause cancer cells to die. PARP inhibitor therapy is being studied in treating ovarian epithelial cancer that remains after chemotherapy.

New types of treatment are being tested in clinical trials.

This section describes treatments that are being studied in clinical trials. It may not mention every new treatment being studied.

Biologic therapy

Biologic therapy is a treatment that uses the patient's immune system to fight cancer. Substances made by the body or made in a laboratory are used to boost, direct, or restore the body's natural defenses against cancer. This type of cancer treatment is also called biotherapy or immunotherapy.

331

Patients may want to think about taking part in a clinical trial.

For some patients, taking part in a clinical trial may be the best treatment choice. Clinical trials are part of the cancer research process. Clinical trials are done to find out if new cancer treatments are safe and effective or better than the standard treatment.

Many of today's standard treatments for cancer are based on earlier clinical trials. Patients who take part in a clinical trial may receive the standard treatment or be among the first to receive a new treatment.

Patients who take part in clinical trials also help improve the way cancer will be treated in the future. Even when clinical trials do not lead to effective new treatments, they often answer important questions and help move research forward.

Patients can enter clinical trials before, during, or after starting their cancer treatment.

Some clinical trials only include patients who have not yet received treatment. Other trials test treatments for patients whose cancer has not gotten better. There are also clinical trials that test new ways to stop cancer from recurring (coming back) or reduce the side effects of cancer treatment.

Clinical trials are taking place in many parts of the country.

Follow-up tests may be needed.

Some of the tests that were done to diagnose the cancer or to find out the stage of the cancer may be repeated. Some tests will be repeated in order to see how well the treatment is working. Decisions about whether to continue, change, or stop treatment may be based on the results of these tests.

Some of the tests will continue to be done from time to time after treatment has ended. The results of these tests can show if your condition has changed or if the cancer has recurred (come back). These tests are sometimes called follow-up tests or check-ups.

Section 25.7

Drugs Approved for Ovarian, Fallopian Tube, or Primary Peritoneal Cancer

Text in this section is excerpted from "Drugs Approved for Ovarian, Fallopian Tube, or Primary Peritoneal Cancer (PDQ®)," National Cancer Institute (NCI), February 23, 2015.

Drugs Approved for Ovarian, Fallopian Tube, or Primary Peritoneal Cancer

This page lists cancer drugs approved by the Food and Drug Administration (FDA) for ovarian, fallopian tube, or primary peritoneal cancer. The list includes generic and brand names. This page also lists common drug combinations used in these cancer types. The individual drugs in the combinations are FDA-approved. However, drug combinations themselves usually are not approved, but are widely used.

The drug names link to NCI's Cancer Drug Information summaries. There may be drugs used in ovarian, fallopian tube, or primary peritoneal cancer that are not listed here.

Avastin (Bevacizumab)

- **Bevacizumab** is approved to be used alone or with other drugs to treat:

- **Cervical cancer** that has not gotten better with other treatment, has metastasized (spread to other parts of the body), or has recurred (come back).

- **Colorectal cancer** that has metastasized.

- **Glioblastoma** (a type of brain cancer) in patients whose disease has not gotten better with other treatment.

- **Non-small cell lung cancer** that is locally advanced, cannot be removed by surgery, has metastasized, or has recurred.

- **Ovarian epithelial, fallopian tube, or primary peritoneal cancer** that has recurred. It is used in patients whose disease does not respond to platinum chemotherapy.

- **Renal cell cancer** that has metastasized.

Bevacizumab

- **Bevacizumab** is approved to be used alone or with other drugs to treat:

- **Cervical cancer** that has not gotten better with other treatment, has metastasized (spread to other parts of the body), or has recurred (come back).

- **Colorectal cancer** that has metastasized.

- **Glioblastoma** (a type of brain cancer) in patients whose disease has not gotten better with other treatment.

- **Non-small cell lung cancer** that is locally advanced, cannot be removed by surgery, has metastasized, or has recurred.

- **Ovarian epithelial, fallopian tube, or primary peritoneal cancer** that has recurred. It is used in patients whose disease does not respond to platinum chemotherapy.

- **Renal cell cancer** that has metastasized.

Bevacizumab is also being studied in the treatment of other types of cancer.

Carboplatin

Carboplatin is approved to be used alone or with other drugs to treat:

- **Non-small cell lung cancer** that is locally advanced, cannot be treated with surgery, has metastasized (spread to other parts of the body), or has recurred (come back).

- **Ovarian cancer** that has recurred after treatment with other chemotherapy or is advanced and has never been treated. Carboplatin is also used for palliative treatment of ovarian cancer that has recurred after earlier chemotherapy.

Carboplatin is also being studied in the treatment of other types of cancer.

Clafen (Cyclophosphamide)

Cyclophosphamide is approved to be used alone or with other drugs to treat:

- **Acute lymphoblastic leukemia** (ALL) in children.
- **Acute myeloid leukemia** (AML).
- **Breast cancer.**
- **Chronic lymphocytic leukemia** (CLL).
- **Chronic myelogenous leukemia** (CML).
- **Hodgkin lymphoma.**
- **Multiple myeloma.**
- **Mycosis fungoides.**
- **Neuroblastoma.**
- **Non-Hodgkin lymphoma** (NHL).
- **Ovarian cancer.**
- **Retinoblastoma.**

Cyclophosphamide is also being studied in the treatment of other types of cancer.

Cisplatin

Cisplatin is approved to be used alone or with other drugs to treat:

- **Bladder cancer** that cannot be treated with surgery or radiation therapy.
- **Cervical cancer** that is advanced and cannot be treated with surgery or radiation therapy.
- **Malignant mesothelioma** that cannot be treated with surgery.
- **Non-small cell lung cancer** that is locally advanced, advanced, or has metastasized (has spread to other parts of the body) and cannot be treated with surgery.
- **Ovarian cancer** that is advanced or has metastasized in patients whose disease has not gotten better with other types of treatment or chemotherapy.
- **Squamous cell carcinoma of the head and neck** that is locally advanced and cannot be treated with surgery.

- **Testicular cancer** in patients who have already had surgery or radiation therapy.

Cisplatin is also being studied in the treatment of other types of cancer.

Cyclophosphamide

Cyclophosphamide is approved to be used alone or with other drugs to treat:

- **Acute lymphoblastic leukemia** (ALL) in children.
- **Acute myeloid leukemia** (AML).
- **Breast cancer.**
- **Chronic lymphocytic leukemia** (CLL).
- **Chronic myelogenous leukemia** (CML).
- **Hodgkin lymphoma.**
- **Multiple myeloma.**
- **Mycosis fungoides.**
- **Neuroblastoma.**
- **Non-Hodgkin lymphoma** (NHL).
- **Ovarian cancer.**
- **Retinoblastoma.**

Cyclophosphamide is also being studied in the treatment of other types of cancer.

Cytoxan (Cyclophosphamide)

Cyclophosphamide is approved to be used alone or with other drugs to treat:

- **Acute lymphoblastic leukemia** (ALL) in children.
- **Acute myeloid leukemia** (AML).
- **Breast cancer.**
- **Chronic lymphocytic leukemia** (CLL).
- **Chronic myelogenous leukemia** (CML).

- **Hodgkin lymphoma.**
- **Multiple myeloma.**
- **Mycosis fungoides.**
- **Neuroblastoma.**
- **Non-Hodgkin lymphoma** (NHL).
- **Ovarian cancer.**
- **Retinoblastoma.**

Cyclophosphamide is also being studied in the treatment of other types of cancer.

Doxorubicin Hydrochloride

Doxorubicin hydrochloride is approved to be used alone or with other drugs to treat:

- **Acute lymphoblastic leukemia** (ALL).
- **Acute myeloid leukemia** (AML).
- **Breast cancer.** It is also used as adjuvant therapy for breast cancer that has spread to the lymph nodes after surgery.
- **Gastric (stomach) cancer.**
- **Hodgkin lymphoma.**
- **Neuroblastoma.**
- **Non-Hodgkin lymphoma.**
- **Ovarian cancer.**
- **Small cell lung cancer.**
- **Soft tissue and bone sarcomas.**
- **Thyroid cancer.**
- **Transitional cell bladder cancer.**
- **Wilms tumor.**

Doxorubicin hydrochloride is also being studied in the treatment of other types of cancer.

Dox-SL (Doxorubicin Hydrochloride Liposome)

Doxorubicin hydrochloride liposome is approved to be used alone or with other drugs to treat:

- **AIDS-related Kaposi sarcoma** that has gotten worse after treatment with other chemotherapy, or in patients who are not able to use other drugs.

- **Multiple myeloma.** It is used with bortezomib in patients who have already been treated with other chemotherapy.

- **Ovarian cancer** that has gotten worse or recurred (come back) after treatment with other chemotherapy.

Doxorubicin hydrochloride liposome is also being studied in the treatment of other types of cancer.

DOXIL (Doxorubicin Hydrochloride Liposome)

Doxorubicin hydrochloride liposome is approved to be used alone or with other drugs to treat:

- **AIDS-related Kaposi sarcoma** that has gotten worse after treatment with other chemotherapy, or in patients who are not able to use other drugs.

- **Multiple myeloma.** It is used with bortezomib in patients who have already been treated with other chemotherapy.

- **Ovarian cancer** that has gotten worse or recurred (come back) after treatment with other chemotherapy.

Doxorubicin hydrochloride liposome is also being studied in the treatment of other types of cancer.

Doxorubicin Hydrochloride Liposome

Doxorubicin hydrochloride liposome is approved to be used alone or with other drugs to treat:

- **AIDS-related Kaposi sarcoma** that has gotten worse after treatment with other chemotherapy, or in patients who are not able to use other drugs.

- **Multiple myeloma.** It is used with bortezomib in patients who have already been treated with other chemotherapy.

- **Ovarian cancer** that has gotten worse or recurred (come back) after treatment with other chemotherapy.

Doxorubicin hydrochloride liposome is also being studied in the treatment of other types of cancer.

Evacet (Doxorubicin Hydrochloride Liposome)

Doxorubicin hydrochloride liposome is approved to be used alone or with other drugs to treat:

- **AIDS-related Kaposi sarcoma** that has gotten worse after treatment with other chemotherapy, or in patients who are not able to use other drugs.
- **Multiple myeloma.** It is used with bortezomib in patients who have already been treated with other chemotherapy.
- **Ovarian cancer** that has gotten worse or recurred (come back) after treatment with other chemotherapy.

Doxorubicin hydrochloride liposome is also being studied in the treatment of other types of cancer.

Gemcitabine Hydrochloride

Gemcitabine hydrochloride is approved to be used alone or with other drugs to treat:

- Breast cancer that has metastasized (spread to other parts of the body) and has not gotten better with other chemotherapy. It is used with paclitaxel.
- Non-small cell lung cancer that is advanced or has metastasized. It is used in patients whose disease cannot be removed by surgery. It is used with cisplatin.
- Ovarian cancer that is advanced and has not gotten better with other chemotherapy. It is used with carboplatin.
- Pancreatic cancer that is advanced or has metastatsized. It is used in patients whose disease cannot be removed by surgery and who have already been treated with other chemotherapy. It is used with paclitaxel albumin-stabilized nanoparticle formulation.

339

Gemcitabine hydrochloride is also being studied in the treatment of other types of cancer.

Gemcitabine Hydrochloride

Gemcitabine hydrochloride is approved to be used alone or with other drugs to treat:

- Breast cancer that has metastasized (spread to other parts of the body) and has not gotten better with other chemotherapy. It is used with paclitaxel.

- Non-small cell lung cancer that is advanced or has metastasized. It is used in patients whose disease cannot be removed by surgery. It is used with cisplatin.

- Ovarian cancer that is advanced and has not gotten better with other chemotherapy. It is used with carboplatin.

- Pancreatic cancer that is advanced or has metastatsized. It is used in patients whose disease cannot be removed by surgery and who have already been treated with other chemotherapy. It is used with paclitaxel albumin-stabilized nanoparticle formulation.

Gemcitabine hydrochloride is also being studied in the treatment of other types of cancer.

Topotecan Hydrochloride

Topotecan hydrochloride is approved to be used alone or with other drugs to treat:

- Cervical cancer that has not gotten better with other treatment or has recurred (come back). It is used with another drug, called cisplatin.

- Ovarian cancer in patients whose disease has not gotten better with other chemotherapy.

- Small cell lung cancer in patients whose disease has not gotten better with other chemotherapy.

Topotecan hydrochloride is also being studied in the treatment of other types of cancer.

Doxorubicin Hydrochloride Liposome

Doxorubicin hydrochloride liposome is approved to be used alone or with other drugs to treat:

- AIDS-related Kaposi sarcoma that has gotten worse after treatment with other chemotherapy, or in patients who are not able to use other drugs.

- Multiple myeloma. It is used with bortezomib in patients who have already been treated with other chemotherapy.

- Ovarian cancer that has gotten worse or recurred (come back) after treatment with other chemotherapy.

Doxorubicin hydrochloride liposome is also being studied in the treatment of other types of cancer.

Doxorubicin hydrochloride liposome is a form of doxorubicin hydrochloride contained inside liposomes (very tiny particles of fat). This form may work better than other forms of doxorubicin hydrochloride and have fewer side effects. Also, because its effects last longer in the body, it doesn't need to be given as often. For more information about doxorubicin hydrochloride that may apply to doxorubicin hydrochloride liposome.

Cyclophosphamide

Cyclophosphamide is approved to be used alone or with other drugs to treat:

- Acute lymphoblastic leukemia (ALL) in children.

- Acute myeloid leukemia (AML).

- Breast cancer.

- Chronic lymphocytic leukemia (CLL).

- Chronic myelogenous leukemia (CML).

- Hodgkin lymphoma.

- Multiple myeloma.

- Mycosis fungoides.

- Neuroblastoma.

- Non-Hodgkin lymphoma (NHL).

- Ovarian cancer.

- Retinoblastoma.

Cyclophosphamide is also being studied in the treatment of other types of cancer.

Olaparib

Olaparib is approved to treat:

- Ovarian cancer that is advanced. It is used in patients who have certain mutations in the BRCA1 and BRCA2 genes and have already been treated with at least three other types of chemotherapy.

Olaparib is also being studied in the treatment of other types of cancer.

Paclitaxel

Paclitaxel is approved to be used alone or with other drugs to treat:

- AIDS-related Kaposi sarcoma.

- Breast cancer.

- Non-small cell lung cancer.

- Ovarian cancer.

Paclitaxel is also being studied in the treatment of other types of cancer.

Paclitaxel is also available in a different form called paclitaxel albumin-stabilized nanoparticle formulation.

Carboplatin

Carboplatin is approved to be used alone or with other drugs to treat:

- Non-small cell lung cancer that is locally advanced, cannot be treated with surgery, has metastasized (spread to other parts of the body), or has recurred (come back).

- Ovarian cancer that has recurred after treatment with other chemotherapy or is advanced and has never been treated. Carboplatin is also used for palliative treatment of ovarian cancer that has recurred after earlier chemotherapy.

Carboplatin is also being studied in the treatment of other types of cancer.

Carboplatin

Carboplatin is approved to be used alone or with other drugs to treat:

- Non-small cell lung cancer that is locally advanced, cannot be treated with surgery, has metastasized (spread to other parts of the body), or has recurred (come back).

- Ovarian cancer that has recurred after treatment with other chemotherapy or is advanced and has never been treated. Carboplatin is also used for palliative treatment of ovarian cancer that has recurred after earlier chemotherapy.

Carboplatin is also being studied in the treatment of other types of cancer.

Cisplatin

Cisplatin is approved to be used alone or with other drugs to treat:

- Bladder cancer that cannot be treated with surgery or radiation therapy.

- Cervical cancer that is advanced and cannot be treated with surgery or radiation therapy.

- Malignant mesothelioma that cannot be treated with surgery.

- Non-small cell lung cancer that is locally advanced, advanced, or has metastasized (has spread to other parts of the body) and cannot be treated with surgery.

- Ovarian cancer that is advanced or has metastasized in patients whose disease has not gotten better with other types of treatment or chemotherapy.

- Squamous cell carcinoma of the head and neck that is locally advanced and cannot be treated with surgery.

- Testicular cancer in patients who have already had surgery or radiation therapy.

Cisplatin is also being studied in the treatment of other types of cancer.

Paclitaxel

Paclitaxel is approved to be used alone or with other drugs to treat:

- AIDS-related Kaposi sarcoma.

- Breast cancer.

- Non-small cell lung cancer.

- Ovarian cancer.

Paclitaxel is also being studied in the treatment of other types of cancer.

Paclitaxel is also available in a different form called paclitaxel albumin-stabilized nanoparticle formulation.

Thiotepa

Thiotepa is approved to treat:

- Bladder cancer.

- Breast cancer.

- Malignant pleural effusion, malignant pericardial effusion, and malignant peritoneal effusion.

- Ovarian cancer.

Thiotepa is also being studied in the treatment of other types of cancer and as part of a regimen to prepare patients for bone marrow and stem cell transplants.

Topotecan Hydrochloride

Topotecan hydrochloride is approved to be used alone or with other drugs to treat:

- Cervical cancer that has not gotten better with other treatment or has recurred (come back). It is used with another drug, called cisplatin.

- Ovarian cancer in patients whose disease has not gotten better with other chemotherapy.

- Small cell lung cancer in patients whose disease has not gotten better with other chemotherapy.

Topotecan hydrochloride is also being studied in the treatment of other types of cancer.

Drug Combinations Used in Ovarian, Fallopian Tube, or Primary Peritoneal Cancer

BEP

BEP is used to treat:

- Ovarian germ cell tumors that are malignant.

- Testicular germ cell tumors that are malignant.

This combination may also be used with other drugs or treatments or to treat other types of cancer.

CARBOPLATIN-TAXOL

Drugs in the CARBOPLATIN-TAXOL combination:
Chemotherapy is often given as a combination of drugs. Combinations usually work better than single drugs because different drugs kill cancer cells in different ways.

Each of the drugs in this combination is approved by the Food and Drug Administration (FDA) to treat cancer or conditions related to cancer.

CARBOPLATIN-TAXOL is used to treat:

- Non-small cell lung cancer that has spread.

- Ovarian cancer.

This combination may also be used with other drugs or treatments or to treat other types of cancer.

GEMCITABINE-CISPLATIN

The drugs in the combination called GEMCITABINE-CISPLATIN are listed, and links to individual drug summaries are included.

Drugs in the GEMCITABINE-CISPLATIN combination:

- Gemcitabine Hydrochloride
- Cisplatin

Chemotherapy is often given as a combination of drugs. Combinations usually work better than single drugs because different drugs kill cancer cells in different ways.

Each of the drugs in this combination is approved by the Food and Drug Administration (FDA) to treat cancer or conditions related to cancer.

GEMCITABINE-CISPLATIN is used to treat:

- Biliary tract cancer.
- Bladder cancer.
- Cervical cancer.
- Malignant mesothelioma.
- Non-small cell lung cancer (NSCLC).
- Ovarian cancer.
- Pancreatic cancer.

This combination may also be used with other drugs or treatments or to treat other types of cancer.

VeIP

Drugs in the VeIP combination:

- Ve = Vinblastine Sulfate (Velban)
- I = Ifosfamide
- P = Cisplatin (Platinol)

Chemotherapy is often given as a combination of drugs. Combinations usually work better than single drugs because different drugs kill cancer cells in different ways.

Each of the drugs in this combination is approved by the Food and Drug Administration (FDA) to treat cancer or conditions related to cancer.

VeIP is used to treat advanced disease in:

- Ovarian germ cell cancer.
- Testicular cancer.

This combination may also be used with other drugs or treatments or to treat other types of cancer.

Chapter 26

Ovarian Germ Cell Tumors

Chapter Contents

Section 26.1

General Information about Ovarian Germ Cell Tumors

Text in this section is excerpted from "Ovarian Germ Cell Tumors Treatment (PDQ®)," National Cancer Institute (NCI), May 29, 2015.

Ovarian germ cell tumor is a disease in which malignant (cancer) cells form in the germ (egg) cells of the ovary.

Germ cell tumors begin in the reproductive cells (egg or sperm) of the body. Ovarian germ cell tumors usually occur in teenage girls or young women and most often affect just one ovary.

The ovaries are a pair of organs in the female reproductive system. They are in the pelvis, one on each side of the uterus (the hollow, pear-shaped organ where a fetus grows). Each ovary is about the size and shape of an almond. The ovaries make eggs and female hormones.

Ovarian germ cell tumor is a general name that is used to describe several different types of cancer. The most common ovarian germ cell tumor is called dysgerminoma.

Signs of ovarian germ cell tumor are swelling of the abdomen or vaginal bleeding after menopause.

Ovarian germ cell tumors can be hard to diagnose (find) early. Often there are no symptoms in the early stages, but tumors may be found during regular gynecologic exams (checkups). Check with your doctor if you have either of the following:

- Swollen abdomen without weight gain in other parts of the body.

- Bleeding from the vagina after menopause (when you are no longer having menstrual periods).

Tests that examine the ovaries, pelvic area, blood, and ovarian tissue are used to detect (find) and diagnose ovarian germ cell tumor.

The following tests and procedures may be used:

- **Physical exam and history:** An exam of the body to check general signs of health, including checking for signs of disease, such as lumps or anything else that seems unusual. A history of the patient's health habits and past illnesses and treatments will also be taken.

- **Pelvic exam:** An exam of the vagina, cervix, uterus, fallopian tubes, ovaries, and rectum. A speculum is inserted into the vagina and the doctor or nurse looks at the vagina and cervix for signs of disease. A Pap test of the cervix is usually done. The doctor or nurse also inserts one or two lubricated, gloved fingers of one hand into the vagina and places the other hand over the lower abdomen to feel the size, shape, and position of the uterus and ovaries. The doctor or nurse also inserts a lubricated, gloved finger into the rectum to feel for lumps or abnormal areas.

- **Laparotomy:** A surgical procedure in which an incision (cut) is made in the wall of the abdomen to check the inside of the abdomen for signs of disease. The size of the incision depends on the reason the laparotomy is being done. Sometimes organs are removed or tissue samples are taken and checked under a microscope for signs of disease.

- **CT scan (CAT scan):** A procedure that makes a series of detailed pictures of areas inside the body, taken from different angles. The pictures are made by a computer linked to an x-ray machine. A dye may be injected into a vein or swallowed to help the organs or tissues show up more clearly. This procedure is also called computed tomography, computerized tomography, or computerized axial tomography.

- **Serum tumor marker test:** A procedure in which a sample of blood is checked to measure the amounts of certain substances released into the blood by organs, tissues, or tumor cells in the body. Certain substances are linked to specific types of cancer when found in increased levels in the blood. These are called tumor markers. An increased level of alpha fetoprotein (AFP) or human chorionic gonadotropin (HCG) in the blood may be a sign of ovarian germ cell tumor.

Certain factors affect prognosis (chance of recovery and treatment options).

The prognosis (chance of recovery) and treatment options depend on the following:

- The type of cancer.
- The size of the tumor.
- The stage of cancer (whether it affects part of the ovary, involves the whole ovary, or has spread to other places in the body).
- The way the cancer cells look under a microscope.
- The patient's general health.

Ovarian germ cell tumors are usually cured if found and treated early.

Section 26.2

Stages of Ovarian Germ Cell Tumors

Text in this section is excerpted from "Ovarian Germ Cell Tumors Treatment (PDQ®)," National Cancer Institute (NCI), May 29, 2015.

After ovarian germ cell tumor has been diagnosed, tests are done to find out if cancer cells have spread within the ovary or to other parts of the body.

The process used to find out whether cancer has spread within the ovary or to other parts of the body is called staging. The information gathered from the staging process determines the stage of the disease. Unless a doctor is sure the cancer has spread from the ovaries to other parts of the body, an operation called a laparotomy is done to see if the cancer has spread. The doctor must cut into the abdomen and carefully look at all the organs to see if they have cancer in them. The doctor will cut out small pieces of tissue so they can be checked under a microscope for signs of cancer. The doctor may also wash the abdominal cavity with fluid, which is also checked under a microscope to see if it has cancer cells in it. Usually the doctor will remove the cancer and other organs that have cancer in them during the laparotomy. It is important to know the stage in order to plan treatment.

Many of the tests used to diagnose ovarian germ cell tumor are also used for staging. The following tests and procedures may also be used for staging:

- **PET scan (positron emission tomography scan):** A procedure to find malignant tumor cells in the body. A small amount of radioactive glucose (sugar) is injected into a vein. The PET scanner rotates around the body and makes a picture of where glucose is being used in the body. Malignant tumor cells show up brighter in the picture because they are more active and take up more glucose than normal cells do.

- **MRI (magnetic resonance imaging):** A procedure that uses a magnet, radio waves, and a computer to make a series of detailed pictures of areas inside the body. This procedure is also called nuclear magnetic resonance imaging (NMRI).

- **Transvaginal ultrasound exam:** A procedure used to examine the vagina, uterus, fallopian tubes, and bladder. An ultrasound transducer (probe) is inserted into the vagina and used to bounce high-energy sound waves (ultrasound) off internal tissues or organs and make echoes. The echoes form a picture of body tissues called a sonogram. The doctor can identify tumors by looking at the sonogram.

There are three ways that cancer spreads in the body.

Cancer can spread through tissue, the lymph system, and the blood:

- Tissue. The cancer spreads from where it began by growing into nearby areas.

- Lymph system. The cancer spreads from where it began by getting into the lymph system. The cancer travels through the lymph vessels to other parts of the body.

- Blood. The cancer spreads from where it began by getting into the blood. The cancer travels through the blood vessels to other parts of the body.

Cancer may spread from where it began to other parts of the body.

When cancer spreads to another part of the body, it is called metastasis. Cancer cells break away from where they began (the primary tumor) and travel through the lymph system or blood.

- Lymph system. The cancer gets into the lymph system, travels through the lymph vessels, and forms a tumor (metastatic tumor) in another part of the body.

- Blood. The cancer gets into the blood, travels through the blood vessels, and forms a tumor (metastatic tumor) in another part of the body.

The metastatic tumor is the same type of tumor as the primary tumor. For example, if an ovarian germ cell tumor spreads to the liver, the tumor cells in the liver are actually cancerous ovarian germ cells. The disease is metastatic ovarian germ cell tumor, not liver cancer.

The following stages are used for ovarian germ cell tumors:

Stage I

In stage I, cancer is found in one or both ovaries. Stage I is divided into stage IA, stage IB, and stage IC.

- Stage IA: Cancer is found inside a single ovary.

- Stage IB: Cancer is found inside both ovaries.

- Stage IC: Cancer is found inside one or both ovaries and one of the following is true:

- cancer is also found on the outside surface of one or both ovaries; or

- the capsule (outer covering) of the ovary has ruptured (broken open); or

- cancer cells are found in the fluid of the peritoneal cavity (the body cavity that contains most of the organs in the abdomen) or in washings of the peritoneum (tissue lining the peritoneal cavity).

Stage II

In stage II, cancer is found in one or both ovaries and has spread into other areas of the pelvis. Stage II is divided into stage IIA, stage IIB, and stage IIC.

- Stage IIA: Cancer has spread to the uterus and/or fallopian tubes (the long slender tubes through which eggs pass from the ovaries to the uterus).

- Stage IIB: Cancer has spread to other tissue within the pelvis.

- Stage IIC: Cancer is found inside one or both ovaries and has spread to the uterus and/or fallopian tubes, or to other tissue within the pelvis. Also, one of the following is true:

- cancer is found on the outside surface of one or both ovaries; or

- the capsule (outer covering) of the ovary has ruptured (broken open); or

- cancer cells are found in the fluid of the peritoneal cavity (the body cavity that contains most of the organs in the abdomen) or in washings of the peritoneum (tissue lining the peritoneal cavity).

Stage III

In stage III, cancer is found in one or both ovaries and has spread outside the pelvis to other parts of the abdomen and/or nearby lymph nodes. Stage III is divided into stage IIIA, stage IIIB, and stage IIIC.

- Stage IIIA: The tumor is found in the pelvis only, but cancer cells that can be seen only with a microscope have spread to the surface of the peritoneum (tissue that lines the abdominal wall and covers most of the organs in the abdomen), the small intestines, or the tissue that connects the small intestines to the wall of the abdomen.

- Stage IIIB: Cancer has spread to the peritoneum and the cancer in the peritoneum is 2 centimeters or smaller.

- Stage IIIC: Cancer has spread to the peritoneum and the cancer in the peritoneum is larger than 2 centimeters and/or cancer has spread to lymph nodes in the abdomen.

Cancer that has spread to the surface of the liver is also considered stage III ovarian cancer.

Stage IV

In stage IV, cancer has spread beyond the abdomen to other parts of the body, such as the lungs or tissue inside the liver.

Cancer cells in the fluid around the lungs is also considered stage IV ovarian cancer.

Section 26.3

Treatment Options for Ovarian Germ Cell Tumors

Text in this section is excerpted from "Ovarian Germ Cell Tumors Treatment (PDQ®)," National Cancer Institute (NCI), May 29, 2015.

There are different types of treatment for patients with ovarian germ cell tumors.

Different types of treatment are available for patients with ovarian germ cell tumor. Some treatments are standard (the currently used treatment), and some are being tested in clinical trials. A treatment clinical trial is a research study meant to help improve current treatments or obtain information on new treatments for patients with cancer. When clinical trials show that a new treatment is better than the standard treatment, the new treatment may become the standard treatment. Patients may want to think about taking part in a clinical trial. Some clinical trials are open only to patients who have not started treatment.

Four types of standard treatment are used:

Surgery

Surgery is the most common treatment of ovarian germ cell tumor. A doctor may take out the cancer using one of the following types of surgery.

- Unilateral salpingo-oophorectomy: A surgical procedure to remove one ovary and one fallopian tube.

- Total hysterectomy: A surgical procedure to remove the uterus, including the cervix. If the uterus and cervix are taken out through the vagina, the operation is called a vaginal hysterectomy. If the uterus and cervix are taken out through a large incision (cut) in the abdomen, the operation is called a total abdominal hysterectomy. If the uterus and cervix are taken out through a small incision (cut) in the abdomen using a laparoscope, the operation is called a total laparoscopic hysterectomy.

- Bilateral salpingo-oophorectomy: A surgical procedure to remove both ovaries and both fallopian tubes.

- Tumor debulking: A surgical procedure in which as much of the tumor as possible is removed. Some tumors cannot be completely removed.

Even if the doctor removes all the cancer that can be seen at the time of the operation, some patients may be offered chemotherapy or radiation therapy after surgery to kill any cancer cells that are left. Treatment given after the surgery, to lower the risk that the cancer will come back, is called adjuvant therapy.

After chemotherapy for an ovarian germ cell tumor, a second-look laparotomy may be done. This is similar to the laparotomy that is done to find out the stage of the cancer. Second-look laparotomy is a surgical procedure to find out if tumor cells are left after primary treatment. During this procedure, the doctor will take samples of lymph nodes and other tissues in the abdomen to see if any cancer is left. This procedure is not done for dysgerminomas.

Observation
Observation is closely watching a patient's condition without giving any treatment unless signs or symptoms appear or change.

Chemotherapy
Chemotherapy is a cancer treatment that uses drugs to stop the growth of cancer cells, either by killing the cells or by stopping them from dividing. When chemotherapy is taken by mouth or injected into a vein or muscle, the drugs enter the bloodstream and can reach cancer cells throughout the body (systemic chemotherapy). When chemotherapy is placed directly into the cerebrospinal fluid, an organ, or a body cavity such as the abdomen, the drugs mainly affect cancer cells in those areas (regional chemotherapy). The way the chemotherapy is given depends on the type and stage of the cancer being treated.

Radiation therapy
Radiation therapy is a cancer treatment that uses high-energy x-rays or other types of radiation to kill cancer cells. There are two types of radiation therapy. External radiation therapy uses a machine outside the body to send radiation toward the cancer. Internal radiation therapy uses a radioactive substance sealed in needles, seeds, wires, or catheters that are placed directly into or near the cancer. The way the radiation therapy is given depends on the type and stage of the cancer being treated.

New types of treatment are being tested in clinical trials.

High-dose chemotherapy with bone marrow transplant

High-dose chemotherapy with bone marrow transplant is a method of giving very high doses of chemotherapy and replacing blood -forming cells destroyed by the cancer treatment. Stem cells (immature blood cells) are removed from the bone marrow of the patient or a donor and are frozen and stored. After the chemotherapy is completed, the stored stem cells are thawed and given back to the patient through an infusion. These reinfused stem cells grow into (and restore) the body's blood cells.

New treatment options

Combination chemotherapy (the use of more than one anticancer drug) is being tested in clinical trials.

Patients may want to think about taking part in a clinical trial.

For some patients, taking part in a clinical trial may be the best treatment choice. Clinical trials are part of the cancer research process. Clinical trials are done to find out if new cancer treatments are safe and effective or better than the standard treatment.

Many of today's standard treatments for cancer are based on earlier clinical trials. Patients who take part in a clinical trial may receive the standard treatment or be among the first to receive a new treatment.

Patients who take part in clinical trials also help improve the way cancer will be treated in the future. Even when clinical trials do not lead to effective new treatments, they often answer important questions and help move research forward.

Patients can enter clinical trials before, during, or after starting their cancer treatment.

Some clinical trials only include patients who have not yet received treatment. Other trials test treatments for patients whose cancer has not gotten better. There are also clinical trials that test new ways to stop cancer from recurring (coming back) or reduce the side effects of cancer treatment.

Clinical trials are taking place in many parts of the country.

Follow-up tests may be needed.

Some of the tests that were done to diagnose the cancer or to find out the stage of the cancer may be repeated. Some tests will be repeated in order to see how well the treatment is working. Decisions about whether to continue, change, or stop treatment may be based on the results of these tests.

Some of the tests will continue to be done from time to time after treatment has ended. The results of these tests can show if your condition has changed or if the cancer has recurred (come back). These tests are sometimes called follow-up tests or check-ups.

Chapter 27

Ovarian Low Malignant Potential Tumors

Chapter Contents

Section 27.1

General Information about Ovarian Low Malignant Potential Tumors

Text in this section is excerpted from "Ovarian Low Malignant Potential Tumors Treatment (PDQ®)," National Cancer Institute (NCI), July 2, 2015.

Ovarian low malignant potential tumor is a disease in which abnormal cells form in the tissue covering the ovary.

Ovarian low malignant potential tumors have abnormal cells that may become cancer, but usually do not. This disease usually remains in the ovary. When disease is found in one ovary, the other ovary should also be checked carefully for signs of disease.

The ovaries are a pair of organs in the female reproductive system. They are in the pelvis, one on each side of the uterus (the hollow, pear-shaped organ where a fetus grows). Each ovary is about the size and shape of an almond. The ovaries make eggs and female hormones.

Signs and symptoms of ovarian low malignant potential tumor include pain or swelling in the abdomen.

Ovarian low malignant potential tumor may not cause early signs or symptoms. If you do have signs or symptoms, they may include the following:

- Pain or swelling in the abdomen.

- Pain in the pelvis.

- Gastrointestinal problems, such as gas, bloating, or constipation.

These signs and symptoms may be caused by other conditions. If they get worse or do not go away on their own, check with your doctor.

Tests that examine the ovaries are used to detect (find), diagnose, and stage ovarian low malignant potential tumor.

The following tests and procedures may be used:

- **Physical exam and history:** An exam of the body to check general signs of health, including checking for signs of disease, such as lumps or anything else that seems unusual. A history of the patient's health habits and past illnesses and treatments will also be taken.

- **Pelvic exam:** An exam of the vagina, cervix, uterus, fallopian tubes, ovaries, and rectum. A speculum is inserted into the vagina and the doctor or nurse looks at the vagina and cervix for signs of disease. A Pap test of the cervix is usually done. The doctor or nurse also inserts one or two lubricated, gloved fingers of one hand into the vagina and places the other hand over the lower abdomen to feel the size, shape, and position of the uterus and ovaries. The doctor or nurse also inserts a lubricated, gloved finger into the rectum to feel for lumps or abnormal areas.

- **Ultrasound exam:** A procedure in which high-energy sound waves (ultrasound) are bounced off internal tissues or organs and make echoes. The echoes form a picture of body tissues called a sonogram. The picture can be printed to be looked at later.Other patients may have a transvaginal ultrasound.

- **CT scan (CAT scan):** A procedure that makes a series of detailed pictures of areas inside the body, taken from different angles. The pictures are made by a computer linked to an x-ray machine. A dye may be injected into a vein or swallowed to help the organs or tissues show up more clearly. This procedure is also called computed tomography, computerized tomography, or computerized axial tomography.

- **CA 125 assay:** A test that measures the level of CA 125 in the blood. CA 125 is a substance released by cells into the bloodstream. An increased CA 125 level is sometimes a sign of cancer or other condition.

- **Chest x-ray:** An x-ray of the organs and bones inside the chest. An x-ray is a type of energy beam that can go through the body and onto film, making a picture of areas inside the body.

- **Biopsy:** The removal of cells or tissues so they can be viewed under a microscope by a pathologist to check for signs of cancer. The tissue is usually removed during surgery to remove the tumor.

Certain factors affect prognosis (chance of recovery) and treatment options.

The prognosis (chance of recovery) and treatment options depend on the following:

- The stage of the disease (whether it affects part of the ovary, involves the whole ovary, or has spread to other places in the body).

- What type of cells make up the tumor.

- The size of the tumor.

- The patient's general health.

Patients with ovarian low malignant potential tumors have a good prognosis, especially when the tumor is found early.

Section 27.2

Stages of Ovarian Low Malignant Potential Tumors

Text in this section is excerpted from "Ovarian Low Malignant Potential Tumors Treatment (PDQ®)," National Cancer Institute (NCI), July 2, 2015.

After ovarian low malignant potential tumor has been diagnosed, tests are done to find out if abnormal cells have spread within the ovary or to other parts of the body.

The process used to find out whether abnormal cells have spread within the ovary or to other parts of the body is called staging. The information gathered from the staging process determines the stage of the disease. It is important to know the stage in order to plan treatment. Certain tests or procedures are used for staging. Staging laparotomy (a surgical incision made in the wall of the abdomen to remove ovarian tissue) may be used. Most patients are diagnosed with stage I disease.

The following stages are used for ovarian low malignant potential tumor:

Stage I

In stage I, the tumor is found in one or both ovaries. Stage I is divided into stage IA, stage IB, and stage IC.

- Stage IA: The tumor is found inside a single ovary.

- Stage IB: The tumor is found inside both ovaries.

- Stage IC: The tumor is found inside one or both ovaries and one of the following is true:

- tumor cells are found on the outside surface of one or both ovaries; or

- the capsule (outer covering) of the ovary has ruptured (broken open); or

- tumor cells are found in the fluid of the peritoneal cavity (the body cavity that contains most of the organs in the abdomen) or in washings of the peritoneum (tissue lining the peritoneal cavity).

Stage II

In stage II, the tumor is found in one or both ovaries and has spread into other areas of the pelvis. Stage II is divided into stage IIA, stage IIB, and stage IIC.

- Stage IIA: The tumor has spread to the uterus and/or fallopian tubes (the long slender tubes through which eggs pass from the ovaries to the uterus).

- Stage IIB: The tumor has spread to other tissue within the pelvis.

- Stage IIC: The tumor is found inside one or both ovaries and has spread to the uterus and/or fallopian tubes, or to other tissue within the pelvis. Also, one of the following is true:

- tumor cells are found on the outside surface of one or both ovaries; or

- the capsule (outer covering) of the ovary has ruptured (broken open); or

- tumor cells are found in the fluid of the peritoneal cavity (the body cavity that contains most of the organs in the abdomen) or in washings of the peritoneum (tissue lining the peritoneal cavity).

Stage III

In stage III, the tumor is found in one or both ovaries and has spread outside the pelvis to other parts of the abdomen and/or nearby lymph nodes. Stage III is divided into stage IIIA, stage IIIB, and stage IIIC.

- Stage IIIA: The tumor is found in the pelvis only, but tumor cells that can be seen only with a microscope have spread to the surface of the peritoneum (tissue that lines the abdominal wall and covers most of the organs in the abdomen), the small intestines, or the tissue that connects the small intestines to the wall of the abdomen.

- Stage IIIB: The tumor has spread to the peritoneum and the tumor in the peritoneum is 2 centimeters or smaller.

- Stage IIIC: The tumor has spread to the peritoneum and the tumor in the peritoneum is larger than 2 centimeters and/or has spread to lymph nodes in the abdomen.

The spread of tumor cells to the surface of the liver is also considered stage III disease.

Stage IV

In stage IV, tumor cells have spread beyond the abdomen to other parts of the body, such as the lungs or tissue inside the liver.

Tumor cells in the fluid around the lungs is also considered stage IV disease.

Ovarian low malignant potential tumors almost never reach stage IV.

Section 27.3

Treatment Options for Ovarian Low Malignant Potential Tumors

Text in this section is excerpted from "Ovarian Low Malignant Potential Tumors Treatment (PDQ®)," National Cancer Institute (NCI), July 2, 2015.

There are different types of treatment for patients with ovarian low malignant potential tumor.

Different types of treatment are available for patients with ovarian low malignant potential tumor. Some treatments are standard (the currently used treatment), and some are being tested in clinical trials. A treatment clinical trial is a research study meant to help improve current treatments or obtain information on new treatments for patients with cancer, tumors, and related conditions. When clinical trials show that a new treatment is better than the standard treatment, the new treatment may become the standard treatment. Patients may want to think about taking part in a clinical trial. Some clinical trials are open only to patients who have not started treatment.

Two types of standard treatment are used:

Surgery
The type of surgery (removing the tumor in an operation) depends on the size and spread of the tumor and the woman's plans for having children. Surgery may include the following:

- Unilateral salpingo-oophorectomy: Surgery to remove one ovary and one fallopian tube.

- Bilateral salpingo-oophorectomy: Surgery to remove both ovaries and both fallopian tubes.

- Total hysterectomy and bilateral salpingo-oophorectomy: Surgery to remove the uterus, cervix, and both ovaries and fallopian

367

tubes. If the uterus and cervix are taken out through the vagina, the operation is called a vaginal hysterectomy. If the uterus and cervix are taken out through a large incision (cut) in the abdomen, the operation is called a total abdominal hysterectomy. If the uterus and cervix are taken out through a small incision (cut) in the abdomen using a laparoscope, the operation is called a total laparoscopic hysterectomy.

- Partial oophorectomy: Surgery to remove part of one ovary or part of both ovaries.

- Omentectomy: Surgery to remove the omentum (a piece of the tissue lining the abdominal wall).

Even if the doctor removes all disease that can be seen at the time of the operation, the patient may be given chemotherapy after surgery to kill any tumor cells that are left. Treatment given after the surgery, to lower the risk that the tumor will come back, is called adjuvant therapy.

Chemotherapy

Chemotherapy is a cancer treatment that uses drugs to stop the growth of cancer cells, either by killing the cells or by stopping them from dividing. When chemotherapy is taken by mouth or injected into a vein or muscle, the drugs enter the bloodstream and can reach cancer cells throughout the body (systemic chemotherapy). When chemotherapy is placed directly into the cerebrospinal fluid, an organ, or a body cavity such as the abdomen, the drugs mainly affect cancer cells in those areas (regional chemotherapy). The way the chemotherapy is given depends on the type and stage of the cancer being treated.

Patients may want to think about taking part in a clinical trial.

For some patients, taking part in a clinical trial may be the best treatment choice. Clinical trials are part of the medical research process. Clinical trials are done to find out if new treatments are safe and effective or better than the standard treatment.

Many of today's standard treatments for disease are based on earlier clinical trials. Patients who take part in a clinical trial may receive the standard treatment or be among the first to receive a new treatment.

Patients who take part in clinical trials also help improve the way diseases will be treated in the future. Even when clinical trials do not lead to effective new treatments, they often answer important questions and help move research forward.

Patients can enter clinical trials before, during, or after starting their treatment.

Some clinical trials only include patients who have not yet received treatment. Other trials test treatments for patients whose disease has not gotten better. There are also clinical trials that test new ways to stop a disease from recurring (coming back) or reduce the side effects of treatment.

Clinical trials are taking place in many parts of the country.

Follow-up tests may be needed.

Some of the tests that were done to diagnose the disease may be repeated. Some tests will be repeated in order to see how well the treatment is working. Decisions about whether to continue, change, or stop treatment may be based on the results of these tests. This is sometimes called re-staging.

Some of the tests will continue to be done from time to time after treatment has ended. The results of these tests can show if your condition has changed or if the disease has recurred (come back). These tests are sometimes called follow-up tests or check-ups.

Chapter 28

Urethral Cancer

Chapter Contents

Section 28.1

General Information about Urethral Cancer

Text in this section is excerpted from "Urethral Cancer Treatment
(PDQ®)," National Cancer Institute (NCI), July 7, 2015.

*Urethral cancer is a disease in which malignant (cancer)
cells form in the tissues of the urethra.*

The urethra is the tube that carries urine from the bladder to outside the body. In women, the urethra is about 1½ inches long and is
just above the vagina. In men, the urethra is about 8 inches long, and
goes through the prostate gland and the penis to the outside of the
body. In men, the urethra also carries semen.

Urethral cancer is a rare cancer that occurs more often in men
than in women.

*There are different types of urethral cancer that begin in
cells that line the urethra.*

These cancers are named for the types of cells that become malignant (cancer):

- Squamous cell carcinoma is the most common type of urethral
  cancer. It forms in cells in the part of the urethra near the bladder in women, and in the lining of the urethra in the penis in
  men.

- Transitional cell carcinoma forms in the area near the urethral
  opening in women, and in the part of the urethra that goes
  through the prostate gland in men.

- Adenocarcinoma forms in the glands that are around the urethra in both men and women.

Urethral cancer can metastasize (spread) quickly to tissues around
the urethra and is often found in nearby lymph nodes by the time it
is diagnosed.

A history of bladder cancer can affect the risk of urethral cancer.

Anything that increases your chance of getting a disease is called a risk factor. Having a risk factor does not mean that you will get cancer; not having risk factors doesn't mean that you will not get cancer. Talk with your doctor if you think you may be at risk. Risk factors for urethral cancer include the following:

- Having a history of bladder cancer.
- Having conditions that cause chronic inflammation in the urethra, including:
- Sexually transmitted diseases (STDs), including *human papillomavirus* (HPV), especially HPV type 16.
- Frequent urinary tract infections (UTIs).

Signs of urethral cancer include bleeding or trouble with urination.

These and other signs and symptoms may be caused by urethral cancer or by other conditions. There may be no signs or symptoms in the early stages. Check with your doctor if you have any of the following:

- Trouble starting the flow of urine.
- Weak or interrupted ("stop-and-go") flow of urine.
- Frequent urination, especially at night.
- Incontinence.
- Discharge from the urethra.
- Bleeding from the urethra or blood in the urine.
- A lump or thickness in the perineum or penis.
- A painless lump or swelling in the groin.

Tests that examine the urethra and bladder are used to detect (find) and diagnose urethral cancer.

The following tests and procedures may be used:

- **Physical exam and history:** An exam of the body to check general signs of health, including checking for signs of disease, such as lumps or anything else that seems unusual. A history of the patient's health habits and past illnesses and treatments will also be taken.

- **Pelvic exam:** An exam of the vagina, cervix, uterus, fallopian tubes, ovaries, and rectum. A speculum is inserted into the vagina and the doctor or nurse looks at the vagina and cervix for signs of disease. The doctor or nurse also inserts one or two lubricated, gloved fingers of one hand into the vagina and places the other hand over the lower abdomen to feel the size, shape, and position of the uterus and ovaries. The doctor or nurse also inserts a lubricated, gloved finger into the rectum to feel for lumps or abnormal areas.

- **Digital rectal exam:** An exam of the rectum. The doctor or nurse inserts a lubricated, gloved finger into the lower part of the rectum to feel for lumps or anything else that seems unusual.

- **Urine cytology**: A laboratory test in which a sample of urine is checked under a microscope for abnormal cells.

- **Urinalysis:** A test to check the color of urine and its contents, such as sugar, protein, blood, and white blood cells. If white blood cells (a sign of infection) are found, a urine culture is usually done to find out what type of infection it is.

- **Blood chemistry studies:** A procedure in which a blood sample is checked to measure the amounts of certain substances released into the blood by organs and tissues in the body. An unusual (higher or lower than normal) amount of a substance can be a sign of disease.

- **Complete blood count (CBC):** A procedure in which a sample of blood is drawn and checked for the following:

  - The number of red blood cells, white blood cells, and platelets.

  - The amount of hemoglobin (the protein that carries oxygen) in the red blood cells.

  - The portion of the blood sample made up of red blood cells.

- **CT scan (CAT scan):** A procedure that makes a series of detailed pictures of areas inside the body, such as the pelvis and abdomen, taken from different angles. The pictures are made by a computer linked to an x-ray machine. A dye may be injected into a vein or swallowed to help the organs or tissues show up more clearly. This procedure is also called computed tomography, computerized tomography, or computerized axial tomography.

- **Ureteroscopy:** A procedure to look inside the ureter and renal pelvis to check for abnormal areas. A ureteroscope is a thin, tube-like instrument with a light and a lens for viewing. The ureteroscope is inserted through the urethra into the bladder, ureter, and renal pelvis. A tool may be inserted through the ureteroscope to take tissue samples to be checked under a microscope for signs of disease.

- **Biopsy:** The removal of cell or tissue samples from the urethra, bladder, and, sometimes, the prostate gland. The samples are viewed under a microscope by a pathologist to check for signs of cancer.

Certain factors affect prognosis (chance of recovery) and treatment options.

The prognosis (chance of recovery) and treatment options depend on the following:

- Where the cancer formed in the urethra.

- Whether the cancer has spread through the mucosa lining the urethra to nearby tissue, to lymph nodes, or to other parts of the body.

- Whether the patient is a male or female.

- The patient's general health.

- Whether the cancer has just been diagnosed or has recurred (come back).

Section 28.2

Stages of Urethral Cancer

Text in this section is excerpted from "Urethral Cancer Treatment
(PDQ®)," National Cancer Institute (NCI), July 7, 2015.

*After urethral cancer has been diagnosed, tests are done to
find out if cancer cells have spread within the urethra or to
other parts of the body.*

The process used to find out if cancer has spread within the urethra
or to other parts of the body is called staging. The information gathered from the staging process determines the stage of the disease. It
is important to know the stage in order to plan treatment.

The following procedures may be used in the staging process:

- **Chest x-ray:** An x-ray of the organs and bones inside the chest.
  An x-ray is a type of energy beam that can go through the body
  and onto film, making a picture of areas inside the body.

- **CT scan (CAT scan) of the pelvis and abdomen:** A procedure
  that makes a series of detailed pictures of the pelvis and abdomen, taken from different angles. The pictures are made by a
  computer linked to an x-ray machine. A dye may be injected into
  a vein or swallowed to help the organs or tissues show up more
  clearly. This procedure is also called computed tomography, computerized tomography, or computerized axial tomography.

- **MRI (magnetic resonance imaging):** A procedure that uses a
  magnet, radio waves, and a computer to make a series of detailed
  pictures of the urethra, nearby lymph nodes, and other soft tissue
  and bones in the pelvis. A substance called gadolinium is injected
  into the patient through a vein. The gadolinium collects around
  the cancer cells so they show up brighter in the picture. This procedure is also called nuclear magnetic resonance imaging (NMRI).

- **Urethrography:** A series of x-rays of the urethra. An x-ray is
  a type of energy beam that can go through the body and onto
  film, making a picture of areas inside the body. A dye is injected

through the urethra into the bladder. The dye coats the bladder and urethra and x-rays are taken to see if the urethra is blocked and if cancer has spread to nearby tissue.

There are three ways that cancer spreads in the body.

Cancer can spread through tissue, the lymph system, and the blood:

- Tissue. The cancer spreads from where it began by growing into nearby areas.
- Lymph system. The cancer spreads from where it began by getting into the lymph system. The cancer travels through the lymph vessels to other parts of the body.
- Blood. The cancer spreads from where it began by getting into the blood. The cancer travels through the blood vessels to other parts of the body.

Cancer may spread from where it began to other parts of the body.

When cancer spreads to another part of the body, it is called metastasis. Cancer cells break away from where they began (the primary tumor) and travel through the lymph system or blood.

- Lymph system. The cancer gets into the lymph system, travels through the lymph vessels, and forms a tumor (metastatic tumor) in another part of the body.
- Blood. The cancer gets into the blood, travels through the blood vessels, and forms a tumor (metastatic tumor) in another part of the body.

The metastatic tumor is the same type of cancer as the primary tumor. For example, if urethral cancer spreads to the lung, the cancer cells in the lung are actually urethral cancer cells. The disease is metastatic urethral cancer, not lung cancer.

Urethral cancer is staged and treated based on the part of the urethra that is affected.

Urethral cancer is staged and treated based on the part of the urethra that is affected and how deeply the tumor has spread into tissue around the urethra. Urethral cancer can be described as distal or proximal.

Distal urethral cancer

In distal urethral cancer, the cancer usually has not spread deeply into the tissue. In women, the part of the urethra that is closest to the outside of the body (about ½ inch) is affected. In men, the part of the urethra that is in the penis is affected.

Proximal urethral cancer

Proximal urethral cancer affects the part of the urethra that is not the distal urethra. In women and men, proximal urethral cancer usually has spread deeply into tissue.

Bladder and / or prostate cancer may occur at the same time as urethral cancer.

In men, cancer that forms in the proximal urethra (the part of the urethra that passes through the prostate to the bladder) may occur at the same time as cancer of the bladder and/or prostate. Sometimes this occurs at diagnosis and sometimes it occurs later.

Section 28.3

Treatment Options for Urethral Cancer

Text in this section is excerpted from "Urethral Cancer Treatment (PDQ®)," National Cancer Institute (NCI), July 7, 2015.

There are different types of treatment for patients with urethral cancer.

Different types of treatments are available for patients with urethral cancer. Some treatments are standard (the currently used treatment), and some are being tested in clinical trials. A treatment clinical trial is a research study meant to help improve current treatments or obtain information on new treatments for patients with cancer. When clinical trials show that a new treatment is better than the standard treatment, the new treatment may become the standard treatment. Patients may want to think about taking part in a clinical trial. Some clinical trials are open only to patients who have not started treatment.

Four types of standard treatment are used:

Surgery

Surgery to remove the cancer is the most common treatment for cancer of the urethra. One of the following types of surgery may be done:

- Open excision: Removal of the cancer by surgery.

- Transurethral resection (TUR): Surgery to remove the cancer using a special tool inserted into the urethra.

- Electroresection with fulguration: Surgery to remove the cancer by electric current. A lighted tool with a small wire loop on the end is used to remove the cancer or to burn the tumor away with high-energy electricity.

- Laser surgery: A surgical procedure that uses a laser beam (a narrow beam of intense light) as a knife to make bloodless cuts in tissue or to remove or destroy tissue.

- Lymph node dissection: Lymph nodes in the pelvis and groin may be removed.

- Cystourethrectomy: Surgery to remove the bladder and the urethra.

- Cystoprostatectomy: Surgery to remove the bladder and the prostate.

- Anterior exenteration: Surgery to remove the urethra, the bladder, and the vagina. Plastic surgery may be done to rebuild the vagina.

- Partial penectomy: Surgery to remove the part of the penis surrounding the urethra where cancer has spread. Plastic surgery may be done to rebuild the penis.

- Radical penectomy: Surgery to remove the entire penis. Plastic surgery may be done to rebuild the penis.

If the urethra is removed, the surgeon will make a new way for the urine to pass from the body. This is called urinary diversion. If the bladder is removed, the surgeon will make a new way for urine to be stored and passed from the body. The surgeon may use part of the small intestine to make a tube that passes urine through an opening (stoma). This is called an ostomy or urostomy. If a patient has an ostomy, a disposable bag to collect urine is worn under clothing.

The surgeon may also use part of the small intestine to make a new storage pouch (continent reservoir) inside the body where the urine can collect. A tube (catheter) is then used to drain the urine through a stoma.

Even if the doctor removes all the cancer that can be seen at the time of the surgery, some patients may be given chemotherapy or radiation therapy after surgery to kill any cancer cells that are left. Treatment given after the surgery, to lower the risk that the cancer will come back, is called adjuvant therapy.

Radiation therapy

Radiation therapy is a cancer treatment that uses high-energy x-rays or other types of radiation to kill cancer cells. There are two types of radiation therapy. External radiation therapy uses a machine outside the body to send radiation toward the cancer. Internal radiation therapy uses a radioactive substance sealed in needles, seeds, wires, or catheters that are placed directly into or near the cancer. The way the radiation therapy is given depends on the type of cancer and where the cancer formed in the urethra.

Chemotherapy

Chemotherapy is a cancer treatment that uses drugs to stop the growth of cancer cells, either by killing the cells or by stopping the cells from dividing. When chemotherapy is taken by mouth or injected into a vein or muscle, the drugs enter the bloodstream and can reach cancer cells throughout the body (systemic chemotherapy). When chemotherapy is placed directly into the cerebrospinal fluid, an organ, or a body cavity such as the abdomen, the drugs mainly affect cancer cells in those areas (regional chemotherapy). The way the chemotherapy is given depends on the type of cancer and where the cancer formed in the urethra.

Active surveillance

Active surveillance is following a patient's condition without giving any treatment unless there are changes in test results. It is used to find early signs that the condition is getting worse. In active surveillance, patients are given certain exams and tests, including biopsies, on a regular schedule.

Patients may want to think about taking part in a clinical trial.

For some patients, taking part in a clinical trial may be the best treatment choice. Clinical trials are part of the cancer research process.

Clinical trials are done to find out if new cancer treatments are safe and effective or better than the standard treatment.

Many of today's standard treatments for cancer are based on earlier clinical trials. Patients who take part in a clinical trial may receive the standard treatment or be among the first to receive a new treatment.

Patients who take part in clinical trials also help improve the way cancer will be treated in the future. Even when clinical trials do not lead to effective new treatments, they often answer important questions and help move research forward.

Patients can enter clinical trials before, during, or after starting their cancer treatment.

Some clinical trials only include patients who have not yet received treatment. Other trials test treatments for patients whose cancer has not gotten better. There are also clinical trials that test new ways to stop cancer from recurring (coming back) or reduce the side effects of cancer treatment.

Clinical trials are taking place in many parts of the country.

Follow-up tests may be needed.

Some of the tests that were done to diagnose the cancer or to find out the stage of the cancer may be repeated. Some tests will be repeated in order to see how well the treatment is working. Decisions about whether to continue, change, or stop treatment may be based on the results of these tests.

Some of the tests will continue to be done from time to time after treatment has ended. The results of these tests can show if your condition has changed or if the cancer has recurred (come back). These tests are sometimes called follow-up tests or check-ups.

Chapter 29

Uterine Sarcoma

Chapter Contents

Section 29.1

General Information about Uterine Sarcoma

Text in this section is excerpted from "Uterine Sarcoma Treatment
(PDQ®)," National Cancer Institute (NCI), July 30, 2015.

Uterine sarcoma is a disease in which malignant (cancer) cells form
in the muscles of the uterus or other tissues that support the uterus.

The uterus is part of the female reproductive system. The uterus is
the hollow, pear-shaped organ in the pelvis, where a fetus grows. The
cervix is at the lower, narrow end of the uterus, and leads to the vagina.

Uterine sarcoma is a very rare kind of cancer that forms in the
uterine muscles or in tissues that support the uterus. Uterine sarcoma
is different from cancer of the endometrium, a disease in which cancer
cells start growing inside the lining of the uterus.

Being exposed to x-rays can increase the risk of uterine sarcoma.

Anything that increases your risk of getting a disease is called a
risk factor. Having a risk factor does not mean that you will get cancer; not having risk factors doesn't mean that you will not get cancer.
Talk with your doctor if you think you may be at risk. Risk factors for
uterine sarcoma include the following:

- Past treatment with radiation therapy to the pelvis.

- Treatment with tamoxifen for breast cancer. If you are taking
  this drug, have a pelvic exam every year and report any vaginal
  bleeding (other than menstrual bleeding) as soon as possible.

Signs of uterine sarcoma include abnormal bleeding.

Abnormal bleeding from the vagina and other signs and symptoms
may be caused by uterine sarcoma or by other conditions. Check with
your doctor if you have any of the following:

- Bleeding that is not part of menstrual periods.

- Bleeding after menopause.

- A mass in the vagina.

- Pain or a feeling of fullness in the abdomen.

- Frequent urination.

Tests that examine the uterus are used to detect (find) and diagnose uterine sarcoma.

The following tests and procedures may be used:

- **Physical exam and history:** An exam of the body to check general signs of health, including checking for signs of disease, such as lumps or anything else that seems unusual. A history of the patient's health habits and past illnesses and treatments will also be taken.

- **Pelvic exam:** An exam of the vagina, cervix, uterus, fallopian tubes, ovaries, and rectum. A speculum is inserted into the vagina and the doctor or nurse looks at the vagina and cervix for signs of disease. A Pap test of the cervix is usually done. The doctor or nurse also inserts one or two lubricated, gloved fingers of one hand into the vagina and places the other hand over the lower abdomen to feel the size, shape, and position of the uterus and ovaries. The doctor or nurse also inserts a lubricated, gloved finger into the rectum to feel for lumps or abnormal areas.

- **Pap test:** A procedure to collect cells from the surface of the cervix and vagina. A piece of cotton, a brush, or a small wooden stick is used to gently scrape cells from the cervix and vagina. The cells are viewed under a microscope to find out if they are abnormal. This procedure is also called a Pap smear. Because uterine sarcoma begins inside the uterus, this cancer may not show up on the Pap test.

- **Transvaginal ultrasound exam:** A procedure used to examine the vagina, uterus, fallopian tubes, and bladder. An ultrasound transducer (probe) is inserted into the vagina and used to bounce high-energy sound waves (ultrasound) off internal tissues or organs and make echoes. The echoes form a picture of body tissues called a sonogram. The doctor can identify tumors by looking at the sonogram.

- **Dilatation and curettage:** A procedure to remove samples of tissue from the inner lining of the uterus. The cervix is dilated and a curette (spoon-shaped instrument) is inserted into the uterus to remove tissue. The tissue samples are checked under a microscope for signs of disease. This procedure is also called a D&C.

- **Endometrial biopsy:** The removal of tissue from the endometrium (inner lining of the uterus) by inserting a thin, flexible tube through the cervix and into the uterus. The tube is used to gently scrape a small amount of tissue from the endometrium and then remove the tissue samples. A pathologist views the tissue under a microscope to look for cancer cells.

Certain factors affect prognosis (chance of recovery) and treatment options.

The prognosis (chance of recovery) and treatment options depend on the following:

- The stage of the cancer.

- The type and size of the tumor.

- The patient's general health.

- Whether the cancer has just been diagnosed or has recurred (come back).

Section 29.2

Stages of Uterine Sarcoma

Text in this section is excerpted from "Uterine Sarcoma Treatment (PDQ®)," National Cancer Institute (NCI), July 30, 2015.

After uterine sarcoma has been diagnosed, tests are done to find out if cancer cells have spread within the uterus or to other parts of the body.

The process used to find out if cancer has spread within the uterus or to other parts of the body is called staging. The information gathered from the staging process determines the stage of the disease. It is important to know the stage in order to plan treatment. The following procedures may be used in the staging process:

- **Blood chemistry studies:** A procedure in which a blood sample is checked to measure the amounts of certain substances released into the blood by organs and tissues in the body. An unusual (higher or lower than normal) amount of a substance can be a sign of disease.

- **CA 125 assay:** A test that measures the level of CA 125 in the blood. CA 125 is a substance released by cells into the bloodstream. An increased CA 125 level is sometimes a sign of cancer or other condition.

- **Chest x-ray:** An x-ray of the organs and bones inside the chest. An x-ray is a type of energy beam that can go through the body and onto film, making a picture of areas inside the body.

- **Transvaginal ultrasound exam:** A procedure used to examine the vagina, uterus, fallopian tubes, and bladder. An ultrasound transducer (probe) is inserted into the vagina and used to bounce high-energy sound waves (ultrasound) off internal tissues or organs and make echoes. The echoes form a picture of body tissues called a sonogram. The doctor can identify tumors by looking at the sonogram.

- **CT scan (CAT scan):** A procedure that makes a series of detailed pictures of areas inside the body, such as the abdomen and pelvis, taken from different angles. The pictures are made by a computer linked to an x-ray machine. A dye may be injected into a vein or swallowed to help the organs or tissues to show up more clearly. This procedure is also called computed tomography, computerized tomography, or computerized axial tomography.

- **Cystoscopy:** A procedure to look inside the bladder and urethra to check for abnormal areas. A cystoscope is inserted through the urethra into the bladder. A cystoscope is a thin, tube-like instrument with a light and a lens for viewing. It may also have a tool to remove tissue samples, which are checked under a microscope for signs of cancer.

Uterine sarcoma may be diagnosed, staged, and treated in the same surgery.

Surgery is used to diagnose, stage, and treat uterine sarcoma. During this surgery, the doctor removes as much of the cancer as possible. The following procedures may be used to diagnose, stage, and treat uterine sarcoma:

- Laparotomy: A surgical procedure in which an incision (cut) is made in the wall of the abdomen to check the inside of the abdomen for signs of disease. The size of the incision depends on the reason the laparotomy is being done. Sometimes organs are removed or tissue samples are taken and checked under a microscope for signs of disease.

- Abdominal and pelvic washings: A procedure in which a saline solution is placed into the abdominal and pelvic body cavities. After a short time, the fluid is removed and viewed under a microscope to check for cancer cells.

- Total abdominal hysterectomy: A surgical procedure to remove the uterus and cervix through a large incision (cut) in the abdomen.

- Bilateral salpingo-oophorectomy: Surgery to remove both ovaries and both fallopian tubes.

- Lymphadenectomy: A surgical procedure in which lymph nodes are removed and checked under a microscope for signs of cancer. For a regional lymphadenectomy, some of the lymph nodes in the tumor area are removed. For a radical lymphadenectomy, most or all of the lymph nodes in the tumor area are removed. This procedure is also called lymph node dissection.

Treatment in addition to surgery may be given, as described in the Treatment Option Overview section of this summary.

There are three ways that cancer spreads in the body.

Cancer can spread through tissue, the lymph system, and the blood:

- Tissue. The cancer spreads from where it began by growing into nearby areas.

- Lymph system. The cancer spreads from where it began by getting into the lymph system. The cancer travels through the lymph vessels to other parts of the body.

- Blood. The cancer spreads from where it began by getting into the blood. The cancer travels through the blood vessels to other parts of the body.

Cancer may spread from where it began to other parts of the body.

When cancer spreads to another part of the body, it is called metastasis. Cancer cells break away from where they began (the primary tumor) and travel through the lymph system or blood.

- Lymph system. The cancer gets into the lymph system, travels through the lymph vessels, and forms a tumor (metastatic tumor) in another part of the body.

- Blood. The cancer gets into the blood, travels through the blood vessels, and forms a tumor (metastatic tumor) in another part of the body.

The metastatic tumor is the same type of cancer as the primary tumor. For example, if uterine sarcoma spreads to the lung, the cancer cells in the lung are actually uterine sarcoma cells. The disease is metastatic uterine sarcoma, not lung cancer.

The following stages are used for uterine sarcoma:

Stage I

In stage I, cancer is found in the uterus only. Stage I is divided into stages IA and IB, based on how far the cancer has spread.

- Stage IA: Cancer is in the endometrium only or less than halfway through the myometrium (muscle layer of the uterus).

- Stage IB: Cancer has spread halfway or more into the myometrium.

Stage II

In stage II, cancer has spread into connective tissue of the cervix, but has not spread outside the uterus.

Stage III

In stage III, cancer has spread beyond the uterus and cervix, but has not spread beyond the pelvis. Stage III is divided into stages IIIA, IIIB, and IIIC, based on how far the cancer has spread within the pelvis.

- Stage IIIA: Cancer has spread to the outer layer of the uterus and/or to the fallopian tubes, ovaries, and ligaments of the uterus.

- Stage IIIB: Cancer has spread to the vagina or to the parametrium (connective tissue and fat around the uterus).

- Stage IIIC: Cancer has spread to lymph nodes in the pelvis and/ or around the aorta (largest artery in the body, which carries blood away from the heart).

Stage IV

In stage IV, cancer has spread beyond the pelvis. Stage IV is divided into stages IVA and IVB, based on how far the cancer has spread.

- Stage IVA: Cancer has spread to the bladder and/or bowel wall.

- Stage IVB: Cancer has spread to other parts of the body beyond the pelvis, including the abdomen and/or lymph nodes in the groin.

Section 29.3

Treatment Options for Uterine Sarcoma

Text in this section is excerpted from "Uterine Sarcoma Treatment (PDQ®)," National Cancer Institute (NCI), July 30, 2015.

There are different types of treatment for patients with uterine sarcoma.

Different types of treatments are available for patients with uterine sarcoma. Some treatments are standard (the currently used treatment), and some are being tested in clinical trials. A treatment clinical trial is a research study meant to help improve current treatments or obtain information on new treatments for patients with cancer. When clinical trials show that a new treatment is better than the standard treatment, the new treatment may become the standard treatment. Patients may want to think about taking part in a clinical trial. Some clinical trials are open only to patients who have not started treatment.

Four types of standard treatment are used:

Surgery

Surgery is the most common treatment for uterine sarcoma, as described in the Stages of Uterine Sarcoma section of this summary.

Even if the doctor removes all the cancer that can be seen at the time of the surgery, some patients may be given chemotherapy or radiation therapy after surgery to kill any cancer cells that are left. Treatment given after the surgery, to lower the risk that the cancer will come back, is called adjuvant therapy.

Radiation therapy

Radiation therapy is a cancer treatment that uses high energy x-rays or other types of radiation to kill cancer cells or keep them from growing. There are two types of radiation therapy. External radiation therapy uses a machine outside the body to send radiation toward the cancer. Internal radiation therapy uses a radioactive substance sealed in needles, seeds, wires, or catheters that are placed directly into or near the cancer. The way the radiation therapy is given depends on the type and stage of the cancer being treated.

Chemotherapy

Chemotherapy is a cancer treatment that uses drugs to stop the growth of cancer cells, either by killing the cells or by stopping them from dividing. When chemotherapy is taken by mouth or injected into a vein or muscle, the drugs enter the bloodstream and can reach cancer cells throughout the body (systemic chemotherapy). When chemotherapy is placed directly into the cerebrospinal fluid, an organ, or a body cavity such as the abdomen, the drugs mainly affect cancer cells in those areas (regional chemotherapy). The way the chemotherapy is given depends on the type and stage of the cancer being treated.

Hormone therapy

Hormone therapy is a cancer treatment that removes hormones or blocks their action and stops cancer cells from growing. Hormones are substances produced by glands in the body and circulated in the bloodstream. Some hormones can cause certain cancers to grow. If tests show the cancer cells have places where hormones can attach (receptors), drugs, surgery, or radiation therapy is used to reduce the production of hormones or block them from working.

New types of treatment are being tested in clinical trials.

Patients may want to think about taking part in a clinical trial.

For some patients, taking part in a clinical trial may be the best treatment choice. Clinical trials are part of the cancer research process. Clinical trials are done to find out if new cancer treatments are safe and effective or better than the standard treatment.

Many of today's standard treatments for cancer are based on earlier clinical trials. Patients who take part in a clinical trial may receive the standard treatment or be among the first to receive a new treatment.

Patients who take part in clinical trials also help improve the way cancer will be treated in the future. Even when clinical trials do not lead to effective new treatments, they often answer important questions and help move research forward.

Patients can enter clinical trials before, during, or after starting their cancer treatment.

Some clinical trials only include patients who have not yet received treatment. Other trials test treatments for patients whose cancer has not gotten better. There are also clinical trials that test new ways to stop cancer from recurring (coming back) or reduce the side effects of cancer treatment.

Clinical trials are taking place in many parts of the country.

Follow-up tests may be needed.

Some of the tests that were done to diagnose the cancer or to find out the stage of the cancer may be repeated. Some tests will be repeated in order to see how well the treatment is working. Decisions about whether to continue, change, or stop treatment may be based on the results of these tests.

Some of the tests will continue to be done from time to time after treatment has ended. The results of these tests can show if your condition has changed or if the cancer has recurred (come back). These tests are sometimes called follow-up tests or check-ups.

Chapter 30

Vaginal Cancer

Chapter Contents

Section 30.1

General Information about Vaginal Cancer

Text in this section is excerpted from "Vaginal Cancer Treatment
(PDQ®)," National Cancer Institute (NCI), July 30, 2015.

Vaginal cancer is a disease in which malignant (cancer) cells form in the vagina.

Vaginal cancer is a disease in which malignant (cancer) cells form
in the vagina.

The vagina is the canal leading from the cervix (the opening of
uterus) to the outside of the body. At birth, a baby passes out of the
body through the vagina (also called the birth canal).

Vaginal cancer is not common. There are two main types of vaginal
cancer:

- Squamous cell carcinoma: Cancer that forms in squamous cells,
  the thin, flat cells lining the vagina. Squamous cell vaginal cancer spreads slowly and usually stays near the vagina, but may
  spread to the lungs, liver, or bone. This is the most common type
  of vaginal cancer.

- Adenocarcinoma: Cancer that begins in glandular (secretory)
  cells. Glandular cells in the lining of the vagina make and
  release fluids such as mucus. Adenocarcinoma is more likely
  than squamous cell cancer to spread to the lungs and lymph
  nodes. A rare type of adenocarcinoma is linked to being exposed
  to diethylstilbestrol (DES) before birth. Adenocarcinomas that
  are not linked with being exposed to DES are most common in
  women after menopause.

Age and being exposed to the drug DES (diethylstilbestrol) before birth affect a woman's risk of vaginal cancer.

Anything that increases your risk of getting a disease is called a
risk factor. Having a risk factor does not mean that you will get cancer; not having risk factors doesn't mean that you will not get cancer.

Talk with your doctor if you think you may be at risk. Risk factors for vaginal cancer include the following:

- Being aged 60 or older.
- Being exposed to DES while in the mother's womb. In the 1950s, the drug DES was given to some pregnant women to prevent miscarriage (premature birth of a fetus that cannot survive). Women who were exposed to DES before birth have an increased risk of vaginal cancer. Some of these women develop a rare form of vaginal cancer called clear cell adenocarcinoma.
- *Having human papilloma virus* (HPV) infection.
- Having a history of abnormal cells in the cervix or cervical cancer.
- Having a history of abnormal cells in the uterus or cancer of the uterus.
- Having had a hysterectomy for health problems that affect the uterus.

Signs and symptoms of vaginal cancer include pain or abnormal vaginal bleeding.

Vaginal cancer often does not cause early signs or symptoms. It may be found during a routine pelvic exam and Pap test. Signs and symptoms may be caused by vaginal cancer or by other conditions. Check with your doctor if you have any of the following:

- Bleeding or discharge not related to menstrual periods.
- Pain during sexual intercourse.
- Pain in the pelvic area.
- A lump in the vagina.
- Pain when urinating.
- Constipation.

Tests that examine the vagina and other organs in the pelvis are used to detect (find) and diagnose vaginal cancer.

The following tests and procedures may be used:

- **Physical exam and history:** An exam of the body to check general signs of health, including checking for signs of disease, such as lumps or anything else that seems unusual. A history of the patient's health habits and past illnesses and treatments will also be taken.

- **Pelvic exam:** An exam of the vagina, cervix, uterus, fallopian tubes, ovaries, and rectum. A speculum is inserted into the vagina and the doctor or nurse looks at the vagina and cervix for signs of disease. A Pap test of the cervix is usually done. The doctor or nurse also inserts one or two lubricated, gloved fingers of one hand into the vagina and places the other hand over the lower abdomen to feel the size, shape, and position of the uterus and ovaries. The doctor or nurse also inserts a lubricated, gloved finger into the rectum to feel for lumps or abnormal areas.

- **Pap test:** A procedure to collect cells from the surface of the cervix and vagina. A piece of cotton, a brush, or a small wooden stick is used to gently scrape cells from the cervix and vagina. The cells are viewed under a microscope to find out if they are abnormal. This procedure is also called a Pap smear.

- **Colposcopy:** A procedure in which a colposcope (a lighted, magnifying instrument) is used to check the vagina and cervix for abnormal areas. Tissue samples may be taken using a curette (spoon-shaped instrument) or a brush and checked under a microscope for signs of disease.

- **Biopsy:** The removal of cells or tissues from the vagina and cervix so they can be viewed under a microscope by a pathologist to check for signs of cancer. If a Pap test shows abnormal cells in the vagina, a biopsy may be done during a colposcopy.

Certain factors affect prognosis (chance of recovery) and treatment options.

The prognosis (chance of recovery) depends on the following:

- The stage of the cancer (whether it is in the vagina only or has spread to other areas).

- The size of the tumor.

- The grade of tumor cells (how different they look from normal cells under a microscope).

- Where the cancer is within the vagina.

- Whether there are signs or symptoms at diagnosis.

- The patient's age and general health.

- Whether the cancer has just been diagnosed or has recurred (come back).

When found in early stages, vaginal cancer can often be cured.

Treatment options depend on the following:

- The stage and size of the cancer.
- Whether the cancer is close to other organs that may be damaged by treatment.
- Whether the tumor is made up of squamous cells or is an adenocarcinoma.
- Whether the patient has a uterus or has had a hysterectomy.
- Whether the patient has had past radiation treatment to the pelvis.

Section 30.2

Stages of Vaginal Cancer

Text in this section is excerpted from "Vaginal Cancer Treatment (PDQ®)," National Cancer Institute (NCI), July 30, 2015.

After vaginal cancer has been diagnosed, tests are done to find out if cancer cells have spread within the vagina or to other parts of the body.

The process used to find out if cancer has spread within the vagina or to other parts of the body is called staging. The information gathered from the staging process determines the stage of the disease. It is important to know the stage in order to plan treatment. The following procedures may be used in the staging process:

- **Chest x-ray:** An x-ray of the organs and bones inside the chest. An x-ray is a type of energy beam that can go through the body and onto film, making a picture of areas inside the body.

- **CT scan (CAT scan):** A procedure that makes a series of detailed pictures of areas inside the body, taken from different angles. The pictures are made by a computer linked to an x-ray machine. A dye may be injected into a vein or swallowed to help the organs or tissues show up more clearly. This procedure is also called computed tomography, computerized tomography, or computerized axial tomography.

- **MRI (magnetic resonance imaging):** A procedure that uses a magnet, radio waves, and a computer to make a series of detailed pictures of areas inside the body. This procedure is also called nuclear magnetic resonance imaging (NMRI).

- **PET scan (positron emission tomography scan):** A procedure to find malignant tumor cells in the body. A small amount of radioactive glucose (sugar) is injected into a vein. The PET scanner rotates around the body and makes a picture of where glucose is being used in the body. Malignant tumor cells show up brighter in the picture because they are more active and take up more glucose than normal cells do.

- **Cystoscopy:** A procedure to look inside the bladder and urethra to check for abnormal areas. A cystoscope is inserted through the urethra into the bladder. A cystoscope is a thin, tube-like instrument with a light and a lens for viewing. It may also have a tool to remove tissue samples, which are checked under a microscope for signs of cancer.

- **Ureteroscopy:** A procedure to look inside the ureters to check for abnormal areas. A ureteroscope is inserted through the bladder and into the ureters. A ureteroscope is a thin, tube-like instrument with a light and a lens for viewing. It may also have a tool to remove tissue to be checked under a microscope for signs of disease. A ureteroscopy and cystoscopy may be done during the same procedure.

- **Proctoscopy:** A procedure to look inside the rectum to check for abnormal areas. A proctoscope is inserted through the rectum. A proctoscope is a thin, tube-like instrument with a light and a lens for viewing. It may also have a tool to remove tissue to be checked under a microscope for signs of disease.

- **Biopsy:** A biopsy may be done to find out if cancer has spread to the cervix. A sample of tissue is removed from the cervix and viewed under a microscope. A biopsy that removes only a small amount of tissue is usually done in the doctor's office. A cone biopsy (removal of a larger, cone-shaped piece of tissue from the cervix and cervical canal) is usually done in the hospital. A biopsy of the vulva may also be done to see if cancer has spread there.

There are three ways that cancer spreads in the body.

Cancer can spread through tissue, the lymph system, and the blood:

- Tissue. The cancer spreads from where it began by growing into nearby areas.
- Lymph system. The cancer spreads from where it began by getting into the lymph system. The cancer travels through the lymph vessels to other parts of the body.
- Blood. The cancer spreads from where it began by getting into the blood. The cancer travels through the blood vessels to other parts of the body.

Cancer may spread from where it began to other parts of the body.

When cancer spreads to another part of the body, it is called metastasis. Cancer cells break away from where they began (the primary tumor) and travel through the lymph system or blood.

- Lymph system. The cancer gets into the lymph system, travels through the lymph vessels, and forms a tumor (metastatic tumor) in another part of the body.
- Blood. The cancer gets into the blood, travels through the blood vessels, and forms a tumor (metastatic tumor) in another part of the body.

The metastatic tumor is the same type of cancer as the primary tumor. For example, if vaginal cancer spreads to the lung, the cancer cells in the lung are actually vaginal cancer cells. The disease is metastatic vaginal cancer, not lung cancer.

In vaginal intraepithelial neoplasia (VAIN), abnormal cells are found in tissue lining the inside of the vagina.

These abnormal cells are not cancer. Vaginal intraepithelial neoplasia (VAIN) is grouped based on how deep the abnormal cells are in the tissue lining the vagina:

- VAIN 1: Abnormal cells are found in the outermost one third of the tissue lining the vagina.
- VAIN 2: Abnormal cells are found in the outermost two-thirds of the tissue lining the vagina.

- VAIN 3: Abnormal cells are found in more than two-thirds of the tissue lining the vagina. When abnormal cells are found throughout the tissue lining, it is called carcinoma in situ.

VAIN may become cancer and spread into the vaginal wall. VAIN is sometimes called stage 0.

The following stages are used for vaginal cancer:

Stage I
In stage I, cancer is found in the vaginal wall only.

Stage II
In stage II, cancer has spread through the wall of the vagina to the tissue around the vagina. Cancer has not spread to the wall of the pelvis.

Stage III
In stage III, cancer has spread to the wall of the pelvis.

Stage IV
Stage IV is divided into stage IVA and stage IVB:

- Stage IVA: Cancer may have spread to one or more of the following areas:

- The lining of the bladder.

- The lining of the rectum.

- Beyond the area of the pelvis that has the bladder, uterus, ovaries, and cervix.

- Stage IVB: Cancer has spread to parts of the body that are not near the vagina, such as the lung or bone.

Section 30.3

Treatment Options for Vaginal Cancer

Text in this section is excerpted from "Vaginal Cancer Treatment (PDQ®)," National Institute (NCI), July 30, 2015.

There are different types of treatment for patients with vaginal cancer.

Different types of treatments are available for patients with vaginal cancer. Some treatments are standard (the currently used treatment), and some are being tested in clinical trials. A treatment clinical trial is a research study meant to help improve current treatments or obtain information on new treatments for patients with cancer. When clinical trials show that a new treatment is better than the standard treatment, the new treatment may become the standard treatment. Patients may want to think about taking part in a clinical trial. Some clinical trials are open only to patients who have not started treatment.

Three types of standard treatment are used:

Surgery

Surgery is the most common treatment of vaginal cancer. The following surgical procedures may be used:

- Laser surgery: A surgical procedure that uses a laser beam (a narrow beam of intense light) as a knife to make bloodless cuts in tissue or to remove a surface lesion such as a tumor.

- Wide local excision: A surgical procedure that takes out the cancer and some of the healthy tissue around it.

- Vaginectomy: Surgery to remove all or part of the vagina.

- Total hysterectomy: Surgery to remove the uterus, including the cervix. If the uterus and cervix are taken out through the vagina, the operation is called a vaginal hysterectomy. If the uterus and cervix are taken out through a large incision (cut) in the abdomen, the operation is called a total abdominal hysterectomy. If the uterus and cervix are taken out through a small incision in the abdomen using a laparoscope, the operation is called a total laparoscopic hysterectomy.

• Lymph node dissection: A surgical procedure in which lymph nodes are removed and a sample of tissue is checked under a microscope for signs of cancer. This procedure is also called lymphadenectomy. If the cancer is in the upper vagina, the pelvic lymph nodes may be removed. If the cancer is in the lower vagina, lymph nodes in the groin may be removed.

• Pelvic exenteration: Surgery to remove the lower colon, rectum, bladder, cervix, vagina, and ovaries. Nearby lymph nodes are also removed. Artificial openings (stoma) are made for urine and stool to flow from the body into a collection bag.

Skin grafting may follow surgery, to repair or reconstruct the vagina. Skin grafting is a surgical procedure in which skin is moved from one part of the body to another. A piece of healthy skin is taken from a part of the body that is usually hidden, such as the buttock or thigh, and used to repair or rebuild the area treated with surgery.

Even if the doctor removes all the cancer that can be seen at the time of the surgery, some patients may be given radiation therapy after surgery to kill any cancer cells that are left. Treatment given after the surgery, to lower the risk that the cancer will come back, is called adjuvant therapy.

Radiation therapy

Radiation therapy is a cancer treatment that uses high-energy x-rays or other types of radiation to kill cancer cells or keep them from growing. There are two types of radiation therapy. External radiation therapy uses a machine outside the body to send radiation toward the cancer. Internal radiation therapy uses a radioactive substance sealed in needles, seeds, wires, or catheters that are placed directly into or near the cancer. The way the radiation therapy is given depends on the type and stage of the cancer being treated.

Chemotherapy

Chemotherapy is a cancer treatment that uses drugs to stop the growth of cancer cells, either by killing the cells or by stopping them from dividing. When chemotherapy is taken by mouth or injected into a vein or muscle, the drugs enter the bloodstream and can affect cancer cells throughout the body (systemic chemotherapy). When chemotherapy is placed directly into the cerebrospinal fluid, an organ, or a body cavity such as the abdomen, the drugs mainly affect cancer cells in those areas (regional chemotherapy). The way the chemotherapy is given depends on the type and stage of the cancer being treated.

Topical chemotherapy for squamous cell vaginal cancer may be applied to the vagina in a cream or lotion.

New types of treatment are being tested in clinical trials.

Radiosensitizers

Radiosensitizers are drugs that make tumor cells more sensitive to radiation therapy. Combining radiation therapy with radiosensitizers may kill more tumor cells.

Patients may want to think about taking part in a clinical trial.

For some patients, taking part in a clinical trial may be the best treatment choice. Clinical trials are part of the cancer research process. Clinical trials are done to find out if new cancer treatments are safe and effective or better than the standard treatment.

Many of today's standard treatments for cancer are based on earlier clinical trials. Patients who take part in a clinical trial may receive the standard treatment or be among the first to receive a new treatment.

Patients who take part in clinical trials also help improve the way cancer will be treated in the future. Even when clinical trials do not lead to effective new treatments, they often answer important questions and help move research forward.

Patients can enter clinical trials before, during, or after starting their cancer treatment.

Some clinical trials only include patients who have not yet received treatment. Other trials test treatments for patients whose cancer has not gotten better. There are also clinical trials that test new ways to stop cancer from recurring (coming back) or reduce the side effects of cancer treatment.

Clinical trials are taking place in many parts of the country.

Follow-up tests may be needed.

Some of the tests that were done to diagnose the cancer or to find out the stage of the cancer may be repeated. Some tests will be repeated in order to see how well the treatment is working. Decisions about whether to continue, change, or stop treatment may be based on the results of these tests.

Chapter 31

Vulvar Cancer

Chapter Contents

Section 31.1

General Information about Vulvar Cancer

Text in this section is excerpted from "Vulvar Cancer Treatment
(PDQ®)," National Cancer Institute (NCI), July 30, 2015.

*Vulvar cancer is a rare disease in which malignant (cancer)
cells form in the tissues of the vulva.*

Vulvar cancer forms in a woman's external genitalia. The vulva
includes:

- Inner and outer lips of the vagina.

- Clitoris (sensitive tissue between the lips).

- Opening of the vagina and its glands.

- Mons pubis (the rounded area in front of the pubic bones that
becomes covered with hair at puberty).

- Perineum (the area between the vulva and the anus).

Vulvar cancer most often affects the outer vaginal lips. Less often,
cancer affects the inner vaginal lips, clitoris, or vaginal glands.

Vulvar cancer usually forms slowly over a number of years. Abnormal
cells can grow on the surface of the vulvar skin for a long time. This condition is called vulvar intraepithelial neoplasia (VIN). Because it is possible
for VIN to become vulvar cancer, it is very important to get treatment.

*Having vulvar intraepithelial neoplasia or HPV infection
can affect the risk of vulvar cancer.*

Anything that increases your risk of getting a disease is called a
risk factor. Having a risk factor does not mean that you will get cancer; not having risk factors doesn't mean that you will not get cancer.
Talk with your doctor if you think you may be at risk. Risk factors for
vulvar cancer include the following:

- Having vulvar intraepithelial neoplasia (VIN).

- *Having human papillomavirus* (HPV) infection.

- Having a history of genital warts.

Other possible risk factors include the following:

- Having many sexual partners.
- Having first sexual intercourse at a young age.
- Having a history of abnormal Pap tests (Pap smears).

Signs of vulvar cancer include bleeding or itching.

Vulvar cancer often does not cause early signs or symptoms. Signs and symptoms may be caused by vulvar cancer or by other conditions. Check with your doctor if you have any of the following:

- A lump or growth on the vulva.
- Changes in the vulvar skin, such as color changes or growths that look like a wart or ulcer.
- Itching in the vulvar area, that does not go away.
- Bleeding not related to menstruation (periods).
- Tenderness in the vulvar area.

Tests that examine the vulva are used to detect (find) and diagnose vulvar cancer.

The following tests and procedures may be used:

- **Physical exam and history** : An exam of the body to check general signs of health, including checking the vulva for signs of disease, such as lumps or anything else that seems unusual. A history of the patient's health habits and past illnesses and treatments will also be taken.
- **Biopsy** : The removal of samples of cells or tissues from the vulva so they can be viewed under a microscope by a pathologist to check for signs of cancer.

Certain factors affect prognosis (chance of recovery) and treatment options.

The prognosis (chance of recovery) and treatment options depend on the following:

- The stage of the cancer.
- The patient's age and general health.
- Whether the cancer has just been diagnosed or has recurred (come back).

Section 31.2

Stages of Vulvar Cancer

Text in this section is excerpted from "Vulvar Cancer Treatment
(PDQ®)," National Cancer Institute (NCI), July 30, 2015.

*After vulvar cancer has been diagnosed, tests are done to
find out if cancer cells have spread within the vulva or to
other parts of the body.*

The process used to find out if cancer has spread within the vulva
or to other parts of the body is called staging. The information gathered from the staging process determines the stage of the disease. It is
important to know the stage in order to plan treatment. The following
tests and procedures may be used in the staging process:

- **Pelvic exam** : An exam of the vagina, cervix, uterus, fallopian
  tubes, ovaries, and rectum. A speculum is inserted into the
  vagina and the doctor or nurse looks at the vagina and cervix
  for signs of disease. A Pap test of the cervix is usually done.
  The doctor or nurse also inserts one or two lubricated, gloved
  fingers of one hand into the vagina and places the other hand
  over the lower abdomen to feel the size, shape, and position of
  the uterus and ovaries. The doctor or nurse also inserts a lubricated, gloved finger into the rectum to feel for lumps or abnormal areas.

- **Colposcopy** : A procedure in which a colposcope (a lighted,
  magnifying instrument) is used to check the vagina and cervix for abnormal areas. Tissue samples may be taken using a
  curette (spoon-shaped instrument) or a brush and checked under
  a microscope for signs of disease.

- **Cystoscopy** : A procedure to look inside the bladder and urethra to check for abnormal areas. A cystoscope is inserted
  through the urethra into the bladder. A cystoscope is a thin,
  tube-like instrument with a light and a lens for viewing. It may
  also have a tool to remove tissue samples, which are checked
  under a microscope for signs of cancer.

- **Proctoscopy :** A procedure to look inside the rectum and anus to check for abnormal areas. A proctoscope is inserted into the anus and rectum. A proctoscope is a thin, tube-like instrument with a light and a lens for viewing. It may also have a tool to remove tissue samples, which are checked under a microscope for signs of cancer.

- **X-rays :** An x-ray is a type of energy beam that can go through the body and onto film, making a picture of areas inside the body. To stage vulvar cancer, x-rays may be taken of the organs and bones inside the chest, and the pelvic bones.

- **Intravenous pyelogram (IVP):** A series of x-rays of the kidneys, ureters, and bladder to find out if cancer has spread to these organs. A contrast dye is injected into a vein. As the contrast dye moves through the kidneys, ureters and bladder, x-rays are taken to see if there are any blockages. This procedure is also called intravenous urography.

- **CT scan (CAT scan):** A procedure that makes a series of detailed pictures of areas inside the body, taken from different angles. The pictures are made by a computer linked to an x-ray machine. A dye may be injected into a vein or swallowed to help the organs or tissues show up more clearly. This procedure is also called computed tomography, computerized tomography, or computerized axial tomography.

- **MRI (magnetic resonance imaging):** A procedure that uses a magnet, radio waves, and a computer to make a series of detailed pictures of areas inside the body. This procedure is also called nuclear magnetic resonance imaging (NMRI).

- **PET scan (positron emission tomography scan):** A procedure to find malignant tumor cells in the body. A small amount of radioactive glucose (sugar) is injected into a vein. The PET scanner rotates around the body and makes a picture of where glucose is being used in the body. Malignant tumor cells show up brighter in the picture because they are more active and take up more glucose than normal cells do.

- **Sentinel lymph node biopsy :** The removal of the sentinel lymph node during surgery. The sentinel lymph node is the first lymph node to receive lymphatic drainage from a tumor. It is the first lymph node the cancer is likely to spread to from the tumor. A radioactive substance and/or blue dye is injected near the tumor. The substance or dye flows through the lymph ducts to the lymph nodes. The first lymph node to receive the substance or dye is removed. A pathologist views the tissue under a microscope to look for cancer cells. If cancer cells are not found, it may not be necessary to remove more lymph nodes. Sentinel lymph node biopsy may be done during surgery to remove the tumor for early-stage vulvar cancer.

There are three ways that cancer spreads in the body.

Cancer can spread through tissue, the lymph system, and the blood:

- Tissue. The cancer spreads from where it began by growing into nearby areas.
- Lymph system. The cancer spreads from where it began by getting into the lymph system. The cancer travels through the lymph vessels to other parts of the body.
- Blood. The cancer spreads from where it began by getting into the blood. The cancer travels through the blood vessels to other parts of the body.

Cancer may spread from where it began to other parts of the body.

When cancer spreads to another part of the body, it is called metastasis. Cancer cells break away from where they began (the primary tumor) and travel through the lymph system or blood.

- Lymph system. The cancer gets into the lymph system, travels through the lymph vessels, and forms a tumor (metastatic tumor) in another part of the body.
- Blood. The cancer gets into the blood, travels through the blood vessels, and forms a tumor (metastatic tumor) in another part of the body.

The metastatic tumor is the same type of cancer as the primary tumor. For example, if vulvar cancer spreads to the lung, the cancer cells in the lung are actually vulvar cancer cells. The disease is metastatic vulvar cancer, not lung cancer.

In vulvar intraepithelial neoplasia (VIN), abnormal cells are found on the surface of the vulvar skin.

These abnormal cells are not cancer. Vulvar intraepithelial neoplasia (VIN) may become cancer and spread into nearby tissue. VIN is sometimes called stage 0 or carcinoma in situ.

The following stages are used for vulvar cancer:

The following stages are used for vulvar cancer:

Stage I

In stage I, cancer has formed. The tumor is found only in the vulva or perineum (area between the rectum and the vagina). Stage I is divided into stages IA and IB.

- In stage IA, the tumor is 2 centimeters or smaller and has spread 1 millimeter or less into the tissue of the vulva. Cancer has not spread to the lymph nodes.

- In stage IB, the tumor is larger than 2 centimeters or has spread more than 1 millimeter into the tissue of the vulva. Cancer has not spread to the lymph nodes.

Stage II

In stage II, the tumor is any size and has spread into the lower part of the urethra, the lower part of the vagina, or the anus. Cancer has not spread to the lymph nodes.

Stage III

In stage III, the tumor is any size and may have spread into the lower part of the urethra, the lower part of the vagina, or the anus. Cancer has spread to one or more nearby lymph nodes. Stage III is divided into stages IIIA, IIIB, and IIIC.

- In stage IIIA, cancer is found in 1 or 2 lymph nodes that are smaller than 5 millimeters or in one lymph node that is 5 millimeters or larger.

- In stage IIIB, cancer is found in 2 or more lymph nodes that are 5 millimeters or larger, or in 3 or more lymph nodes that are smaller than 5 millimeters.

- In stage IIIC, cancer is found in lymph nodes and has spread to the outside surface of the lymph nodes.

Stage IV

In stage IV, the tumor has spread into the upper part of the urethra, the upper part of the vagina, or to other parts of the body. Stage IV is divided into stages IVA and IVB.

- In stage IVA:
- cancer has spread into the lining of the upper urethra, the upper vagina, the bladder, or the rectum, or has attached to the pelvic bone; or

- cancer has spread to nearby lymph nodes and the lymph nodes are not moveable or have formed an ulcer.

- In stage IVB, cancer has spread to lymph nodes in the pelvis or to other parts of the body.

Section 31.3

Treatment Options for Vulvar Sarcoma

Text in this section is excerpted from "Vulvar Cancer Treatment (PDQ®)," National Cancer Institute (NCI), July 30, 2015.

There are different types of treatment for patients with vulvar cancer.

Different types of treatments are available for patients with vulvar cancer. Some treatments are standard (the currently used treatment), and some are being tested in clinical trials. A treatment clinical trial is a research study meant to help improve current treatments or obtain information on new treatments for patients with cancer. When clinical trials show that a new treatment is better than the standard treatment, the new treatment may become the standard treatment. Patients may want to think about taking part in a clinical trial. Some clinical trials are open only to patients who have not started treatment.

Four types of standard treatment are used:

Surgery

Surgery is the most common treatment for vulvar cancer. The goal of surgery is to remove all the cancer without any loss of the woman's sexual function. One of the following types of surgery may be done:

- Laser surgery: A surgical procedure that uses a laser beam (a narrow beam of intense light) as a knife to make bloodless cuts in tissue or to remove a surface lesion such as a tumor.

- Wide local excision: A surgical procedure to remove the cancer and some of the normal tissue around the cancer.

- Radical local excision: A surgical procedure to remove the cancer and a large amount of normal tissue around it. Nearby lymph nodes in the groin may also be removed.

- Ultrasound surgical aspiration (USA): A surgical procedure to break the tumor up into small pieces using very fine vibrations. The small pieces of tumor are washed away and removed by suction. This procedure causes less damage to nearby tissue.

- Vulvectomy: A surgical procedure to remove part or all of the vulva:

- Skinning vulvectomy: The top layer of vulvar skin where the cancer is found is removed. Skin grafts from other parts of the body may be needed to cover the area where the skin was removed.

- Modified radical vulvectomy: Surgery to remove part of the vulva. Nearby lymph nodes may also be removed.

- Radical vulvectomy: Surgery to remove the entire vulva. Nearby lymph nodes are also removed.

- Pelvic exenteration: A surgical procedure to remove the lower colon, rectum, and bladder. The cervix, vagina, ovaries, and nearby lymph nodes are also removed. Artificial openings (stoma) are made for urine and stool to flow from the body into a collection bag.

Even if the doctor removes all the cancer that can be seen at the time of the surgery, some patients may have chemotherapy or radiation therapy after surgery to kill any cancer cells that are left. Treatment given after the surgery, to lower the risk that the cancer will come back, is called adjuvant therapy.

Radiation therapy

Radiation therapy is a cancer treatment that uses high-energy x-rays or other types of radiation to kill cancer cells. There are two types of radiation therapy. External radiation therapy uses a machine outside the body to send radiation toward the cancer. Internal radiation therapy uses a radioactive substance sealed in needles, seeds, wires, or catheters that are placed directly into or near the cancer. The way the radiation therapy is given depends on the type and stage of the cancer being treated.

Chemotherapy

Chemotherapy is a cancer treatment that uses drugs to stop the growth of cancer cells, either by killing the cells or by stopping the cells from dividing. When chemotherapy is taken by mouth or injected into a vein or muscle, the drugs enter the bloodstream and can reach cancer cells throughout the body (systemic chemotherapy). When chemotherapy is placed directly into the cerebrospinal fluid, an organ, a body cavity such as the abdomen, or onto the skin, the drugs mainly affect cancer cells in those areas (regional chemotherapy). The way the chemotherapy is given depends on the type and stage of the cancer being treated.

Topical chemotherapy for vulvar cancer may be applied to the skin in a cream or lotion.

Biologic therapy

Biologic therapy is a treatment that uses the patient's immune system to fight cancer. Substances made by the body or made in a laboratory are used to boost, direct, or restore the body's natural defenses against cancer. This type of cancer treatment is also called biotherapy or immunotherapy.

Imiquimod is a biologic therapy that may be used to treat vulvar lesions and is applied to the skin in a cream.

Patients may want to think about taking part in a clinical trial.

For some patients, taking part in a clinical trial may be the best treatment choice. Clinical trials are part of the cancer research process. Clinical trials are done to find out if new cancer treatments are safe and effective or better than the standard treatment.

Many of today's standard treatments for cancer are based on earlier clinical trials. Patients who take part in a clinical trial may receive the standard treatment or be among the first to receive a new treatment.

Patients who take part in clinical trials also help improve the way cancer will be treated in the future. Even when clinical trials do not lead to effective new treatments, they often answer important questions and help move research forward.

Patients can enter clinical trials before, during, or after starting their cancer treatment.

Some clinical trials only include patients who have not yet received treatment. Other trials test treatments for patients whose cancer has not gotten better. There are also clinical trials that test new ways to stop cancer from recurring (coming back) or reduce the side effects of cancer treatment.

Clinical trials are taking place in many parts of the country.

Follow-up tests may be needed.

Some of the tests that were done to diagnose the cancer or to find out the stage of the cancer may be repeated. Some tests will be repeated in order to see how well the treatment is working. Decisions about whether to continue, change, or stop treatment may be based on the results of these tests.

Some of the tests will continue to be done from time to time after treatment has ended. The results of these tests can show if your condition has changed or if the cancer has recurred (come back). These tests are sometimes called follow-up tests or check-ups.

It is important to have regular follow-up exams to check for recurrent vulvar cancer.

Part Five

Other Cancers of Special Concern to Women

Chapter 32

Anal Cancer

Chapter Contents

419

Section 32.1

General Information about Anal Cell Cancer

Text in this section is excerpted from "Anal Cancer Treatment,"
National Cancer Institute (NCI), May 12, 2015.

*Anal cancer is a disease in which malignant (cancer) cells
form in the tissues of the anus.*

The anus is the end of the large intestine, below the rectum, through
which stool (solid waste) leaves the body. The anus is formed partly from
the outer skin layers of the body and partly from the intestine. Two ring-
like muscles, called sphincter muscles, open and close the anal opening
and let stool pass out of the body. The anal canal, the part of the anus
between the rectum and the anal opening, is about 1-1½ inches long.

The skin around the outside of the anus is called the perianal area.
Tumors in this area are skin tumors, not anal cancer.

Being infected with the **human papillomavirus** *(HPV)*
increases the risk of developing anal cancer.

Risk factors include the following:

- Being infected with *human papillomavirus* (HPV).
- Having many sexual partners.
- Having receptive anal intercourse (anal sex).
- Being older than 50 years.
- Frequent anal redness, swelling, and soreness.
- Having anal fistulas (abnormal openings).
- Smoking cigarettes.

*Signs of anal cancer include bleeding from the anus or rec-
tum or a lump near the anus.*

These and other signs and symptoms may be caused by anal cancer
or by other conditions. Check with your doctor if you have any of the
following:

- Bleeding from the anus or rectum.

- Pain or pressure in the area around the anus.

- Itching or discharge from the anus.

- A lump near the anus.

- A change in bowel habits.

Tests that examine the rectum and anus are used to detect (find) and diagnose anal cancer.

The following tests and procedures may be used:

- **Physical exam and history**: An exam of the body to check general signs of health, including checking for signs of disease, such as lumps or anything else that seems unusual. A history of the patient's health habits and past illnesses and treatments will also be taken.

- **Digital rectal examination (DRE)**: An exam of the anus and rectum. The doctor or nurse inserts a lubricated, gloved finger into the lower part of the rectum to feel for lumps or anything else that seems unusual.

- **Anoscopy**: An exam of the anus and lower rectum using a short, lighted tube called an anoscope.

- **Proctoscopy**: An exam of the rectum using a short, lighted tube called a proctoscope.

- **Endo-anal or endorectal ultrasound:** A procedure in which an ultrasound transducer (probe) is inserted into the anus or rectum and used to bounce high-energy sound waves (ultrasound) off internal tissues or organs and make echoes. The echoes form a picture of body tissues called a sonogram.

- **Biopsy**: The removal of cells or tissues so they can be viewed under a microscope by a pathologist to check for signs of cancer. If an abnormal area is seen during the anoscopy, a biopsy may be done at that time.

Certain factors affect the prognosis (chance of recovery) and treatment options.

The prognosis (chance of recovery) depends on the following:

- The size of the tumor.

- Where the tumor is in the anus.

- Whether the cancer has spread to the lymph nodes.

The treatment options depend on the following:

- The stage of the cancer.

- Where the tumor is in the anus.

- Whether the patient has *human immunodeficiency virus* (HIV).

- Whether cancer remains after initial treatment or has recurred.

Section 32.2

Stages of Anal Cell Cancer

Text in this section is excerpted from "Anal Cancer Treatment,"
National Cancer Institute (NCI), May 12, 2015.

After anal cancer has been diagnosed, tests are done to find out if cancer cells have spread within the anus or to other parts of the body.

The process used to find out if cancer has spread within the anus or to other parts of the body is called staging. The information gathered from the staging process determines the stage of the disease. It is important to know the stage in order to plan treatment. The following tests may be used in the staging process:

- **CT scan (CAT scan)**: A procedure that makes a series of detailed pictures of areas inside the body, such as the abdomen or chest, taken from different angles. The pictures are made by a computer linked to an x-ray machine. A dye may be injected into a vein or swallowed to help the organs or tissues show up more clearly. This procedure is also called computed tomography, computerized tomography, or computerized axial tomography. For anal cancer, a CT scan of the pelvis and abdomen may be done.

- **Chest x-ray**: An x-ray of the organs and bones inside the chest. An x-ray is a type of energy beam that can go through the body and onto film, making a picture of areas inside the body.

- **MRI (magnetic resonance imaging)**: A procedure that uses a magnet, radio waves, and a computer to make a series of detailed pictures of areas inside the body. This procedure is also called nuclear magnetic resonance imaging (NMRI).

- **PET scan (positron emission tomography scan)**: A procedure to find malignant tumor cells in the body. A small amount of radioactive glucose (sugar) is injected into a vein. The PET scanner rotates around the body and makes a picture of where glucose is being used in the body. Malignant tumor cells show up brighter in the picture because they are more active and take up more glucose than normal cells do.

There are three ways that cancer spreads in the body.

Cancer can spread through tissue, the lymph system, and the blood:

- Tissue. The cancer spreads from where it began by growing into nearby areas.

- Lymph system. The cancer spreads from where it began by getting into the lymph system. The cancer travels through the lymph vessels to other parts of the body.

- Blood. The cancer spreads from where it began by getting into the blood. The cancer travels through the blood vessels to other parts of the body.

Cancer may spread from where it began to other parts of the body.

When cancer spreads to another part of the body, it is called metastasis. Cancer cells break away from where they began (the primary tumor) and travel through the lymph system or blood.

- Lymph system. The cancer gets into the lymph system, travels through the lymph vessels, and forms a tumor (metastatic tumor) in another part of the body.

- Blood. The cancer gets into the blood, travels through the blood vessels, and forms a tumor (metastatic tumor) in another part of the body.

The metastatic tumor is the same type of cancer as the primary tumor. For example, if anal cancer spreads to the lung, the cancer cells in the lung are actually anal cancer cells. The disease is metastatic anal cancer, not lung cancer.

The following stages are used for anal cancer:

Stage 0 (Carcinoma in Situ)

In stage 0, abnormal cells are found in the innermost lining of the anus. These abnormal cells may become cancer and spread into nearby normal tissue. Stage 0 is also called carcinoma in situ.

Stage I

In stage I, cancer has formed and the tumor is 2 centimeters or smaller.

Stage II

In stage II, the tumor is larger than 2 centimeters.

Stage IIIA

In stage IIIA, the tumor may be any size and has spread to either:

- lymph nodes near the rectum; or
- nearby organs, such as the vagina, urethra, and bladder.

Stage IIIB

In stage IIIB, the tumor may be any size and has spread:

- to nearby organs and to lymph nodes near the rectum; or
- to lymph nodes on one side of the pelvis and/or groin, and may have spread to nearby organs; or
- to lymph nodes near the rectum and in the groin, and/or to lymph nodes on both sides of the pelvis and/or groin, and may have spread to nearby organs.

Stage IV

In stage IV, the tumor may be any size and cancer may have spread to lymph nodes or nearby organs and has spread to distant parts of the body.

Section 32.3

Treatment Options for Anal Cancer

Text in this section is excerpted from "Anal Cancer Treatment,"
National Cancer Institute (NCI), May 12, 2015.

There are different types of treatment for patients with anal cancer.

Different types of treatments are available for patients with anal cancer. Some treatments are standard (the currently used treatment), and some are being tested in clinical trials. A treatment clinical trial is a research study meant to help improve current treatments or obtain information on new treatments for patients with cancer. When clinical trials show that a new treatment is better than the standard treatment, the new treatment may become the standard treatment. Patients may want to think about taking part in a clinical trial. Some clinical trials are open only to patients who have not started treatment.

Three types of standard treatment are used:

Radiation therapy

Radiation therapy is a cancer treatment that uses high-energy x-rays or other types of radiation to kill cancer cells. There are two types of radiation therapy. External radiation therapy uses a machine outside the body to send radiation toward the cancer. Internal radiation therapy uses a radioactive substance sealed in needles, seeds, wires, or catheters that are placed directly into or near the cancer. The way the radiation therapy is given depends on the type and stage of the cancer being treated.

Chemotherapy

Chemotherapy is a cancer treatment that uses drugs to stop the growth of cancer cells, either by killing the cells or by stopping the cells from dividing. When chemotherapy is taken by mouth or injected into a vein or muscle, the drugs enter the bloodstream and can reach cancer cells throughout the body (systemic chemotherapy). When chemotherapy is placed directly into the cerebrospinal fluid, an organ, or a body cavity such as the abdomen, the drugs mainly affect cancer cells in those areas (regional chemotherapy). The way the chemotherapy is given depends on the type and stage of the cancer being treated.

Surgery

- Local resection: A surgical procedure in which the tumor is cut from the anus along with some of the healthy tissue around it. Local resection may be used if the cancer is small and has not spread. This procedure may save the sphincter muscles so the patient can still control bowel movements. Tumors that form in the lower part of the anus can often be removed with local resection.

- Abdominoperineal resection: A surgical procedure in which the anus, the rectum, and part of the sigmoid colon are removed through an incision made in the abdomen. The doctor sews the end of the intestine to an opening, called a stoma, made in the surface of the abdomen so body waste can be collected in a disposable bag outside of the body. This is called a colostomy. Lymph nodes that contain cancer may also be removed during this operation.

Having the **human immunodeficiency virus** *can affect treatment of anal cancer.*

Cancer therapy can further damage the already weakened immune systems of patients who have the *human immunodeficiency virus* (HIV). For this reason, patients who have anal cancer and HIV are usually treated with lower doses of anticancer drugs and radiation than patients who do not have HIV.

New types of treatment are being tested in clinical trials.

Radiosensitizers

Radiosensitizers are drugs that make tumor cells more sensitive to radiation therapy. Combining radiation therapy with radiosensitizers may kill more tumor cells.

Patients may want to think about taking part in a clinical trial.

For some patients, taking part in a clinical trial may be the best treatment choice. Clinical trials are part of the cancer research process.

Clinical trials are done to find out if new cancer treatments are safe and effective or better than the standard treatment.

Many of today's standard treatments for cancer are based on earlier clinical trials. Patients who take part in a clinical trial may receive the standard treatment or be among the first to receive a new treatment.

Patients who take part in clinical trials also help improve the way cancer will be treated in the future. Even when clinical trials do not lead to effective new treatments, they often answer important questions and help move research forward.

Patients can enter clinical trials before, during, or after starting their cancer treatment.

Some clinical trials only include patients who have not yet received treatment. Other trials test treatments for patients whose cancer has not gotten better. There are also clinical trials that test new ways to stop cancer from recurring (coming back) or reduce the side effects of cancer treatment.

Clinical trials are taking place in many parts of the country.

Follow-up tests may be needed.

Some of the tests that were done to diagnose the cancer or to find out the stage of the cancer may be repeated. Some tests will be repeated in order to see how well the treatment is working. Decisions about whether to continue, change, or stop treatment may be based on the results of these tests.

Some of the tests will continue to be done from time to time after treatment has ended. The results of these tests can show if your condition has changed or if the disease has recurred (come back). These tests are sometimes called follow-up tests or check-ups.

Chapter 33

Bladder Cancer

Chapter Contents

Section 33.1

General Information about Bladder Cancer

Text in this section is excerpted from "Bladder Cancer Treatment,"
National Cancer Institute (NCI), July 1, 2015.

*Bladder cancer is a disease in which malignant (cancer)
cells form in the tissues of the bladder.*

The bladder is a hollow organ in the lower part of the abdomen. It
is shaped like a small balloon and has a muscular wall that allows it
to get larger or smaller to store urine made by the kidneys. There are
two kidneys, one on each side of the backbone, above the waist. Tiny
tubules in the kidneys filter and clean the blood. They take out waste
products and make urine. The urine passes from each kidney through a
long tube called a ureter into the bladder. The bladder holds the urine
until it passes through the urethra and leaves the body.

There are three types of bladder cancer that begin in cells in the
lining of the bladder. These cancers are named for the type of cells that
become malignant (cancerous):

- Transitional cell carcinoma: Cancer that begins in cells in the
  innermost tissue layer of the bladder. These cells are able to
  stretch when the bladder is full and shrink when it is emptied.
  Most bladder cancers begin in the transitional cells. Transitional
  cell carcinoma can be low-grade or high-grade:

  - Low-grade transitional cell carcinoma often recurs (comes
    back) after treatment, but rarely spreads into the muscle
    layer of the bladder or to other parts of the body.

  - High-grade transitional cell carcinoma often recurs (comes
    back) after treatment and often spreads into the muscle layer
    of the bladder, to other parts of the body, and to lymph nodes.
    Almost all deaths from bladder cancer are due to high-grade
    disease.

- Squamous cell carcinoma: Cancer that begins in squamous cells,
  which are thin, flat cells that may form in the bladder after long-
  term infection or irritation.

- Adenocarcinoma: Cancer that begins in glandular (secretory) cells that are found in the lining of the bladder. This is a very rare type of bladder cancer.

Cancer that is in the lining of the bladder is called superficial bladder cancer. Cancer that has spread through the lining of the bladder and invades the muscle wall of the bladder or has spread to nearby organs and lymph nodes is called invasive bladder cancer.

Smoking can affect the risk of bladder cancer.

Anything that increases your chance of getting a disease is called a risk factor. Having a risk factor does not mean that you will get cancer; not having risk factors doesn't mean that you will not get cancer. Talk to your doctor if you think you may be at risk for bladder cancer.

Other risk factors for bladder cancer include:
- Using tobacco, especially smoking cigarettes.
- Having a family history of bladder cancer.
- Having certain changes in the genes that are linked to bladder cancer.
- Being exposed to paints, dyes, metals, or petroleum products in the workplace.
- Past treatment with radiation therapy to the pelvis or with certain anticancer drugs, such as cyclophosphamide or ifosfamide.
- Taking Aristolochia fangchi, a Chinese herb.
- Drinking water from a well that has high levels of arsenic.
- Drinking water that has been treated with chlorine.
- Having a history of bladder infections, including bladder infections caused by Schistosoma haematobium.
- Using urinary catheters for a long time.

Older age is a risk factor for most cancers. The chance of getting cancer increases as you get older.

Signs and symptoms of bladder cancer include blood in the urine and pain during urination.

These and other signs and symptoms may be caused by bladder cancer or by other conditions. Check with your doctor if you have any of the following:

- Blood in the urine (slightly rusty to bright red in color).

- Frequent urination.
- Pain during urination.
- Lower back pain.

Tests that examine the urine and bladder are used to help detect (find) and diagnose bladder cancer.

The following tests and procedures may be used:

- **Physical exam and history:** An exam of the body to check general signs of health, including checking for signs of disease, such as lumps or anything else that seems unusual. A history of the patient's health habits and past illnesses and treatments will also be taken.
- **Internal exam:** An exam of the vagina and/or rectum. The doctor inserts lubricated, gloved fingers into the vagina and/or rectum to feel for lumps.
- **Urinalysis:** A test to check the color of urine and its contents, such as sugar, protein, red blood cells, and white blood cells.
- **Urine cytology:** A laboratory test in which a sample of urine is checked under a microscope for abnormal cells.
- **Cystoscopy:** A procedure to look inside the bladder and urethra to check for abnormal areas. A cystoscope is inserted through the urethra into the bladder. A cystoscope is a thin, tube-like instrument with a light and a lens for viewing. It may also have a tool to remove tissue samples, which are checked under a microscope for signs of cancer.
- **Intravenous pyelogram (IVP):** A series of x-rays of the kidneys, ureters, and bladder to find out if cancer is present in these organs. A contrast dye is injected into a vein. As the contrast dye moves through the kidneys, ureters, and bladder, x-rays are taken to see if there are any blockages.
- **Biopsy:** The removal of cells or tissues so they can be viewed under a microscope by a pathologist to check for signs of cancer. A biopsy for bladder cancer is usually done during cystoscopy. It may be possible to remove the entire tumor during biopsy.

Certain factors affect prognosis (chance of recovery) and treatment options.

The prognosis (chance of recovery) depends on the following:

- The stage of the cancer (whether it is superficial or invasive bladder cancer, and whether it has spread to other places in the body). Bladder cancer in the early stages can often be cured.

- The type of bladder cancer cells and how they look under a microscope.

- Whether there is carcinoma in situ in other parts of the bladder.

- The patient's age and general health.

If the cancer is superficial, prognosis also depends on the following:

- How many tumors there are.

- The size of the tumors.

- Whether the tumor has recurred (come back) after treatment.

Treatment options depend on the stage of bladder cancer.

Section 33.2

Stages of Bladder Cancer

Text in this section is excerpted from "Bladder Cancer Treatment,"
National Cancer Institute (NCI), July 1, 2015.

After bladder cancer has been diagnosed, tests are done to find out if cancer cells have spread within the bladder or to other parts of the body.

The process used to find out if cancer has spread within the bladder lining and muscle or to other parts of the body is called staging. The information gathered from the staging process determines the stage of the disease. It is important to know the stage in order to plan treatment. The following tests and procedures may be used in the staging process:

- **CT scan (CAT scan):** A procedure that makes a series of detailed pictures of areas inside the body, taken from different angles. The pictures are made by a computer linked to an x-ray machine. A dye may be injected into a vein or swallowed to help the organs or tissues show up more clearly. This procedure is also called computed tomography, computerized tomography, or computerized axial tomography. To stage bladder cancer, the CT scan may take pictures of the chest, abdomen, and pelvis.

- **MRI (magnetic resonance imaging):** A procedure that uses a magnet, radio waves, and a computer to make a series of detailed pictures of areas inside the body. This procedure is also called nuclear magnetic resonance imaging (NMRI).

- **Chest x-ray:** An x-ray of the organs and bones inside the chest. An x-ray is a type of energy beam that can go through the body and onto film, making a picture of areas inside the body.

- **Bone scan:** A procedure to check if there are rapidly dividing cells, such as cancer cells, in the bone. A very small amount of radioactive material is injected into a vein and travels through the bloodstream. The radioactive material collects in the bones and is detected by a scanner.

There are three ways that cancer spreads in the body.

Cancer can spread through tissue, the lymph system, and the blood:

- Tissue. The cancer spreads from where it began by growing into nearby areas.

- Lymph system. The cancer spreads from where it began by getting into the lymph system. The cancer travels through the lymph vessels to other parts of the body.

- Blood. The cancer spreads from where it began by getting into the blood. The cancer travels through the blood vessels to other parts of the body.

Cancer may spread from where it began to other parts of the body.

When cancer spreads to another part of the body, it is called metastasis. Cancer cells break away from where they began (the primary tumor) and travel through the lymph system or blood.

- Lymph system. The cancer gets into the lymph system, travels through the lymph vessels, and forms a tumor (metastatic tumor) in another part of the body.

- Blood. The cancer gets into the blood, travels through the blood vessels, and forms a tumor (metastatic tumor) in another part of the body.

The metastatic tumor is the same type of cancer as the primary tumor. For example, if bladder cancer spreads to the bone, the cancer cells in the bone are actually bladder cancer cells. The disease is metastatic bladder cancer, not bone cancer.

The following stages are used for bladder cancer:

Stage 0 (Papillary Carcinoma and Carcinoma in Situ)

In stage 0, abnormal cells are found in tissue lining the inside of the bladder. These abnormal cells may become cancer and spread into nearby normal tissue. Stage 0 is divided into stage 0a and stage 0is, depending on the type of the tumor:

- Stage 0a is also called papillary carcinoma, which may look like tiny mushrooms growing from the lining of the bladder.

- Stage 0is is also called carcinoma in situ, which is a flat tumor on the tissue lining the inside of the bladder.

Stage I

In stage I, cancer has formed and spread to the layer of connective tissue next to the inner lining of the bladder.

Stage II

In stage II, cancer has spread to the layers of muscle tissue of the bladder.

Stage III

In stage III, cancer has spread from the bladder to the layer of fat surrounding it and may have spread to the reproductive organs (prostate, seminal vesicles, uterus, or vagina).

Stage IV

In stage IV, one or more of the following is true:

- Cancer has spread from the bladder to the wall of the abdomen or pelvis.

- Cancer has spread to one or more lymph nodes.

- Cancer has spread to other parts of the body, such as the lung, bone, or liver.

Section 33.3

Treatment Options for Bladder Cancer

Text in this section is excerpted from "Bladder Cancer Treatment,"
National Cancer Institute (NCI), July 1, 2015.

There are different types of treatment for patients with bladder cancer.

Different types of treatment are available for patients with bladder
cancer. Some treatments are standard (the currently used treatment),
and some are being tested in clinical trials. A treatment clinical trial is
a research study meant to help improve current treatments or obtain
information on new treatments for patients with cancer. When clinical trials show that a new treatment is better than the standard
treatment, the new treatment may become the standard treatment.
Patients may want to think about taking part in a clinical trial. Some
clinical trials are open only to patients who have not started treatment.

Four types of standard treatment are used:

Surgery

One of the following types of surgery may be done:

- Transurethral resection (TUR) with fulguration: Surgery in
  which a cystoscope (a thin lighted tube) is inserted into the bladder through the urethra. A tool with a small wire loop on the
  end is then used to remove the cancer or to burn the tumor away
  with high-energy electricity. This is known as fulguration.

- Radical cystectomy: Surgery to remove the bladder and any
  lymph nodes and nearby organs that contain cancer. This surgery
  may be done when the bladder cancer invades the muscle wall,
  or when superficial cancer involves a large part of the bladder. In
  men, the nearby organs that are removed are the prostate and the
  seminal vesicles. In women, the uterus, the ovaries, and part of
  the vagina are removed. Sometimes, when the cancer has spread
  outside the bladder and cannot be completely removed, surgery to

remove only the bladder may be done to reduce urinary symptoms caused by the cancer. When the bladder must be removed, the surgeon creates another way for urine to leave the body.

- Partial cystectomy: Surgery to remove part of the bladder. This surgery may be done for patients who have a low-grade tumor that has invaded the wall of the bladder but is limited to one area of the bladder. Because only a part of the bladder is removed, patients are able to urinate normally after recovering from this surgery. This is also called segmental cystectomy.

- Urinary diversion: Surgery to make a new way for the body to store and pass urine.

Even if the doctor removes all the cancer that can be seen at the time of the surgery, some patients may be given chemotherapy after surgery to kill any cancer cells that are left. Treatment given after surgery, to lower the risk that the cancer will come back, is called adjuvant therapy.

Radiation therapy

Radiation therapy is a cancer treatment that uses high-energy x-rays or other types of radiation to kill cancer cells or keep them from growing. There are two types of radiation therapy. External radiation therapy uses a machine outside the body to send radiation toward the cancer. Internal radiation therapy uses a radioactive substance sealed in needles, seeds, wires, or catheters that are placed directly into or near the cancer. The way the radiation therapy is given depends on the type and stage of the cancer being treated.

Chemotherapy

Chemotherapy is a cancer treatment that uses drugs to stop the growth of cancer cells, either by killing the cells or by stopping them from dividing. When chemotherapy is taken by mouth or injected into a vein or muscle, the drugs enter the bloodstream and can reach cancer cells throughout the body (systemic chemotherapy). When chemotherapy is placed directly into the cerebrospinal fluid, an organ, or a body cavity such as the abdomen, the drugs mainly affect cancer cells in those areas (regional chemotherapy). For bladder cancer, regional chemotherapy may be intravesical (put into the bladder through a tube inserted into the urethra). The way the chemotherapy is given depends on the type and stage of the cancer being treated. Combination chemotherapy is treatment using more than one anticancer drug.

Biologic therapy

Biologic therapy is a treatment that uses the patient's immune system to fight cancer. Substances made by the body or made in a laboratory are used to boost, direct, or restore the body's natural defenses against cancer. This type of cancer treatment is also called biotherapy or immunotherapy.

Bladder cancer may be treated with an intravesical biologic therapy called BCG (bacillus Calmette-Guérin). The BCG is given in a solution that is placed directly into the bladder using a catheter (thin tube).

Patients may want to think about taking part in a clinical trial.

For some patients, taking part in a clinical trial may be the best treatment choice. Clinical trials are part of the cancer research process. Clinical trials are done to find out if new cancer treatments are safe and effective or better than the standard treatment.

Many of today's standard treatments for cancer are based on earlier clinical trials. Patients who take part in a clinical trial may receive the standard treatment or be among the first to receive a new treatment.

Patients who take part in clinical trials also help improve the way cancer will be treated in the future. Even when clinical trials do not lead to effective new treatments, they often answer important questions and help move research forward.

Patients can enter clinical trials before, during, or after starting their cancer treatment.

Some clinical trials only include patients who have not yet received treatment. Other trials test treatments for patients whose cancer has not gotten better. There are also clinical trials that test new ways to stop cancer from recurring (coming back) or reduce the side effects of cancer treatment.

Clinical trials are taking place in many parts of the country.

Follow-up tests may be needed.

Some of the tests that were done to diagnose the cancer or to find out the stage of the cancer may be repeated. Some tests will be repeated in order to see how well the treatment is working. Decisions about whether to continue, change, or stop treatment may be based on the results of these tests.

Some of the tests will continue to be done from time to time after treatment has ended. The results of these tests can show if your condition has changed or if the cancer has recurred (come back). These tests are sometimes called follow-up tests or check-ups.

Bladder cancer often recurs (comes back), even when the cancer is superficial. Surveillance of the urinary tract to check for recurrence is standard after a diagnosis of bladder cancer. Surveillance is closely watching a patient's condition but not giving any treatment unless there are changes in test results that show the condition is getting worse. During active surveillance, certain exams and tests are done on a regular schedule. Surveillance may include ureteroscopy and imaging tests.

Chapter 34

Colorectal Cancer

Chapter Contents

Section 34.1

General Information about Colon Cancer

Text in this section is excerpted from "Colon Cancer Treatment,"
National Cancer Institute (NCI), July 22, 2015.

Colon cancer is a disease in which malignant (cancer) cells form in the tissues of the colon.

The colon is part of the body's digestive system. The digestive system removes and processes nutrients (vitamins, minerals, carbohydrates, fats, proteins, and water) from foods and helps pass waste material out of the body. The digestive system is made up of the esophagus, stomach, and the small and large intestines. The colon (large bowel) is the first part of the large intestine and is about 5 feet long. Together, the rectum and anal canal make up the last part of the large intestine and are about 6-8 inches long. The anal canal ends at the anus (the opening of the large intestine to the outside of the body).

Gastrointestinal stromal tumors can occur in the colon.

Health history can affect the risk of developing colon cancer.

Anything that increases your chance of getting a disease is called a risk factor. Having a risk factor does not mean that you will get cancer; not having risk factors doesn't mean that you will not get cancer. Talk with your doctor if you think you may be at risk. Risk factors include the following:

- A family history of cancer of the colon or rectum.
- Certain hereditary conditions, such as familial adenomatous polyposis and hereditary nonpolyposis colon cancer (HNPCC; Lynch Syndrome).
- A history of ulcerative colitis (ulcers in the lining of the large intestine) or Crohn disease.
- A personal history of cancer of the colon, rectum, ovary, endometrium, or breast.
- A personal history of polyps (small areas of bulging tissue) in the colon or rectum.

Signs of colon cancer include blood in the stool or a change in bowel habits.

These and other signs and symptoms may be caused by colon cancer or by other conditions. Check with your doctor if you have any of the following:

- A change in bowel habits.
- Blood (either bright red or very dark) in the stool.
- Diarrhea, constipation, or feeling that the bowel does not empty all the way.
- Stools that are narrower than usual.
- Frequent gas pains, bloating, fullness, or cramps.
- Weight loss for no known reason.
- Feeling very tired.
- Vomiting.

Tests that examine the colon and rectum are used to detect (find) and diagnose colon cancer.

The following tests and procedures may be used:

- **Physical exam and history:** An exam of the body to check general signs of health, including checking for signs of disease, such as lumps or anything else that seems unusual. A history of the patient's health habits and past illnesses and treatments will also be taken.

- **Digital rectal exam:** An exam of the rectum. The doctor or nurse inserts a lubricated, gloved finger into the rectum to feel for lumps or anything else that seems unusual.

- **Fecal occult blood test :** A test to check stool (solid waste) for blood that can only be seen with a microscope. Small samples of stool are placed on special cards and returned to the doctor or laboratory for testing.

- **Barium enema :** A series of x-rays of the lower gastrointestinal tract. A liquid that contains barium (a silver-white metallic compound) is put into the rectum. The barium coats the lower gastrointestinal tract and x-rays are taken. This procedure is also called a lower GI series.

- **Sigmoidoscopy:** A procedure to look inside the rectum and sigmoid (lower) colon for polyps (small areas of bulging tissue), other abnormal areas, or cancer. A sigmoidoscope is inserted through the rectum into the sigmoid colon. A sigmoidoscope is a thin, tube-like instrument with a light and a lens for viewing. It may also have a tool to remove polyps or tissue samples, which are checked under a microscope for signs of cancer.

- **Colonoscopy:** A procedure to look inside the rectum and colon for polyps, abnormal areas, or cancer. A colonoscope is inserted through the rectum into the colon. A colonoscope is a thin, tube-like instrument with a light and a lens for viewing. It may also have a tool to remove polyps or tissue samples, which are checked under a microscope for signs of cancer.

- **Virtual colonoscopy:** A procedure that uses a series of x-rays called computed tomography to make a series of pictures of the colon. A computer puts the pictures together to create detailed images that may show polyps and anything else that seems unusual on the inside surface of the colon. This test is also called colonography or CT colonography.

- **Biopsy:** The removal of cells or tissues so they can be viewed under a microscope by a pathologist to check for signs of cancer.

Certain factors affect prognosis (chance of recovery) and treatment options.

The prognosis (chance of recovery) and treatment options depend on the following:

- The stage of the cancer (whether the cancer is in the inner lining of the colon only or has spread through the colon wall, or has spread to lymph nodes or other places in the body).
- Whether the cancer has blocked or made a hole in the colon.
- Whether there are any cancer cells left after surgery.
- Whether the cancer has recurred.
- The patient's general health.

The prognosis also depends on the blood levels of carcinoembryonic antigen (CEA) before treatment begins. CEA is a substance in the blood that may be increased when cancer is present.

Section 34.2

Stages of Colon Cancer

Text in this section is excerpted from "Colon Cancer Treatment,"
National Cancer Institute (NCI), July 22, 2015.

*After colon cancer has been diagnosed, tests are done to find
out if cancer cells have spread within the colon or to other
parts of the body.*

The process used to find out if cancer has spread within the colon
or to other parts of the body is called staging. The information gathered from the staging process determines the stage of the disease. It
is important to know the stage in order to plan treatment.

The following tests and procedures may be used in the staging
process:

- **CT scan (CAT scan):** A procedure that makes a series of
  detailed pictures of areas inside the body, such as the abdomen
  or chest, taken from different angles. The pictures are made by a
  computer linked to an x-ray machine. A dye may be injected into
  a vein or swallowed to help the organs or tissues show up more
  clearly. This procedure is also called computed tomography,
  computerized tomography, or computerized axial tomography.

- **MRI (magnetic resonance imaging):** A procedure that uses
  a magnet, radio waves, and a computer to make a series of
  detailed pictures of areas inside the colon. A substance called
  gadolinium is injected into the patient through a vein. The gadolinium collects around the cancer cells so they show up brighter
  in the picture. This procedure is also called nuclear magnetic
  resonance imaging (NMRI).

- **PET scan (positron emission tomography scan):** A procedure to find malignant tumor cells in the body. A small amount
  of radioactive glucose (sugar) is injected into a vein. The PET
  scanner rotates around the body and makes a picture of where
  glucose is being used in the body. Malignant tumor cells show up

445

brighter in the picture because they are more active and take up more glucose than normal cells do.

- **Chest x-ray:** An x-ray of the organs and bones inside the chest. An x-ray is a type of energy beam that can go through the body and onto film, making a picture of areas inside the body.

- **Surgery:** A procedure to remove the tumor and see how far it has spread through the colon.

- **Lymph node biopsy:** The removal of all or part of a lymph node. A pathologist views the tissue under a microscope to look for cancer cells.

- **Complete blood count (CBC):** A procedure in which a sample of blood is drawn and checked for the following:

- The number of red blood cells, white blood cells, and platelets.

- The amount of hemoglobin (the protein that carries oxygen) in the red blood cells.

- The portion of the blood sample made up of red blood cells.

- **Carcinoembryonic antigen (CEA) assay**: A test that measures the level of CEA in the blood. CEA is released into the bloodstream from both cancer cells and normal cells. When found in higher than normal amounts, it can be a sign of colon cancer or other conditions.

There are three ways that cancer spreads in the body.

Cancer can spread through tissue, the lymph system, and the blood:

- Tissue. The cancer spreads from where it began by growing into nearby areas.

- Lymph system. The cancer spreads from where it began by getting into the lymph system. The cancer travels through the lymph vessels to other parts of the body.

- Blood. The cancer spreads from where it began by getting into the blood. The cancer travels through the blood vessels to other parts of the body.

Cancer may spread from where it began to other parts of the body.

When cancer spreads to another part of the body, it is called metastasis. Cancer cells break away from where they began (the primary tumor) and travel through the lymph system or blood.

- Lymph system. The cancer gets into the lymph system, travels through the lymph vessels, and forms a tumor (metastatic tumor) in another part of the body.

- Blood. The cancer gets into the blood, travels through the blood vessels, and forms a tumor (metastatic tumor) in another part of the body.

The metastatic tumor is the same type of cancer as the primary tumor. For example, if colon cancer spreads to the lung, the cancer cells in the lung are actually colon cancer cells. The disease is metastatic colon cancer, not lung cancer.

The following stages are used for colon cancer:

Stage 0 (Carcinoma in Situ)

In stage 0, abnormal cells are found in the mucosa (innermost layer) of the colon wall. These abnormal cells may become cancer and spread. Stage 0 is also called carcinoma in situ.

Stage I

In stage I, cancer has formed in the mucosa (innermost layer) of the colon wall and has spread to the submucosa (layer of tissue under the mucosa). Cancer may have spread to the muscle layer of the colon wall.

Stage II

Stage II colon cancer is divided into stage IIA, stage IIB, and stage IIC.

- Stage IIA: Cancer has spread through the muscle layer of the colon wall to the serosa (outermost layer) of the colon wall.

- Stage IIB: Cancer has spread through the serosa (outermost layer) of the colon wall but has not spread to nearby organs.

- Stage IIC: Cancer has spread through the serosa (outermost layer) of the colon wall to nearby organs.

Stage III

Stage III colon cancer is divided into stage IIIA, stage IIIB, and stage IIIC.
In stage IIIA:

- Cancer has spread through the mucosa (innermost layer) of the colon wall to the submucosa (layer of tissue under the mucosa) and may have spread to the muscle layer of the colon wall. Cancer has spread to at least one but not more than 3 nearby lymph nodes or cancer cells have formed in tissues near the lymph nodes; or

- Cancer has spread through the mucosa (innermost layer) of the colon wall to the submucosa (layer of tissue under the mucosa). Cancer has spread to at least 4 but not more than 6 nearby lymph nodes.

In stage IIIB:

- Cancer has spread through the muscle layer of the colon wall to the serosa (outermost layer) of the colon wall or has spread through the serosa but not to nearby organs. Cancer has spread to at least one but not more than 3 nearby lymph nodes or cancer cells have formed in tissues near the lymph nodes; or

- Cancer has spread to the muscle layer of the colon wall or to the serosa (outermost layer) of the colon wall. Cancer has spread to at least 4 but not more than 6 nearby lymph nodes; or

- Cancer has spread through the mucosa (innermost layer) of the colon wall to the submucosa (layer of tissue under the mucosa) and may have spread to the muscle layer of the colon wall. Cancer has spread to 7 or more nearby lymph nodes.

In stage IIIC:

- Cancer has spread through the serosa (outermost layer) of the colon wall but has not spread to nearby organs. Cancer has spread to at least 4 but not more than 6 nearby lymph nodes; or

- Cancer has spread through the muscle layer of the colon wall to the serosa (outermost layer) of the colon wall or has spread through the serosa but has not spread to nearby organs. Cancer has spread to 7 or more nearby lymph nodes; or

- Cancer has spread through the serosa (outermost layer) of the colon wall and has spread to nearby organs. Cancer has spread to one or more nearby lymph nodes or cancer cells have formed in tissues near the lymph nodes.

Stage IV

Stage IV colon cancer is divided into stage IVA and stage IVB.

- Stage IVA: Cancer may have spread through the colon wall and may have spread to nearby organs or lymph nodes. Cancer has spread to one organ that is not near the colon, such as the liver, lung, or ovary, or to a distant lymph node.

- Stage IVB: Cancer may have spread through the colon wall and may have spread to nearby organs or lymph nodes. Cancer has spread to more than one organ that is not near the colon or into the lining of the abdominal wall.

Section 34.3

Treatment Options for Colon Cancer

Text in this section is excerpted from "Colon Cancer Treatment," National Cancer Institute (NCI), July 22, 2015.

There are different types of treatment for patients with colon cancer.

Different types of treatment are available for patients with colon cancer. Some treatments are standard (the currently used treatment), and some are being tested in clinical trials. A treatment clinical trial is a research study meant to help improve current treatments or obtain information on new treatments for patients with cancer. When clinical trials show that a new treatment is better than the standard treatment, the new treatment may become the standard treatment. Patients may want to think about taking part in a clinical trial. Some clinical trials are open only to patients who have not started treatment.

Six types of standard treatment are used:

Surgery

Surgery (removing the cancer in an operation) is the most common treatment for all stages of colon cancer. A doctor may remove the cancer using one of the following types of surgery:

- Local excision: If the cancer is found at a very early stage, the doctor may remove it without cutting through the abdominal wall. Instead, the doctor may put a tube with a cutting tool through the rectum into the colon and cut the cancer out. This is called a local excision. If the cancer is found in a polyp (a small bulging area of tissue), the operation is called a polypectomy.

- Resection of the colon with anastomosis: If the cancer is larger, the doctor will perform a partial colectomy (removing the cancer and a small amount of healthy tissue around it). The doctor may then perform an anastomosis (sewing the healthy parts of the colon together). The doctor will also usually remove lymph nodes near the colon and examine them under a microscope to see whether they contain cancer.

- Resection of the colon with colostomy: If the doctor is not able to sew the 2 ends of the colon back together, a stoma (an opening) is made on the outside of the body for waste to pass through. This procedure is called a colostomy. A bag is placed around the stoma to collect the waste. Sometimes the colostomy is needed only until the lower colon has healed, and then it can be reversed. If the doctor needs to remove the entire lower colon, however, the colostomy may be permanent.

Even if the doctor removes all the cancer that can be seen at the time of the operation, some patients may be given chemotherapy or radiation therapy after surgery to kill any cancer cells that are left. Treatment given after the surgery, to lower the risk that the cancer will come back, is called adjuvant therapy.

Radiofrequency ablation

Radiofrequency ablation is the use of a special probe with tiny electrodes that kill cancer cells. Sometimes the probe is inserted directly through the skin and only local anesthesia is needed. In other cases, the probe is inserted through an incision in the abdomen. This is done in the hospital with general anesthesia.

Cryosurgery

Cryosurgery is a treatment that uses an instrument to freeze and destroy abnormal tissue. This type of treatment is also called cryotherapy.

Chemotherapy

Chemotherapy is a cancer treatment that uses drugs to stop the growth of cancer cells, either by killing the cells or by stopping them from dividing. When chemotherapy is taken by mouth or injected into a vein or muscle, the drugs enter the bloodstream and can reach cancer cells throughout the body (systemic chemotherapy). When chemotherapy is placed directly into the cerebrospinal fluid, an organ, or a body cavity such as the abdomen, the drugs mainly affect cancer cells in those areas (regional chemotherapy).

Chemoembolization of the hepatic artery may be used to treat cancer that has spread to the liver. This involves blocking the hepatic artery (the main artery that supplies blood to the liver) and injecting anticancer drugs between the blockage and the liver. The liver's arteries then deliver the drugs throughout the liver. Only a small amount of the drug reaches other parts of the body. The blockage may be temporary or permanent, depending on what is used to block the artery. The liver continues to receive some blood from the hepatic portal vein, which carries blood from the stomach and intestine.

The way the chemotherapy is given depends on the type and stage of the cancer being treated.

Radiation therapy

Radiation therapy is a cancer treatment that uses high-energy x-rays or other types of radiation to kill cancer cells or keep them from growing. There are two types of radiation therapy. External radiation therapy uses a machine outside the body to send radiation toward the cancer. Internal radiation therapy uses a radioactive substance sealed in needles, seeds, wires, or catheters that are placed directly into or near the cancer. The way the radiation therapy is given depends on the type and stage of the cancer being treated.

Targeted therapy

Targeted therapy is a type of treatment that uses drugs or other substances to identify and attack specific cancer cells without harming normal cells.

Types of targeted therapies used in the treatment of colon cancer include the following:

- Monoclonal antibodies: Monoclonal antibodies are made in the laboratory from a single type of immune system cell. These antibodies can identify substances on cancer cells or normal substances that may help cancer cells grow. The antibodies attach to the substances and kill the cancer cells, block their growth, or keep them from spreading. Monoclonal antibodies are given by infusion. They may be used alone or to carry drugs, toxins, or radioactive material directly to cancer cells.

- Angiogenesis inhibitors: Angiogenesis inhibitors stop the growth of new blood vessels that tumors need to grow.

Patients may want to think about taking part in a clinical trial.

For some patients, taking part in a clinical trial may be the best treatment choice. Clinical trials are part of the cancer research process. Clinical trials are done to find out if new cancer treatments are safe and effective or better than the standard treatment.

Many of today's standard treatments for cancer are based on earlier clinical trials. Patients who take part in a clinical trial may receive the standard treatment or be among the first to receive a new treatment.

Patients who take part in clinical trials also help improve the way cancer will be treated in the future. Even when clinical trials do not lead to effective new treatments, they often answer important questions and help move research forward.

Patients can enter clinical trials before, during, or after starting their cancer treatment.

Some clinical trials only include patients who have not yet received treatment. Other trials test treatments for patients whose cancer has not gotten better. There are also clinical trials that test new ways to stop cancer from recurring (coming back) or reduce the side effects of cancer treatment.

Clinical trials are taking place in many parts of the country.

Follow-up tests may be needed.

Some of the tests that were done to diagnose the cancer or to find out the stage of the cancer may be repeated. Some tests will be repeated in order to see how well the treatment is working. Decisions about whether to continue, change, or stop treatment may be based on the results of these tests.

Some of the tests will continue to be done from time to time after treatment has ended. The results of these tests can show if your condition has changed or if the cancer has recurred (come back). These tests are sometimes called follow-up tests or check-ups.

Chapter 35

Esophageal Cancer

Chapter Contents

Section 35.1

General Information about Esophageal Cancer

Text in this section is excerpted from "Esophageal Cancer Treatment
(PDQ®)," National Cancer Institute (NCI), May 12, 2015.

Esophageal cancer is a disease in which malignant (cancer) cells form in the tissues of the esophagus.

The esophagus is the hollow, muscular tube that moves food and liquid from the throat to the stomach. The wall of the esophagus is made up of several layers of tissue, including mucous membrane, muscle, and connective tissue. Esophageal cancer starts at the inside lining of the esophagus and spreads outward through the other layers as it grows.

The two most common forms of esophageal cancer are named for the type of cells that become malignant (cancerous):

- Squamous cell carcinoma: Cancer that forms in squamous cells, the thin, flat cells lining the esophagus. This cancer is most often found in the upper and middle part of the esophagus, but can occur anywhere along the esophagus. This is also called epidermoid carcinoma.

- Adenocarcinoma: Cancer that begins in glandular (secretory) cells. Glandular cells in the lining of the esophagus produce and release fluids such as mucus. Adenocarcinomas usually form in the lower part of the esophagus, near the stomach.

Smoking, heavy alcohol use, and Barrett esophagus can increase the risk of developing esophageal cancer.

Anything that increases your risk of getting a disease is called a risk factor. Having a risk factor does not mean that you will get cancer; not having risk factors doesn't mean that you will not get cancer. Talk with your doctor if you think you may be at risk. Risk factors include the following:

- Tobacco use.

- Heavy alcohol use.

- Barrett esophagus: A condition in which the cells lining the lower part of the esophagus have changed or been replaced with abnormal cells that could lead to cancer of the esophagus. Gastric reflux (the backing up of stomach contents into the lower section of the esophagus) may irritate the esophagus and, over time, cause Barrett esophagus.
- Older age.
- Being male.
- Being African-American.

Signs and symptoms of esophageal cancer are weight loss and painful or difficult swallowing.

These and other signs and symptoms may be caused by esophageal cancer or by other conditions. Check with your doctor if you have any of the following:

- Painful or difficult swallowing.
- Weight loss.
- Pain behind the breastbone.
- Hoarseness and cough.
- Indigestion and heartburn.

Tests that examine the esophagus are used to detect (find) and diagnose esophageal cancer.

The following tests and procedures may be used:

- **Physical exam and history:** An exam of the body to check general signs of health, including checking for signs of disease, such as lumps or anything else that seems unusual. A history of the patient's health habits and past illnesses and treatments will also be taken.

- **Chest x-ray:** An x-ray of the organs and bones inside the chest. An x-ray is a type of energy beam that can go through the body and onto film, making a picture of areas inside the body.

- **Barium swallow:** A series of x-rays of the esophagus and stomach. The patient drinks a liquid that contains barium (a silver-white metallic compound). The liquid coats the esophagus and stomach, and x-rays are taken. This procedure is also called an upper GI series.

- **Esophagoscopy**: A procedure to look inside the esophagus to check for abnormal areas. An esophagoscope is inserted through the mouth or nose and down the throat into the esophagus. An esophagoscope is a thin, tube-like instrument with a light and a lens for viewing. It may also have a tool to remove tissue samples, which are checked under a microscope for signs of cancer. When the esophagus and stomach are looked at, it is called an upper endoscopy.

- **Biopsy:** The removal of cells or tissues so they can be viewed under a microscope by a pathologist to check for signs of cancer. The biopsy is usually done during an esophagoscopy. Sometimes a biopsy shows changes in the esophagus that are not cancer but may lead to cancer.

Certain factors affect prognosis (chance of recovery) and treatment options.

The prognosis (chance of recovery) and treatment options depend on the following:

- The stage of the cancer (whether it affects part of the esophagus, involves the whole esophagus, or has spread to other places in the body).

- The size of the tumor.

- The patient's general health.

When esophageal cancer is found very early, there is a better chance of recovery. Esophageal cancer is often in an advanced stage when it is diagnosed. At later stages, esophageal cancer can be treated but rarely can be cured. Taking part in one of the clinical trials being done to improve treatment should be considered.

Section 35.2

Stages of Esophageal Cancer

Text in this section is excerpted from "Esophageal Cancer Treatment (PDQ®)," National Cancer Institute (NCI), May 12, 2015.

After esophageal cancer has been diagnosed, tests are done to find out if cancer cells have spread within the esophagus or to other parts of the body.

The process used to find out if cancer cells have spread within the esophagus or to other parts of the body is called staging. The information gathered from the staging process determines the stage of the disease. It is important to know the stage in order to plan treatment. The following tests and procedures may be used in the staging process:

- **Bronchoscopy**: A procedure to look inside the trachea and large airways in the lung for abnormal areas. A bronchoscope is inserted through the nose or mouth into the trachea and lungs. A bronchoscope is a thin, tube-like instrument with a light and a lens for viewing. It may also have a tool to remove tissue samples, which are checked under a microscope for signs of cancer.

- **CT scan (CAT scan)**: A procedure that makes a series of detailed pictures of areas inside the body, such as the chest, abdomen, and pelvis, taken from different angles. The pictures are made by a computer linked to an x-ray machine. A dye may be injected into a vein or swallowed to help the organs or tissues show up more clearly. This procedure is also called computed tomography, computerized tomography, or computerized axial tomography.

- **PET scan (positron emission tomography scan)**: A procedure to find malignant tumor cells in the body. A small amount of radioactive glucose (sugar) is injected into a vein. The PET scanner rotates around the body and makes a picture of where glucose is being used in the body. Malignant tumor cells show up brighter in the picture because they are more active and take up more glucose than normal cells do. A PET scan and CT scan may be done at the same time. This is called a PET-CT.

- **MRI (magnetic resonance imaging)**: A procedure that uses a magnet, radio waves, and a computer to make a series of detailed pictures of areas inside the body. This procedure is also called nuclear magnetic resonance imaging (NMRI).

- **Endoscopic ultrasound (EUS)**: A procedure in which an endoscope is inserted into the body, usually through the mouth or rectum. An endoscope is a thin, tube-like instrument with a light and a lens for viewing. A probe at the end of the endoscope is used to bounce high-energy sound waves (ultrasound) off internal tissues or organs and make echoes. The echoes form a picture of body tissues called a sonogram. This procedure is also called endosonography.

- **Thoracoscopy**: A surgical procedure to look at the organs inside the chest to check for abnormal areas. An incision (cut) is made between two ribs and a thoracoscope is inserted into the chest. A thoracoscope is a thin, tube-like instrument with a light and a lens for viewing. It may also have a tool to remove tissue or lymph node samples, which are checked under a microscope for signs of cancer. In some cases, this procedure may be used to remove part of the esophagus or lung.

- **Laparoscopy**: A surgical procedure to look at the organs inside the abdomen to check for signs of disease. Small incisions (cuts) are made in the wall of the abdomen and a laparoscope (a thin, lighted tube) is inserted into one of the incisions. Other instruments may be inserted through the same or other incisions to perform procedures such as removing organs or taking tissue samples to be checked under a microscope for signs of disease.

There are three ways that cancer spreads in the body.

Cancer can spread through tissue, the lymph system, and the blood:

- Tissue. The cancer spreads from where it began by growing into nearby areas.

- Lymph system. The cancer spreads from where it began by getting into the lymph system. The cancer travels through the lymph vessels to other parts of the body.

- Blood. The cancer spreads from where it began by getting into the blood. The cancer travels through the blood vessels to other parts of the body.

Cancer may spread from where it began to other parts of the body.

When cancer spreads to another part of the body, it is called metastasis. Cancer cells break away from where they began (the primary tumor) and travel through the lymph system or blood.

- Lymph system. The cancer gets into the lymph system, travels through the lymph vessels, and forms a tumor (metastatic tumor) in another part of the body.

- Blood. The cancer gets into the blood, travels through the blood vessels, and forms a tumor (metastatic tumor) in another part of the body.

The metastatic tumor is the same type of cancer as the primary tumor. For example, if esophageal cancer spreads to the lung, the cancer cells in the lung are actually esophageal cancer cells. The disease is metastatic esophageal cancer, not lung cancer.

The grade of the tumor is also used to describe the cancer and plan treatment.

The grade of the tumor describes how abnormal the cancer cells look under a microscope and how quickly the tumor is likely to grow and spread. Grades 1 to 3 are used to describe esophageal cancer:

- In grade 1, the cancer cells look more like normal cells under a microscope and grow and spread more slowly than grade 2 and 3 cancer cells.

- In grade 2, the cancer cells look more abnormal under a microscope and grow and spread more quickly than grade 1 cancer cells.

- In grade 3, the cancer cells look more abnormal under a microscope and grow and spread more quickly than grade 1 and 2 cancer cells.

The following stages are used for squamous cell carcinoma of the esophagus:

Stage 0 (High-grade Dysplasia)

In stage 0, abnormal cells are found in the mucosa or submucosa layer of the esophagus wall. These abnormal cells may become cancer and spread into nearby normal tissue. Stage 0 is also called high-grade dysplasia.

Stage I squamous cell carcinoma of the esophagus

Stage I is divided into Stage IA and Stage IB, depending on where the cancer is found.

- Stage IA: Cancer has formed in the mucosa or submucosa layer of the esophagus wall. The cancer cells are grade 1. Grade 1 cancer cells look more like normal cells under a microscope and grow and spread more slowly than grade 2 and 3 cancer cells.

- Stage IB: Cancer has formed:
  - in the mucosa or submucosa layer of the esophagus wall. The cancer cells are grade 2 and 3; or
  - in the mucosa or submucosa layer and spread into the muscle layer or the connective tissue layer of the esophagus wall. The cancer cells are grade 1. The tumor is in the lower esophagus or it is not known where the tumor is.

Grade 1 cancer cells look more like normal cells under a microscope and grow and spread more slowly than grade 2 and 3 cancer cells.

Stage II squamous cell carcinoma of the esophagus

Stage II is divided into Stage IIA and Stage IIB, depending on where the cancer has spread.

- Stage IIA: Cancer has spread into the muscle layer of the esophagus wall. The cancer cells are grade 3. Grade 3 cancer cells look more abnormal under a microscope and grow and spread more quickly than grade 1 and 2 cancer cells.

  - Stage IIB: Cancer: has spread into the connective tissue layer of the esophagus wall; or
  - is in the mucosa or submucosa layer and may have spread into the muscle layer of the esophagus wall. Cancer is found in 1 or 2 lymph nodes near the tumor.

Stage III adenocarcinoma of the esophagus

Stage III is divided into Stage IIIA, Stage IIIB, and Stage IIIC, depending on where the cancer has spread.

- Stage IIIA: Cancer:
  - is in the mucosa or submucosa layer and may have spread into the muscle layer of the esophagus wall. Cancer is found in 3 to 6 lymph nodes near the tumor; or

- has spread into the connective tissue layer of the esophagus wall. Cancer is found in 1 or 2 lymph nodes near the tumor; or

- has spread into the diaphragm, pleura (tissue that covers the lungs and lines the inner wall of the chest cavity), or sac around the heart. The cancer can be removed by surgery.

- Stage IIIB: Cancer has spread into the connective tissue layer of the esophagus wall. Cancer is found in 3 to 6 lymph nodes near the tumor.

- Stage IIIC: Cancer has spread:

  - into the diaphragm, pleura (tissue that covers the lungs and lines the inner wall of the chest cavity), or sac around the heart. The cancer can be removed by surgery. Cancer is found in 1 to 6 lymph nodes near the tumor; or

  - into other nearby organs such as the aorta, trachea, or spine, and the cancer cannot be removed by surgery; or

  - to 7 or more lymph nodes near the tumor.

Stage IV adenocarcinoma of the esophagus

In Stage IV, cancer has spread to other parts of the body.

Section 35.3

Treatment Options for Esophageal Cancer

Text in this section is excerpted from "Esophageal Cancer Treatment (PDQ®)," National Cancer Institute (NCI), May 12, 2015.

There are different types of treatment for patients with esophageal cancer.

Different types of treatment are available for patients with esophageal cancer. Some treatments are standard (the currently used treatment), and some are being tested in clinical trials. A treatment clinical trial is a research study meant to help improve current treatments or obtain information on new treatments for patients with cancer. When clinical trials show that a new treatment is better than the standard treatment, the new treatment may become the standard treatment. Patients may want to think about taking part in a clinical trial. Some clinical trials are open only to patients who have not started treatment.

Patients have special nutritional needs during treatment for esophageal cancer.

Many people with esophageal cancer find it hard to eat because they have trouble swallowing. The esophagus may be narrowed by the tumor or as a side effect of treatment. Some patients may receive nutrients directly into a vein. Others may need a feeding tube (a flexible plastic tube that is passed through the nose or mouth into the stomach) until they are able to eat on their own.

Six types of standard treatment are used:

Surgery

Surgery is the most common treatment for cancer of the esophagus. Part of the esophagus may be removed in an operation called an esophagectomy.

The doctor will connect the remaining healthy part of the esophagus to the stomach so the patient can still swallow. A plastic tube or part of the intestine may be used to make the connection. Lymph nodes near the esophagus may also be removed and viewed under a microscope to see if they contain cancer. If the esophagus is partly blocked by the tumor, an expandable metal stent (tube) may be placed inside the esophagus to help keep it open.

Radiation therapy

Radiation therapy is a cancer treatment that uses high-energy x-rays or other types of radiation to kill cancer cells or keep them from growing. There are two types of radiation therapy. External radiation therapy uses a machine outside the body to send radiation toward the cancer. Internal radiation therapy uses a radioactive substance sealed in needles, seeds, wires, or catheters that are placed directly into or near the cancer. The way the radiation therapy is given depends on the type and stage of the cancer being treated.

A plastic tube may be inserted into the esophagus to keep it open during radiation therapy. This is called intraluminal intubation and dilation.

Chemotherapy

Chemotherapy is a cancer treatment that uses drugs to stop the growth of cancer cells, either by killing the cells or by stopping them from dividing. When chemotherapy is taken by mouth or injected into a vein or muscle, the drugs enter the bloodstream and can reach cancer cells throughout the body (systemic chemotherapy). When chemotherapy is placed directly into the cerebrospinal fluid, an organ, or a body cavity such as the abdomen, the drugs mainly affect cancer cells in those areas (regional chemotherapy). The way the chemotherapy is given depends on the type and stage of the cancer being treated.

Chemoradiation therapy

Chemoradiation therapy combines chemotherapy and radiation therapy to increase the effects of both.

Laser therapy

Laser therapy is a cancer treatment that uses a laser beam (a narrow beam of intense light) to kill cancer cells.

Electrocoagulation

Electrocoagulation is the use of an electric current to kill cancer cells.

Patients may want to think about taking part in a clinical trial.

For some patients, taking part in a clinical trial may be the best treatment choice. Clinical trials are part of the cancer research process. Clinical trials are done to find out if new cancer treatments are safe and effective or better than the standard treatment.

Many of today's standard treatments for cancer are based on earlier clinical trials. Patients who take part in a clinical trial may receive the standard treatment or be among the first to receive a new treatment.

Patients who take part in clinical trials also help improve the way cancer will be treated in the future. Even when clinical trials do not lead to effective new treatments, they often answer important questions and help move research forward.

Patients can enter clinical trials before, during, or after starting their cancer treatment.

Some clinical trials only include patients who have not yet received treatment. Other trials test treatments for patients whose cancer has not gotten better. There are also clinical trials that test new ways to stop cancer from recurring (coming back) or reduce the side effects of cancer treatment.

Clinical trials are taking place in many parts of the country.

Follow-up tests may be needed.

Some of the tests that were done to diagnose the cancer or to find out the stage of the cancer may be repeated. Some tests will be repeated in order to see how well the treatment is working. Decisions about whether to continue, change, or stop treatment may be based on the results of these tests.

Some of the tests will continue to be done from time to time after treatment has ended. The results of these tests can show if your condition has changed or if the disease has recurred (come back). These tests are sometimes called follow-up tests or check-ups.

Chapter 36

Gallbladder and Extrahepatic Bile Duct Cancer

Chapter Contents

Section 36.1

General Information about Gallbladder Cancer

This section includes excerpts from "Gallbladder Cancer Treatment (PDQ®)," National Cancer Institute (NCI), April 23, 2014.

Gallbladder cancer is a disease in which malignant (cancer) cells form in the tissues of the gallbladder.

Gallbladder cancer is a rare disease in which malignant (cancer) cells are found in the tissues of the gallbladder. The gallbladder is a pear-shaped organ that lies just under the liver in the upper abdomen. The gallbladder stores bile, a fluid made by the liver to digest fat. When food is being broken down in the stomach and intestines, bile is released from the gallbladder through a tube called the common bile duct, which connects the gallbladder and liver to the first part of the small intestine.

The wall of the gallbladder has 3 main layers of tissue.

- Mucosal (inner) layer.

- Muscularis (middle, muscle) layer.

- Serosal (outer) layer.

Between these layers is supporting connective tissue. Primary gallbladder cancer starts in the inner layer and spreads through the outer layers as it grows.

Being female can increase the risk of developing gallbladder cancer.

Anything that increases your chance of getting a disease is called a risk factor. Having a risk factor does not mean that you will get cancer; not having risk factors doesn't mean that you will not get cancer. Talk with your doctor if you think you may be at risk. Risk factors for gallbladder cancer include the following:

- Being female.

- Being Native American.

Signs and symptoms of gallbladder cancer include jaundice, fever, and pain.

These and other signs and symptoms may be caused by gallbladder cancer or by other conditions. Check with your doctor if you have any of the following:

- Jaundice (yellowing of the skin and whites of the eyes).
- Pain above the stomach.
- Fever.
- Nausea and vomiting.
- Bloating.
- Lumps in the abdomen.

Gallbladder cancer is difficult to detect (find) and diagnose early.

Gallbladder cancer is difficult to detect and diagnose for the following reasons:

- There are no signs or symptoms in the early stages of gallbladder cancer.
- The symptoms of gallbladder cancer, when present, are like the symptoms of many other illnesses.
- The gallbladder is hidden behind the liver.

Gallbladder cancer is sometimes found when the gallbladder is removed for other reasons. Patients with gallstones rarely develop gallbladder cancer.

Tests that examine the gallbladder and nearby organs are used to detect (find), diagnose, and stage gallbladder cancer.

Procedures that make pictures of the gallbladder and the area around it help diagnose gallbladder cancer and show how far the cancer has spread. The process used to find out if cancer cells have spread within and around the gallbladder is called staging.

In order to plan treatment, it is important to know if the gallbladder cancer can be removed by surgery. Tests and procedures to detect, diagnose, and stage gallbladder cancer are usually done at the same time. The following tests and procedures may be used:

- **Physical exam and history:** An exam of the body to check general signs of health, including checking for signs of disease, such as lumps or anything else that seems unusual. A history of the patient's health habits and past illnesses and treatments will also be taken.

- **Liver function tests:** A procedure in which a blood sample is checked to measure the amounts of certain substances released into the blood by the liver. A higher than normal amount of a substance can be a sign of liver disease that may be caused by gallbladder cancer.

- **Carcinoembryonic antigen (CEA) assay:** A test that measures the level of CEA in the blood. CEA is released into the bloodstream from both cancer cells and normal cells. When found in higher than normal amounts, it can be a sign of gallbladder cancer or other conditions.

- **CA 19-9 assay:** A test that measures the level of CA 19-9 in the blood. CA 19-9 is released into the bloodstream from both cancer cells and normal cells. When found in higher than normal amounts, it can be a sign of gallbladder cancer or other conditions.

- **Blood chemistry studies:** A procedure in which a blood sample is checked to measure the amounts of certain substances released into the blood by organs and tissues in the body. An unusual (higher or lower than normal) amount of a substance can be a sign of disease in the organ or tissue that makes it.

- **CT scan (CAT scan):** A procedure that makes a series of detailed pictures of areas inside the body, such as the chest, abdomen, and pelvis, taken from different angles. The pictures are made by a computer linked to an x-ray machine. A dye may be injected into a vein or swallowed to help the organs or tissues show up more clearly. This procedure is also called computed tomography, computerized tomography, or computerized axial tomography.

- **Ultrasound exam:** A procedure in which high-energy sound waves (ultrasound) are bounced off internal tissues or organs and make echoes. The echoes form a picture of body tissues called a sonogram. An abdominal ultrasound is done to diagnose gallbladder cancer.

- **PTC (percutaneous transhepatic cholangiography):** A procedure used to x-ray the liver and bile ducts. A thin needle is inserted through the skin below the ribs and into the liver. Dye is injected into the liver or bile ducts and an x-ray is taken. If a blockage is found, a thin, flexible tube called a stent is sometimes left in the liver to drain bile into the small intestine or a collection bag outside the body.

- **Chest x-ray:** An x-ray of the organs and bones inside the chest. An x-ray is a type of energy beam that can go through the body and onto film, making a picture of areas inside the body.

- **ERCP (endoscopic retrograde cholangiopancreatography):** A procedure used to x-ray the ducts (tubes) that carry bile from the liver to the gallbladder and from the gallbladder to the small intestine. Sometimes gallbladder cancer causes these ducts to narrow and block or slow the flow of bile, causing jaundice. An endoscope (a thin, lighted tube) is passed through the mouth, esophagus, and stomach into the first part of the small intestine. A catheter (a smaller tube) is then inserted through the endoscope into the bile ducts. A dye is injected through the catheter into the ducts and an x-ray is taken. If the ducts are blocked by a tumor, a fine tube may be inserted into the duct to unblock it. This tube (or stent) may be left in place to keep the duct open. Tissue samples may also be taken.

- **Laparoscopy:** A surgical procedure to look at the organs inside the abdomen to check for signs of disease. Small incisions (cuts) are made in the wall of the abdomen and a laparoscope (a thin, lighted tube) is inserted into one of the incisions. Other instruments may be inserted through the same or other incisions to perform procedures such as removing organs or taking tissue samples for biopsy. The laparoscopy helps to find out if the cancer is within the gallbladder only or has spread to nearby tissues and if it can be removed by surgery.

- **Biopsy:** The removal of cells or tissues so they can be viewed under a microscope by a pathologist to check for signs of cancer. The biopsy may be done after surgery to remove the tumor. If the tumor clearly cannot be removed by surgery, the biopsy may be done using a fine needle to remove cells from the tumor.

Certain factors affect the prognosis (chance of recovery) and treatment options.

The prognosis (chance of recovery) and treatment options depend on the following:

- The stage of the cancer (whether the cancer has spread from the gallbladder to other places in the body).

- Whether the cancer can be completely removed by surgery.

- The type of gallbladder cancer (how the cancer cell looks under a microscope).

- Whether the cancer has just been diagnosed or has recurred (come back).

Treatment may also depend on the age and general health of the patient and whether the cancer is causing signs or symptoms.

Gallbladder cancer can be cured only if it is found before it has spread, when it can be removed by surgery. If the cancer has spread, palliative treatment can improve the patient's quality of life by controlling the symptoms and complications of this disease.

Taking part in one of the clinical trials being done to improve treatment should be considered.

Section 36.2

Stages of Gallbladder Cancer

This section includes excerpts from "Gallbladder Cancer Treatment (PDQ®)," National Cancer Institute (NCI), April 23, 2014.

There are three ways that cancer spreads in the body.

Cancer can spread through tissue, the lymph system, and the blood:

- Tissue. The cancer spreads from where it began by growing into nearby areas.

- Lymph system. The cancer spreads from where it began by getting into the lymph system. The cancer travels through the lymph vessels to other parts of the body.

- Blood. The cancer spreads from where it began by getting into the blood. The cancer travels through the blood vessels to other parts of the body.

Cancer may spread from where it began to other parts of the body.

When cancer spreads to another part of the body, it is called metastasis. Cancer cells break away from where they began (the primary tumor) and travel through the lymph system or blood.

- Lymph system. The cancer gets into the lymph system, travels through the lymph vessels, and forms a tumor (metastatic tumor) in another part of the body.

- Blood. The cancer gets into the blood, travels through the blood vessels, and forms a tumor (metastatic tumor) in another part of the body.

The metastatic tumor is the same type of cancer as the primary tumor. For example, if gallbladder cancer spreads to the liver, the cancer cells in the liver are actually gallbladder cancer cells. The disease is metastatic gallbladder cancer, not liver cancer.

The following stages are used for gallbladder cancer:

Stage 0 (Carcinoma in Situ)

In stage 0, abnormal cells are found in the inner (mucosal) layer of the gallbladder. These abnormal cells may become cancer and spread into nearby normal tissue. Stage 0 is also called carcinoma in situ.

Stage I

In stage I, cancer has formed and has spread beyond the inner (mucosal) layer to a layer of tissue with blood vessels or to the muscle layer.

Stage II

In stage II, cancer has spread beyond the muscle layer to the connective tissue around the muscle.

Stage IIIA

In stage IIIA, cancer has spread through the thin layers of tissue that cover the gallbladder and/or to the liver and/or to one nearby organ (such as the stomach, small intestine, colon, pancreas, or bile ducts outside the liver).

Stage IIIB

In stage IIIB, cancer has spread to nearby lymph nodes and:

- beyond the inner layer of the gallbladder to a layer of tissue with blood vessels or to the muscle layer; or

- beyond the muscle layer to the connective tissue around the muscle; or

- through the thin layers of tissue that cover the gallbladder and/or to the liver and/or to one nearby organ (such as the stomach, small intestine, colon, pancreas, or bile ducts outside the liver).

Stage IVA

In stage IVA, cancer has spread to a main blood vessel of the liver or to 2 or more nearby organs or areas other than the liver. Cancer may have spread to nearby lymph nodes.

Stage IVB

In stage IVB, cancer has spread to either:

- lymph nodes along large arteries in the abdomen and/or near the lower part of the backbone; or

- to organs or areas far away from the gallbladder.

For gallbladder cancer, stages are also grouped according to how the cancer may be treated. There are two treatment groups:

Localized (Stage I)

Cancer is found in the wall of the gallbladder and can be completely removed by surgery.

Unresectable, recurrent, or metastatic (Stage II, Stage III, and Stage IV)

Unresectable cancer cannot be removed completely by surgery. Most patients with gallbladder cancer have unresectable cancer.

Recurrent cancer is cancer that has recurred (come back) after it has been treated. Gallbladder cancer may come back in the gallbladder or in other parts of the body.

Metastasis is the spread of cancer from the primary site (place where it started) to other places in the body. Metastatic gallbladder cancer may spread to surrounding tissues, organs, throughout the abdominal cavity, or to distant parts of the body.

Section 36.3

Treatment Options for Gallbladder Cancer

This section includes excerpts from "Gallbladder Cancer Treatment (PDQ®)," National Cancer Institute (NCI), April 23, 2014.

There are different types of treatment for patients with gallbladder cancer.

Different types of treatments are available for patients with gallbladder cancer. Some treatments are standard (the currently used treatment), and some are being tested in clinical trials. A treatment clinical trial is a research study meant to help improve current treatments or obtain information on new treatments for patients with cancer. When clinical trials show that a new treatment is better than the standard treatment, the new treatment may become the standard treatment. Patients may want to think about taking part in a clinical trial. Some clinical trials are open only to patients who have not started treatment.

Three types of standard treatment are used:

Surgery

Gallbladder cancer may be treated with a cholecystectomy, surgery to remove the gallbladder and some of the tissues around it. Nearby lymph nodes may be removed. A laparoscope is sometimes used to guide gallbladder surgery. The laparoscope is attached to a video camera and inserted through an incision (port) in the abdomen. Surgical instruments are inserted through other ports to perform the surgery. Because there is a risk that gallbladder cancer cells may spread to these ports, tissue surrounding the port sites may also be removed.

473

If the cancer has spread and cannot be removed, the following types of palliative surgery may relieve symptoms:

- Surgical biliary bypass: If the tumor is blocking the small intestine and bile is building up in the gallbladder, a biliary bypass may be done. During this operation, the gallbladder or bile duct will be cut and sewn to the small intestine to create a new pathway around the blocked area.

- Endoscopic stent placement: If the tumor is blocking the bile duct, surgery may be done to put in a stent (a thin, flexible tube) to drain bile that has built up in the area. The stent may be placed through a catheter that drains to the outside of the body or the stent may go around the blocked area and drain the bile into the small intestine.

- Percutaneous transhepatic biliary drainage: A procedure done to drain bile when there is a blockage and endoscopic stent placement is not possible. An x-ray of the liver and bile ducts is done to locate the blockage. Images made by ultrasound are used to guide placement of a stent, which is left in the liver to drain bile into the small intestine or a collection bag outside the body. This procedure may be done to relieve jaundice before surgery.

Radiation therapy

Radiation therapy is a cancer treatment that uses high-energy x-rays or other types of radiation to kill cancer cells. There are two types of radiation therapy. External radiation therapy uses a machine outside the body to send radiation toward the cancer. Internal radiation therapy uses a radioactive substance sealed in needles, seeds, wires, or catheters that are placed directly into or near the cancer. The way the radiation therapy is given depends on the type and stage of the cancer being treated.

Chemotherapy

Chemotherapy is a cancer treatment that uses drugs to stop the growth of cancer cells, either by killing the cells or by stopping the cells from dividing. When chemotherapy is taken by mouth or injected into a vein or muscle, the drugs enter the bloodstream and can reach cancer cells throughout the body (systemic chemotherapy). When chemotherapy is placed directly into the cerebrospinal fluid, an organ, or a body cavity such as the abdomen, the drugs mainly affect cancer cells in those areas (regional chemotherapy). The way the chemotherapy is given depends on the type and stage of the cancer being treated.

New types of treatment are being tested in clinical trials.

Radiation sensitizers

Clinical trials are studying ways to improve the effect of radiation therapy on tumor cells, including the following:

- Hyperthermia therapy: A treatment in which body tissue is exposed to high temperatures to damage and kill cancer cells or to make cancer cells more sensitive to the effects of radiation therapy and certain anticancer drugs.

- Radiosensitizers: Drugs that make tumor cells more sensitive to radiation therapy. Giving radiation therapy together with radiosensitizers may kill more tumor cells.

Patients may want to think about taking part in a clinical trial.

For some patients, taking part in a clinical trial may be the best treatment choice. Clinical trials are part of the cancer research process. Clinical trials are done to find out if new cancer treatments are safe and effective or better than the standard treatment.

Many of today's standard treatments for cancer are based on earlier clinical trials. Patients who take part in a clinical trial may receive the standard treatment or be among the first to receive a new treatment.

Patients who take part in clinical trials also help improve the way cancer will be treated in the future. Even when clinical trials do not lead to effective new treatments, they often answer important questions and help move research forward.

Patients can enter clinical trials before, during, or after starting their cancer treatment.

Some clinical trials only include patients who have not yet received treatment. Other trials test treatments for patients whose cancer has not gotten better. There are also clinical trials that test new ways to stop cancer from recurring (coming back) or reduce the side effects of cancer treatment.

Clinical trials are taking place in many parts of the country.

Follow-up tests may be needed.

Some of the tests that were done to diagnose the cancer or to find out the stage of the cancer may be repeated. Some tests will be repeated in order to see how well the treatment is working. Decisions about whether to continue, change, or stop treatment may be based on the results of these tests.

Some of the tests will continue to be done from time to time after treatment has ended. The results of these tests can show if your condition has changed or if the cancer has recurred (come back). These tests are sometimes called follow-up tests or check-ups.

Section 36.4

General Information about Extrahepatic Bile Duct Cancer

This section includes excerpts from "Extrahepatic Bile Duct Cancer Treatment (PDQ®)," National Cancer Institute (NCI), July 15, 2015.

Extrahepatic bile duct cancer is a rare disease in which malignant (cancer) cells form in the ducts that are outside the liver.

The extrahepatic bile duct is made up of two parts:

- Common hepatic duct, which is also called the perihilar part of the extrahepatic duct.

- Common bile duct, which is also called the distal part of the extrahepatic duct.

The extrahepatic bile duct is part of a network of ducts (tubes) that connect the liver, gallbladder, and small intestine. This network begins in the liver where many small ducts collect bile (a fluid made by the liver to break down fats during digestion). The small ducts come together to form the right and left hepatic ducts, which lead out of the liver. The two ducts join outside the liver and form the common hepatic duct. Bile from the liver passes through the hepatic ducts, common hepatic duct and cystic duct and is stored in the gallbladder.

When food is being digested, bile stored in the gallbladder is released and passes through the cystic duct to the common bile duct and into the small intestine.

Having colitis or certain liver diseases can increase the risk of extrahepatic bile duct cancer.

Anything that increases your risk of getting a disease is called a risk factor. Having a risk factor does not mean that you will get cancer; not having risk factors doesn't mean that you will not get cancer. Talk with your doctor if you think you may be at risk. Risk factors include having any of the following disorders:

- Primary sclerosing cholangitis.
- Chronic ulcerative colitis.
- Choledochal cysts.
- Infection with a Chinese liver fluke parasite.

Signs and symptoms of extrahepatic bile duct cancer include jaundice and pain.

These and other signs and symptoms may be caused by extrahepatic bile duct cancer or by other conditions. Check with your doctor if you have any of the following:

- Jaundice (yellowing of the skin or whites of the eyes).
- Pain in the abdomen.
- Fever.
- Itchy skin.

Tests that examine the bile duct and liver are used to detect (find) and diagnose extrahepatic bile duct cancer.

The following tests and procedures may be used:

- **Physical exam and history:** An exam of the body to check general signs of health, including checking for signs of disease, such as lumps or anything else that seems unusual. A history of the patient's health habits and past illnesses and treatments will also be taken.

- **Ultrasound exam:** A procedure in which high-energy sound waves (ultrasound) are bounced off internal tissues or organs and make echoes. The echoes form a picture of body tissues called a sonogram. The picture can be printed to be looked at later.

- **CT scan (CAT scan):** A procedure that makes a series of detailed pictures of areas inside the body, taken from different angles. The pictures are made by a computer linked to an x-ray machine. A dye may be injected into a vein or swallowed to help the organs or tissues show up more clearly. This procedure is also called computed tomography, computerized tomography, or computerized axial tomography. A spiral or helical CT scan makes detailed pictures of areas inside the body using an x-ray machine that scans the body in a spiral path.

- **MRI (magnetic resonance imaging):** A procedure that uses a magnet, radio waves, and a computer to make a series of detailed pictures of areas inside the body. This procedure is also called nuclear magnetic resonance imaging (NMRI).

- **PET scan (positron emission tomography scan):** A procedure to find malignant tumor cells in the body. A small amount of radioactive glucose (sugar) is injected into a vein. The PET scanner rotates around the body and makes a picture of where glucose is being used in the body. Malignant tumor cells show up brighter in the picture because they are more active and take up more glucose than normal cells do.

- **ERCP (endoscopic retrograde cholangiopancreatography):** A procedure used to x-ray the ducts (tubes) that carry bile from the liver to the gallbladder and from the gallbladder to the small intestine. Sometimes bile duct cancer causes these ducts to narrow and block or slow the flow of bile, causing jaundice. An endoscope is passed through the mouth, esophagus, and stomach into the first part of the small intestine. An endoscope is a thin, tube-like instrument with a light and a lens for viewing. A catheter (a smaller tube) is then inserted through the endoscope into the pancreatic ducts. A dye is injected through the catheter into the ducts and an x-ray is taken. If the ducts are blocked by a tumor, a fine tube may be inserted into the duct to unblock it. This tube (or stent) may be left in place to keep the duct open. Tissue samples may also be taken and checked under a microscope for signs of cancer.

- **PTC (percutaneous transhepatic cholangiography):** A procedure used to x-ray the liver and bile ducts. A thin needle is inserted through the skin below the ribs and into the liver. Dye is injected into the liver or bile ducts and an x-ray is taken. If a blockage is found, a thin, flexible tube called a stent is sometimes left in the liver to drain bile into the small intestine or a collection bag outside the body.

- **Biopsy:** The removal of cells or tissues so they can be viewed under a microscope to check for signs of cancer. The sample may be taken using a thin needle inserted into the duct during an x-ray or ultrasound. This is called a fine-needle aspiration (FNA) biopsy. The biopsy is usually done during PTC or ERCP. Tissue, including part of a lymph node, may also be removed during surgery.

- **Liver function tests:** A procedure in which a blood sample is checked to measure the amounts of certain substances released into the blood by the liver. A higher than normal amount of a substance can be a sign of liver disease that may be caused by extrahepatic bile duct cancer.

- **Tumor marker test:** A procedure in which a sample of blood, urine, or tissue is checked to measure the amounts of certain substances made by organs, tissues, or tumor cells in the body. Certain substances are linked to specific types of cancer when found in increased levels in the body. These are called tumor markers. Carcinoembryonic antigen (CEA) and CA 19-9 are associated with extrahepatic bile duct cancer when found in increased levels in the body.

Certain factors affect prognosis (chance of recovery) and treatment options.

The prognosis (chance of recovery) and treatment options depend on the following:

- The stage of the cancer (whether it affects only the bile duct or has spread to other places in the body).

- Whether the tumor can be completely removed by surgery.

- Whether the tumor is in the upper or lower part of the duct.

- Whether the cancer has just been diagnosed or has recurred (come back).

Treatment options may also depend on the symptoms caused by the tumor. Extrahepatic bile duct cancer is usually found after it has spread and can rarely be removed completely by surgery. Palliative therapy may relieve symptoms and improve the patient's quality of life.

Section 36.5

Stages of Extrahepatic Bile Duct Cancer

This section includes excerpts from "Extrahepatic Bile Duct Cancer Treatment (PDQ®)," National Cancer Institute (NCI), July 15, 2015.

After extrahepatic bile duct cancer has been diagnosed, tests are done to find out if cancer cells have spread within the bile duct or to other parts of the body.

The process used to find out if cancer has spread within the extrahepatic bile duct or to other parts of the body is called staging. The information gathered from the staging process determines the stage of the disease. It is important to know the stage in order to plan treatment.

Extrahepatic bile duct cancer may be staged following a laparotomy. A surgical incision is made in the wall of the abdomen to check the inside of the abdomen for signs of disease and to remove tissue and fluid for examination under a microscope. The results of the diagnostic imaging tests, laparotomy, and biopsy are viewed together to determine the stage of the cancer. Sometimes, a laparoscopy will be done before the laparotomy to see if the cancer has spread. If the cancer has spread and cannot be removed by surgery, the surgeon may decide not to do a laparotomy.

There are three ways that cancer spreads in the body.

Cancer can spread through tissue, the lymph system, and the blood:

- Tissue. The cancer spreads from where it began by growing into nearby areas.

- Lymph system. The cancer spreads from where it began by getting into the lymph system. The cancer travels through the lymph vessels to other parts of the body.

- Blood. The cancer spreads from where it began by getting into the blood. The cancer travels through the blood vessels to other parts of the body.

Cancer may spread from where it began to other parts of the body.

When cancer spreads to another part of the body, it is called metastasis. Cancer cells break away from where they began (the primary tumor) and travel through the lymph system or blood.

- Lymph system. The cancer gets into the lymph system, travels through the lymph vessels, and forms a tumor (metastatic tumor) in another part of the body.

- Blood. The cancer gets into the blood, travels through the blood vessels, and forms a tumor (metastatic tumor) in another part of the body.

The metastatic tumor is the same type of cancer as the primary tumor. For example, if extrahepatic bile duct cancer spreads to the liver, the cancer cells in the liver are actually extrahepatic bile duct cancer cells. The disease is metastatic extrahepatic bile duct cancer, not liver cancer.

There are two staging systems for extrahepatic bile duct cancer.

Extrahepatic bile duct cancer has two staging systems. The staging system used depends on where in the extrahepatic bile duct the cancer first formed.

- *Perihilar* or proximal extrahepatic bile duct tumors (perihilar bile duct tumors) form in the area where the bile duct leaves the liver. This type of tumor is also called a Klatskin tumor.

- Distal extrahepatic bile duct tumors (distal bile duct tumors) form in the area where the bile duct empties into the small intestine.

The following stages are used for perihilar extrahepatic bile duct cancer:

Stage 0 (Carcinoma in Situ)

In stage 0, abnormal cells are found in the innermost layer of tissue lining the perihilar bile duct. These abnormal cells may become cancer and spread into nearby normal tissue. Stage 0 is also called carcinoma in situ.

Stage I

In stage I, cancer has formed in the innermost layer of the wall of the perihilar bile duct and has spread into the muscle and fibrous tissue of the wall.

Stage II

In stage II, cancer has spread through the wall of the perihilar bile duct to nearby fatty tissue or to the liver.

Stage III

Stage III is divided into stages IIIA and IIIB.

- Stage IIIA: The tumor has spread to one branch of the hepatic artery or of the portal vein.

- Stage IIIB: The tumor has spread to nearby lymph nodes. Cancer has also spread into the wall of the perihilar bile duct and may have spread through the wall to nearby fatty tissue, the liver, or to one branch of the hepatic artery or of the portal vein.

Stage IV

Stage IV is divided into stages IVA and IVB.

- Stage IVA: The tumor may have spread to nearby lymph nodes and has spread to one or more of the following:
  - the main part of the portal vein or both branches of the portal vein;
  - the hepatic artery;
  - the right and left hepatic ducts;
  - the right hepatic duct and the left branch of the hepatic artery or of the portal vein;
  - the left hepatic duct and the right branch of the hepatic artery or of the portal vein.

- Stage IVB: The tumor has spread to other parts of the body, such as the liver.

The following stages are used for distal extrahepatic bile duct cancer:

Stage 0 (Carcinoma in Situ)

In stage 0, abnormal cells are found in the innermost layer of tissue lining the distal bile duct. These abnormal cells may become cancer and spread into nearby normal tissue. Stage 0 is also called carcinoma in situ.

Stage I

In stage I, cancer has formed. Stage I is divided into stages IA and IB.

- Stage IA: Cancer is found in the distal bile duct only.

- Stage IB: Cancer has spread all the way through the wall of the distal bile duct.

Stage II

Stage II is divided into stages IIA and IIB.

- Stage IIA: Cancer has spread from the distal bile duct to the gallbladder, pancreas, small intestine, or other nearby organs.

- Stage IIB: Cancer has spread from the distal bile duct to nearby lymph nodes. Cancer may have spread through the wall of the distal bile duct or to the gallbladder, pancreas, small intestine, or other nearby organs.

Stage III

In stage III, cancer has spread to the large vessels that carry blood to the organs in the abdomen. Cancer may have spread to nearby lymph nodes.

Stage IV

In stage IV, cancer has spread to other parts of the body, such as the liver or lungs.

Extrahepatic bile duct cancer can also be grouped according to how the cancer may be treated. There are two treatment groups:

Localized (and resectable)

The cancer is in an area where it can be removed completely by surgery.

Unresectable, recurrent, or metastatic

Unresectable cancer cannot be removed completely by surgery. Most patients with extrahepatic bile duct cancer have unresectable cancer.

Recurrent cancer is cancer that has recurred (come back) after it has been treated. Extrahepatic bile duct cancer may come back in the bile duct or in other parts of the body.

Metastasis is the spread of cancer from the primary site (place where it started) to other places in the body. Metastatic extrahepatic bile duct cancer may have spread to nearby blood vessels, the liver, the common bile duct, nearby lymph nodes, other parts of the abdominal cavity, or to distant parts of the body.

Section 36.6

Treatment Options for Extrahepatic Bile Duct Cancer

This section includes excerpts from "Extrahepatic Bile Duct Cancer Treatment (PDQ®)," National Cancer Institute (NCI), July 15, 2015.

There are different types of treatment for patients with extrahepatic bile duct cancer.

Different types of treatment are available for patients with extrahepatic bile duct cancer. Some treatments are standard (the currently used treatment), and some are being tested in clinical trials. A treatment clinical trial is a research study meant to help improve current treatments or obtain information on new treatments for patients with cancer. When clinical trials show that a new treatment is better than the standard treatment, the new treatment may become the standard treatment. Patients may want to think about taking part in a clinical trial. Some clinical trials are open only to patients who have not started treatment.

Three types of standard treatment are used:

Surgery

The following types of surgery are used to treat extrahepatic bile duct cancer:

- Removal of the bile duct: If the tumor is small and only in the bile duct, the entire bile duct may be removed. A new duct is made by connecting the duct openings in the liver to the intestine. Lymph nodes are removed and viewed under a microscope to see if they contain cancer.

- Partial hepatectomy: Removal of the part of the liver where cancer is found. The part removed may be a wedge of tissue, an entire lobe, or a larger part of the liver, along with some normal tissue around it.

- Whipple procedure: A surgical procedure in which the head of the pancreas, the gallbladder, part of the stomach, part of the small intestine, and the bile duct are removed. Enough of the pancreas is left to make digestive juices and insulin.

- Surgical biliary bypass: If the tumor cannot be removed but is blocking the small intestine and causing bile to build up in the gallbladder, a biliary bypass may be done. During this operation, the gallbladder or bile duct will be cut and sewn to the small intestine to create a new pathway around the blocked area. This procedure helps to relieve jaundice caused by the build-up of bile.

- Stent placement: If the tumor is blocking the bile duct, a stent (a thin tube) may be placed in the duct to drain bile that has built up in the area. The stent may drain to the outside of the body or it may go around the blocked area and drain the bile into the small intestine. The doctor may place the stent during surgery or PTC, or with an endoscope.

Radiation therapy

Radiation therapy is a cancer treatment that uses high-energy x-rays or other types of radiation to kill cancer cells or keep them from growing. There are two types of radiation therapy. External radiation therapy uses a machine outside the body to send radiation toward the cancer. Internal radiation therapy uses a radioactive substance sealed in needles, seeds, wires, or catheters that are placed directly into or near the cancer. The way the radiation therapy is given depends on the type and stage of the cancer being treated.

Chemotherapy

Chemotherapy is a cancer treatment that uses drugs to stop the growth of cancer cells, either by killing the cells or by stopping them from dividing. When chemotherapy is taken by mouth or injected into a vein or muscle, the drugs enter the bloodstream and can reach cancer cells throughout the body (systemic chemotherapy). When chemotherapy is placed directly into the cerebrospinal fluid, an organ, or a body cavity such as the abdomen, the drugs mainly affect cancer cells in those areas (regional chemotherapy). The way the chemotherapy is given depends on the type and stage of the cancer being treated.

New types of treatment are being tested in clinical trials.

Radiation sensitizers

Clinical trials are studying ways to improve the effect of radiation therapy on tumor cells, including the following:

- **Hyperthermia therapy:** A treatment in which body tissue is exposed to high temperatures to damage and kill cancer cells or to make cancer cells more sensitive to the effects of radiation therapy and certain anticancer drugs.

- **Radiosensitizers:** Drugs that make tumor cells more sensitive to radiation therapy. Combining radiation therapy with radiosensitizers may kill more tumor cells.

Patients may want to think about taking part in a clinical trial.

For some patients, taking part in a clinical trial may be the best treatment choice. Clinical trials are part of the cancer research process. Clinical trials are done to find out if new cancer treatments are safe and effective or better than the standard treatment.

Many of today's standard treatments for cancer are based on earlier clinical trials. Patients who take part in a clinical trial may receive the standard treatment or be among the first to receive a new treatment.

Patients who take part in clinical trials also help improve the way cancer will be treated in the future. Even when clinical trials do not lead to effective new treatments, they often answer important questions and help move research forward.

Patients can enter clinical trials before, during, or after starting their cancer treatment.

Some clinical trials only include patients who have not yet received treatment. Other trials test treatments for patients whose cancer has not gotten better. There are also clinical trials that test new ways to stop cancer from recurring (coming back) or reduce the side effects of cancer treatment.

Clinical trials are taking place in many parts of the country.

Follow-up tests may be needed.

Some of the tests that were done to diagnose the cancer or to find out the stage of the cancer may be repeated. Some tests will be repeated in order to see how well the treatment is working. Decisions about whether to continue, change, or stop treatment may be based on the results of these tests.

Some of the tests will continue to be done from time to time after treatment has ended. The results of these tests can show if your condition has changed or if the cancer has recurred (come back). These tests are sometimes called follow-up tests or check-ups.

Chapter 37

Lung Cancer

Chapter Contents

Section 37.1

General Information about Non-Small Cell Lung Cancer

This section includes excerpts from "Non-Small Cell Lung Cancer Treatment (PDQ®)," National Cancer Institute (NCI), May 12, 2015.

Non-small cell lung cancer is a disease in which malignant (cancer) cells form in the tissues of the lung.

The lungs are a pair of cone-shaped breathing organs in the chest. The lungs bring oxygen into the body as you breathe in. They release carbon dioxide, a waste product of the body's cells, as you breathe out. Each lung has sections called lobes. The left lung has two lobes. The right lung is slightly larger and has three lobes. Two tubes called bronchi lead from the trachea (windpipe) to the right and left lungs. The bronchi are sometimes also involved in lung cancer. Tiny air sacs called alveoli and small tubes called bronchioles make up the inside of the lungs.

A thin membrane called the pleura covers the outside of each lung and lines the inside wall of the chest cavity. This creates a sac called the pleural cavity. The pleural cavity normally contains a small amount of fluid that helps the lungs move smoothly in the chest when you breathe.

There are two main types of lung cancer: non-small cell lung cancer and small cell lung cancer.

There are several types of non-small cell lung cancer.

Each type of non-small cell lung cancer has different kinds of cancer cells. The cancer cells of each type grow and spread in different ways. The types of non-small cell lung cancer are named for the kinds of cells found in the cancer and how the cells look under a microscope:

- Squamous cell carcinoma: Cancer that begins in squamous cells, which are thin, flat cells that look like fish scales. This is also called epidermoid carcinoma.

- Large cell carcinoma: Cancer that may begin in several types of large cells.

- Adenocarcinoma: Cancer that begins in the cells that line the alveoli and make substances such as mucus.

Other less common types of non-small cell lung cancer are: pleomorphic, carcinoid tumor, salivary gland carcinoma, and unclassified carcinoma.

Smoking increases the risk of non-small cell lung cancer.

Smoking cigarettes, pipes, or cigars is the most common cause of lung cancer. The earlier in life a person starts smoking, the more often a person smokes, and the more years a person smokes, the greater the risk of lung cancer. If a person has stopped smoking, the risk becomes lower as the years pass.

Anything that increases your chance of getting a disease is called a risk factor. Having a risk factor does not mean that you will get cancer; not having risk factors doesn't mean that you will not get cancer. Talk with your doctor if you think you may be at risk.

Risk factors for lung cancer include the following:

- Smoking cigarettes, pipes, or cigars, now or in the past.
- Being exposed to secondhand smoke.
- Having a family history of lung cancer.
- Being treated with radiation therapy to the breast or chest.
- Being exposed to asbestos, chromium, nickel, arsenic, soot, or tar in the workplace.
- Being exposed to radon in the home or workplace.
- Living where there is air pollution.
- Being infected with the *human immunodeficiency virus* (HIV).
- Using beta carotene supplements and being a heavy smoker.

When smoking is combined with other risk factors, the risk of lung cancer is increased.

Signs of non-small cell lung cancer include a cough that doesn't go away and shortness of breath.

Sometimes lung cancer does not cause any signs or symptoms. It may be found during a chest x-ray done for another condition. Signs

491

and symptoms may be caused by lung cancer or by other conditions. Check with your doctor if you have any of the following:

- Chest discomfort or pain.

- A cough that doesn't go away or gets worse over time.

- Trouble breathing.

- Wheezing.

- Blood in sputum (mucus coughed up from the lungs).

- Hoarseness.

- Loss of appetite.

- Weight loss for no known reason.

- Feeling very tired.

- Trouble swallowing.

- Swelling in the face and/or veins in the neck.

Tests that examine the lungs are used to detect (find), diagnose, and stage non-small cell lung cancer.

Tests and procedures to detect, diagnose, and stage non-small cell lung cancer are often done at the same time. Some of the following tests and procedures may be used:

- **Physical exam and history:** An exam of the body to check general signs of health, including checking for signs of disease, such as lumps or anything else that seems unusual. A history of the patient's health habits, including smoking, and past jobs, illnesses, and treatments will also be taken.

- **Laboratory tests:** Medical procedures that test samples of tissue, blood, urine, or other substances in the body. These tests help to diagnose disease, plan and check treatment, or monitor the disease over time.

- **Chest x-ray:** An x-ray of the organs and bones inside the chest. An x-ray is a type of energy beam that can go through the body and onto film, making a picture of areas inside the body.

- **CT scan (CAT scan):** A procedure that makes a series of detailed pictures of areas inside the body, such as the chest, taken from different angles. The pictures are made by a computer linked to an x-ray machine. A dye may be injected into a vein or swallowed to help the organs or tissues show up more clearly. This procedure is also called computed tomography, computerized tomography, or computerized axial tomography.

- **Sputum cytology:** A procedure in which a pathologist views a sample of sputum (mucus coughed up from the lungs) under a microscope, to check for cancer cells.

- **Fine-needle aspiration (FNA) biopsy of the lung:** The removal of tissue or fluid from the lung using a thin needle. A CT scan, ultrasound, or other imaging procedure is used to locate the abnormal tissue or fluid in the lung. A small incision may be made in the skin where the biopsy needle is inserted into the abnormal tissue or fluid. A sample is removed with the needle and sent to the laboratory. A pathologist then views the sample under a microscope to look for cancer cells. A chest x-ray is done after the procedure to make sure no air is leaking from the lung into the chest.

- **Bronchoscopy:** A procedure to look inside the trachea and large airways in the lung for abnormal areas. A bronchoscope is inserted through the nose or mouth into the trachea and lungs. A bronchoscope is a thin, tube-like instrument with a light and a lens for viewing. It may also have a tool to remove tissue samples, which are checked under a microscope for signs of cancer.

- **Thoracoscopy:** A surgical procedure to look at the organs inside the chest to check for abnormal areas. An incision (cut) is made between two ribs, and a thoracoscope is inserted into the chest. A thoracoscope is a thin, tube-like instrument with a light and a lens for viewing. It may also have a tool to remove tissue or lymph node samples, which are checked under a microscope for signs of cancer. In some cases, this procedure is used to remove part of the esophagus or lung. If certain tissues, organs, or lymph nodes can't be reached, a thoracotomy may be done. In this procedure, a larger incision is made between the ribs and the chest is opened.

- **Thoracentesis:** The removal of fluid from the space between the lining of the chest and the lung, using a needle. A pathologist views the fluid under a microscope to look for cancer cells.

- **Light and electron microscopy**: A laboratory test in which cells in a sample of tissue are viewed under regular and high-powered microscopes to look for certain changes in the cells.

- **Immunohistochemistry:** A test that uses antibodies to check for certain antigens in a sample of tissue. The antibody is usually linked to a radioactive substance or a dye that causes the tissue to light up under a microscope. This type of test may be used to tell the difference between different types of cancer.

Certain factors affect prognosis (chance of recovery) and treatment options.

The prognosis (chance of recovery) and treatment options depend on the following:

- The stage of the cancer (the size of the tumor and whether it is in the lung only or has spread to other places in the body).

- The type of lung cancer.

- Whether the cancer has mutations (changes) in certain genes, such as the epidermal growth factor receptor (EGFR) gene or the anaplastic lymphoma kinase (ALK) gene.

- Whether there are signs and symptoms such as coughing or trouble breathing.

- The patient's general health.

For most patients with non-small cell lung cancer, current treatments do not cure the cancer.

If lung cancer is found, taking part in one of the many clinical trials being done to improve treatment should be considered. Clinical trials are taking place in most parts of the country for patients with all stages of non-small cell lung cancer.

Section 37.2

Stages of Non-Small Cell Lung Cancer

This section includes excerpts from "Non-Small Cell Lung Cancer Treatment (PDQ®)," National Cancer Institute (NCI), May 12, 2015.

After lung cancer has been diagnosed, tests are done to find out if cancer cells have spread within the lungs or to other parts of the body.

The process used to find out if cancer has spread within the lungs or to other parts of the body is called staging. The information gathered from the staging process determines the stage of the disease. It is important to know the stage in order to plan treatment. Some of the tests used to diagnose non-small cell lung cancer are also used to stage the disease. Other tests and procedures that may be used in the staging process include the following:

- **MRI (magnetic resonance imaging):** A procedure that uses a magnet, radio waves, and a computer to make a series of detailed pictures of areas inside the body, such as the brain. This procedure is also called nuclear magnetic resonance imaging (NMRI).

- **CT scan (CAT scan):** A procedure that makes a series of detailed pictures of areas inside the body, such as the brain and abdomen, taken from different angles. The pictures are made by a computer linked to an x-ray machine. A dye may be injected into a vein or swallowed to help the organs or tissues show up more clearly. This procedure is also called computed tomography, computerized tomography, or computerized axial tomography.

- **PET scan (positron emission tomography scan):** A procedure to find malignant tumor cells in the body. A small amount of radioactive glucose (sugar) is injected into a vein. The PET scanner rotates around the body and makes a picture of where glucose is being used in the body. Malignant tumor cells show up brighter in the picture because they are more active and take up more glucose than normal cells do.

- **Radionuclide bone scan:** A procedure to check if there are rapidly dividing cells, such as cancer cells, in the bone. A very small amount of radioactive material is injected into a vein and travels through the bloodstream. The radioactive material collects in the bones and is detected by a scanner.

- **Pulmonary function test (PFT):** A test to see how well the lungs are working. It measures how much air the lungs can hold and how quickly air moves into and out of the lungs. It also measures how much oxygen is used and how much carbon dioxide is given off during breathing. This is also called lung function test.

- **Endoscopic ultrasound (EUS):** A procedure in which an endoscope is inserted into the body. An endoscope is a thin, tube-like instrument with a light and a lens for viewing. A probe at the end of the endoscope is used to bounce high-energy sound waves (ultrasound) off internal tissues or organs and make echoes. The echoes form a picture of body tissues called a sonogram. This procedure is also called endosonography. EUS may be used to guide fine needle aspiration (FNA) biopsy of the lung, lymph nodes, or other areas.

- **Mediastinoscopy:** A surgical procedure to look at the organs, tissues, and lymph nodes between the lungs for abnormal areas. An incision (cut) is made at the top of the breastbone and a mediastinoscope is inserted into the chest. A mediastinoscope is a thin, tube-like instrument with a light and a lens for viewing. It may also have a tool to remove tissue or lymph node samples, which are checked under a microscope for signs of cancer.

- **Anterior mediastinotomy:** A surgical procedure to look at the organs and tissues between the lungs and between the breastbone and heart for abnormal areas. An incision (cut) is made next to the breastbone and a mediastinoscope is inserted into the chest. A mediastinoscope is a thin, tube-like instrument with a light and a lens for viewing. It may also have a tool to remove tissue or lymph node samples, which are checked under a microscope for signs of cancer. This is also called the Chamberlain procedure.

- **Lymph node biopsy:** The removal of all or part of a lymph node. A pathologist views the tissue under a microscope to look for cancer cells.

- **Bone marrow aspiration and biopsy:** The removal of bone marrow, blood, and a small piece of bone by inserting a hollow needle into the hipbone or breastbone. A pathologist views the bone marrow, blood, and bone under a microscope to look for signs of cancer.

There are three ways that cancer spreads in the body.

Cancer can spread through tissue, the lymph system, and the blood:

- Tissue. The cancer spreads from where it began by growing into nearby areas.
- Lymph system. The cancer spreads from where it began by getting into the lymph system. The cancer travels through the lymph vessels to other parts of the body.
- Blood. The cancer spreads from where it began by getting into the blood. The cancer travels through the blood vessels to other parts of the body.

Cancer may spread from where it began to other parts of the body.

When cancer spreads to another part of the body, it is called metastasis. Cancer cells break away from where they began (the primary tumor) and travel through the lymph system or blood.

- Lymph system. The cancer gets into the lymph system, travels through the lymph vessels, and forms a tumor (metastatic tumor) in another part of the body.
- Blood. The cancer gets into the blood, travels through the blood vessels, and forms a tumor (metastatic tumor) in another part of the body.

The metastatic tumor is the same type of cancer as the primary tumor. For example, if non-small cell lung cancer spreads to the brain, the cancer cells in the brain are actually lung cancer cells. The disease is metastatic lung cancer, not brain cancer.

The following stages are used for non-small cell lung cancer:

Occult (hidden) stage

In the occult (hidden) stage, cancer cannot be seen by imaging or bronchoscopy. Cancer cells are found in sputum (mucus coughed up from the lungs) or bronchial washing (a sample of cells taken from inside the airways that lead to the lung). Cancer may have spread to other parts of the body.

Stage 0 (carcinoma in situ)

In stage 0, abnormal cells are found in the lining of the airways. These abnormal cells may become cancer and spread into nearby normal tissue. Stage 0 is also called carcinoma in situ.

Stage I

In stage I, cancer has formed. Stage I is divided into stages IA and IB:

- Stage IA: The tumor is in the lung only and is 3 centimeters or smaller.

- Stage IB: Cancer has not spread to the lymph nodes and one or more of the following is true:

  - The tumor is larger than 3 centimeters but not larger than 5 centimeters.

  - Cancer has spread to the main bronchus and is at least 2 centimeters below where the trachea joins the bronchus.

  - Cancer has spread to the innermost layer of the membrane that covers the lung.

  - Part of the lung has collapsed or developed pneumonitis (inflammation of the lung) in the area where the trachea joins the bronchus.

Stage II

Stage II is divided into stages IIA and IIB. Stage IIA and IIB are each divided into two sections depending on the size of the tumor, where the tumor is found, and whether there is cancer in the lymph nodes.

- Stage IIA:

(1) Cancer has spread to lymph nodes on the same side of the chest as the tumor. The lymph nodes with cancer are within the lung or near the bronchus. Also, one or more of the following is true:

  - The tumor is not larger than 5 centimeters.

  - Cancer has spread to the main bronchus and is at least 2 centimeters below where the trachea joins the bronchus.

  - Cancer has spread to the innermost layer of the membrane that covers the lung.

- Part of the lung has collapsed or developed pneumonitis (inflammation of the lung) in the area where the trachea joins the bronchus.

or

(2) Cancer has not spread to lymph nodes and one or more of the following is true:

- The tumor is larger than 5 centimeters but not larger than 7 centimeters.

- Cancer has spread to the main bronchus and is at least 2 centimeters below where the trachea joins the bronchus.

- Cancer has spread to the innermost layer of the membrane that covers the lung.

- Part of the lung has collapsed or developed pneumonitis (inflammation of the lung) in the area where the trachea joins the bronchus.

- Stage IIB:

(1) Cancer has spread to nearby lymph nodes on the same side of the chest as the tumor. The lymph nodes with cancer are within the lung or near the bronchus. Also, one or more of the following is true:

- The tumor is larger than 5 centimeters but not larger than 7 centimeters.

- Cancer has spread to the main bronchus and is at least 2 centimeters below where the trachea joins the bronchus.

- Cancer has spread to the innermost layer of the membrane that covers the lung.

- Part of the lung has collapsed or developed pneumonitis (inflammation of the lung) in the area where the trachea joins the bronchus.

or

(2) Cancer has not spread to lymph nodes and one or more of the following is true:

- The tumor is larger than 7 centimeters.

- Cancer has spread to the main bronchus (and is less than 2 centimeters below where the trachea joins the bronchus),

the chest wall, the diaphragm, or the nerve that controls
the diaphragm.

- Cancer has spread to the membrane around the heart or lining
the chest wall.

- The whole lung has collapsed or developed pneumonitis (inflammation of the lung).

- There are one or more separate tumors in the same lobe of the
lung.

- Stage IIIA

Stage IIIA is divided into three sections depending on the size of
the tumor, where the tumor is found, and which lymph nodes have
cancer (if any).

(1) Cancer has spread to lymph nodes on the same side of the chest
as the tumor. The lymph nodes with cancer are near the sternum (chest
bone) or where the bronchus enters the lung. Also:

- The tumor may be any size.

- Part of the lung (where the trachea joins the bronchus) or
the whole lung may have collapsed or developed pneumonitis
(inflammation of the lung).

- There may be one or more separate tumors in the same lobe of
the lung.

- Cancer may have spread to any of the following:

  - Main bronchus, but not the area where the trachea joins the
  bronchus.

  - Chest wall.

  - Diaphragm and the nerve that controls it.

  - Membrane around the lung or lining the chest wall.

  - Membrane around the heart.

or

(2) Cancer has spread to lymph nodes on the same side of the chest
as the tumor. The lymph nodes with cancer are within the lung or near
the bronchus. Also:

- The tumor may be any size.

- The whole lung may have collapsed or developed pneumonitis (inflammation of the lung).

- There may be one or more separate tumors in any of the lobes of the lung with cancer.

- Cancer may have spread to any of the following:
  - Main bronchus, but not the area where the trachea joins the bronchus.
  - Chest wall.
  - Diaphragm and the nerve that controls it.
  - Membrane around the lung or lining the chest wall.
  - Heart or the membrane around it.
  - Major blood vessels that lead to or from the heart.
  - Trachea.
  - Esophagus.
  - Nerve that controls the larynx (voice box).
  - Sternum (chest bone) or backbone.
  - Carina (where the trachea joins the bronchi).

or

(2) Cancer has spread to lymph nodes on the same side of the chest as the tumor. The lymph nodes with cancer are near the sternum (chest bone) or where the bronchus enters the lung. Also:

- The tumor may be any size.

- There may be separate tumors in different lobes of the same lung.

- Cancer has spread to any of the following:
  - Heart.
  - Major blood vessels that lead to or from the heart.
  - Trachea.
  - Esophagus.
  - Nerve that controls the larynx (voice box).
  - Sternum (chest bone) or backbone.
  - Carina (where the trachea joins the bronchi).

- Stage IV

In stage IV, the tumor may be any size and cancer may have spread to lymph nodes. One or more of the following is true:

- There are one or more tumors in both lungs.

- Cancer is found in fluid around the lungs or the heart.

- Cancer has spread to other parts of the body, such as the brain, liver, adrenal glands, kidneys, or bone.

Section 37.3

Treatment Options for Non-Small Cell Lung Cancer

This section includes excerpts from "Non-Small Cell Lung Cancer Treatment (PDQ®)," National Cancer Institute (NCI), May 12, 2015.

There are different types of treatment for patients with non-small cell lung cancer.

Different types of treatments are available for patients with non-small cell lung cancer. Some treatments are standard (the currently used treatment), and some are being tested in clinical trials. A treatment clinical trial is a research study meant to help improve current treatments or obtain information on new treatments for patients with cancer. When clinical trials show that a new treatment is better than the standard treatment, the new treatment may become the standard treatment. Patients may want to think about taking part in a clinical trial. Some clinical trials are open only to patients who have not started treatment.

Nine types of standard treatment are used:

Surgery

Four types of surgery are used to treat lung cancer:

- Wedge resection: Surgery to remove a tumor and some of the normal tissue around it. When a slightly larger amount of tissue is taken, it is called a segmental resection.

502

- Lobectomy: Surgery to remove a whole lobe (section) of the lung.

- Pneumonectomy: Surgery to remove one whole lung.

- Sleeve resection: Surgery to remove part of the bronchus.

Even if the doctor removes all the cancer that can be seen at the time of the surgery, some patients may be given chemotherapy or radiation therapy after surgery to kill any cancer cells that are left. Treatment given after the surgery, to lower the risk that the cancer will come back, is called adjuvant therapy.

Radiation therapy

Radiation therapy is a cancer treatment that uses high-energy x-rays or other types of radiation to kill cancer cells or keep them from growing. There are two types of radiation therapy. External radiation therapy uses a machine outside the body to send radiation toward the cancer. Internal radiation therapy uses a radioactive substance sealed in needles, seeds, wires, or catheters that are placed directly into or near the cancer.

Radiosurgery is a method of delivering radiation directly to the tumor with little damage to healthy tissue. It does not involve surgery and may be used to treat certain tumors in patients who cannot have surgery.

The way the radiation therapy is given depends on the type and stage of the cancer being treated. It also depends on where the cancer is found. For tumors in the airways, radiation is given directly to the tumor through an endoscope.

Chemotherapy

Chemotherapy is a cancer treatment that uses drugs to stop the growth of cancer cells, either by killing the cells or by stopping them from dividing. When chemotherapy is taken by mouth or injected into a vein or muscle, the drugs enter the bloodstream and can reach cancer cells throughout the body (systemic chemotherapy). When chemotherapy is placed directly into the cerebrospinal fluid, an organ, or a body cavity such as the abdomen, the drugs mainly affect cancer cells in those areas (regional chemotherapy). The way the chemotherapy is given depends on the type and stage of the cancer being treated.

Targeted therapy

Targeted therapy is a type of treatment that uses drugs or other substances to attack specific cancer cells. Targeted therapies usually cause less harm to normal cells than chemotherapy or radiation therapy do. Monoclonal antibodies and small-molecule tyrosine kinase inhibitors are the two main types of targeted therapy being used in the treatment of non-small cell lung cancer.

Monoclonal antibody therapy is a cancer treatment that uses antibodies made in the laboratory from a single type of immune system cell. These antibodies can identify substances on cancer cells or normal substances in the blood or tissues that may help cancer cells grow. The antibodies attach to the substances and kill the cancer cells, block their growth, or keep them from spreading. Monoclonal antibodies are given by infusion. They may be used alone or to carry drugs, toxins, or radioactive material directly to cancer cells.

Monoclonal antibodies used to treat non-small cell lung cancer include bevacizumab and cetuximab. Bevacizumab binds to vascular endothelial growth factor (VEGF) in the blood and tissues and may prevent the growth of new blood vessels that tumors need to grow. Cetuximab is a monoclonal antibody that acts as a tyrosine kinase inhibitor. It binds to epidermal growth factor receptor (EGFR), which is a tyrosine kinase protein, on the surface of cancer cells and works to stop the cells from growing and dividing.

Small-molecule tyrosine kinase inhibitors are targeted therapy drugs that work inside cancer cells and block signals needed for tumors to grow. Small-molecule tyrosine kinase inhibitors may be used with other anticancer drugs as adjuvant therapy.

Small-molecule tyrosine kinase inhibitors used to treat non-small cell lung cancer include erlotinib and gefitinib. They are types of epidermal growth factor receptor (EGFR) tyrosine kinase inhibitors.

Crizotinib is another type of small-molecule tyrosine kinase inhibitor that is used to treat non-small cell lung cancer. It is used to treat non-small cell lung cancer that has certain mutations (changes) in the anaplastic lymphoma kinase (ALK) gene. The protein made by the ALK gene has tyrosine kinase activity.

Laser therapy

Laser therapy is a cancer treatment that uses a laser beam (a narrow beam of intense light) to kill cancer cells.

Photodynamic therapy (PDT)

Photodynamic therapy (PDT) is a cancer treatment that uses a drug and a certain type of laser light to kill cancer cells. A drug that is not active until it is exposed to light is injected into a vein. The drug collects more in cancer cells than in normal cells. Fiberoptic tubes are then used to carry the laser light to the cancer cells, where the drug becomes active and kills the cells. Photodynamic therapy causes little damage to healthy tissue. It is used mainly to treat tumors on or just under the skin or in the lining of internal organs. When the tumor is in the airways, PDT is given directly to the tumor through an endoscope.

Cryosurgery

Cryosurgery is a treatment that uses an instrument to freeze and destroy abnormal tissue, such as carcinoma in situ. This type of treatment is also called cryotherapy. For tumors in the airways, cryosurgery is done through an endoscope.

Electrocautery

Electrocautery is a treatment that uses a probe or needle heated by an electric current to destroy abnormal tissue. For tumors in the airways, electrocautery is done through an endoscope.

Watchful waiting

Watchful waiting is closely monitoring a patient's condition without giving any treatment until signs or symptoms appear or change. This may be done in certain rare cases of non-small cell lung cancer.

New types of treatment are being tested in clinical trials.

Chemoprevention

Chemoprevention is the use of drugs, vitamins, or other substances to reduce the risk of cancer or to reduce the risk cancer will recur (come back).

New combinations

New combinations of treatments are being studied in clinical trials.

Patients may want to think about taking part in a clinical trial.

For some patients, taking part in a clinical trial may be the best treatment choice. Clinical trials are part of the cancer research process. Clinical trials are done to find out if new cancer treatments are safe and effective or better than the standard treatment.

Many of today's standard treatments for cancer are based on earlier clinical trials. Patients who take part in a clinical trial may receive the standard treatment or be among the first to receive a new treatment.

Patients who take part in clinical trials also help improve the way cancer will be treated in the future. Even when clinical trials do not lead to effective new treatments, they often answer important questions and help move research forward.

Patients can enter clinical trials before, during, or after starting their cancer treatment.

Some clinical trials only include patients who have not yet received treatment. Other trials test treatments for patients whose cancer has not gotten better. There are also clinical trials that test new ways to stop cancer from recurring (coming back) or reduce the side effects of cancer treatment.

Clinical trials are taking place in many parts of the country.

Follow-up tests may be needed.

Some of the tests that were done to diagnose the cancer or to find out the stage of the cancer may be repeated. Some tests will be repeated in order to see how well the treatment is working. Decisions about whether to continue, change, or stop treatment may be based on the results of these tests.

Some of the tests will continue to be done from time to time after treatment has ended. The results of these tests can show if your condition has changed or if the cancer has recurred (come back). These tests are sometimes called follow-up tests or check-ups.

Section 37.4

General Information about Small Cell Lung Cancer

This section includes excerpts from "Small Cell Lung Cancer Treatment (PDQ®)," National Cancer Institute (NCI), May 12, 2015.

Small cell lung cancer is a disease in which malignant (cancer) cells form in the tissues of the lung.

The lungs are a pair of cone-shaped breathing organs that are found in the chest. The lungs bring oxygen into the body when you breathe in and take out carbon dioxide when you breathe out. Each lung has sections called lobes. The left lung has two lobes. The right lung, which is slightly larger, has three. A thin membrane called the pleura surrounds the lungs. Two tubes called bronchi lead from the trachea (windpipe) to the right and left lungs. The bronchi are sometimes also affected by lung cancer. Small tubes called bronchioles and tiny air sacs called alveoli make up the inside of the lungs.

There are two types of lung cancer: small cell lung cancer and non-small cell lung cancer.

There are two main types of small cell lung cancer.

These two types include many different types of cells. The cancer cells of each type grow and spread in different ways. The types of small cell lung cancer are named for the kinds of cells found in the cancer and how the cells look when viewed under a microscope:

- Small cell carcinoma (oat cell cancer).
- Combined small cell carcinoma.

Smoking increases the risk of small cell lung cancer.

Smoking cigarettes, pipes, or cigars is the most common cause of lung cancer. The earlier in life a person starts smoking, the more often a person smokes, and the more years a person smokes, the greater the risk of lung cancer. If a person has stopped smoking, the risk becomes lower as the years pass.

Anything that increases your chance of getting a disease is called a risk factor. Having a risk factor does not mean that you will get cancer; not having risk factors doesn't mean that you will not get cancer. Talk to your doctor if you think you may be at risk.

Risk factors for small cell lung cancer include:

- Smoking cigarettes, pipes, or cigars now or in the past.
- Being exposed to secondhand smoke.
- Having a family history of lung cancer.
- Being treated with radiation therapy to the breast or chest.
- Being exposed to asbestos, chromium, nickel, arsenic, soot, or tar in the workplace.
- Being exposed to radon in the home or workplace.
- Living where there is air pollution.
- Being infected with the *human immunodeficiency virus* (HIV).
- Using beta carotene supplements and being a heavy smoker.

When smoking is combined with other risk factors, the risk of lung cancer is increased.

Signs and symptoms of small cell lung cancer include coughing, shortness of breath, and chest pain.

These and other signs and symptoms may be caused by small cell lung cancer or by other conditions. Check with your doctor if you have any of the following:

- Chest discomfort or pain.
- A cough that doesn't go away or gets worse over time.
- Trouble breathing.
- Wheezing.
- Blood in sputum (mucus coughed up from the lungs).
- Hoarseness.
- Trouble swallowing.
- Loss of appetite.
- Weight loss for no known reason.

- Feeling very tired.

- Swelling in the face and/or veins in the neck.

Tests and procedures that examine the lungs are used to detect (find), diagnose, and stage small cell lung cancer.

The following tests and procedures may be used:

- **Physical exam and history:** An exam of the body to check general signs of health, including checking for signs of disease, such as lumps or anything else that seems unusual. A history of the patient's health habits, including smoking, and past jobs, illnesses, and treatments will also be taken.

- **Laboratory tests:** Medical procedures that test samples of tissue, blood, urine, or other substances in the body. These tests help to diagnose disease, plan and check treatment, or monitor the disease over time.

- **Chest x-ray:** An x-ray of the organs and bones inside the chest. An x-ray is a type of energy beam that can go through the body and onto film, making a picture of areas inside the body.

- **CT scan (CAT scan) of the brain, chest, and abdomen:** A procedure that makes a series of detailed pictures of areas inside the body, taken from different angles. The pictures are made by a computer linked to an x-ray machine. A dye may be injected into a vein or swallowed to help the organs or tissues show up more clearly. This procedure is also called computed tomography, computerized tomography, or computerized axial tomography.

- **Sputum cytology:** A microscope is used to check for cancer cells in the sputum (mucus coughed up from the lungs).

- **Biopsy:** The removal of cells or tissues so they can be viewed under a microscope by a pathologist to check for signs of cancer. The different ways a biopsy can be done include the following:

  - **Fine-needle aspiration (FNA) biopsy of the lung:** The removal of tissue or fluid from the lung, using a thin needle. A CT scan, ultrasound, or other imaging procedure is used to find the abnormal tissue or fluid in the lung. A small incision may be made in the skin where the biopsy needle is inserted into the abnormal tissue or fluid. A sample is removed with the needle and sent to the laboratory. A pathologist then views the sample under a microscope to look for cancer cells.

A chest x-ray is done after the procedure to make sure no air is leaking from the lung into the chest.

- **Bronchoscopy:** A procedure to look inside the trachea and large airways in the lung for abnormal areas. A broncho-scope is inserted through the nose or mouth into the trachea and lungs. A bronchoscope is a thin, tube-like instrument with a light and a lens for viewing. It may also have a tool to remove tissue samples, which are checked under a micro-scope for signs of cancer.

- **Thoracoscopy:** A surgical procedure to look at the organs inside the chest to check for abnormal areas. An incision (cut) is made between two ribs, and a thoracoscope is inserted into the chest. A thoracoscope is a thin, tube-like instrument with a light and a lens for viewing. It may also have a tool to remove tissue or lymph node samples, which are checked under a microscope for signs of cancer. In some cases, this procedure is used to remove part of the esophagus or lung. If certain tissues, organs, or lymph nodes can't be reached, a thoracotomy may be done. In this procedure, a larger incision is made between the ribs and the chest is opened.

- **Thoracentesis:** The removal of fluid from the space between the lining of the chest and the lung, using a needle. A patholo-gist views the fluid under a microscope to look for cancer cells.

- **Mediastinoscopy:** A surgical procedure to look at the organs, tissues, and lymph nodes between the lungs for abnormal areas. An incision (cut) is made at the top of the breastbone and a mediastinoscope is inserted into the chest. A mediastinoscope is a thin, tube-like instrument with a light and a lens for viewing. It may also have a tool to remove tissue or lymph node samples, which are checked under a microscope for signs of cancer.

- **Light and electron microscopy:** A laboratory test in which cells in a sample of tissue are viewed under regular and high-powered microscopes to look for certain changes in the cells.

- **Immunohistochemistry:** A test that uses antibodies to check for certain antigens in a sample of tissue. The antibody is usu-ally linked to a radioactive substance or a dye that causes the tissue to light up under a microscope. This type of test may be used to tell the difference between different types of cancer.

Certain factors affect prognosis (chance of recovery) and treatment options.

The prognosis (chance of recovery) and treatment options depend on the following:

- The stage of the cancer (whether it is in the chest cavity only or has spread to other places in the body).
- The patient's age, gender, and general health.

For certain patients, prognosis also depends on whether the patient is treated with both chemotherapy and radiation.

For most patients with small cell lung cancer, current treatments do not cure the cancer.

If lung cancer is found, patients should think about taking part in one of the many clinical trials being done to improve treatment. Clinical trials are taking place in most parts of the country for patients with all stages of small cell lung cancer.

Section 37.5

Stages of Small Cell Lung Cancer

This section includes excerpts from "Small Cell Lung Cancer Treatment (PDQ®)," National Cancer Institute (NCI), May 12, 2015.

After small cell lung cancer has been diagnosed, tests are done to find out if cancer cells have spread within the chest or to other parts of the body.

The process used to find out if cancer has spread within the chest or to other parts of the body is called staging. The information gathered from the staging process determines the stage of the disease. It is important to know the stage in order to plan treatment. Some of the tests used to diagnose small cell lung cancer are also used to stage the disease.

Other tests and procedures that may be used in the staging process include the following:

- **MRI (magnetic resonance imaging) of the brain:** A procedure that uses a magnet, radio waves, and a computer to make

a series of detailed pictures of areas inside the body. This procedure is also called nuclear magnetic resonance imaging (NMRI).

- **CT scan (CAT scan):** A procedure that makes a series of detailed
  pictures of areas inside the body, such as the brain, chest or upper
  abdomen, taken from different angles. The pictures are made by a
  computer linked to an x-ray machine. A dye may be injected into
  a vein or swallowed to help the organs or tissues show up more
  clearly. This procedure is also called computed tomography, computerized tomography, or computerized axial tomography.

- **PET scan (positron emission tomography scan):** A procedure to find malignant tumor cells in the body. A small amount
  of radioactive glucose (sugar) is injected into a vein. The PET
  scanner rotates around the body and makes a picture of where
  glucose is being used in the body. Malignant tumor cells show up
  brighter in the picture because they are more active and take up
  more glucose than normal cells do. A PET scan and CT scan may
  be done at the same time. This is called a PET-CT.

- **Bone scan:** A procedure to check if there are rapidly dividing
  cells, such as cancer cells, in the bone. A very small amount of
  radioactive material is injected into a vein and travels through
  the bloodstream. The radioactive material collects in the bones
  and is detected by a scanner.

There are three ways that cancer spreads in the body.

Cancer can spread through tissue, the lymph system, and the blood:

- Tissue. The cancer spreads from where it began by growing into
  nearby areas.

- Lymph system. The cancer spreads from where it began by
  getting into the lymph system. The cancer travels through the
  lymph vessels to other parts of the body.

- Blood. The cancer spreads from where it began by getting into
  the blood. The cancer travels through the blood vessels to other
  parts of the body.

Cancer may spread from where it began to other parts of the body.

When cancer spreads to another part of the body, it is called metastasis. Cancer cells break away from where they began (the primary
tumor) and travel through the lymph system or blood.

- Lymph system. The cancer gets into the lymph system, travels through the lymph vessels, and forms a tumor (metastatic tumor) in another part of the body.

- Blood. The cancer gets into the blood, travels through the blood vessels, and forms a tumor (metastatic tumor) in another part of the body.

The metastatic tumor is the same type of cancer as the primary tumor. For example, if small cell lung cancer spreads to the brain, the cancer cells in the brain are actually lung cancer cells. The disease is metastatic small cell lung cancer, not brain cancer.

The following stages are used for small cell lung cancer:

Limited-Stage Small Cell Lung Cancer

In limited-stage, cancer is in the lung where it started and may have spread to the area between the lungs or to the lymph nodes above the collarbone.

Extensive-Stage Small Cell Lung Cancer

In extensive-stage, cancer has spread beyond the lung or the area between the lungs or the lymph nodes above the collarbone to other places in the body.

Section 37.6

Treatment Options for Small Cell Lung Cancer

This section includes excerpts from "Small Cell Lung Cancer Treatment (PDQ®)," National Cancer Institute (NCI), May 12, 2015.

There are different types of treatment for patients with small cell lung cancer.

Different types of treatment are available for patients with small cell lung cancer. Some treatments are standard (the currently used treatment), and some are being tested in clinical trials. A treatment clinical trial is a research study meant to help improve current treatments or obtain information on new treatments for patients with cancer. When clinical trials show that a new treatment is better than the standard treatment, the new treatment may become the standard treatment. Patients may want to think about taking part in a clinical trial. Some clinical trials are open only to patients who have not started treatment.

Five types of standard treatment are used:

Surgery

Surgery may be used if the cancer is found in one lung and in nearby lymph nodes only. Because this type of lung cancer is usually found in both lungs, surgery alone is not often used. During surgery, the doctor will also remove lymph nodes to find out if they have cancer in them. Sometimes, surgery may be used to remove a sample of lung tissue to find out the exact type of lung cancer.

Even if the doctor removes all the cancer that can be seen at the time of the operation, some patients may be given chemotherapy or radiation therapy after surgery to kill any cancer cells that are left. Treatment given after the surgery, to lower the risk that the cancer will come back, is called adjuvant therapy.

Chemotherapy

Chemotherapy is a cancer treatment that uses drugs to stop the growth of cancer cells, either by killing the cells or by stopping them from dividing. When chemotherapy is taken by mouth or injected into a vein or muscle, the drugs enter the bloodstream and can reach cancer cells throughout the body (systemic chemotherapy). When chemotherapy is placed directly into the cerebrospinal fluid, an organ, or a body cavity such as the abdomen, the drugs mainly affect cancer cells in those areas (regional chemotherapy). The way the chemotherapy is given depends on the type and stage of the cancer being treated.

Radiation therapy

Radiation therapy is a cancer treatment that uses high-energy x-rays or other types of radiation to kill cancer cells or keep them from growing. There are two types of radiation therapy. External radiation therapy uses a machine outside the body to send radiation toward the cancer. Internal radiation therapy uses a radioactive substance sealed in needles, seeds, wires, or catheters that are placed directly into or near the cancer. Prophylactic cranial irradiation (radiation therapy to the brain to reduce the risk that cancer will spread to the brain) may also be given. The way the radiation therapy is given depends on the type and stage of the cancer being treated.

Laser therapy

Laser therapy is a cancer treatment that uses a laser beam (a narrow beam of intense light) to kill cancer cells.

Endoscopic stent placement

An endoscope is a thin, tube-like instrument used to look at tissues inside the body. An endoscope has a light and a lens for viewing and may be used to place a stent in a body structure to keep the structure open. An endoscopic stent can be used to open an airway blocked by abnormal tissue.

Patients may want to think about taking part in a clinical trial.

For some patients, taking part in a clinical trial may be the best treatment choice. Clinical trials are part of the cancer research process. Clinical trials are done to find out if new cancer treatments are safe and effective or better than the standard treatment.

Many of today's standard treatments for cancer are based on earlier clinical trials. Patients who take part in a clinical trial may receive the standard treatment or be among the first to receive a new treatment.

Patients who take part in clinical trials also help improve the way cancer will be treated in the future. Even when clinical trials do not lead to effective new treatments, they often answer important questions and help move research forward.

Patients can enter clinical trials before, during, or after starting their cancer treatment.

Some clinical trials only include patients who have not yet received treatment. Other trials test treatments for patients whose cancer has not gotten better. There are also clinical trials that test new ways to stop cancer from recurring (coming back) or reduce the side effects of cancer treatment.

Clinical trials are taking place in many parts of the country.

Follow-up tests may be needed.

Some of the tests that were done to diagnose the cancer or to find out the stage of the cancer may be repeated. Some tests will be repeated in order to see how well the treatment is working. Decisions about whether to continue, change, or stop treatment may be based on the results of these tests.

Some of the tests will continue to be done from time to time after treatment has ended. The results of these tests can show if your condition has changed or if the cancer has recurred (come back). These tests are sometimes called follow-up tests or check-ups.

Chapter 38

Pancreatic Cancer

Chapter Contents

Section 38.1

General Information about Pancreatic Cancer

This section includes excerpts from "Pancreatic Cancer Treatment
(PDQ®)," National Cancer Institute (NCI), July 2, 2015.

*Pancreatic cancer is a disease in which malignant (cancer)
cells form in the tissues of the pancreas.*

The pancreas is a gland about 6 inches long that is shaped like a
thin pear lying on its side. The wider end of the pancreas is called
the head, the middle section is called the body, and the narrow end is
called the tail. The pancreas lies between the stomach and the spine.

The pancreas has two main jobs in the body:

- To make juices that help digest (break down) food.
- To make hormones, such as insulin and glucagon, that help control blood sugar levels. Both of these hormones help the body use
  and store the energy it gets from food.

The digestive juices are made by exocrine pancreas cells and the
hormones are made by endocrine pancreas cells. about 95% of pancreatic cancers begin in exocrine cells.

*Smoking and health history can affect the risk of pancreatic
cancer.*

Anything that increases your risk of getting a disease is called a
risk factor. Having a risk factor does not mean that you will get cancer;
not having risk factors doesn't mean that you will not get cancer. Talk
with your doctor if you think you may be at risk.

Risk factors for pancreatic cancer include the following:

- Smoking.
- Being very overweight.
- Having a personal history of diabetes or chronic pancreatitis.
- Having a family history of pancreatic cancer or pancreatitis.
- Having certain hereditary conditions, such as:

- Multiple endocrine neoplasia type 1 (MEN1) syndrome.
- Hereditary nonpolyposis colon cancer (HNPCC; Lynch syndrome).
- von Hippel-Lindau syndrome.
- Peutz-Jeghers syndrome.
- Hereditary breast and ovarian cancer syndrome.
- Familial atypical multiple mole melanoma (FAMMM) syndrome.

Signs and symptoms of pancreatic cancer include jaundice, pain, and weight loss.

Pancreatic cancer may not cause early signs or symptoms. Signs and symptoms may be caused by pancreatic cancer or by other conditions. Check with your doctor if you have any of the following:

- Jaundice (yellowing of the skin and whites of the eyes).
- Light-colored stools.
- Dark urine.
- Pain in the upper or middle abdomen and back.
- Weight loss for no known reason.
- Loss of appetite.
- Feeling very tired.

Pancreatic cancer is difficult to detect (find) and diagnose early.

Pancreatic cancer is difficult to detect and diagnose for the following reasons:

- There aren't any noticeable signs or symptoms in the early stages of pancreatic cancer.
- The signs and symptoms of pancreatic cancer, when present, are like the signs and symptoms of many other illnesses.
- The pancreas is hidden behind other organs such as the stomach, small intestine, liver, gallbladder, spleen, and bile ducts.

Tests that examine the pancreas are used to detect (find), diagnose, and stage pancreatic cancer.

Pancreatic cancer is usually diagnosed with tests and procedures that make pictures of the pancreas and the area around it. The process used to find out if cancer cells have spread within and around the pancreas is called staging. Tests and procedures to detect, diagnose, and stage pancreatic cancer are usually done at the same time. In order to plan treatment, it is important to know the stage of the disease and whether or not the pancreatic cancer can be removed by surgery.

The following tests and procedures may be used:

- **Physical exam and history:** An exam of the body to check general signs of health, including checking for signs of disease, such as lumps or anything else that seems unusual. A history of the patient's health habits and past illnesses and treatments will also be taken.

- **Blood chemistry studies:** A procedure in which a blood sample is checked to measure the amounts of certain substances, such as bilirubin, released into the blood by organs and tissues in the body. An unusual (higher or lower than normal) amount of a substance can be a sign of disease.

- **Tumor marker test:** A procedure in which a sample of blood, urine, or tissue is checked to measure the amounts of certain substances, such as CA 19-9, and carcinoembryonic antigen (CEA), made by organs, tissues, or tumor cells in the body. Certain substances are linked to specific types of cancer when found in increased levels in the body. These are called tumor markers.

- **MRI (magnetic resonance imaging):** A procedure that uses a magnet, radio waves, and a computer to make a series of detailed pictures of areas inside the body. This procedure is also called nuclear magnetic resonance imaging (NMRI).

- **CT scan (CAT scan):** A procedure that makes a series of detailed pictures of areas inside the body, taken from different angles. The pictures are made by a computer linked to an x-ray machine. A dye may be injected into a vein or swallowed to help the organs or tissues show up more clearly. This procedure is also called computed tomography, computerized tomography, or computerized axial tomography. A spiral or helical CT scan makes a series of very detailed pictures of areas inside the body using an x-ray machine that scans the body in a spiral path.

- **PET scan (positron emission tomography scan):** A procedure to find malignant tumor cells in the body. A small amount of radioactive glucose (sugar) is injected into a vein. The PET scanner rotates around the body and makes a picture of where glucose is being used in the body. Malignant tumor cells show up brighter in the picture because they are more active and take up more glucose than normal cells do. A PET scan and CT scan may be done at the same time. This is called a PET-CT.

- **Abdominal ultrasound:** An ultrasound exam used to make pictures of the inside of the abdomen. The ultrasound transducer is pressed against the skin of the abdomen and directs high-energy sound waves (ultrasound) into the abdomen. The sound waves bounce off the internal tissues and organs and make echoes. The transducer receives the echoes and sends them to a computer, which uses the echoes to make pictures called sonograms. The picture can be printed to be looked at later.

- **Endoscopic ultrasound (EUS):** A procedure in which an endoscope is inserted into the body, usually through the mouth or rectum. An endoscope is a thin, tube-like instrument with a light and a lens for viewing. A probe at the end of the endoscope is used to bounce high-energy sound waves (ultrasound) off internal tissues or organs and make echoes. The echoes form a picture of body tissues called a sonogram. This procedure is also called endosonography.

- **Endoscopic retrograde cholangiopancreatography (ERCP):** A procedure used to x-ray the ducts (tubes) that carry bile from the liver to the gallbladder and from the gallbladder to the small intestine. Sometimes pancreatic cancer causes these ducts to narrow and block or slow the flow of bile, causing jaundice. An endoscope (a thin, lighted tube) is passed through the mouth, esophagus, and stomach into the first part of the small intestine. A catheter (a smaller tube) is then inserted through the endoscope into the pancreatic ducts. A dye is injected through the catheter into the ducts and an x-ray is taken. If the ducts are blocked by a tumor, a fine tube may be inserted into the duct to unblock it. This tube (or stent) may be left in place to keep the duct open. Tissue samples may also be taken.

- **Percutaneous transhepatic cholangiography (PTC):** A procedure used to x-ray the liver and bile ducts. A thin needle is inserted through the skin below the ribs and into the liver. Dye is injected into the liver or bile ducts and an x-ray is taken. If a blockage is found, a thin, flexible tube called a stent is sometimes left in the liver to drain bile into the small intestine or a collection bag outside the body. This test is done only if ERCP cannot be done.

- **Laparoscopy:** A surgical procedure to look at the organs inside the abdomen to check for signs of disease. Small incisions (cuts) are made in the wall of the abdomen and a laparoscope (a thin, lighted tube) is inserted into one of the incisions. The laparoscope may have an ultrasound probe at the end in order to bounce high-energy sound waves off internal organs, such as the pancreas. This is called laparoscopic ultrasound. Other instruments may be inserted through the same or other incisions to perform procedures such as taking tissue samples from the pancreas or a sample of fluid from the abdomen to check for cancer.

- **Biopsy:** The removal of cells or tissues so they can be viewed under a microscope by a pathologist to check for signs of cancer. There are several ways to do a biopsy for pancreatic cancer. A fine needle or a core needle may be inserted into the pancreas during an x-ray or ultrasound to remove cells. Tissue may also be removed during a laparoscopy.

Certain factors affect prognosis (chance of recovery) and treatment options.

The prognosis (chance of recovery) and treatment options depend on the following:

- Whether or not the tumor can be removed by surgery.
- The stage of the cancer (the size of the tumor and whether the cancer has spread outside the pancreas to nearby tissues or lymph nodes or to other places in the body).
- The patient's general health.
- Whether the cancer has just been diagnosed or has recurred (come back).

Pancreatic cancer can be controlled only if it is found before it has spread, when it can be completely removed by surgery. If the cancer has spread, palliative treatment can improve the patient's quality of life by controlling the symptoms and complications of this disease.

Section 38.2

Stages of Pancreatic Cancer

This section includes excerpts from "Pancreatic Cancer Treatment
(PDQ®)," National Cancer Institute (NCI), July 2, 2015.

Tests and procedures to stage pancreatic cancer are usually done at the same time as diagnosis.

The process used to find out if cancer has spread within the pancreas or to other parts of the body is called staging. The information gathered from the staging process determines the stage of the disease. It is important to know the stage of the disease in order to plan treatment. The results of some of the tests used to diagnose pancreatic cancer are often also used to stage the disease. See the General Information section for more information.

There are three ways that cancer spreads in the body.

Cancer can spread through tissue, the lymph system, and the blood:

- Tissue. The cancer spreads from where it began by growing into nearby areas.
- Lymph system. The cancer spreads from where it began by getting into the lymph system. The cancer travels through the lymph vessels to other parts of the body.
- Blood. The cancer spreads from where it began by getting into the blood. The cancer travels through the blood vessels to other parts of the body.

Cancer may spread from where it began to other parts of the body.

When cancer spreads to another part of the body, it is called metastasis. Cancer cells break away from where they began (the primary tumor) and travel through the lymph system or blood.

- Lymph system. The cancer gets into the lymph system, travels through the lymph vessels, and forms a tumor (metastatic tumor) in another part of the body.

- Blood. The cancer gets into the blood, travels through the blood vessels, and forms a tumor (metastatic tumor) in another part of the body.

The metastatic tumor is the same type of cancer as the primary tumor. For example, if pancreatic cancer spreads to the liver, the cancer cells in the liver are actually pancreatic cancer cells. The disease is metastatic pancreatic cancer, not liver cancer.

The following stages are used for pancreatic cancer:

Stage 0 (Carcinoma in Situ)

In stage 0, abnormal cells are found in the lining of the pancreas. These abnormal cells may become cancer and spread into nearby normal tissue. Stage 0 is also called carcinoma in situ.

Stage I

In stage I, cancer has formed and is found in the pancreas only. Stage I is divided into stage IA and stage IB, based on the size of the tumor.

- Stage IA: The tumor is 2 centimeters or smaller.
- Stage IB: The tumor is larger than 2 centimeters.

Stage II

In stage II, cancer may have spread to nearby tissue and organs, and may have spread to lymph nodes near the pancreas. Stage II is divided into stage IIA and stage IIB, based on where the cancer has spread.

- Stage IIA pancreatic cancer. Cancer has spread to nearby tissue and organs but has not spread to nearby lymph nodes.
- Stage IIB: Cancer has spread to nearby lymph nodes and may have spread to nearby tissue and organs.

Stage III

In stage III, cancer has spread to the major blood vessels near the pancreas and may have spread to nearby lymph nodes.

Stage IV

In stage IV, cancer may be of any size and has spread to distant organs, such as the liver, lung, and peritoneal cavity. It may have also spread to organs and tissues near the pancreas or to lymph nodes.

Section 38.3

Treatment Options for Pancreatic Cancer

This section includes excerpts from "Pancreatic Cancer Treatment (PDQ®)," National Cancer Institute (NCI), July 2, 2015.

There are different types of treatment for patients with pancreatic cancer.

Different types of treatment are available for patients with pancreatic cancer. Some treatments are standard (the currently used treatment), and some are being tested in clinical trials. A treatment clinical trial is a research study meant to help improve current treatments or obtain information on new treatments for patients with cancer. When clinical trials show that a new treatment is better than the standard treatment, the new treatment may become the standard treatment. Patients may want to think about taking part in a clinical trial. Some clinical trials are open only to patients who have not started treatment.

Five types of standard treatment are used:

Surgery

One of the following types of surgery may be used to take out the tumor:

- Whipple procedure: A surgical procedure in which the head of the pancreas, the gallbladder, part of the stomach, part of the small intestine, and the bile duct are removed. Enough of the pancreas is left to produce digestive juices and insulin.

- Total pancreatectomy: This operation removes the whole pancreas, part of the stomach, part of the small intestine, the common bile duct, the gallbladder, the spleen, and nearby lymph nodes.

- Distal pancreatectomy: The body and the tail of the pancreas and usually the spleen are removed.

If the cancer has spread and cannot be removed, the following types of palliative surgery may be done to relieve symptoms and improve quality of life:

- Surgical biliary bypass: If cancer is blocking the small intestine and bile is building up in the gallbladder, a biliary bypass may be done. During this operation, the doctor will cut the gallbladder or bile duct and sew it to the small intestine to create a new pathway around the blocked area.

- Endoscopic stent placement: If the tumor is blocking the bile duct, surgery may be done to put in a stent (a thin tube) to drain bile that has built up in the area. The doctor may place the stent through a catheter that drains to the outside of the body or the stent may go around the blocked area and drain the bile into the small intestine.

- Gastric bypass: If the tumor is blocking the flow of food from the stomach, the stomach may be sewn directly to the small intestine so the patient can continue to eat normally.

Radiation therapy

Radiation therapy is a cancer treatment that uses high-energy x-rays or other types of radiation to kill cancer cells or keep them from growing. There are two types of radiation therapy. External radiation therapy uses a machine outside the body to send radiation toward the cancer. Internal radiation therapy uses a radioactive substance sealed in needles, seeds, wires, or catheters that are placed directly into or near the cancer. The way the radiation therapy is given depends on the type and stage of the cancer being treated.

Chemotherapy

Chemotherapy is a cancer treatment that uses drugs to stop the growth of cancer cells, either by killing the cells or by stopping them from dividing. When chemotherapy is taken by mouth or injected into a vein or muscle, the drugs enter the bloodstream and can reach cancer cells throughout the body (systemic chemotherapy). When chemotherapy is placed directly into the cerebrospinal fluid, an organ, or a body cavity such as the abdomen, the drugs mainly affect cancer cells in those areas (regional chemotherapy). Combination chemotherapy is treatment using more than one anticancer drug. The way the chemotherapy is given depends on the type and stage of the cancer being treated.

Chemoradiation therapy

Chemoradiation therapy combines chemotherapy and radiation therapy to increase the effects of both.

Targeted therapy

Targeted therapy is a type of treatment that uses drugs or other substances to identify and attack specific cancer cells without harming normal cells. Tyrosine kinase inhibitors (TKIs) are targeted therapy drugs that block signals needed for tumors to grow. Erlotinib is a type of TKI used to treat pancreatic cancer.

There are treatments for pain caused by pancreatic cancer.

Pain can occur when the tumor presses on nerves or other organs near the pancreas. When pain medicine is not enough, there are treatments that act on nerves in the abdomen to relieve the pain. The doctor may inject medicine into the area around affected nerves or may cut the nerves to block the feeling of pain. Radiation therapy with or without chemotherapy can also help relieve pain by shrinking the tumor.

Patients with pancreatic cancer have special nutritional needs.

Surgery to remove the pancreas may affect its ability to make pancreatic enzymes that help to digest food. As a result, patients may have problems digesting food and absorbing nutrients into the body. To prevent malnutrition, the doctor may prescribe medicines that replace these enzymes.

New types of treatment are being tested in clinical trials.

Biologic therapy

Biologic therapy is a treatment that uses the patient's immune system to fight cancer. Substances made by the body or made in a laboratory are used to boost, direct, or restore the body's natural defenses against cancer. This type of cancer treatment is also called biotherapy or immunotherapy.

Patients may want to think about taking part in a clinical trial.

For some patients, taking part in a clinical trial may be the best treatment choice. Clinical trials are part of the cancer research process.

Clinical trials are done to find out if new cancer treatments are safe and effective or better than the standard treatment.

Many of today's standard treatments for cancer are based on earlier clinical trials. Patients who take part in a clinical trial may receive the standard treatment or be among the first to receive a new treatment.

Patients who take part in clinical trials also help improve the way cancer will be treated in the future. Even when clinical trials do not lead to effective new treatments, they often answer important questions and help move research forward.

Patients can enter clinical trials before, during, or after starting their cancer treatment.

Some clinical trials only include patients who have not yet received treatment. Other trials test treatments for patients whose cancer has not gotten better. There are also clinical trials that test new ways to stop cancer from recurring (coming back) or reduce the side effects of cancer treatment.

Clinical trials are taking place in many parts of the country. See the Treatment Options section that follows for links to current treatment clinical trials. These have been retrieved from NCI's listing of clinical trials.

Follow-up tests may be needed

Some of the tests that were done to diagnose the cancer or to find out the stage of the cancer may be repeated. Some tests will be repeated in order to see how well the treatment is working. Decisions about whether to continue, change, or stop treatment may be based on the results of these tests.

Some of the tests will continue to be done from time to time after treatment has ended. The results of these tests can show if your condition has changed or if the cancer has recurred (come back). These tests are sometimes called follow-up tests or check-ups.

Chapter 39

Skin Cancer

Chapter Contents

Section 39.1

General Information about Skin Cancer

This section includes excerpts from "Skin Cancer Treatment
(PDQ®)," National Cancer Institute (NCI), April 2, 2015.

Skin cancer is a disease in which malignant (cancer) cells form in the tissues of the skin.

The skin is the body's largest organ. It protects against heat, sunlight, injury, and infection. Skin also helps control body temperature and stores water, fat, and vitamin D. The skin has several layers, but the two main layers are the epidermis (upper or outer layer) and the dermis (lower or inner layer). Skin cancer begins in the epidermis, which is made up of three kinds of cells:

- Squamous cells: Thin, flat cells that form the top layer of the epidermis.

- Basal cells: Round cells under the squamous cells.

- Melanocytes: Cells that make melanin and are found in the lower part of the epidermis. Melanin is the pigment that gives skin its natural color. When skin is exposed to the sun, melanocytes make more pigment and cause the skin to darken.

Skin cancer can occur anywhere on the body, but it is most common in skin that is often exposed to sunlight, such as the face, neck, hands, and arms.

There are different types of cancer that start in the skin.

The most common types are basal cell carcinoma and squamous cell carcinoma, which are nonmelanoma skin cancers. Nonmelanoma skin cancers rarely spread to other parts of the body. Melanoma is the rarest form of skin cancer. It is more likely to invade nearby tissues and spread to other parts of the body. Actinic keratosis is a skin condition that sometimes becomes squamous cell carcinoma.

Skin color and being exposed to sunlight can increase the risk of nonmelanoma skin cancer and actinic keratosis.

Anything that increases your chance of getting a disease is called a risk factor. Having a risk factor does not mean that you will get cancer; not having risk factors doesn't mean that you will not get cancer. Talk with your doctor if you think you may be at risk. Risk factors for basal cell carcinoma and squamous cell carcinoma include the following:

- Being exposed to natural sunlight or artificial sunlight (such as from tanning beds) over long periods of time.

- Having a fair complexion, which includes the following:

  - Fair skin that freckles and burns easily, does not tan, or tans poorly.

  - Blue or green or other light-colored eyes.

  - Red or blond hair.

- Having actinic keratosis.

- Past treatment with radiation.

- Having a weakened immune system.

- Having certain changes in the genes that are linked to skin cancer.

- Being exposed to arsenic.

Risk factors for actinic keratosis include the following:

- Being exposed to natural sunlight or artificial sunlight (such as from tanning beds) over long periods of time.

- Having a fair complexion, which includes the following:

  - Fair skin that freckles and burns easily, does not tan, or tans poorly.

  - Blue or green or other light-colored eyes.

  - Red or blond hair.

Nonmelanoma skin cancer and actinic keratosis often appear as a change in the skin.

Not all changes in the skin are a sign of nonmelanoma skin cancer or actinic keratosis. Check with your doctor if you notice any changes in your skin.

Signs of nonmelanoma skin cancer include the following:

- A sore that does not heal.
- Areas of the skin that are:
    - Raised, smooth, shiny, and look pearly.
    - Firm and look like a scar, and may be white, yellow, or waxy.
    - Raised, and red or reddish-brown.
    - Scaly, bleeding or crusty.

Signs of actinic keratosis include the following:

- A rough, red, pink, or brown, raised, scaly patch on the skin that may be flat or raised.
- Cracking or peeling of the lower lip that is not helped by lip balm or petroleum jelly.

Tests or procedures that examine the skin are used to detect (find) and diagnose nonmelanoma skin cancer and actinic keratosis.

The following procedures may be used:

- Skin exam: A doctor or nurse checks the skin for bumps or spots that look abnormal in color, size, shape, or texture.
- Skin biopsy: All or part of the abnormal-looking growth is cut from the skin and viewed under a microscope by a pathologist to check for signs of cancer. There are four main types of skin biopsies:
    - Shave biopsy: A sterile razor blade is used to "shave-off" the abnormal-looking growth.
    - Punch biopsy: A special instrument called a punch or a trephine is used to remove circle of tissue from the abnormal-looking growth.
    - Incisional biopsy: A scalpel is used to remove part of a growth.
    - Excisional biopsy: A scalpel is used to remove the entire growth.

Certain factors affect prognosis (chance of recovery) and treatment options.

The prognosis (chance of recovery) depends mostly on the stage of the cancer and the type of treatment used to remove the cancer.

Treatment options depend on the following:

- The stage of the cancer (whether it has spread deeper into the skin or to other places in the body).

- The type of cancer.

- The size of the tumor and what part of the body it affects.

- The patient's general health.

Section 39.2

Stages of Skin Cancer

This section includes excerpts from "Skin Cancer Treatment (PDQ®)," National Cancer Institute (NCI), April 2, 2015.

After nonmelanoma skin cancer has been diagnosed, tests are done to find out if cancer cells have spread within the skin or to other parts of the body.

The process used to find out if cancer has spread within the skin or to other parts of the body is called staging. The information gathered from the staging process determines the stage of the disease. It is important to know the stage in order to plan treatment.

The following tests and procedures may be used in the staging process:

- **CT scan (CAT scan):** A procedure that makes a series of detailed pictures of areas inside the body, taken from different angles. The pictures are made by a computer linked to an x-ray machine. A dye may be injected into a vein or swallowed to help the organs or tissues show up more clearly. This procedure is also called computed tomography, computerized tomography, or computerized axial tomography.

- **MRI (magnetic resonance imaging):** A procedure that uses a magnet, radio waves, and a computer to make a series of detailed pictures of areas inside the body. This procedure is also called nuclear magnetic resonance imaging (NMRI).

- **Lymph node biopsy:** For squamous cell carcinoma, the lymph nodes may be removed and checked to see if cancer has spread to them.

There are three ways that cancer spreads in the body.

Cancer can spread through tissue, the lymph system, and the blood:

- Tissue. The cancer spreads from where it began by growing into nearby areas.

- Lymph system. The cancer spreads from where it began by getting into the lymph system. The cancer travels through the lymph vessels to other parts of the body.

- Blood. The cancer spreads from where it began by getting into the blood. The cancer travels through the blood vessels to other parts of the body.

Cancer may spread from where it began to other parts of the body.

When cancer spreads to another part of the body, it is called metastasis. Cancer cells break away from where they began (the primary tumor) and travel through the lymph system or blood.

- Lymph system. The cancer gets into the lymph system, travels through the lymph vessels, and forms a tumor (metastatic tumor) in another part of the body.

- Blood. The cancer gets into the blood, travels through the blood vessels, and forms a tumor (metastatic tumor) in another part of the body.

The metastatic tumor is the same type of cancer as the primary tumor. For example, if skin cancer spreads to the lung, the cancer cells in the lung are actually skin cancer cells. The disease is metastatic skin cancer, not lung cancer.

Staging of nonmelanoma skin cancer depends on whether the tumor has certain "high-risk" features and if the tumor is on the eyelid.

Staging for nonmelanoma skin cancer that is on the eyelid is different from staging for nonmelanoma skin cancer that affects other parts of the body.

The following are high-risk features for nonmelanoma skin cancer that is not on the eyelid:

- The tumor is thicker than 2 millimeters.

- The tumor is described as Clark level IV (has spread into the lower layer of the dermis) or Clark level V (has spread into the layer of fat below the skin).

- The tumor has grown and spread along nerve pathways.

- The tumor began on an ear or on a lip that has hair on it.

- The tumor has cells that look very different from normal cells under a microscope.

The following stages are used for nonmelanoma skin cancer that is not on the eyelid:

Stage 0 (Carcinoma in Situ)

In stage 0, abnormal cells are found in the squamous cell or basal cell layer of the epidermis (topmost layer of the skin). These abnormal cells may become cancer and spread into nearby normal tissue. Stage 0 is also called carcinoma in situ.

Stage I

In stage I, cancer has formed. The tumor is not larger than 2 centimeters at its widest point and may have one high-risk feature.

Stage II

In stage II, the tumor is either:

- larger than 2 centimeters at its widest point; or

- any size and has two or more high-risk features.

Stage III

In stage III:

- The tumor has spread to the jaw, eye socket, or side of the skull. Cancer may have spread to one lymph node on the same side of the body as the tumor. The lymph node is not larger than 3 centimeters.

  or

- Cancer has spread to one lymph node on the same side of the body as the tumor. The lymph node is not larger than 3 centimeters and one of the following is true:

  - the tumor is not larger than 2 centimeters at its widest point and may have one high-risk feature; or

  - the tumor is larger than 2 centimeters at its widest point; or

  - the tumor is any size and has two or more high-risk features.

Stage IV

In stage IV, one of the following is true:

- The tumor is any size and may have spread to the jaw, eye socket, or side of the skull. Cancer has spread to one lymph node on the same side of the body as the tumor and the affected node is larger than 3 centimeters but not larger than 6 centimeters, or cancer has spread to more than one lymph node on one or both sides of the body and the affected nodes are not larger than 6 centimeters; or

- The tumor is any size and may have spread to the jaw, eye socket, skull, spine, or ribs. Cancer has spread to one lymph node that is larger than 6 centimeters; or

- The tumor is any size and has spread to the base of the skull, spine, or ribs. Cancer may have spread to the lymph nodes; or

- Cancer has spread to other parts of the body, such as the lung.

The following stages are used for nonmelanoma skin cancer on the eyelid:

Stage 0 (Carcinoma in Situ)

In stage 0, abnormal cells are found in the epidermis (topmost layer of the skin). These abnormal cells may become cancer and spread into nearby normal tissue. Stage 0 is also called carcinoma in situ.

Stage I

Stage I is divided into stages IA, IB, and IC.

- Stage IA: The tumor is 5 millimeters or smaller and has not spread to the connective tissue of the eyelid or to the edge of the eyelid where the lashes are.

- Stage IB: The tumor is larger than 5 millimeters but not larger than 10 millimeters or has spread to the connective tissue of the eyelid or to the edge of the eyelid where the lashes are.

- Stage IC: The tumor is larger than 10 millimeters but not larger than 20 millimeters or has spread through the full thickness of the eyelid.

Stage II

In stage II, one of the following is true:

- The tumor is larger than 20 millimeters.

- The tumor has spread to nearby parts of the eye or eye socket.

- The tumor has spread to spaces around the nerves in the eyelid.

Stage III

Stage III is divided into stages IIIA, IIIB, and IIIC.

- Stage IIIA: To remove all of the tumor, the whole eye and part of the optic nerve must be removed. The bone, muscles, fat, and connective tissue around the eye may also be removed.

- Stage IIIB: The tumor may be anywhere in or near the eye and has spread to nearby lymph nodes.

- Stage IIIC: The tumor has spread to structures around the eye or in the face, or to the brain, and cannot be removed in surgery.

Stage IV

The tumor has spread to distant parts of the body.

Treatment is based on the type of nonmelanoma skin cancer or other skin condition diagnosed:

Basal cell carcinoma

Basal cell carcinoma is the most common type of skin cancer. It usually occurs on areas of the skin that have been in the sun, most often the nose. Often this cancer appears as a raised bump that looks smooth and pearly. Another type looks like a scar and is flat and firm and may be white, yellow, or waxy. Basal cell carcinoma may spread to tissues around the cancer, but it usually does not spread to other parts of the body.

Squamous cell carcinoma

Squamous cell carcinoma occurs on areas of the skin that have been in the sun, such as the ears, lower lip, and the back of the hands. Squamous cell carcinoma may also appear on areas of the skin that have been burned or exposed to chemicals or radiation. Often this cancer appears as a firm red bump. The tumor may feel scaly, bleed, or form a crust. Squamous cell tumors may spread to nearby lymph nodes. Squamous cell carcinoma that has not spread can usually be cured.

Actinic keratosis

Actinic keratosis is a skin condition that is not cancer, but sometimes changes into squamous cell carcinoma. It usually occurs in areas that have been exposed to the sun, such as the face, the back of the hands, and the lower lip. It looks like rough, red, pink, or brown scaly patches on the skin that may be flat or raised, or the lower lip cracks and peels and is not helped by lip balm or petroleum jelly.

Section 39.3

Treatment Options for Skin Cancer

This section includes excerpts from "Skin Cancer Treatment (PDQ®)," National Cancer Institute (NCI), April 2, 2015.

There are different types of treatment for patients with non-melanoma skin cancer and actinic keratosis.

Different types of treatment are available for patients with non-melanoma skin cancer and actinic keratosis. Some treatments are standard (the currently used treatment), and some are being tested in clinical trials. A treatment clinical trial is a research study meant to help improve current treatments or obtain information on new treatments for patients with cancer. When clinical trials show that a new treatment is better than the standard treatment, the new treatment may become the standard treatment. Patients may want to think about taking part in a clinical trial. Some clinical trials are open only to patients who have not started treatment.

Five types of standard treatment are used:

Surgery

One or more of the following surgical procedures may be used to treat nonmelanoma skin cancer or actinic keratosis:

- Mohs micrographic surgery: The tumor is cut from the skin in thin layers. During surgery, the edges of the tumor and each layer of tumor removed are viewed through a microscope to check for cancer cells. Layers continue to be removed until no more cancer cells are seen. This type of surgery removes as little normal tissue as possible and is often used to remove skin cancer on the face.

- Simple excision: The tumor is cut from the skin along with some of the normal skin around it.

- Shave excision: The abnormal area is shaved off the surface of the skin with a small blade.

- Electrodesiccation and curettage: The tumor is cut from the skin with a curette (a sharp, spoon-shaped tool). A needle-shaped electrode is then used to treat the area with an electric current that stops the bleeding and destroys cancer cells that remain around the edge of the wound. The process may be repeated one to three times during the surgery to remove all of the cancer.

- Cryosurgery: A treatment that uses an instrument to freeze and destroy abnormal tissue, such as carcinoma in situ. This type of treatment is also called cryotherapy.

- Laser surgery: A surgical procedure that uses a laser beam (a narrow beam of intense light) as a knife to make bloodless cuts in tissue or to remove a surface lesion such as a tumor.

- Dermabrasion: Removal of the top layer of skin using a rotating wheel or small particles to rub away skin cells.

Radiation therapy

Radiation therapy is a cancer treatment that uses high-energy x-rays or other types of radiation to kill cancer cells or keep them from growing. There are two types of radiation therapy. External radiation therapy uses a machine outside the body to send radiation toward the cancer. Internal radiation therapy uses a radioactive substance sealed in needles, seeds, wires, or catheters that are placed directly into or near the cancer. The way the radiation therapy is given depends on the type and stage of the cancer being treated.

Chemotherapy

Chemotherapy is a cancer treatment that uses drugs to stop the growth of cancer cells, either by killing the cells or by stopping them from dividing. When chemotherapy is taken by mouth or injected into a vein or muscle, the drugs enter the bloodstream and can reach cancer cells throughout the body (systemic chemotherapy). When chemotherapy is placed directly into the cerebrospinal fluid, an organ, or a body cavity such as the abdomen, the drugs mainly affect cancer cells in those areas (regional chemotherapy). Chemotherapy for nonmelanoma skin cancer and actinic keratosis is usually topical (applied to the skin in a cream or lotion). The way the chemotherapy is given depends on the condition being treated.

Retinoids (drugs related to vitamin A) are sometimes used to treat squamous cell carcinoma of the skin.

Photodynamic therapy

Photodynamic therapy (PDT) is a cancer treatment that uses a drug and a certain type of laser light to kill cancer cells. A drug that is not active until it is exposed to light is injected into a vein. The drug collects more in cancer cells than in normal cells. For skin cancer, laser light is shined onto the skin and the drug becomes active and kills the cancer cells. Photodynamic therapy causes little damage to healthy tissue.

Biologic therapy

Biologic therapy is a treatment that uses the patient's immune system to fight cancer. Substances made by the body or made in a laboratory are used to boost, direct, or restore the body's natural defenses against cancer. This type of cancer treatment is also called biotherapy or immunotherapy.

Interferon and imiquimod are biologic agents used to treat skin cancer. Interferon (by injection) may be used to treat squamous cell carcinoma of the skin. Topical imiquimod therapy (a cream applied to the skin) may be used to treat some small basal cell carcinomas.

Patients may want to think about taking part in a clinical trial.

For some patients, taking part in a clinical trial may be the best treatment choice. Clinical trials are part of the cancer research process.

Clinical trials are done to find out if new cancer treatments are safe and effective or better than the standard treatment.

Many of today's standard treatments for cancer are based on earlier clinical trials. Patients who take part in a clinical trial may receive the standard treatment or be among the first to receive a new treatment.

Patients who take part in clinical trials also help improve the way cancer will be treated in the future. Even when clinical trials do not lead to effective new treatments, they often answer important questions and help move research forward.

Patients can enter clinical trials before, during, or after starting their cancer treatment.

Some clinical trials only include patients who have not yet received treatment. Other trials test treatments for patients whose cancer has not gotten better. There are also clinical trials that test new ways to stop cancer from recurring (coming back) or reduce the side effects of cancer treatment.

Clinical trials are taking place in many parts of the country.

Follow-up tests may be needed.

Some of the tests that were done to diagnose the cancer or to find out the stage of the cancer may be repeated. Some tests will be repeated in order to see how well the treatment is working. Decisions about whether to continue, change, or stop treatment may be based on the results of these tests.

Some of the tests will continue to be done from time to time after treatment has ended. The results of these tests can show if your condition has changed or if the cancer has recurred (come back). These tests are sometimes called follow-up tests or check-ups.

Basal cell carcinoma and squamous cell carcinoma are likely to recur (come back), usually within 5 years, or new tumors may form. Talk to your doctor about how often you should have your skin checked for signs of cancer.

Chapter 40

Thyroid Cancer

Chapter Contents

Section 40.1

General Information about Thyroid Cancer

Text in this section is excerpted from "Thyroid Cancer Treatment (PDQ®)," National Cancer Institue (NCI), June 17, 2015.

Thyroid cancer is a disease in which malignant (cancer) cells form in the tissues of the thyroid gland.

The thyroid is a gland at the base of the throat near the trachea (windpipe). It is shaped like a butterfly, with a right lobe and a left lobe. The isthmus, a thin piece of tissue, connects the two lobes. A healthy thyroid is a little larger than a quarter. It usually cannot be felt through the skin.

The thyroid uses iodine, a mineral found in some foods and in iodized salt, to help make several hormones. Thyroid hormones do the following:

- Control heart rate, body temperature, and how quickly food is changed into energy (metabolism).

- Control the amount of calcium in the blood.

There are four main types of thyroid cancer:

- Papillary thyroid cancer: The most common type of thyroid cancer.

- Follicular thyroid cancer. Hurthle cell carcinoma is a form of follicular thyroid cancer and is treated the same way.

- Medullary thyroid cancer.

- Anaplastic thyroid cancer.

Age, gender, and exposure to radiation can affect the risk of thyroid cancer.

Anything that increases your risk of getting a disease is called a risk factor. Having a risk factor does not mean that you will get cancer; not having risk factors doesn't mean that you will not get cancer.

Talk with your doctor if you think you may be at risk. Risk factors for thyroid cancer include the following:

- Being between 25 and 65 years old.

- Being female.

- Being exposed to radiation to the head and neck as a child or being exposed to radiation from an atomic bomb. The cancer may occur as soon as 5 years after exposure.

- Having a history of goiter (enlarged thyroid).

- Having a family history of thyroid disease or thyroid cancer.

- Having certain genetic conditions such as familial medullary thyroid cancer (FMTC), multiple endocrine neoplasia type 2A syndrome, and multiple endocrine neoplasia type 2B syndrome.

- Being Asian.

Medullary thyroid cancer is sometimes caused by a change in a gene that is passed from parent to child.

The genes in cells carry hereditary information from parent to child. A certain change in a gene that is passed from parent to child (inherited) may cause medullary thyroid cancer. A test has been developed that can find the changed gene before medullary thyroid cancer appears. The patient is tested first to see if he or she has the changed gene. If the patient has it, other family members may also be tested. Family members, including young children, who have the changed gene can decrease the chance of developing medullary thyroid cancer by having a thyroidectomy (surgery to remove the thyroid).

Signs of thyroid cancer include a swelling or lump in the neck.

Thyroid cancer may not cause early signs or symptoms. It is sometimes found during a routine physical exam. Signs or symptoms may occur as the tumor gets bigger. Other conditions may cause the same signs or symptoms. Check with your doctor if you have any of the following:

- A lump in the neck.

- Trouble breathing.

- Trouble swallowing.

- Hoarseness.

Tests that examine the thyroid, neck, and blood are used to detect (find) and diagnose thyroid cancer.

The following tests and procedures may be used:

- **Physical exam and history:** An exam of the body to check general signs of health, including checking for signs of disease, such as lumps or swelling in the neck, voice box, and lymph nodes, and anything else that seems unusual. A history of the patient's health habits and past illnesses and treatments will also be taken.

- **Laryngoscopy:** A procedure in which the doctor checks the larynx (voice box) with a mirror or with a laryngoscope. A laryngoscope is a thin, tube-like instrument with a light and a lens for viewing. A thyroid tumor may press on vocal cords. The laryngoscopy is done to see if the vocal cords are moving normally.

- **Blood hormone studies:** A procedure in which a blood sample is checked to measure the amounts of certain hormones released into the blood by organs and tissues in the body. An unusual (higher or lower than normal) amount of a substance can be a sign of disease in the organ or tissue that makes it. The blood may be checked for abnormal levels of thyroid-stimulating hormone (TSH). TSH is made by the pituitary gland in the brain. It stimulates the release of thyroid hormone and controls how fast follicular thyroid cells grow. The blood may also be checked for high levels of the hormone calcitonin and antithyroid antibodies.

- **Blood chemistry studies:** A procedure in which a blood sample is checked to measure the amounts of certain substances, such as calcium, released into the blood by organs and tissues in the body. An unusual (higher or lower than normal) amount of a substance can be a sign of disease.

- **Ultrasound exam:** A procedure in which high-energy sound waves (ultrasound) are bounced off internal tissues or organs and make echoes. The echoes form a picture of body tissues called a sonogram. The picture can be printed to be looked at later. This procedure can show the size of a thyroid tumor and whether it is solid or a fluid -filled cyst. Ultrasound may be used to guide a fine-needle aspiration biopsy.

- **CT scan (CAT scan):** A procedure that makes a series of detailed pictures of areas inside the body, taken from different angles. The pictures are made by a computer linked to an x-ray machine. A dye may be injected into a vein or swallowed to help the organs or tissues show up more clearly. This procedure is also called computed tomography, computerized tomography, or computerized axial tomography.

- **Fine-needle aspiration biopsy of the thyroid:** The removal of thyroid tissue using a thin needle. The needle is inserted through the skin into the thyroid. Several tissue samples are removed from different parts of the thyroid. A pathologist views the tissue samples under a microscope to look for cancer cells. Because the type of thyroid cancer can be hard to diagnose, patients should ask to have biopsy samples checked by a pathologist who has experience diagnosing thyroid cancer.

- **Surgical biopsy:** The removal of the thyroid nodule or one lobe of the thyroid during surgery so the cells and tissues can be viewed under a microscope by a pathologist to check for signs of cancer. Because the type of thyroid cancer can be hard to diagnose, patients should ask to have biopsy samples checked by a pathologist who has experience diagnosing thyroid cancer.

Certain factors affect prognosis (chance of recovery) and treatment options.

The prognosis (chance of recovery) and treatment options depend on the following:

- The age of the patient.
- The type of thyroid cancer.
- The stage of the cancer.
- The patient's general health.
- Whether the patient has multiple endocrine neoplasia type 2B (MEN 2B).
- Whether the cancer has just been diagnosed or has recurred (come back).

Section 40.2

Stages of Thyroid Cancer

Text in this section is excerpted from "Thyroid Cancer Treatment
(PDQ®)," National Cancer Institue (NCI), June 17, 2015.

*After thyroid cancer has been diagnosed, tests are done to
find out if cancer cells have spread within the thyroid or to
other parts of the body.*

The process used to find out if cancer has spread within the thyroid
or to other parts of the body is called staging. The information gathered from the staging process determines the stage of the disease. It is
important to know the stage in order to plan treatment. The following
tests and procedures may be used in the staging process:

- **CT scan (CAT scan):** A procedure that makes a series of
  detailed pictures of areas inside the body, taken from different
  angles. The pictures are made by a computer linked to an x-ray
  machine. A dye may be injected into a vein or swallowed to help
  the organs or tissues show up more clearly. This procedure is
  also called computed tomography, computerized tomography, or
  computerized axial tomography.

- **Ultrasound exam:** A procedure in which high-energy sound
  waves (ultrasound) are bounced off internal tissues or organs and
  make echoes. The echoes form a picture of body tissues called a
  sonogram. The picture can be printed to be looked at later.

- **Chest x-ray:** An x-ray of the organs and bones inside the chest.
  An x-ray is a type of energy beam that can go through the body
  and onto film, making a picture of areas inside the body.

- **Sentinel lymph node biopsy:** The removal of the sentinel
  lymph node during surgery. The sentinel lymph node is the first
  lymph node to receive lymphatic drainage from a tumor. It is the
  first lymph node the cancer is likely to spread to from the tumor.
  A radioactive substance and/or blue dye is injected near the
  tumor. The substance or dye flows through the lymph ducts to
  the lymph nodes. The first lymph node to receive the substance

or dye is removed. A pathologist views the tissue under a microscope to look for cancer cells. If cancer cells are not found, it may not be necessary to remove more lymph nodes.

There are three ways that cancer spreads in the body.

Cancer can spread through tissue, the lymph system, and the blood:

- Tissue. The cancer spreads from where it began by growing into nearby areas.

- Lymph system. The cancer spreads from where it began by getting into the lymph system. The cancer travels through the lymph vessels to other parts of the body.

- Blood. The cancer spreads from where it began by getting into the blood. The cancer travels through the blood vessels to other parts of the body.

Cancer may spread from where it began to other parts of the body.

When cancer spreads to another part of the body, it is called metastasis. Cancer cells break away from where they began (the primary tumor) and travel through the lymph system or blood.

- Lymph system. The cancer gets into the lymph system, travels through the lymph vessels, and forms a tumor (metastatic tumor) in another part of the body.

- Blood. The cancer gets into the blood, travels through the blood vessels, and forms a tumor (metastatic tumor) in another part of the body.

The metastatic tumor is the same type of cancer as the primary tumor. For example, if thyroid cancer spreads to the lung, the cancer cells in the lung are actually thyroid cancer cells. The disease is metastatic thyroid cancer, not lung cancer.

Stages are used to describe thyroid cancer according to the type of thyroid cancer and age of the patient:

Papillary and follicular thyroid cancer in patients younger than 45 years

- Stage I: In stage I papillary and follicular thyroid cancer, the tumor is any size, may be in the thyroid, or may have spread to nearby tissues and lymph nodes. Cancer has not spread to other parts of the body.

- Stage II: In stage II papillary and follicular thyroid cancer, the tumor is any size and cancer has spread from the thyroid to other parts of the body, such as the lungs or bone, and may have spread to lymph nodes.

Papillary and follicular thyroid cancer in patients 45 years and older

- Stage I: In stage I papillary and follicular thyroid cancer, cancer is found only in the thyroid and the tumor is 2 centimeters or smaller.

- Stage II: In stage II papillary and follicular thyroid cancer, cancer is only in the thyroid and the tumor is larger than 2 centimeters but not larger than 4 centimeters.

- Stage III: In stage III papillary and follicular thyroid cancer, either of the following is found:

  - the tumor is larger than 4 centimeters and only in the thyroid or the tumor is any size and cancer has spread to tissues just outside the thyroid, but not to lymph nodes; or

  - the tumor is any size and cancer may have spread to tissues just outside the thyroid and has spread to lymph nodes near the trachea or the larynx (voice box).

- Stage IV: Stage IV papillary and follicular thyroid cancer is divided into stages IVA, IVB, and IVC.

- In stage IVA, either of the following is found:

  - the tumor is any size and cancer has spread outside the thyroid to tissues under the skin, the trachea, the esophagus, the larynx (voice box), and/or the recurrent laryngeal nerve (a nerve with 2 branches that go to the larynx); cancer may have spread to lymph nodes near the trachea or the larynx; or

  - the tumor is any size and cancer may have spread to tissues just outside the thyroid. Cancer has spread to lymph nodes on one or both sides of the neck or between the lungs.

- In stage IVB, cancer has spread to tissue in front of the spinal column or has surrounded the carotid artery or the blood vessels in the area between the lungs. Cancer may have spread to lymph nodes.

- In stage IVC, the tumor is any size and cancer has spread to other parts of the body, such as the lungs and bones, and may have spread to lymph nodes.

Medullary thyroid cancer for all ages

- Stage 0: Stage 0 medullary thyroid cancer is found only with a special screening test. No tumor can be found in the thyroid.

- Stage I: Stage I medullary thyroid cancer is found only in the thyroid and is 2 centimeters or smaller.

- Stage II: In stage II medullary thyroid cancer, either of the following is found:

  - the tumor is larger than 2 centimeters and only in the thyroid; or

  - the tumor is any size and has spread to tissues just outside the thyroid, but not to lymph nodes.

- Stage III: In stage III medullary thyroid cancer, the tumor is any size, has spread to lymph nodes near the trachea and the larynx (voice box), and may have spread to tissues just outside the thyroid.

- Stage IV: Stage IV medullary thyroid cancer is divided into stages IVA, IVB, and IVC.

- In stage IVA, either of the following is found:

  - the tumor is any size and cancer has spread outside the thyroid to tissues under the skin, the trachea, the esophagus, the larynx (voice box), and/or the recurrent laryngeal nerve (a nerve with 2 branches that go to the larynx); cancer may have spread to lymph nodes near the trachea or the larynx; or

  - the tumor is any size and cancer may have spread to tissues just outside the thyroid. Cancer has spread to lymph nodes on one or both sides of the neck or between the lungs.

- In stage IVB, cancer has spread to tissue in front of the spinal column or has surrounded the carotid artery or the blood vessels in the area between the lungs. Cancer may have spread to lymph nodes.

- In stage IVC, the tumor is any size and cancer has spread to other parts of the body, such as the lungs and bones, and may have spread to lymph nodes.

Anaplastic thyroid cancer is considered stage IV thyroid cancer.

Anaplastic thyroid cancer grows quickly and has usually spread within the neck when it is found. Stage IV anaplastic thyroid cancer is divided into stages IVA, IVB, and IVC.

- In stage IVA, cancer is found in the thyroid and may have spread to lymph nodes.

- In stage IVB, cancer has spread to tissue just outside the thyroid and may have spread to lymph nodes.

- In stage IVC, cancer has spread to other parts of the body, such as the lungs and bones, and may have spread to lymph nodes.

Section 40.3

Treatment Options for Thyroid Cancer

Text in this section is excerpted from "Thyroid Cancer Treatment (PDQ®)," National Cancer Institue (NCI), June 17, 2015.

There are different types of treatment for patients with thyroid cancer.

Different types of treatment are available for patients with thyroid cancer. Some treatments are standard (the currently used treatment), and some are being tested in clinical trials. A treatment clinical trial is a research study meant to help improve current treatments or obtain information on new treatments for patients with cancer. When clinical trials show that a new treatment is better than the standard treatment, the new treatment may become the standard treatment. Patients may want to think about taking part in a clinical trial. Some clinical trials are open only to patients who have not started treatment.

Five types of standard treatment are used:

Surgery

Surgery is the most common treatment of thyroid cancer. One of the following procedures may be used:

- Lobectomy: Removal of the lobe in which thyroid cancer is found. Biopsies of lymph nodes in the area may be done to see if they contain cancer.

- Near-total thyroidectomy: Removal of all but a very small part of the thyroid.

- Total thyroidectomy: Removal of the whole thyroid.

- Lymphadenectomy: Removal of lymph nodes in the neck that contain cancer.

Radiation therapy, including radioactive iodine therapy

Radiation therapy is a cancer treatment that uses high-energy x-rays or other types of radiation to kill cancer cells or keep them from growing. There are two types of radiation therapy. External radiation therapy uses a machine outside the body to send radiation toward the cancer. Internal radiation therapy uses a radioactive substance sealed in needles, seeds, wires, or catheters that are placed directly into or near the cancer. The way the radiation therapy is given depends on the type and stage of the cancer being treated.

Radiation therapy may be given after surgery to kill any thyroid cancer cells that were not removed. Follicular and papillary thyroid cancers are sometimes treated with radioactive iodine (RAI) therapy. RAI is taken by mouth and collects in any remaining thyroid tissue, including thyroid cancer cells that have spread to other places in the body. Since only thyroid tissue takes up iodine, the RAI destroys thyroid tissue and thyroid cancer cells without harming other tissue. Before a full treatment dose of RAI is given, a small test-dose is given to see if the tumor takes up the iodine.

Chemotherapy

Chemotherapy is a cancer treatment that uses drugs to stop the growth of cancer cells, either by killing the cells or by stopping them from dividing. When chemotherapy is taken by mouth or injected into a vein or muscle, the drugs enter the bloodstream and can reach cancer cells throughout the body (systemic chemotherapy). When chemotherapy is placed directly into the cerebrospinal fluid, an organ, or a body cavity such as the abdomen, the drugs mainly affect cancer cells in those areas (regional chemotherapy). The way the chemotherapy is given depends on the type and stage of the cancer being treated.

Thyroid hormone therapy

Hormone therapy is a cancer treatment that removes hormones or blocks their action and stops cancer cells from growing. Hormones are substances made by glands in the body and circulated in the bloodstream. In the treatment of thyroid cancer, drugs may be given to prevent the body from making thyroid-stimulating hormone (TSH), a hormone that can increase the chance that thyroid cancer will grow or recur.

Also, because thyroid cancer treatment kills thyroid cells, the thyroid is not able to make enough thyroid hormone. Patients are given thyroid hormone replacement pills.

Targeted therapy

Targeted therapy is a type of treatment that uses drugs or other substances to identify and attack specific cancer cells without harming normal cells. Tyrosine kinase inhibitor therapy is a type of targeted therapy that blocks signals needed for tumors to grow.

Vandetanib and sorafenib are tyrosine kinase inhibitors that are used to treat certain types of thyroid cancer.

Patients may want to think about taking part in a clinical trial.

For some patients, taking part in a clinical trial may be the best treatment choice. Clinical trials are part of the cancer research process. Clinical trials are done to find out if new cancer treatments are safe and effective or better than the standard treatment.

Many of today's standard treatments for cancer are based on earlier clinical trials. Patients who take part in a clinical trial may receive the standard treatment or be among the first to receive a new treatment.

Patients who take part in clinical trials also help improve the way cancer will be treated in the future. Even when clinical trials do not lead to effective new treatments, they often answer important questions and help move research forward.

Patients can enter clinical trials before, during, or after starting their cancer treatment.

Some clinical trials only include patients who have not yet received treatment. Other trials test treatments for patients whose cancer has not gotten better. There are also clinical trials that test new ways to stop cancer from recurring (coming back) or reduce the side effects of cancer treatment.

Clinical trials are taking place in many parts of the country.

Follow-up tests may be needed.

Some of the tests that were done to diagnose the cancer or to find out the stage of the cancer may be repeated. Some tests will be repeated in order to see how well the treatment is working. Decisions about whether to continue, change, or stop treatment may be based on the results of these tests.

Some of the tests will continue to be done from time to time after treatment has ended. The results of these tests can show if your condition has changed or if the cancer has recurred (come back). These tests are sometimes called follow-up tests or check-ups.

Part Six

Diagnosing and Treating Cancer

Chapter 41

Diagnosis and Staging

Chapter Contents

Section 41.1

Symptoms

Text in this section is excerpted from "Symptoms," National Cancer
Institute (NCI), March 5, 2015.

Cancer can cause many different symptoms. These are some of them:

- Skin changes, such as:
  - A new mole or a change in an existing mole
  - A sore that does not heal
- Breast changes, such as:
  - Change in size or shape of the breast or nipple
  - Change in texture of breast skin
- A thickening or lump on or under the skin
- Hoarseness or cough that does not go away
- Changes in bowel habits
- Difficult or painful urination
- Problems with eating, such as:
  - Discomfort after eating
  - A hard time swallowing
- Changes in appetite
- Weight gain or loss with no known reason
- Abdominal pain
- Unexplained night sweats
- Unusual bleeding or discharge, including:
  - Blood in the urine
  - Vaginal bleeding
  - Blood in the stool
- Feeling weak or very tired

Most often, these symptoms are not due to cancer. They may also be caused by benign tumors or other problems. If you have symptoms that last for a couple of weeks, it is important to see a doctor so that problems can be diagnosed and treated as early as possible.

Usually, early cancer does not cause pain. If you have symptoms, do not wait to feel pain before seeing a doctor.

Section 41.2

Diagnosis

Text in this section is excerpted from "Diagnosis," National Cancer Institute (NCI), March 9, 2015.

If you have a symptom or your screening test result suggests cancer, the doctor must find out whether it is due to cancer or some other cause. The doctor may ask about your personal and family medical history and do a physical exam. The doctor also may order lab tests, scans, or other tests or procedures.

Lab Tests

High or low levels of certain substances in your body can be a sign of cancer. So, lab tests of the blood, urine, or other body fluids that measure these substances can help doctors make a diagnosis. However, abnormal lab results are not a sure sign of cancer. Lab tests are an important tool, but doctors cannot rely on them alone to diagnose cancer.

Imaging Procedures

Imaging procedures create pictures of areas inside your body that help the doctor see whether a tumor is present. These pictures can be made in several ways:

- **CT scan:** An x-ray machine linked to a computer takes a series of detailed pictures of your organs. You may receive a dye or other contrast material to highlight areas inside the body. Contrast material helps make these pictures easier to read.

- **Nuclear scan:** For this scan, you receive an injection of a small amount of radioactive material, which is sometimes called a tracer. It flows through your bloodstream and collects in certain bones or organs. A machine called a scanner detects and measures the radioactivity. The scanner creates pictures of bones or organs on a computer screen or on film. Your body gets rid of the radioactive substance quickly. This type of scan may also be called radionuclide scan.

- **Ultrasound:** An ultrasound device sends out sound waves that people cannot hear. The waves bounce off tissues inside your body like an echo. A computer uses these echoes to create a picture of areas inside your body. This picture is called a sonogram.

- **MRI**: A strong magnet linked to a computer is used to make detailed pictures of areas in your body. Your doctor can view these pictures on a monitor and print them on film.

- **PET scan:** For this scan, you receive an injection of a tracer. Then, a machine makes 3-D pictures that show where the tracer collects in the body. These scans show how organs and tissues are working.

- **X-rays:** X-rays use low doses of radiation to create pictures of the inside of your body.

Biopsy

In most cases, doctors need to do a biopsy to make a diagnosis of cancer. A biopsy is a procedure in which the doctor removes a sample of tissue. A pathologist then looks at the tissue under a microscope to see if it is cancer. The sample may be removed in several ways:

- **With a needle:** The doctor uses a needle to withdraw tissue or fluid.

- **With an endoscope:** The doctor looks at areas inside the body using a thin, lighted tube called an endoscope. The scope is inserted through a natural opening, such as the mouth. Then, the doctor uses a special tool to remove tissue or cells through the tube.

- **With surgery:** Surgery may be excisional or incisional.

  - In an excisional biopsy, the surgeon removes the entire tumor. Often some of the normal tissue around the tumor also is removed.

- In an incisional biopsy, the surgeon removes just part of the tumor.

Section 41.3

Staging

Text in this section is excerpted from "Staging," National Cancer Institute (NCI), March 9, 2015.

Stage refers to the extent of your cancer, such as how large the tumor is, and if it has spread. Knowing the stage of your cancer helps your doctor plan the best treatment for you. He or she may order x-rays, lab tests, and other tests or procedures to learn the stage of your disease.

There are many staging systems. Some cover many types of cancer. Others are specific to a particular type of cancer. Most staging systems include information about:

- Where the tumor is located in the body

- The cell type (such as, adenocarcinoma or squamous cell carcinoma)

- Tumor size

- Whether the cancer has spread to nearby lymph nodes

- Whether the cancer has spread to a different part of the body

- Tumor grade, which refers to how abnormal the cancer cells look and how likely the tumor is to grow and spread

The TNM Staging System

The TNM system is the most widely used cancer staging system. Most hospitals and medical centers use the TNM system as their main method for cancer reporting. You are likely to see your cancer described by this staging system in your pathology report, unless you have a cancer for which a different staging system is used. Examples of cancers with different staging systems include brain and spinal cord tumors and blood cancers. In the TNM system:

- The T refers to the size and extent of the main tumor. The main tumor is usually called the primary tumor.

- The N refers to the amount of cancer that has spread to nearby lymph nodes.

- The M refers to whether the cancer has metastasized. This means that the cancer has spread from the primary tumor to other parts of the body.

The TNM system also includes numbers that tell more details about the cancer. Here is the basic TNM system:

Primary tumor (T)

- TX: Main tumor cannot be measured
- T0: Main tumor cannot be found
- T1, T2, T3, T4: Size and/or extent of the main tumor. The higher the number after the T, the larger the tumor or the more it has grown into nearby tissues.

Regional lymph nodes (N)

- NX: Cancer in nearby lymph nodes cannot be measured
- N0: There is no cancer in nearby lymph nodes
- N1, N2, N3: Number and location of lymph nodes that contain cancer. The higher the number after the N, the more lymph nodes that contain cancer.

Distant metastasis (M)

- MX: Metastasis cannot be measured
- M0: Cancer has not spread to other parts of the body
- M1: Cancer has spread to other parts of the body

For many cancers, the TNM combinations correspond to one of five stages. The TNM system helps describe your cancer in great detail.

But, when talking about your cancer, your doctor or nurse is likely to describe it using one of the following:

Table 41.1. TNM combinations correspond to one of five stages

Stage	What it means
Stage 0	Carcinoma in situ, also called CIS. Means that abnormal cells are present but have not spread to nearby tissue. CIS is not cancer, but it may become cancer.
Stage I, Stage II, and Stage III	The higher the number, the larger the cancer tumor and the more it has spread into nearby tissues.
Stage IV	The cancer has spread to other parts of the body.

Section 41.4

Prognosis

Text in this section is excerpted from "Understanding Cancer Prognosis," National Cancer Institute (NCI), November 24, 2014.

If you have cancer, you may have questions about how serious your cancer is and your chances of survival. The estimate of how the disease will go for you is called prognosis. It can be hard to understand what prognosis means and also hard to talk about, even for doctors.

Many Factors Can Affect Your Prognosis

Some of the factors that affect prognosis include:

- The type of cancer and where it is in your body

- The stage of the cancer, which refers to the size of the cancer and if it has spread to other parts of your body

- The cancer's grade, which refers to how abnormal the cancer cells look under a microscope. Grade provides clues about how quickly the cancer is likely to grow and spread.

- Certain traits of the cancer cells

- Your age and how healthy you were before cancer

- How you respond to treatment

Seeking Information about Your Prognosis Is a Personal Decision

When you have cancer, you and your loved ones face many unknowns. Understanding your cancer and knowing what to expect can help you and your loved ones make decisions. Some of the decisions you may face include:

- Which treatment is best for you

- If you want treatment

- How to best take care of yourself and manage treatment side effects

- How to deal with financial and legal matters

Many people want to know their prognosis. They find it easier to cope when they know more about their cancer. You may ask your doctor about survival statistics or search for this information on your own. Or, you may find statistics confusing and frightening, and think they are too impersonal to be of value to you. It is up to you to decide how much information you want.

If you do decide you want to know more, the doctor who knows the most about your situation is in the best position to discuss your prognosis and explain what the statistics may mean.

Understanding Statistics about Survival

Doctors estimate prognosis by using statistics that researchers have collected over many years about people with the same type of cancer. Several types of statistics may be used to estimate prognosis. The most commonly used statistics include:

Cancer-specific survival

This is the percentage of patients with a specific type and stage of cancer who have not died from their cancer during a certain period of time after diagnosis. The period of time may be 1 year, 2 years, 5 years, etc., with 5 years being the time period most often used. Cancer-specific survival is also called disease-specific survival. In most cases, cancer-specific survival is based on causes of death listed in medical records.

Relative survival

This statistic is another method used to estimate cancer-specific survival that does not use information about the cause of death. It is the percentage of cancer patients who have survived for a certain period of time after diagnosis compared to people who do not have cancer.

Overall survival

This is the percentage of people with a specific type and stage of cancer who have not died from any cause during a certain period of time after diagnosis.

Disease-free survival

This statistic is the percentage of patients who have no signs of cancer during a certain period of time after treatment. Other names for this statistic are recurrence-free or progression-free survival.

Because statistics are based on large groups of people, they cannot be used to predict exactly what will happen to you. Everyone is different. Treatments and how people respond to treatment can differ greatly. Also, it takes years to see the benefit of new treatments and ways of finding cancer. So, the statistics your doctor uses to make a prognosis may not be based on treatments being used today.

Still, your doctor may tell you that you have a good prognosis if statistics suggest that your cancer is likely to respond well to treatment. Or, he may tell you that you have a poor prognosis if the cancer is harder to control. Whatever your doctor tells you, keep in mind that a prognosis is an educated guess. Your doctor cannot be certain how it will go for you.

If You Decide Not to Have Treatment

If you decide not to have treatment, the doctor who knows your situation best is in the best position to discuss your prognosis.

Survival statistics most often come from studies that compare treatments with each other, rather than treatment with no treatment. So, it may not be easy for your doctor to give you an accurate prognosis.

Understanding the Difference Between Cure and Remission

Cure means that there are no traces of your cancer after treatment and the cancer will never come back.

Remission means that the signs and symptoms of your cancer are reduced. Remission can be partial or complete. In a complete remission, all signs and symptoms of cancer have disappeared.

If you remain in complete remission for 5 years or more, some doctors may say that you are cured. Still, some cancer cells can remain in your body for many years after treatment. These cells may cause the cancer to come back one day. For cancers that return, most do so within the first 5 years after treatment. But, there is a chance that cancer will come back later. For this reason, doctors cannot say for sure that you are cured. The most they can say is that there are no signs of cancer at this time.

Because of the chance that cancer can come back, your doctor will monitor you for many years and do tests to look for signs of cancer's return. They will also look for signs of late side effects from the cancer treatments you received.

Section 41.5

Tumor Grade

Text in this section is excerpted from "Tumor Grade," National Cancer Institute (NCI), May 3, 2013.

What is tumor grade?

Tumor grade is the description of a tumor based on how abnormal the tumor cells and the tumor tissue look under a microscope. It is an indicator of how quickly a tumor is likely to grow and spread. If the cells of the tumor and the organization of the tumor's tissue are close to those of normal cells and tissue, the tumor is called "well-differentiated." These tumors tend to grow and spread at a slower rate than tumors that are "undifferentiated" or "poorly differentiated," which have abnormal-looking cells and may lack normal tissue structures. Based on these and other differences in microscopic appearance, doctors assign a numerical "grade" to most cancers. The factors used to determine tumor grade can vary between different types of cancer.

Tumor grade is not the same as the stage of a cancer. Cancer stage refers to the size and/or extent (reach) of the original (primary) tumor and whether or not cancer cells have spread in the body. Cancer stage is based on factors such as the location of the primary tumor, tumor size, regional lymph node involvement (the spread of cancer to nearby lymph nodes), and the number of tumors present.

How is tumor grade determined?

If a tumor is suspected to be malignant, a doctor removes all or part of it during a procedure called a biopsy. A pathologist (a doctor who identifies diseases by studying cells and tissues under a microscope) then examines the biopsied tissue to determine whether the tumor is benign or malignant. The pathologist also determines the tumor's grade and identifies other characteristics of the tumor. The NCI fact sheet Pathology Reports describes the type of information that can be found in a pathologist's report about the visual and microscopic examination of tissue removed during a biopsy or other surgery.

How are tumor grades classified?

Grading systems differ depending on the type of cancer. In general, tumors are graded as 1, 2, 3, or 4, depending on the amount of abnormality. In Grade 1 tumors, the tumor cells and the organization of the tumor tissue appear close to normal. These tumors tend to grow and spread slowly. In contrast, the cells and tissue of Grade 3 and Grade 4 tumors do not look like normal cells and tissue. Grade 3 and Grade 4 tumors tend to grow rapidly and spread faster than tumors with a lower grade.

If a grading system for a tumor type is not specified, the following system is generally used

- GX: Grade cannot be assessed (undetermined grade)
- G1: Well differentiated (low grade)
- G2: Moderately differentiated (intermediate grade)
- G3: Poorly differentiated (high grade)
- G4: Undifferentiated (high grade)

What are some of the cancer type-specific grading systems?

Breast and prostate cancers are the most common types of cancer that have their own grading systems.

Breast cancer. Doctors most often use the Nottingham grading system (also called the Elston-Ellis modification of the Scarff-Bloom-Richardson grading system) for breast cancer. This system grades breast tumors based on the following features:

- Tubule formation: how much of the tumor tissue has normal breast (milk) duct structures

- Nuclear grade: an evaluation of the size and shape of the nucleus in the tumor cells

- Mitotic rate: how many dividing cells are present, which is a measure of how fast the tumor cells are growing and dividing

Each of the categories gets a score between 1 and 3; a score of "1" means the cells and tumor tissue look the most like normal cells and tissue, and a score of "3" means the cells and tissue look the most abnormal. The scores for the three categories are then added, yielding a total score of 3 to 9. Three grades are possible:

- Total score = 3–5: G1 (Low grade or well differentiated)

- Total score = 6–7: G2 (Intermediate grade or moderately differentiated)

- Total score = 8–9: G3 (High grade or poorly differentiated)

Prostate cancer. The Gleason scoring system is used to grade prostate cancer. The Gleason score is based on biopsy samples taken from the prostate. The pathologist checks the samples to see how similar the tumor tissue looks to normal prostate tissue. Both a primary and a secondary pattern of tissue organization are identified. The primary pattern represents the most common tissue pattern seen in the tumor, and the secondary pattern represents the next most common pattern. Each pattern is given a grade from 1 to 5, with 1 looking the most like normal prostate tissue and 5 looking the most abnormal. The two grades are then added to give a Gleason score. The American Joint Committee on Cancer recommends grouping Gleason scores into the following categories:

- Gleason X: Gleason score cannot be determined

- Gleason 2–6: The tumor tissue is well differentiated

- Gleason 7: The tumor tissue is moderately differentiated

- Gleason 8–10: The tumor tissue is poorly differentiated or undifferentiated

How does tumor grade affect a patient's treatment options?

Doctors use tumor grade and other factors, such as cancer stage and a patient's age and general health, to develop a treatment plan and to determine a patient's prognosis (the likely outcome or course of a disease; the chance of recovery or recurrence). Generally, a lower grade indicates a better prognosis. A higher-grade cancer may grow and spread more quickly and may require immediate or more aggressive treatment.

The importance of tumor grade in planning treatment and determining a patient's prognosis is greater for certain types of cancer, such as soft tissue sarcoma, primary brain tumors, and breast and prostate cancer.

Patients should talk with their doctor for more information about tumor grade and how it relates to their treatment and prognosis.

Section 41.6

Understanding Laboratory Tests

Text in this section is excerpted from "Understanding Laboratory Tests," National Cancer Institute (NCI), December 11, 2013.

What are laboratory tests?

A laboratory test is a procedure in which a sample of blood, urine, other bodily fluid, or tissue is examined to get information about a person's health. Some laboratory tests provide precise and reliable information about specific health problems. Other tests provide more general information that helps doctors identify or rule out possible health problems. Doctors often use other types of tests, such as imaging tests, in addition to laboratory tests to learn more about a person's health.

How are laboratory tests used in cancer medicine?

Laboratory tests are used in cancer medicine in many ways:

- To screen for cancer or precancerous conditions before a person has any symptoms of disease

- To help diagnose cancer

- To provide information about the stage of a cancer (that is, its severity); for malignant tumors, this includes the size and/or extent (reach) of the original (primary) tumor and whether or not the tumor has spread (metastasized) to other parts of the body

- To plan treatment

- To monitor a patient's general health during treatment and to check for potential side effects of the treatment

- To determine whether a cancer is responding to treatment

- To find out whether a cancer has recurred (come back)

Which laboratory tests are used in cancer medicine?

Categories of some common laboratory tests used in cancer medicine are listed below in alphabetical order.

Blood chemistry test

What it measures: The amounts of certain substances that are released into the blood by the organs and tissues of the body, such as metabolites, electrolytes, fats, and proteins, including enzymes. Blood chemistry tests usually include tests for blood urea nitrogen (BUN) and creatinine.

How it is used: Diagnosis and monitoring of patients during and after treatment. High or low levels of some substances can be signs of disease or side effects of treatment.

Cancer gene mutation testing

What it measures: The presence or absence of specific inherited mutations in genes that are known to play a role in cancer development. Examples include tests to look for BRCA1 and BRCA2 gene mutations, which play a role in development of breast, ovarian, and other cancers.

How it is used: Assessment of cancer risk

Complete blood count (CBC)

What it measures: Numbers of the different types of blood cells, including red blood cells, white blood cells, and platelets, in a sample of blood. This test also measures the amount of hemoglobin (the protein that carries oxygen) in the blood, the percentage of the total blood volume that is taken up by red blood cells (hematocrit), the size of the red blood cells, and the amount of hemoglobin in red blood cells.

How it is used: Diagnosis, particularly in leukemias, and monitoring during and after treatment

Cytogenetic analysis

What it measures: Changes in the number and/or structure of chromosomes in a patient's white blood cells or bone marrow cells

How it is used: Diagnosis, deciding on appropriate treatment

Immunophenotyping

What it measures: Identifies cells based on the types of antigens present on the cell surface

How it is used: Diagnosis, staging, and monitoring of cancers of the blood system and other hematologic disorders, including leukemias, lymphomas, myelodysplastic syndromes, and myeloproliferative disorders. It is most often done on blood or bone marrow samples, but it may also be done on other bodily fluids or biopsy tissue samples.

Sputum cytology (also called sputum culture)

What it measures: The presence of abnormal cells in sputum (mucus and other matter brought up from the lungs by coughing)

How it is used: Diagnosis of lung cancer

Tumor marker tests

What they measure: Some measure the presence, levels, or activity of specific proteins or genes in tissue, blood, or other bodily fluids that may be signs of cancer or certain benign (noncancerous) conditions. A tumor that has a greater than normal level of a tumor marker may respond to treatment with a drug that targets that marker. For example, cancer cells that have high levels of the HER2/neu gene or protein may respond to treatment with a drug that targets the HER2/neu protein.

Some tumor marker tests analyze DNA to look for specific gene mutations that may be present in cancers but not normal tissues. Examples include EGFR gene mutation analysis to help determine treatment and assess prognosis in non-small cell lung cancer and BRAF gene mutation analysis to predict response to targeted therapies in melanoma and colorectal cancer.

Still other tumor marker tests, called multigene tests (or multiparameter gene expression tests), analyze the expression of a specific group of genes in tumor samples. These tests are used for prognosis and treatment planning. For example, the 21-gene signature can help patients with lymph node–negative, estrogen receptor–positive breast cancer decide if there may be benefit to treating with chemotherapy in addition to hormone therapy, or not.

How they are used: Diagnosis, deciding on appropriate treatment, assessing response to treatment, and monitoring for cancer recurrence

Urinalysis

What it measures: The color of urine and its contents, such as sugar, protein, red blood cells, and white blood cells.

How it is used: Detection and diagnosis of kidney cancer and urothelial cancers

Urine cytology

What it measures: The presence of abnormal cells shed from the urinary tract into urine to detect disease.

How it is used: Detection and diagnosis of bladder cancer and other urothelial cancers, monitoring patients for cancer recurrence

How do I interpret my test results?

With some laboratory tests, the results obtained for healthy people can vary somewhat from person to person. Factors that can cause person-to-person variation in laboratory test results include a person's age, sex, race, medical history, and general health. In fact, the results obtained from a single person given the same test on different days can also vary. For these tests, therefore, the results are considered normal if they fall between certain lower and upper limits or values. This range of normal values is known as the "normal range," the "reference range," and the "reference interval." When healthy people take such tests, it is expected that their results will fall within the normal range 95 percent of the time. (Five percent of the time, the results from healthy people will fall outside the normal range and will be marked as "abnormal.") Reference ranges are based on test results from large numbers of people who have been tested in the past.

Some test results can be affected by certain foods and medications. For this reason, people may be asked to not eat or drink for several hours before a laboratory test or to delay taking medications until after the test.

For many tests, it is possible for someone with cancer to have results that fall within the normal range. Likewise, it is possible for someone who doesn't have cancer to have test results that fall outside the normal range. This is one reason that many laboratory tests alone cannot provide a definitive diagnosis of cancer or other diseases.

In general, laboratory test results must be interpreted in the context of the overall health of the patient and are considered along with the results of other examinations, tests, and procedures. A doctor who is familiar with a patient's medical history and current situation is the best person to explain test results and what they mean.

What if a laboratory test result is unclear or inconclusive?

If a test result is unclear or inconclusive, the doctor will likely repeat the test to be certain of the result and may order additional tests. The doctor may also compare the latest test result to previous results, if available, to get a better idea of what is normal for that person.

What are some questions to ask the doctor about laboratory tests?

It can be helpful to take a list of questions to the doctor's office. Questions about a laboratory test might include:

- What will this test measure?
- Why is this test being ordered?
- Does this test have any risks or side effects?
- How should I prepare for the test?
- When will the test results be available?
- How will the results be given (a letter, a phone call, online)?
- Will this test need to be done more than once?

How reliable are laboratory tests and their results?

The results of laboratory tests affect many of the decisions a doctor makes about a person's health care, including whether additional tests are necessary, developing a treatment plan, or monitoring a person's response to treatment. It is very important, therefore, that the laboratory tests themselves are trustworthy and that the laboratory that performs the tests meets rigorous state and federal regulatory standards.

The Food and Drug Administration (FDA) regulates the development and marketing of all laboratory tests that use test kits and equipment that are commercially manufactured in the United States. After the FDA approves a laboratory test, other federal and state agencies make sure that the test materials and equipment meet strict standards while they are being manufactured and then used in a medical or clinical laboratory.

All laboratory testing that is performed on humans in the United States (except testing done in clinical trials and other types of human research) is regulated through the Clinical Laboratory Improvement Amendments (CLIA), which were passed by Congress in 1988. The CLIA laboratory certification program is administered by the Centers for Medicare & Medicaid Services (CMS) in conjunction with the FDA and the Centers for Disease Control and Prevention. CLIA ensures that laboratory staff are appropriately trained and supervised and that testing laboratories have quality control programs in place so that test results are accurate and reliable.

To enroll in the CLIA program, laboratories must complete a certification process that is based on the level of complexity of tests that the laboratory will perform. The more complicated the test, the more demanding the requirements for certification. Laboratories must demonstrate that they can perform tests as accurately and as precisely as the manufacturer did to gain FDA approval of the test. Laboratories must also evaluate the tests regularly to make sure that they continue to meet the manufacturer's specifications. Laboratories undergo regular unannounced on-site inspections to ensure they are following the requirements outlined in CLIA to receive and maintain certification.

Some states have additional requirements that are equal to or more stringent than those outlined in CLIA. CMS has determined that Washington and New York have state licensure programs that are exempt from CLIA program requirements. Therefore, licensing authorities in Washington and New York have primary responsibility for oversight of their state's laboratory practices.

What new laboratory tests for cancer medicine are on the horizon?

Tests that measure the number of cancer cells in a sample of blood (circulating tumors cells) or examine the DNA of such cells are of great interest in cancer medicine because research suggests that levels of these cells might be useful for evaluating response to treatment and detecting cancer recurrence. One circulating tumor cell test has been approved by the Food and Drug Administration (FDA) to monitor patients with breast, colorectal, or prostate cancer. However, such tests are still being studied in clinical trials and are not routinely used in clinical practice.

Tests that determine the sequences of a large number of genes at one time using next generation DNA sequencing methods are being developed to provide gene mutation profiles of solid tumors (e.g., lung cancer). Some of these tests are being used to help choose the best treatment, but none are FDA approved.

Chapter 42

Managing Cancer Care

Chapter Contents

579

Section 42.1

How To Find a Doctor or Treatment Facility If You Have Cancer

Text in this section is excerpted from "Managing Cancer Care,"
National Cancer Institute (NCI), March 10, 2015.

How are doctors trained and certified to treat cancer patients?

When choosing a doctor for your cancer care, you may find it helpful to know some of the terms used to describe a doctor's training and credentials. Most physicians who treat people with cancer are medical doctors (they have an M.D. degree) or osteopathic doctors (they have a D.O. degree). The basic training for both types of physicians includes 4 years of premedical education at a college or university, 4 years of medical school to earn an M.D. or D.O. degree, and postgraduate medical education through internships and residences. This training usually lasts 3 to 7 years. Physicians must pass an exam to become licensed (legally permitted) to practice medicine in their state. Each state or territory has its own procedures and general standards for licensing physicians.

Specialists are physicians who have completed their residency training in a specific area, such as internal medicine. Independent specialty boards certify physicians after they have fulfilled certain requirements. These requirements include meeting specific education and training criteria, being licensed to practice medicine, and passing an examination given by the specialty board. Doctors who have met all of the requirements are given the status of "Diplomate" and are board certified as specialists. Doctors who are board eligible have obtained the required education and training but have not completed the specialty board examination.

After being trained and certified as a specialist, a physician may choose to become a subspecialist. A subspecialist has at least 1 additional year of full-time education in a particular area of a specialty. This training is designed to increase the physician's expertise in a specific field. Specialists can be board certified in their subspecialty as well.

The following are some specialties and subspecialties that pertain to cancer treatment:

- **Medical Oncology** is a subspecialty of internal medicine. Doctors who specialize in internal medicine treat a wide range of medical problems. Medical oncologists treat cancer and manage the patient's course of treatment. A medical oncologist may also consult with other physicians about the patient's care or refer the patient to other specialists.

- **Hematology** is a subspecialty of internal medicine. Hematologists focus on diseases of the blood and related tissues, including the bone marrow, spleen, and lymph nodes.

- **Radiation Oncology** is a subspecialty of radiology. Radiology is the use of x-rays and other forms of radiation to diagnose and treat disease. Radiation oncologists specialize in the use of radiation to treat cancer.

- **Surgery** is a specialty that pertains to the treatment of disease by surgical operation. General surgeons perform operations on almost any area of the body. Physicians can also choose to specialize in a certain type of surgery; for example, thoracic surgeons are specialists who perform operations specifically in the chest area, including the lungs and the esophagus.

The American Board of Medical Specialties® (ABMS) is a not-for-profit organization that assists medical specialty boards with the development and use of standards for evaluation and certification of physicians. Information about other specialties that treat cancer is available from the ABMS website.

Almost all board-certified specialists are members of their medical specialty society. Physicians can attain Fellowship status in a specialty society, such as the American College of Surgeons (ACS), if they demonstrate outstanding achievement in their profession. Criteria for Fellowship status may include the number of years of membership in the specialty society, years practicing in the specialty, and professional recognition by peers.

How can I find a doctor who specializes in cancer care?

One way to find a doctor who specializes in cancer care is to ask for a referral from your primary care physician. You may know a specialist yourself, or through the experience of a family member, coworker, or friend.

The following resources may also be able to provide you with names of doctors who specialize in treating specific diseases or conditions. However, these resources may not have information about the quality of care that the doctors provide.

- Your local hospital or its patient referral service may be able to provide you with a list of specialists who practice at that hospital.

- Your nearest NCI-designated cancer center can provide information about doctors who practice at that center. The NCI-Designated Cancer Centers Find a Cancer Center page provides contact information to help health care providers and cancer patients with referrals to NCI-designated cancer centers located throughout the United States.

- The ABMS has a list of doctors who have met certain education and training requirements and have passed specialty examinations. Is Your Doctor Board Certified lists doctors' names along with their specialty and their educational background? Users must register to use this online self-serve resource, which allows users to conduct searches by a physician's name or area of certification and a state name. The directory is available in most libraries.

- The American Medical Association (AMA) DoctorFinder database provides basic information on licensed physicians in the United States. Users can search for physicians by name or by medical specialty.

- The American Society of Clinical Oncology (ASCO) provides an online list of doctors who are members of ASCO. The member database has the names and affiliations of nearly 30,000 oncologists worldwide. It can be searched by doctor's name, institution, location, oncology specialty, and/or type of board certification.

- The American College of Surgeons (ACS) membership database is an online list of surgeons who are members of the ACS. The list can be searched by doctor's name, geographic location, or medical specialty. The ACS can be contacted by telephone at 1–800–621–4111.

- The American Osteopathic Association (AOA) Find a Doctor database provides an online list of practicing osteopathic

physicians who are AOA members. The information can
be searched by doctor's name, geographic location, or medical specialty. The AOA can be contacted by telephone at
1–800–621–1773.

- Local medical societies may maintain lists of doctors in each
  specialty.

- Public and medical libraries may have print directories of doctors' names listed geographically by specialty.

- Your local Yellow Pages or Yellow Book may have doctors listed
  by specialty under "Physicians."

If you are a member of a health insurance plan, your choice may
be limited to doctors who participate in your plan. Your insurance
company can provide you with a list of participating primary care
doctors and specialists. It is important to ask whether the doctor you
are considering is accepting new patients through your health plan.
You also have the option of seeing a doctor outside your health plan
and paying the costs yourself. If you have the option to change health
insurance plans, you may first wish to consider which doctor or doctors you would like to use, and then choose a plan that includes your
chosen physician(s).

If you are using a federal or state health insurance program such
as Medicare or Medicaid, you may want to ask whether the doctor you
are considering is accepting patients who use these programs.

You will have many factors to consider when choosing a doctor. To
make an informed decision, you may wish to speak with several doctors
before choosing one. When you meet with each doctor, you might want
to consider the following:

- Does the doctor have the education and training to meet my
  needs?

- Does the doctor use the hospital that I have chosen?

- Does the doctor listen to me and treat me with respect?

- Does the doctor explain things clearly and encourage me to ask
  questions?

- What are the doctor's office hours?

- Who covers for the doctor when he or she is unavailable? Will
  that person have access to my medical records?

- How long does it take to get an appointment with the doctor?

If you are choosing a surgeon, you may wish to ask additional questions about the surgeon's background and experience with specific procedures. These questions may include:

- Is the surgeon board certified?

- Has the surgeon been evaluated by a national professional association of surgeons, such as the ACS?

- At which treatment facility or facilities does the surgeon practice?

- How often does the surgeon perform the type of surgery I need?

- How many of these procedures has the surgeon performed? What was the success rate?

It is important for you to feel comfortable with the specialist that you choose because you will be working closely with that person to make decisions about your cancer treatment. Trust your own observations and feelings when deciding on a doctor for your medical care.

How can I get another doctor's opinion about the diagnosis and treatment plan?

After your doctor gives you advice about the diagnosis and treatment plan, you may want to get another doctor's opinion before you begin treatment. This is known as getting a second opinion. You can do this by asking another specialist to review all of the materials related to your case. The doctor who gives the second opinion can confirm or suggest modifications to your doctor's proposed treatment plan, provide reassurance that you have explored all of your options, and answer any questions you may have.

Getting a second opinion is done frequently, and most physicians welcome another doctor's views. In fact, your doctor may be able to recommend a specialist for this consultation. However, some people find it uncomfortable to request a second opinion. When discussing this issue with your doctor, it may be helpful to express satisfaction with your doctor's decision and care and to mention that you want your decision about treatment to be as thoroughly informed as possible. You may also wish to bring a family member along for support when asking for a second opinion. It is best to involve your doctor in the process of getting a second opinion, because your doctor will need to make your medical records (such as your test results and x-rays) available to the specialist who is giving the second opinion.

Some health care plans require a second opinion, particularly if a doctor recommends surgery. Other health care plans will pay for a second opinion if the patient requests it. If your plan does not cover a second opinion, you can still obtain one if you are willing to cover the cost.

If your doctor is unable to recommend a specialist for a second opinion, or if you prefer to choose one on your own, the following resources can help:

- Many of the resources listed above for finding a doctor can also help you find a specialist for a consultation.

- The NIH Clinical Center in Bethesda, Maryland, is the research hospital for the NIH, including NCI. Several branches of the NCI provide second opinion services. The NCI fact sheet Cancer Clinical Trials at the NIH Clinical Center describes these NCI branches and their services.

- The R. A. Bloch Cancer Foundation, Inc., can refer cancer patients to institutions that are willing to provide multidisciplinary second opinions. A list of these institutions is available on the organization's website. You can also contact the R. A. Bloch Cancer Foundation, Inc., by telephone at 816–854–5050 or 1–800–433–0464.

How can U.S. residents find treatment facilities?

Choosing a treatment facility is another important consideration for getting the best medical care possible. Although you may not be able to choose which hospital treats you in an emergency, you can choose a facility for scheduled and ongoing care. If you have already found a doctor for your cancer treatment, you may need to choose a facility based on where your doctor practices. Your doctor may be able to recommend a facility that provides quality care to meet your needs. You may wish to ask the following questions when considering a treatment facility:

- Has the facility had experience and success in treating my condition?

- Has the facility been rated by state, consumer, or other groups for its quality of care?

- How does the facility check on and work to improve its quality of care?

- Has the facility been approved by a nationally recognized accrediting body, such as the ACS Commission on Cancer and/or The Joint Commission?

- Does the facility explain patients' rights and responsibilities? Are copies of this information available to patients?

- Does the treatment facility offer support services, such as social workers and resources, to help me find financial assistance if I need it?

- Is the facility conveniently located?

If you are a member of a health insurance plan, your choice of treatment facilities may be limited to those that participate in your plan. Your insurance company can provide you with a list of approved facilities. Although the costs of cancer treatment can be very high, you do have the option of paying out-of-pocket if you want to use a treatment facility that is not covered by your insurance plan. If you are considering paying for treatment yourself, you may wish to discuss the possible costs with your doctor beforehand. You may also want to speak with the person who does the billing for the treatment facility. Nurses and social workers may also be able to provide you with more information about coverage, eligibility, and insurance issues.

The following resources may help you find a hospital or treatment facility for your care:

- The NCI-Designated Cancer Centers Find a Cancer Center page provides contact information for NCI-designated cancer centers located throughout the country.

- The ACS's Commission on Cancer (CoC) accredits cancer programs at hospitals and other treatment facilities. More than 1,430 programs in the United States have been designated by the CoC as Approved Cancer Programs. The ACS website offers a searchable database of these programs. The CoC can be contacted by telephone at 312–202–5085 or by e-mail at CoC@facs.org.

- The Joint Commission is an independent not-for-profit organization that evaluates and accredits health care organizations and programs in the United States. It also offers information for the general public about choosing a treatment facility. The Joint Commission can be contacted by telephone at 630–792–5000.

- The Joint Commission offers an online Quality Check® service that patients can use to determine whether a specific facility has been accredited by the Joint Commission and to view the organization's performance reports.

How can people who live outside the United States find treatment facilities in or near their countries?

If you live outside the United States, facilities that offer cancer treatment may be located in or near your country. Cancer information services are available in many countries to provide information and answer questions about cancer; they may also be able to help you find a cancer treatment facility close to where you live. A list of these cancer information services is available on the website of the International Cancer Information Service Group, an independent international organization of cancer information services. A list may also be requested by writing to the NCI Public Inquiries Office at:

Cancer Information Service
BG 9609 MSC 9760
9609 Medical Center Drive
Bethesda, MD 20892-9760
USA

The Union for International Cancer Control (UICC) is another resource for people living outside the United States who want to find a cancer treatment facility. The UICC consists of international cancer-related organizations devoted to the worldwide fight against cancer. UICC membership includes research facilities and treatment centers and, in some countries, ministries of health. Other members include volunteer cancer leagues, associations, and societies. These organizations serve as resources for the public and may have helpful information about cancer and treatment facilities. To find a resource in or near your country, contact the UICC at:

Union for International Cancer Control (UICC)
62 route de Frontenex
1207 Geneva
Switzerland
+ 41 22 809 1811
http://www.uicc.org

How can people who live outside the United States get a second opinion or have cancer treatment in the United States?

Some people living outside the United States may wish to obtain a second opinion or have their cancer treatment in this country. Many facilities in the United States offer these services to international cancer patients. These facilities may also provide support services, such

587

as language interpretation, assistance with travel, and guidance in finding accommodations near the treatment facility for patients and their families.

If you live outside the United States and would like to obtain cancer treatment in this country, you should contact cancer treatment facilities directly to find out whether they have an international patient office. The NCI-Designated Cancer Centers Find a Cancer Center page offers contact information for NCI-designated cancer centers throughout the United States.

Citizens of other countries who are planning to travel to the United States for cancer treatment generally must first obtain a nonimmigrant visa for medical treatment from the U.S. Embassy or Consulate in their home country. Visa applicants must demonstrate that the purpose of their trip is to enter the United States for medical treatment; that they plan to remain for a specific, limited period; that they have funds to cover expenses in the United States; that they have a residence and social and economic ties outside the United States; and that they intend to return to their home country.

To determine the specific fees and documentation required for the nonimmigrant visa and to learn more about the application process, contact the U.S. Embassy or Consulate in your home country. A list of links to the websites of U.S. Embassies and Consulates worldwide can be found on the U.S. Department of State's website.

Section 42.2

People in Health Care

Text in this section is excerpted from "Managing Cancer Care," National Cancer Institute (NCI), March 10, 2015.

Most cancer patients have a team of health care providers who work together to help them. This team may include doctors, nurses, social workers, pharmacists, dietitians, and other people in health care. Chances are that you will never see all of these people at the same time. In fact, there may be health care providers on your team who you never meet.

Doctors

While most people have two or more doctors, chances are you will see one doctor most often. This doctor is the leader of your treatment team, who will meet and work closely with all of your health care providers. It's important to let your doctor know how you're feeling so your team can figure out whether you're getting better or worse, decide if other drugs or treatments are needed, and ensure that you get the extra support you need.

Nurses

Most likely, you will see nurses more often than other people on your treatment team. Besides giving medical care, nurses can answer questions, and offer hope and support. They may also suggest ways to talk with family and friends about your feelings. Nurses work with all other health care providers on your treatment team.

Pharmacists

Pharmacists not only fill your prescriptions but also teach you about the drugs you're taking (proper usage, side effects, foods to avoid, and warnings about sun exposure and the dangers of mixing drugs).

Dietitians

People with cancer often have trouble eating or digesting food. These problems can be a side effect of cancer drugs or treatments. Dietitians can help by teaching you about foods that are healthy, taste good, and are easy to eat.

Oncology Social Workers

These professionals are trained to counsel you about ways to cope with the emotional and physical issues related to your cancer. They can also tell you about other resources that can help you deal with your cancer, such as community programs and support materials. In addition, they can connect you with financial, legal, and insurance services in your area.

Psychologists

Psychologists can talk to you and your family about your worries and teach you ways to cope with these feelings and concerns. Let your doctor or nurse know if you want to talk with a psychologist who is trained to help people with cancer. Many social workers can also fill this role.

Psychiatrists

Psychiatrists are medical doctors who diagnose and prescribe drugs for mental and emotional disorders. They can also talk with you about your feelings and help you find the mental health services you need.

Licensed Counselors and Other Mental Health Professionals

Licensed counselors, pastoral care professionals, spiritual leaders, and other mental health professionals also help people deal with their feelings, worries, and concerns. Talk with your doctor or contact your local cancer center to find mental health professionals near you.

Patient Educators

Patient or health educators help you and your family learn more about your cancer by finding information that fits your needs. Patient educators typically run the resource centers in hospitals and treatment centers. They can offer you tools to help you and your family understand your type of cancer, your treatment choices, and side effects. They can also give you tips for living with and beyond your cancer. Ask your doctor or nurse about talking to a patient educator.

Occupational Therapists

Occupational therapists can help you regain, develop, and build skills that are important for day-to-day living. They can help you relearn how to do daily activities, such as bathing, dressing, or feeding yourself, after cancer treatment.

Physical Therapists

Physical therapists are trained to understand how different parts of your body work together. They can teach you about proper exercises and body motions that can help you gain strength and move better after treatment. They can also advise you about proper postures that help prevent injuries.

Speech Therapists

Speech therapists can evaluate and treat any speech, language, or swallowing problems you may have after treatment.

Section 42.3

Support Services

Text in this section is excerpted from "Managing Cancer Care,"
National Cancer Institute (NCI), March 10, 2015.

There are a number of services available to help you cope during and after your treatment. Talk with your doctor to help you locate services such as these:

Counseling

Trained specialists can help you talk about your feelings, problems and concerns. Some forms of counseling available to you may include individual, couples, family, and faith and spiritual counseling.

Genetic Counseling

Trained specialists can advise you on whether to have genetic testing for cancer and how to deal with the results. It can be helpful for you and for family members who have concerns about their own health.

Long-Term Follow-up Clinics

All doctors can offer follow-up care, but there are also clinics that specialize in long-term follow-up care for cancer survivors. These clinics most often see people who are no longer being treated by an oncologist and who are considered free of disease. Ask your doctor if there are any follow-up cancer clinics in your area.

Pain Clinics (also called Pain and Palliative Care Services)

These are centers with professionals who are trained in helping people get relief from pain.

Quitting Smoking (Smoking Cessation Services)

Research shows that the more support you have in quitting smoking, the greater your chance for success. Ask your doctor, nurse, social worker, or hospital about available programs, or call NCI's Smoking Quitline at 1-877-44-U-QUIT (1-877-448-7848).

Stress Management Programs

These programs teach ways to help you relax and take more control over stress. Hospitals, clinics, or local cancer organizations may offer these programs and classes.

Support Groups

In-person and online groups enable cancer survivors to interact with others in similar situations.

Survivor Wellness Programs

These types of programs are growing in number, and they are meant for people who have finished their cancer treatment and are interested in redefining their life beyond cancer. The programs help cancer survivors take steps to lead a healthy lifestyle, improve the quality and meaningfulness of their lives, and potentially reduce the risk of recurrence.

Vocational Rehabilitation

If you have disabilities or other special needs, vocational rehabilitation specialists can help you find suitable jobs. They offer services such as counseling, education and skills training, and help in obtaining and using assistive technology and tools.

Section 42.4

Advance Directives

Text in this section is excerpted from "Managing Cancer Care,"
National Cancer Institute (NCI), March 10, 2015.

Advance directives are legal papers that tell your loved ones and doctors what kind of medical care you want if you can't tell them yourself. The papers let you say ahead of time how you want to be treated and to select someone who will make sure your wishes are carried out. It's best to fill these out when you're healthy in case you become ill or unable to make these decisions in the future. Think about taking action now to give someone you trust the right to make medical decisions for you. This is one of the most important things you can do.

Types of Advance Directives

Living Will

This is a document used for people to state whether or not they would like to receive certain types of medical care if they become unable to speak for themselves. The most common types of care addressed by a living will are:

- The use of machines to keep you alive. Examples include dialysis machines and ventilators (also called respirators).

- "Do not resuscitate" (DNR) orders. These instruct the health care team not to use cardiopulmonary resuscitation (CPR) if your breathing or heartbeat stops.

- Tube feeding

- Withholding food and fluids

- Organ and tissue donation

Medical Power of Attorney

This is a document that allows people to name another person to make decisions about their medical care if they are unable to make these decisions for themselves. (It is also called a health care proxy or durable power of attorney for health care.) People often appoint someone they know well and trust to carry out their wishes. This person may be called a health care agent, surrogate, or proxy.

Why Advance Directives Are Important

Filling out advance directives gives people control over their health care. Choices about end-of-life care can be hard to make even when people are healthy. But if they are already seriously ill, such decisions can seem overwhelming. Some cancer patients want to try every drug or treatment in the hope that something will be effective. Others will choose to stop treatment. Although patients may turn to family and friends for advice, ultimately it is the patient's decision.

It's important to keep in mind that if a day comes where you choose not to receive or to stop treatment to control your disease, medical care to promote your well-being (palliative care) continues. This type of care includes treatment to manage pain and other physical symptoms, as well as support for psychosocial and spiritual needs. You have the right to make your own decisions about treatment. Filling out advance directives gives you a way to be in control.

When to Fill Out Advance Directives

Ideally, these documents should be completed when you're healthy. Yet many people connect filling out advance directives to making decisions near the end of life. But you don't need to wait until being diagnosed with a serious illness to think about your wishes for care. In fact, making these choices when you're healthy can reduce the burden on you and your loved ones later on. Talking about these issues ensures that when the time comes, you will face the end of your life with dignity and with treatment that reflects your values.

Talk to your doctor, nurse, or social worker for advice or help with filling out advance directives. Most health care facilities have someone who can help. As you prepare your advance directives, you should talk about your decisions with family members and loved ones and explain the reasons behind your choices.

It's hard to talk about these issues. But the benefits of talking to the people close to you about the kind of care you want are:

- Your wishes are known and can be followed.

- It often comforts family members to know what you want.

- It saves family members from having to bring up the subject themselves.

- You may also gain peace of mind. You are making the choices for yourself instead of leaving them to your loved ones.

- It can help you and your loved ones worry less about the future and live each day to the fullest.

If talking with your family and other loved ones is too hard, consider having a family meeting and invite a social worker or member of the faith community to guide the discussion.

Reviewing and Signing Your Advance Directives

Once your advance directives have been completed, the next steps are:

- Review them with a member of your health care team or other health care professional for accuracy before signing. Most states require a witness to be present at the signing of the documents.

- Provide copies to your doctor, hospital, and family members after you sign them.

- Store copies in a safe, accessible place.

- Consider keeping a card in your wallet with a written statement declaring you have a living will and medical power of attorney and describing where the documents can be found.

Some organizations will store advance directives and make them available on the patient's behalf. Contact the National Hospice and Palliative Care Organization for more information about companies that provide this service.

Changing Your Advance Directives

Even after advance directives have been signed, you can change your mind at any time. As a matter of fact, the process of discussing advance directives should be ongoing, rather than taking place just once. This way you can review the documents from time to time and modify them if your situation or wishes change.

To update your document, you should talk to your health care providers and loved ones about the new decisions you would like to make. When new advance directives have been signed, the old ones should be destroyed.

Advance Directives and State Laws

Each state has its own laws regarding advance directives. Therefore, special care should be taken to follow the laws of the state where you live or are being treated. A living will or medical power of attorney that is accepted in one state may not be accepted in another state. State-specific advance directives can be downloaded from the National Hospice and Palliative Care Organization.

More Information about Advance Directives

There are a number of organizations that can answer questions and give you more information about advance directives. Two well-known ones are:

Aging with Dignity

Aging with Dignity is a national nonprofit organization that worked with the American Bar Association to develop an easy-to-read living will called Five Wishes. This document is legal in 42 states and the District of Columbia, and is available in 26 languages, including Spanish and Braille. The organization has also created an advance care planning guide for adolescents and young adults called Voicing My Choices. Both these, and other resources, can be accessed online or ordered in hard copy format.

http://www.agingwithdignity.org
1–888–594–7437 (1-888-5WISHES)
1-850–681–2010

National Hospice and Palliative Care Organization

The National Hospice and Palliative Care Organization (NHPCO) represents programs and professionals that provide hospice and palliative care in the United States. Caring Connections is a national consumer and community engagement program of NHPCO that works to improve care at the end of life. Caring Connections provides a toll-free number, website, and a wide range of free materials about end-of-life care (such as hospice and palliative care information, advance care planning, and caregiving). Caring Connections provides free advance directives with instructions for each state. Some Spanish-language publications are available, and staff can answer calls in Spanish.

> 1–800–658–8898 (helpline)
> 1–877–658–8896 (multilingual line)
> caringinfo@nhpco.org
> http://www.caringinfo.org

Section 42.5

Using Trusted Resources

Text in this section is excerpted from "Managing Cancer Care,"
National Cancer Institute (NCI), March 10, 2015.

Health information, whether in print or online, should come from a trusted, credible source. Government agencies, hospitals, universities, and medical journals and books that provide evidenced-based information are sources you can trust. Too often, other sources can provide misleading or incorrect information. If a source makes claims that are too good to be true, remember—they usually are.

There are many websites, books, and magazines that provide health information to the public, but not all of them are trustworthy. Use the resources provided below to safeguard yourself when reviewing sources of health information.

Websites

Online sources of health information should make it easy for people to learn who is responsible for posting the information. They should make clear the original source of the information, along with the medical credentials of the people who prepare or review the posted material.

Use the following questions to determine the credibility of health information published online.

- **Who manages this information?**

  The person or group that has published health information online should be identified somewhere.

- **Who is paying for the project, and what is their purpose?**

  You should be able to find this information in the "About Us" section.

- **What is the original source of the information that they have posted?**

  If the information was originally published in a research journal or a book, they should say which one(s) so that you can find it.

- **How is information reviewed before it gets posted?**

  Most health information publications have someone with medical or research credentials (e.g., someone who has earned an M.D., D.O., or Ph.D.) review the information before it gets posted, to make sure it is correct.

- **How current is the information?**

  Online health information sources should show you when the information was posted or last reviewed.

- **If they are asking for personal information, how will they use that information and how will they protect your privacy?**

  This is very important. Do not share personal information until you understand the policies under which it will be used and you are comfortable with any risk involved in sharing your information online.

Books

A number of books have been written about cancer, cancer treatment, and complementary and alternative medicine (CAM). Some books contain trustworthy content, while others do not.

It's important to know that information is always changing and that new research results are reported every day. Be aware that if a book is written by only one person, you may only be getting that one person's view.

If you go to the library, ask the staff for suggestions. Or if you live near a college or university, there may be a medical library available. Local bookstores may also have people on staff who can help you. If you find a book online, look very carefully at the author's credentials, background, and expertise. Questions you may want to ask yourself are:

- Is the author an expert on this subject?

- Do you know anyone else who has read the book?

- Has the book been reviewed by other experts?

- Was it published in the past 5 years?

- Does the book offer different points of view, or does it seem to hold one opinion?

- Has the author researched the topic in full?

- Are the references listed in the back?

Magazines

If you want to look for articles you can trust, search online medical journal databases or ask your librarian to help you look for medical journals, books, and other research that has been done by experts.

Articles in popular magazines are usually not written by experts. Rather, the authors speak with experts, gather information, and then write the article. If claims are made in a magazine, remember:

- The authors may not have expert knowledge in this area.

- They may not say where they found their information.

- The articles have not been reviewed by experts.

- The publisher may have ties to advertisers or other organizations. Therefore, the article may be one-sided in the information or view(s) it presents.

When you read these articles, you can use the same process that the magazine writer uses:

- Speak with experts

- Ask lots of questions

- Then decide if the therapy is right for you

Where to Get More Help

Cancer Treatment Scams

A page from the Federal Trade Commission (FTC) that advises people to ask their health care provider about products that claim to cure or treat cancer and offers tips for spotting treatment scams.

For Consumers: Protecting Yourself

A page from the Food and Drug Administration (FDA) that includes links to several resources that have tips about buying medicines and other products online.

Evaluating Cancer Information on the Internet

Developed by the American Society of Clinical Oncology (ASCO), Cancer.Net provides information, including common misconceptions about cancer and tips to evaluate the credibility of online cancer information.

Rumors, Myths, and Truths

The American Cancer Society (ACS) offers a variety of services and programs for patients and their families, including educational programs and links to information about possible cancer hoaxes.

Chapter 43

Getting Cancer Treatment – An Overview

Cancer Treatment

There are many types of cancer treatment. The types of treatment that you have will depend on the type of cancer you have and how advanced it is. Some people with cancer will have only one treatment. But most people have a combination of treatments, such as surgery with chemotherapy and/or radiation therapy. You may also have immunotherapy, targeted therapy, or hormone therapy.

Clinical trials might also be an option for you. Clinical trials are research studies that involve people. Understanding what they are and how they work can help you decide if taking part in a trial is a good option for you.

When you need treatment for cancer, you have a lot to learn and think about. It is normal to feel overwhelmed and confused. But, talking with your doctor and learning all you can about all your treatment options, including clinical trials, can help you make a decision you feel good about.

Text in this chapter is excerpted from "Cancer Treatment," National Cancer Institute (NCI), April 29, 2015.

Types of Treatment

There are many types of cancer treatment. The types of treatment that you receive will depend on the type of cancer you have and how advanced it is.

The main types of cancer treatment include:

Surgery

A procedure in which a doctor with special training, called a surgeon, removes cancer from your body.

Radiation Therapy

Uses high doses of radiation to kill cancer cells and shrink tumors.

Chemotherapy

Uses drugs to kill cancer cells.

Immunotherapy

Helps your immune system fight cancer.

Targeted Therapy

Targets the changes in cancer cells that help them grow, divide, and spread.

Hormone Therapy

Slows or stops the growth of cancer that uses hormones to grow.

Stem Cell Transplant

Procedures that restore blood-forming stem cells in people who have had theirs destroyed by high doses of cancer treatments, such as chemotherapy and radiation therapy.

Some people with cancer will have only one treatment. But most people have a combination of treatments, such as surgery with chemotherapy and/or radiation therapy. When you need treatment for cancer, you have a lot to learn and think about. It is normal to feel overwhelmed and confused.

Chapter 44

Types of Cancer Treatment

Chapter Contents

Section 44.1

Surgery

Text in this section is excerpted from "Types of Treatment," National
Cancer Institute (NCI), April 29, 2015.

How Surgery Is Performed

Surgeons often use small, thin knives, called scalpels, and other
sharp tools to cut your body during surgery. Surgery often requires
cuts through skin, muscles, and sometimes bone. After surgery, these
cuts can be painful and take some time to recover from.

Anesthesia keeps you from feeling pain during surgery. Anesthesia
refers to drugs or other substances that cause you to lose feeling or
awareness. There are three types of anesthesia:

- Local anesthesia causes loss of feeling in one small area of the body.

- Regional anesthesia causes loss of feeling in a part of the body,
  such as an arm or leg.

- General anesthesia causes loss of feeling and a complete loss of
  awareness that seems like a very deep sleep.

There are other ways of performing surgery that do not involve cuts
with scalpels. Some of these include:

- **Cryosurgery**

  Cryosurgery is a type of treatment in which extreme cold produced by liquid nitrogen or argon gas is used to destroy abnormal tissue. Cryosurgery may be used to treat early-stage skin
  cancer, retinoblastoma, and precancerous growths on the skin
  and cervix. Cryosurgery is also called cryotherapy.

- **Lasers**

  This is a type of treatment in which powerful beams of light are
  used to cut through tissue. Lasers can focus very accurately on
  tiny areas, so they can be used for precise surgeries. Lasers can
  also be used to shrink or destroy tumors or growths that might
  turn into cancer.

Lasers are most often used to treat tumors on the surface of the body or on the inside lining of internal organs. Examples include basal cell carcinoma, cervical changes that might turn into cancer, and cervical, vaginal, esophageal, and non-small cell lung cancer.

- **Hyperthermia**

  Hyperthermia is a type of treatment in which small areas of body tissue are exposed to high temperatures. The high heat can damage and kill cancer cells or make them more sensitive to radiation and certain chemotherapy drugs. Radiofrequency ablation is one type of hyperthermia that uses high-energy radio waves to generate heat. Hyperthermia is not widely available and is being studied in clinical trials.

- **Photodynamic Therapy**

  Photodynamic therapy is a type of treatment that uses drugs which react to a certain type of light. When the tumor is exposed to this light, these drugs become active and kill nearby cancer cells. Photodynamic therapy is used most often to treat or relieve symptoms caused by skin cancer, mycosis fungoides, and non-small cell lung cancer.

Types of Surgery

There are many types of surgery. The types differ based on the purpose of the surgery, the part of the body that requires surgery, the amount of tissue to be removed, and, in some cases, what the patient prefers.

Surgery may be open or minimally invasive.

- In open surgery, the surgeon makes one large cut to remove the tumor, some healthy tissue, and maybe some nearby lymph nodes.

- In minimally invasive surgery, the surgeon makes a few small cuts instead of one large one. She inserts a long, thin tube with a tiny camera into one of the small cuts. This tube is called a laparoscope. The camera projects images from the inside of the body onto a monitor, which allows the surgeon to see what she is doing. She uses special surgery tools that are inserted through the other small cuts to remove the tumor and some healthy tissue.

605

Because minimally invasive surgery requires smaller cuts, it takes less time to recover from than open surgery.

Who Has Surgery

Many people with cancer are treated with surgery. Surgery works best for solid tumors that are contained in one area. It is a local treatment, meaning that it treats only the part of your body with the cancer. It is not used for leukemia (a type of blood cancer) or for cancers that have spread.

Sometimes surgery will be the only treatment you need. But most often, you will also have other cancer treatments.

How Surgery Works against Cancer

Depending on your type of cancer and how advanced it is, surgery can be used to:

- **Remove the entire tumor**

  Surgery removes cancer that is contained in one area.

- **Debulk a tumor**

  Surgery removes some, but not all, of a cancer tumor. Debulking is used when removing an entire tumor might damage an organ or the body. Removing part of a tumor can help other treatments work better.

- **Ease cancer symptoms**

  Surgery is used to remove tumors that are causing pain or pressure.

Risks of Surgery

Surgeons are highly trained and will do everything they can to prevent problems during surgery. Even so, sometimes problems do occur. Common problems are:

- **Pain**

  After surgery, most people will have pain in the part of the body that was operated on. How much pain you feel will depend on the extent of the surgery, the part of your body where you had surgery, and how you feel pain.

Your doctor or nurse can help you manage pain after surgery. Talk with your doctor or nurse before surgery about ways to control pain. After surgery, tell them if your pain is not controlled.

- **Infection**

  Infection is another problem that can happen after surgery. To help prevent infection, follow your nurse's instructions about caring for the area where you had surgery. If you do develop an infection, your doctor can prescribe a medicine (called an antibiotic) to treat it. Other risks of surgery include bleeding, damage to nearby tissues, and reactions to the anesthesia. Talk to your doctor about possible risks for the type of surgery you will have.

How Much Surgery Costs

The cost of surgery depends on many factors, including:

- The type of surgery you have

- How many specialists are involved in your surgery

- If you need local, regional, or general anesthesia

- Where you have surgery—at an outpatient clinic, a doctor's office, or the hospital

- If you need to stay in the hospital, and for how long

- The part of the country where you live

Talk with your health insurance company about what services it will pay for. Most insurance plans pay for surgery to treat cancer. To learn more, talk with the business office of the clinic or hospital where you go for treatment. If you need financial assistance, there are organizations that may be able to help. To find such organizations, go to the NCI database, Organizations that Offer Support Services and search for "financial assistance." Or call toll-free 1-800-4-CAN-CER (1-800-422-6237) to ask for information on organizations that may help.

Where You Have Surgery

Where you have surgery depends on:

- The type of surgery

- How extensive it is

- Where the surgeon practices

- The type of facility your insurance will cover

You can have outpatient surgery in a doctor's office, surgery center, or hospital. Outpatient means that you do not spend the night. Or, you may have surgery in the hospital and stay the night. How many nights you stay will depend on the type of surgery you have and how quickly you recover.

What to Expect before, during, and after Surgery

Before Surgery

Before surgery, a nurse may call you to tell you how to prepare. He or she may tell you about tests and exams you need to have before the surgery. Common tests that you may need, if you have not had them lately, are:

- Blood tests

- Chest x-ray

- Electrocardiogram (ECG)

You may not be able to eat or drink for a certain period of time before the surgery. It is important to follow the instructions about eating and drinking. If you don't, your surgery may need to be rescheduled.

You may also be asked to have supplies on hand for taking care of your wounds after surgery. Supplies might include antiseptic ointment and bandages.

During Surgery

Once you are under anesthesia, the surgeon removes the cancer, usually along with some healthy tissue around it. Removing this healthy tissue helps improve the chances that all the cancer has been removed.

Sometimes, the surgeon might also remove lymph nodes or other tissues near the tumor. These tissues will be checked under a microscope to see if the cancer has spread. Knowing if the nearby tissue contains cancer will help your doctors suggest the best treatment plan for you after surgery.

After Surgery

Once you are ready to go home after surgery, the nurse will tell you how to take care of yourself. He or she will explain:

- How to control pain

- Activities you should and should not do

- How to take care of your wound

- How to spot signs of infection and steps to take if you do

- When you can return to work

You will have at least one more visit with the surgeon a week or two after you go home. For more complex surgeries, you may need to see the surgeon more often. You may have stitches removed, and the surgeon will check to make sure you are healing as you should.

Special Diet Needs before and after Surgery

Surgery increases your need for good nutrition. If you are weak or underweight, you may need to eat a high-protein, high-calorie diet before surgery.

Some types of surgery may change how your body uses food. Surgery can also affect eating if you have surgery of the mouth, stomach, intestines, or throat. If you have trouble eating after surgery, you may be given nutrients through a feeding tube or IV (through a needle directly into a vein).

Talk with a dietitian for help with eating problems caused by surgery.

Working after Surgery

You will need to take time off from work to have and recover from surgery. You may need only 1 day or many weeks. How long you need to recover depends on many factors, such as:

- The type of anesthesia you have. If you have local or regional anesthesia, you will probably return to work more quickly than if you have general anesthesia.

- The type of surgery you have, and how extensive it is

- The type of work you do. If you have an active job, you may need to take off more time than if you sit at a desk. If your job allows, you may want to see if you can work at home, or start back part time, to help you ease back into a full work day.

Ask your doctor how long you will need to recover from your surgery. If you expect a longer recovery time, talk with your employer to find out if you can take medical leave. Check to make sure your health insurance will cover costs if you are on medical leave and not working for a time.

Section 44.2

Radiation Therapy

Text in this section is excerpted from "Types of Treatment," National Cancer Institute (NCI), April 29, 2015.

Radiation Therapy

Radiation therapy (also called radiotherapy) is a cancer treatment that uses high doses of radiation to kill cancer cells and shrink tumors. At low doses, radiation is used in x-rays to see inside your body, as with x-rays of your teeth or broken bones.

How Radiation Therapy Works against Cancer

At high doses, radiation kills cancer cells or slows their growth. Radiation therapy is used to:

- **Treat cancer**

  Radiation can be used to cure cancer, to prevent it from returning, or to stop or slow its growth.

- **Ease cancer symptoms**

  Radiation may be used to shrink a tumor to treat pain and other problems caused by the tumor. Or, it can lessen problems that may be caused by a growing tumor, such as trouble breathing or loss of bowel and bladder control.

Radiation therapy does not kill cancer cells right away. It takes days or weeks of treatment before cancer cells start to die. Then, cancer cells keep dying for weeks or months after radiation therapy ends.

Types of Radiation Therapy

There are two main types of radiation therapy, external beam and internal.

External Beam Radiation Therapy

External beam radiation therapy comes from a machine that aims radiation at your cancer. The machine is large and may be noisy. It does not touch you, but can move around you, sending radiation to a part of your body from many directions.

External beam radiation therapy treats a specific part of your body. For example, if you have cancer in your lung, you will have radiation only to your chest, not to your whole body.

Internal Radiation Therapy

Internal radiation therapy is a treatment in which a source of radiation is put inside your body. The radiation source can be solid or liquid.

Internal radiation therapy with a solid source is called brachytherapy. In this type of treatment, radiation in the form of seeds, ribbons, or capsules is placed in your body in or near the cancer.

You receive liquid radiation through an IV line. Liquid radiation travels throughout your body, seeking out and killing cancer cells.

Who Receives Radiation Therapy

External beam radiation therapy is used to treat many types of cancer. For some people, radiation may be the only treatment you need. But, most often, you will have radiation therapy and other cancer treatments, such as surgery and chemotherapy.

Brachytherapy is used to treat cancers of the head and neck, breast, cervix, prostate, and eye.

Liquid forms of internal radiation are most often used to treat thyroid cancer.

How Radiation Is Used with Other Cancer Treatments

Radiation may be given before, during, or after surgery. Doctors may use radiation:

- Before surgery, to shrink the size of the cancer.

- During surgery, so that it goes straight to the cancer without passing through the skin. Radiation therapy used this way is called intraoperative radiation.

- After surgery, to kill any cancer cells that may remain.

Radiation may also be given before, during, or after other cancer treatments to shrink the cancer or to kill any cancer cells that might remain.

Radiation Therapy Can Cause Side Effects

Radiation not only kills or slows the growth of cancer cells, it can also affect nearby healthy cells. Damage to healthy cells can cause side effects. External radiation and brachytherapy cause side effects only in the part of the body being treated.

The most common side effect of radiation therapy is fatigue, which is feeling exhausted and worn out. Fatigue can happen all at once or little by little. People feel fatigue in different ways. You may feel more or less fatigue than someone else who is also getting radiation therapy.

You can prepare for fatigue by:

- Asking someone to drive you to and from radiation therapy
- Planning time to rest
- Asking for help with meals and childcare

Healthy cells that are damaged during radiation treatment almost always recover after it is over. But sometimes people may have side effects that are severe or do not improve. Other side effects may show up months or years after radiation therapy is over. These are called late effects.

Doctors try to protect healthy cells during treatment by:

- **Using as low a dose of radiation as possible**

  The radiation dose is balanced between being high enough to kill cancer cells, yet low enough to limit damage to healthy cells.

- **Spreading out treatment over time**

  You may get radiation therapy once a day, or in smaller doses twice a day for several weeks. Spreading out the radiation dose allows normal cells to recover while cancer cells die.

- **Aiming radiation at a precise part of your body**

  With external radiation therapy, for example, your doctor is able to aim high doses of radiation at your cancer while reducing the amount of radiation that reaches nearby healthy tissue. These treatments use a computer to deliver precise radiation doses to a tumor or to specific areas within the tumor.

How Much Radiation Therapy Costs

Radiation therapy can be expensive. It uses complex machines and involves the services of many health care providers. The exact cost of your radiation therapy depends on the cost of health care where you live, what kind of radiation therapy you get, and how many treatments you need.

Talk with your health insurance company about what services it will pay for. Most insurance plans pay for radiation therapy. To learn more, talk with the business office at the clinic or hospital where you go for treatment. If you need financial assistance, there are organizations that may be able to help. To find such organizations, go to the National Cancer Institute database, Organizations that Offer Support Services and search for "financial assistance." Or call toll-free 1-800-4-CANCER (1-800-422-6237) to ask for information on organizations that may help.

What to Expect When Having External Beam Radiation Therapy

How Often Will You Have Treatment

Most people have external beam radiation therapy with the same dose of radiation once a day, 5 days a week, Monday through Friday. Treatment lasts up to 6 weeks, depending on the type of cancer you have and the treatment goal. This span of time is called a course of treatment.

Sometimes, the radiation dose or schedule is changed to reach the total dose of radiation more quickly. This can be done in one of these ways:

* Accelerated fractionation, which gives the half of the usual daily dose of radiation twice each day.

* Hyperfractionation, which is a smaller than usual daily dose of radiation given twice each day.

* Hypofractionation, which is a larger than usual daily dose of radiation given once a day for up to 3 weeks.

The doctor may prescribe one of these treatment schedules if he or she feels that it will work better for the type of cancer you have.

Where You Go for Treatment

Most of the time, you will get external beam radiation therapy as an outpatient. This means that you will have treatment at a clinic or radiation therapy center and will not stay the night in the hospital.

What Happens before Your First Treatment

You will have a 1- to 2-hour meeting with your doctor or nurse before you begin radiation therapy. At this time, you will have a physical exam, talk about your medical history, and maybe have imaging tests. Your doctor or nurse will discuss external beam radiation therapy, its benefits and side effects, and ways you can care for yourself during and after treatment. You can then choose whether to have external beam radiation therapy.

If you decide to have external beam radiation therapy, you will be scheduled for a treatment planning session called a simulation. At this time:

- A radiation oncologist (a doctor who specializes in using radiation to treat cancer) and radiation therapist will figure out your treatment area. You may also hear the treatment area referred to as the treatment port or treatment field. These terms refer to the places in your body that will get radiation. You will be asked to lie very still while x-rays or scans are taken.

- The radiation therapist will tattoo or draw small dots of colored ink on your skin to mark the treatment area. These dots will be needed throughout your course of radiation therapy. The radiation therapist will use them to make sure you are in exactly the same position for every treatment. The dots are about the size of a freckle. If the dots are tattooed, they will remain on your skin for the rest of your life. Ink markings will fade over time. Be careful not to remove them and tell the radiation therapist if they have faded or lost color.

- A body mold may be made of the part of the body that is being treated. This is a plastic or plaster form that keeps you from moving during treatment. It also helps make sure that you are in exactly the same position for each treatment.

- If you are getting radiation to the head and neck area you may be fitted for a mask. The mask has many air holes. It attaches to the table where you will lie for your treatments. The mask helps keep your head from moving so that you are in exactly the same position for each treatment.

What to wear for your treatments

Wear clothes that are comfortable and made of soft fabric, such as fleece or cotton. Choose clothes that are easy to take off, since you may need to expose the treatment area or change into a hospital gown. Do not wear clothes that are tight, such as close-fitting collars or waistbands, near your treatment area. Also, do not wear jewelry, adhesive bandages, or powder in the treatment area.

What happens during a treatment session

- You may be asked to change into a hospital gown or robe.

- You will go to the treatment room where you will receive radiation. The temperature in this room will be very cool.

- Depending on where your cancer is, you will either lie down on a treatment table or sit in a special chair. The radiation therapist will use the dots on your skin and body mold or face mask, if you have one, to help you get into the right position.

- You may see colored lights pointed at your skin marks. These lights are harmless and help the therapist position you for treatment.

- You will need to stay very still so the radiation goes to the exact same place each time. You will get radiation for 1 to 5 minutes. During this time, you can breathe normally.

The radiation therapist will leave the room just before your treatment begins. He or she will go to a nearby room to control the radiation machine. The therapist watches you on a TV screen or through a window and talks with you through a speaker in the treatment room. Make sure to tell the therapist if you feel sick or are uncomfortable. He or she can stop the radiation machine at any time. You will hear the radiation machine and see it moving around, but you won't be able to feel, hear, see, or smell the radiation.

Most visits last from 30 minutes to an hour, with most of that time spent helping you get into the correct position.

How to Relax for Treatment Sessions

Keep yourself busy while you wait:

- Read a book or magazine.

- Work on crossword puzzles or needlework.

- Use headphones to listen to music or recorded books.

- Meditate, breathe deeply, pray, use imagery, or find other ways to relax.

External Beam Radiation Therapy Will Not Make You Radioactive

People often wonder if they will be radioactive when they are having treatment with radiation. External beam radiation therapy will not make you radioactive. You may safely be around other people, even pregnant women, babies, and young children.

615

What to Expect When Having Internal Radiation Therapy

What Happens before Your First Treatment

You will have a 1- to 2-hour meeting with your doctor or nurse to plan your treatment before you begin internal radiation therapy. At this time, you will have a physical exam, talk about your medical history, and maybe have imaging tests. Your doctor will discuss the type of internal radiation therapy that is best for you, its benefits and side effects, and ways you can care for yourself during and after treatment. You can then decide whether to have internal radiation therapy.

How Brachytherapy Is Put in Place

Most brachytherapy is put in place through a catheter, which is a small, stretchy tube. Sometimes, brachytherapy is put in place through a larger device called an applicator. The way the brachytherapy is put in place depends on your type of cancer. Your doctor will place the catheter or applicator into your body before you begin treatment.

Once the catheter or applicator is in place, the radiation source is placed inside it. The radiation source may be kept in place for a few minutes, for many days, or for the rest of your life. How long it remains in place depends on the type of radiation source, your type of cancer, where the cancer is in your body, your health, and other cancer treatments you have had.

Types of Brachytherapy

There are three types of brachytherapy:

- **Low-dose rate (LDR) implants**

  In this type of brachytherapy, the radiation source stays in place for 1 to 7 days. You are likely to be in the hospital during this time. Once your treatment is finished, your doctor will remove the radiation source and the catheter or applicator.

- **High-dose rate (HDR) implants**

  In this type of brachytherapy, the radiation source is left in place for just 10 to 20 minutes at a time and then taken out. You may have treatment twice a day for 2 to 5 days or once a week for 2 to 5 weeks. The schedule depends on your type of cancer. During the course of treatment, your catheter or applicator may stay in place, or it may be put in place before each treatment. You may be in the hospital during this time, or you may make daily trips to the hospital to have the radiation source put in place. As with LDR implants, your doctor will remove the catheter or applicator once you have finished treatment.

616

- **Permanent implants**

  After the radiation source is put in place, the catheter is removed. The implants remain in your body for the rest of your life, but the radiation gets weaker each day. As time goes on, almost all the radiation will go away. When the radiation is first put in place, you may need to limit your time around other people and take other safety measures. Be extra careful not to spend time with children or pregnant women.

Internal Radiation Therapy Makes You Give Off Radiation

With liquid radiation, your body fluids (urine, sweat, and saliva) will give off radiation for a while. With brachytherapy, your body fluids will not give off radiation, but the radiation source in your body will. If the radiation you receive is a very high dose, you may need to follow some safety measures.

These measures may include:

- Staying in a private hospital room to protect others from radiation coming from your body

- Being treated quickly by nurses and other hospital staff. They will provide all the care you need, but may stand at a distance, talk with you from the doorway of your room, and wear protective clothing.

Your visitors will also need to follow safety measures, which may include:

- Not being allowed to visit when the radiation is first put in

- Needing to check with the hospital staff before they go to your room

- Standing by the doorway rather than going into your hospital room

- Keeping visits short (30 minutes or less each day). The length of visits depends on the type of radiation being used and the part of your body being treated.

- Not having visits from pregnant women and children younger than a year old

You may also need to follow safety measures once you leave the hospital, such as not spending much time with other people. Your doctor or nurse will talk with you about any safety measures you should follow when you go home.

What to Expect When the Catheter Is Removed

Once you finish treatment with LDR or HDR implants, the catheter will be removed. Here are some things to expect:

- You will get medicine for pain before the catheter or applicator is removed.

- The area where the catheter or applicator was might be tender for a few months.

- There is no radiation in your body after the catheter or applicator is removed. It is safe for people to be near you—even young children and pregnant women.

For a week or two, you may need to limit activities that take a lot of effort. Ask your doctor what kinds of activities are safe for you and which ones you should avoid.

Special Diet Needs

Radiation can cause side effects that make it hard to eat, such as nausea, mouth sores, and throat problems called esophagitis. Since your body uses a lot of energy to heal during radiation therapy, it is important that you eat enough calories and protein to maintain your weight during treatment.

If you are having trouble eating and maintaining your weight, talk to your doctor or nurse. You might also find it helpful to speak with a dietitian.

Working during Radiation Therapy

Some people are able to work full-time during radiation therapy. Others can work only part-time or not at all. How much you are able to work depends on how you feel. Ask your doctor or nurse what you may expect from the treatment you will have.

You are likely to feel well enough to work when you first start your radiation treatments. As time goes on, do not be surprised if you are more tired, have less energy, or feel weak. Once you have finished treatment, it may take just a few weeks for you to feel better—or it could take months.

You may get to a point during your radiation therapy when you feel too sick to work. Talk with your employer to find out if you can go on medical leave. Check that your health insurance will pay for treatment while you are on medical leave.

Section 44.3

Chemotherapy

Text in this section is excerpted from "Types of Treatment," National Cancer Institute (NCI), April 29, 2015.

How Chemotherapy Works against Cancer

Chemotherapy works by stopping or slowing the growth of cancer cells, which grow and divide quickly. Chemotherapy is used to:

- **Treat cancer**

  Chemotherapy can be used to cure cancer, lessen the chance it will return, or stop or slow its growth.

- **Ease cancer symptoms**

  Chemotherapy can be used to shrink tumors that are causing pain and other problems.

Who Receives Chemotherapy

Chemotherapy is used to treat many types of cancer. For some people, chemotherapy may be the only treatment you receive. But most often, you will have chemotherapy and other cancer treatments. The types of treatment that you need depends on the type of cancer you have, if it has spread and where, and if you have other health problems.

How Chemotherapy Is Used with Other Cancer Treatments

When used with other treatments, chemotherapy can:

- Make a tumor smaller before surgery or radiation therapy. This is called neoadjuvant chemotherapy.

- Destroy cancer cells that may remain after treatment with surgery or radiation therapy. This is called adjuvant chemotherapy.

- Help other treatments work better.

- Kill cancer cells that have returned or spread to other parts of your body.

Chemotherapy Can Cause Side Effects

Chemotherapy not only kills fast-growing cancer cells, but also kills or slows the growth of healthy cells that grow and divide quickly. Examples are cells that line your mouth and intestines and those that cause your hair to grow. Damage to healthy cells may cause side effects, such as mouth sores, nausea, and hair loss. Side effects often get better or go away after you have finished chemotherapy.

The most common side effect is fatigue, which is feeling exhausted and worn out. You can prepare for fatigue by:

- Asking someone to drive you to and from chemotherapy
- Planning time to rest on the day of and day after chemotherapy
- Asking for help with meals and childcare on the day of and at least one day after chemotherapy

There are many ways you can help manage chemotherapy side effects.

How Much Chemotherapy Costs

The cost of chemotherapy depends on:

- The types and doses of chemotherapy used
- How long and how often chemotherapy is given
- Whether you get chemotherapy at home, in a clinic or office, or during a hospital stay
- The part of the country where you live

Talk with your health insurance company about what services it will pay for. Most insurance plans pay for chemotherapy. To learn more, talk with the business office where you go for treatment.

If you need financial assistance, there are organizations that may be able to help. To find such organizations, go to the National Cancer Institute database, Organizations that Offer Support Services and search for "financial assistance." Or call toll-free 1-800-4-CANCER (1-800-422-6237) to ask for information on organizations that may help.

What to Expect When Receiving Chemotherapy

How Chemotherapy Is Given

Chemotherapy may be given in many ways. Some common ways include:

- **Oral**

  The chemotherapy comes in pills, capsules, or liquids that you swallow

- **Intravenous (IV)**

  The chemotherapy goes directly into a vein

- **Injection**

  The chemotherapy is given by a shot in a muscle in your arm, thigh, or hip, or right under the skin in the fatty part of your arm, leg, or belly

- **Intrathecal**

  The chemotherapy is injected into the space between the layers of tissue that cover the brain and spinal cord

- **Intraperitoneal (IP)**

  The chemotherapy goes directly into the peritoneal cavity, which is the area in your body that contains organs such as your intestines, stomach, and liver

- **Intra-arterial (IA)**

  The chemotherapy is injected directly into the artery that leads to the cancer

- **Topical**

  The chemotherapy comes in a cream that you rub onto your skin. Chemotherapy is often given through a thin needle that is placed in a vein on your hand or lower arm. Your nurse will put the needle in at the start of each treatment and remove it when treatment is over. IV chemotherapy may also be given through catheters or ports, sometimes with the help of a pump.

- **Catheter**

  A catheter is a thin, soft tube. A doctor or nurse places one end of the catheter in a large vein, often in your chest area. The other end of the catheter stays outside your body. Most catheters stay in place until you have finished your chemotherapy treatments. Catheters can also be used to give you other drugs and to draw blood. Be sure to watch for signs of infection around your catheter. See the section about infection for more information.

621

- **Port**

    A port is a small, round disc that is placed under your skin during minor surgery. A surgeon puts it in place before you begin your course of treatment, and it remains there until you have finished. A catheter connects the port to a large vein, most often in your chest. Your nurse can insert a needle into your port to give you chemotherapy or draw blood. This needle can be left in place for chemotherapy treatments that are given for longer than one day. Be sure to watch for signs of infection around your port.

- **Pump**

    Pumps are often attached to catheters or ports. They control how much and how fast chemotherapy goes into a catheter or port, allowing you to receive your chemotherapy outside of the hospital. Pumps can be internal or external. External pumps remain outside your body. Internal pumps are placed under your skin during surgery.

How Your Doctor Decides Which Chemotherapy Drugs to Give You

There are many different chemotherapy drugs. Which ones are included in your treatment plan depends mostly on:

- The type of cancer you have and how advanced it is

- Whether you have had chemotherapy before

- Whether you have other health problems, such as diabetes or heart disease

Where You Go for Treatment

You may receive chemotherapy during a hospital stay, at home, or as an outpatient at a doctor's office, clinic, or hospital. Outpatient means you do not stay overnight. No matter where you go for chemotherapy, your doctor and nurse will watch for side effects and help you manage them. For more information on side effects and how to manage them, see the section on side effects.

How Often You Receive Chemotherapy

Treatment schedules for chemotherapy vary widely. How often and how long you get chemotherapy depends on:

- Your type of cancer and how advanced it is

- Whether chemotherapy is used to:

- Cure your cancer

- Control its growth

- Ease symptoms

- The type of chemotherapy you are getting

- How your body responds to the chemotherapy

You may receive chemotherapy in cycles. A cycle is a period of chemotherapy treatment followed by a period of rest. For instance, you might receive chemotherapy every day for 1 week followed by 3 weeks with no chemotherapy. These 4 weeks make up one cycle. The rest period gives your body a chance to recover and build new healthy cells.

Missing a Treatment

It is best not to skip a chemotherapy treatment. But, sometimes your doctor may change your chemotherapy schedule if you are having certain side effects. If this happens, your doctor or nurse will explain what to do and when to start treatment again.

How Chemotherapy May Affect You

Chemotherapy affects people in different ways. How you feel depends on:

- The type of chemotherapy you are getting

- The dose of chemotherapy you are getting

- Your type of cancer

- How advanced your cancer is

- How healthy you are before treatment

Since everyone is different and people respond to chemotherapy in different ways, your doctor and nurses cannot know for sure how you will feel during chemotherapy.

How Will I Know If My Chemotherapy Is Working?

You will see your doctor often. During these visits, she will ask you how you feel, do a physical exam, and order medical tests and scans. Tests might include blood tests. Scans might include MRI, CT, or PET scans.

You cannot tell if chemotherapy is working based on its side effects. Some people think that severe side effects mean that chemotherapy is working well, or that no side effects mean that chemotherapy is not working. The truth is that side effects have nothing to do with how well chemotherapy is fighting your cancer.

Special Diet Needs

Chemotherapy can damage the healthy cells that line your mouth and intestines and cause eating problems. Tell your doctor or nurse if you have trouble eating while you are receiving chemotherapy. You might also find it helpful to speak with a dietitian.

Working during Chemotherapy

Many people can work during chemotherapy, as long as they match their work schedule to how they feel. Whether or not you can work may depend on what kind of job you have. If your job allows, you may want to see if you can work part-time or from home on days you do not feel well.

Many employers are required by law to change your work schedule to meet your needs during cancer treatment. Talk with your employer about ways to adjust your work during chemotherapy. You can learn more about these laws by talking with a social worker.

Section 44.4

Immunotherapy

Text in this section is excerpted from "Types of Treatment," National Cancer Institute (NCI), April 29, 2015.

Immunotherapy

Immunotherapy is a type of cancer treatment that helps your immune system fight cancer. The immune system helps your body fight infections and other diseases. It is made up of white blood cells and organs and tissues of the lymph system.

Immunotherapy is a type of biological therapy. Biological therapy is a type of treatment that uses substances made from living organisms to treat cancer.

Types of Immunotherapy

Many different types of immunotherapy are used to treat cancer. They include:

- **Monoclonal antibodies**, which are drugs that are designed to bind to specific targets in the body. They can cause an immune response that destroys cancer cells.

  Other types of monoclonal antibodies can "mark" cancer cells so it is easier for the immune system to find and destroy them. These types of monoclonal antibodies may also be referred to as targeted therapy.

- **Adoptive cell transfer,** which is a treatment that attempts to boost the natural ability of your T cells to fight cancer. T cells are a type of white blood cell and part of the immune system. Researchers take T cells from the tumor. They then isolate the T cells that are most active against your cancer or modify the genes in them to make them better able to find and destroy your cancer cells. Researchers then grow large batches of these T cells in the lab.

  You may have treatments to reduce your immune cells. After these treatments, the T cells that were grown in the lab will be given back to you via a needle in your vein. The process of growing your T cells in the lab can take 2 to 8 weeks, depending on how fast they grow.

- **Cytokines**, which are proteins that are made by your body's cells. They play important roles in the body's normal immune responses and also in the immune system's ability to respond to cancer. The two main types of cytokines used to treat cancer are called interferons and interleukins.

- **Treatment Vaccines**, which work against cancer by boosting your immune system's response to cancer cells. Treatment vaccines are different from the ones that help prevent disease.

- **BCG**, which stands for Bacillus Calmette-Guérin, is an immunotherapy that is used to treat bladder cancer. It is a weakened form of the bacteria that causes tuberculosis. When inserted directly into the bladder with a catheter, BCG causes an immune response against cancer cells. It is also being studied in other types of cancer.

Who Receives Immunotherapy

Immunotherapy is not yet as widely used as surgery, chemotherapy, and radiation therapy. However, immunotherapies have been approved to treat people with many types of cancer.

Many other immunotherapies are being studied in clinical trials, which are research studies involving people. To find a study that may be an option for you, visit Find a Clinical Trial.

How Immunotherapy Works against Cancer

One reason that cancer cells thrive is because they are able to hide from your immune system. Certain immunotherapies can mark cancer cells so it is easier for the immune system to find and destroy them. Other immunotherapies boost your immune system to work better against cancer.

Immunotherapy Can Cause Side Effects

Immunotherapy can cause side effects. The side effects you may have depend on the type of immunotherapy you receive and how your body reacts to it.

The most common side effects are skin reactions at the needle site. These side effects include:

- Pain
- Swelling
- Soreness
- Redness
- Itchiness
- Rash

You may have flu-like symptoms, which include:

- Fever
- Chills
- Weakness
- Dizziness
- Nausea or vomiting
- Muscle or joint aches

- Fatigue
- Headache
- Trouble breathing
- Low or high blood pressure

Other side effects might include:

- Swelling
- Weight gain from retaining fluid
- Heart palpitations
- Sinus congestion
- Diarrhea
- Risk of infection

Immunotherapies may also cause severe or even fatal allergic reactions. However, these reactions are rare.

How Immunotherapy Is Given

Different forms of immunotherapy may be given in different ways. These include:

- **Intravenous (IV)**

  The immunotherapy goes directly into a vein.

- **Oral**

  The immunotherapy comes in pills or capsules that you swallow.

- **Topical**

  The immunotherapy comes in a cream that you rub onto your skin. This type of immunotherapy can be used for very early skin cancer.

- **Intravesical**

  The immunotherapy goes directly into the bladder.

Where You Go for Your Treatment

You may receive immunotherapy in a doctor's office, clinic, or outpatient unit in a hospital. Outpatient means you do not spend the night in the hospital.

How Often You Will Receive Treatment

How often and how long you receive immunotherapy depends on:

- Your type of cancer and how advanced it is
- The type of immunotherapy you get
- How your body reacts to treatment

You may have treatment every day, week, or month. Some immuno-therapies are given in cycles. A cycle is a period of treatment followed by a period of rest. The rest period gives your body a chance to recover, respond to the immunotherapy, and build new healthy cells.

How Immunotherapy Makes You Feel

Immunotherapy affects people in different ways. How you feel depends on how healthy you are before treatment, your type of cancer, how advanced it is, the type of therapy you are getting, and the dose. Doctors and nurses cannot know for certain how you will feel during treatment.

How to Tell Whether Immunotherapy Is Working

You will see your doctor often. He or she will give you physical exams and ask you how you feel. You will have medical tests, such as blood tests and different types of scans. These tests will measure the size of your tumor and look for changes in your blood work.

Section 44.5

Targeted Therapy

Text in this section is excerpted from "Types of Treatment," National Cancer Institute (NCI), April 29, 2015.

What Is Precision Medicine?

Precision medicine refers to the use of information about the genes, proteins, and other features of a person's cancer to diagnose or treat their disease.

What Is Targeted Therapy?

Targeted therapy is the foundation of precision medicine. It is a type of cancer treatment that targets the changes in cancer cells that help them grow, divide, and spread. As researchers learn more about the cell changes that drive cancer, they are better able to design promising therapies that target these changes or block their effects.

Types of Targeted Therapy

Most targeted therapies are either small-molecule drugs or monoclonal antibodies.

Small-molecule drugs are small enough to enter cells easily, so they are used for targets that are inside cells.

Monoclonal antibodies are drugs that are not able to enter cells easily. Instead, they attach to specific targets on the outer surface of cancer cells.

Who Receives Targeted Therapy

For some types of cancer, most patients with that cancer will have a target for a certain drug, so they can be treated with that drug. But, most of the time, your tumor will need to be tested to see if it contains targets for which we have drugs.

To have your tumor tested for targets, you may need to have a biopsy. A biopsy is a procedure in which your doctor removes a piece of the tumor for testing. There are some risks to having a biopsy. These risks vary depending on the size of the tumor and where it is located. Your doctor will explain the risks of having a biopsy for your type of tumor.

How Targeted Therapy Works Against Cancer

Most targeted therapies help treat cancer by interfering with specific proteins that help tumors grow and spread throughout the body. They treat cancer in many different ways. They can:

- **Help the immune system destroy cancer cells.** One reason that cancer cells thrive is because they are able to hide from your immune system. Certain targeted therapies can mark cancer cells so it is easier for the immune system to find and destroy them. Other targeted therapies help boost your immune system to work better against cancer.

- **Stop cancer cells from growing.** Healthy cells in your body usually divide to make new cells only when they receive strong signals to do so. These signals bind to proteins on the cell surface, telling the cells to divide. This process helps new cells form only as your body needs them. But, some cancer cells have changes in the proteins on their surface that tell them to divide whether or not signals are present. Some targeted therapies interfere with these proteins, preventing them from telling the cells to divide. This process helps slow cancer's uncontrolled growth.

- **Stop signals that help form blood vessels**. Tumors need to form new blood vessels to grow beyond a certain size. These new blood vessels form in response to signals from the tumor. Some targeted therapies are designed to interfere with these signals to prevent a blood supply from forming. Without a blood supply, tumors stay small. Or, if a tumor already has a blood supply, these treatments can cause blood vessels to die, which causes the tumor to shrink.

- **Deliver cell-killing substances to cancer cells**. Some monoclonal antibodies are combined with toxins, chemotherapy drugs, and radiation. Once these monoclonal antibodies attach to targets on the surface of cancer cells, the cells take up the cell-killing substances, causing them to die. Cells that don't have the target will not be harmed.

- **Cause cancer cell death**. Healthy cells die in an orderly manner when they become damaged or are no longer needed. But, cancer cells have ways of avoiding this dying process. Some targeted therapies can cause cancer cells to go through this process of cell death.

- **Starve cancer of the hormones it needs to grow**. Some breast and prostate cancers require certain hormones to grow. Hormone therapies are a type of targeted therapy that can work in two ways. Some hormone therapies prevent your body from making specific hormones. Others prevent the hormones from acting on your cells, including cancer cells.

Drawbacks of Targeted Therapy

Targeted therapies do have some drawbacks. These include:

- Cancer cells can become resistant to them. For this reason, targeted therapies may work best when used with other targeted therapies or with other cancer treatments, such as chemotherapy and radiation.

- Drugs for some targets are hard to develop. Reasons include the target's structure, the target's function in the cell, or both.

Targeted Therapy Can Cause Side Effects

Targeted therapy can cause side effects. The side effects you may have depend on the type of targeted therapy you receive and how your body reacts to the therapy.

The most common side effects of targeted therapy include diarrhea and liver problems. Other side effects might include problems with blood clotting and wound healing, high blood pressure, fatigue, mouth sores, nail changes, the loss of hair color, and skin problems. Skin problems might include rash or dry skin. Very rarely, a hole might form through the wall of the esophagus, stomach, small intestine, large bowel, rectum, or gallbladder.

There are medicines for many of these side effects. These medicines may prevent the side effects from happening or treat them once they occur.

Most side effects of targeted therapy go away after treatment ends.

Other Risks

Since your tumor may be tested to find targets for treatment, there may be risks to the privacy of your personal information. The privacy of all information found from these tests is protected by law. But, there is a slight risk that genetic or other information from your health records may be obtained by people outside of the medical team.

Having Targeted Therapy

How Targeted Therapies Are Given

- Small-molecule drugs are pills or capsules that you can swallow.

- Monoclonal antibodies are usually given through a needle in a blood vein.

Where You Go For Your Treatment

Where you go for treatment depends on which drugs you are getting and how they are given. You may take targeted therapy at home. Or, you may receive targeted therapy in a doctor's office, clinic, or outpatient unit in a hospital. Outpatient means you do not spend the night in the hospital.

How Often You Will Receive Treatment

How often and how long you receive targeted therapy depends on:

- Your type of cancer and how advanced it is

- The type of targeted therapy

- How your body reacts to treatment

You may have treatment every day, every week, or every month. Some targeted therapies are given in cycles. A cycle is a period of treatment followed by a period of rest. The rest period gives your body a chance to recover and build new healthy cells.

How Targeted Therapy May Affect You

Targeted therapy affects people in different ways. How you feel depends on how healthy you are before treatment, your type of cancer, how advanced it is, the kind of targeted therapy you are getting, and the dose. Doctors and nurses cannot know for certain how you will feel during treatment.

How to Tell Whether Targeted Therapy Is Working

You will see your doctor often. He or she will give you physical exams and ask you how you feel. You will have medical tests, such as blood tests, x-rays, and different types of scans.

Section 44.6

Hormone Therapy

Text in this section is excerpted from "Types of Treatment," National Cancer Institute (NCI), April 29, 2015.

Hormone Therapy

Hormone therapy is a cancer treatment that slows or stops the growth of cancer that uses hormones to grow. Hormone therapy is also called hormonal therapy, hormone treatment, or endocrine therapy.

How Hormone Therapy Works against Cancer

Hormone therapy is used to:

- **Treat cancer.** Hormone therapy can lessen the chance that cancer will return or stop or slow its growth.

- **Ease cancer symptoms.** Hormone therapy may be used to reduce or prevent symptoms in men with prostate cancer who are not able to have surgery or radiation therapy.

Types of Hormone Therapy

Hormone therapy falls into two broad groups, those that block the body's ability to produce hormones and those that interfere with how hormones behave in the body

Who Receives Hormone Therapy

Hormone therapy is used to treat prostate and breast cancers that use hormones to grow. Hormone therapy is most often used along with other cancer treatments. The types of treatment that you need depend on the type of cancer, if it has spread and how far, if it uses hormones to grow, and if you have other health problems.

How Hormone Therapy Is Used with Other Cancer Treatments

When used with other treatments, hormone therapy can:

- Make a tumor smaller before surgery or radiation therapy. This is called neo-adjuvant therapy.

- Lower the risk that cancer will come back after the main treatment. This is called adjuvant therapy.

- Destroy cancer cells that have returned or spread to other parts of your body.

Hormone Therapy Can Cause Side Effects

Because hormone therapy blocks your body's ability to produce hormones or interferes with how hormones behave, it can cause unwanted side effects. The side effects you have will depend on the type of hormone therapy you receive and how your body responds to it. People respond differently to the same treatment, so not everyone gets the same side effects. Some side effects also differ if you are a man or a woman.

Some common side effects for men who receive hormone therapy for prostate cancer include:

- Hot flashes
- Loss of interest in or ability to have sex
- Weakened bones
- Diarrhea
- Nausea
- Enlarged and tender breasts
- Fatigue

Some common side effects for women who receive hormone therapy for breast cancer include:

- Hot flashes
- Vaginal dryness
- Changes in your periods if you have not yet reached menopause
- Loss of interest in sex
- Nausea
- Mood changes
- Fatigue

How Much Hormone Therapy Costs

The cost of hormone therapy depends on:

- The types of hormone therapy you receive
- How long and how often you receive hormone therapy
- The part of the country where you live

Talk with your health insurance company about what services it will pay for. Most insurance plans pay for hormone therapy for their members. To learn more, talk with the business office where you go for treatment. You can also go to the National Cancer Institute database, Organizations that Offer Support Services and search "financial assistance." Or call toll-free 1-800-4-CANCER (1-800-422-6237) to ask for help.

What to Expect When Receiving Hormone Therapy

How Hormone Therapy Is Given

Hormone therapy may be given in many ways. Some common ways include:

- **Oral**. Hormone therapy comes in pills that you swallow.

- **Injection**. The hormone therapy is given by a shot in a muscle in your arm, thigh, or hip, or right under the skin in the fatty part of your arm, leg, or belly.

- **Surgery**. You may have surgery to remove organs that produce hormones. In women, the ovaries are removed. In men, the testicles are removed.

Where You Receive Treatment

Where you receive treatment depends on which hormone therapy you are getting and how it is given. You may take hormone therapy at home. Or, you may receive hormone therapy in a doctor's office, clinic, or hospital.

How Hormone Therapy May Affect You

Hormone therapy affects people in different ways. How you feel depends on the type of cancer you have, how advanced it is, the type of hormone therapy you are getting, and the dose. Your doctors and nurses cannot know for certain how you will feel during hormone therapy.

How to Tell If Hormone Therapy Is Working

If you are taking hormone therapy for prostate cancer, you will have regular PSA tests. If hormone therapy is working, your PSA levels will stay the same or may even go down. But, if your PSA levels go up, this may be a sign that the treatment is no longer working. If this happens, your doctor will discuss treatment options with you.

If you are taking hormone therapy for breast cancer, you will have regular checkups. Checkups usually include an exam of the neck, underarm, chest, and breast areas. You will have regular mammograms, though you probably won't need a mammogram of a reconstructed breast. Your doctor may also order other imaging procedures or lab tests.

Special Diet Needs

Hormone therapy for prostate cancer may cause weight gain. Talk with your doctor, nurse, or dietitian if weight gain becomes a problem for you.

Working during Hormone Therapy

Hormone therapy should not interfere with your ability to work.

Section 44.7

Stem Cell Transplant

Text in this section is excerpted from "Types of Treatment," National Cancer Institute (NCI), April 29, 2015.

Stem Cell Transplant

Stem cell transplants are procedures that restore blood-forming stem cells in people who have had theirs destroyed by the very high doses of chemotherapy or radiation therapy that are used to treat certain cancers.

Blood-forming stem cells are important because they grow into different types of blood cells. The main types of blood cells are:

- White blood cells, which are part of your immune system and help your body fight infection

- Red blood cells, which carry oxygen throughout your body

- Platelets, which help the blood clot

You need all three types of blood cells to be healthy.

Types of Stem Cell Transplants

In a stem cell transplant, you receive healthy blood-forming stem cells through a needle in your vein. Once they enter your bloodstream, the stem cells travel to the bone marrow, where they take the place of the cells that were destroyed by treatment. The blood-forming stem cells that are used in transplants can come from the bone marrow, bloodstream, or umbilical cord. Transplants can be:

- Autologous, which means the stem cells come from you, the patient

- Allogeneic, which means the stem cells come from someone else. The donor may be a blood relative but can also be someone who is not related.

- Syngeneic, which means the stem cells come from your identical twin, if you have one

To reduce possible side effects and improve the chances that an allogeneic transplant will work, the donor's blood-forming stem cells must match yours in certain ways.

How Stem Cell Transplants Work against Cancer

Stem cell transplants do not usually work against cancer directly. Instead, they help you recover your ability to produce stem cells after treatment with very high doses of radiation therapy, chemotherapy, or both.

However, in multiple myeloma and some types of leukemia, the stem cell transplant may work against cancer directly. This happens because of an effect called graft-versus-tumor that can occur after allogeneic transplants. Graft-versus-tumor occurs when white blood cells from your donor (the graft) attack any cancer cells that remain in your body (the tumor) after high-dose treatments. This effect improves the success of the treatments.

Who Receives Stem Cell Transplants

Stem cell transplants are most often used to help people with leukemia and lymphoma. They may also be used for neuroblastoma and multiple myeloma.

Stem cell transplants for other types of cancer are being studied in clinical trials, which are research studies involving people.

Stem Cell Transplants Can Cause Side Effects

The high doses of cancer treatment that you have before a stem cell transplant can cause problems such as bleeding and an increased risk of infection. Talk with your doctor or nurse about other side effects that you might have and how serious they might be. For more information about side effects and how to manage them, see the section on side effects.

If you have an allogeneic transplant, you might develop a serious problem called graft-versus-host disease. Graft-versus-host disease can occur when white blood cells from your donor (the graft) recognize cells in your body (the host) as foreign and attack them. This problem can cause damage to your skin, liver, intestines, and many other organs. It can occur a few weeks after the transplant or much later. Graft-versus-host disease can be treated with steroids or other drugs that suppress your immune system.

The closer your donor's blood-forming stem cells match yours, the less likely you are to have graft-versus-host disease. Your doctor may also try to prevent it by giving you drugs to suppress your immune system.

How Much Stem Cell Transplants Cost

Stem cells transplants are complicated procedures that are very expensive. Most insurance plans cover some of the costs of transplants for certain types of cancer. Talk with your health plan about which services it will pay for. Talking with the business office where you go for treatment may help you understand all the costs involved.

To learn about groups that may be able to provide financial help, go to the National Cancer Institute database, Organizations that Offer Support Services and search "financial assistance." Or call toll-free 1-800-4-CANCER (1-800-422-6237) for information about groups that may be able to help.

What to Expect When Receiving a Stem Cell Transplant

Where You Go for Treatment

When you need an allogeneic stem cell transplant, you will need to go to a hospital that has a specialized transplant center. The National Marrow Donor Program® maintains a list of transplant centers in the United States that can help you find a transplant center.

Unless you live near a transplant center, you may need to travel from home for your treatment. You might need to stay in the hospital during your transplant, you may be able to have it as an outpatient, or you may need to be in the hospital only part of the time. When you are not in the hospital, you will need to stay in a hotel or apartment nearby. Many transplant centers can assist with finding nearby housing.

How Long It Takes to Have a Stem Cell Transplant

A stem cell transplant can take a few months to complete. The process begins with treatment of high doses of chemotherapy, radiation therapy, or a combination of the two. This treatment goes on for a week or two. Once you have finished, you will have a few days to rest.

Next, you will receive the blood-forming stem cells. The stem cells will be given to you through an IV catheter. This process is like receiving a blood transfusion. It takes 1 to 5 hours to receive all the stem cells.

After receiving the stem cells, you begin the recovery phase. During this time, you wait for the blood cells you received to start making new blood cells.

Even after your blood counts return to normal, it takes much longer for your immune system to fully recover—several months for autologous transplants and 1 to 2 years for allogeneic or syngeneic transplants.

How Stem Cell Transplants May Affect You

Stem cell transplants affect people in different ways. How you feel depends on:

- The type of transplant that you have

- The doses of treatment you had before the transplant

- How you respond to the high-dose treatments

- Your type of cancer

- How advanced your cancer is

- How healthy you were before the transplant

Since people respond to stem cell transplants in different ways, your doctor or nurses cannot know for sure how the procedure will make you feel.

How to tell if your Stem Cell Transplant worked

Doctors will follow the progress of the new blood cells by checking your blood counts often. As the newly transplanted stem cells produce blood cells, your blood counts will go up.

Special Diet Needs

The high-dose treatments that you have before a stem cell transplant can cause side effects that make it hard to eat, such as mouth sores and nausea. Tell your doctor or nurse if you have trouble eating while you are receiving treatment. You might also find it helpful to speak with a dietitian.

Working during your Stem Cell Transplant

Whether or not you can work during a stem cell transplant may depend on the type of job you have. The process of a stem cell transplant, with the high-dose treatments, the transplant, and recovery, can take weeks or months. You will be in and out of the hospital during this time. Even when you are not in the hospital, sometimes you will need to stay near it, rather than staying in your own home. So, if your job allows, you may want to arrange to work remotely part-time.

Many employers are required by law to change your work schedule to meet your needs during cancer treatment. Talk with your employer about ways to adjust your work during treatment. You can learn more about these laws by talking with a social worker.

Section 44.8

Biological Therapies for Cancer

Text in this section is excerpted from "Types of Treatment," National Cancer Institute (NCI), April 29, 2015.

What is biological therapy?

Biological therapy involves the use of living organisms, substances derived from living organisms, or laboratory-produced versions of such substances to treat disease. Some biological therapies for cancer use vaccines or bacteria to stimulate the body's immune system to act against cancer cells. These types of biological therapy, which are sometimes referred to collectively as "immunotherapy" or "biological response modifier therapy," do not target cancer cells directly. Other biological therapies, such as antibodies or segments of genetic material (RNA or DNA), do target cancer cells directly. Biological therapies that interfere with specific molecules involved in tumor growth and progression are also referred to as targeted therapies.

For patients with cancer, biological therapies may be used to treat the cancer itself or the side effects of other cancer treatments. Although many forms of biological therapy have been approved by the U.S. Food and Drug Administration (FDA), others remain experimental and are available to cancer patients principally through participation in clinical trials (research studies involving people).

What is the immune system and what role does it have in biological therapy for cancer?

The immune system is a complex network of organs, tissues, and specialized cells. It recognizes and destroys foreign invaders, such as bacteria or viruses, as well as some damaged, diseased, or abnormal cells in the body, including cancer cells. An immune response is triggered when the immune system encounters a substance, called an antigen, it recognizes as "foreign."

White blood cells are the primary players in immune system responses. Some white blood cells, including macrophages and natural killer cells, patrol the body, seeking out foreign invaders and diseased, damaged, or dead cells. These white blood cells provide a general—or nonspecific—level of immune protection.

Other white blood cells, including cytotoxic T cells and B cells, act against specific targets. Cytotoxic T cells release chemicals that can directly destroy microbes or abnormal cells. B cells make antibodies that latch onto foreign intruders or abnormal cells and tag them for destruction by another component of the immune system. Still other white blood cells, including dendritic cells, play supporting roles to ensure that cytotoxic T cells and B cells do their jobs effectively.

It is generally believed that the immune system's natural capacity to detect and destroy abnormal cells prevents the development of many cancers. Nevertheless, some cancer cells are able to evade detection by using one or more strategies. For example, cancer cells can undergo genetic changes that lead to the loss of cancer-associated antigens, making them less "visible" to the immune system. They may also use several different mechanisms to suppress immune responses or to avoid being killed by cytotoxic T cells.

The goal of immunotherapy for cancer is to overcome these barriers to an effective anticancer immune response. These biological therapies restore or increase the activities of specific immune-system components or counteract immunosuppressive signals produced by cancer cells.

641

What are monoclonal antibodies, and how are they used in cancer treatment?

Monoclonal antibodies, or MAbs, are laboratory-produced antibodies that bind to specific antigens expressed by cells, such as a protein that is present on the surface of cancer cells but is absent from (or expressed at lower levels by) normal cells.

To create MAbs, researchers inject mice with an antigen from human cells. They then harvest the antibody-producing cells from the mice and individually fuse them with a myeloma cell (cancerous B cell) to produce a fusion cell known as a hybridoma. Each hybridoma then divides to produce identical daughter cells or clones—hence the term "monoclonal"—and antibodies secreted by different clones are tested to identify the antibodies that bind most strongly to the antigen. Large quantities of antibodies can be produced by these immortal hybridoma cells. Because mouse antibodies can themselves elicit an immune response in humans, which would reduce their effectiveness, mouse antibodies are often "humanized" by replacing as much of the mouse portion of the antibody as possible with human portions. This is done through genetic engineering.

Some MAbs stimulate an immune response that destroys cancer cells. Similar to the antibodies produced naturally by B cells, these MAbs "coat" the cancer cell surface, triggering its destruction by the immune system. FDA-approved MAbs of this type include rituximab, which targets the CD20 antigen found on non-Hodgkin lymphoma cells, and alemtuzumab, which targets the CD52 antigen found on B-cell chronic lymphocytic leukemia (CLL) cells. Rituximab may also trigger cell death (apoptosis) directly.

Another group of MAbs stimulates an anticancer immune response by binding to receptors on the surface of immune cells and inhibiting signals that prevent immune cells from attacking the body's own tissues, including cancer cells. One such MAb, ipilimumab, has been approved by the FDA for treatment of metastatic melanoma, and others are being investigated in clinical studies.

Other MAbs interfere with the action of proteins that are necessary for tumor growth. For example, bevacizumab targets vascular endothelial growth factor (VEGF), a protein secreted by tumor cells and other cells in the tumor's microenvironment that promotes the development of tumor blood vessels. When bound to bevacizumab, VEGF cannot interact with its cellular receptor, preventing the signaling that leads to the growth of new blood vessels.

Similarly, cetuximab and panitumumab target the epidermal growth factor receptor (EGFR), and trastuzumab targets the human epidermal growth factor receptor 2 (HER-2). MAbs that bind to cell surface growth factor receptors prevent the targeted receptors from sending their normal growth-promoting signals. They may also trigger apoptosis and activate the immune system to destroy tumor cells.

Another group of cancer therapeutic MAbs are the immunoconjugates. These MAbs, which are sometimes called immunotoxins or antibody-drug conjugates, consist of an antibody attached to a cell-killing substance, such as a plant or bacterial toxin, a chemotherapy drug, or a radioactive molecule. The antibody latches onto its specific antigen on the surface of a cancer cell, and the cell-killing substance is taken up by the cell. FDA-approved conjugated MAbs that work this way include Y-ibritumomab tiuxetan, which targets the CD20 antigen to deliver radioactive yttrium-90 to B-cell non-Hodgkin lymphoma cells, and ado-trastuzumab emtansine, which targets the HER-2 molecule to deliver the drug DM1, which inhibits cell proliferation, to HER-2 expressing metastatic breast cancer cells.

What are cytokines, and how are they used in cancer treatment?

Cytokines are signaling proteins that are produced by white blood cells. They help mediate and regulate immune responses, inflammation, and hematopoiesis (new blood cell formation). Two types of cytokines are used to treat patients with cancer: interferons (INFs) and interleukins (ILs). A third type, called hematopoietic growth factors, is used to counteract some of the side effects of certain chemotherapy regimens.

Researchers have found that one type of INF, INF-alfa, can enhance a patient's immune response to cancer cells by activating certain white blood cells, such as natural killer cells and dendritic cells. INF-alfa may also inhibit the growth of cancer cells or promote their death. INF-alfa has been approved for the treatment of melanoma, Kaposi sarcoma, and several hematologic cancers.

Like INFs, ILs play important roles in the body's normal immune response and in the immune system's ability to respond to cancer. Researchers have identified more than a dozen distinct ILs, including IL-2, which is also called T-cell growth factor. IL-2 is naturally produced by activated T cells. It increases the proliferation of white blood cells, including cytotoxic T cells and natural killer cells, leading to an enhanced anticancer immune response. IL-2 also facilitates the production of antibodies by B cells to further target cancer cells. Aldesleukin, IL-2 that is made in a laboratory, has been approved for the treatment of metastatic kidney cancer and metastatic melanoma. Researchers are currently investigating whether combining aldesleukin treatment with other types of biological therapies may enhance its anticancer effects.

Hematopoietic growth factors are a special class of naturally occurring cytokines. All blood cells arise from hematopoietic stem cells in the bone marrow. Because chemotherapy drugs target proliferating cells, including normal blood stem cells, chemotherapy depletes these stem cells and the blood cells that they produce. Loss of red blood cells, which transport oxygen and nutrients throughout the body, can cause anemia. A decrease in platelets, which are responsible for blood clotting, often leads to abnormal bleeding. Finally, lower white blood cell counts leave chemotherapy patients vulnerable to infections.

Several growth factors that promote the growth of these various blood cell populations have been approved for clinical use. Erythropoietin stimulates red blood cell formation, and IL-11 increases platelet production. Granulocyte-macrophage colony-stimulating factor (GM-CSF) and granulocyte colony-stimulating factor (G-CSF) both increase the number of white blood cells, reducing the risk of infections. Treatment with these factors allows patients to continue chemotherapy regimens that might otherwise be stopped temporarily or modified to reduce the drug doses because of low blood cell numbers.

G-CSF and GM-CSF can also enhance the immune system's specific anticancer responses by increasing the number of cancer-fighting T cells. Thus, GM-CSF and G-CSF are used in combination with other biological therapies to strengthen anticancer immune responses.

What are cancer treatment vaccines?

Cancer treatment vaccines are designed to treat cancers that have already developed rather than to prevent them in the first place. Cancer treatment vaccines contain cancer-associated antigens to enhance the immune system's response to a patient's tumor cells. The cancer-associated antigens can be proteins or another type of molecule found on the surface of or inside cancer cells that can stimulate B cells or killer T cells to attack them.

Some vaccines that are under development target antigens that are found on or in many types of cancer cells. These types of cancer vaccines are being tested in clinical trials in patients with a variety of cancers, including prostate, colorectal, lung, breast, and thyroid cancers. Other cancer vaccines target antigens that are unique to a specific cancer type. Still other vaccines are designed against an antigen specific to one patient's tumor and need to be customized for each patient. The one cancer treatment vaccine that has received FDA approval, sipuleucel-T, is this type of vaccine.

Because of the limited toxicity seen with cancer vaccines, they are also being tested in clinical trials in combination with other forms of therapy, such as hormonal therapy, chemotherapy, radiation therapy, and targeted therapies.

What is bacillus Calmette-Guérin therapy?

Bacillus Calmette-Guérin (BCG) was the first biological therapy to be approved by the FDA. It is a weakened form of a live tuberculosis bacterium that does not cause disease in humans. It was first used medically as a vaccine against tuberculosis. When inserted directly into the bladder with a catheter, BCG stimulates a general immune response that is directed not only against the foreign bacterium itself but also against bladder cancer cells. How and why BCG exerts this anticancer effect is not well understood, but the efficacy of the treatment is well documented. Approximately 70 percent of patients with early-stage bladder cancer experience a remission after BCG therapy.

BCG is also being studied in the treatment of other types of cancer.

What is oncolytic virus therapy?

Oncolytic virus therapy is an experimental form of biological therapy that involves the direct destruction of cancer cells. *Oncolytic viruses* infect both cancer and normal cells, but they have little effect on normal cells. In contrast, they readily replicate, or reproduce, inside cancer cells and ultimately cause the cancer cells to die. Some viruses, such as *reovirus*, Newcastle disease virus, and *mumps virus*, are naturally oncolytic, whereas others, including *measles virus, adenovirus*, and *vaccinia virus*, can be adapted or modified to replicate efficiently only in cancer cells. In addition, *oncolytic viruses* can be genetically engineered to preferentially infect and replicate in cancer cells that produce a specific cancer-associated antigen, such as EGFR or HER-2.

One of the challenges in using *oncolytic viruses* is that they may themselves be destroyed by the patient's immune system before they have a chance to attack the cancer. Researchers have developed several strategies to overcome this challenge, such as administering a combination of immune-suppressing chemotherapy drugs like cyclophosphamide along with the virus or "cloaking" the virus within a protective envelope. But an immune reaction in the patient may actually have benefits: although it may hamper *oncolytic virus* therapy at the time of viral delivery, it may enhance cancer cell destruction after the virus has infected the tumor cells.

No *oncolytic virus* has been approved for use in the United States, although H101, a modified form of *adenovirus*, was approved in China in 2006 for the treatment of patients with head and neck cancer. Several *oncolytic viruses* are currently being tested in clinical trials. Researchers are also investigating whether *oncolytic viruses* can be combined with other types of cancer therapies or can be used to sensitize patients' tumors to additional therapy.

What is gene therapy?

Still an experimental form of treatment, gene therapy attempts to introduce genetic material (DNA or RNA) into living cells. Gene therapy is being studied in clinical trials for many types of cancer.

In general, genetic material cannot be inserted directly into a person's cells. Instead, it is delivered to the cells using a carrier, or "vector." The vectors most commonly used in gene therapy are viruses, because they have the unique ability to recognize certain cells and insert genetic material into them. Scientists alter these viruses to make them more safe for humans (e.g., by inactivating genes that enable them to reproduce or cause disease) and/or to improve their ability to recognize and enter the target cell. A variety of liposomes (fatty particles) and nanoparticles are also being used as gene therapy vectors, and scientists are investigating methods of targeting these vectors to specific cell types.

Researchers are studying several methods for treating cancer with gene therapy. Some approaches target cancer cells, to destroy them or prevent their growth. Others target healthy cells to enhance their ability to fight cancer. In some cases, researchers remove cells from the patient, treat the cells with the vector in the laboratory, and return the cells to the patient. In others, the vector is given directly to the patient. Some gene therapy approaches being studied are described below.

- Replacing an altered tumor suppressor gene that produces a nonfunctional protein (or no protein) with a normal version of the gene. Because tumor suppressor genes (e.g., TP53) play a role in preventing cancer, restoring the normal function of these genes may inhibit cancer growth or promote cancer regression.

- Introducing genetic material to block the expression of an oncogene whose product promotes tumor growth. Short RNA or DNA molecules with sequences complementary to the gene's messenger RNA (mRNA) can be packaged into vectors or given to cells directly. These short molecules, called oligonucleotides, can bind to the target mRNA, preventing its translation into protein or even causing its degradation.

- Improving a patient's immune response to cancer. In one approach, gene therapy is used to introduce cytokine-producing genes into cancer cells to stimulate the immune response to the tumor.

- Inserting genes into cancer cells to make them more sensitive to chemotherapy, radiation therapy, or other treatments

- Inserting genes into healthy blood-forming stem cells to make them more resistant to the side effects of cancer treatments, such as high doses of anticancer drugs

- Introducing "suicide genes" into a patient's cancer cells. A suicide gene is a gene whose product is able to activate a "pro-drug" (an inactive form of a toxic drug), causing the toxic drug to be produced only in cancer cells in patients given the pro-drug. Normal cells, which do not express the suicide genes, are not affected by the pro-drug.

- Inserting genes to prevent cancer cells from developing new blood vessels (angiogenesis)

Proposed gene therapy clinical trials, or protocols, must be approved by at least two review boards at the researchers' institution before they can be conducted. Gene therapy protocols must also be approved by the FDA, which regulates all gene therapy products. In addition, gene therapy trials that are funded by the National Institutes of Health must be registered with the NIH Recombinant DNA Advisory Committee.

What is adoptive T-cell transfer therapy?

Adoptive cell transfer is an experimental anticancer therapy that attempts to enhance the natural cancer-fighting ability of a patient's T cells. In one form of this therapy, researchers first harvest cytotoxic T cells that have invaded a patient's tumor. They then identify the cells with the greatest antitumor activity and grow large populations of those cells in a laboratory. The patients are then treated to deplete their immune cells, and the laboratory-grown T cells are infused into the patients.

In another, more recently developed form of this therapy, which is also a kind of gene therapy, researchers isolate T cells from a small sample of the patient's blood. They genetically modify the cells by inserting the gene for a receptor that recognizes an antigen specific to the patient's cancer cells and grow large numbers of these modified cells in culture. The genetically modified cells are then infused into patients whose immune cells have been depleted. The receptor expressed by the modified T cells allows these cells to attach to antigens on the surface of the tumor cells, which activates the T cells to attack and kill the tumor cells.

Adoptive T-cell transfer was first studied for the treatment of metastatic melanoma because melanomas often cause a substantial immune response, with many tumor-invading cytotoxic T cells. Adoptive cell transfer with genetically modified T cells is also being investigated as a treatment for other solid tumors, as well as for hematologic cancers.

What are the side effects of biological therapies?

The side effects associated with various biological therapies can differ by treatment type. However, pain, swelling, soreness, redness, itchiness, and rash at the site of infusion or injection are fairly common with these treatments.

Less common but more serious side effects tend to be more specific to one or a few types of biological therapy. For example, therapies intended to prompt an immune response against cancer can cause an array of flu-like symptoms, including fever, chills, weakness, dizziness, nausea or vomiting, muscle or joint aches, fatigue, headache, occasional breathing difficulties, and lowered or heightened blood pressure. Biological therapies that provoke an immune system response also pose a risk of severe or even fatal hypersensitivity (allergic) reactions.

Potential serious side effects of specific biological therapies are as follows:

MAbs

- Flu-like symptoms
- Severe allergic reaction
- Lowered blood counts

- Changes in blood chemistry
- Organ damage (usually to heart, lungs, kidneys, liver or brain)

Cytokines (interferons, interleukins, hematopoietic growth factors)

- Flu-like symptoms
- Severe allergic reaction
- Lowered blood counts
- Changes in blood chemistry
- Organ damage (usually to heart, lungs, kidneys, liver or brain)

Treatment vaccines

- Flu-like symptoms
- Severe allergic reaction

BCG

- Flu-like symptoms
- Severe allergic reaction
- Urinary side effects
  - Pain or burning sensation during urination
  - Increased urgency or frequency of urination
  - Blood in the urine

Oncolytic viruses

- Flu-like symptoms
- Tumor lysis syndrome: severe, sometimes life-threatening alterations in blood chemistry following the release of materials formerly contained within cancer cells into the bloodstream

Gene therapy

- Flu-like symptoms
- Secondary cancer: techniques that insert DNA into a host cell chromosome can cause cancer to develop if the insertion inhibits expression of a tumor suppressor gene or activates an oncogene; researchers are working to minimize this possibility

- Mistaken introduction of a gene into healthy cells, including reproductive cells

- Overexpression of the introduced gene may harm healthy tissues

- Virus vector transmission to other individuals or into the environment

How can people obtain information about clinical trials of biological therapies for cancer?

Both FDA-approved and experimental biological therapies for specific types of cancer are being studied in clinical trials. The names of the biological therapy types listed below are links to descriptions of ongoing clinical trials that are testing those types of biological therapies in cancer patients. These trial descriptions can also be accessed by searching NCI's list of cancer clinical trials on the NCI website. NCI's list of cancer clinical trials includes all NCI-funded clinical trials as well as studies conducted by investigators at hospitals and medical centers throughout the United States and around the world.

Section 44.9

Nutrition Therapy in Cancer Care

Text in this section is excerpted from "Nutrition in Cancer Care
(PDQ®)," National Cancer Institute (NCI), April 29, 2015.

Screening and assessment are done before cancer treatment begins, and assessment continues during treatment.

Screening is used to look for nutrition risks in a patient who has
no symptoms. This can help find out if the patient is likely to become
malnourished, so that steps can be taken to prevent it.

Assessment checks the nutritional health of the patient and helps
to decide if nutrition therapy is needed to correct a problem.

Screening and assessment may include questions about the
following:

- Weight changes over the past year.

- Changes in the amount and type of food eaten compared to what
  is usual for the patient.

- Problems that have affected eating, such as loss of appetite, nausea, vomiting, diarrhea, constipation, mouth sores, dry mouth,
  changes in taste and smell, or pain.

- Ability to walk and do other activities of daily living (dressing,
  getting into or out of a bed or chair, taking a bath or shower, and
  using the toilet).

A physical exam is also done to check the body for general health
and signs of disease. The doctor will look for loss of weight, fat, and
muscle, and for fluid buildup in the body.

Finding and treating nutrition problems early may improve the patient's prognosis (chance of recovery).

Early nutrition screening and assessment help find problems that
may affect how well the patient's body can deal with the effects of
cancer treatment. Patients who are underweight or malnourished

may not be able to get through treatment as well as a well-nourished patient. Finding and treating nutrition problems early can help the patient gain weight or prevent weight loss, decrease problems with the treatment, and help recovery.

A healthcare team of nutrition specialists will continue to watch for nutrition problems.

A nutrition support team will check the patient's nutritional health often during cancer treatment and recovery. The team may include the following specialists:

- Physician.
- Nurse.
- Registered dietitian.
- Social worker.
- Psychologist.

A patient whose religion doesn't allow eating certain foods may want to talk with a religious advisor about allowing those foods during cancer treatment and recovery.

There are three main goals of nutrition therapy for cancer patients in active treatment and recovery.

The main goals of nutrition therapy for patients in active treatment and recovery are to provide nutrients that are missing, maintain nutritional health, and prevent problems. The health care team will use nutrition therapy to do the following:

- Prevent or treat nutrition problems, including preventing muscle and bone loss.
- Decrease side effects of cancer treatment and problems that affect nutrition.
- Keep up the patient's strength and energy.
- Help the immune system fight infection.
- Help the body recover and heal.
- Keep up or improve the patient's quality of life.

Good nutrition continues to be important for patients who are in remission or whose cancer has been cured.

The goal of nutrition therapy for patients who have advanced cancer is to help with the patient's quality of life.

The goals of nutrition therapy for patients who have advanced cancer include the following:

- Control side effects.

- Lower the risk of infection.

- Keep up strength and energy.

- Improve or maintain quality of life.

Chapter 45

Complementary and Alternative Medicine for Cancer

Complementary and alternative medicine (CAM) is any medical and health care systems, practices, or products that are not thought of as standard medical care.

- **Standard treatments** are based on scientific evidence from research studies.

- **Complementary medicine** refers to treatments that are used with standard medical treatments, like using acupuncture to help with side effects of cancer treatment.

- **Alternative medicine** refers to treatments that are used instead of standard medical treatments.

- **Integrative medicine** is a total approach to care that combines standard medical treatment with the CAM practices that have shown to be safe and effective.

Although claims made by CAM treatment providers about the benefits of the treatments can sound promising, we do not know how safe many CAM treatments are or how well they work. If you are using or

Text in this chapter is excerpted from "Complementary and Alternative Medicine for Patients," National Cancer Institute (NCI), June 1, 2015.

considering using a complementary or alternative therapy, you should talk with your doctor or nurse. Some CAM therapies may interfere with standard treatment or even be harmful.

Acupuncture

- Acupuncture applies needles, heat, pressure, and other treatments to one or more places on the skin known as acupuncture points.

- Acupuncture has been used in China and other Asian countries for thousands of years as part of traditional Chinese medicine.

- Acupuncture has been used in the United States for about 200 years.

- Acupuncture is used to treat many illnesses and ailments and in cancer patients. Patients use it to control pain and to relieve nausea and vomiting, fatigue, hot flashes, xerostomia, neuropathy, anxiety, depression, and sleeping problems.

- Acupuncture may work by causing physical responses in nerve cells, the pituitary gland, and parts of the brain, affecting blood pressure and body temperature.

- Laboratory and animal studies of acupuncture for cancer treatment suggest acupuncture may also help the immune system be stronger during chemotherapy.

- The strongest evidence of the effect of acupuncture has come from clinical trials on the use of acupuncture to relieve nausea and vomiting, but acupuncture appears to be more effective in preventing vomiting than in reducing nausea.

- It is important that acupuncture treatment be given by a qualified practitioner who uses a new set of disposable (single-use) needles for each patient.

Antineoplastons

- Antineoplastons are chemical compounds that are found normally in urine and blood. For use in medical research, antineoplastons can be made from chemicals in a laboratory.

- Antineoplaston therapy was developed by Dr. S. R. Burzynski, who proposed the use of antineoplastons as a possible cancer treatment in 1976.

- No randomized, controlled trials showing the effectiveness of antineoplastons have been published in peer-reviewed scientific journals.

- Nonrandomized clinical trials are ongoing at Dr. Burzynski's clinic to study the effect of antineoplastons on cancer.

- Antineoplastons have caused mild side effects and some serious nervous system problems.

- Antineoplastons are not approved by the U. S. Food and Drug Administration for the prevention or treatment of any disease.

Aromatherapy and Essential Oils

- Aromatherapy is the use of essential oils from plants (flowers, herbs, or trees) as therapy to improve physical, emotional, and spiritual well-being.

- Patients with cancer use aromatherapy mainly to improve their quality of life, such as reducing stress and anxiety.

- Aromatherapy may be combined with other complementary treatments as well as with standard treatments for symptom management.

- Essential oils like Roman chamomile, geranium, lavender, or cedarwood are the basic materials of aromatherapy.

- Interest in aromatherapy grew in the late 20th century as a form of complementary medicine.

- Aromatherapy may work by sending chemical messages to the part of the brain that affects moods and emotions.

- Essential oils are most often used by inhaling them or by applying them in diluted form to the skin.

- Laboratory studies and animal studies have shown that certain essential oils have antibacterial, antiviral, antifungal, calming, or energizing effects.

- Aromatherapy research with cancer patients has mainly studied its effect on other health conditions and quality-of-life issues such as cancer-related symptoms, stress, and anxiety. There are no studies discussing aromatherapy as a treatment for cancer.

- Safety testing on essential oils has found very few bad side effects. Lavender and tea tree oils have been found to have some hormone -like effects.

- Aromatherapy products do not need approval by the U.S. Food and Drug Administration because no specific medical claims are made.

Cancell/Cantron/Protocel

- Cancell is a trademarked name of a liquid mixture long promoted as a treatment for people with cancer and other diseases.

- The U.S. Food and Drug Administration (FDA) has listed the ingredients of Cancell as the chemicals inositol, nitric acid, sodium sulfite, potassium hydroxide, sulfuric acid, and catechol.

- Cantron and Protocel are other products that are said to be similar to Cancell.

- None of the common chemicals in these products is known to be effective in treating any type of cancer.

- In the early 1990s, the National Cancer Institute (NCI) tested these ingredients against cancer cells in the laboratory and based on the results decided not to continue studying Cancell.

- No clinical trials have been published in peer-reviewed journals. Only testimonials and anecdotal reports have been made available.

- The U.S. Food and Drug Administration has not approved Cancell to treat cancer or any disease in the United States. In 1989, the FDA requested and received a court order making it illegal for manufacturers to send Cancell across state lines.

Cannabis and Cannabinoids

- Cannabis, also known as marijuana, is a plant grown in many parts of the world which produces a resin containing compounds called cannabinoids. Some cannabinoids are psychoactive (acting on the brain and changing mood or consciousness).

- The use of Cannabis for medicinal purposes dates back to ancient times.

- By federal law, the use, sale, and possession of Cannabis is illegal in the United States. However, a growing number of states and the District of Columbia have enacted laws to legalize medical marijuana.

- In the United States, Cannabis is a controlled substance requiring special licensing for its use.

- Cannabinoids are active chemicals in Cannabis that cause drug -like effects throughout the body, including the central nervous system and the immune system.

- Cannabinoids can be taken by mouth, inhaled, or sprayed under the tongue.

- Cannabis and cannabinoids have been studied in the laboratory and the clinic for relief of pain, nausea and vomiting, anxiety, and loss of appetite.

- Cannabis and cannabinoids may have benefits in treating the symptoms of cancer or the side effects of cancer therapies. There is growing interest in treating children for symptoms such as nausea with Cannabis and cannabinoids, although studies are limited.

- Two cannabinoids (dronabinol and nabilone) are drugs approved by the U.S. Food and Drug Administration (FDA) for the prevention or treatment of chemotherapy -related nausea and vomiting.

- Cannabis has been shown to kill cancer cells in the laboratory.

- At this time, there is not enough evidence to recommend that patients inhale or ingest Cannabis as a treatment for cancer-related symptoms or side effects of cancer therapy.

- Cannabis is not approved by the FDA for use as a cancer treatment.

Cartilage (Bovine and Shark)

- Cartilage is a type of tough, flexible connective tissue.

- Cartilage from cows (bovine cartilage) and sharks has been studied as a treatment for people with cancer and other medical conditions for more than 30 years.

- Laboratory and animal studies have looked at whether bovine and shark cartilage products can kill cancer cells, make the immune system more active against cancer, and prevent the body from making the new blood vessels that a tumor needs to grow.

- The results have been mixed in the human studies of cartilage as a treatment for cancer reported to date.

- The US Food and Drug Administration (FDA) has not approved cartilage as a treatment for cancer.

Coenzyme Q10

- Coenzyme Q10 (commonly known as CoQ10) is a compound that is made naturally in the body. The body uses it for cell growth and to protect cells from damage that could lead to cancer.

- Animal studies have shown that CoQ10 helps the immune system work better and makes the body better able to resist certain infections and types of cancer.

- Clinical trials have shown that CoQ10 helps protect the heart from the damaging side effects of doxorubicin, a drug used to treat cancer.

- In 3 small studies of CoQ10 in breast cancer patients, some patients appeared to be helped by the treatment. Weaknesses in study design and reporting, however, made it unclear if benefits were caused by CoQ10 or by something else.

- CoQ10 may not mix safely with other treatments. It is important that patients tell their health care providers about all therapies they are currently using or thinking of using.

- CoQ10 has not been carefully tested in combination with chemotherapy to see if it is safe and effective. Because CoQ10 is sold as a dietary supplement rather than a drug, it is not regulated by the US Food and Drug Administration.

- **Essiac/Flor Essence**
- Essiac and Flor Essence are herbal tea mixtures that are sold worldwide as health tonics or herbal dietary supplements.

- Essiac was first promoted as a cancer treatment in the 1920s. Flor Essence was created a number of years later.

- Supporters of Essiac and Flor Essence say that these products make the immune system stronger, have anti-inflammatory effects, relieve pain, decrease side effects, and show anticancer activity.

- Laboratory, animal, and clinical (human) studies with Essiac and Flor Essence have not reported clear evidence of an anticancer effect.

- The U.S. Food and Drug Administration has not approved Essiac or Flor Essence as a cancer treatment.

- **Gerson Therapy**

- The Gerson therapy is a complex regimen that has been used to treat people with cancer and other diseases.

- The key parts of the Gerson therapy are a strict diet, dietary supplements, and enemas.

- The theory is that disease can be cured by removing toxins from the body, boosting the immune system, and replacing excess salt in the body's cells with potassium.

- The Gerson therapy requires that the many details of its treatment plan be followed exactly.

- Few clinical studies of the Gerson therapy have been published.

- Taking too many enemas of any kind can be harmful

- The US Food and Drug Administration has not approved the Gerson therapy for the treatment of cancer or other diseases.

- Cancer patients should talk with their health care providers about an appropriate diet to follow.

Gonzalez Regimen

- The Gonzalez regimen, developed by Dr. Nicholas Gonzalez, involves taking pancreatic enzymes thought to have anticancer activity. The regimen also includes prescribed diets, nutritional supplements, and coffee enemas.

- The Gonzalez regimen is based on the theory that pancreatic enzymes help the body get rid of toxins (harmful substances) that lead to cancer.

- A few studies have examined the effect of pancreatic enzymes in animals with implanted cancers, but it is not possible to test many other parts of the Gonzalez regimen this way.

- In an early small study of Dr. Gonzalez's patients with advanced pancreatic cancer, he reported that patients on his regimen lived longer than most people with the same type of cancer.

- A later nonrandomized, controlled clinical trial compared the effectiveness of standard treatment with that of the Gonzalez regimen in patients whose pancreatic cancer could not be removed by surgery. Patients treated with standard chemotherapy survived an average of 14 months and patients treated with the Gonzalez regimen survived only an average of 4.3 months. In addition, patients treated with chemotherapy reported a better quality of life than those treated with the Gonzalez regimen.

- The US Food and Drug Administration has not approved the Gonzalez regimen or any of its components as a cancer treatment.

High-Dose Vitamin C

- Vitamin C is a nutrient found in food and dietary supplements. It is an antioxidant and also plays a key role in making collagen.

- High-dose vitamin C may be given by intravenous (IV) infusion (through a vein into the bloodstream) or orally (taken by mouth). When taken by intravenous infusion, vitamin C can reach much higher levels in the blood than when the same amount is taken by mouth.

- High-dose vitamin C has been studied as a treatment for patients with cancer since the 1970s.

- Laboratory studies have shown that high doses of vitamin C may slow the growth and spread of prostate, pancreatic, liver, colon, and other types of cancer cells.

- Some laboratory and animal studies have shown that combining vitamin C with anticancer therapies may be helpful, while other studies have shown that certain forms of vitamin C may make chemotherapy less effective.

- Animal studies have shown that high-dose vitamin C treatment blocks tumor growth in certain models of pancreatic, liver, prostate, and ovarian cancers, sarcoma, and malignant mesothelioma.

- Some human studies of high-dose IV vitamin C in patients with cancer have shown improved quality of life, as well as improvements in physical, mental, and emotional functions, symptoms of fatigue, nausea and vomiting, pain, and appetite loss.

- Intravenous high-dose ascorbic acid has caused very few side effects in clinical.

- While generally approved as a dietary supplement, the U.S. Food and Drug Administration (FDA) has not approved the use of IV high-dose vitamin C as a treatment for cancer or any other medical condition.

Hydrazine Sulfate

- Hydrazine sulfate is a chemical compound that has been studied as a treatment for cancer and certain side effects caused by cancer.

- Hydrazine sulfate may block the tumor from taking in glucose, which is a type of sugar that tumor cells need to grow.

- In randomized clinical trials (a type of research study), hydrazine sulfate did not make tumors shrink or go away. In some randomized trials, however, hydrazine sulfate was reported to be helpful in treating anorexia and cachexia caused by cancer.

- Hydrazine sulfate is sold as a dietary supplement in the United States. The US Food and Drug Administration has not approved the use of hydrazine sulfate as a cancer treatment, except in clinical trials.

Laetrile/Amygdalin

- Laetrile is another name for a chemical called amygdalin. Amygdalin is found in the pits of many fruits, raw nuts, and plants.

- It is believed that the active anticancer ingredient in laetrile is cyanide.

- Laetrile is given by mouth as a pill or by intravenous injection.

- Laetrile has shown little anticancer effect in laboratory studies, animal studies, or human studies.

- The side effects of laetrile are like the symptoms of cyanide poisoning.

- Laetrile is not approved by the U.S. Food and Drug Administration (FDA).

Milk Thistle

- Milk thistle is a plant whose fruit and seeds are used to make remedies for liver and bile duct ailments.

- The active ingredient found in milk thistle is silymarin, an antioxidant that, among other things, protects against cell damage and stimulates repair of liver tissue.

- Milk thistle has been studied in laboratory cell lines and animal tumors for its potential to make chemotherapy less toxic and more effective, and to slow the growth of cancer cells.

- Milk thistle is usually taken in capsules or tablets.

- Milk thistle has been studied in a clinical trial of children with leukemia.

- Very few bad side effects from the use of milk thistle or silymarin have been reported.

- It is not known if milk thistle may make anticancer medications or other drugs more or less effective when taken with them.

- The U.S. Food and Drug Administration has not approved the use of milk thistle as a treatment for cancer or any other medical condition.

- Milk thistle is available in the United States as an herbal dietary supplement.

Mistletoe Extracts

- Mistletoe is a semiparasitic plant that grows on several types of common trees such as apple, oak, pine, and elm. Mistletoe extract has been used since ancient times to treat many ailments.

- Mistletoe is one of the most widely studied complementary and alternative medicine therapies in people with cancer. In certain European countries, preparations made from European mistletoe are among the most prescribed drugs for patients with cancer.

- Mistletoe extract has been shown to kill cancer cells in the laboratory and to affect the immune system. However, there is limited evidence that mistletoe's effects on the immune system help the body fight cancer.

- Mistletoe extracts are usually given by injection under the skin or, less often, into a vein, into the pleural cavity, or into the tumor.

- Animal studies have suggested that mistletoe may be useful in decreasing the side effects of standard anticancer therapy, such as chemotherapy and radiation.

- A large number of human studies using mistletoe to treat cancer have been done since the early 1960s, but major weaknesses in many of these have raised doubts about their findings.

- Very few harmful side effects have been reported from the use of mistletoe extract.

- The U.S. Food and Drug Administration (FDA) has not approved mistletoe as a treatment for cancer or any other medical condition.

- The FDA does not allow injectable mistletoe to be imported, sold, or used except for clinical research.

Newcastle Disease Virus

- *Newcastle disease virus* (NDV) is a virus that is of interest because it replicates (makes copies of itself) more quickly in human cancer cells than in most normal human cells and because it can kill these host cells.

- NDV can be used to directly kill cancer cells, or it can be given as a cancer vaccine. Cancer vaccines cause the body's natural immune system to seek out and destroy cancer cells.

- The results of clinical trials (research studies with people) of NDV as a cancer treatment have not proved that it works (see Question 6)

- The US Food and Drug Administration has not approved NDV as a treatment for cancer.

PC-SPES

- PC-SPES is a mixture of 8 herbs that was sold as a dietary supplement to keep the prostate healthy.

- Some batches of PC-SPES were found to contain prescription medicines. It was taken off the market and is no longer being made.

- Herbs in PC-SPES have been used in traditional Chinese medicine for many health problems, including prostate problems, for hundreds of years.

- The herbs used in PC-SPES have been reported to help keep cancer cells from growing or help prevent cell damage that can lead to cancer.

- Laboratory and animal studies suggested that PC-SPES might slow the growth of prostate cancer cells, but it is not known if these results were caused by the herbs in PC-SPES, prescription medicines that were found in the mixture, or both.

- Clinical trials suggested that PC-SPES lowers PSA (prostate specific antigen) and testosterone levels in humans and has some anticancer effects. It is not known if these results were caused by the herbs in PC-SPES, prescription medicines that were found in the mixture, or both.

- The U.S. Food and Drug Administration has not approved PC-SPES for use in cancer treatment.

Overview of CAM Use in Prostate Cancer

- Studies of CAM use to treat prostate cancer have shown the following:

- Men who have prostate cancer are more likely to take dietary supplements than men who do not have prostate cancer.

- Prostate cancer patients with the healthiest eating habits (for example, eating lots of fish rich in omega-3 fatty acids and vegetables) are the most likely to take dietary supplements.

- Reasons given by prostate cancer patients for using CAM treatments include boosting the immune system, improving quality of life, and lowering the risk of the cancer coming back.

- Studies of CAM use to lower the risk of developing prostate cancer or to prevent it from coming back have shown the following:

- A study of men with a family history of prostate cancer found that over half used vitamins or other dietary supplements, including those sold for prostate health or cancer prevention, such as some of those listed in this summary.

- A study of men at a prostate cancer screening clinic found that well over half took multivitamins and a smaller number took herbal supplements.

- A study of prostate cancer survivors found that up to one-third took vitamins or minerals.

- Although many prostate cancer patients use CAM therapies, only about half of them tell their doctors about their use of CAM.

- Studies of why prostate cancer patients do or don't decide to use CAM show that their choice is based on many factors, including their medical history, their beliefs about the safety and side effects of CAM compared to standard treatments, and their need to feel in control of their treatment.

Selected Vegetables/Sun's Soup

- "Selected Vegetables" and "Sun's Soup" are different mixtures of vegetables and herbs that are being studied as treatments for people with cancer.

- Dried and frozen forms of Selected Vegetables are sold in the United States as dietary supplements.

- The vegetables and herbs in Selected Vegetables/Sun's Soup may contain substances that block the growth of cancer cells and/or help the body's immune system kill cancer cells.

- Researchers reported that the growth of tumors was slower in the mice that were fed ingredients in Selected Vegetables/Sun's Soup, compared to the mice that ate standard food.

- Researchers reported that some cancer patients lived longer and had better quality of life when they received Selected Vegetables/Sun's Soup along with other treatments. Randomized controlled trials, enrolling larger numbers of people, are needed to confirm the results.

- No mixture of Selected Vegetables/Sun's Soup has been approved by the U. S. Food and Drug Administration for the treatment of cancer or any other medical condition.

Topics in CAM

Complementary and alternative medicine (CAM) includes a wide variety of therapies, botanicals, nutritional products, and practices. These forms of treatment are used in addition to (complementary) or instead of (alternative) standard treatments. The 2007 National Health Interview Survey reported that about 4 out of 10 adults use a CAM therapy, naming natural products and deep breathing exercises as the most commonly used treatments.

One large survey reported on the use of complementary therapies in cancer survivors. The therapies used most often were prayer and spiritual practice, relaxation, faith and spiritual healing, and nutritional supplements and vitamins. CAM therapies are used often by children with cancer, both in and outside clinical trials. CAM therapies have been used to manage side effects caused by cancer or cancer treatment.

Part Seven

Coping with the Side Effects of Cancer and Cancer Treatments

Chapter 46

Common Side Effects of Cancer Treatment

Common side effects caused by cancer treatments include the following:

- Nausea
- Vomiting
- Constipation
- Diarrhea
- Pain
- Fatigue

Nausea and Vomiting

Nausea is when you feel sick to your stomach, as if you are going to throw up. Vomiting is when you throw up. There are different types of nausea and vomiting caused by cancer treatment, including anticipatory, acute, and delayed nausea and vomiting. Controlling nausea and vomiting will help you to feel better and prevent more serious problems such as malnutrition and dehydration.

Text in this chapter is excerpted from "Side Effects," National Cancer Institute (NCI), April 29, 2015.

Your doctor or nurse will determine what is causing your symptoms and advise you on ways to prevent them. Medicines called anti-nausea drugs or antiemetics are effective in preventing or reducing many types of nausea and vomiting. The medicine is taken at specific times to prevent and/or control symptoms of nausea and vomiting. There are also practical steps you may be advised to take to feel better, including those listed below.

Ways to Manage

You may be advised to take these steps to feel better:

- **Take an anti-nausea medicine.** Talk with your doctor or nurse to learn when to take your medicine. Most people need to take an anti-nausea medicine even on days when they feel well. Tell your doctor or nurse if the medicine doesn't help. There are different kinds of medicine and one may work better than another for you.

- **Drink plenty of water and fluids.** Drinking will help to prevent dehydration, a serious problem that happens when your body loses too much fluid and you are not drinking enough. Try to sip on water, fruit juices, ginger ale, tea, and/or sports drinks throughout the day.

- **Avoid certain foods.** Don't eat greasy, fried, sweet, or spicy foods if you feel sick after eating them. If the smell of food bothers you, ask others to make your food. Try cold foods that do not have strong smells, or let food cool down before you eat it.

- **Try these tips on treatment days.** Some people find that it helps to eat a small snack before treatment. Others avoid eating or drinking right before or after treatment because it makes them feel sick. After treatment, wait at least 1 hour before you eat or drink.

- **Learn about complementary medicine practices that may help.** Acupuncture relieves nausea and/or vomiting cause by chemotherapy in some people. Deep breathing, guided imagery, hypnosis, and other relaxation techniques (such as listening to music, reading a book, or meditating) also help some people.

Talking with Your Health Care Team

Prepare for your visit by making a list of questions to ask. Consider adding these questions to your list:

- What symptoms or problems should I call you about?
- What medicine could help me? When should I take this medicine?
- How much liquid should I drink each day? What should I do if I throw up?
- What foods would be easy on my stomach? What foods should I avoid?
- Could I meet with a registered dietitian to learn more?
- What specialists could I see to learn about acupuncture and other practices that could help to lower my symptoms?

Acute and delayed nausea and vomiting are common in patients being treated for cancer.

Chemotherapy is the most common cause of nausea and vomiting that is related to cancer treatment.

How often nausea and vomiting occur and how severe they are may be affected by the following:

- The specific drug.
- The dose of the drug or if it is given with other drugs.
- How often the drug is given.
- The way the drug is given.
- The individual patient.

Acute nausea and vomiting are more likely in patients who:

- Have had nausea and vomiting after previous chemotherapy sessions.
- Are female.
- Drink little or no alcohol.
- Are young.

Delayed nausea and vomiting are more likely in patients who:

- Are receiving high-dose chemotherapy.
- Are receiving chemotherapy two or more days in a row.
- Have had acute nausea and vomiting with chemotherapy.
- Are female.

- Drink little or no alcohol.
- Are young.

Acute and delayed nausea and vomiting are usually treated with drugs.

Acute and delayed nausea and vomiting are usually treated with antinausea drugs. Some types of chemotherapy are more likely to cause acute nausea and vomiting. Drugs may be given before each treatment to prevent nausea and vomiting. After chemotherapy, drugs may be given to prevent delayed vomiting. Some drugs last only a short time in the body and need to be given more often. Others last a long time and are given less often.

Ginger is being studied in the treatment of nausea and vomiting.

The following table shows drugs that are commonly used to treat nausea and vomiting caused by cancer treatment:

Table 47.1. Drugs Used to Treat Nausea and Vomiting Caused by Cancer Treatment

Drug Name	Type of Drug
Droperidol, haloperidol, metoclopramide, prochlorperazine and other phenothiazines	Dopamine receptor antagonists
Dolasetron, granisetron, ondansetron, palonosetron	Serotonin receptor antagonists
Aprepitant	Substance P/NK-1 antagonists
Dexamethasone. methylprednisolone, dronabinol	Corticosteroids
Marijuana, nabilone	Cannabinoids
Alprazolam, lorazepam, midazolam	Benzodiazepines
Olanzapine	Antipsychotic /monoamine antagonists

Constipation

Constipation is when you have infrequent bowel movements and stool that may be hard, dry, and difficult to pass. You may also have stomach cramps, bloating, and nausea when you are constipated.

Cancer treatments such as chemotherapy can cause constipation. Certain medicines (such as pain medicines), changes in diet, not drinking enough fluids, and being less active may also cause constipation.

There are steps you can take to prevent constipation. It is easier to prevent constipation than to treat its complications which may include fecal impaction or bowel obstruction.

Ways to Prevent or Treat

Take these steps to prevent or treat constipation:

- **Eat high-fiber foods.** Adding bran to foods such as cereals or smoothies is an easy way to get more fiber in your diet. Ask your health care team how many grams of fiber you should have each day. If you have had an intestinal obstruction or intestinal surgery, you should not eat a high-fiber diet.

- **Drink plenty of liquids.** Most people need to drink at least 8 cups of liquid each day. You may need more based on your treatment, medications you are taking, or other health factors. Drinking warm or hot liquids may also help.

- **Try to be active every day.** Ask your health care team about exercises that you can do. Most people can do light exercise, even in a bed or chair. Other people choose to walk or ride an exercise bike for 15 to 30 minutes each day.

- **Learn about medicine.** Use only medicines and treatments for constipation that are prescribed by your doctor, since some may lead to bleeding, infection, or other harmful side effects in people being treated for cancer. Keep a record of your bowel movements to share with your doctor or nurse.

Talking with Your Health Care Team

Prepare for your visit by making a list of questions to ask. Consider adding these questions to your list:

- What problems should I call you about?
- What information should I keep track of and share with you? (For example, you may be asked to keep track of your bowel movements, meals that you have, and exercise that you do each day.)
- How much liquid should I drink each day?
- What steps can I take to feel better?
- Would you give me the name of a registered dietitian who can tell me about foods that might help?

- Should I take medicine for constipation? If so, what medicine should I take? What medicine should I avoid?

Diarrhea

Diarrhea means having bowel movements that are soft, loose, or watery more often than normal. If diarrhea is severe or lasts a long time, the body does not absorb enough water and nutrients. This can cause you to become dehydrated or malnourished. Cancer treatments, or the cancer itself, may cause diarrhea or make it worse. Some medicines, infections, and stress can also cause diarrhea. Tell your health care team if you have diarrhea.

Diarrhea that leads to dehydration (the loss of too much fluid from the body) and low levels of salt and potassium (important minerals needed by the body) can be life threatening. Call your health care team if you feel dizzy or light headed, have dark yellow urine or are not urinating, or have a fever of 100.5 °F (38 °C) or higher.

Ways to Manage

You may be advised to take steps to prevent complications from diarrhea:

- Drink plenty of fluid each day. Most people need to drink 8 to 12 cups of fluid each day. Ask your doctor or nurse how much fluid you should drink each day. For severe diarrhea, only clear liquids or IV (intravenous) fluids may be advised for a short period.

- Eat small meals that are easy on your stomach. Eat six to eight small meals throughout the day, instead of three large meals. Foods high in potassium and sodium (minerals you lose when you have diarrhea) are good food choices, for most people. Limit or avoid foods and drinks that can make your diarrhea worse.

- Check before taking medicine. Check with your doctor or nurse before taking medicine for diarrhea. Your doctor will prescribe the correct medicine for you.

- Keep your anal area clean and dry. Try using warm water and wipes to stay clean. It may help to take warm, shallow baths. These are called sitz baths.

Talking with Your Health Care Team

Prepare for your visit by making a list of questions to ask. Consider adding these questions to your list:

- What is causing the diarrhea?

- What symptoms should I call you about?

- How much liquid should I drink each day?

- Can I speak to a registered dietitian to learn more about foods and drinks that are best for me?

- What medicine or other steps can I take to prevent diarrhea and to decrease rectal pain?

Pain

Cancer itself and the side effects of cancer treatment can sometimes cause pain. Pain is not something that you have to "put up with." Controlling pain is an important part of your cancer treatment plan. Pain can suppress the immune system, increase the time it takes your body to heal, interfere with sleep, and affect your mood.

Talk with your health care team about pain, especially if:

- the pain isn't getting better or going away with pain medicine

- the pain comes on quickly

- the pain makes it hard to eat, sleep, or perform your normal activities

- you feel new pain

- you have side effects from the pain medicine such as sleepiness, nausea, or constipation

Your doctor will work with you to develop a pain control plan that is based on your description of the pain. Taking pain medicine is an important part of the plan. Your doctor will talk with you about using drugs to control pain and prescribe medicine (including opioids and nonopioid medicines) to treat the pain.

Ways to Treat or Lessen Pain

Here are some steps you can take, as you work with your health care team to prevent, treat, or lessen pain:

- **Keep track of your pain levels.** Each day, write about any pain you feel. Writing down answers to the questions below will help you describe the pain to your doctor or nurse.

- What part of your body feels painful?

- What does the pain feel like (is it sharp, burning, shooting, or throbbing) and where do you feel the pain?

- When does the pain start? How long does the pain last?

- What activities (such as eating, sleeping, or other activities) does pain interfere with?

- What makes the pain feel better or worse? For example, do ice packs, heating pads, or exercises help? Does pain medicine help? How much do you take? How often do you take it?

- How bad is the pain, on a scale of 1 to 10, where "10" is the most pain and "1" is the least pain?

- **Take the prescribed pain medicine.** Take the right amount of medicine at the right time. Do not wait until your pain gets too bad before taking pain medicine. Waiting to take your medicine could make it take longer for the pain to go away or increase the amount of medicine needed to lower pain. Do not stop taking the pain medicine unless your doctor advises you to. Tell your doctor or nurse if the medicine no longer lowers the pain, or if you are in pain, but it's not yet time to take the pain medicine.

- **Meet with a pain specialist.** Specialists who treat pain often work together as part of a pain or palliative care team. These specialists may include a neurologist, surgeon, physiatrist, psychiatrist, psychologist, or pharmacist. Talk with your health care team to find a pain specialist.

- **Ask about integrative medicine.** Treatments such as acupuncture, biofeedback, hypnosis, massage therapy and physical therapy may also be used to treat pain.

Talking with Your Health Care Team

- Prepare for your visit by making a list of questions to ask. Consider adding these questions to your list:

- What problems or levels of pain should I call you about?

- What is most likely causing the pain?

- What can I do to lessen the pain?

- What medicine should I take? If the pain doesn't go away, how much more medicine can I take, and when can I take it?

- What are the side effects of this pain medicine? How long will they last?

- Is there a pain specialist I could meet with to get more support to lower my pain?

Fatigue

Fatigue is the most common side effect of cancer treatment.

Cancer treatments such as chemotherapy, radiation therapy, and biologic therapy can cause fatigue in cancer patients. Fatigue is also a common symptom of some types of cancer. Patients describe fatigue as feeling tired, weak, worn-out, heavy, slow, or that they have no energy or get-up-and-go. Fatigue in cancer patients may be called cancer fatigue, cancer-related fatigue, and cancer treatment-related fatigue.

Fatigue related to cancer is different from fatigue that healthy people feel.

When a healthy person is tired by day-to-day activities, their fatigue can be relieved by sleep and rest. Cancer-related fatigue is different. Cancer patients get tired after less activity than people who do not have cancer. Also, cancer-related fatigue is not completely relieved by sleep and rest and may last for a long time. Fatigue usually decreases after cancer treatment ends, but patients may still feel some fatigue for months or years.

Fatigue can decrease a patient's quality of life.

Fatigue can affect all areas of life by making the patient too tired to take part in daily activities, relationships, social events, and community activities. Patients may miss work or school, spend less time with friends and family, or spend more time sleeping. In some cases, physical fatigue leads to mental fatigue and mood changes. This can make it hard for the patient to pay attention, remember things, and think clearly. Money may become a problem if the patient needs to take leave from a job or stop working completely. Job loss can lead to the loss of health insurance. All these things can lessen the patient's quality of life and self-esteem.

Getting help with fatigue may prevent some of these problems and improve quality of life.

Chapter 47

Cancer Treatment and Physical Appearance

Chapter Contents

Section 47.1

Hair Loss

Text in this section is excerpted from "Hair Loss (Alopecia)," National
Cancer Institute (NCI), April 29, 2015.

Hair Loss (Alopecia)

Some types of chemotherapy cause the hair on your head and
other parts of your body to fall out. Radiation therapy can also cause
hair loss on the part of the body that is being treated. Hair loss is
called alopecia. Talk with your health care team to learn if the cancer treatment you will be receiving causes hair loss. Your doctor or
nurse will share strategies that have help others, including those
listed below.

Ways to Manage

Talk with your health care team about ways to manage before and
after hair loss:

- **Treat your hair gently**. You may want to use a hairbrush with
  soft bristles or a wide-tooth comb. Do not use hair dryers, irons,
  or products such as gels or clips that may hurt your scalp. Wash
  your hair with a mild shampoo. Wash it less often and be very
  gentle. Pat it dry with a soft towel.

- **You have choices**. Some people choose to cut their hair short
  to make it easier to deal with when it starts to fall out. Others
  choose to shave their head. If you choose to shave your head, use
  an electric shaver so you won't cut yourself. If you plan to buy a
  wig, get one while you still have hair so you can match it to the
  color of your hair. If you find wigs to be itchy and hot, try wearing a comfortable scarf or turban.

- **Protect and care for your scalp**. Use sunscreen or wear a hat
  when you are outside. Choose a comfortable scarf or hat that you
  enjoy and that keeps your head warm. If your scalp itches or feels
  tender, using lotions and conditioners can help it feel better.

- **Talk about your feelings**. Many people feel angry, depressed, or embarrassed about hair loss. It can help to share these feelings with someone who understands. Some people find it helpful to talk with other people who have lost their hair during cancer treatment. Talking openly and honestly with your children and close family members can also help you all. Tell them that you expect to lose your hair during treatment.

Ways to Care for Your Hair When It Grows Back

- **Be gentle**. When your hair starts to grow back, you will want to be gentle with it. Avoid too much brushing, curling, and blow-drying. You may not want to wash your hair as frequently.

- **After chemotherapy**. Hair often grows back in 2 to 3 months after treatment has ended. Your hair will be very fine when it starts to grow back. Sometimes your new hair can be curlier or straighter—or even a different color. In time, it may go back to how it was before treatment.

- **After radiation therapy**. Hair often grows back in 3 to 6 months after treatment has ended. If you received a very high dose of radiation your hair may grow back thinner or not at all on the part of your body that received radiation.

Talking with Your Health Care Team

Prepare for your visit by making a list of questions to ask. Consider adding these questions to your list:

- Is treatment likely to cause my hair to fall out?

- How should I protect and care for my head? Are there products that you recommend? Ones I should avoid?

- Where can I get a wig or hairpiece?

- What support groups could I meet with that might help?

- When will my hair grow back?

Section 47.2

Skin and Nail Changes

Text in this section is excerpted from "Skin and Nail Changes,"
National Cancer Institute (NCI), April 29, 2015.

Skin and Nail Changes

Cancer treatments may cause a range of skin and nail changes.
Talk with your health care team to learn whether or not you will have
these changes, based on the treatment you are receiving.

- Radiation therapy can cause the skin on the part of your body
  receiving radiation therapy to become dry and peel, itch (called
  pruritus), and turn red or darker. It may look sunburned or tan
  and be swollen or puffy.

- Chemotherapy may damage fast growing skin and nail cells. This
  can cause problems such as skin that is dry, itchy, red, and/or that
  peels. Some people may develop a rash or sun sensitivity, causing
  you to sunburn easily. Nail changes may include dark, yellow, or
  cracked nails and/or cuticles that are red and hurt. Chemotherapy in people who have received radiation therapy in the past can
  cause skin to become red, blister, peel, or hurt on the part of the
  body that received radiation therapy; this is called radiation recall.

- Biological therapy may cause itching (pruritus).

- Targeted therapy may cause a dry skin, a rash, and nail
  problems.

These skin problems are more serious and need urgent medical
attention:

- Sudden or severe itching, a rash, or hives during chemotherapy.
  These may be signs of an allergic reaction.

- Sores on the part of your body where you are receiving treatment that become painful, wet, and/or infected. This is called a
  moist reaction and may happen in areas where the skin folds,
  such as around your ears, breast, or bottom.

Your doctor or nurse will talk with about possible skin and nail changes and advise you on ways to treat or prevent them.

Ways to Manage

Depending on what treatment you are receiving, you may be advised to take these steps to protect your skin, prevent infection, and reduce itching:

- **Use only recommended skin products.** Use mild soaps that are gentle on your skin. Ask your nurse to recommend specific lotions and creams. Ask when and how often to use them. Ask what skin products to avoid. For example, you may be advised to not use powders or antiperspirants before radiation therapy.

- **Protect your skin.** Ask about lotions or antibiotics for dry, itchy, infected or swollen skin. Don't use heating pads, ice packs, or bandages on the area receiving radiation therapy. Shave less often and use an electric razor or stop shaving if your skin is sore. Wear sunscreen and lip balm or a loose-fitting long-sleeved shirt, pants, and a hat with a wide brim when outdoors.

- **Prevent or treat dry, itchy skin (pruritus).** Your doctor will work to assess the cause of pruritus. There are also steps you can take to feel better. Avoid products with alcohol or perfume, which can dry or irritate your skin. Take short showers or baths in lukewarm, not hot, water. Put on lotion after drying off from a shower, while your skin is still slightly damp. Keep your home cool and humid. Eat a healthy diet and drink plenty of fluids to help keep your skin moist and healthy. Applying a cool washcloth or ice to the affected area may also help. Acupuncture also helps some people.

- **Prevent or treat minor nail problems.** Keep your nails clean and cut short. Wear gloves when you wash the dishes, work in the garden, or clean the house. Check with your nurse about products that can help your nails.

If your skin hurts in the area where you get treatment, tell your doctor or nurse. Your skin might have a moist reaction. Most often this happens in areas where the skin folds, such as behind the ears or under the breasts. It can lead to an infection if not properly treated. Ask your doctor or nurse how to care for these areas.

Talking with Your Health Care Team

Prepare for your visit by making a list of questions to ask. Consider adding these questions to your list:

- What symptoms or problems should I call you about?

- What steps can I take to feel better?

- What brands of soap and lotion are best for me to use? What products can help my nails stay healthy?

- What skin and nail products should I avoid?

- When will these problems go away?

Chapter 48

The Effects of Cancer Treatments on Blood Cells

Chapter Contents

Section 48.1

Anemia due to Chemotherapy

This section includes excerpts from "Side Effects," from National
Cancer Institute (NCI), April 29, 2015.

Anemia

Anemia is a condition that can make you feel very tired, short of
breath, and lightheaded. Other signs of anemia may include feeling
dizzy or faint, headaches, a fast heartbeat, and/or pale skin.

Cancer treatments, such as chemotherapy and radiation therapy,
as well as cancers that affect the bone marrow, can cause anemia.
When you are anemic, your body does not have enough red blood cells.
Red blood cells are the cells that that carry oxygen from the lungs
throughout your body to help it work properly. You will have blood
tests to check for anemia. Treatment for anemia is also based on your
symptoms and on what is causing the anemia.

Ways to Manage

Here are some steps you can take if you have fatigue caused by
anemia:

- Save your energy and ask for help. Choose the most important
  things to do each day. When people offer to help, let them do so.
  They can take you to the doctor, make meals, or do other things
  you are too tired to do.

- Balance rest with activity. Take short naps during the day, but
  keep in mind that too much bed rest can make you feel weak.
  You may feel better if you take short walks or exercise a little
  every day.

- Eat and drink well. Talk with your doctor, nurse, or a registered dietitian to learn what foods and drinks are best for
  you. You may need to eat foods that are high in protein or
  iron.

Talking with Your Health Care Team

Prepare for your visit by making a list of questions to ask. Consider adding these questions to your list:

- What is causing the anemia?

- What problems should I call you about?

- What steps can I take to feel better?

- Would medicine, iron pills, a blood transfusion, or other treatments help me?

- Would you give me the name of a registered dietitian who could also give me advice?

Section 48.2

Bleeding and Bruising

Text in this section is excerpted from "Bleeding and Bruising (Thrombocytopenia)," National Cancer Institute (NCI), April 29, 2015.

Bleeding and Bruising (Thrombocytopenia)

Some cancer treatments, such as chemotherapy and targeted therapy, can increase your risk of bleeding and bruising. These treatments can lower the number of platelets in the blood. Platelets are the cells that help your blood to clot and stop bleeding. When your platelet count is low, you may bruise or bleed a lot or very easily and have tiny purple or red spots on your skin. This condition is called thrombocytopenia. It is important to tell your doctor or nurse if you notice any of these changes.

Call your doctor or nurse if you have more serious problems, such as:

- Bleeding that doesn't stop after a few minutes; bleeding from your mouth, nose, or when you vomit; bleeding from your vagina when you are not having your period (menstruation); urine that is red or pink; stools that are black or bloody; or bleeding during your period that is heavier or lasts longer than normal.

- Head or vision changes such as bad headaches or changes in how well you see, or if you feel confused or very sleepy.

Ways to Manage

Steps to take if you are at increased risk of bleeding and bruising:

- **Avoid certain medicines.** Many over-the-counter medicines contain aspirin or ibuprofen, which can increase your risk of bleeding. When in doubt, be sure to check the label. Get a list of medicines and products from your health care team that you should avoid taking. You may also be advised to limit or avoid alcohol if your platelet count is low.

- **Take extra care to prevent bleeding.** Brush your teeth gently, with a very soft toothbrush. Wear shoes, even when you are inside. Be extra careful when using sharp objects. Use an electric shaver, not a razor. Use lotion and a lip balm to prevent dry, chapped skin and lips. Tell your doctor or nurse if you are constipated or notice bleeding from your rectum.

- **Care for bleeding or bruising.** If you start to bleed, press down firmly on the area with a clean cloth. Keep pressing until the bleeding stops. If you bruise, put ice on the area.

Talking with Your Health Care Team

Prepare for your visit by making a list of questions to ask. Consider adding these questions to your list:

- What steps can I take to prevent bleeding or bruising?

- How long should I wait for the bleeding to stop before I call you or go the emergency room?

- Do I need to limit or avoid things that could increase my risk of bleeding, such as alcohol or sexual activity?

- What medicines, vitamins, or herbs should I avoid? Could I get a list from you of medicines to avoid?

Section 48.3

Infection and Neutropenia

Text in this section is excerpted from "Infection and Neutropenia,"
National Cancer Institute (NCI), April 29, 2015.

Infection and Neutropenia

An infection is the invasion and growth of germs in the body, such as bacteria, viruses, yeast, or other fungi. An infection can begin anywhere in the body, may spread throughout the body, and can cause one or more of these signs:

- fever of 100.5 °F (38 °C) or higher or chills

- cough or sore throat

- diarrhea

- ear pain, headache or sinus pain, or a stiff or sore neck

- skin rash

- sores or white coating in your mouth or on your tongue

- swelling or redness, especially where a catheter enters your body

- urine that is bloody or cloudy, or pain when you urinate

Call your health care team if you have signs of an infection. Infections during cancer treatment can be life threatening and require urgent medical attention. Be sure to talk with your doctor or nurse before taking medicine—even aspirin, acetaminophen (such as Tylenol®), or ibuprofen (such as Advil®) for a fever. These medicines can lower a fever but may also mask or hide signs of a more serious problem.

Some types of cancer and treatments such as chemotherapy may increase your risk of infection. This is because they lower the number of white blood cells, the cells that help your body to fight infection. During chemotherapy, there will be times in your treatment cycle when the number of white blood cells (called neutrophils) is particularly low and you are at increased risk of infection. Stress, poor nutrition, and not enough sleep can also weaken the immune system, making infection more likely.

You will have blood tests to check for neutropenia (a condition in which there is a low number of neutrophils). Medicine may sometimes be given to help prevent infection or to increase the number of white blood cells.

Ways to Prevent Infection

Talking with Your Health Care Team

Prepare for your visit by making a list of questions to ask. Consider adding these questions to your list:

- Am I at increased risk of infection during treatment? When am I at increased risk?

- What steps should I take to prevent infection?

- What signs of infection should I look for?

- Which signs signal that I need urgent medical care at the emergency room? Which should I call you about?

Chapter 49

Losing Sleep and Appetite

Sleep Disturbance in Cancer Patients

Cancer patients are at great risk of developing insomnia and disorders of the sleep-wake cycle. Insomnia is the most common sleep disturbance in this population and is most often secondary to physical and/or psychological factors related to cancer and/or cancer treatment. Anxiety and depression common psychological responses to the diagnosis of cancer, cancer treatment, and hospitalization are highly correlated with insomnia.

Sleep disturbances may be exacerbated by paraneoplastic syndromes associated with steroid production and by symptoms associated with tumor invasion, such as draining lesions, gastrointestinal (GI) and genitourinary (GU) alterations, pain, fever, cough, dyspnea, pruritus, and fatigue. Medications—including vitamins, corticosteroids, neuroleptics for nausea and vomiting, and sympathomimetics for the treatment of dyspnea—as well as other treatment factors can negatively impact sleep patterns.

Side effects of treatment that may affect the sleep-wake cycle include the following:

- Pain.

- Anxiety.

This chapter includes excerpts from "Sleep Disorders–for health professionals (PDQ®)," National Cancer Institute (NCI), June 17, 2015; and text from "Appetite Loss," National Cancer Institute (NCI), April 29, 2015.

- Night sweats/hot flashes.
- GI disturbances (e.g., incontinence, diarrhea, constipation, or nausea).
- GU disturbances (e.g., incontinence, retention, or GU irritation).
- Respiratory disturbances.
- Fatigue.

Sustained use of the following can cause insomnia:

- Sedatives and hypnotics (e.g., glutethimide, benzodiazepines, pentobarbital, chloral hydrate, secobarbital sodium, and amobarbital sodium).
- Cancer chemotherapeutic agents (especially antimetabolites).
- Anticonvulsants (e.g., phenytoin).
- Corticosteroids.
- Oral contraceptives.
- Monoamine oxidase inhibitors.
- Methyldopa.
- Propranolol.
- Atenolol.
- Alcohol.
- Thyroid preparations.

In addition, withdrawal from the following substances may cause insomnia:

- Central nervous system depressants (e.g., barbiturates, opioids, glutethimide, chloral hydrate, methaqualone, ethchlorvynol, alcohol, and over-the-counter and prescription antihistamine sedatives).
- Benzodiazepines.
- Major tranquilizers.
- Tricyclic and monamine oxidase inhibitor antidepressants.
- Illicit drugs (e.g., marijuana, cocaine, phencyclidine, and opioids).

Hypnotics can interfere with rapid eye movement (REM) sleep, resulting in increased irritability, apathy, and diminished mental alertness. Abrupt withdrawal of hypnotics and sedatives may lead to symptoms such as nervousness, jitteriness, seizures, and REM rebound. REM rebound has been defined as a marked increase in REM sleep with increased frequency and intensity of dreaming, including nightmares. The increased physiologic arousal that occurs during REM rebound may be dangerous for patients with peptic ulcers or a history of cardiovascular problems. Newer medications for insomnia have reduced adverse effects.

The sleep of hospitalized patients is likely to be frequently interrupted by treatment schedules, hospital routines, and roommates, which singularly or collectively alter the sleep-wake cycle. Other factors influencing sleep-wake cycles in the hospital setting include patient age, comfort, pain, and anxiety; and environmental noise and temperature.

Consequences of sleep disturbances can influence outcomes of therapeutic and supportive care measures. The patient with mild to moderate sleep disturbances may experience irritability and inability to concentrate, which may in turn affect the patient's compliance with treatment protocols, ability to make decisions, and relationships with significant others. Depression and anxiety can also be caused by sleep disturbances. Supportive care measures are directed toward promoting quality of life and adequate rest.

Appetite Loss

Cancer treatments may lower your appetite or change the way food tastes or smells. Side effects such as mouth and throat problems, or nausea and vomiting can also make eating difficult. Cancer-related fatigue can also lower your appetite.

Talk with your health care team if you are not hungry or if your find it difficult to eat. Don't wait until you feel weak, have lost too much weight, or are dehydrated, to talk with your doctor or nurse. It's important to eat well, especially during treatment for cancer.

Ways to Manage

Take these steps to get the nutrition you need to stay strong during treatment:

Drink plenty of liquids. Drinking plenty of liquids is important, especially if you have less of an appetite. Losing fluid can lead to dehydration, a dangerous condition. You may become weak or dizzy and have dark yellow urine if you are not drinking enough liquids.

Choose healthy and high-nutrient foods. Eat a little, even if you are not hungry. It may help to have five or six small meals throughout the day instead of three large meals. Most people need to eat a variety of nutrient-dense foods that are high in protein and calories.

Be active. Being active can actually increase your appetite. Your appetite may increase when you take a short walk each day.

Talking with Your Health Care Team

Prepare for your visit by making a list of questions to ask. Consider adding these questions to your list:

- What symptoms or problems should I call you about?
- What steps can I take to feel better?
- What food and drink choices are best for me?
- Do you recommend supplemental nutrition drinks for me?
- Are there vitamins and supplements that I should avoid? Are there any I should take?
- Would you recommend a registered dietitian who could also help me?

Chapter 50

Sexual, Reproductive, and Fertility Problems

Sexual and Fertility Problems (Women)

Many cancer treatments and some types of cancer can cause sexual and fertility-related side effects. Whether or not you have these problems depends on the type of treatment(s) you receive, your age at time of treatment, and the length of time since treatment.

It is important to get information about how the treatment recommended for you may affect your fertility before you start treatment. Many women also find it helpful to talk with their doctor or nurse about sexual problems they may have during treatment. Learning about these issues will help you make decisions that are best for you.

Treatments That May Cause Sexual and Fertility Problems

- Some types of chemotherapy may cause symptoms of early menopause (hot flashes, vaginal dryness, irregular or no periods, and feeling irritable) or lead to vaginal infections. It may also cause temporary or permanent infertility.

This chapter includes excerpts from "Sexual and Fertility Problems (Women)," National Cancer Institute (NCI), April 29, 2015; and text from "Sexuality and Reproductive Issues," National Cancer Institute (NCI), December 9, 2013.

- Hormone therapy can stop or slow the growth of certain cancers, such as breast cancer. However, lower hormone levels can cause problems (hot flashes, vaginal discharge or pain, and trouble reaching orgasm). These problems are more likely in women over the age of 45.

- Radiation therapy to the pelvic area (vagina, uterus, or ovaries) can cause:

  - infertility

  - symptoms of menopause (hot flashes, vaginal dryness, and no periods)

  - pain or discomfort during sex

  - increased risk of birth defects; use a method of birth control to avoid pregnancy

  - vaginal stenosis (less elastic, narrow, shorter vagina)

  - vaginal itching, burning, or dryness

  - vaginal atrophy (weak vaginal muscles and thin vaginal wall)

- Surgery for cancers of the uterus, bladder, vulvar, endometrium, cervix, or ovaries may cause sexual and infertility-related side effects, depending on the size and location of the tumor.

- Other side effects of cancer and its treatment, such as fatigue and anxiety, can also lower your interest in sexual activity.

What to Expect

Before starting treatment talk with your health care team to learn what to expect, based on the type of treatment you will be receiving. Get answers to questions about:

- **Infertility.** Ask if treatment could lower your fertility or make you infertile. If you would like to have children after treatment, talk with your doctor or nurse before you start treatment. Learn ahead of time about options such as embryo banking, ovarian tissue banking, ovarian transposition, and clinical trials for egg banking. Talk with your doctor or a fertility specialist to learn more about these procedures and others that may be available through a clinical trial.

- **Pregnancy.** It is important to prevent pregnancy during treatment and for some time after treatment. Ask your doctor or nurse about different methods of birth control, to choose one that may be best for you and your partner.

- **Sexual activity.** Ask your doctor or nurse if it is okay for you to be sexually active during your treatment period. Most women can be sexually active, but you will want to confirm this with your health care team.

Talking with Your Health Care Team

Prepare for your visit by making a list of questions. Consider adding these questions to your list:

Sexual and Sexuality-Related Questions

- What problems or changes might I have during treatment?
- How long might these problems last? Will any be permanent?
- Is there treatment for these problems?
- Would you give me the name of a specialist that I could meet with?
- Is there a support group for women that you would recommend?

Fertility-Related Questions

- Will my fertility be affected by the treatment I receive?
- What are all of my options now if I would like to have children in the future?
- Could you give me the name of a fertility specialist who I can talk with to learn more?
- After treatment, how long should I use birth control?

Sexual and Reproductive Issues (Men)

Good communication can help you and your partner continue sex after cancer treatment.

You may be afraid or anxious about having sex after cancer treatment. Fear and anxiety can cause you to avoid intimacy, touch, and sexual activity. Your partner may also be afraid and anxious that starting sexual activity will make you feel pressured or cause you pain. Even when a couple has been together a long time, talking about these things is important. Honest communication of feelings, concerns, and preferences can help.

You can learn ways to adapt to changes in sexual function.

Health professionals who specialize in treating sexual problems can give you the names of organizations that offer support. They can also tell you about educational materials such as Internet sources, books, pamphlets, and DVDs. These resources can help you learn ways to adapt to changes in sexual function.

Counseling may make it easier for you to cope with changes in your body and your sex life after cancer.

Sexual counseling may help you. Counseling may be for you alone, with you and your partner, or in a group.

Medical treatments may help improve sexual function.

You may be helped by medical treatments such as hormone replacement, drugs, medical devices, or surgery.

Chapter 51

Edema and Lymphedema

Edema

Edema, a condition in which fluid builds up in your body's tissues, may be caused by some types of chemotherapy, certain cancers, and conditions not related to cancer.

Signs of edema may include:

- swelling in your feet, ankles, and legs

- swelling in your hands and arms

- swelling in your face or abdomen

- skin that is puffy, shiny, or looks slightly dented after being pressed

- shortness of breath, a cough, or irregular heartbeat

Tell your health care team if you notice swelling. Your doctor or nurse will determine what is causing your symptoms, advise you on steps to take, and may prescribe medicine.

Some problems related to edema are serious. Call your doctor or nurse if you feel short of breath, have a heartbeat that seems different or is not regular, have sudden swelling or swelling that is getting

This chapter includes excerpts from "Edema," National Cancer Institute (NCI), April 29, 2015; and text from "Lymphedema," National Cancer Institute (NCI), April 29, 2015.

worse or is moving up your arms or legs, you gain weight quickly, or you don't urinate at all or urinate only a little.

Ways to Prevent or Lessen Edema

Steps you can take to prevent or lessen edema-related swelling include:

- **Get comfortable.** Wear loose clothing and shoes that are not too tight. When you sit or lie down, raise your feet with a stool or pillows. Avoid crossing your legs when you sit. Talk with your health care team about wearing special stockings, sleeves, or gloves that help with circulation if your swelling is severe.

- **Exercise.** Moving the part of your body with edema can help. Your doctor may give you specific exercises, including walking, to improve circulation. However, you may be advised not to stand or walk too much at one time.

- **Limit salt (sodium) in your diet.** Avoid foods such as chips, bacon, ham, and canned soup. Check food labels for the sodium content. Don't add salt or soy sauce to your food.

- **Take your medicine.** If your doctor prescribes a medicine called a diuretic, take it exactly as instructed. The medicine will help move the extra fluid and salt out of your body.

Talking with Your Health Care Team

Prepare for your visit by making a list of questions to ask. Consider adding these questions to your list:

- Are my medications or treatment likely to increase my risk of developing edema?

- Are there steps I can take to prevent edema?

- What symptoms or problems should I call you about?

- What steps can I take to feel better if I notice swelling?

- Are there foods, drinks, or activities I should avoid?

Lymphedema

Lymphedema is a condition in which the lymph fluid does not drain properly. It may build up in the tissues and causes swelling. This can happen when part of the lymph system is damaged or blocked, such as during surgery to remove lymph nodes, or radiation therapy. Cancers that block lymph vessels can also cause lymphedema.

Lymphedema usually affects an arm or leg, but it can also affect other parts of the body, such as the head and neck. You may notice symptoms of lymphedema at the part of your body where you had surgery or received radiation therapy. Swelling usually develops slowly, over time. It may develop during treatment or it may start years after treatment.

At first, lymphedema in an arm or leg may cause symptoms such as:

- swelling and a heavy or achy feeling in your arms or legs that may spread to your fingers and toes

- a dent when you press on the swollen area

- swelling that is soft to the touch and is usually not painful at first

Lymphedema that is not controlled may cause:

- more swelling, weakness, and difficulty moving your arm or leg

- itchy, red, warm skin, and sometimes a rash

- wounds that don't heal, and an increased risk of skin infections that may cause pain, redness, and swelling

- thickening or hardening of the skin

- tight feeling in the skin; pressing on the swollen area does not leave a dent

- hair loss

Lymphedema in the head or neck may cause:

- swelling and a tight uncomfortable feeling on your face, neck, or under your chin

- difficulty moving your head or neck

Tell your health care team as soon as you notice symptoms. Early treatment may prevent or reduce the severity of problems caused by lymphedema.

Ways to Manage

Steps you may be advised to take to prevent lymphedema or to keep it from getting worse:

- **Protect your skin.** Use lotion to avoid dry skin. Use sunscreen. Wear plastic gloves with cotton lining when working in order to prevent scratches, cuts, or burns. Keep your feet clean and dry. Keep your nails clean and short to prevent ingrown nails and infection. Avoid tight shoes and tight jewelry.

- **Exercise.** Work to keep body fluids moving, especially in places where lymphedema has developed. Start with gentle exercises that help you to move and contract your muscles. Ask your doctor or nurse what exercises are best for you.

- **Manual lymph drainage.** See a trained specialist (a certified lymphedema therapist) to receive a type of therapeutic massage called manual lymph drainage. Therapeutic massage works best to lower lymphedema when given early, before symptoms progress.

Ways to Treat

Your doctor or nurse may advise you to take these and other steps to treat lymphedema:

- **Wear compression garments or bandages.** Wear special garments, such as sleeves, stockings, bras, compression shorts, gloves, bandages, and face or neck compression wear. Some garments are meant to be worn during the day, while others are to be worn at night.

- **Other practices**. Your health care team may advise you to use compression devices (special pumps that apply pressure periodically) or have laser therapy or other treatments.

Talking with Your Health Care Team

Prepare for your visit by making a list of questions to ask. Consider adding these questions to your list:

- What can I do to prevent these problems?

- What symptoms should I call you about?

- What steps can I take to feel better?

- Would you recommend that I see a certified lymphedema therapist?

- If lymphedema advances, what special garments should I wear during the day? During the night?

Chapter 52

Cognitive-Related Effects of Cancer Treatment

Memory or Concentration Problems

Whether you have memory or concentration problems (sometimes described as a mental fog or chemo brain) depends on the type of treatment you receive, your age, and other health-related factors. Cancer treatments such as chemotherapy may cause difficulty with thinking, concentrating, or remembering things. So can some types of biological therapies and radiation therapy to the brain.

These cognitive problems may start during or after cancer treatment. Some people notice very small changes, such as a bit more difficulty remembering things, whereas others have much greater memory or concentration problems.

Your doctor will assess your symptoms and advise you about ways to manage or treat these problems. Treating conditions such as poor nutrition, anxiety, depression, fatigue, and insomnia may also help.

Ways to Manage

It's important for you or a family member to tell your health care team if you have difficulty remembering things, thinking, or

This chapter includes excerpts from "Memory or Concentration Problems," National Cancer Institute (NCI), April 29, 2015; and text from "Delirium (PDQ®)," National Cancer Institute (NCI), December 12, 2013.

concentrating. Here are some steps you can take to manage minor memory or concentration problems:

- **Plan your day.** Do things that need the most concentration at the time of day when you feel best. Get extra rest and plenty of sleep at night. If you need to rest during the day, short naps of less than 1 hour are best. Long naps can make it more difficult to sleep at night. Keep a daily routine.

- **Exercise your body and mind.** Exercise can help to decrease stress and help you to feel more alert. Exercise releases endorphins, also known as "feel-good chemicals," which give people a feeling of well-being. Ask what light physical exercises may be helpful for you. Mind–body practices such as meditation or mental exercises such as puzzles or games also help some people.

- **Get help to remember things.** Write down and keep a list handy of important information. Use a daily planner, recorder, or other electronic device to help you remember important activities. Make a list of important names and phone numbers. Keep it in one place so it's easy to find.

Talking with Your Health Care Team

It's important for you or a family member to talk with your doctor or nurse about any memory or cognitive changes you may have. Prepare for your visit by making a list of questions to ask. Consider adding these questions to your list:

- Am I at increased risk of cognitive problems based on the treatment I am receiving?

- When might these problems start to occur? How long might they last?

- Are there steps I can take to decrease these problems?

- What symptoms or other problems should I, or a family member, call you about?

- Could I meet with a social worker to get ideas about additional support and resources?

- Are there specialists who could assess, treat, or advise me on these problems (such as neuropsychologists, occupational therapists, vocational therapists, and others)?

Treatment of Delirium

Treatment includes looking at the causes and symptoms of delirium.

Both the causes and the symptoms of delirium may be treated. Treatment depends on the following:

- Where the patient is living, such as home, hospital, or nursing home.

- How advanced the cancer is.

- How the delirium symptoms are affecting the patient.

- The wishes of the patient and family.

Treating the causes of delirium usually includes the following:

- Stopping or lowering the dose of medicines that cause delirium.

- Giving fluids to treat dehydration.

- Giving drugs to treat hypercalcemia (too much calcium in the blood).

- Giving antibiotics for infections.

In a terminally ill patient with delirium, the doctor may treat just the symptoms. The doctor will continue to watch the patient closely during treatment.

Treatment without medicines can also help relieve symptoms.

Controlling the patient's surroundings may help with mild symptoms of delirium. The following may help:

- Keep the patient's room quiet and well-lit, and put familiar objects in it.

- Put a clock or calendar where the patient can see it.

- Have family members around.

- Keep the same caregivers as much as possible.

Patients who may hurt themselves or others may need to have physical restraints.

Treatment may include medicines.

Medicines may be used to treat the symptoms of delirium depending on the patient's condition and heart health. These medicines have serious side effects and the patient will be watched closely by a doctor. These medicines include the following:

- Haloperidol.

- Olanzapine.

- Risperidone.

- Lorazepam.

- Midazolam.

Sedation may be used for delirium at the end of life or when delirium does not get better with treatment.

When the symptoms of delirium are not relieved with standard treatments and the patient is near death, in pain, or has trouble breathing, other treatment may be needed. Sometimes medicines that will sedate (calm) the patient will be used. The family and the health care team will make this decision together.

The decision to use sedation for delirium may be guided by the following:

- The patient will have repeated assessments by experts before the delirium is considered to be refractory (doesn't respond to treatment).

- The decision to sedate the patient is reviewed by a team of health care professionals and not made by one doctor.

- Temporary sedation, for short periods of time such as overnight, is considered before continuous sedation is used.

- The team of health care professionals will work with the family to make sure the team understands the family's views and that the family understands palliative sedation.

Chapter 53

Nerve Problems

Nerve Problems (Peripheral Neuropathy)

Some cancer treatments cause peripheral neuropathy, a result of damage to the peripheral nerves. These nerves carry information from the brain to other parts of the body. Side effects depend on which peripheral nerves (sensory, motor, or autonomic) are affected.

Damage to sensory nerves (nerves that help you feel pain, heat, cold, and pressure) can cause:

- tingling, numbness, or a pins-and-needles feeling in your feet and hands that may spread to your legs and arms

- inability to feel a hot or cold sensation, such as a hot stove

- inability to feel pain, such as from a cut or sore on your foot

Damage to motor nerves (nerves that help your muscles to move) can cause:

- weak or achy muscles. You may lose your balance or trip easily. It may also be difficult to button shirts or open jars.

- muscles that twitch and cramp or muscle wasting (if you don't use your muscles regularly).

Text in this chapter is excerpted from "Nerve Problems (Peripheral Neuropathy)," National Cancer Institute (NCI), April 29, 2015.

- swallowing or breathing difficulties (if your chest or throat muscles are affected)

Damage to autonomic nerves (nerves that control functions such as blood pressure, digestion, heart rate, temperature, and urination) can cause:

- digestive changes such as constipation or diarrhea

- dizzy or faint feeling, due to low blood pressure

- sexual problems; men may be unable to get an erection and women may not reach orgasm

- sweating problems (either too much or too little sweating)

- urination problems, such as leaking urine or difficulty emptying your bladder

If you start to notice any of the problems listed above, talk with your doctor or nurse. Getting these problems diagnosed and treated early is the best way to control them, prevent further damage, and to reduce pain and other complications.

Ways to Prevent or Manage Problems Related to Nerve Changes

You may be advised to take these steps:

- **Prevent falls**. Have someone help you prevent falls around the house. Move rugs out of your path so you will not trip on them. Put rails on the walls and in the bathroom, so you can hold on to them and balance yourself. Put bathmats in the shower or tub. Wear sturdy shoes with soft soles. Get up slowly after sitting or lying down, especially if you feel dizzy.

- **Take extra care in the kitchen and shower**. Use potholders in the kitchen to protect your hands from burns. Be careful when handling knives or sharp objects. Ask someone to check the water temperature, to make sure it's not too hot.

- **Protect your hands and feet**. Wear shoes, both inside and outside. Check your arms, legs, and feet for cuts or scratches every day. When it's cold, wear warm clothes to protect your hands and feet.

- **Ask for help and slow down**. Let people help you with difficult tasks. Slow down and give yourself more time to do things.

- **Ask about pain medicine and integrative medicine practices**. You may be prescribed pain medicine. Sometimes practices such as acupuncture, massage, physical therapy, yoga, and others may also be advised to lower pain. Talk with your health care team to learn what is advised for you.

Talking with Your Health Care Team

Prepare for your visit by making a list of questions to ask. Consider adding these questions to your list:

- What symptoms or problems might I have? Which ones should I call you about?

- When will these problems start? How long might they last?

- What medicine, treatments, and integrative medicine practices could help me to feel better?

- What steps can I take to feel better? What precautions should I take to stay safe?

- Could you refer me to a specialist who could give me additional advice?

Chapter 54

Urinary and Bladder Problems

Urinary and Bladder Problems

Some cancer treatments, such as those listed below, may cause the urinary and bladder problems:

- Radiation therapy to the pelvis (including reproductive organs, the bladder, colon and rectum) can irritate the bladder and urinary tract. These problems often start several weeks after radiation therapy begins and go away several weeks after treatment has been completed.

- Some types of chemotherapy and biological therapy can also affect or damage cells in the bladder and kidneys.

- Surgery to remove the prostate (prostatectomy), bladder cancer surgery, and surgery to remove a woman's uterus, the tissue on the sides of the uterus, the cervix, and the top part of the vagina (radical hysterectomy) can also cause urinary problems. These types of surgery may also increase the risk of a urinary tract infection.

Text in this chapter is excerpted from "Urinary and Bladder Problems," National Cancer Institute (NCI), April 29, 2015.

Symptoms of a Urinary Problem

Talk with your doctor or nurse to learn what symptoms you may experience and ask which ones to call about. Some urinary or bladder changes may be normal, such as changes to the color or smell of your urine caused by some types of chemotherapy. Your health care team will determine what is causing your symptoms and will advise on steps to take to feel better.

Irritation of the bladder lining (radiation cystitis):

- pain or a burning feeling when you before or after you urinate
- blood in your urine
- trouble starting to urinate
- trouble emptying your bladder completely
- feeling that you need to urinate urgently or frequently
- leaking a little urine when you sneeze or cough
- bladder spasms, cramps, or discomfort in the pelvic area

Urinary tract infection (UTI):

- pain or a burning feeling when you urinate
- urine that is cloudy or red
- a fever of 100.5 °F (38 °C) or higher, chills, and fatigue
- pain in your back or abdomen
- difficulty urinating or not being able to urinate

In people being treated for cancer, a UTI can turn into a serious condition that needs immediate medical care. Antibiotics will be prescribed if you have a bacterial infection.

Symptoms that may occur after surgery:

- leaking urine (incontinence)
- trouble emptying your bladder completely

Ways to Prevent or Manage

Here are some steps you may be advised to take to feel better and to prevent problems:

- **Have plenty of liquids.** Drink plenty of liquids. Most people need to drink at least 8 cups of fluid each day, so that urine is light yellow or clear. You'll want to stay away from things that can make bladder problems worse. These include caffeine, drinks with alcohol, spicy foods, and tobacco products.

- **Prevent urinary tract infections.** Your doctor or nurse will talk with you about ways to lower your chances of getting a urinary tract infection. These may include going to the bathroom often, wearing cotton underwear and loose fitting pants, learning about safe and sanitary practices for catheterization, taking showers instead of baths, and checking with your nurse before using products such as creams or lotions near your genital area.

Talking with Your Health Care Team

Prepare for your visit by making a list of questions to ask. Consider adding these questions to your list:

- What symptoms or problems should I call you about?
- What steps can I take to feel better?
- How much should I drink each day? What liquids are best for me?
- Are there certain drinks or foods that I should avoid?

Chapter 55

Hot Flashes and Night Sweats

Hot flashes and night sweats may be side effects of cancer or its treatment.

Sweating is the body's way of lowering body temperature by causing heat loss through the skin. In patients with cancer, sweating may be caused by fever, a tumor, or cancer treatment.

Hot flashes can also cause too much sweating. They may occur in natural menopause or in patients who have been treated for breast cancer or prostate cancer.

Hot flashes combined with sweats that happen while sleeping are often called night sweats or hot flushes.

Hot flashes and night sweats affect quality of life in many patients with cancer.

A treatment plan to help manage hot flashes and night sweats is based on the patient's condition and goals of care. For some patients, relieving symptoms and improving quality of life is the most important goal.

This chapter describes the causes and treatment of hot flashes and night sweats in cancer patients.

Text in this chapter is excerpted from "Hot Flashes and Night Sweats (PDQ®)," National Cancer Institute (NCI), October 15, 2014.

Causes of Hot Flashes and Night Sweats in Patients with Cancer

In patients with cancer, hot flashes and night sweats may be caused by the tumor, its treatment, or other conditions.

Sweating happens with disease conditions such as fever and may occur without disease in warm climates, during exercise, and during hot flashes in menopause. Sweating helps balance body temperature by allowing heat to evaporate through the skin.

Hot flashes and night sweats are common in patients with cancer and in cancer survivors. They are more common in women but can also occur in men.

Many patients treated for breast cancer and prostate cancer have hot flashes.

Menopause in women can have natural, surgical, or chemical causes. Chemical menopause in women with cancer is caused by certain types of chemotherapy, radiation, or hormone therapy with androgen (a male hormone).

"Male menopause" in men with cancer can be caused by orchiectomy (surgery to remove one or both testicles) or hormone therapy with gonadotropin-releasing hormone or estrogen.

Treatment for breast cancer and prostate cancer can cause menopause or menopause-like effects, including severe hot flashes.

Certain types of drugs can cause night sweats.

Drugs that may cause night sweats include the following:

- Tamoxifen.
- Aromatase inhibitors.
- Opioids.
- Tricyclic antidepressants.
- Steroids.

Chapter 56

Feelings and Cancer

Feelings and Cancer

Dealing with the different side effects and life changes of cancer treatment can be hard on you emotionally as well as physically. Just as cancer affects your physical health, it can bring up a wide range of feelings you're not used to dealing with. It can also make many feelings seem more intense. They may change daily, hourly, or even minute to minute. This is true whether you're currently in treatment, done with treatment, or a friend or family member. These feelings are all normal.

Often the values you grew up with affect how you think about and deal with cancer. For example some people:

- Feel they have to be strong and protect their friends and families

- Seek support and turn to loved ones or other cancer survivors

- Ask for help from counsellors or other professionals

- Turn to their faith to help them cope

Whatever you decide, it's important to do what's right for you and not to compare yourself with others. Your friends and family members may share some of the same feelings. If you feel comfortable, share this information with them.

Text in this chapter is excerpted from "Feelings and Cancer," National Cancer Institute (NCI), December 2, 2014.

Overwhelmed

When you first learn that you have cancer, you may feel as if your life is out of control. This could be because:

- You wonder if you're going to live.
- Your normal routine is disrupted by doctor visits and treatments.
- People use medical terms that you don't understand.
- You feel like you can't do the things you enjoy.
- You feel helpless and lonely.

Even if you feel out of control, there are ways you can take charge. Try to learn as much as you can about your cancer. Ask your doctor questions and don't be afraid to say when you don't understand. Also, many people feel better if they stay busy. You can take part in activities such as music, crafts, reading, or learning something new.

Denial

When you were first diagnosed, you may have had trouble believing or accepting the fact that you have cancer. This is called denial. It can be helpful because it can give you time to adjust to your diagnosis. It can also give you time to feel hopeful and better about the future.

Sometimes, denial is a serious problem. If it lasts too long, it can keep you from getting the treatment you need.

The good news is that most people work through denial. Usually by the time treatment begins, most people accept the fact that they have cancer and move forward. This is true for those with cancer as well as the people they love and care about.

Anger

People with cancer often feel angry. It's normal to ask, "Why me?" and be angry at the cancer. You may also feel anger or resentment towards your health care providers, your healthy friends and your loved ones. And if you're religious, you may even feel angry with God.

Anger often comes from feelings that are hard to show, such as fear, panic, frustration, anxiety, or helplessness. If you feel angry, you don't have to pretend that everything is okay. Anger can be helpful in that it may motivate you to take action. Talk with your family and friends about your anger. Or, ask your doctor to refer you to a counsellor.

Fear and Worry

It's scary to hear that you have cancer. You may be afraid or worried about:

- Being in pain, either from the cancer or the treatment
- Feeling sick or looking different as a result of your treatment
- Taking care of your family
- Paying your bills
- Keeping your job
- Dying

Some fears about cancer are based on stories, rumors, or wrong information. To cope with fears and worries, it often helps to be informed. Most people feel better when they learn the facts. They feel less afraid and know what to expect. Learn about your cancer and understand what you can do to be an active partner in your care. Some studies even suggest that people who are well-informed about their illness and treatment are more likely to follow their treatment plans and recover from cancer more quickly than those who are not.

Hope

Once people accept that they have cancer, they often feel a sense of hope. There are many reasons to feel hopeful. Millions of people who have had cancer are alive today. Your chances of living with cancer—and living beyond it—are better now than they have ever been before. And people with cancer can lead active lives, even during treatment.

Some doctors think that hope may help your body deal with cancer. So, scientists are studying whether a hopeful outlook and positive attitude helps people feel better. Here are some ways you can build your sense of hope:

- Plan your days as you've always done.
- Don't limit the things you like to do just because you have cancer.
- Look for reasons to have hope. If it helps, write them down or talk to others about them.
- Spend time in nature,
- Reflect on your religious or spiritual beliefs.
- Listen to stories about people with cancer who are leading active lives.

Stress and Anxiety

Both during and after treatment, it's normal to have stress over all the life changes you are going through. Anxiety means you have extra worry, can't relax, and feel tense. You may notice that:

- Your heart beats faster.
- You have headaches or muscle pains.
- You don't feel like eating. Or you eat more.
- You feel sick to your stomach or have diarrhaea.
- You feel shaky, weak, or dizzy.
- You have a tight feeling in your throat and chest.
- You sleep too much or too little.
- You find it hard to concentrate.

If you have any of these feelings, talk to your doctor. Though they are common signs of stress, you will want to make sure they aren't due to medicines or treatment.

Stress can keep your body from healing as well as it should.

If you're worried about your stress, ask your doctor to suggest a counsellor for you to talk to. You could also take a class that teaches ways to deal with stress. The key is to find ways to control your stress and not to let it control you.

Sadness and Depression

Many people with cancer feel sad. They feel a sense of loss of their health, and the life they had before they learned they had the disease. Even when you're done with treatment, you may still feel sad. This is a normal response to any serious illness. It may take time to work through and accept all the changes that are taking place.

When you're sad, you may have very little energy, feel tired, or not want to eat. For some, these feelings go away or lessen over time. But for others, these emotions can become stronger. The painful feelings don't get any better, and they get in the way of daily life. This may be a medical condition called **depression**. For some, cancer treatment may have added to this problem by changing the way the brain works.

Getting Help for Depression

Depression can be treated. Below are common signs of depression. If you have any of the following signs for more than 2 weeks, talk to your doctor about treatment. Be aware that some of these symptoms could be due to physical problems, so it's important to talk about them with your doctor.

Emotional signs:

- Feelings of sadness that don't go away
- Feeling emotionally numb
- Feeling nervous or shaky
- Having a sense of guilt or feeling unworthy
- Feeling helpless or hopeless, as if life has no meaning
- Feeling short-tempered, moody
- Having a hard time concentrating, feeling scatter-brained
- Crying for long periods of time or many times each day
- Focusing on worries and problems
- No interest in the hobbies and activities you used to enjoy
- Finding it hard to enjoy everyday things, such as food or being with family and friends
- Thinking about hurting yourself
- Thoughts about killing yourself

Body changes:

- Unintended weight gain or loss not due to illness or treatment
- Sleep problems, such as not being able to sleep, having nightmares, or sleeping too much
- Racing heart, dry mouth, increased perspiration, upset stomach, diarrhaea
- Changes in energy level
- Fatigue that doesn't go away
- Headaches, other aches and pains

If your doctor thinks that you suffer from depression, he or she may give you medicine to help you feel less tense. Or, he or she may refer you to other experts. Don't feel that you should have to control these feelings on your own. Getting the help you need is important for your life and your health.

Guilt

If you feel guilty, know that many people with cancer feel this way. You may blame yourself for upsetting the people you love, or worry that you're a burden in some way. Or, you may envy other people's good health and be ashamed of this feeling. You might even blame yourself for lifestyle choices that you think could have led to your cancer.

These feelings are all very common. It may help you to share them with someone. Let your doctor know if you would like to talk with a counsellor or go to a support group.

Loneliness

People with cancer often feel lonely or distant from others. This may be for a number of reasons:

- Friends sometimes have a hard time dealing with cancer and may not visit or call you.

- You may feel too sick to take part in the hobbies and activities you used to enjoy.

- Sometimes, even when you're with people you care about, you may feel that no one understands what you're going through.

It's also normal to feel alone after treatment.

You may miss the support you got from your health care team. Many people have a sense that their safety net has been pulled away, and they get less attention. It's common to still feel cut off from certain friends or family members. Some of them may think that now that treatment is over, you will be back to normal soon, even though this may not be true. Others may want to help but don't know how.

Look for emotional support in different ways. It could help you to talk to other people who have cancer or to join a support group. Or, you may feel better talking only to a close friend or family member, or counsellor, or a member of your faith or spiritual community. Do what feels right for you.

Gratitude

Some people see their cancer as a "wake-up call." They realize the importance of enjoying the little things in life. They go places they've never been. They finish projects they had started but put aside.

They spend more time with friends and family. They mend broken relationships.

It may be hard at first, but you can find joy in your life if you have cancer. Pay attention to the things you do each day that make you smile. They can be as simple as drinking a good cup of coffee or talking to a friend.

You can also do things that are more special to you, like being in nature or praying in a place that has meaning for you. Or, it could be playing a sport you love or cooking a good meal. Whatever you choose, embrace the things that bring you joy when you can.

Other Ways to Cope with Your Emotions

Express Your Feelings

People have found that when they express strong feelings like anger or sadness, they're more able to let go of them. Some sort out their feelings by talking to friends or family, other cancer survivors, a support group, or a counsellor. But even if you prefer not to discuss your cancer with others, you can still sort out your feelings by thinking about them or writing them down.

Look for the Positive

Sometimes this means looking for the good even in a bad time or trying to be hopeful instead of thinking the worst. Try to use your energy to focus on wellness and what you can do now to stay as healthy as possible.

Don't Blame Yourself for Your Cancer

Some people believe that they got cancer because of something they did or did not do. Remember, cancer can happen to anyone.

Don't Try to Be Upbeat If You're Not

Many people say they want to have the freedom to give in to their feelings sometimes. As one woman said, "When it gets really bad, I just tell my family I'm having a bad cancer day and go upstairs and crawl into bed."

You Choose When to Talk about Your Cancer

It can be hard for people to know how to talk to you about your cancer. Often loved ones mean well, but they don't know what to say or how to act. You can make them feel more at ease by asking them what they think or how they feel.

Find Ways to Help Yourself Relax

Whatever activity helps you unwind, you should take some time to do it. Meditation, guided imagery and relaxation exercises are just a few ways that have been shown to help others, these may help you relax when you feel worried.

Be as Active as You Can

Getting out of the house and doing something can help you focus on other things besides cancer and the worries it brings. Exercise or gentle yoga and stretching can help too.

Look for Things You Enjoy

You may like hobbies such as woodworking, photography, reading, or crafts. Or find creative outlets such as art, music, or dance.

Look at What You Can Control

Some people say that putting their lives in order helps. Being involved in your health care, keeping your appointments, and making changes in your lifestyle are among the things you can control. Even setting a daily schedule can give you a sense of control. And while no one can control every thought, some say that they try not to dwell on the fearful ones. And while no one can control every thought, some say that they try not to dwell on the fearful ones.

Chapter 57

Adjusting to Cancer

Adjusting to Cancer

When you learn you have cancer, you may feel like your life has been turned upside down. Once the shock wears off, the process of making changes begins. You may have to rearrange things in your life as you start treatment. The symptoms and side effects may take a toll on both your body and your emotions. You may have to learn new ways of talking to your loved ones and to your health care team. And you probably have a lot of questions to ask about adjusting to all the new issues that cancer brings.

It can seem overwhelming at first, but knowing what to expect may help you feel more at ease. The following sections have tips to help you deal with these changes:

Talking with Your Health Care Team

There is a lot to learn about cancer and your treatment. There are many things to remember. And if you're scared or confused, it can be even harder to take it all in. But, there are things you can do to make it easier to learn.

Express yourself clearly. Describe your problem or concern briefly.

Text in this chapter is excerpted from "Adjusting to Cancer," National Cancer Institute (NCI), December 2, 2014.

Ask your doctor or nurse to write down the name and stage of your cancer. There are many different types of cancer. "Stage" refers to the size of the cancer tumor and how far it has spread in your body. Knowing the name and stage of your cancer will help you find out more about your cancer and help your doctor decide which treatment choices you have.

Learn about your treatment choices. Ask your doctor to tell you about your treatment options. Ask how each treatment can help and which side effects you might have. Try to learn all you can about each choice. Let your doctor know if you need more time to think about these issues before you choose one.

Ask as many questions as you need to. Your doctor needs to know your questions and concerns. Write down your questions and bring them with you to your visit. Ask your most important questions first, in case the doctor runs out of time. If you have a lot of questions, you may want to plan extra time to talk.

Don't worry if your questions seem silly or don't make sense. All your questions are important and deserve an answer. It's okay to ask the same question more than once. It's also okay to ask your doctor to use simpler words and explain terms that are new to you. To make sure you understand, use your own words to repeat back what you heard the doctor say.

Take someone with you when you see the doctor. Ask a family member or friend to go with you when you see your doctor. This person can help by listening, taking notes, and asking questions. If you can't find someone to go with you, ask your doctor if he or she will talk with a friend or family member over the phone.

Take notes or ask to record your conversation with your doctor. Many patients have trouble remembering what they talk about with their doctor. Take notes or ask if you can record the conversation.

Changes for the Family

Cancer affects family and friends, not just the person with the disease. The people in your life may also feel worried, angry, or afraid. Family members may be very supportive, or they may start acting differently towards you. Some may feel guilty that they're not sick, or they may feel helpless, not knowing how to help you.

Adjusting to the new situation

When you find out you have cancer, daily routines may change for everyone. Schedules may be focused around treatment. Someone in your family may need to take time off from work to drive you to treatments. Or, perhaps you need help paying bills or cooking meals. You may need help with chores and errands. Other issues that often come up are:

Changing Roles

When someone has cancer, everyone in the family has to take on new roles and responsibilities. A child may have to do more chores, or a spouse may have to help shop or do carpool. It can be hard for some to adjust to these changes.

Money

Most people find it stressful to keep up with money matters. Cancer can reduce the amount of money your family has to spend or save. If you're not able to work, someone else in your family may need to get a job. You and your family may need to learn more about health insurance and find out what will be covered and what you need to pay for. These and other money issues can be hard to deal with.

Living Arrangements

People with cancer sometimes need to change where they live or whom they live with. You may need to move in with someone else to get the care you need. Or, you may need to travel far from home for treatment. This can be stressful because you may feel that you're losing your independence, even if it's just for a little while.

Daily Activities

You may need help with duties such as paying bills, cooking meals, or coaching your children's teams. Asking others to do these things for you can be hard. But most people want to help and like to do so when you ask.

While some families find it easy to talk about these changes, it's also common for others to find the challenges hard to discuss. If your family is having trouble talking about these issues, ask for help from your health care team or request a family meeting. Your doctor or nurse can refer you to someone who can help families talk about cancer.

Help from Other Family and Friends

Once people learn of your cancer, some will ask you how they can help. Others will wonder what they can do for you, but aren't sure how to ask. You can help your friends cope with the news by letting them assist you in some way. For example, ask them to drive your carpool or go to the store. Make a list of things you think you might need help with, so they can pick something they're able to do for you.

Do What You Can

You probably can, and want to keep doing things on your own. It's important to let people know that you can still do some things for yourself. As much as you're able, keep up with your normal routine by making decisions, doing chores and errands, and taking part in things you enjoy.

Ask for Help

It's okay to ask for help if you need to. Asking for help is not a sign of weakness. Most likely your loved ones want to help you. You can also find volunteers to help you through churches or community groups. Professional helpers can be hired to assist you with physical care and other needs. You could also ask your doctor about respite care, which is when someone comes to your home and takes care of you while your family member goes out for a while.

Show Gratitude for Your Caregivers

Cancer and its treatment are hard on everyone, especially the people who take care of you. Sometimes loved ones become run down and get sick from the stress. Because of this, they need to have balance in their life—time to take care of personal chores and errands, rest, be with friends, or enjoy hobbies. Your caregivers will also need time to sort through their feelings about cancer. Let them know that you want them to have a break, and that it's okay for other people to take care of you for a while.

Facing Cancer with Your Spouse or Partner

Your spouse or partner may feel just as scared by cancer as you do. You both may feel anxious, helpless, or afraid. You may even find it hard to be taken care of by someone you love.

Some relationships get stronger during cancer treatment. Others are weakened. Nearly all couples feel more stress than usual when cancer occurs. They often feel stress about:

- Knowing how to best support each other and how to communicate

- Dealing with new feelings that come up

- Making decisions

- Juggling lots of roles (such as childcare, housekeeping, work, and caregiving)
- Changing their social life
- Changing their daily routine
- Not feeling connected sexually

It helps to know that people express their emotions in different ways. Some like to talk things out or focus on others. Others like to focus inward by doing things, such as washing the dishes or fixing things around the house. These differences can cause tension because each person may expect the other to act the way they would in their place. To reduce stress, it may help to remind yourself that everyone reacts differently.

Ways to Improve Communication

Some couples find it easier to talk about serious issues than other couples. Only you and your partner know how you feel about this. The sections below may help you think about ways to communicate that work for both of you.

Share the Decisions

Including your spouse or partner in treatment decisions is important. Together you can meet with your doctor and learn about common symptoms, your treatment choices, and their side effects. This will help you plan for the upcoming weeks and months.

Help Each Other

Everyone needs to feel needed and loved. You may have always been the "strong one" in your family, but now is the time to let your loved one help you. This can be as simple as letting the other person fluff your pillow, bring you a cool drink, or read to you. And in turn, make sure you help your partner. You can simply express gratitude and let them know you understand it's a tough time for them too.

Be Open about Stress

Some things that cause stress for you and your partner can't be solved right now. And yet sometimes talking about these things can be helpful. Look at the issues that bother you such as dealing with the unknown or feeling a strain between you. You may want to say up front, "I know we can't solve this today. But I'd like to just talk about how it's going and how we're feeling." Getting things out into the open may help you both.

Be a Team

You and your partner may need to be a team now more than ever. It may help to think things through together. Talk about what decisions you should make together and which ones you should make alone. You may want to decide what tasks to share and if other people in your life could help with them.

Make Dates

Many couples find that it helps to plan special occasions. Some days may end up being better than others, depending on how your partner feels. So you may need to be okay with last-minute changes.

Your dates don't have to be fancy. It's about spending time together. That can mean watching a video, going out to eat, or looking through old photos. It can be whatever you both like to do. You can also plan these dates to include other people, if you miss being around others.

Talking to Children about Your Cancer

Even though your children will be upset when they learn about your cancer, don't pretend that everything is okay. Even very young children can sense when something is wrong. They will see that you don't feel well, are away from home more often, or can't spend as much time with them as you used to. Children as young as 18 months old begin to notice what's going on around them. It's important to be honest. Telling the truth is better than letting them imagine the worst. Give your kids time to ask questions and express their feelings.

What Children of All Ages Need to Know

About Cancer

- Nothing your child did, thought, or said caused you to get cancer.

- Just because you have cancer doesn't mean you'll die from it. In fact, many people live with cancer for a long time.

- Your child can't make you well. But there are ways he or she can make you feel better.

- Scientists are finding many new ways to treat cancer.

About Living with Cancer in the Family

- Your child is not alone. Other children have parents who have cancer.

- It's okay to be upset, angry, or scared.

- Your child can't do anything to change the fact that you have cancer.

- Family members may act differently because they're worried about you.

- You will make sure that your children are taken care of, no matter what happens to you.

About What They Can Do

- They can help you by doing nice things like washing dishes or drawing you a picture.

- They should still go to school and take part in sports and other fun activities.

- They can talk to other adults for support, such as teachers, family members, and religious or spiritual leaders.

How Kids May Act When You Have Cancer

Children can react to cancer in many different ways. For example, they may:

- Be confused, scared, lonely, or overwhelmed

- Feel guilty and think that something they did or said caused your cancer

- Feel angry when they are asked to be quiet or to do more chores around the house

- Miss the amount of attention they're used to getting

- Regress and behave as they did when they were much younger

- Get into trouble at school or at home

- Be clingy and afraid to leave the house

Teens

If you have a teenager, know that they're at a time in their lives when they're trying to break away and be independent from their parents. Try to get them to talk about their feelings and ask questions. Tell them as much as they want to know about your cancer. Ask them for their opinions and, if possible, let them help you make decisions.

Teens may want to talk with other people in their lives. Friends can be a great source of support for them, especially those who also have a serious illness in their family. Other family members, teachers, coaches, and spiritual leaders can also help. Encourage your teenage children to talk about their fears and feelings with people they trust.

Adult Children

If you have adult children, your relationship with them may change now that you have cancer. You may:

- Ask them to help with making health care decisions, paying bills, or taking care of the house
- Ask them to explain medical information
- Need them to go to the doctor with you or pick up medicines
- Rely on them for emotional support
- Feel awkward when they help with your physical care

For some parents, it may be hard to ask for comfort and care from their grown children. But it's important to talk about cancer with your family members, even if they get upset or worry about you. Try to include them when talking about your treatment. Let them know the choices you would like them to make about your care, in case you're too sick to make the choices yourself. Recognize that it may be hard for your children to have this talk and that, like you, they're trying to adjust to your illness.

Cancer Support Groups

Cancer support groups are meetings for people with cancer and those touched by the disease. They can have many benefits. Even though a lot of people receive support from friends and family, the number one reason they join a support group is to be with others with similar cancer experiences. Some research shows that joining a support group improves both quality of life and survival.

Support groups can:

- Help you feel better, more hopeful, and not so alone
- Give you a chance to talk about your feelings and work through them
- Help you deal with practical problems, such as problems at work or school
- Help you cope with side effects of treatment

Types of Support Groups

Some groups focus on all kinds of cancer. Others talk about just one kind, such as a group for women with breast cancer or one for men with prostate cancer. Some can be open to everyone or just for people of a certain age, sex, culture, or religion. For instance, some groups are just for teens or young children.

Support groups can also be helpful for children or family members. These groups focus on family concerns such as role changes, relationship changes, financial worries, and how to support the person with cancer. Some groups include both cancer survivors and family members.

Telephone support groups are when everyone dials in to a phone line that is linked together, like a conference call. They can share and talk to others with similar experiences from all over the country. There is usually little or no charge.

Online support groups are "meetings" that take place online. People meet through chat rooms, listservs, or moderated discussion groups and talk with each other over email. People often like online support groups because they can take part in them any time of the day or night. They're also good for people who can't travel to meetings. But always talk with your doctor about cancer information you learn from the Internet.

Where to Find a Support Group

Many hospitals, cancer centers, community groups, and schools offer cancer support groups. Here are some ways to find groups near you:

- Call your local hospital and ask about its cancer support programs.

- Ask your social worker to suggest groups.

- Do an online search for groups.

Is a Support Group Right for Me?

A support group may not be right for everyone. For some people, hearing about others' problems can make them feel worse. Or you may find that your need for a support group changes over time.

If you have a choice of support groups, visit a few and see what they are like. See which ones make sense for you. Although many groups are free, some charge a small fee. Find out if your health insurance pays for support groups.

If you're thinking about joining a support group, here are some questions you may want to ask the group's contact person:

- How large is the group?

- Who attends (survivors, family members, types of cancer, age range)?

- How long are the meetings?

- How often does the group meet?

- How long has the group been together?

- Who leads the meetings - a professional or a survivor?

- What is the format of the meetings?

- Is the main purpose to share feelings, or do people also offer tips to solve common problems?

- If I go, can I just sit and listen?

- Before joining a group, here are questions you may want to ask yourself:

- Am I comfortable talking about personal issues?

- Do I have something to offer to the group?

- What do I hope to gain by joining a group?

Support groups vary greatly, and if you have one bad experience, it doesn't mean these groups aren't a good option for you. You may also want to find another cancer survivor with whom you can discuss your cancer experience. Many organizations can pair you with someone who had your type of cancer and is close to your age and background.

Chapter 58

Self-Image and Sexuality

Self-Image and Sexuality

Each of us has a mental picture of how we look, our "self-image." Although we may not always like how we look, we're used to our self-image and accept it. But cancer and its treatment can change how you look and feel about yourself. Know you aren't alone in how you feel. Many others have similar feelings.

Body Changes during and after Treatment

Some body changes are short-term while others will last forever. Either way, your looks may be a big concern during or after treatment. For example, people with ostomies after colon or rectal surgery are sometimes afraid to go out. They worry about carrying equipment around or fear that it may leak. Some may feel ashamed or afraid that others will reject them.

Every person changes in different ways. Some will be noticeable to other people, but some changes only you will notice. For some of these you may need time to adjust. Issues you may face include:

- Hair loss or skin changes

- Scars or changes in the way you look caused by surgery

Text in this chapter is excerpted from "Self-Image and Sexuality," National Cancer Institute (NCI), December 2, 2014.

- Weight changes

- Loss of limbs

- Loss of fertility, which means it can be hard to get pregnant or father a child

Even if others can't see them, your body changes may trouble you. Feelings of anger and grief about changes in your body are natural. Feeling bad about your body can also lower your sex drive. This loss may make you feel even worse about yourself.

Changes in the way you look can also be hard for your loved ones, which in turn, can be hard on you. For example, parents and grand-parents often worry about how they look to a child or grandchild. They fear that changes in their appearance may scare the child or get in the way of their staying close.

Getting Help

How do you cope with body changes?

- Mourn your losses. They are real, and you have a right to grieve.

- Try to focus on the ways that coping with cancer has made you stronger, wiser, and more realistic.

- If you find that your skin has changed from radiation, ask your doctor about ways you can care for it.

- Look for new ways to enhance your appearance. A new haircut, hair color, makeup, or clothing may give you a lift. If you're wearing a wig, you can take it to a hairdresser to shape and style.

- If you choose to wear a breast form (prosthesis), make sure it fits you well. Don't be afraid to ask the clerk or someone close to you for help. And check your health insurance plan to see if it will pay for it.

Coping with these changes can be hard. But, over time, most people learn to accept them and move on. If you need to, ask your doctor to suggest a counsellor who you can talk with about your feelings.

Staying Active

Many people find that staying active can help their self-image. Whether you swim, play a sport, or take an exercise class, you may find that being active helps you cope with changes. Talk with your doctor about ways you can stay active.

Hobbies and volunteer work can also help improve your self-image. You may like to read, listen to music, or knit for example. Or you could become a mentor or tutor, teach someone how to read or volunteer at a homeless shelter. You may find that you feel better about yourself when you get involved in helping others and doing things you enjoy.

Changes in Your Sex Life

It's common for people to have problems with sex because of cancer and its treatment. When your treatment is over, you may feel like having sex again. Until then, you and your spouse or partner may need to find new ways to show that you care about each other. This can include touching, holding, hugging, and cuddling.

Treatment-Related Problems

Sexual problems are often caused by changes to your body. Depending on the cancer you had, you may have short-term or long-term problems with sex after treatment. These changes result from chemotherapy, radiation surgery, or certain medicines. Sometimes emotional issues may cause problems with sex. Some examples include anxiety, depression, worry, and stress.

What types of problems occur? Common concerns are:

- **Worries about intimacy after treatment.** Some may struggle with their body image after treatment. Even thinking about being seen without clothes may be stressful. People may worry that having sex will hurt or that they won't be able to perform or will feel less attractive. Pain, loss of interest, depression, or cancer medicines can also affect sex drive.

- **Not being able to have sex as you did before.** Some cancer treatments cause changes in sex organs that also change your sex life.

  - Some men can no longer get or keep an erection after treatment for prostate cancer, cancer of the penis, or cancer of the testes. Some treatments can also weaken a man's orgasm or make it dry.

  - Some women find it harder, or even painful, to have sex after cancer treatment. Some cancer treatments can cause these problems, but there may be no clear cause. Some women also have a loss of sensation in their genital area.

741

- **Having menopause symptoms.** When women stop getting their periods, they can get hot flashes, dryness or tightness in the vagina, and/or other problems that can affect their desire to have sex.

- **Losing the ability to have children.** Some cancer treatments can cause infertility, making it impossible for cancer survivors to have children. Depending on the type of treatment, age, and length of time since treatment, you may still be able to have children.

Ask for Help

Even though you may feel awkward, let your doctor or nurse know if you're having problems. There may be treatments or other ways you and your loved one can give each other pleasure. If your doctor can't talk with you about sexual problems, ask for the name of a doctor who can. Some people also find it helpful to talk with other couples.

Sexual problems may not always get better on their own. Sometimes there can be an underlying medical problem that causes changes, such as:

- **Erection problems.** Medicine, assistive devices, counselling, surgery, or other approaches may help.

- **Vaginal dryness.** Dryness or tightness in the vagina can be caused by menopause. Ask whether using a water-based lubricant during sex, using vaginal dilators before sex, and/or taking hormones or using a hormone cream are options for you.

- **Muscle weakness.** You can help strengthen muscles in your genital area by doing **Kegel** exercises. This is when you practice controlling your muscles to stop the flow of urine. You can do these exercises even when you are not urinating. Just tighten and relax the muscles as you sit, stand, or go about your day.

Other issues you may want to talk about include:

- **Concerns about having children.** Discuss family planning concerns with your doctor. If you're a woman, ask if you still need to use birth control, even if you are not getting your period.

- **Talking with a counsellor.** Some people find that sexual problems related to cancer start to strain their relationship with their partner. If this is the case, ask a nurse or social worker if you can talk to a counsellor. Talking to someone alone, or with your partner, may help.

- **Seeing a specialist. A sex therapist may** be able to help you talk openly about your problems, work through your concerns, and come up with new ways to help you and your partner.

Tell Your Partner How You Feel

Talking to your loved one and sharing your feelings and concerns is very important. Even for a couple that has been together a long time, it can be hard to stay connected.

Let your partner know if you want to have sex or would rather just hug, kiss, and cuddle. He or she may be afraid to have sex with you. Or your partner may be worried about hurting you or think that you're not feeling well.

Talk to your partner about any concerns you have about your sex life. Be open about your feelings and stay positive to avoid blame.

Finding Ways to Be Intimate

You can still have an intimate relationship in spite of cancer. Intimacy isn't just physical. It also involves feelings. Here are some ways to improve your intimate relationship:

- Focus on just talking and renewing your connection.

- Protect your time together. Turn off the phone and TV. If needed, find someone to take care of the kids for a few hours.

- Take it slow. Plan an hour or so to be together without being physical. For example, you may want to listen to music or take a walk.

- Try new touch. Cancer treatment or surgery can change a patient's body. Areas where touch used to feel good may now be numb or painful. Some of these changes will go away. Some will stay. For now, you can figure out together what kinds of touch feel good, such as holding, hugging, and cuddling.

Feeling Intimate after Treatment

Although cancer treatment may be over, sexual problems may remain for a while. But you can find other ways to show that you care about each other. Feeling close to your partner is important.

743

- Be proud of your body. It got you through treatment!

- Think of things that help you feel more attractive and confident.

- Focus on the positive. Try to be aware of your thoughts, since they can affect your sex life.

- Be open to change. You may find new ways to enjoy intimacy.

Dating

If you're single, body changes and concerns about sex can affect how you feel about dating. As you struggle to accept the changes yourself, you may also worry about how others will feel. For example, you may wonder how someone will react to physical things, such as hair loss, scars or ostomies. Or it can feel awkward to bring up sexual problems or loss of fertility, which can make feeling close even harder.

You may wonder how and when to tell a new person in your life about your cancer and body changes. For some cancer survivors, the fear of being rejected keeps them from seeking the social life they would like to have. Others who choose not to date may face pressure from friends or family to be more sociable. Here are some ideas that can make it easier to get back into social situations:

- Focus on activities that you have time to enjoy, such as taking a class or joining a club.

- Try not to let cancer be an excuse for not dating and trying to meet people.

- Wait until you feel a sense of trust and friendship before telling a new date about your cancer.

Think about dating as a learning process with the goal of having a social life you enjoy. Not every date has to be perfect. If some people reject you (which can happen with or without cancer), you have not failed. Try to remember that not all dates worked out before you had cancer.

Think about dating as a learning process with the goal of having a social life you enjoy. Not every date has to be perfect. If some people reject you (which can happen with or without cancer), you have not failed.

Chapter 59

Day-to-Day Life

Day-to-Day Life

Dealing with cancer is a life-changing event for most people. For many, it can be a time to minimize regrets and make new priorities. Try to live each day as normally as you can. Enjoy the simple things you like to do and take pleasure in big events.

Keep Up with Your Daily Routine

If you feel well enough, keep up with your daily routine. This includes:

- Going to work
- Spending time with family and friends
- Taking part in activities
- Going on trips

Think about how you want to spend your time and who you like to be with. What makes you happy? What types of things do you enjoy the most?

Text in this chapter is excerpted from "Day-to-Day Life," National Cancer Institute (NCI), December 2, 2014.

Have Fun

You can still have joy in your life while having cancer. Sometimes people with cancer try new, fun things that they have never done before. For instance, have you always wanted to ride in a hot air balloon or go on a boat cruise? What fun things have you always wanted to try, but have never taken the time to do?

Try to do something just for fun, not because you have to do it. But be careful not to tire yourself out. Some people get depressed when they are too tired. Make sure to get enough rest so you feel strong and can enjoy these fun activities.

Finding Humor and Laughing

If you like to joke with your friends and family don't stop now. For many people, humor is a way to gain a sense of control. Laughter can help you relax. When you laugh, your brain releases chemicals that produce pleasure and relax your muscles. Even a smile can fight off stressful thoughts. Of course, you may not always feel like laughing, but other people have found that these ideas can help:

- Ask people to send you funny cards
- Enjoy the funny things children and pets do
- Watch funny movies or TV shows
- Listen to comedy recordings
- Buy a funny desk calendar
- Read humor-related books or articles
- Check out websites and videos on the Internet. If you don't own a computer, use one at your local library

You may even find that you can laugh at yourself. "I went by to help a friend this summer, and it was really hot, so I took my wig off," one woman said. "I got ready to go and I couldn't find it. After searching high and low, I found it hanging from her dog's mouth. But I just stuck it on my head and went home. My husband said, 'What happened?' Needless to say that wig has never been the same."

Physical Activities

Research shows many people find they have more energy when they take part in physical activities such as swimming, walking, yoga, and biking. They find that these types of activities help them keep strong and make them feel good. A bit of exercise every day:

- Improves your chances of feeling better
- Keeps your muscles toned
- Speeds your healing
- Decreases fatigue
- Controls stress
- Increases appetites
- Decreases constipation
- Helps free your mind of bad thoughts

Even if you have never done physical activities before, you can start now. Choose something you think you'd like to do, and get your doctor's okay to try it. There are exercises you can do even if you have to stay in bed.

Set Goals

You may find it helpful to look beyond your treatment and think about what you want to do when you feel well again. Many people set goals so that they can work toward something. For example, they research and plan a trip, or they think about classes and learning things they've always meant to learn. They may look forward to going to a wedding or meeting a new grandchild.

Your Faith and Spirituality

Many people with cancer look more deeply for meaning in their lives. They want to understand their purpose in life or why they got cancer. Spirituality means the way you look at the world and how you make sense of your place in it. Spirituality can include faith or religion, beliefs, values, and "reasons for being."

What It Means to You

Being spiritual can mean different things to everyone. It's a very personal issue. Everyone has their own beliefs about it. Some people find it through religion or faith. Others may be spiritual through meditating, teaching, volunteer work, or reading. It can mean something different for each person. Some people look for a sense of peace or bond with other people. Others seek to forgive themselves or others for past actions.

Your Cancer May Affect Your Spirituality

Having cancer may cause you to think about what you believe, whether or not you're connected to a traditional religion. It's normal to view the experience both negatively and positively at the same time. Some people find that cancer brings more meaning to their faith. Others feel that their faith has let them down and they struggle to understand why they have cancer. For example, they might question their relationship with God.

Your Values May Change

Many people also find that cancer changes their values. They make changes to reflect what matters most to them now. The things you own and your daily duties may seem less important. You may decide to spend more time with loved ones or do something to help others. Or you may take more time to do things in the outdoors or learn about something new. For some, faith can be an important part of both coping with and recovering from cancer.

Finding Comfort and Meaning

If you want to find faith-based or spiritual support, many hospitals have chaplains who are trained to give support to people of different faiths, as well as those who aren't religious at all. You could also ask your health care team about local experts or organizations that help cancer patients and survivors.

Some ideas that have helped others find comfort and meaning are:

- Praying or meditating
- Reading uplifting stories about the human spirit
- Talking with others with similar experiences
- Taking time alone to reflect on life and relationships
- Writing in a journal
- Finding a special place where you find beauty or a sense of calm
- Taking part in community or social gatherings for support and to support others

Going Back to Work

People with cancer often want to get back to work. Their jobs not only give them an income but also a sense of routine. Work helps people feel good about themselves.

Before you go back to work, talk with your doctor as well as your boss. You will all want to make sure you're well enough to do your job. You may need to work fewer hours or do your job in a different way. Some people feel well enough to work while they're having chemo or radiation treatment. Others need to take time off until their treatments are over.

Talking with Your Boss and Co-workers

The response of co-workers about your cancer treatment may differ. Some people may be a huge source of support, while others may be a source of anger or frustration. Some people mean well, but they don't know the right thing to say. Maybe they just don't know how to offer support. Others don't want to deal with your cancer at all. They may think that you aren't able to work as hard as before.

If co-workers seem unsupportive, it could be because they're anxious for you or for themselves. Your cancer experience may threaten them because it reminds them that cancer can happen to anyone. Try to understand their fears and be patient as you try to regain a good relationship. But some people with cancer say that they get tired of trying to act cheerful around others. Many say that friendships change as they let go of their casual ones and give more time to the meaningful ones.

Relating to Others at Work

How do you relate to other people in your life when you go back to work? Does it feel good to return or do you worry how others will react? Here are some tips for returning to work:

- **Accept help.** When people offer to help, say yes, and have in mind some things that they could do to make your life easier. In this way, you will get the support you need, and they will feel helpful.

- **Talk to others.** If you find that a co-worker's feelings about cancer are hurting you, try to resolve the problem with that person face-to-face. If it's still affecting your work after that, your manager, employee assistance counsellor, or personnel office may be able to help.

749

- **Address problems that come up from the start.** Supervisors or co-workers may be able to help those around you understand how you want to be treated.

- **Try to keep up contacts during your recovery.** Co-workers will worry about you. But if they are kept up-to-date about your progress, they will be less anxious and scared. Talk to them on the phone, send email, or appoint a trusted friend or family member to do this for you. Your return to work or other activities will be easier for you and others if you stay in touch.

- **Plan what you'll say about your cancer.** There is no right way to deal with others about your illness, but you do need to think about what you'll say when you're back on the job. Some people don't want to focus on their cancer or be linked in people's minds with the disease. Others are very open about it, speaking frankly with their boss or other workers to air concerns, correct wrong ideas, and decide how to work together. The best approach is the one that feels right to you.

Your Legal Rights at Work

Some people with cancer face roadblocks when they try to go back to work or get a new job. Even people who had cancer many years ago may still have trouble. Employers may not treat them fairly because of false beliefs about cancer. For example, an employer may think cancer can be spread from person to person or that people with cancer take too many sick days. Some employers also think that people with cancer are poor insurance risks.

It is against the law to discriminate against (treat unfairly) workers who have disabilities such as cancer. There are national laws that protect your rights as a worker. And if you're looking for a new job, you have no legal obligation to talk about your cancer history unless your past health has a direct impact on the job you seek.

Handling Problems at Work

- Decide how to handle the problem.

- What are your rights as an employee?

- Are you willing to take action to correct a problem?

- Do you still want to work there? Or would you rather look for a new job?

- If necessary, ask your employer to adjust to your needs.

- Start by talking informally to your supervisor, personnel office, employee assistance counsellor, shop steward, or union representative.

- Ask for a change that would make it easier for you to keep your job (for example, flextime, working at home, special equipment at work).

- Document each request and its outcome for your records.

- Get help working with your employer if you need it.

- Ask your doctor or nurse to find times for follow-up visits that don't conflict with your other responsibilities.

- Get your doctor to write a letter to your employer or personnel officer explaining how, if at all, your cancer may affect your work or your schedule.

Talk with your social worker about laws in your state. Your social worker can give you the name of the state agency that protects your rights as an employee. You may also want to ask about benefits you can get as a person with cancer.

Money Worries

The financial challenges that people with cancer and their families face are very real. During an illness, you may find it hard to find the time or energy to review your options. Yet it's important to keep your family financially healthy.

For hospital bills, you or your loved one may want to talk with a hospital financial counsellor. You may be able to work out a monthly payment plan or get a reduced rate. You may also want to stay in touch with the insurance company to make sure certain treatment costs are covered.

Chapter 60

Nutrition in Cancer Care

Chapter Contents

Section 60.1

Nutrition in Cancer Care – Overview

Text in this section is excerpted from "Nutrition in Cancer Care,"
National Cancer Institute (NCI), July 16, 2015.

Good nutrition is important for cancer patients.

Nutrition is a process in which food is taken in and used by the
body for growth, to keep the body healthy, and to replace tissue. Good
nutrition is important for good health. Eating the right kinds of foods
before, during, and after cancer treatment can help the patient feel
better and stay stronger. A healthy diet includes eating and drinking
enough of the foods and liquids that have the important nutrients (vitamins, minerals, protein, carbohydrates, fat, and water) the body needs.

When the body does not get or cannot absorb the nutrients needed
for health, it causes a condition called malnutrition or malnourishment.

Healthy eating habits are important during cancer treatment.

Nutrition therapy is used to help cancer patients get the nutrients
they need to keep up their body weight and strength, keep body tissue
healthy, and fight infection. Eating habits that are good for cancer
patients can be very different from the usual healthy eating guidelines.

Healthy eating habits and good nutrition can help patients deal
with the effects of cancer and its treatment. Some cancer treatments
work better when the patient is well nourished and gets enough calories and protein in the diet. Patients who are well nourished may have
a better prognosis (chance of recovery) and quality of life.

Cancer can change the way the body uses food.

Some tumors make chemicals that change the way the body uses
certain nutrients. The body's use of protein, carbohydrates, and fat
may be affected, especially by tumors of the stomach or intestines. A
patient may seem to be eating enough, but the body may not be able
to absorb all the nutrients from the food.

Cancer and cancer treatments may affect nutrition.

For many patients, the effects of cancer and cancer treatments make it hard to eat well. Cancer treatments that affect nutrition include:

- Surgery.
- Chemotherapy.
- Radiation therapy.
- Immunotherapy.
- Stem cell transplant.

When the head, neck, esophagus, stomach, or intestines are affected by the cancer treatment, it is very hard to take in enough nutrients to stay healthy.

The side effects of cancer and cancer treatment that can affect eating include:

- Anorexia (loss of appetite).
- Mouth sores.
- Dry mouth.
- Trouble swallowing.
- Nausea.
- Vomiting.
- Diarrhea.
- Constipation.
- Pain.
- Depression.
- Anxiety.

Cancer and cancer treatments may affect taste, smell, appetite, and the ability to eat enough food or absorb the nutrients from food. This can cause malnutrition (a condition caused by a lack of key nutrients). Malnutrition can cause the patient to be weak, tired, and unable to fight infections or get through cancer treatment. Malnutrition may be made worse if the cancer grows or spreads. Eating too little protein and calories is a very common problem for cancer patients. Having enough protein and calories is important for healing, fighting infection, and having enough energy.

Anorexia and cachexia are common causes of malnutrition in cancer patients.

Anorexia (the loss of appetite or desire to eat) is a common symptom in people with cancer. Anorexia may occur early in the disease or later, if the cancer grows or spreads. Some patients already have anorexia when they are diagnosed with cancer. Almost all patients who have advanced cancer will have anorexia. Anorexia is the most common cause of malnutrition in cancer patients.

Cachexia is a condition marked by a loss of appetite, weight loss, muscle loss, and general weakness. It is common in patients with tumors of the lung, pancreas, and upper gastrointestinal tract. It is important to watch for and treat cachexia early in cancer treatment because it is hard to correct.

Cancer patients may have anorexia and cachexia at the same time. Weight loss can be caused by eating fewer calories, using more calories, or both.

It is important to treat weight loss caused by cancer and its treatment.

It is important that cancer symptoms and side effects that affect eating and cause weight loss are treated early. Both nutrition therapy and medicine can help the patient stay at a healthy weight. Medicine may be used for the following:

- To help increase appetite.

- To help digest food.

- To help the muscles of the stomach and intestines contract (to keep food moving along).

- To prevent or treat nausea and vomiting.

- To prevent or treat diarrhaea.

- To prevent or treat constipation.

- To prevent and treat mouth problems (such as dry mouth, infection, pain, and sores).

- To prevent and treat pain.

Section 60.2

Types of Nutrition Care

Text in this section is excerpted from "Nutrition in Cancer Care,"
National Cancer Institute (NCI), July 16, 2015.

Nutrition support gives nutrition to patients who cannot eat or digest normally.

It is best to take in food by mouth whenever possible. Some patients may not be able to take in enough food by mouth because of problems from cancer or cancer treatment. Medicine to increase appetite may be used.

Nutrition support for patients who cannot eat can be given in different ways.

A patient who is not able to take in enough food by mouth may be fed using enteral nutrition (through a tube inserted into the stomach or intestines) or parenteral nutrition (infused into the bloodstream). The nutrients are given in liquid formulas that have water, protein, fats, carbohydrates, vitamins, and/or minerals.

Nutrition support can improve a patient's quality of life during cancer treatment, but there are harms that should be considered before making the decision to use it. The patient and health care providers should discuss the harms and benefits of each type of nutrition support.

Enteral Nutrition

Enteral nutrition is also called tube feeding.

Enteral nutrition is giving the patient nutrients in liquid form (formula) through a tube that is placed into the stomach or small intestine. The following types of feeding tubes may be used:

- A nasogastric tube is inserted through the nose and down the throat into the stomach or small intestine. This kind of tube is used when enteral nutrition is only needed for a few weeks.

- A gastrostomy tube is inserted into the stomach or a jejunostomy tube is inserted into the small intestine through an

757

opening made on the outside of the abdomen. This kind of tube is usually used for long-term enteral feeding or for patients who cannot use a tube in the nose and throat.

The type of formula used is based on the specific needs of the patient. There are formulas for patients who have special health conditions, such as diabetes. Formula may be given through the tube as a constant drip (continuous feeding) or 1 to 2 cups of formula can be given 3 to 6 times a day (bolus feeding).

Enteral nutrition is sometimes used when the patient is able to eat small amounts by mouth, but cannot eat enough for health. Nutrients given through a tube feeding add the calories and nutrients needed for health.

Enteral nutrition may continue after the patient leaves the hospital.

If enteral nutrition is to be part of the patient's care after leaving the hospital, the patient and caregiver will be trained to do the nutrition support care at home.

Parenteral Nutrition

Parenteral nutrition carries nutrients directly into the blood stream.

Parenteral nutrition is used when the patient cannot take food by mouth or by enteral feeding. Parenteral feeding does not use the stomach or intestines to digest food. Nutrients are given to the patient directly into the blood, through a catheter (thin tube) inserted into a vein. These nutrients include proteins, fats, vitamins, and minerals.

Parenteral nutrition is used only in patients who need nutrition support for five days or more.

The catheter may be placed into a vein in the chest or in the arm.

A central venous catheter is placed beneath the skin and into a large vein in the upper chest. The catheter is put in place by a surgeon. This type of catheter is used for long-term parenteral feeding.

A peripheral venous catheter is placed into a vein in the arm. A peripheral venous catheter is put in place by trained medical staff. This type of catheter is usually used for short-term parenteral feeding.

The patient is checked often for infection or bleeding at the place where the catheter enters the body.

Parenteral nutrition support may continue after the patient leaves the hospital.

If parenteral nutrition is to be part of the patient's care after leaving the hospital, the patient and caregiver will be trained to do the nutrition support care at home.

Ending parenteral nutrition support must be done under medical supervision.

Going off parenteral nutrition support needs to be done slowly and is supervised by a medical team. The parenteral feedings are decreased by small amounts over time until they can be stopped, or as the patient is changed over to enteral or oral feeding.

Section 60.3

Effects of Cancer Treatment on Nutrition

Text in this section is excerpted from "Nutrition in Cancer Care," National Cancer Institute (NCI), July 16, 2015.

Surgery and Nutrition

Surgery increases the body's need for nutrients and energy.

The body needs extra energy and nutrients to heal wounds, fight infection, and recover from surgery. If the patient is malnourished before surgery, it may cause problems during recovery, such as poor healing or infection. For these patients, nutrition care may begin before surgery.

Surgery to the head, neck, esophagus, stomach, or intestines may affect nutrition.

Most cancer patients are treated with surgery. Surgery that removes all or part of certain organs can affect a patient's ability to eat and digest food. The following are nutrition problems caused by specific types of surgery:

- Surgery to the head and neck may cause problems with:

  - Chewing.

  - Swallowing.

- Tasting or smelling food.

- Making saliva.

- Seeing.

- Surgery that affects the esophagus, stomach, or intestines may keep these organs from working as they should to digest food and absorb nutrients.

All of these can affect the patient's ability to eat normally. Emotional stress about the surgery itself also may affect appetite.

Nutrition therapy can help relieve nutrition problems caused by surgery.

Nutrition therapy can relieve or decrease the side effects of surgery and help cancer patients get the nutrients they need. Nutrition therapy may include the following:

- Nutritional supplement drinks.

- Enteral nutrition (feeding liquid through a tube into the stomach or intestines).

- Parenteral nutrition (feeding through a catheter into the bloodstream).

- Medicines to increase appetite.

It is common for patients to have pain, tiredness, and/or loss of appetite after surgery. For a short time, some patients may not be able to eat what they usually do because of these symptoms. Following certain tips about food may help. These include:

- Stay away from carbonated drinks (such as sodas) and foods that cause gas, such as:

  - Beans.

  - Peas.

  - Broccoli.

  - Cabbage.

  - Brussels sprouts.

  - Green peppers.

  - Radishes.

  - Cucumbers.

- Increase calories by frying foods and using gravies, mayonnaise, and salad dressings. Supplements high in calories and protein can also be used.
- Choose high-protein and high-calorie foods to increase energy and help wounds heal. Good choices include:
  - Eggs.
  - Cheese.
  - Whole milk.
  - Ice cream.
  - Nuts.
  - Peanut butter.
  - Meat.
  - Poultry.
  - Fish.

If constipation is a problem, increase fibre by small amounts and drink lots of water. Good sources of fibre include:

- Whole-grain cereals (such as oatmeal and bran).
- Beans.
- Vegetables.
- Fruit.
- Whole-grain breads.

Chemotherapy and Nutrition

Chemotherapy affects cells all through the body.

Chemotherapy affects fast-growing cells and is used to treat cancer because cancer cells grow and divide quickly. Healthy cells that normally grow and divide quickly may also be killed. These include cells in the mouth, digestive tract, and hair follicles.

Chemotherapy may affect nutrition.

Chemotherapy may cause side effects that cause problems with eating and digestion. When more than one anticancer drug is given, more side effects may occur or they may be more severe. The following side effects are common:

- Loss of appetite.
- Inflammation and sores in the mouth.

761

- Changes in the way food tastes.

- Feeling full after only a small amount of food.

- Nausea.

- Vomiting.

- Diarrhea.

- Constipation.

Nutrition therapy can help relieve nutrition problems caused by chemotherapy.

Patients who have side effects from chemotherapy may not be able to eat normally and get all the nutrients they need to restore healthy blood counts between treatments. Nutrition therapy can help relieve these side effects, help patients recover from chemotherapy, prevent delays in treatment, prevent weight loss, and maintain general health. Nutrition therapy may include the following:

- Nutrition supplement drinks between meals.

- Enteral nutrition (tube feedings).

- Changes in the diet, such as eating small meals throughout the day.

Radiation Therapy and Nutrition

Radiation therapy can affect cancer cells and healthy cells in the treatment area.

Radiation therapy can kill cancer cells and healthy cells in the treatment area. The amount of damage depends on the following:

- The part of the body that is treated.

- The total dose of radiation and how it is given.

Radiation therapy may affect nutrition.

Radiation therapy to any part of the digestive system often has side effects that cause nutrition problems. Most of the side effects begin a few weeks after radiation therapy begins and go away a few weeks after it is finished. Some side effects can continue for months or years after treatment ends.

The following are some of the more common side effects:

- For radiation therapy to the head and neck

- Loss of appetite.
- Changes in the way food tastes.
- Pain when swallowing.
- Dry mouth or thick saliva.
- Sore mouth and gums.
- Narrowing of the upper esophagus, which can cause choking, breathing, and swallowing problems.
- For radiation therapy to the chest
- Infection of the esophagus.
- Trouble swallowing.
- Esophageal reflux (a backward flow of the stomach contents into the esophagus).
- For radiation therapy to the abdomen or pelvis
- Diarrhea.
- Nausea.
- Vomiting.
- Inflamed intestines or rectum.
- A decrease in the amount of nutrients absorbed by the intestines.

Radiation therapy may also cause tiredness, which can lead to a decrease in appetite.

Nutrition therapy can help relieve the nutrition problems caused by radiation therapy.
Nutrition therapy during radiation treatment can help the patient get enough protein and calories to get through treatment, prevent weight loss, help wound and skin healing, and maintain general health. Nutrition therapy may include the following:

- Nutritional supplement drinks between meals.
- Enteral nutrition (tube feedings).
- Changes in the diet, such as eating small meals throughout the day.

Patients who receive high-dose radiation therapy to prepare for a bone marrow transplant may have many nutrition problems and should see a dietitian for nutrition support.

Biologic Therapy and Nutrition

Biologic therapy may affect nutrition.

The side effects of biologic therapy are different for each patient and each type of biologic agent. The following nutrition problems are common:

- Fever.
- Nausea.
- Vomiting.
- Diarrhea.
- Loss of appetite.
- Tiredness.
- Weight gain.

Nutrition therapy can help relieve nutrition problems caused by biologic therapy.

The side effects of biologic therapy can cause weight loss and malnutrition if they are not treated. Nutrition therapy can help patients receiving biologic therapy get the nutrients they need to get through treatment, prevent weight loss, and maintain general health.

Stem Cell Transplant and Nutrition

Stem cell transplant patients have special nutrition needs.

Chemotherapy, radiation therapy, and medicines used for a stem cell transplant may cause side effects that keep a patient from eating and digesting food as usual. Common side effects include the following:

- Changes in the way food tastes.
- Dry mouth or thick saliva.
- Mouth and throat sores.
- Nausea.
- Vomiting.
- Diarrhea.
- Constipation.
- Weight loss and loss of appetite.
- Weight gain.

Nutrition therapy is very important for patients who have a stem cell transplant.

Transplant patients have a very high risk of infection. High doses of chemotherapy or radiation therapy decrease the number of white blood cells, which fight infection. It is especially important that transplant patients avoid getting infections.

Patients who have a transplant need plenty of protein and calories to get through and recover from the treatment, prevent weight loss, fight infection, and maintain general health. It is also important to avoid infection from bacteria in food. Nutrition therapy during transplant treatment may include the following:

- A diet of cooked and processed foods only, because raw vegetables and fresh fruit may carry harmful bacteria.

- Guidelines on safe food handling.

- A specific diet based on the type of transplant and the part of the body affected by cancer.

- Parenteral nutrition (feeding through the bloodstream) during the first few weeks after the transplant, to give the patient the calories, protein, vitamins, minerals, and fluids they need to recover.

Section 60.4

Nutrition in Advanced Cancer

Text in this section is excerpted from "Nutrition in Cancer Care," National Cancer Institute (NCI), July 16, 2015.

Palliative care helps relieve symptoms that bother the patient and helps improve the patient's quality of life.

The goal of palliative care is to improve the quality of life of patients who have a serious or life-threatening disease. Palliative care is meant to prevent or treat symptoms, side effects, and psychological, social, and spiritual problems caused by a disease or its treatment.

Palliative care for patients with advanced cancer includes nutrition therapy and/or drug therapy.

Nutrition needs are different for patients with advanced cancer.

It is common for patients with advanced cancer to want less food. Patients usually prefer soft foods and clear liquids. Those who have problems swallowing may do better with thick liquids than with thin liquids. Patients often do not feel much hunger at all and may need very little food.

In patients with advanced cancer, most foods are allowed. During this time, eating can be focused on pleasure rather than getting enough nutrients. Patients usually cannot eat enough of any food that might cause a problem. However, some patients may need to stay on a special diet. For example, patients with cancer that affects the abdomen may need a soft diet to keep the bowel from getting blocked.

The benefits and harms of nutrition support are different for each patient.

Answering the following questions may help to make decisions about using nutrition support:

- What are the wishes and needs of the patient and family?

- Will the patient's quality of life be improved?

- Do the possible benefits outweigh the risks and costs?

- Is there an advance directive? An advance directive is a legal document that states the treatment or care a person wishes to receive or not receive if he or she becomes unable to make medical decisions. One type of advance directive is a living will.

Cancer patients and their caregivers have the right to make informed decisions. The healthcare team and a registered dietitian can explain the benefits and risks of using nutrition support for patients with advanced cancer. In most cases, there are more harms than benefits, especially with parenteral nutrition support. However, for someone who still has good quality of life but is unable to get enough food and water by mouth, enteral feedings may be best. The benefits and risks of enteral nutrition during advanced cancer include the following:

Benefits

- May make the patient more alert.

- May be a comfort to the family.

- May relieve nausea.
- May make the patient feel more hopeful.

Harms

- Surgery may be needed to place a tube through the abdomen.
- May increase the amount of saliva in the mouth and throat. This may cause choking or pneumonia.
- May cause diarrhaea or constipation.
- May cause nausea.
- May cause infection.
- Makes patient care harder for caregiver.

Chapter 61

For Family and Friends

For Family and Friends

If you are helping your family member or friend through cancer treatment, you are a caregiver. This may mean helping with daily activities such as going to the doctor or making meals. It could also mean coordinating services and care. Or it may be giving emotional and spiritual support.

Adjusting to Being a Caregiver

Giving care and support during this time can be a challenge. Many caregivers put their own needs and feelings aside to focus on the person with cancer. This can be hard to maintain for a long time, and it's not good for your health. If you don't take care of yourself, you won't be able to take care of others. It's important for everyone that you give care to you.

Changing Roles

Whether you're younger or older, you may find yourself in a new role as a caregiver. You may have been an active part of someone's life before cancer, but perhaps now the way you support that person is different. It may be in a way in which you haven't had much experience,

Text in this chapter is excerpted from "For Family and Friends," National Cancer Institute (NCI), December 2, 2014.

or in a way that feels more intense than before. Even though caregiving may feel new to you now, many caregivers say that they learn more as they go through their loved one's cancer experience. Common situations that they describe:

- Your spouse or partner may feel comfortable with only you taking care of him.

- Your parent may have a hard time accepting help from you (her adult child) since she's always been used to caring for you.

- Your adult child with cancer may not want to rely on his parents for care.

- You may have health problems yourself, making it hard physically and emotionally to take care of someone else.

Whatever your roles are now, accepting the changes may be tough. It's very common to feel confused and stressed at this time. If you can, try to share your feelings with others or a join support group. Or you may choose to seek help from a counsellor.

Ask for Help

Many caregivers say that, looking back, they took too much on themselves. Or they wish they had asked for help sooner. Take an honest look at what you can and can't do. What things do you need or want to do yourself? What tasks can you turn over or share with others? Be willing to let go of things that aren't essential for you to do. Some examples may be:

- Helping with chores, such as cooking , cleaning, shopping, or yard work

- Taking care of the kids or picking them up from school or activities

- Driving your loved one to appointments or picking up medicines

- Being the contact person to keep others updated

Accepting help from others isn't always easy. When tough things happen, many people tend to pull away. They think, "We can handle this on our own." But things can get harder as the patient goes through treatment. You may need to change your schedule and take on new tasks. As a result, many caregivers have said, "There's just too much on my plate."

Remember that getting help for yourself can also help your loved one because:

- You may stay healthier.

- Your loved one may feel less guilty about all the things that you're doing.

- Some of your helpers may offer time and skills that you don't have.

Be Prepared for Some People to Say No

Sometimes people may not be able to help. This may hurt your feelings or make you angry. It may be especially hard coming from people that you expected help from. You might wonder why someone wouldn't offer to help you. Some common reasons are:

- Some people may be coping with their own problems.

- Some may have a lack of time.

- They are afraid of cancer or may have already had a bad experience with cancer. They don't want to get involved and feel pain all over again.

- Some people believe it's best to keep a distance when people are struggling.

- Sometimes people don't realize how hard things really are for you. Or they don't understand that you need help unless you ask them for it directly.

- Some people feel awkward because they don't know how to show they care.

If someone isn't giving you the help you need, you may want to talk to them and explain your needs. Or you can just let it go. But if the relationship is important, you may want to tell the person how you feel. This can help prevent resentment or stress from building up. These feelings could hurt your relationship in the long run.

Caring for Your Mind, Body, and Spirit

You may feel that your needs aren't important right now. Or maybe by the time you've taken care of everything else, there's no time left for yourself. Or you may feel guilty that you can enjoy things that your loved one can't right now.

Most caregivers say they have those same feelings. But caring for your own needs, hopes, and desires can give you the strength you need to carry on.

Make Time for Yourself

Taking time to recharge your mind, body, and spirit can help you be a better caregiver. You may want to think about:

- Finding nice things you can do for yourself--even just a few minutes can help

- Cutting back on personal activities, rather than cutting them out entirely

- Finding things others can do or arrange for you, such as appointments or errands

- Looking for easy ways to connect with friends

- Finding larger chunks of "off-duty" time

Take Stock of Your Own Feelings

Giving yourself an outlet for your own thoughts and feelings is important. Think about what would help lift your spirits. Would talking with others help ease your load? Or would you rather have quiet time by yourself? Maybe you need both, depending on what's going on in your life. It's helpful for you and others to know what you need.

Find Time to Relax

Your mind needs a break from the demands of caregiving. Think about what gives you comfort or helps you relax. Caregivers say that even a few minutes a day without interruptions helps them to cope and focus.

Take 15–30 minutes each day to do something for yourself, no matter how small it is. Try to make time for a nap, exercise, yard work, a hobby, watching a movie, or whatever you find relaxing. If you find it hard to relax even when you have time for it, you're not alone. But, some caregivers find it helpful to simply do gentle exercises, such as stretching or yoga. Or, take deep breaths or just sit still for a minute.

Join a Support Group

Support groups can meet in person, by phone, or over the Internet. They may help you gain new insights into what is happening, get ideas about how to cope, and help you know that you're not alone. In a support group, people may talk about their feelings, trade advice, and try to help others who are dealing with the same kinds of issues. Some people like to go and just listen. And others prefer not to join support groups at all. Some people aren't comfortable with this kind of sharing.

If you can't find a group in your area, try a support group on the Internet. Some caregivers say websites with support groups have helped them a lot.

Talk to a Counsellor

You may be feeling overwhelmed and feel like talking to someone outside your inner circle. Some caregivers find it helpful to talk to a counsellor, such as a social worker, psychologist, or other mental health professional. Others also find it helpful to turn to a leader in their faith or spiritual community. These types of experts may be able to help you talk about things that you don't feel you can talk about with friends or family. They can also help you find ways to express your feelings and learn ways to cope that you hadn't thought of before.

Connect with Your Loved One

Cancer may bring you and your loved one closer together than ever before. Often people become closer as they face challenges together. If you can, take time to share special moments with one another. Try to gain strength from all you are going through together, and what you have dealt with so far. This may help you move toward the future with a positive outlook and feelings of hope.

Connect with Others

Studies show that connecting with other people is very important to most caregivers. It's especially helpful when you feel overwhelmed or want to say things that you can't say to your loved one. Try to find someone you can really open up to about your feelings or fears. You may find it helpful to talk with someone outside the situation. Also, it may help to have an informal network of people to contact, either by phone or in person.

Look for the Positive

It can be hard finding positive moments when you're busy caregiving. It can be also hard to adjust to your role as a caregiver. Caregivers say that looking for the good things in life helps them feel better. For example, think about something that you found rewarding about caregiving, such as gratitude you've received, or extra support from others. You might also take a moment to feel good about anything else from the day that is positive; a nice sunset, a hug, or something funny that you heard or read.

Let Yourself Laugh

It's okay to laugh, even when your loved one is in treatment. In fact, it's healthy. Laughter releases tension and makes you feel better. You can read and watch humor columns, watch comedy shows, or talk with upbeat friends. Or just remember funny things that have happened to you in the past. Keeping your sense of humor in trying times is a good coping skill.

Write in a Journal

Research shows that writing or journaling can help relieve negative thoughts and feelings. And it may actually help improve your own health. You might write about your most stressful experiences. Or you may want to express your deepest thoughts and feelings. You can also write about things that make you feel good, such as a pretty day or a kind co-worker or friend.

Be Thankful

You may feel thankful that you can be there for your loved one. You may be glad for a chance to do something positive and give to another person in a way you never knew you could. Some caregivers feel that they've been given the chance to build or strengthen a relationship. This doesn't mean that caregiving is easy or stress-free. But finding meaning in caregiving can make it easier to manage.

Keep Up Your Routine

If you can, try to keep doing some of your regular activities. If you don't, studies show that it can increase the stress you feel. Keep it simple and stick with things you do well. Be willing to change your routines. You may have to do things at a different time of day or for less time than you normally would, but try to still do them.

Learn More about Cancer

Sometimes understanding your loved one's medical situation can make you feel more confident and in control. For example, you may want to know more about his stage of cancer. It may help you to know what to expect during treatment, such as the tests and procedures that will be done, as well as the side effects that will result.

Caring for Your Body

You may find yourself so busy and concerned about your loved one that you don't pay attention to your own physical health. But it's very important that you take care of your health, too. Doing so will give you strength to help others.

New stresses and daily demands often add to any health problems caregivers already have. And if you are sick or have an injury that requires you to be careful, it's even more important that you take care of yourself. Here are some changes caregivers often have:

- Fatigue (feeling tired)

- Weaker immune system (poor ability to fight off illness)

- Sleep problems

- Slower healing of wounds

- Higher blood pressure

- Changes in appetite or weight

- Headaches

- Anxiety, depression, or other mood changes

Taking Care of Yourself

The ideas below for taking care of yourself may sound easy. But they're a challenge for most caregivers. They are so used to taking care of someone else it's hard for them to change focus. You'll need to pay attention to how you're feeling, in both body and mind. Even though you may be putting someone else's needs first, it's important to:

- **Keep up with your own checkups, screenings, and other medical needs.**

- **Watch for signs of depression or anxiety.** Stress can cause many different feelings or body changes. But if they last for more than two weeks, talk to your doctor.

- **Take your medicines as prescribed.** Ask your doctor to give you a larger prescription to save trips to the pharmacy. Find out if your grocery store or pharmacy delivers.

- **Try to eat healthy meals.** Eating well will help you keep up your strength. If your loved one is in the hospital or has long doctor's appointments, bring easy-to-prepare food from home. For example, sandwiches, salads, or packaged foods and canned meats fit easily into a lunch container.

- **Get enough rest.** Listening to soft music or doing breathing exercises may help you fall asleep. Short naps can energize you if you aren't getting enough sleep. Be sure to talk with your doctor if lack of sleep becomes an ongoing problem.

- **Exercise.** Walking, swimming, running, or bike riding are only a few ways to get your body moving. Any kind of exercise (including working in the garden, cleaning, mowing, or going up stairs) can help you keep your body healthy. Finding at least 15-30 minutes a day to exercise may make you feel better and help manage your stress.

- **Make time for yourself.** You may choose to stretch, read, watch television, or talk on the phone. Whatever helps you unwind, you should take the time to do it. It's important to tend to your own needs and reduce your own stress levels.

Long Distance Caregiving

It can be really tough to be away from a loved one who has cancer. You may feel like you're a step behind in knowing what is happening with his or her care. Yet even if you live far away, it's possible for you to give support and be a problem-solver and care coordinator.

Caregivers who live more than an hour away from their loved ones most often rely on the telephone or email as their communication link. But either of these methods can be rather limiting when trying to assess someone's needs. Aside from true medical emergencies, long-distance caregivers often need to judge whether situations can be dealt with over the phone or require an in-person visit.

Finding Contacts

Develop a relationship with one or two key members of the health care team, such as a social worker or patient educator. It may help you feel more at ease to have direct contact with someone involved in the medical care of your loved one. Also, many long-distance caregivers say that it helps to explore both paid and volunteer support. Ways you can do this are:

- Create a list of people who live near your loved one whom you could call day or night in a crisis or just to check in.

- Look into volunteer visitors, adult day care centers, or meal delivery services in the area.

- Make a list of web sites in your loved one's area to give you quick access to resources.

- Keep a copy of the local phone book available for reference.

Remember to share a list of home, work, and cell phone numbers with the health care team. You should also give this to loved ones and others in case of an emergency.

Other Tips

- Ask a local family member or friend to update you daily by email. Or, consider creating a web site to share news about your loved one's condition and needs.

- Talk to electronic or computer experts to learn about other ways to connect with people. New advances using video and the Internet are being made every day. For example, Skype and Facetime are ways people connect from a distance.

- Airlines or bus lines may have special deals for patients or family members. The hospital social worker may also know of other resources, such as private pilots, advocacy organizations, or companies that help people with cancer and their families with transportation.

- If you are traveling to see your loved one, time your flights or drives so that you have time to rest when you return. Many long-distance caregivers say that they don't allow themselves enough time to rest after their visits.

- Consider getting a phone card from a discount store to cut down on long-distance bills. Or, review your long-distance and cell phone plans. See if you can make any changes that would reduce your bills.

Caregiving after Treatment

It's important for caregivers to understand that even though treatment has ended, cancer survivors are still coping with a lot.

Often they're dealing with side effects from treatment and learning how to adjust to the many other changes they have gone through. They may not be returning back to normal life as soon as they had hoped.

Once treatment ends, most people want to put the cancer experience behind them. Still, one of the most common reactions by caregivers is to ask themselves, "Now what do I do?" Many have to think about how to adjust to this "new normal." Until now, your focus has been on getting the patient through treatment. So it can be a time of mixed emotions - you may be happy treatment is over. But at the same time, the full impact of what you've gone through with your loved one may start to hit you.

Be Aware of Your Feelings

It's normal to have many different feelings after treatment ends. Some caregivers say that their feelings are even more intense after treatment, since they have more time to process it all.

You may be glad and relieved that your loved one is through with treatment. But you could also feel anxious because you're no longer doing something directed at fighting the cancer. You may feel a sense of sadness and loss at still seeing your friend or family member in a weakened state. This can also be a time when you feel more lonely and isolated than before.

Common feelings that you may have include:

- Missing the support you had from the patient's health care team.

- Feeling pressure to return to your old self.

- Feeling lonely. Friends and family may go back to their daily lives, leaving you with more to do. They may not be checking in with you as they did when your loved one was getting treatment.

- Avoiding going out with others for fear of something happening to your loved one while you are gone.

- Finding it hard to relate to people who haven't been through what you have.

- Having mixed feelings as you see your loved one struggle with moodiness, depression, or loss of self-esteem.

- Worrying that any physical problem is a sign of the cancer returning. Yet at the same time, feel thankful that this person is here and part of your life.

- Looking forward to putting more energy into the things that mean the most to you.

These feelings are all normal. You can manage them by giving yourself time to reflect on your experience with cancer. People need different amounts of time to work through the challenges that they're facing.

Make Time for Yourself

If you've been putting your own needs aside, this may be a good time to think about how you can best care for yourself. Having some down time to recharge your mind and spirit can help you cope. You may want to think about:

- Getting back to activities that you enjoy

- Finding ways others can help you

- Finding new ways to connect with friends

For example, some caregivers feel the need to give back to others who are facing cancer. They turn their energy to helping people in their community, joining support groups, or volunteering with cancer organizations. For many, making a difference in the lives of others helps them to help themselves.

Let Others Help You

You may feel tempted to tell people that you and your loved one are doing fine and don't need help. It may be that you don't want to trouble people any longer. Chances are that both of you are tired and are still getting used to life after treatment. It may help to tell others that you're still adjusting and let them know ways they can help. Family, friends, neighbors, and coworkers who stayed away during treatment may now be willing or able to support you. However, be aware that others may not be there to help. They may feel awkward about helping or assume that you're getting back to your routine and don't need help any more. Or they may have personal reasons, such as lack of time or things going on in their own lives.

Teens Who Have a Family Member with Cancer

If you are a teen – and your parent or sibling has cancer – this information can help prepare you for some of the things you may face in the coming months. While there is a team of people working hard to help your family member get better -- there are also people available to help you. No one should go through this alone.

You may want to talk with others in your family about the information you find here. It may help you bring up something that's on your mind. For starters, focus on these facts:

- **Many people survive cancer.** There are over 14 million cancer survivors in the U.S. and scientists are discovering better cancer treatments.

- **You are not alone.** Right now, it might seem that no one else in the world feels the way you do. In a way, you are right. No one can feel exactly like you do. But it might help to know that many teens have a family member with cancer. Talking to other teens, who are facing similar challenges, may help you sort out your feelings.

- **Balance is important.** Many teens feel like the experience of having a sibling or parent with cancer is always on their mind. Others try to avoid it all together. Try to strike a balance. You can be concerned and still stay connected with friends and activities that you care about.

- **Knowledge is power.** It can help to learn more about the type of cancer your family member has, and how it will be treated. Sometimes what you imagine is actually worse than the reality.

- **You can give comfort.** Sometimes you will be strong for your family and sometimes people in your family will be strong for you.

Finding Ways to Cope

If your parent or sibling has cancer, you may have range of feeling. Some days will be good, and things might seem like they used to. Other days may be harder. There is no one "right" way to feel. When someone in your family has cancer – it can change the way you look at things in life. In this section we look at some common emotions and ways to cope.

It may be hard to share your feelings. You may ignore them and hope they will go away. Holding your feelings inside can prevent you from getting the help you need. Some emotions that teens feel when a family member has cancer are:

- **Scared:** It's normal to feel scared. Some of your fears may be real. Others may be based on things that won't happen. Some fears may lessen over time.

- **Angry:** Anger often covers up other feelings that are harder to show. If having cancer in your family means you can't do what you like to do, it's tough. Don't let anger build up.

- **Neglected:** Your family's focus may be changing. Find a time to tell your parents how you feel and what you think may help. Remember that you are important and loved and that you deserve to feel that way, even though you might not get as much attention now.

- **Lonely:** Try to remember that these feelings won't last forever.

- **Embarrassed:** Many teens who felt embarrassed about having a family member with cancer say it gets easier to deal with over time.

- **Guilty:** You might feel bad about having fun when your sibling or parent is sick. This shows how much you care about them. However, having fun doesn't mean that you care any less. It's both okay and important for you to do things that make you happy.

Some teens try to be perfect and not cause trouble. They want to protect their parents and not give them one more thing to worry about. If you feel this way, remember that no one can be perfect all the time. You need time to vent, to feel sad, and to be happy. Other teens may get the wrong kind of attention from the wrong people – which ends up hurting them and their family in the long run.

Try to let your parents, or other trusted adult, know how you feel. It is probably hard to imagine right now, but, if you let yourself, you can grow stronger as a person through this experience. Some teens have found that having a family member with cancer changes the way they look at life. Some said this experience helped them to become stronger and more appreciative, over time.

These tips can help you cope during this difficult situation:

- Write down your thoughts in a journal. Research has found this really works!

- Join a support group to meet other kids who are facing some of the same things you are. Who knows, you might get some good advice.

- Find a friend who's a really good listener and who cares about you. Talk with a teacher at school. Meet with a counsellor either in or out of school.

Managing Stress

You may be so focused on your family member with cancer that you don't think about your own needs, or if you do, they don't seem important. But, they are! It's important to "stay fit"; both inside and out.

These tips have helped others deal with stress. Pick one or two things to do each week:

- **Stay connected.** Stay involved with sports, clubs, or other activities you enjoy.

- **Relax and get enough sleep.** Take breaks. You will have more energy and be in a better frame of mind. Get at least 8 hours of sleep. Pray or meditate. Make or listen to music.

- **Help others.** Join a walk against cancer. Plan a charity event to collect money.

- **Avoid risky behaviors.** Stay away from smoking, drinking, and other risky behaviors.

- **Put your creative side to work.** Keep a journal to write down your thoughts and experiences. Draw, paint, or take photographs. Read about people who have made it through tough times. Get inspired by what they achieved and who they became.

- **Eat and drink well.** Drink plenty of water each day. Grab fresh fruit, whole-grain breads, and lean meats like chicken or turkey when you have a choice. Avoid foods that have a lot of sugar.

- **Be active.** Exercise can make you feel better. Play a sport or walk to improve your mood.

It's normal to feel sad or "blue" during difficult times. However, if these feelings last for 2 weeks or more and you no long enjoy things you used to love, you may be depressed.

Learning What to Expect

Learning about cancer and how it's treated can help you prepare for the days ahead. This may help you to feel less anxious. Some of what you have seen or heard about cancer may not apply to your family member. Keep in mind that cancer is a group of related diseases – not just one disease. Doctors have found more than 100 different types of cancer. Each has different treatments and different outcomes.

You and Your Family

Your family may be going through many changes. You may be the oldest, youngest, or middle child in your family. You may live with one parent or two. Whatever your family situation, chances are things have changed since your sibling or parent, was diagnosed with cancer. You may be asked to take on more responsibility. You might resent it at first. Then again, you may learn a lot from the experience and grow to appreciate the trust your parents have in you.

Do any of these sound familiar?

- Are you doing more chores?

- Are you home alone more?

- Are you spending more time with relatives?

- Are you spending more time making dinner or doing laundry?

- Do you want to hang out with friends when you are needed at home?

- Do you try to protect your parents from anything that might worry them?

Changing Routines and Responsibilities

Whatever your family situation – chances are that things have changed since your sibling or parent got sick. Let your parents know if you feel that there is more to do than you can handle. Together, you can work it out. Teens who said that their families grew closer say that it happened because people in their family:

- Tried to put themselves in the other person's position and thought about how they would feel if they were the other person

- Understood that even though people react differently to situations, they were all hurting. Some cried a lot. Others showed little emotion. Some used humor to get by.

- Learned to respect and talk about differences. The more they asked about how others were feeling, the more they could help each other.

Staying Connected

Families say that it helps to make time to talk together, even if it's only for a short time each week. Talking can help your family stay connected and sort things out. Some teens want to know a lot, while others only want to know a little. Tell your parents how much you want to know.

- Expect your parents to feel some stress, just as you do. Your parent may not always do or say the right thing. Show your sick parent or sibling that you care. Maybe he or she is sick or very tired. Or maybe he or she feels okay and wants your company.

- Help your siblings. If you are the oldest child, your younger siblings may look to you for support. It's okay to let them know that you are having a tough time, too. If you are looking to your older sibling for help, tell them how you feel. They can help, but may not have all the answers.

Helping Your Parent or Sibling Who Has Cancer

Just like everyone else, the person in your family who has cancer may be worried, scared, or confused. They may also feel tired and sick because of the treatment. You may both have many of the same feelings. Knowing how another person is feeling can help you figure out how to help them, or at least understand where they are coming from.

People with cancer may feel afraid. Depending on how your sibling or parent reacts to tough situations they may be more or less afraid. Others may feel sad. People with cancer sometimes cannot do things they used to do. They may miss certain activities and friends. Cancer and treatment side effects can sometimes cause a person to be mad or grumpy. Chances are your family member is angry at the disease, not at you. Many people with cancer are hopeful. Ways to help a family member who has cancer include:

- **Hang out together.** Watch a movie, television show, or read together. Decorate their bedroom. Say, "I love you." Just be with them.

- **Help your brother or sister stay in touch with friends.** Encourage your sibling's friends to text notes or send pictures. Help your sibling to stay connected with their friends.

- **Keep your parent in the loop.** Tell your parent about your day. Ask your parent how his or her day was.

- **Share a laugh.** You have probably heard that laughter is good medicine. Watch a comedy or tell jokes together.

- **Talk about your family.** Look through pictures. Talk about what you're both most proud of, your best memories, and how you both have met challenges.

- **Try to be upbeat, but be "real," too.** Being positive can be good for you and your whole family. But don't feel like you have to act cheerful all the time if that's not how you really feel.

- **Keep a journal together.** Take turns writing in a journal with people in your family. This can help you share your thoughts when it might be hard to talk about them.

You and Your Friends

Your friends are important to you, and you are important to them. In the past, you could tell them everything. Now, it may seem like a lot of things are changing - even your friendships. It may be hard to talk with your friends. But when someone in your family is sick, you really need friends you can talk with. Here are some things to think about:

- **Friends may not know what to say.** It's hard for some friends, even those who care, to know what to say. They may be afraid of upsetting you. You may need to take the first step.

- **Friends may not understand.** It may feel like your friends don't care anymore. It might seem as though their lives are moving on and yours is not. It can be hard to watch them. Since they aren't facing the situation you are right now, it may be hard for them to relate.

- **Friends – old and new.** You may not have as much in common with some friends as you used to. However you may also make new friends through this experience. Kids you used to just pass you in the halls may now ask how you're doing. Be open to new friendships – perhaps through a support group. Support groups can help connect you with other teens who are going through some of the same things that you are.

Finding Support

Don't be shy about asking for help. When faced with tough situations, we all need support from others. It may not be easy to reach out to others, but if you do you will find that there are people who can help. You may want to start with your parent, or a trusted adult such as a teacher or coach.

Tips for Talking with Your Parents

You may or may not have a great relationship with your parents. It may or may not be easy to talk with them. But, you and your parents really can help each other. These steps can help:

- **Prepare before you talk.** Think about what you want to say and about some solutions to the problem. Think about how your parents might react. How will you respond to them?

- **Suggest a place.** Whether it's in your room, on the front steps, or while taking a walk – find a place that feels comfortable.

- **Take things slowly.** Don't expect to solve everything right away. Difficult problems often don't have quick and easy solutions. Some conversations will go better than others.

- **Keep it up.** Don't think you have to have just one big conversation. Have many small ones. Make time to talk a little each day if you can, even if it's just for a few minutes.

Tips for Asking Others for Help

You and your family need support from others. It can be hard to ask. Yet most of the time people really want to help, so don't hesitate to ask. Help your family to make a plan that considers:

- **People who may be able to help:** Grandparents, aunts, uncles, family friends, neighbors, teachers, coaches, people in your religious community, school nurses, and guidance counsellors are all people you can ask for help.

- **Ways people can help:** People can help by giving rides to school or sports events, helping with homework, or giving your family practical help – such as grocery shopping, making meals, or mowing the lawn.

Make a list with your parents of what needs to get done. Talk about people who might be able to help. Keep the list by the phone. When people ask what they can do, pull out the list. Ask about websites you can use to get practical support from people who care and can help.

Tips for Joining a Support Group

A good way to connect with others who are going through similar things is a support group. Some groups meet in person. Others meet online. At first, this may not sound like something you want to do. Other teens have thought the same thing, until they went to a support group meeting. They were often surprised that so many others felt the same way they did and had helpful advice. Many support groups meet online these days.

Tips for Meeting with a Counsellor

Sometimes talking to friends and your parents may not be enough. When you are having a hard time, it may help to talk with a counsellor. Going to a counsellor means you have the courage to recognize that you are going through a tough time and need some help. Teens who have talked with a counsellor say it helped to talk with someone outside their circle of friends and family who didn't take sides, who they could trust.

The Road Ahead

It can be hard to stay calm when you aren't sure what the future holds. You may be thinking – will my sibling or parent live? Will the cancer come back? Will life ever be the same?

While no one can know the future, there are things you can do to make your life a little easier:

- **Keep talking and pulling together as a family.** You may find that cancer has drawn you closer together and made you appreciate each other more.

- **Discover your own needs.** Don't let others tell you how you should feel. Allow yourself to cope at your own pace and in your own way.

- **You are growing as a person.** Many teens say that having a family member with cancer has made them more sympathetic, more responsible, and stronger.

- **Accept people's help.** Right now you may feel lonelier than you ever have in your life. But you are not alone. Many people are there to lend a helping hand. Accept their help.

- **Appreciate each day.** Many teens who have a family member with cancer say that they learned to see the world more clearly. In time you may come to appreciate things you once took for granted. Take some time to write your thoughts down, even if they seem small.

After Treatment

After treatment, you and your family may feel a whole range of emotions. Part of you is glad it is over. Another part of you may miss the freedom or new responsibilities you had. You may be afraid the cancer will come back. You may look to find more meaning in your life now. All these feelings are normal.

Getting back to a more carefree life may take a long time - or it may not happen as you expect.

If Treatment Doesn't Help

If treatment does not help your sibling or parent – you and your family will face even more challenges. You may feel many of the same emotions you felt when you first learned that your family member had cancer.

When the future is uncertain, teens say that it helps to:

- **Make the most of the time you have.** Do special things as a family. Call and visit as much as you can if they are in the hospital. Write notes and draw pictures. If possible, have some special times together. Let your family member know how much you love them.

- **Stay on track.** When people get bad news, they often feel like they are living outside of themselves – that life is moving along without them. Keep a schedule and stay involved in things that matter to you.

- **Have hope.** Never stop believing in tomorrow. Don't be too hard on yourself. There is more good than bad in this world - even though you might not feel that way right now.

- **Get help when you feel alone.** Make sure you find people who can help you. In addition to your family, it may help to talk to a social worker, counsellor, or people in a support group. It's important to get your feelings out.

If Your Loved One Passes Away

- **You will always have memories**. Your sibling or parent will always be part of your life. Hold on to your memories. It's okay to think about something funny that he or she did or said. By smiling you are bringing back just a little of what was so special about them.

- **The pain will lessen with time.** At first, the pain may be so strong that you might wonder whether you will ever feel happy again. Time has a way of healing. And when you find yourself not being sad every day – it doesn't mean that you have forgotten. It just means you are starting to heal.

- **Everyone grieves in his or her own way.** Some teens grieve by crying. Others get quiet and spend time by themselves. Some find that they need to be around friends and talk. Others get angry. Most people find it helps to keep a regular routine. There is no right or wrong way to grieve. It's okay to deal with loss at your own pace.

- **Life will change.** Stay open to new experiences. Make small changes that give your life new meaning. Write down what you are feeling. It won't be the same, but it can be rich and full again. Keep believing this.

Facing cancer in your family is probably the toughest thing you've ever had to do. It will change your life. But you will get through it. Why? Because you are strong, and you are capable - even if you don't always feel that way.

Learning More

It is great that you want to learn more. Make sure that what you read is accurate. You can get information from your school, the public library, or the patient education office at the hospital. Keep in mind that you may also find a lot of cancer-related information online. Some of what you find might not be accurate. Check with your parent or another trusted adult to learn if what you found applies to your family member.

If you are a teen, and your parent or sibling has cancer, it's normal to feel a range of emotions. It may be hard to share your feelings, but talking with your friends and family can help.

Chapter 62

Cancer Support Groups and Caregivers

Cancer support groups are meetings for people with cancer and those touched by the disease. They can have many benefits. Even though a lot of people receive support from friends and family, the number one reason they join a support group is to be with others with similar cancer experiences. Some research shows that joining a support group improves both quality of life and survival.

Support groups can:

- Help you feel better, more hopeful, and not so alone

- Give you a chance to talk about your feelings and work through them

- Help you deal with practical problems, such as problems at work or school

- Help you cope with side effects of treatment

Types of Support Groups

Some groups focus on all kinds of cancer. Others talk about just one kind, such as a group for women with breast cancer or one for men

Text in this chapter is excerpted from "Cancer Support Groups," National Cancer Institute (NCI), December 2, 2014; and text from "Caregivers for Cancer Patients and Survivors," Centers for Disease Control and Prevention (CDC), November 3, 2013.

with prostate cancer. Some can be open to everyone or just for people of a certain age, sex, culture, or religion. For instance, some groups are just for teens or young children.

Support groups can also be helpful for children or family members. These groups focus on family concerns such as role changes, relationship changes, financial worries, and how to support the person with cancer. Some groups include both cancer survivors and family members.

Telephone support groups are when everyone dials in to a phone line that is linked together, like a conference call. They can share and talk to others with similar experiences from all over the country. There is usually little or no charge.

Online support groups are "meetings" that take place online. People meet through chat rooms, listservs, or moderated discussion groups and talk with each other over email. People often like online support groups because they can take part in them any time of the day or night. They're also good for people who can't travel to meetings. But always talk with your doctor about cancer information you learn from the Internet.

Where to Find a Support Group

Many hospitals, cancer centers, community groups, and schools offer cancer support groups. Here are some ways to find groups near you:

- Call your local hospital and ask about its cancer support programs.

- Ask your social worker to suggest groups.

- Do an online search for groups.

Is a Support Group Right for Me?

A support group may not be right for everyone. For some people, hearing about others' problems can make them feel worse. Or you may find that your need for a support group changes over time.

If you have a choice of support groups, visit a few and see what they are like. See which ones make sense for you. Although many groups are free, some charge a small fee. Find out if your health insurance pays for support groups.

If you're thinking about joining a support group, here are some questions you may want to ask the group's contact person:

- How large is the group?

- Who attends (survivors, family members, types of cancer, age range)?

- How long are the meetings?

- How often does the group meet?

- How long has the group been together?

- Who leads the meetings - a professional or a survivor?

- What is the format of the meetings?

- Is the main purpose to share feelings, or do people also offer tips to solve common problems?

- If I go, can I just sit and listen?

- Before joining a group, here are questions you may want to ask yourself:

- Am I comfortable talking about personal issues?

- Do I have something to offer to the group?

- What do I hope to gain by joining a group?

Support groups vary greatly, and if you have one bad experience, it doesn't mean these groups aren't a good option for you. You may also want to find another cancer survivor with whom you can discuss your cancer experience. Many organizations can pair you with someone who had your type of cancer and is close to your age and background.

Caregivers for Cancer Patients and Survivors

Although the rate of people who get cancer is decreasing, the overall number of people who have cancer is going up. The number of people who are 65 years old or older is expected to grow to 71 million by 2030—twice the number of people in this age group in 2000. Also, people are living longer after being told they have cancer, due to improvements in finding cancer early and better cancer treatments.

People who have cancer often live at home, and get help from informal caregivers—people who help them without being paid. Informal caregivers are usually the cancer patient's spouse, family members, friends, or neighbors. Researchers are studying what informal caregivers do and the problems and benefits of caregiving, so they can suggest ways in which caregivers can be supported.

Although the rate of people who get cancer is decreasing, the overall number of people who have cancer is going up. The number of people who are 65 years old or older is expected to grow to 71 million by 2030—twice the number of people in this age group in 2000. Also, people are living longer after being told they have cancer, due to improvements in finding cancer early and better cancer treatments.1

People who have cancer often live at home, and get help from informal caregivers—people who help them without being paid. Informal caregivers are usually the cancer patient's spouse, family members, friends, or neighbors. Researchers are studying what informal caregivers do and the problems and benefits of caregiving, so they can suggest ways in which caregivers can be supported.

Who Are Informal Caregivers?

While the most common type of informal caregiving relationship is an adult child caring for an elderly parent, other common informal caregiving relationships include parents or grandparents caring for a child with cancer, a spouse caring for a spouse, or a neighbor, close friend, or members of the same house of worship caring for the cancer patient.

The cancer patient may also receive care from a formal caregiver a trained person who is paid to provide care, such as a nurse, therapist, social worker, or home health aide. Formal caregivers usually work for home care agencies, community or social service agencies, or for-profit providers.

What Do Informal Caregivers Do?

The types of care that informal caregivers provide ranges from simple, occasional tasks like driving the cancer patient to the doctor, to full-time care. The demands on caregivers often change over time. Some of the types of help caregivers provide include

- Cooking, cleaning, and other household chores.
- Running errands such as buying groceries and getting prescriptions filled.

- Helping the cancer patient bathe, get dressed, use the bathroom, eat, and take medicine.

- Paying bills and filing insurance claims.

- Providing encouragement and support to the patient, and helping him or her stay in touch with friends and family members.

- Telling the doctor if the patient gets worse or has side effects from treatment.

What Problems Do Informal Caregivers Experience?

Many people get a sense of personal fulfillment from taking care of a loved one who has cancer. But informal caregivers usually face physical, emotional, and financial problems that vary according to the amount and kind of care the patient needs.

Physical problems. Many caregivers develop physical problems from stress and not taking care of themselves. Stress can cause aches and pains, sleep problems, and appetite changes. About half of caregivers often don't get enough restful, continuous sleep, making them feel tired. Caregivers often don't have the time and energy to prepare proper meals and exercise, and they may skip doctor's appointments.

Emotional problems. Depression is common among caregivers. They may also feel lonely if the demands of caring for their loved one leave them little time to spend visiting friends and family, and if they have to quit their jobs. Caregiver stress can lead to feelings of anxiety, frustration, anger, and guilt. These problems increase as the time spent with the patient and the intensity of care increases. Stress is higher among caregivers who feel they have no choice but to take care of the patient.

Financial problems. Caregiving can create immediate and long-term financial problems for caregivers. Many caregivers give money to the patient—$200 per month on average—and spend an average of $5,531 per year out-of-pocket on expenses related to caregiving. At the same time, caregivers frequently are forced to reduce their work hours or quit their job entirely to care for their loved one, reducing their retirement savings and Social Security benefits, and often losing their health insurance.

What Can Be Done to Help Caregivers?

Caregiver assessment. A caregiver assessment is a systematic process of gathering information to describe a caregiving situation. It identifies the particular problems, needs, resources, and strengths of the family caregiver and approaches issues from the caregiver's perspective and culture to help the caregiver maintain her or his health and well-being.

Based on the caregiver assessment, health care professionals can inform the caregiver about community resources, professional services, and state and federal agencies that may help. The health care professional also can make sure the caregiver is educated about the patient's condition and trained to give medications and use medical devices properly.

Chapter 63

Survivorship

There are millions of people in the United States who are cancer survivors. Many say that they felt they had lots of support during their treatment, but once it ended, it was hard to make a transition to a new way of life. It was like entering a whole new world where they had to adjust to new feelings, new problems and different ways of looking at the world.

A New Normal

The end of cancer treatment is often a time to rejoice. Most likely you're relieved to be finished with the demands of treatment. You may be ready to put the experience behind you and have life return to the way it used to be. Yet at the same time, you may feel sad and worried. It can take time to recover. And it's very common to be thinking about whether the cancer will come back and what happens now. Often this time is called adjusting to a "new normal." You will have many different feelings during this time.

One of the hardest things after treatment is not knowing what happens next. Those who have gone through cancer treatment describe the first few months as a time of change. It's not so much "getting back to normal" as it is finding out what's normal for you

Text in this chapter is excerpted from "Survivorship," National Cancer Institute (NCI), December 2, 2014.

now. People often say that life has new meaning or that they look at things differently.

Your new normal may include:

- Making changes in the way you eat and the things you do

- New or different sources of support

- Permanent scars on your body

- Not be able to do some things you used to do more easily

- Emotional scars from going through so much

You may see yourself in a different way, or find that others think of you differently now. Whatever your new normal may be, give yourself time to adapt to the changes. Take it one day at a time.

Coping with Fear of Recurrence

It's normal to worry that your cancer will come back. Almost all cancer survivors have this fear, so you are not alone. It's common for people to feel a lack of control over their lives or have trouble trusting their bodies. Every ache or pain brings up the fear that the cancer is back. Some tips on how to cope with this are:

- **Be informed.** Understand what you can do for your health now, and find out about the services available to you. Doing this can give you a greater sense of control. Some studies even suggest that people who are well-informed about their cancer are more likely to recover more quickly than those who are not.

- **Be open and talk to your health care team about your fears.** They can assure you that they're looking out for you and help you feel less worried.

- **Express your feelings of fear, anger, or sadness.** People have found that when they express strong feelings like anger or sadness, they're more able to let go of them.

- **Look for the positive.** Sometimes this means looking for the good even in a bad time or trying to be hopeful instead of thinking the worst. Try to use your energy to focus on wellness and what you can do now to stay as healthy as possible.

- **Find ways to help yourself relax.** Relaxation exercises have been proven to help others and may help you relax when you feel worried.

- **Be as active as you can.** Getting out of the house can help you focus on other things besides cancer and the worries it brings.

- **Focus on what you can control.** Being involved in your health care, keeping your appointments, and making changes in your lifestyle are some of the things you can control. Even setting a daily schedule can help. And while no one can control every thought, some say that they try not to dwell on the fearful ones.

For some it can be hard to let go of the fear and lack of trust your body. If your fears of recurrence seem overwhelming, talk to a counsellor. He or she may be able to help you reduce your anxiety and calm your fears.

Getting Follow-Up Medical Care

All cancer survivors should have follow-up care. Follow-up care means seeing a doctor for regular medical check-ups once you're finished with treatment. It's important to look for any changes in your health or any problems that may occur due to cancer treatment. These check-ups are also a time to check for physical and emotional effects that may develop months or years after treatment ends.

Knowing what to expect after cancer treatment can help you and your family make plans, lifestyle changes, and important decisions about the future. Common questions you may have are:

- What symptoms should I tell the doctor about?

- Which doctors should I see after treatment?

- How often should I see my doctor?

- What tests do I need?

- What can be done to relieve pain, fatigue, or other problems after treatment?

- How long will it take for me to recover and feel more like myself?

- Is there anything I can do to keep the cancer from coming back?

- Will I have trouble with health insurance?

- Are there any support groups I can go to?

Coping with these issues can be a challenge. Yet many say that getting involved in decisions about their medical care and lifestyle was a good way for them to regain some of the control they felt they lost during cancer treatment. Being an active partner with your doctor and getting help from other members of your health care team is the first step.

Your Follow-Up Care Plan

Once you're done with cancer treatment, you should receive a follow-up cancer care plan from your doctor. The National Cancer Institute and other cancer organizations recommend this document for people who have finished treatment. The details of your plan will depend on the type of cancer and type of treatment you had, along with your overall health. It is usually different for each person. In general, survivors return to the doctor every 3 to 4 months at first, and once or twice a year after that. At these visits, your doctor may give you a physical exam along with blood tests and other follow-up tests that are necessary.

For follow-up care, you may see the same doctor who treated you for cancer. Or you may decide to go to your primary care doctor. This is something you can discuss with your health care team. Your oncologist should give you a written summary of your treatment. Keep this with you to share with your primary care doctor and any other doctors you see. Many people keep this along with their medical records in a binder or folder. This way, key facts about your treatment will always be in the same place. Types of health information to include may be:

- The date you were diagnosed
- The type of cancer you had
- Pathology report(s) that describe the type and stage of cancer in detail
- Places and dates of specific treatment, such as:
  - Details of all surgeries
  - Sites and total amounts of radiation therapy
  - Names and doses of chemotherapy and all other drugs
  - Key lab reports, x-ray reports, CT scans, and MRI reports
- List of signs to watch for and possible long-term effects of treatment
- Contact information for all health professionals involved in your treatment and follow-up care
- Any problems that occurred during or after treatment

- Information about supportive care you received (such as special medicines, emotional support, and nutritional supplements)

When you meet with your doctor about follow-up care, it's important to talk openly about any physical or emotional problems you're having. Always mention any symptoms or concerns that are new to you or that won't go away. And keep in mind, just because you have certain symptoms, it doesn't always mean the cancer has come back. Symptoms can be due to other problems that still need to be addressed. Questions about your follow-up care should include:

- How often should I see the doctor?

- What follow-up tests should be done? How often?

- Are there symptoms I should watch out for?

- If I develop any of the symptoms, whom should I call?

You might find it helpful to write these questions down. When you meet with the doctor, you can take notes or record your talks to refer to later.

Getting a Wellness Plan

After cancer treatment, many survivors want to find ways to reduce the chances of their cancer coming back. Some worry that the way they eat, the stress in their lives, or their exposure to chemicals may put them at risk. Cancer survivors find that this is a time when they take a good look at how they take care of themselves. This is an important start to living a healthier life.

Ask your doctor about developing a survivorship care plan that includes ways you can take care of your physical, emotional, social, and spiritual needs. As with the follow-up cancer care plan, the National Cancer Institute and other cancer organizations recommend this document for people who have finished treatment.

If you find that it's hard to talk with your doctor about these wellness issues, it may be helpful to know that the more you do it, the easier it becomes. Your doctor may also suggest other members of the health care team for you to talk with, such as a social worker, nutritionist, clergy member, or nurse.

Guidelines for a Healthy Lifestyle

- **Quit smoking.** Research shows that smoking can increase the chances of getting cancer at the same or a different site.

- **Cut down on how much alcohol you drink.** Research shows that drinking alcohol increases your chances of getting certain types of cancers.

- **Maintain a healthy weight.** Eating well and staying active can help you reach a healthy weight and stay there.

- **Eat well.** Healthy food choices may help reduce the risk of cancer or recurrence. Talk with your doctor or a dietitian to find out about any special dietary needs that you may have. The American Cancer Society and the American Institute for Cancer Research have developed similar diet and fitness guidelines that may help reduce the risk of cancer:

  - Eat a plant-based diet that includes at least 5-9 servings of fruit and vegetables daily. Try to include beans in your diet, and eat whole grains (such as cereals, breads, and pasta) several times daily.

  - Choose foods low in fat and salt.

- **Exercise and stay active.** Research suggests that staying active after cancer can help lower the risk of recurrence and lead to longer survival. Moderate exercise (walking, biking, swimming) for about 30 minutes every—or almost every—day can:

  - Reduce anxiety and depression

  - Improve mood and boost self-esteem

  - Reduce fatigue, nausea, pain, and diarrhea

It is important to start an exercise program slowly and increase activity over time. Work with your doctor or a specialist (such as a physical therapist) if needed. If you need to stay in bed during your recovery, even doing small activities can help. Stretching or moving your arms or legs can help you stay flexible, relieve muscle tension, and help you feel better. Some people may need to take special care in exercising. Talk with your doctor before you begin any exercise program.

Physical Changes

Some have described survivorship as being "disease-free, but not free of your disease." What you experience with your body may be related to the type of cancer you had and the treatment you received. You may find that you're still coping with the effects of treatment on your body. It can take time to get over these effects.

It's important to remember that no two people are alike. You may experience changes that are very different from someone else's, even if that person had the same type of cancer and treatment

Some of the most common problems that people report are:

- Fatigue

- Memory or concentration problems

- Pain

- Nervous system changes (neuropathy)

- Lymphedema (swelling)

- Mouth or throat problems

- Changes in weight and eating habits

- Bladder or bowel control problems

- Menopause symptoms

Many of these changes can be controlled. Talk to your doctor at the first sign of any problems you have.

Late Effects of Cancer Treatment

Cancer treatment can also cause side effects that may not show up for months or years after cancer treatment. These are called long-term side effects or late effects. Chemotherapy, radiation, and certain cancer drugs may cause problems with the:

- Heart

- Lungs

- Endocrine system (hormones)

- Bone loss

- Hearing loss

- Teeth and gums

- Eyes

Long term side effects are very specific to certain types of treatments and the amount received. Therefore, many survivors won't have them. Your doctor should talk to you about long term effects when you discuss your follow-up care.

Family Issues after Treatment

When treatment ends, families are often unprepared for the fact that recovery takes time. In general, your recovery will take much longer than your treatment did. Survivors often say that they didn't realize how much time they needed to recover. This can lead to disappointment, worry, and frustration for everyone.

Families also may not realize that the way their family works may have changed permanently as a result of cancer. They may need help dealing with the changes and keeping the "new" family strong.

Some survivors say they would not have been able to cope without the help and love of their family members. And even though treatment has ended, they still receive a lot of support. For other families, problems that were present before the cancer diagnosis may still exist, or new ones may develop. You may receive less support than you had hoped.

Common problems with loved ones:

- **People expect you to do what you did before your cancer.** For instance, if you used to take care of the house or yard before your treatment, you may find that these jobs are still too much for you to handle. Yet family members who took over for you may want life to go back to normal. They may expect you to do what you used to do around the house.

- **You may expect more from your family than you receive.** They may disappoint you, which might make you angry or frustrated. For example you may get less attention and concern than you did during treatment.

- **You may still need to depend on others during this time.** Even though you want to get back to the role you had in your family before, it may take a while to get into a routine.

At the same time you're going through these things, your family is still adjusting too. It may be hard for all of you to express feelings or know how to talk about your cancer.

Getting Help with Family Issues

After treatment, you may want to consider getting help from someone to help you and your family adjust. Ask your doctor or social worker to refer you to a counselor. An expert on family roles and concerns after cancer treatment may help your family work on your problems.

How do you cope with family issues? Here are some ideas that have helped others deal with family concerns:

- **Let others know what you're able to do as you heal – and what not to expect.** For example, don't feel like you have to keep the house or yard in perfect order because you always did in the past.

- **Know that this is a new time in your life so it may take time to adjust.** Roles in the family may change again and different emotions may get triggered. This is normal.

Give yourself time. You and your family will be able to adjust over time to the changes cancer brings. Just being open with each other can help ensure that each person's needs are met. Good communication is still very important.

Talking with Children and Teens

Help the children in your family understand that it may take a while for you to have the energy you used to have now that you are finished with treatment. Be open about what you can and can't do.

You don't have to tell your kids about every check-up or every symptom that occurs. But do tell them if you still have side effects that make certain things hard for you to do. If you're not able to do an activity or go to an event, the children may think that you're unhappy or mad at them.

Children of cancer survivors have said that these things are important once their parent has finished treatment. That you:

- Be honest with them

- Speak as directly and openly as possible

- Keep them informed about your cancer and involved in your recovery

- Spend extra time with them

With your permission, other family members should also be open with your children about your cancer and its treatment.

As hard as treatment is, many cancer survivors say that the experience led them to make important changes in their lives. It helped them learn the value of being grateful for each day and for the people in their lives.

Part Eight

Clinical Trials and Cancer Research

Chapter 64

Clinical Trials – The Basics

What Are Clinical Trials and Why Do People Participate?

Clinical trials are part of clinical research and at the heart of all medical advances. Clinical trials look at new ways to prevent, detect, or treat disease. Treatments might be new drugs or new combinations of drugs, new surgical procedures or devices, or new ways to use existing treatments. The goal of clinical trials is to determine if a new test or treatment works and is safe. Clinical trials can also look at other aspects of care, such as improving the quality of life for people with chronic illnesses.

People participate in clinical trials for a variety of reasons. Healthy volunteers say they participate to help others and to contribute to moving science forward. Participants with an illness or disease also participate to help others, but also to possibly receive the newest treatment and to have the additional care and attention from the clinical trial staff. Clinical trials offer hope for many people and an opportunity to help researchers find better treatments for others in the future.

What Is Clinical Research?

Clinical research is medical research that involves people like you. People volunteer to participate in carefully conducted investigations that ultimately uncover better ways to treat, prevent, diagnose, and understand human disease. Clinical research includes trials that test

Text in this chapter is excerpted from "Clinical Research Trials and You," National Institutes of Health (NIH), June 12, 2015.

new treatments and therapies as well as long-term natural history studies, which provide valuable information about how disease and health progress.

The idea

The idea for a clinical research study—also known as a clinical trial—often originates in the laboratory. After researchers test new therapies or procedures in the laboratory and in animal studies, the most promising experimental treatments are moved into clinical trials, which are conducted in phases. During a trial, more information is gained about an experimental treatment, its risks, and its effectiveness.

The protocol

Clinical research is conducted according to a plan known as a protocol. The protocol is carefully designed to safeguard the participants' health and answer specific research questions. A protocol describes the following:

- Who is eligible to participate in the trial

- Details about tests, procedures, medications, and dosages

- The length of the study and what information will be gathered

A clinical study is led by a principal investigator (PI), who is often a doctor. Members of the research team regularly monitor the participants' health to determine the study's safety and effectiveness.

Institutional Review Board (IRB) review

Most, but not all, clinical trials in the United States are approved and monitored by an Institutional Review Board (IRB) in order to ensure that the risks are minimal and are worth any potential benefits. An IRB is an independent committee that consists of physicians, statisticians, and members of the community who ensure that clinical trials are ethical and that the rights of participants are protected. Potential research participants should ask the sponsor or research coordinator whether the research they are considering participating in was reviewed by an IRB.

Sponsors

Clinical trials are sponsored or funded by various organizations or individuals, including physicians, foundations, medical institutions, voluntary groups, and pharmaceutical companies, as well as federal agencies such as the National Institutes of Health and the Department of Veterans Affairs.

Informed consent

Informed consent is the process of providing potential participants with the key facts about a clinical trial before they decide whether to participate. The process of informed consent (providing additional information) continues throughout the study. To help someone decide whether or not to participate, members of the research team explain the details of the study. Translation or interpretive assistance can be provided for participants with limited English proficiency. The research team provides an informed consent document that includes details about the study, such as its purpose, duration, required procedures, and who to contact for further information. The informed consent document also explains risks and potential benefits. The participant then decides whether to sign the document. Informed consent is not a contract. Volunteers are free to withdraw from the study completely or to refuse particular treatments or tests at any time. Sometimes, however, this will make them ineligible to continue the study.

Types of clinical trials

There are different types of clinical trials.

- **Natural history studies** provide valuable information about how disease and health progress.

- **Prevention trials** look for better ways to prevent a disease in people who have never had the disease or to prevent the disease from returning. Better approaches may include medicines, vaccines, or lifestyle changes, among other things.

- **Screening trials** test the best way to detect certain diseases or health conditions.

- **Diagnostic trials** determine better tests or procedures for diagnosing a particular disease or condition.

- **Treatment trials** test new treatments, new combinations of drugs, or new approaches to surgery or radiation therapy.

- **Quality of life trials** (or supportive care trials) explore and measure ways to improve the comfort and quality of life of people with a chronic illness.

Phases of clinical trials

Clinical trials are conducted in "phases." Each phase has a different purpose and helps researchers answer different questions.

- **Phase I trials:** Researchers test an experimental drug or treatment in a small group of people (20–80) for the first time. The purpose is to evaluate its safety and identify side effects.

- **Phase II trials:** The experimental drug or treatment is administered to a larger group of people (100–300) to determine its effectiveness and to further evaluate its safety.

- **Phase III trials:** The experimental drug or treatment is administered to large groups of people (1,000–3,000) to confirm its effectiveness, monitor side effects, compare it with standard or equivalent treatments, and collect information that will allow the experimental drug or treatment to be used safely.

- **Phase IV trials:** After a drug is approved by the FDA and made available to the public, researchers track its safety, seeking more information about a drug or treatment's risks, benefits, and optimal use.

Some concepts to understand

Typically, clinical trials compare a new product or therapy with another that already exists to determine if the new one is as successful as, or better than, the existing one. In some studies, participants may be assigned to receive a **placebo** (an inactive product that resembles the test product, but without its treatment value).

Comparing a new product with a placebo can be the fastest and most reliable way to demonstrate the new product's therapeutic effectiveness. However, placebos are not used if a patient would be put at risk — particularly in the study of treatments for serious illnesses — by not having effective therapy. Most of these studies compare new products with an approved therapy. Potential participants are told if placebos will be used in the study before they enter a trial.

Randomization is the process by which two or more alternative treatments are assigned to volunteers by chance rather than by choice. This is done to avoid any bias with investigators assigning volunteers to one group or another. The results of each treatment are compared at specific points during a trial, which may last for years. When one treatment is found superior, the trial is stopped so that the fewest volunteers receive the less beneficial treatment.

In **single-blind** or **double-blind studies**, also called single-masked or double-masked studies, the participants do not know which medicine is being used, so they can describe what happens without bias. "Blind" (or "masked") studies are designed to prevent members of the research team or study participants from influencing the results. This allows scientifically accurate conclusions. In single-blind ("single-masked") studies, only the patient is not told what is being administered. In a double-blind study, only the pharmacist knows; members of the research team are not told which patients are getting which medication, so that their observations will not be biased. If medically necessary, however, it is always possible to find out what the patient is taking.

Who Participates in Clinical Trials?

Many different types of people participate in clinical trials. Some are healthy, while others may have illnesses. A **healthy volunteer** is a person with no known significant health problems who participates in clinical research to test a new drug, device, or intervention. Research procedures with healthy volunteers are designed to develop new knowledge, not to provide direct benefit to study participants. Healthy volunteers have always played an important role in research.

Healthy volunteers are needed for several reasons. When developing a new technique, such as a blood test or imaging device, healthy volunteers (formerly called "normal volunteers") help define the limits of "normal." These volunteers serve as controls for patient groups and are often matched to patients on characteristics such as age, gender, or family relationship. They receive the same test, procedure, or drug the patient group receives. Investigators learn about the disease process by comparing the patient group to the healthy volunteers.

Factors like how much of your time is needed, discomfort you may feel, or risk involved depends on the trial. While some require minimal amounts of time and effort, other studies may require a major commitment in time and effort on behalf of the volunteer, and may involve some discomfort. The research procedure may also carry some risk. The consent process for healthy volunteers includes a detailed discussion of the study's procedures and tests.

A **patient volunteer** has a known health problem and participates in research to better understand, diagnose, treat, or cure that disease or condition. Research procedures with a patient volunteer help develop new knowledge. These procedures may or may not benefit the study participants.

Patient volunteers may be involved in studies similar to those in which healthy volunteers participate. These studies involve drugs, devices, or interventions designed to prevent, treat, or cure disease. Although these studies may provide direct benefit to patient volunteers, the main aim is to prove, by scientific means, the effects and limitations of the experimental treatment. Consequently, some patients serve as controls by not taking the test drug, or by receiving test doses of the drug large enough only to show that it is present, but not at a level that can treat the condition. A study's benefits may be indirect for the volunteers but may help others.

All clinical trials have guidelines about who can participate, called **Inclusion/Exclusion Criteria**. Factors that allow someone to participate in a clinical trial are "inclusion criteria." Those that exclude or not allow participation are "exclusion criteria." These criteria are based on factors such as age, gender, the type and stage of a disease, previous treatment history, and other medical conditions. Before joining a clinical trial, a participant must qualify for the study. Some research studies seek participants with illnesses or conditions to be studied in the clinical trial, while others need healthy volunteers.

Some studies need both types. Inclusion and exclusion criteria are not used to reject people personally; rather, the criteria are used to identify appropriate participants and keep them safe, and to help ensure that researchers can find new information they need.

What Do I Need to Know if I Am Thinking about Participating

Risks and benefits

Clinical trials involve risks, just as routine medical care and the activities of daily living. When weighing the risks of research, you can consider two important factors:

1. the degree of harm that could result from participating in the study and

2. the chance of any harm occurring.

Most clinical studies pose the risk of minor discomfort, which lasts only a short time. However, some study participants experience complications that require medical attention. In rare cases, participants have been seriously injured or have died of complications resulting from their participation in trials of experimental therapies. The specific risks associated with a research protocol are described in detail in the informed consent document, which participants are asked to sign before participating in research. Also, a member of the research team explains the major risks of participating in a study and will answer any questions you have about the study. Before deciding to participate, carefully consider possible risks and benefits.

Potential benefits

Well-designed and well-executed clinical trials provide the best approach for participants to:

- Play an active role in their health care.
- Gain access to new research treatments before they are widely available.
- Receive regular and careful medical attention from a research team that includes doctors and other health professionals.
- Help others by contributing to medical research.

Potential risks

Risks to participating in clinical trials include the following:

- There may be unpleasant, serious, or even life-threatening side effects to experimental treatment.
- The study may require more time and attention than standard treatment would, including visits to the study site, more blood tests, more treatments, hospital stays, or complex dosage requirements.

What Questions Should I Ask if Offered a Clinical Trial

If you are offered a clinical trial, feel free to ask any questions or bring up any issues concerning the trial at any time. The following suggestions may give you some ideas as you think about your own questions.

The study

- What is the purpose of the study?
- Why do researchers think the approach may be effective?
- Who will fund the study?
- Who has reviewed and approved the study?

- How are study results and safety of participants being checked?
- How long will the study last?
- What will my responsibilities be if I participate?

Possible risks and benefits

- What are my possible short-term benefits?
- What are my possible long-term benefits?
- What are my short-term risks, such as side effects?
- What are my possible long-term risks?
- What other options do people with my disease have?
- How do the possible risks and benefits of this trial compare with those options?

Participation and care

- What kinds of therapies, procedures and/or tests will I have during the trial?
- Will they hurt, and if so, for how long?
- How do the tests in the study compare with those I would have outside of the trial?
- Will I be able to take my regular medications while in the clinical trial?
- Where will I have my medical care?
- Who will be in charge of my care?

Personal issues

- How could being in this study affect my daily life?
- Can I talk to other people in the study?

Cost issues

- Will I have to pay for any part of the trial such as tests or the study drug?
- If so, what will the charges likely be?
- What is my health insurance likely to cover?
- Who can help answer any questions from my insurance company or health plan?

- Will there be any travel or child care costs that I need to consider while I am in the trial?

Tips for asking your doctor about trials

- Consider taking a family member or friend along, for support and for help in asking questions or recording answers.

- Plan ahead what to ask—but don't hesitate to ask any new questions you think of while you're there.

- Write down your questions in advance, to make sure you remember to ask them all.

- Write down the answers, so that you can review them whenever you want.

- Ask about bringing a tape recorder to make a taped record of what's said (even if you write down answers).

How Am I Protected?

Ethical guidelines

The goal of clinical research is to develop knowledge that improves human health or increases understanding of human biology. People who participate in clinical research make it possible for this to occur. The path to finding out if a new drug is safe or effective is to test it on patient volunteers. By placing some people at risk of harm for the good of others, clinical research has the potential to exploit patient volunteers. The purpose of ethical guidelines is both to protect patient volunteers and to preserve the integrity of the science. Ethical guidelines in place today were primarily a response to past research abuses.

Informed consent

Informed consent is the process of learning the key facts about a clinical trial before deciding whether to participate. The process of providing information to participants continues throughout the study. To help someone decide whether to participate, members of the research team explain details of the study. The research team provides an informed consent document, which includes such details about the study as its purpose, duration, required procedures, and who to contact for various purposes. The informed consent document also explains risks and potential benefits.

If the participant decides to enroll in the trial, the informed consent document will be signed. Informed consent is not a contract. Volunteers are free to withdraw from the study at any time.

Institutional Review Board (IRB)

Most, but not all, clinical trials in the United States are approved and monitored by an Institutional Review Board (IRB) in order to ensure that the risks are minimal and are worth any potential benefits. An IRB is an independent committee that consists of physicians, statisticians, and members of the community who ensure that clinical trials are ethical and that the rights of participants are protected. Potential research participants should ask the sponsor or research coordinator whether the research they are considering participating in was reviewed by an IRB.

What Happens after a Clinical Trial Is Completed?

After a clinical trial is completed, the researchers carefully examine information collected during the study before making decisions about the meaning of the findings and about further testing. After a phase I or II trial, the researchers decide whether to move on to the next phase or to stop testing the agent or intervention because it was unsafe or ineffective. When a phase III trial is completed, the researchers examine the data and decide whether the results have medical importance.

Results from clinical trials are often published in peer-reviewed scientific journals. **Peer review** is a process by which experts review the report before it is published to ensure that the analysis and conclusions are sound. If the results are particularly important, they may be featured in news media and discussed at scientific meetings and by patient advocacy groups before they are published. Once a new approach has been proven safe and effective in a clinical trial, it may become the standard of medical practice.

How Does the Outcome of Clinical Research Make a Difference?

Only through clinical research can we gain insights and answers about the safety and effectiveness of drugs and therapies. Ground breaking scientific advances in the present and the past were possible only because of participation of volunteers, both healthy and those diagnosed with an illness, in clinical research. Clinical research requires complex and rigorous testing in collaboration with communities that are affected by the disease. As clinical research opens new doors to finding ways to diagnose, prevent, treat, or cure disease and disability, clinical trial participation of volunteers is essential to help us find the answers.

Chapter 65

How to Find a Cancer Treatment Trial?

A 10-Step Guide

This chapter will help you look for a cancer treatment clinical trial. It does not provide medical advice and should not be used in place of advice from your doctor or other members of your health care team. If you wish, your health care team and your loved ones can assist you in deciding whether or not a clinical trial is right for you. But, the decision to take part in a clinical trial is yours alone to make.

A Word about Timing:

Some treatment trials will not accept people who have already been treated for their cancer. The researchers conducting these trials are hoping to find improved cancer treatments for people with newly diagnosed disease.

- **If you have just found out that you have cancer**, the time to think about joining a trial is before you have any treatment. Talk with your doctor about how quickly you need to make a treatment decision.

Other treatment trials are looking for people who have already been treated for their cancer.

Text in this chapter is excerpted from "How to Find a Cancer Treatment Trial: A 10-Step Guide," National Cancer Institute (NCI), June 4, 2015.

- **If you have already had cancer treatment** and are looking for a new treatment option, there are still clinical trials for you to think about.

Step 1: Understand Clinical Trials

Clinical trials are research studies that involve people. They are the final step in a long process that begins with laboratory research and testing in animals. Many treatments used today are the result of past clinical trials.

Step 2: Talk with Your Doctor

When thinking about clinical trials, **your best starting point is your doctor or another member of your health care team.**

Usually, it is a doctor who may know about a clinical trial, or search for one, that could be a good option for you and your type of cancer. He or she can provide information and answer questions while you think about joining a clinical trial.

In some cases, your doctor may not be familiar with clinical trials. If so, you may want to get a second opinion about your treatment options, including taking part in a clinical trial.

Step 3: Complete the Checklist

If you decide to look for a clinical trial, **you must know certain details about your cancer diagnosis**. You will need to compare these details with the eligibility criteria of any trial that interests you. Eligibility criteria are the guidelines for who can and cannot take part in a certain clinical trial. They are also called entry criteria or enrollment criteria.

To help you know which trials you may be eligible to join, **complete the** Cancer Details Checklist available at http://www.cancer.gov/about-cancer/treatment/clinical-trials/search/trial-guide/detailschecklist.pdf. This form asks questions about your cancer and provides space to write down your answers. Keep the form with you during your search for a clinical trial.

To get the information you need for the form, ask **your doctor, a nurse, or social worker at your doctor's office for help.** Explain to them that you are interested in looking for a clinical trial and that you need these details before starting to look. They may be able to review your medical records and help you fill out the form. The more information you can find to complete the form, the easier it will be to find a clinical trial to fit your situation.

Step 4: Search National Cancer Institute's (NCI) List of Trials

Many web sites have lists of cancer clinical trials that are taking place in the United States. Some trials are sponsored by non-profit organizations, including the U.S. federal government. Others are sponsored by for-profit groups, such as drug companies. In addition, there are hospitals and academic medical centers that sponsor trials conducted by their own researchers. Unfortunately, because of the many types of sponsors, no single list of clinical trials is complete.

How to Search NCI's List of Cancer Clinical Trials:

- **Look for trials yourself** using NCI's clinical trials search form. A related web page, Help Using the NCI Clinical Trials Search Form, provides more information about how to use the form.

- **Call NCI's Cancer Information Service (CIS)** at 1-800-4-CANCER (1-800-422-6237). The CIS provides free help in English and Spanish from 8:00 a.m. to 8:00 p.m. Eastern time in the United States. All calls are strictly confidential.

  - **Have your Cancer Details Checklist** ready when you call the CIS.

  - The CIS is staffed with understanding and knowledgeable **cancer information specialists who will search NCI's list of cancer clinical trials for you.** They can send you the search results and clinical trial summaries by e-mail, fax, or regular mail. The CIS can also give you reliable information about your type of cancer and the usual treatment for the type of cancer you have.

  - If you would like help searching NCI's list of cancer clinical trials while you are on the Internet, **think about using LiveHelp**. Through LiveHelp, you can communicate confidentially and in real time with a CIS information specialist. This service is available Monday through Friday from 8:00 a.m. to 11:00 p.m. Eastern time.

Step 5: Other Lists of Trials

In addition to NCI's list of cancer clinical trials, you may want to check a few other trial lists. Why? Because:

- Some may include a few trials not found in NCI's list.

- You may prefer the way you can search those lists.

Other places to look for lists of cancer clinical trials include the web sites of:

- Research Organizations that Conduct Cancer Clinical Trials

- Drug and Biotechnology Companies

- Clinical Trial Listing Services

- Cancer Advocacy Groups

Web Sites of Research Organizations that Conduct Cancer Clinical Trials

Many cancer centers across the United States, including NCI-designated Cancer Centers, sponsor or take part in cancer clinical trials. The web sites of these centers usually have a list of the clinical trials taking place at their location. Some of the trials included in these lists, mainly phase I clinical trials, may not be in NCI's list.

Keep in mind that the amount of information about clinical trials on these web sites can vary considerably. You may have to contact a cancer center's clinical trials office to get more information about the trials that interest you.

Another place to look is TrialCheck. This web site is managed by an organization called the Coalition of Cancer Cooperative Groups (CCCG). The CCCG includes groups of doctors and other health professionals who conduct many of the large cancer clinical trials sponsored by NCI. The TrialCheck web site has a clinical trials questionnaire that helps you search for trials based on your cancer type and the treatment(s) you have already received. Most of the clinical trials listed on the Trial-Check web site are the same as those found in NCI's clinical trials list.

Drug and Biotechnology Company Web Sites

Drug and biotechnology companies also sponsor cancer clinical trials. Many of these trials are included in NCI's list of cancer clinical trials, but some are not.

How to search for company-sponsored trials:

- Search the U.S. web sites of drug and biotechnology companies. Many companies provide lists of the clinical trials that they sponsor on their web sites. Sometimes, a company's web site may refer you to the web site of another organization that helps the company find patients for its trials. The other organization may be paid fees for this service.

The web site of the Pharmaceutical Research and Manufacturers of America (PhRMA) includes a list of its member companies, many of which sponsor cancer clinical trials. PhRMA is a trade organization that represents drug and biotechnology companies in the United States.

- Search the Clinical Trials Portal of the International Federation of Pharmaceutical Manufacturers & Associations (IFPMA). The IFPMA web portal includes trials found in NCI's list of cancer clinical trials, as well as some other trials. You can search for clinical trials based on cancer type or other medical condition, drug name, and where the trial is taking place.

Clinical Trial Listing Services

Other organizations provide lists of clinical trials as a major part of their business. These organizations generally do not sponsor or take part in clinical trials. Some of them may receive fees from drug or biotechnology company sponsors of trials for listing their trials or helping them find patients for their trials.

Keep the following points in mind:

- The trial lists provided by these organizations often rely heavily on trial lists that are available at no cost from the U.S. federal government (NCI and ClinicalTrials.gov).

- The trial lists provided by these organizations may have a few more trials than NCI's list, or they may have fewer trials.

- Unlike the NCI web site (and ClinicalTrials.gov), the web sites of these organizations may not be updated regularly.

- Unlike the NCI web site (and ClinicalTrials.gov), the web sites of these organizations may require you to register to search for clinical trials or obtain trial contact information for trials that interest you.

Cancer Advocacy Group Web sites

Cancer advocacy groups work on behalf of people diagnosed with cancer and their loved ones. They provide education, support, financial assistance, and advocacy to help patients and families who are dealing with cancer, its treatment, and survivorship. These organizations recognize that clinical trials are important to improving cancer care.

They work to educate and empower people to find information and obtain access to appropriate treatment.

Advocacy groups work hard to know about the latest advances in cancer research. They will sometimes have information about certain government-sponsored clinical trials, as well as some trials sponsored by cancer centers or drug and biotechnology companies.

How to search for trials through a cancer advocacy group:

- Search the web sites of advocacy groups for specific types of cancer. Many of these web sites have lists of clinical trials or refer you to the web sites of organizations that match patients to trials. CancerActionNow, managed by the non-profit Marti Nelson Cancer Foundation, provides a partial list of cancer advocacy groups. Or, you can contact an advocacy group directly for assistance in finding clinical trials.

Step 6: Identify Potential Trials

At this point, you should have completed the Cancer Details Checklist, found one or more trials of interest to you, and printed out or saved a summary for each trial.

Key questions to ask about each trial:

- **Trial objective:** What is the main purpose of the trial? Is it to cure your cancer? To slow its growth or spread? To lessen the severity of cancer symptoms or the side effects of treatment? To determine whether a new treatment is safe and well-tolerated? Read this information carefully to learn whether the trial's main objective matches your goals for treatment.

- **Eligibility criteria:** Do the details of your cancer diagnosis and your current overall state of health match the trial's entry criteria? This may tell you whether or not you can qualify for the trial. If you're not sure, keep the trial on your list for now.

- **Trial location:** Is the location of the trial manageable for you? Some trials take place at more than one location. Look carefully at how often you will need to receive treatment during the course of the trial. Decide how far and how often you are willing to travel. You will also need to ask whether the sponsoring organization will pay for some or all of your travel costs.

- **Study length:** How long will the trial run? Not all clinical trial summaries provide this information. If they do, consider the time involved and whether it will work for you and your family.

After considering these questions, if you are still interested in one or more of the clinical trials you have found, then you are ready for Step 7.

Step 7: Contact the Trial Team

There are many ways to contact the clinical trial team.

- **Contact the trial team directly.** The clinical trial summary should include the phone number of a person or an office that you can contact for more information. You do not need to talk to the lead researcher (called the "protocol chair" or "principal investigator") at this time, even if his or her name is given along with the telephone number. Instead, call the number and ask to speak with the "trial coordinator," the "referral coordinator," or the "protocol assistant." This person can answer questions from patients and their doctors. It is also this person's job to decide whether you are likely to be eligible to join the trial. (A final decision will probably not be made until you have had a visit with a doctor who is taking part in the trial.)

- **Ask your doctor or another health care team member to contact the trial team for you.** Because the clinical trial coordinator will ask questions about your cancer diagnosis and your current general health, you may want to ask your doctor or someone else on your health care team to contact the clinical trial team for you.

- **The trial team may contact you.** If you have used the web site of a clinical trial listing service and found a trial that interests you, you may have provided your name, phone number, and e-mail address so the clinical trial team can contact you directly.

You will need to refer to the Cancer Details Checklist during this conversation, so keep it handy.

Step 8: Ask Questions

Whether you or someone from your health care team calls the clinical trial team, this is the time to get answers to questions that will help you decide whether or not to take part in this particular clinical trial.

It will be helpful if you can talk about your cancer and your current general health in a manner that is brief and to the point. Before you make the call, you may want to rehearse how you will present key information about your cancer diagnosis and general health with a family member or a friend. This will make you more comfortable when you are talking with the clinical trial team member, and it will help you answer his or her questions more smoothly. Remember to keep your Cancer Details Checklist handy to help you answer some of the questions that may be asked.

Questions to Ask the Trial Coordinator

Is the trial still open?

On occasion, clinical trial listings will be out of date and will include trials that are no longer accepting new participants.

Am I eligible for this trial?

The trial team member will ask you many, if not all, of the questions listed on your Cancer Details Checklist. This is the time to confirm that you are a candidate for this trial. However, a final decision will likely not be made until you have had your first visit with a doctor who is taking part in the clinical trial (Step 10).

Why do researchers think the new treatment might be effective?

Results from previous research have indicated that the new treatment may be effective in people with your type of cancer. Ask about the previous research studies. Results from studies in humans are stronger than results from laboratory or animal studies.

What are the potential risks and benefits associated with the treatments I may receive in this trial?

Every treatment has risks, whether you receive the treatment as part of a clinical trial or from your doctor outside of a clinical trial. Be sure you understand the possible risks and side effects of each treatment you may receive as a participant in this trial. Also, ask for a detailed description of how the treatments you may receive could benefit you.

Who will watch over my care and safety?

Primary responsibility for the care and safety of people taking part in a cancer clinical trial rests with the clinical trial team. Also, clinical trials are governed by safety and ethical regulations set by the Federal government and the organization sponsoring and carrying out the trial. One of these groups is called the Institutional Review Board (IRB). The trial team will be able to give you more information.

Can I get a copy of the trial's protocol document?

A trial's protocol document is an action plan for the trial. It includes the reason(s) for doing the trial, the number of people that will be included, the eligibility criteria for participation, the treatments that will be given, the medical tests that will be done and how often, and what information will be collected. These documents are usually written in highly technical language and are often confidential. In some cases, however, the trial team may be allowed to release the protocol document to you.

Can I get a copy of the informed consent document?

Yes. The U.S. Food and Drug Administration (FDA) and the Office for Human Research Protections (OHRP) require that potential participants in a clinical trial receive detailed, understandable information about the trial. This process is known as "informed consent," and it must be in writing. It may be helpful to see a copy of this document before you make your final decision about joining the trial.

Is there a chance that I will receive a placebo?

Placebos (sham or inactive treatments) are rarely used alone in cancer treatment trials. When they are used, they are most often given along with a standard (usual) treatment. In such cases, a trial will compare a standard treatment plus a new treatment with the same standard treatment plus a placebo. If a placebo is used alone, it's because no standard treatment exists. In this case, a trial will compare the effects of a new treatment with the effects of a placebo. Be sure you understand the treatments that are being used in any trial you are thinking of joining.

Is the trial randomized?

In a randomized clinical trial, participants are assigned by chance to different treatment groups or "arms" of the trial. Neither you nor your doctor can choose which arm you are in. All participants in an arm receive the same treatment. At the end of the trial, the results from the different treatment arms are compared. In a randomized trial, you may or may not receive the new treatment that is being tested.

What is the dose and schedule of the treatments given in each arm of the trial?

Dose refers to the amount of treatment given, and schedule refers to when and how often treatment is given. You will want to think about this information when you are discussing your treatment options with your health care team. Is the treatment schedule manageable for you?

What costs will I or my health insurance plan have to pay?

In many cases, the research costs are paid by the organization sponsoring the trial. Research costs include the treatments being studied and any tests performed purely for research purposes. However, you or your insurance plan would be responsible for paying "routine patient care costs." These are the costs of medical care (for example, doctor visits, hospital stays, x-rays) that you would receive whether or not you were taking part in a clinical trial. Some insurance plans don't cover these costs once you join a trial. Check with your health plan to find out which costs it will and will not pay for. You may also wish to visit Paying for Clinical Trials.

If I have to travel, who will pay for my travel and lodging?

Clinical trials rarely cover travel and lodging expenses. Usually, you will be responsible for these costs. However, you should still ask this question.

Will participation in this trial require more time (hours/days) than standard care? Will participation require a hospital stay?

Understanding how much time is involved and whether a hospital stay is required, compared to the usual treatment for your type of cancer, may influence your decision. This information will also be important if you decide to take part in the trial because it will help you in making plans.

How will participating in this trial affect my everyday life?

A diagnosis of cancer can disrupt the routine of your everyday life. Many people seek to keep their routine intact as they deal with their cancer and its treatment. This information will be useful in making plans and in determining whether you need any additional help at home.

Step 9: Talk to Your Doctor

To make a final decision, you will want to know the potential risks and benefits of all treatment options available to you. Through the research that you have done, you likely have a good idea about the possible risks and benefits of the treatment(s) in clinical trials that interest you. If you have any remaining questions or concerns, you should discuss them with your doctor. You should also ask your doctor about the risks and benefits of standard, or usual, treatment for your type of cancer. Then, you and your doctor can compare the risks and benefits of standard treatment with those of treatment in a clinical trial. You may decide that joining a trial is your best option, or you may decide not to join a trial. It's your choice.

The Questions to Ask in Step 8 can give you ideas of questions to ask your doctor.

Step 10: Make an Appointment

If you decide to join a clinical trial for which you are eligible, schedule a visit with the trial team. Most likely, the same person you spoke with in Step 8.

If you decide to join a clinical trial for which you are eligible, schedule a visit with the trial team.

Chapter 66

Taking Part in Clinical Trials

Deciding to Take Part in a Clinical Trial

When you need treatment for cancer, you may want to think about joining a clinical trial. Like all treatment options, clinical trials have possible benefits and risks. By looking closely at all options, including clinical trials, you are taking an active role in a decision that affects your life. This chapter has information you can use when making your decision.

Possible Benefits

- You will have access to a new treatment that is not available to people outside the trial.

- The research team will watch you closely.

- If the treatment being studied is more effective than the standard treatment, you may be among the first to benefit.

- The trial may help scientists learn more about cancer and help people in the future.

Possible Risks

- The new treatment may not be better than, or even as good as, the standard treatment.

Text in this chapter is excerpted from "Deciding to Take Part in a Clinical Trial," National Cancer Institute (NCI), July 1, 2013.

- New treatments may have side effects that doctors do not expect or that are worse than those of the standard treatment.

- You may be required to make more visits to the doctor than if you were receiving standard treatment. You may have extra expenses related to these extra visits, such as travel and child-care costs.

- You may need extra tests. Some of the tests could be uncomfortable or time consuming.

- Even if a new treatment has benefits in some patients, it may not work for you.

- Health insurance may not cover all patient care costs in a trial.

Who Can Join

Every clinical trial has a protocol, or study plan, that describes what will be done during the trial, how the trial will be conducted, and why each part of the trial is necessary. The protocol also includes guidelines for who can and cannot take part in the trial. These guidelines are called eligibility criteria.

Common eligibility criteria include:

- Having a certain type or stage of cancer

- Having received (or not having received) a certain kind of therapy in the past

- Being in a certain age group

- Medical history

- Current health status

Criteria such as these help reduce the medical differences among people in the trial. When people taking part in a trial are alike in key ways, researchers can be more certain that the results are due to the treatment being tested and not to other factors.

Some people have health problems besides cancer that could be made worse by the treatments in a trial. If you are interested in joining a trial, you will receive medical tests to be sure that you fit for the trial.

If you are interested in joining a trial, you will receive medical tests to be sure that you fit for the trial.

Chapter 67

National Cancer Institute's (NCI) Role in Cancer Research

How Cancer Research Works

When people think about cancer research, they may envision men and women in lab coats, carefully dripping substances into test tubes or peering thoughtfully into microscopes. Of course, those things do happen in biomedical research. But they are just one small part of a much larger research landscape.

In reality, cancer research is a vast, complex enterprise that involves researchers from many different disciplines. It also relies heavily on the participation of patients and healthy volunteers, without whom cancer research would not be possible.

Cancer research happens in many places, such as:

- the lab, with investigators studying the inner workings of cells
- hospitals, with doctors administering treatments to patients as part of clinical trials
- community clinics, with nurses or health educators teaching people how to reduce their cancer risk

Text in this chapter is excerpted from "NCI's Role in Cancer Research," National Cancer Institute (NCI), March 19, 2015.

- universities and academic medical centers across the country and the world, where doctors, professors, fellows, and students unravel the complexity of cancer

- the offices of National Cancer Institute (NCI) staff who analyze data to identify behaviors, exposures, or other factors that influence cancer risk or cancer outcomes

- NCI program offices, where staff review applications from researchers across the country who are hoping to secure funding for their research projects

Research Begins with Ideas

An idea. That's the genesis of a cancer research study. It could be an idea for a large-scale project like The Cancer Genome Atlas, a multi-year effort that involved researchers from institutions across the country working collaboratively to catalogue all of the changes to deoxyribonucleic acid (DNA) and other molecules in more than 30 different cancer types. Or it could be something more modest, such as testing whether a text messaging service can help pregnant women quit smoking.

Ideas for new cancer research studies are often inspired by findings from earlier research, research on other cancers, and even findings from research done on other diseases, such as diabetes or immune disorders.

Findings from basic research, such as studies of cancer cells in the laboratory, can ultimately define research questions to study in humans, such as helping to identify drugs to test in clinical trials. And findings from clinical trials in humans can, conversely, generate hypotheses that need to be further investigated in cells or animal models in the lab. An epidemiologic study can help identify potential risk factors for certain cancers and generate hypotheses about what may cause some cancers or suggest possible preventive measures.

It's all part of a continuum of innovation and knowledge that produces important biomedical advances. Each advance builds on the next, and each advance spurs new ideas.

The Cancer Research Continuum

Although studies of new cancer treatments often receive the most headlines, cancer research involves much more than testing new therapies.

Learning more about how to treat and prevent cancer entails the work of researchers from a wide range of disciplines, many of whom will never handle a frozen tissue sample or don a white lab coat or hospital scrubs.

Generally, biomedical research falls into three categories, each of which is essential to advances in cancer research overall.

Basic Research

Why do cancer cells grow and spread uncontrollably? What causes a cell to become cancerous in the first place?

To answer basic research questions like these, investigators study bacteria, viruses, fungi, animal cells and human cells (both healthy and cancerous) grown in the lab, and tumors in animals, such as mice and rats.

Some examples of basic research in cancer biology might include:

- defining the communication pathways in cells that regulate processes such as cell proliferation and the repair of damaged DNA

- analyzing how healthy cells respond to injury from a suspected cancer-causing toxin

- analyzing how cancer cells and malignant tumors growing in animals respond to an investigational drug

- detailing the physical structure of a protein receptor commonly found on the surface of cancer cells, which may aid in developing drugs that target the protein

- determining the biological differences between immune system cells that attack and kill cancer cells and those that ignore them

Without basic research, it would be impossible to develop new ways to prevent and treat cancer. Basic research is the foundation on which much of the cancer research continuum is built.

Clinical Research

Nearly every new treatment, test, or intervention for cancer must be rigorously tested in clinical trials to be sure that it is safe and effective before it can be used in humans.

In clinical trials, researchers test drugs, medical devices, or other interventions in human volunteers, with the goal of improving all aspects of patient care.

Trials are used to find answers to many different clinical questions, such as:

- Can a new (or old) drug prevent cancer in people at increased risk of the disease (such as those with certain genetic mutations or a family history of a specific cancer)?

- Does a new screening test reduce deaths from the cancer that it is meant to detect?

- Can taking a drug or making a lifestyle change (e.g., exercise, diet) after treatment extend the lives of patients with cancer?

- Which of two commonly used treatments for the same cancer is more effective or safer?

- Can a new drug or intervention improve patients' quality of life?

Initial, or early-phase, clinical trials of a potential new therapy are very small, with just a handful of participants, and are conducted primarily to determine whether a new treatment is safe and to identify the best dose to test in larger trials.

Later-phase clinical trials, which often take several years or more to conduct, often involve hundreds or thousands of patients. These trials are used to determine whether a treatment is more effective and/or better tolerated than current treatments and should be used more broadly.

Increasingly, additional studies (often called correlative studies) are built into clinical trials. These additional studies are intended to help researchers better understand issues such as why some patients in the trial did or didn't respond to a new treatment or how treatments affect patients' quality of life.

Population-Based Research

Studying populations of people—their family histories and genetics, health behaviors and health histories, and environmental exposures— can provide important information about the causes of cancer and its consequences.

Are any risk factors (e.g., gene mutations, environmental exposures) common among people who develop a certain kind of cancer? After completing treatment for cancer, what was the state of the emotional and psychological well-being of the population studied? Often, these types of questions can only be answered by studying large groups of people.

Population studies can involve:

- mining data from cancer registries and databases (such as NCI's SEER registry, one of the largest of its kind in the world)

- studies of large families in which the same cancer was diagnosed in multiple members or registries of families with hereditary cancers

- observational studies, including case-control and cohort studies

- comprehensive surveys of specific population groups

Population-based research can identify associations or highlight trends that would be difficult or impossible to find otherwise. Important data about disparities in diagnosis or survival rates among certain racial or socioeconomic groups or the long-term health of pediatric cancer survivors, for instance, only came to light as a result of population-based research.

Although these different areas of research are distinct in many ways, they also have something in common: they are often performed over a period of years and, in some cases, decades. To take a finding in basic research, such as identifying a mutant protein that drives a particular cancer, and develop a drug that inactivates the protein and performs well in cells in the lab and in animal models can take years if not decades. Even once a drug makes it to late-phase clinical trials, patients must be followed for several years, or even a decade or more, to determine whether the new treatment is more effective than current treatments. And, in population-based studies, researchers typically collect a substantial amount of data on the groups being studied and often follow them (via interviews, surveys, medical records, etc.) for many years.

Technology and Collaboration Fuel Progress

Cancer researchers are increasingly using advanced technologies that are capable of providing far more information and detail than was previously possible, propelling the shift toward precision medicine. Some of these technologies include:

- next-generation DNA sequencing and gene and protein array platforms, which allow researchers to perform more comprehensive molecular analyses of tumors, more quickly and accurately, than was possible with older technology

- advanced imaging technologies that allow researchers to obtain biopsy samples with more precision or measure the inner workings of cancer cells and their microenvironments

- new bioinformatics tools for storing and analyzing the large amounts of data captured in the course of much cancer research today

And cancer research now involves collaborative efforts from researchers in disciplines such as physics, advanced mathematics, structural biology, nanotechnology, and many more, who have introduced new concepts and approaches to studying cancer.

There is also greater collaboration among the chief funders of cancer research: the government, the private sector, and non-profit organizations. This collaboration is allowing patients and advocates to become more involved in guiding and developing studies and allowing researchers to overcome issues related to intellectual property that can sometimes stall or halt important research projects.

NCI: The Largest Funder of Cancer Research

NCI is the largest funder of cancer research in the world. The institute's annual budget, which is set by Congress, is approximately $5 billion. These funds support research performed at NCI and at cancer centers, hospitals, community clinics, and universities across the United States and around the world.

NCI has a number of divisions and centers that either conduct research or manage research programs.

The NCI intramural program is carried out by both government and contract staff, who conduct research at one of several campuses in suburban Maryland. Intramural research spans the research continuum.

The bulk of NCI's budget supports the extramural program—the investigators and institutions across the country who use federal funds to conduct cancer research. The extramural program includes:

- independent investigators at universities and academic medical centers who work on basic and clinical research

- special programs focused on specific research areas, such as genomics and health disparities.

- the NCI-designated Cancer Centers program

- the National Clinical Trials Network and other research networks

In both the intramural and extramural programs, NCI conducts and supports research on rare cancers. This work is an important part of NCI's mission and allows the institute to support research into cancers not typically of interest to the private sector. As a federal agency, NCI is able to study interventions and drugs that also might not be of interest to the private sector, for instance because they are no longer under patent protection or they are not anticipated to be profitable.

Supporting the Cancer Research Enterprise

NCI offers a number of important resources and services for cancer researchers.

Training

NCI offers a variety of training programs for early-career and international investigators that span the research continuum. Training opportunities are available for high school students, graduate students, scientists, clinicians, and health care professionals. Some of these programs include training in:

- basic and translational science
- cancer prevention
- epidemiology
- behavioral research
- genetics
- regulatory science

These programs are run through NCI's divisions and centers, some of which include partnerships with other HHS institutes and universities.

NCI Grants and Peer Review

In order to receive NCI funding, researchers submit proposals for research projects, outlining what the project will entail, the scientific rationale for the project, and what they hope to show. Proposals can be submitted without any solicitation, but some are submitted in response to research requests (RFAs, RFPs, PAs) developed by NCI staff.

These proposals are then subject to peer review, in which independent experts from outside NCI review and score the applications based on factors such as applicability to cancer, scientific merit, and feasibility, among others.

Bioinformatics

Because many cancer research studies produce vast amounts of data, cancer researchers are increasingly reliant on bioinformatics tools to conduct their work. Bioinformatics enables researchers to manage and analyze the very large data sets generated by clinical trials, genomics studies, and population-based research.

Led by the National Cancer Informatics Program, developing and managing bioinformatics resources—including web-based databases and "cloud computing" tools—has become a core component of the NCI's research enterprise.

Advisory Boards

Several independent advisory boards guide decisions by NCI leadership, including funding support for proposed or ongoing research projects and programs.

These advisory boards, which include leading cancer researchers and cancer research advocates, meet regularly throughout the year to review the status and progress of NCI's intramural and extramural programs. During these meetings, the advisory boards often recommend funding levels at which programs should be supported and changes to the composition and/or direction of different programs.

Divisions, Offices, Centers, and Special Programs

The program staff in NCI's divisions, offices, and centers are highly experienced in their respective fields (e.g., cancer biology, prevention, clinical trials, etc.). NCI staff:

- prioritize and develop concepts for research programs

- evaluate research proposals submitted by extramural investigators

- work with investigators to manage their research grants

- conduct training programs for intramural and extramural researchers

- aid in NCI's strategic planning and prioritization process

In addition to conducting and funding research to develop more effective and safer therapies, NCI has thriving research programs in critically important areas like survivorship, delivery of care, primary prevention, screening, and quality of life—areas that are not traditionally supported by the private sector because they have limited commercial value or are not a good fit with traditional pharmaceutical and biotech business models.

Funding for these areas of research is vital to making advances that cut across the spectrum of cancer care. Advances in symptom control, for example, can ensure people undergoing cancer treatment have an improved quality of life and, in many cases, save health care resources. Advances in delivery of care can improve the overall quality of treatment, improving patient outcomes and saving health care dollars.

Funding the Best Science

Like other components of the federal government, NCI must operate within the confines of its budget. Because medical inflation has outpaced general inflation and NCI has had a relatively flat budget over much of the last decade, the institute's purchasing power has declined substantially.

NCI senior leadership has worked closely with its advisory boards to make difficult choices about funding, including whether to fund a project or program at all or adjust their funding levels. Decisions about funding are heavily influenced by the areas of research considered by NCI leadership and its advisory boards to be the highest priority and have the greatest potential to produce important advances and improve patients' lives.

Part Nine

Additional Help and Information

Chapter 68

Glossary of Terms Related to Cancer

Excerpted from "Dictionary of Cancer Terms," National Cancer Institute (http://www.cancer.gov/publications/dictionaries/cancer-terms), 2015.

adjuvant therapy: Additional cancer treatment given after the primary treatment to lower the risk that the cancer will come back. Adjuvant therapy may include chemotherapy, radiation therapy, hormone therapy, targeted therapy, or biological therapy.

alopecia: The lack or loss of hair from areas of the body where hair is usually found. Alopecia can be a side effect of some cancer treatments.

angiogenesis inhibitor: A substance that may prevent the formation of blood vessels. In anticancer therapy, an angiogenesis inhibitor may prevent the growth of new blood vessels that tumors need to grow.

antiestrogen: A substance that keeps cells from making or using estrogen (a hormone that plays a role in female sex characteristics, the menstrual cycle, and pregnancy). Antiestrogens may stop some cancer cells from growing and are used to prevent and treat breast cancer. They are also being studied in the treatment of other types of cancer. An antiestrogen is a type of hormone antagonist. Also called estrogen blocker.

axilla: The underarm or armpit.

basal cell carcinoma: Cancer that begins in the lower part of the epidermis (the outer layer of the skin). It may appear as a small white or flesh-colored bump that grows slowly and may bleed. Basal cell carcinomas are usually found on areas of the body exposed to the sun. Basal cell carcinomas rarely metastasize (spread) to other parts of the body. They are the most common form of skin cancer. Also called basal cell cancer.

benign: Not cancerous. Benign tumors may grow larger but do not spread to other parts of the body. Also called nonmalignant.

bilateral salpingo-oophorectomy: Surgery to remove both ovaries and both fallopian tubes.

biological therapy: Treatment to boost or restore the ability of the immune system to fight cancer, infections, and other diseases. Also used to lessen certain side effects that may be caused by some cancer treatments. Agents used in biological therapy include monoclonal antibodies, growth factors, and vaccines. These agents may also have a direct anti tumor effect. Also called biological response modifier therapy, biotherapy, BRM therapy, and immunotherapy.

biopsy: The removal of cells or tissues for examination by a pathologist. The pathologist may study the tissue under a microscope or perform other tests on the cells or tissue. There are many different types of biopsy procedures. The most common types include: (1) incisional biopsy, in which only a sample of tissue is removed; (2) excisional biopsy, in which an entire lump or suspicious area is removed; and (3) needle biopsy, in which a sample of tissue or fluid is removed with a needle. When a wide needle is used, the procedure is called a core biopsy. When a thin needle is used, the procedure is called a fine-needle aspiration biopsy.

bone marrow: The soft, sponge-like tissue in the center of most bones. It produces white blood cells, red blood cells, and platelets.

BRCA-1: A gene on chromosome 17 that normally helps to suppress cell growth. A person who inherits certain mutations (changes) in a BRCA1 gene has a higher risk of getting breast, ovarian, prostate, and other types of cancer.

BRCA-2: A gene on chromosome 13 that normally helps to suppress cell growth. A person who inherits certain mutations (changes) in a BRCA2 gene has a higher risk of getting breast, ovarian, prostate, and other types of cancer.

breast-conserving surgery: An operation to remove the breast cancer but not the breast itself. Types of breast-conserving surgery include lumpectomy (removal of the lump), quadrantectomy (removal of one quarter, or quadrant, of the breast), and segmental mastectomy (removal of the cancer as well as some of the breast tissue around the tumor and the lining over the chest muscles below the tumor). Also called breast-sparing surgery.

CA-125: A substance that may be found in high amounts in the blood of patients with certain types of cancer, including ovarian cancer. CA-125 levels may also help monitor how well cancer treatments are working or if cancer has come back. Also called cancer antigen 125.

cancer of unknown primary origin: A case in which cancer cells are found in the body, but the place where the cells first started growing (the origin or primary site) cannot be determined. Also called carcinoma of unknown primary and CUP.

carcinoma: Cancer that begins in the skin or in tissues that line or cover internal organs.

carcinoma in situ: A group of abnormal cells that remain in the place where they first formed. They have not spread. These abnormal cells may become cancer and spread into nearby normal tissue. Also called stage 0 disease.

cervical intraepithelial neoplasia (CIN): Growth of abnormal cells on the surface of the cervix. Numbers from 1 to 3 may be used to describe how abnormal the cells are and how much of the cervical tissue is involved. Also called CIN.

cervix: The lower, narrow end of the uterus that forms a canal between the uterus and vagina.

chemotherapy: Treatment with drugs that kill cancer cells.

clinical breast exam: A physical exam of the breast performed by a health care provider to check for lumps or other changes. Also called CBE.

clinical trial: A type of research study that tests how well new medical approaches work in people. These studies test new methods of screening, prevention, diagnosis, or treatment of a disease. Also called clinical study.

colon: The longest part of the large intestine, which is a tube-like organ connected to the small intestine at one end and the anus at the other. The colon removes water and some nutrients and electrolytes from partially digested food. The remaining material, solid waste called stool, moves through the colon to the rectum and leaves the body through the anus.

colonoscopy: Examination of the inside of the colon using a colonoscope, inserted into the rectum. A colonoscope is a thin, tube-like instrument with a light and a lens for viewing. It may also have a tool to remove tissue to be checked under a microscope for signs of disease.

colostomy: An opening into the colon from the outside of the body. A colostomy provides a new path for waste material to leave the body after part of the colon has been removed.

colposcopy: Examination of the vagina and cervix using a lighted magnifying instrument called a colposcope.

complementary and alternative medicine (CAM): Forms of treatment that are used in addition to (complementary) or instead of (alternative) standard treatments. These practices generally are not considered standard medical approaches. Standard treatments go through a long and careful research process to prove they are safe and effective, but less is known about most types of CAM. CAM may include dietary supplements, megadose vitamins, herbal preparations, special teas, acupuncture, massage therapy, magnet therapy, spiritual healing, and meditation. Also called CAM.

computed tomography (CT scan): A series of detailed pictures of areas inside the body taken from different angles. The pictures are created by a computer linked to an x-ray machine. Also called CAT scan, computerized axial tomography scan, computerized tomography, and CT scan.

conization: Surgery to remove a cone-shaped piece of tissue from the cervix and cervical canal. Conization may be used to diagnose or treat a cervical condition. Also called cone biopsy.

cryosurgery: A procedure in which tissue is frozen to destroy abnormal cells. Liquid nitrogen or liquid carbon dioxide is used to freeze the tissue. Also called cryoablation and cryosurgical ablation.

cyst: A sac or capsule in the body. It may be filled with fluid or other material.

diethylstilbestrol (DES): A synthetic form of the hormone estrogen that was prescribed to pregnant women between about 1940 and 1971 because it was thought to prevent miscarriages. Diethylstilbestrol may increase the risk of uterine, ovarian, or breast cancer in women who took it. It also has been linked to an increased risk of clear cell carcinoma of the vagina or cervix in daughters exposed to diethylstilbestrol before birth. Also called DES.

dilation and curettage (D&C): A procedure to remove tissue from the cervical canal or the inner lining of the uterus. The cervix is dilated (made larger) and a curette (spoon-shaped instrument) is inserted into the uterus to remove tissue. Also called D&C and dilatation and curettage.

dilator: A device used to stretch or enlarge an opening.

ductal carcinoma in situ (DCIS): A noninvasive condition in which abnormal cells are found in the lining of a breast duct. The abnormal cells have not spread outside the duct to other tissues in the breast. In some cases, ductal carcinoma in situ may become invasive cancer and spread to other tissues, although it is not known at this time how to predict which lesions will become invasive. Also called DCIS and intraductal carcinoma.

dysplasia: Cells that look abnormal under a microscope but are not cancer.

dysplastic nevus: A type of nevus (mole) that looks different from a common mole. A dysplastic nevus is often larger with borders that are not easy to see. Its color is usually uneven and can range from pink to dark brown. Parts of the mole may be raised above the skin surface. A dysplastic nevus may develop into malignant melanoma (a type of skin cancer).

early-stage breast cancer: Breast cancer that has not spread beyond the breast or the axillary lymph nodes. This includes ductal carcinoma in situ and stage I, stage IIA, stage IIB, and stage IIIA breast cancers.

endometriosis: A benign condition in which tissue that looks like endometrial tissue grows in abnormal places in the abdomen.

endometrium: The layer of tissue that lines the uterus.

estrogen: A type of hormone made by the body that helps develop and maintain female sex characteristics and the growth of long bones. Estrogens can also be made in the laboratory. They may be used as a type of birth control and to treat symptoms of menopause, menstrual disorders, osteoporosis, and other conditions.

excisional biopsy: A surgical procedure in which an entire lump or suspicious area is removed for diagnosis. The tissue is then examined under a microscope.

fallopian tube: A slender tube through which eggs pass from an ovary to the uterus. In the female reproductive tract, there is one ovary and one fallopian tube on each side of the uterus.

fine-needle aspiration: The removal of tissue or fluid with a thin needle for examination under a microscope. Also called FNA biopsy.

gestational trophoblastic tumor: Any of a group of tumors that develops from trophoblastic cells (cells that help an embryo attach to the uterus and help form the placenta) after fertilization of an egg by a sperm. The two main types of gestational trophoblastic tumors are hydatidiform mole and choriocarcinoma. Also called gestational trophoblastic disease.

grade: A description of a tumor based on how abnormal the cancer cells look under a microscope and how quickly the tumor is likely to grow and spread. Grading systems are different for each type of cancer.

graft: Healthy skin, bone, or other tissue taken from one part of the body and used to replace diseased or injured tissue removed from another part of the body.

gynecologic cancer: Cancer of the female reproductive tract, including the cervix, endometrium, fallopian tubes, ovaries, uterus, and vagina.

gynecologic oncologist: A doctor who specializes in treating cancers of the female reproductive organs.

Herceptin: A monoclonal antibody that binds to HER2 (human epidermal growth factor receptor 2), and can kill HER2-positive cancer cells. Monoclonal antibodies are made in the laboratory and can locate and bind to substances in the body, including cancer cells. Herceptin is used to treat breast cancer that is HER2-positive and has spread after treatment with other drugs. It is also used with other anticancer drugs to treat HER2-positive breast cancer after surgery. Herceptin is also being studied in the treatment of other types of cancer. Also called trastuzumab.

hormone: One of many chemicals made by glands in the body. Hormones circulate in the bloodstream and control the actions of certain cells or organs. Some hormones can also be made in the laboratory.

hormone replacement therapy (HRT): Hormones (estrogen, progesterone, or both) given to women after menopause to replace the hormones no longer produced by the ovaries. Also called HRT and menopausal hormone therapy.

human papillomavirus (HPV): A type of virus that can cause abnormal tissue growth (for example, warts) and other changes to cells. Infection for a long time with certain types of *human papillomavirus* can cause cervical cancer. *Human papillomavirus* can also play a role in some other types of cancer, such as anal, vaginal, vulvar, penile, and oropharyngeal cancers. Also called HPV.

hysterectomy: Surgery to remove the uterus and, sometimes, the cervix. When the uterus and the cervix are removed, it is called a total hysterectomy. When only the uterus is removed, it is called a partial hysterectomy.

immunotherapy: Treatment to boost or restore the ability of the immune system to fight cancer, infections, and other diseases. Also used to lessen certain side effects that may be caused by some cancer treatments. Agents used in immunotherapy include monoclonal antibodies, growth factors, and vaccines. These agents may also have a direct anti tumor effect. Also called biological response modifier therapy, biological therapy, biotherapy, and BRM therapy.

intraepithelial: Within the layer of cells that form the surface or lining of an organ.

invasive cancer: Cancer that has spread beyond the layer of tissue in which it developed and is growing into surrounding, healthy tissues. Also called infiltrating cancer.

laser therapy: Treatment that uses intense, narrow beams of light to cut and destroy tissue, such as cancer tissue. Laser therapy may also be used to reduce lymphedema (swelling caused by a buildup of lymph fluid in tissue) after breast cancer surgery.

lobular carcinoma in situ (LCIS): A condition in which abnormal cells are found in the lobules of the breast. Lobular carcinoma in situ seldom becomes invasive cancer; however, having it in one breast increases the risk of developing breast cancer in either breast. Also called LCIS.

local cancer: An invasive malignant cancer confined entirely to the organ where the cancer began.

loop electrosurgical excision procedure (LEEP): A technique that uses electric current passed through a thin wire loop to remove abnormal tissue. Also called LEEP and loop excision.

low grade: A term used to describe cells that look nearly normal under a microscope. These cells are less likely to grow and spread more quickly than cells in high-grade cancer or in growths that may become cancer.

lumpectomy: Surgery to remove abnormal tissue or cancer from the breast and a small amount of normal tissue around it. It is a type of breast-sparing surgery.

lymph node: A rounded mass of lymphatic tissue that is surrounded by a capsule of connective tissue. Lymph nodes filter lymph (lymphatic fluid), and they store lymphocytes (white blood cells). They are located along lymphatic vessels. Also called lymph gland.

lymphatic system: The tissues and organs that produce, store, and carry white blood cells that fight infections and other diseases. This system includes the bone marrow, spleen, thymus, lymph nodes, and lymphatic vessels (a network of thin tubes that carry lymph and white blood cells). Lymphatic vessels branch, like blood vessels, into all the tissues of the body.

lymphedema: A condition in which extra lymph fluid builds up in tissues and causes swelling. It may occur in an arm or leg if lymph vessels are blocked, damaged, or removed by surgery.

magnetic resonance imaging (MRI): A procedure in which radio waves and a powerful magnet linked to a computer are used to create detailed pictures of areas inside the body. These pictures can show the difference between normal and diseased tissue. Magnetic resonance imaging makes better images of organs and soft tissue than other scanning techniques, such as computed tomography (CT) or x-ray. Magnetic resonance imaging is especially useful for imaging the brain, the spine, the soft tissue of joints, and the inside of bones. Also called MRI, NMRI, and nuclear magnetic resonance imaging.

malignant: Cancerous. Malignant tumors can invade and destroy nearby tissue and spread to other parts of the body.

mammography: The use of film or a computer to create a picture of the breast.

mastectomy: Surgery to remove the breast (or as much of the breast tissue as possible).

menopause: The time of life when a woman's ovaries stop producing hormones and menstrual periods stop. Natural menopause usually occurs around age 50. A woman is said to be in menopause when she hasn't had a period for 12 months in a row. Symptoms of menopause include hot flashes, mood swings, night sweats, vaginal dryness, trouble concentrating, and infertility.

metastasis: The spread of cancer from one part of the body to another. A tumor formed by cells that have spread is called a metastatic tumor or a metastasis. The metastatic tumor contains cells that are like those in the original (primary) tumor. The plural form of metastasis is metastases (meh-TAS-tuh-SEEZ).

mutation: Any change in the DNA of a cell. Mutations may be caused by mistakes during cell division, or they may be caused by exposure to DNA-damaging agents in the environment. Mutations can be harmful, beneficial, or have no effect. If they occur in cells that make eggs or sperm, they can be inherited; if mutations occur in other types of cells, they are not inherited. Certain mutations may lead to cancer or other diseases.

neoadjuvant therapy: Treatment given as a first step to shrink a tumor before the main treatment, which is usually surgery, is given. Examples of neoadjuvant therapy include chemotherapy, radiation therapy, and hormone therapy. It is a type of induction therapy.

oncologist: A doctor who specializes in treating cancer. Some oncologists specialize in a particular type of cancer treatment. For example, a radiation oncologist specializes in treating cancer with radiation.

oophorectomy: Surgery to remove one or both ovaries.

ostomy: An operation to create an opening (a stoma) from an area inside the body to the outside. Colostomy and urostomy are types of ostomies.

ovarian ablation: Surgery, radiation therapy, or a drug treatment to stop the functioning of the ovaries. Also called ovarian suppression.

ovary: One of a pair of female reproductive glands in which the ova, or eggs, are formed. The ovaries are located in the pelvis, one on each side of the uterus.

palliative care: Care given to improve the quality of life of patients who have a serious or life-threatening disease. The goal of palliative care is to prevent or treat as early as possible the symptoms of a disease, side effects caused by treatment of a disease, and psychological, social, and spiritual problems related to a disease or its treatment. Also called comfort care, supportive care, and symptom management.

Pap test: A procedure in which cells are scraped from the cervix for examination under a microscope. It is used to detect cancer and changes that may lead to cancer. A Pap test can also show conditions, such as infection or inflammation, that are not cancer. Also called Pap smear and Papanicolaou test.

pathologist: A doctor who identifies diseases by studying cells and tissues under a microscope.

polyp: A growth that protrudes from a mucous membrane.

positron emission tomography scan (PET scan): A procedure in which a small amount of radioactive glucose (sugar) is injected into a vein, and a scanner is used to make detailed, computerized pictures of areas inside the body where the glucose is used. Because cancer cells often use more glucose than normal cells, the pictures can be used to find cancer cells in the body. Also called PET scan.

precancerous: A term used to describe a condition that may (or is likely to) become cancer. Also called premalignant.

progesterone: A type of hormone made by the body that plays a role in the menstrual cycle and pregnancy. Progesterone can also be made in the laboratory. It may be used as a type of birth control and to treat menstrual disorders, infertility, symptoms of menopause, and other conditions.

progestin: Any natural or laboratory-made substance that has some or all of the biologic effects of progesterone, a female hormone.

prophylactic mastectomy: Surgery to reduce the risk of developing breast cancer by removing one or both breasts before disease develops. Also called preventive mastectomy.

radiation therapy: The use of high-energy radiation from x-rays, gamma rays, neutrons, protons, and other sources to kill cancer cells and shrink tumors. Radiation may come from a machine outside the body (external-beam radiation therapy), or it may come from radioactive material placed in the body near cancer cells (internal radiation therapy). Systemic radiation therapy uses a radioactive substance, such as a radio-labeled monoclonal antibody, that travels in the blood to tissues throughout the body. Also called irradiation and radiotherapy.

radical mastectomy: Surgery for breast cancer in which the breast, chest muscles, and all of the lymph nodes under the arm are removed. For many years, this was the breast cancer operation used most often, but it is used rarely now. Doctors consider radical mastectomy only when the tumor has spread to the chest muscles. Also called Halsted radical mastectomy.

raloxifene: The active ingredient in a drug used to reduce the risk of invasive breast cancer in post-menopausal women who are at high risk of the disease or who have osteoporosis. It is also used to prevent and treat osteoporosis in post menopausal women. It is also being studied in the prevention of breast cancer in certain premenopausal women and in the prevention and treatment of other conditions. Raloxifene blocks the effects of the hormone estrogen in the breast and increases the amount of calcium in bone. It is a type of selective estrogen receptor modulator (SERM).

recurrent cancer: Cancer that has recurred (come back), usually after a period of time during which the cancer could not be detected. The cancer may come back to the same place as the original (primary) tumor or to another place in the body. Also called recurrence.

salpingo-oophorectomy: Surgical removal of the fallopian tubes and ovaries.

sarcoma: A cancer of the bone, cartilage, fat, muscle, blood vessels, or other connective or supportive tissue.

selective estrogen receptor modulator: A drug that acts like estrogen on some tissues but blocks the effect of estrogen on other tissues. Tamoxifen and raloxifene are selective estrogen receptor modulators. Also called SERM.

sigmoidoscopy: Examination of the lower colon using a sigmoidoscope, inserted into the rectum. A sigmoidoscope is a thin, tube-like instrument with a light and a lens for viewing. It may also have a tool to remove tissue to be checked under a microscope for signs of disease. Also called proctosigmoidoscopy.

speculum: An instrument used to widen an opening of the body to make it easier to look inside.

squamous cell: Flat cell that looks like a fish scale under a microscope. These cells cover inside and outside surfaces of the body. They are found in the tissues that form the surface of the skin, the lining of the hollow organs of the body (such as the bladder, kidney, and uterus), and the passages of the respiratory and digestive tracts.

stage: The extent of a cancer in the body. Staging is usually based on the size of the tumor, whether lymph nodes contain cancer, and whether the cancer has spread from the original site to other parts of the body.

stem cell transplant: A method of replacing immature blood-forming cells in the bone marrow that have been destroyed by drugs, radiation, or disease. Stem cells are injected into the patient and make healthy blood cells. A stem cell transplant may be autologous (using a patient's own stem cells that were saved before treatment), allogeneic (using stem cells donated by someone who is not an identical twin), or syngeneic (using stem cells donated by an identical twin).

tamoxifen: A drug used to treat certain types of breast cancer in women and men. It is also used to prevent breast cancer in women who have had ductal carcinoma in situ (abnormal cells in the ducts of the breast) and in women who are at a high risk of developing breast cancer. Tamoxifen is also being studied in the treatment of other types of cancer. It blocks the effects of the hormone estrogen in the breast. Tamoxifen is a type of anti estrogen. Also called tamoxifen citrate.

taxane: A type of drug that blocks cell growth by stopping mitosis (cell division). Taxanes interfere with microtubules (cellular structures that help move chromosomes during mitosis). They are used to treat cancer. A taxane is a type of mitotic inhibitor and antimicrotubule agent.

tumor: An abnormal mass of tissue that results when cells divide more than they should or do not die when they should. Tumors may be benign (not cancer), or malignant (cancer). Also called neoplasm.

ultrasound: A procedure in which high-energy sound waves are bounced off internal tissues or organs and make echoes. The echo patterns are shown on the screen of an ultrasound machine, forming a picture of body tissues called a sonogram. Also called ultrasonography.

uterus: The small, hollow, pear-shaped organ in a woman's pelvis. This is the organ in which a fetus develops. Also called womb.

vagina: The muscular canal extending from the uterus to the exterior of the body. Also called birth canal.

vulva: The external female genital organs, including the clitoris, vaginal lips, and the opening to the vagina.

Chapter 69

National Organizations Offering Cancer-Related Services

Support Helplines

American Cancer Society
800-ACS-2345 (227-2345)

CancerCare
800-813-HOPE (4673)
212-302-2400 (outside North America)

Cancer Information and Counseling Line (CICL)
800-525-3777

Cancer Research Foundations of America
800-227-2732

Susan G. Komen
877-GO KOMEN (465-6636)

Living Beyond Breast Cancer
888-753-5222

National Cancer Institute's Cancer Information Service
800-422-6237

SHARE: Self Help for Women with Breast or Ovarian Cancer
866-891-2392

Online Support

Cancer Survivors Network American Cancer Society
csn.cancer.org

LiveHelp National Cancer Institute
www.cancer.gov/livehelp

OncoChat
www.oncochat.org

Support Organizations

American Society of Clinical Oncology
2318 Mill Rd., Ste. 800
Alexandria, VA 22314
571-483-1300; Fax: 703-299-0255
www.asco.org
customerservice@asco.org

Avon Breast Cancer Crusade
Avon Foundation
777 Third Ave.
New York, NY 10017
866-505-2866
www.avonfoundation.org/causes/
breast-cancer-crusade
info@avonfoundation.org.

Black Women's Health Imperative
1726 M St. N.W. Ste. 300
Washington, DC 20036
202-548-4000
www.bwhi.org
Imperative@bwhi.org

Cancer Support Community
1050 17th St., N.W.
Ste. 500
Washington, DC 20036
888-793-9355; Fax: 202-974-7999
www.cancersupportcommunity.
org
help@cancersupportcommunity.
org

Celebrating Life Foundation
12100 Ford Rd., Ste. 100
Dallas, TX 75234
800-207-0992 ext 110
www.celebratinglife.org

Reach to Recovery
American Cancer Society
800-ACS-2345 (227-2345)
www.cancer.org/treatment/
supportprogramsservices/
reach-to-recovery

Look Good Feel Better®
The Personal Care Products
Council Foundation
800-395-LOOK (5665)
www.lookgoodfeelbetter.org

TLC Tender Loving Care
American Cancer Society
P.O. Box 395
Louisiana, MO 63353-0395
800-850-9445; Fax: 800-279-2018
www.tlcdirect.org
customerservice@tlccatalog.org

Vital Options International
TeleSupport Cancer Network
818-508-5657
www.vitaloptions.org
info@vitaloptions.org

Young Survival Coalition
80 Broadway, Ste. 1700
New York, NY 10004
877-972-1011; Fax: 646-257-3030
www.youngsurvival.org
info@youngsurvival.org

National Organizations Offering Cancer-Related Services

Agency for Healthcare Research and Quality
540 Gaither Rd.
Rockville, MD 20850
301-427-1104
www.ahrq.gov
info@ahrq.gov

Air Charity Network
4620 Haygood Rd., Ste. 1
Virginia Beach, VA 23455
800-296-3797; Fax: 757-464-1284
www.angelflightmidatlantic.org
info@angel-flight.org

American Association for Cancer Research
615 Chestnut St., 17th Fl.
Philadelphia, PA 19106-4404
866-423-3965; Fax: 215-440-9313
www.aacr.org
aacr@aacr.org

American Cancer Society
250 Williams St.
Atlanta, GA 30303
800-ACS-2345 (227-2345); Fax: 866-228-4327
www.cancer.org

American Childhood Cancer Organization
10920 Connecticut Ave., Ste. A
Kensington, MD 20895
855-858-2226; Fax: 301-962-3521
www.acco.org
staff@acco.org

American Institute for Cancer Research
1759 R St. N.W.
Washington, DC 20009
800-843-8114; Fax: 202-328-7226
www.aicr.org
aicrweb@aicr.org

Association of Community Cancer Centers
11600 Nebel St., Ste. 201
Rockville, MD 20852-2557
301-984-9496; Fax: 301-770-1949
www.accc-cancer.org

Be The Match®
National Marrow Donor Program (NMDP)
3001 Broadway St., N.E.
Ste. 100
Minneapolis, MN 55413-1753
800-MARROW2 (627-7692)
www.bethematch.org
patientinfo@nmdp.org

Benefits.gov
800-FED-INFO (333-4636)
www.benefits.gov

Bloch (R.A.) Cancer Foundation, Inc.
One H&R Block Way
Kansas City, MO 64105
800-433-0464; Fax: 816-854-8024
www.blochcancer.org
hotline@blochcancer.org

Camp Kesem
P.O. Box 452
Culver City, CA 90232
260-22-KESEM (225-3736)
www.campkesem.org

Canadian Cancer Society
565 W. 10th Ave.
Vancouver, BC V5Z 4J4
604-872-4400
www.bc.cancer.ca
info@cis.cancer.ca

Cancer and Careers.org
212-685-5955
www.cancerandcareers.org

Cancer Care
275 Seventh Ave., 22nd Fl.
New York, NY 10001
800-813- HOPE (4673)
www.cancercare.org
info@cancercare.org

Cancer Financial Assistance Coalition
www.cancerfac.org

Cancer Hope Network
2 N. Rd., Ste. A
Chester, NJ 07930
800-552-4366; Fax: 908-879-6518
www.cancerhopenetwork.org
info@cancerhopenetwork.org

Cancer Research UK
www.cancerhelp.org.uk

Caritas Internationalis
Headquarters
Palazzo San Calisto
Vatican City State, V-00120
www.caritas.org
caritas.internationalis@caritas.va

Centers for Disease Control and Prevention
1600 Clifton Rd.
Atlanta, GA 30329-4027
800-CDC-4636 (232-4636); Fax: 888-232-6348
www.cdc.com

Cleaning for a Reason Foundation
211 S. Stemmons, Ste. G
Lewisville, TX 75067
877-337-7233; Fax: 972-316-4138
www.cleaningforareason.org
info@cleaningforareason.org

Colorectal Cancer Control Program
4770 Buford Hwy, N.E.
Atlanta, GA 30341
800-232-4636; Fax: 888-232-6348
www.cdc.gov/cancer/crccp
cdcinfo@cdc.gov

Colorectal Care Line
421 Butler Farm Rd.
Hampton, VA 23666
866-657-8634; Fax: 757-952-2031
www.colorectalcareline.org

Co-Pay Relief Program
421 Butler Farm Rd.
Hampton, VA 23666
866-512-3861
www.copays.org

Corporate Angel Network
Westchester County Airport
One Loop Rd.
White Plains, NY 10604
866-328-1313; Fax: 914-328-3938
www.corpangelnetwork.org
info@corpangelnetwork.org

Dana-Farber Cancer Institute
44 Binney St.
Boston, MA 02115
866-408-DFCI (408-3324); TDD:
617-632-5330
www.dfci.harvard.edu
Dana-Farber@dfci.harvard.edu

Eldercare Locator
800-677-1116
www.eldercare.gov
eldercarelocator@n4a.org

Facing Our Risk of Cancer Empowered (FORCE)
16057 Tampa Palms Blvd. W
PMB #373
Tampa, FL 33647
866-824-RISK (7475)
www.facingourrisk.org
info@facingourrisk.org

Food and Drug Administration
10903 New Hampshire Ave.
Silver Spring, MD 20993
888-INFO-FDA (463-6332)
www.fda.gov

Good Days
6900 N. Dallas Pkwy, Ste. 200
Plano, TX 75024
877-968-7233; Fax: 214-570-3621
www.gooddaysfromcdf.org
info@cdfund.org

Healthcare.gov
200 Independence Ave., S.W.
Washington, DC 20201
800-318-2596
www.healthcare.gov

Health Well Foundation
P.O. Box 4133
Gaithersburg, MD 20878
800-675-8416
www.healthwellfoundation.org

Hill-Burton Program
5600 Fishers Ln.
Rm. 10-105
Rockville, MD 20857
800-638-0742; Fax: 877-489-4772
www.hrsa.gov

Hospice Education Institute
Three Unity Sq. P.O. Box 98
Machiasport, ME 04655-0098
800-331-1620; Fax: 207-255-8008
www.hospiceworld.org
hospiceall@aol.com

Intercultural Cancer Council
Ste. 1025
1720 Dryden, PMB 25
Houston, TX 77030
877-BIENNIAL (243-6642)
iccnetwork.org
info@iccnetwork.org

International Cancer
Information Service Group
www.icisg.org
info@icisg.org

International Union Against Cancer
www.uicc.org

Joe's House
505 E. 79th St., Ste. 17E
New York, NY 10075
877-JOESHOU (563-7468)
www.joeshouse.org
info@joeshouse.org

Leukemia and Lymphoma Society
1311 Mamaroneck Ave., Ste. 310
White Plains, NY 10605
800-955-4572; Fax: 914-949-6691
www.lls.org
infocenter@lls.org

LIVESTRONG
2201 E. Sixth St.
Austin, TX 78702
855-220-7777
www.livestrong.org

Lymphoma Research Foundation
115 Broadway, Ste. 1301
New York, NY 10006
800-500-9976; Fax: 212-349-2886
www.lymphoma.org
helpline@lymphoma.org

Macmillan Cancer Support
(+44) 0808-88-00-00
www.macmillan.org
webmanager@macmillan.org.uk

Mayo Foundation for Medical Education and Research
200 First St. SW
Rochester, MN 55905
www.mayoclinic.com
comments@mayoclinic.com

M.D. Anderson Cancer Center
1515 Holcombe Blvd.
Houston, TX 77030
800-392-1611
www.mdanderson.org

Medicaid (Medical Assistance)
7500 Security Blvd.
Baltimore, MD 21244
877-267-2323
www.cms.gov/MedicaidGenInfo

Medicare
7500 Security Blvd.
Baltimore, MD 21244
800-633-4227; Fax: 877-486-2048
www.medicare.gov

Melanoma International Foundation
250 Mapleflower Rd.
Glenmoore, PA 19343
866-463-6663
www.safefromthesun.org
cpoole@melanomainternational.org

Memorial Sloan-Kettering Cancer Center
1275 York Ave.
New York, NY 10021
800-525-2225
www.mskcc.org

Mesothelioma Applied Research Foundation
1317 King St.
Alexandria, VA 22314
877-363-6376; Fax: 703-299-0399
www.curemeso.org
info@curemeso.org

Moores Cancer Center
University of California
200 West Arbor Dr.
San Diego, CA 92103
858-657-7000
health.ucsd.edu/cancer

*National Association for
Proton Therapy*
1301 Highland Dr.
Silver Spring, MD 20910
301-587-6100; Fax: 202-530-0659
www.proton-therapy.org

*National Association of
Insurance Commissioners*
1100 Walnut St., Ste. 1500
Kansas City, MO 64108
866-470-6242; Fax: 816-460-7493
www.naic.org
help@naic.org

*National Breast and Cervical
Cancer Early Detection
Program*
4770 Buford Hwy, N.E.
Atlanta, GA 30341
800-CDC-INFO (232-4636)
www.cdc.gov/cancer/nbccedp
cdcinfo@cdc.gov

*National Center for
Complementary and
Alternative Medicine*
NCCAM Clearinghouse
P.O. Box 7923
Gaithersburg, MD 20898-7923
888-644-6226; Fax: 866-464-3616
nccih.nih.gov
info@nccam.nih.gov

*The National Children's
Cancer Society*
500 N. Broadway, Ste. 1850
St. Louis, MO 63102
800-532-6459; Fax: 314-241-1996
www.thenccs.org/contact
pbeck@children-cancer.org

*National Coalition for
Cancer Survivorship*
1010 Wayne Ave., Ste. 770
Silver Spring, MD 20910
888-NCCS.YES (650-9127)
www.canceradvocacy.org
info@canceradvocacy.org

*National Comprehensive
Cancer Network*
275 Commerce Dr., Ste. 300
Fort Washington, PA 19034
215-690-0300; Fax: 215-690-0280
www.nccn.org

*National Institutes of Health
(NIH)*
9000 Rockville Pike
Bethesda, MD 20892
301-496-4000; Fax: 301-402-9612
www.nih.gov
NIHinfo@od.nih.gov

*National Cancer Institute
(NCI)*
Public Inquiries Office
Ste. 300
6116 Executive Blvd.
MSC8322
Bethesda, MD 20892-8322
800-422-6237; Fax: 888-232-6348
www.cancer.gov

*National Foundation for
Cancer Research*
4600 E. W. Hwy
Ste. 525
Bethesda, MD 20814
800-321-CURE (321-2873); Fax:
301-654-5824
www.nfcr.org

National Heart, Lung, and Blood Institute

NHLBI Health Information
Center
P.O. Box 30105
Bethesda, MD 20824-0105
301-592-8573; Fax: 240-629-3246
www.nhlbi.nih.gov
nhlbiinfo@nhlbi.nih.gov

National Hospice and Palliative Care Organization

1731 King St., Ste. 100
Alexandria, VA 22314
800-658-8898; Fax: 703-837-1233
www.nhpco.org
nhpco_info@nhpco.org

National Institute on Aging (NIA)

Bldg. 31, Rm. 5C27
31 Center Dr., MSC 2292
Bethesda, MD 20892
800-222-2225; Fax: 800-222-4225
www.nia.nih.gov
niaic@nia.nih.gov

National Institute on Alcohol Abuse and Alcoholism (NIAAA)

5635 Fishers Ln., MSC 9304
Bethesda, MD 20892-9304
888-MY-NIAAA (696-4222)
www.niaaa.nih.gov
NIAAAPressOffice@mail.nih.gov

National Lymphedema Network

225 Bush St., Ste. 357
San Francisco, CA 94104
800-541-3259; Fax: 415-908-3813
www.lymphnet.org
nln@lymphnet.org

National Marrow Donor Program

3001 Broadway St. N.E.
Ste. 500
Minneapolis, MN 55413-1753
800-MARROW2 (627-7692)
www.marrow-donor.org

Native American Cancer Research

3022 South Nova Rd.
Pine, CO 80470
303-838-9359
natamcancer.org

Needy Meds

P.O. Box 219
Gloucester, MA 01931
800-503-6897; Fax: 206-260-8850
www.needymeds.org
info@needymeds.org

Novartis Oncology

Novartis Pharmaceuticals
Corporation
One Health Plaza
East Hanover, NJ 07936-1080
888-669-6682; Fax: 732-673-5262
www.us.novartisoncology.com

Office On Women's Health
Department of Health and
Human Services
200 Independence Ave., S.W.
Rm. 712E
Washington, DC 20201
202-690-7650; Fax: 202-205-2631
womenshealth.gov

OncoLink
Abramson Cancer Center of the
University of Pennsylvania
Civic Center Blvd.
Ste. 2338
Philadelphia, PA 19104
215-349-8895; Fax: 215-349-5445
www.oncolink.com
hampshire@uphs.upenn.edu

Patient Advocate Foundation
421 Butler Farm Rd.
Hampton, VA 23666
800-532-5274; Fax: 757-873-8999
www.patientadvocate.org
help@patientadvocate.org

The Physicians Committee
5100 Wisconsin Ave.
Ste. 400
Washington, DC 20016
202-686-2210; Fax: 202-686-2216
www.pcrm.org
pcrm@pcrm.org

*Pregnant With Cancer
Network*
P.O. Box 253
Amherst, NY 14226
www.pregnantwithcancer.org

Prevent Cancer Foundation
1600 Duke St., Ste. 500
Alexandria, VA 22314
800-227-2732; Fax: 703-836-4413
www.preventcancer.org

*Ronald McDonald House
Charities*
One Kroc Dr.
Oak Brook, IL 60523
630-623-7048; Fax: 630-623-7488
www.rmhc.org
info@rmhc.org

The Salvation Army
International Headquarters
101 Queen Victoria St.
London EC4V 4EH
United Kingdom
www.salvationarmy.org
websa@salvationarmy.org

The Salvation Army
National Headquarters
615 Slaters Ln.
P.O. Box 269
Alexandria, VA 22313
703-684-5500; Fax: 703-684-5500
www.salvationarmyusa.org
NHQ_Webmaster@USN.
salvationarmy.org

*The SAMFund for Young
Adult Survivors of Cancer*
89 S. St., Ste. LL02
Boston, MA 02211
617-938-3484; Fax: 866-496-8070
www.thesamfund.org
info@thesamfund.org

Sarcoma Alliance
775 E. Blithedale # 334
Mill Valley, CA 94941
415-381-7236; Fax: 415-381-7235
www.sarcomaalliance.org
info@sarcomaalliance.org

Sisters Network, Inc.
2922 Rosedale St.
Houston, TX 77004
866-781-1808; Fax: 713-780-8998
www.sistersnetworkinc.org
infonet@sistersnetworkinc.org

*Social Security
Administration*
Windsor Park Bldg.
Baltimore, MD 21235
800-772-1213; Fax: 800-325-0778
www.ssa.gov
SSA.OMB.515@ssa.gov

*Society of Laparoendoscopic
Surgeons*
7330 S.W. 62nd Place, Ste. 410
Miami, FL 33143-4825
305-665-9959
www.sls.org
info@sls.org

Society of Surgical Oncology
9525 West Bryn Mawr Ave.
Ste. 870
Rosemont, IL 60018
847-427-1400; Fax: 847-427-1411
www.surgonc.org
info@surgonc.org

*State Health Insurance
Assistance Program*
Centers for Medicare and
Medicaid Services
7500 Security Blvd.
Baltimore, MD 21244
www.shiptacenter.org

*State Pharmaceutical
Assistance Programs*
7700 E. First Pl.
Denver, CO 80230
303-364-7700; Fax: 303-364-7800
www.ncsl.org

Susan G. Komen
5005 LBJ Fwy, Ste. 250
Dallas, TX 75244
877-GO KOMEN (465-6636)
www.komen.org
Helpline@komen.org

*The Ulman Cancer Fund for
Young Adults*
6770 Oak Hall Ln., Unit 116
Columbia, MD 21045
888-393-3863
www.ulmanfund.org
info@ulmanfund.org

*U.S. Department of Housing
and Urban Development*
451 Seventh St., S.W.
Washington, DC 20410
800-569-4287; Fax: 202-708-1455
www.hud.gov

Union for International Cancer Control
62 Rt. de Frontenex
Geneva 1207
Switzerland
www.uicc.org
info@uicc.org

United Way Worldwide
701 N. Fairfax St.
Alexandria, VA 22314
703-836-7112
www.liveunited.org

United Healthcare Children's Foundation
MN012-S286
P.O. Box 41
Minneapolis, MN 55440
952-992-4459
www.uhccf.org

Us TOO International, Inc.
2720 S. River Rd., Ste. 112
Des Plaines, IL 60018
800-808-7866; Fax: 630-795-1602
www.ustoo.org
ustoo@ustoo.org

Women's Cancer Resource Center
5741 Telegraph Ave.
Oakland, CA 94609
888-421-7900; Fax: 510-601-4045
www.wcrc.org

Breast Cancer Resources

African American Breast Cancer Alliance
P.O. Box 8981
Minneapolis, MN 55408
612-825-3675; Fax: 612-827-2977
aabcainc.org

American Breast Cancer Foundation
10400 Little Patuxent Pkway
Ste. 480
Columbia, MD 21044
410-730-5105
www.abcf.org
contact@abcf.org

Breast Cancer Action
657 Mission St., Ste. 302
San Francisco, CA 94105
877-2STOPBC (278-6722); Fax:
415-243-3996
www.bcaction.org
info@bcaction.org

Breast Cancer Fund
1388 Sutter St., Ste. 400
San Francisco, CA 94109-5400
866-760-8223; Fax: 415-346-2975
www.breastcancerfund.org
info@breastcancerfund.org

Breast Cancer Research Foundation
60E. 56th St., 8th Fl.
New York, NY 10022
866-FIND-A-CURE (346-3228);
Fax: 646-497-0890
www.bcrfcure.org
bcrf@bcrfcure.org

Healthy Women
P.O. Box 430
Red Bank, NJ 07701
877-986-9472; Fax: 732-530-3347
www.healthywomen.org
mail@winabc.org

Imaginis: The Breast Cancer Resource
25 E. Ct. St.
Ste. 301
Greenville, SC 29601
864-209-1139
www.imaginis.com
learnmore@imaginis.com

Johns Hopkins Breast Cancer Center
601 N. Caroline St.
Rm. 4161
Baltimore, MD 21287
410-955-5000; Fax: 410-614-1947
www.hopkinsbreastcenter.org

Living Beyond Breast Cancer
40 Monument Rd., Ste. 104
Bala Cynwyd, PA 190041
888-753-LBBC (5222); Fax:
610-645-4573
www.lbbc.org

Mayors' Campaign Against Breast Cancer
U.S. Conference of Mayors
1620 Eye St., N.W., 3rd Fl.
Washington, DC 20006
202-293-7330; Fax: 202-293-2352
www.usmayors.org/cancer
info@usmayors.org

National Breast and Cervical Cancer Early Detection Program
www.cdc.gov/cancer/nbccedp/
index.htm

National Breast Cancer Coalition
1600 Clifton Rd.
Atlanta, GA 30329-4027
800-CDC-INFO (232-4636);
Fax: 888-232-6348
www.breastcancerdeadline2020.
org/homepage.html
info@stopbreastcancer.org

National Breast Cancer Foundation
2600 Network Blvd., Ste. 300
Frisco, TX 75034
www.nationalbreastcancer.org

Program on Breast Cancer and Environmental Risk Factors
Cornell University, College of
Veterinary Medicine
Vet Box 31
Ithaca, NY 14853-6401
Fax: 607-254-4730
envirocancer.cornell.edu
breastcancer@cornell.edu

SHARE: Self-Help for Women with Breast or Ovarian Cancer
165 W. 46th St., Ste. 712
New York, NY 10036
866-891-2392
212-719-0364; Fax: 212-869-3431
www.sharecancersupport.org
info@sharecancersupport.org

Gynecologic Cancer Resources

American College of Obstetricians and Gynecologists
P.O. Box 70620
Washington, DC 20024-9998
800-673-8444; Fax: 240-575-9880
www.acog.org

American Society for Colposcopy and Cervical Pathology
1530 Tilco Dr., Ste. C
Frederick, MD 21704
800-787-7227; Fax: 301-733-5775
www.asccp.org

Gynecologic Cancer Foundation
230 W. Monroe St., Ste. 2528
Chicago, IL 60606-4902
312-578-1439; Fax: 312-578-9769
www.thegcf.org

Gynecologic Cancer Foundation / Women's Cancer Network
230 W. Monroe, Ste. 2528
Chicago, IL 60606
312-578-1439
www.wcn.org
info@thegcf.org

International Gynecologic Cancer Society
P.O. Box 6387
Louisville, KY 40206
502-981-4575; Fax: 502-891-4576
www.igcs.org
adminoffice@igcs.org

National Cervical Cancer Coalition
P.O. Box 13827
Research Triangle Park, NC 27709
800-685-5531; Fax: 818-780-8199
www.nccc-online.org
info@nccc-online.org

National HPV and Cervical Cancer Prevention Resource Center
P.O. Box 13827
Research Triangle Park, NC 27713
www.ashastd.org/hpvccrc

National Ovarian Cancer Association
101-145 Front St. E.
Toronto, Ontario M5A 1E3
Canada
877-413-7970 (Canada only);
Fax: 416-962-2701
www.ovariancanada.org
noca@ovariancanada.org

Ovarian Cancer National Alliance
1101 14th St., N.W.
Ste. 850
Washington, DC 20005
202-331-1332; Fax: 202-331-2292
www.ovariancancer.org
ocna@ovariancancer.org

Ovarian Cancer Research Fund, Inc.
14 Pennsylvania Plaza
Ste. 1400
New York, NY 10122
800-873-9569; Fax: 212-947-5652
www.ocrf.org
info@ocrf.org

Resources for Other Types of Cancer

American Gastroenterological Association
4930 Del Ray Ave.
Bethesda, MD 20814
301-654-2055; Fax: 301-654-5920
www.gastro.org
member@gstro.org

American Liver Foundation
75 Maiden Ln., Ste. 603
New York, NY 10038
800-465-4837; Fax: 212-483-8179
www.liverfoundation.org

American Lung Association
55 W. Wacker Dr., Ste. 1150
Chicago, IL 60601
800-LUNGUSA (586-4872)
www.lungusa.org

American Melanoma Foundation
4150 Regents Park Row
Ste. 300
La Jolla, CA 92037
858-882-7712; Fax: 619-448-2902
www.melanomafoundation.org
sunsmartz@
melanomafoundation.org

American Society for Gastrointestinal Endoscopy
3300 Woodcreek Dr.
Downers Grove, IL 60515
630-573-0600; Fax: 630-573-0691
www.asge.org
info@asge.org

American Society of Colon and Rectal Surgeons
85 W. Algonquin Rd.
Ste. 550
Arlington Heights, IL 60005
847-290-9184; Fax: 847-290-9203
www.fascrs.org
ascrs@fascrs.org

Colon Cancer Alliance
1025 Vermont Ave., N.W.
Ste. 1066
Washington, DC 20005
877-422-2030; Fax: 866-304-9075
www.ccalliance.org
info@ccalliance.org

Kidney Cancer Association
P.O. Box 803338 #38269
Chicago, IL 60680-3338
800-850-9132; Fax: 847-332-2978
www.kidneycancer.org

Leukemia and Lymphoma Society
1311 Mamaroneck Ave.
White Plains, NY 10605-5221
800-955-4572; Fax: 914-949-6691
www.leukemia-lymphoma.org
infocenter@leukemia-lymphoma.
org

Lung Cancer Alliance
1700 K St., N.W.
Ste. 660
Washington, DC 20006
800-298-2436
www.lungcanceralliance.org
info@lungcanceralliance.org

*Lung Cancer Online
Foundation*
www.lungcanceronline.org

*Lymphoma Foundation of
America*
1100 N. Main St.
Ann Arbor, MI 48104
800-385-1060; Fax: 734-222-0044
www.lymphomahelp.org
LFA@lymphomahelp.org

*Lymphoma Research
Foundation*
115 Broadway, Ste. 1301
New York, NY 10006
212-349-2910; Fax: 212-349-2886
www.lymphoma.org
helpline@lymphoma.org

*Melanoma Education
Foundation*
P.O. Box 2023
Peabody, MA 01960
978-535-3080; Fax: 978-535-5602
www.skincheck.org
mef@skincheck.org

*Multiple Myeloma Research
Foundation*
383 Main Ave., 5th Fl.
Norwalk, CT 06851
203-972-1250; Fax: 203-972-1259
www.multiplemyeloma.org
info@themmrf.org

*National Brain Tumor
Foundation*
255 Chapel St., Ste. 200
Newton, MA 02458
617-924-9997; Fax: 617-924-9998
www.braintumor.org
nbtf@braintumor.org

*National Lymphedema
Network*
225 Bush St., Ste. 357
San Francisco, CA 94104
800-541-3259; Fax: 510-208-3110
www.lymphnet.org
nln@lymphnet.org

*Pancreatic Cancer Action
Network*
1500 Rosecrans Ave., Ste. 200
Manhattan Beach, CA 90266
877-272-6226; Fax: 310-725-0029
www.pancan.org
info@pancan.org

Skin Cancer Foundation
149 Madison Ave. Ste. 901
New York, NY 10016
800-SKIN490 (754-6490); Fax:
212-725-5751
www.skincancer.org
info@skincancer.org

*Thyroid Cancer Survivors'
Association, Inc.*
P.O. Box 1545
New York, NY 10159-1545
877-588-7904; Fax: 630-604-6078
www.thyca.org
thyca@thyca.org

Index

Index